Florence Nightingale

An Introduction to her Life and Family

Volume 1
of the Collected Works of Florence Nightingale

THE COLLECTED WORKS OF FLORENCE NIGHTINGALE

LIST OF VOLUMES

Note: Short title denoted by bold

FLORENCE NIGHTINGALE

AN INTRODUCTION TO HER
LIFE AND FAMILY

LYNN McDONALD, EDITOR

VOLUME 1
OF THE COLLECTED WORKS OF
FLORENCE NIGHTINGALE

Wilfrid Laurier University Press

We acknowledge the financial support of the Government of Canada through the Book Publishing Industry Development Program for our publishing activities.

National Library of Canada Cataloguing in Publication Data

Nightingale, Florence, 1820-1910.
    Florence Nightingale : an introduction to her life and family

(The collected works of Florence Nightingale ; v. 1)
Includes bibliographical references and index.
ISBN 0-88920-387-3

1. Nightingale, Florence, 1820-1910. 2. Nurses — England — Biography.
I. McDonald, Lynn, 1940-   II. Title. III. Series: Nightingale, Florence, 1820-1910. Collected works of Florence Nightingale ; v. 1.

RT37.N5A2 2001 v. 1   610.73′.092   C2001-903700-7

© 2001 Wilfrid Laurier University Press

Cover design by Leslie Macredie. Cover photography by Dr. Ross Camidge.

Printed in Canada

Wilfrid Laurier University Press
Waterloo, Ontario, Canada N2L 3C5
E-mail: press@wlu.ca
Web: http://www.wlupress.wlu.ca

The Collected Works of Florence Nightingale Web site:
http://www.sociology.uoguelph.ca/fnightingale

CONTENTS

ACKNOWLEDGMENTS

cknowledgments are due to a large number of individuals and organizations for assistance on this volume, and even more for assistance at various stages in the *Collected Works* project. To the Henry Bonham Carter Will Trust thanks go for permission to publish Nightingale original manuscripts, and indeed for treating Nightingale material generally as being in the public domain. To the owners of Nightingale manuscripts thanks are due for their important role in conservation, for permitting scholarly access and for permitting copies to be made for this *Collected Works*. All sources actually used in this volume are indicated at the appropriate place; the more than 150 archives and private collections world wide found to date are listed in Appendix E below.

To the Social Sciences and Humanities Research Council of Canada acknowledgment is due for a grant of $61,500 for support of the research 1997-2000. To the University of Guelph thanks for the provision of an extra faculty office to house the project, computers, technical and administrative support.

Transcriptions were done by: Gwyneth Watkins, Kim Cowan, Maria Schneidersmann, Meredith Risk, Kelly Thomas, Leo Uotila, Victoria Rea and Daniel Phelan. Volunteer verifiers of texts were: Gwyneth Watkins, Joan Enns, Barbara Brooks, Linda Elliot, Cherry Ambrose and Lois Thompson; volunteers assisting me with proofreading: Cherry Ambrose, Aideen Nicholson and Sandra Hunter. Dr Margaret Griffin as project manager oversaw transcriptions and research.

Thanks to Dr Gérard Vallée for assistance with translations from French, Latin and German, for proofreading and the identifying of literary passages. For assistance with Italian and Latin translations thanks to Dr Quirino DiGiulio. For assistance in identifying poems and hymns thanks to Lesley Mann, Toronto, Rev Dr Eric Griffin, Hamilton, ON, Bart Peeren, Netherlands, and for other research information thanks to Essex local historian Jennifer Bobrowski and Dr Mary Jane Mossman, Osgoode Hall Law School.

At the Press thanks are due to Dr Brian Henderson, director, Sandra Woolfrey, former director, Carroll Klein, managing editor, Doreen Armbruster, typesetter, Leslie Macredie and Penelope Grows, marketing, Steve Izma, production, and Elin Edwards, peer review. The copy editing was done by Frances Rooney.

Acknowledgments for photographs and other illustrations are given in the illustrations section.

In spite of the assistance of so many people undoubtedly errors remain, which are the responsibility of the editor. I would be grateful for notification of any errors, and for information on missing identifications. Corrections will be made in the electronic text and any other later publications.

Lynn McDonald
December 2001

Dramatis Personae

Frances "Fanny" (Smith) Nightingale (1788-1880), mother
William Edward Nightingale (1794-1874), father, "WEN"
Parthenope, "Pop," Lady Verney (1819-90), sister
Sir Harry Verney (1801-94), brother-in-law
Captain (later Sir) Edmund Verney (1838-1910), son of Harry Verney
Margaret Verney (1844-1930), wife of Edmund Verney
children of Edmund and Margaret Verney:
   Ellin (1873-1947); Lettice Sarah (1875-1908); Ruth Florence
   (1879-1968); (Sir) Harry Calvert Williams (1881-1974)
Frederick Verney (1846-1913), youngest son of Harry Verney
Maude Verney (d. 1936), wife of Frederick Verney
children of Frederick and Maude Verney:
   Ralph (1879-1959); Gwendolen (1881-1932); Kathleen (1883-1966)
William Smith (1756-1835), maternal grandfather
Mary (Evans) Shore (1758-1853), paternal grandmother
Mary Shore Smith (1798-1889), "Aunt Mai"
Samuel Smith (1794-1880), "Uncle Sam"
Blanche (Smith) Clough (1828-1904), cousin
Arthur Hugh Clough (1819-61) "AHC," husband of Blanche
William Shore Smith (1831-94), "Shore," cousin, Nightingale heir
Louisa Shore Smith, wife of "Shore"
Julia Smith (1799-1883), "Aunt Ju"
Octavius Smith (1796-1871), "Uncle Oc"
Jane (Cooke) Smith (d. 1878) "Aunt Jenny," wife of Uncle Oc
Marianne (Nicholson) Galton, (d. 1909), cousin
Captain Sir Douglas Galton (1822-99), husband of Marianne
George Henry Nicholson (d. 1851), cousin
Rosalind (Smith) Nash (1862-1952), cousin
Hilary Bonham Carter ((1821-65), cousin
Henry Bonham Carter (1827-1921), cousin

LIST OF ILLUSTRATIONS

INTRODUCTION TO THE
COLLECTED WORKS

I t is an astonishing fact that there has been up to now no Collected Works of such an important thinker and influential social reformer as Florence Nightingale. Yet she was a legend in her own time (1820-1910), described as the second most famous woman in Britain after Queen Victoria. She remains known as the heroine of the Crimean War (1854-56), the most eminent founder of the modern profession of nursing and a major hospital reformer. Her signal contribution to public health in India is still recognized there. There are Nightingale streets, schools, hospitals and pubs around the world—after the Crimean War even a racehorse was named after her. Her portrait was on the British ten-pound note in the 1970s. There have been feature films, an opera and many fictional books using Nightingale as a heroine.

In the late twentieth century Nightingale's contribution to the development of the social sciences, the subject that prompted my interest in her, received much attention. In May 1997 Oxford University inaugurated its Florence Nightingale Lectures on Statistics. There is a new interest in her spirituality, prompted likely by the new interest in spirituality outside the bounds of organized religion. The recent more holistic approach to public health and greater emphasis on environmental factors accounts for another surge of interest in Nightingale, a community health pioneer par excellence.

The late twentieth century saw the publication of many Nightingale works, especially on her spirituality, comparative religion and theology, some for the first time, some republication or at least facsimile reproduction. There are new biographies in process, and children's books on her life have never been lacking. Nightingale papers are plentiful at history of nursing conferences. Critical, analytical work has been produced that is of high quality and much interest. Clearly there is a modest Nightingale industry in the scholarly world. Yet, though there have been a number of editions of her correspondence, most of the enormous number of her extant letters remain unpublished. Significant published works have been long out of print or are otherwise unavailable.

The *Collected Works* now being published differs from the usual mode by appearing in both print (sixteen volumes) and electronic form. The printed volumes present a substantial selection from the vast amount of surviving Nightingale writing. The electronic publication will be complete, including all known Nightingale writing, published and archival. Volume references are to the printed volumes.

Early biographies (dating from Nightingale's lifetime and soon after her death) tended to the sycophantic, so that descriptions of her as the "wise, beloved and far-seeing heroine of the Crimean War" are typical.[1] But beginning with Lytton Strachey's irreverent, whimsical and somewhat rude 1918 essay, it became acceptable, even fashionable, to attack. The most hostile treatment is F.B. Smith's *Florence Nightingale: Reputation and Power*, 1982. It is also the most inaccurate treatment of Nightingale's work; some of the more egregious of his errors will be pointed out where relevant. Smith's book in turn has influenced much subsequent writing on Nightingale, so that flagrantly incorrect "facts" about her abound in the secondary literature. This negative literature has become sufficiently large and influential to warrant review: see Appendix B.

Further, although much new material by and about Nightingale has appeared in recent decades, very little has made it into mainstream textbooks or curricula. Nightingale is sometimes given her due in the development of the social sciences, applied statistics,[2] epidemiology,[3] political theory, the public health care system, welfare state or comparative religion. She has a place in my books on theory: *The Early Origins of the Social Sciences* and *Women Founders of the Social Sciences,* and in my anthology, *Women Theorists on Society and Politics.* Otherwise, how-

---

1 Lizzie Aldrich, "Florence Nightingale," in Charles F. Horne, ed., *Great Men and Famous Women* 6:377.
2 Edwin W. Kopf, "Florence Nightingale as Statistician," *Publications of the American Statistical Association*; I. Bernard Cohen, "Florence Nightingale"; Richard Stone, "Florence Nightingale and Hospital Reform," in *Some British Empiricists in the Social Sciences 1650-1900*, ch 11.
3 David J. Spiegelhalter, "Surgical Audit: Statistical Lessons from Nightingale and Codman"; Paul D. Stolley and Tamar Lasky, *Investigating Disease Patterns: The Science of Epidemiology.*

ever, she is absent from histories of the social sciences. Even in the field of nursing she is seldom treated as a serious theoretical contributor. Scholars debate the role and influence of the training school established in her name at St Thomas' Hospital while ignoring her greater role in the more general reform of public health measures.[4]

Nightingale's omission from the literature on peace, war and militarism is similarly remarkable. She is still widely acknowledged as "the lady of the lamp" in the Crimean War. Her contribution to the reform of military nursing and hospital construction[5] is also acknowledged in the scholarly literature. Yet her pertinent and interesting views on the origins of war and the role of military institutions in fomenting it are scarcely known. That she was decorated by both sides in the Franco-Prussian War is known, as is the fact that her example inspired the foundation of the International Red Cross.[6] Her interesting and astute observations on *militarism* are not known, but deserve to be.

The re-emergence of the women's movement in the mid-twentieth century sparked interest in Nightingale, among many other significant women. Anthologies of women of the Victorian period accord her a substantial place.[7] The feminist interest in the *personal* has prompted interest in her relations with her mother and sister.[8] Yet welcome as the new material and its analysis is, much is amiss. Nightingale's reluctance to *work* in the suffrage movement has been mistaken for a refusal to sign a petition. In fact she signed the first suffrage petition in 1866. (It took Beatrice Webb twenty years to acknowledge that she was wrong, after an outright refusal to sign, and that was a generation later!) Nor are the reasons for Nightingale's reluctance always acknowledged, namely that she placed greater importance on

4 Monica Baly, "Shattering the Nightingale Myth"; Anne Summers, *Angels and Citizens: British Women as Military Nurses 1854-1914*; Jean Donnison, *Midwives and Medical Men: A History of Inter-Professional Rivalries and Women's Rights*; Mike Barfoot, "To Catch a Nightingale: Nursing Reforms at the Royal Infirmary of Edinburgh, 1872-1900"; Linda Bryder and Derek A. Dow, eds., *New Countries and Old Medicine*; Evelyn Bolster, *The Sisters of Mercy in the Crimean War*.

5 Notably in Brian Abel-Smith, *The Hospitals 1800-1948: A Study in Social Administration in England and Wales*.

6 Henri Dunant, letter to the *Times* 7 August 1872:3.

7 Penelope Tuson, ed., *The Queen's Daughters: An Anthology of Victorian Feminist Writings on India 1857-1900*; Margaret Forster, "Florence Nightingale 1820-1910."

8 Karen Payne, ed., "Florence Nightingale and Her Mother Fanny, 1851-62."

economic rights for women than on political ones. Similarly the fact that she initially (largely) opposed the entry of women into the medical profession is known, but the reasons for it and that the opposition was never absolute but much more a matter of the right timing and conditions are not known. Nightingale had a poor opinion of the medical profession and sought a *different* role for women as nurses and midwives. That she succeeded in opening up professional work for women as nurses is of course recognized and applauded. But her pioneering practical work for women on childbirth mortality, *Introductory Notes on Lying-in Institutions,* is still scarcely known. Also unfamiliar are her remarkably liberal views on prostitution and the regulation of sexually transmitted diseases—with her total rejection of a double standard and her radical views on gender roles. Altogether, on the status of women, Nightingale appears in the literature in a much less favourable light than she deserves, given her actual contributions.

Nightingale was on the nursing pedestal for decades, often without being taken seriously as a theorist. Generations of nurses received pins with a lamp on them (although not the same as carried by the "lady of the lamp" in the Crimea) at their graduation, but rarely, then or now, has either her *theory of nursing* or the importance of having a clear theoretical basis where none existed before been taught. Nursing professors are now prominent in the "trash Nightingale" movement, followed by Anglican clergy.

Those who denigrate Nightingale have been, in the opinion of the editors of this *Collected Works,* ill-informed. We, too, have had enough of the stereotyped heroine, and we want her now to be understood in all her complexity. Since a collected works tells all, warts, errors of judgment and ill temper will be evident. Overwhelmingly, however, the volumes to follow will portray a woman of extraordinary intellect, utter dedication to her calling, a prodigious appetite for work and touching human qualities, especially fierce loyalty to her co-workers. The spirituality that underlay all her intellectual and practical work will be apparent from beginning to end.

These then are the considerations that led to the project of a collected works. Here the intent is to present Nightingale as a scholar, theorist, intellectual, an original thinker and practical reformer in a diverse range of subjects. This full edition of her work will introduce readers for the first time to the wide scope and significance of her writing: a theory of social organization, theory of the state (including a significant role for government in the provision of services), the family, applied statistics, the role of empire (notably on Britain's relations with India), public administration, her theology and spirituality (including translations of the medieval mystics as well as her own visions), comparative religion, sociology of knowledge, biblical commentary, critique of religious institutions, public health (especially the role of the environment and health promotion), the foundation of the nursing profession and its relations with the medical profession, gender roles and the status of women.

Nightingale's ideas might have more appeal now in the third millennium than in her own day. Certainly her more holistic approach to health care and emphasis on environmental factors and nutrition are popular now. Her highly positive conceptualization of human life will resonate with the present age, where it offended the dour hellfire and damnation adherents of her own. Her unorthodox religious views would offend few people now while her spirituality, nourished from diverse sources and not tied to any one religious institution, would attract rather than appear heretical. The fact that she gave up church attendance in her early thirties would intrigue now rather than scandalize. For today's Christian feminists Nightingale is a great source, fully believing as she did in the equal right of women to develop themselves, their lives and careers. Liberation theologians and Christian socialists, now in a political climate of cutbacks of the welfare state, may be interested in her early vision of public health care and her work to advance it. Experts on India will find a rich trove of unpublished as well as now-hard-to-obtain published material. Although she never visited India, Nightingale became so immersed in Indian material, and such an advocate of Indian causes, that Indian nationalists appreciated her as a model. She was mentor to Gopal Krishna Gokhale, Gandhi's mentor. Her *systemic* approach, the integration of physical, geographical factors with the social—land tenure, taxation, government institution—is as appropriate now as it was when she developed it.

Nightingale might even be a more congenial model for social scientists today than in her own time. Her hard-line quantitative approach will please some and displease others, as in the past. So will her insistence on knowledge for application. Yet her criticism of positivism as being too embedded in the seen, material world will cheer those who seek a greater role for *values* in social science without giving up on the principles of scientific method. Nightingale herself always maintained her commitment to values, religious values at that, while conducting, in some cases pioneering, practical empirical research.

Throughout, Nightingale's theoretical work was integrated with practical application, consistent with the Enlightenment tradition. (The very term "social science" originated in the French Revolution, to describe the intellectual foundation needed for the "social art" that would produce a better society.) Nightingale was acutely aware that knowledge did not apply itself, that the right recommendations from a royal commission would be useless without an implementation policy and a media strategy to promote it. Thus she, with her team of collaborators, always worked out a strategy for application along with the substantive conclusions.

Nightingale herself was a formidable political actor, although she confined her role to the backroom. She *never* spoke in public although she wrote numerous letters to the editor, feature articles for newspapers and scholarly articles for journals. Later in life she wrote letters of endorsement for (a very select list) of political candidates (reproduced in *Society and Politics*). She knew how to threaten a recalcitrant minister or government official with bad publicity, knew the circulation of the various news and opinion outlets and governed her choices accordingly. Early in her reform career she herself briefed witnesses for her royal commissions. She understood the important role of public servants, variously recruiting them to her causes or working out ways to outmanoeuvre them. With her team, she agonized over the appointment of the right people for the royal commission or government department in question. She drafted terms of reference herself to make sure that they would be adequate. The Nightingale method will become clear in the material to come, as correspondence, draft policies and memoranda are presented along with the published political work. The introductions and annotations will show how skillfully she interwove analysis and application.

The very backward state of medicine as a whole, as well as nursing, prevailing in Nightingale's time must be understood as context. Medical doctors were educated, respectable men when there were very few trained nurses at all, and most were disreputable, ill paid and often drunk. Yet very little was known of the causes of most diseases and treatment was limited accordingly. For cancer there was nothing but surgical removal of a, generally well-advanced, tumour. Chloroform was first used as an anaesthetic only in 1847. Leeches were still used to balance the humours (see early correspondence by Nightingale for references). Water cures were prescribed; indeed both Nightingale and her father took several. Epidemics of cholera (1831-32, 1848-49, 1854, 1863), typhus and smallpox (1847) killed large numbers and threatened many more. The fact that cholera was spread by water was only published in 1849 by John Snow, whose map in the 1854 cholera epidemic located the infamous pump at Broad Street as a major source. As will be noted later in discussing Nightingale's approach to health care, the great advances in medical science, such as the discovery of specific bacilli, postdate her own writing and practice.

Thematic Organization

Nightingale's writing covers such a range of topics, with likely quite different readers in the different areas, that the decision was made early on to organize the *Collected Works* thematically rather than by the usual classification by type of work (books, essays, letters) in chronological order. Chronological publication of letters would have resulted in unwieldy volumes, for Nightingale kept up work on most of her great range of topics in most years. The result is that some letters have to be split between volumes, but this seemed to be a reasonable price to pay to have coherent volumes with thorough annotations on the people and events pertaining to them. All the letters can be consulted exactly as they were written in the electronic text.

All of Nightingale's theoretical and practical work was informed by a very particular, even singular, religious faith. This is true of her calling to be a nurse, her heading the nursing team in the Crimean War and all her subsequent years of work to reorganize society. Accordingly, it is no coincidence that the first substantive section of this *Collected Works* presents her spirituality and theological views, beginning (in *Spiritual Journey*) with her biblical annotations, sermons and deeply personal reflections. *Theology* presents her more academic analyses, essays, correspondence, her recommendations for a children's edition of the Bible and some excerpts from her reading notes. *Mysticism and Eastern Religions* gives Nightingale's comments on and translations of the medieval mystics, her *Letters from Egypt*, correspondence and notes on Eastern religions and other religious writing.

The only area of Nightingale's work which did not see successful publication, incidentally, was her religious writing, and this was not for lack of trying. As with the rest of her material, Nightingale sought practical influence; her *Suggestions for Thought* was intended to provide a reasonable and practical faith to the working classes of her own country and time. She hoped to publish her translations of and introductions to the medieval mystics, with her own practical exhortation on the subject: spirituality to nourish the active life of social and political reform. In fact all she published on the subject of religion were two rather abstruse essays. Religious thinking and imagery pervade her writing on all subjects—social science, nursing (especially her letters to student nurses) and social reform.

Society and Politics relates Nightingale's work in these two areas, including such topics as society, government, elections and political parties, empire, family, status of women and gender roles. Here we present substantial unpublished writing as well as papers presented to social science and statistical congresses and journals. The relationship between this material on social science and her religious philosophy will be evident. Similarly the material giving her views on the role of government will provide context for the material to follow on the provision of health care services more particularly. Her expertise on Plato (427-347 BCE) appears here in her extensive comments at the request of her friend, Benjamin Jowett (1817-93), on the introductions to his translations of the *Dialogues of Plato* (he took most of her advice in revising for a second edition). Her comments on major philosophers, on natural science and literature appear here also. This includes notes on classical writers, Shakespeare and on to contemporary novelists and poets.

Public Health Care presents Nightingale's broad, holistic conceptualization of a public health care system, according a powerful role to health promotion and preventive medicine and giving full scope to such socio-economic factors as occupation and housing. The volume begins with her *Notes on Nursing for the Labouring Classes*, 1861, in effect the second edition of *Notes on Nursing*, now with simpler language and a new chapter, "Minding Baby." It covers the introduction of professional nursing into workhouse infirmaries, a crucial and difficult step in the development of public health care. Nightingale's insistence on incorporating an adequate statistical base into the system will be shown. This requirement included specific roles for government, from international co-operation on statistical gathering to the distinct duties of local government.

Nightingale's pioneering work on maternal mortality in childbirth will be presented in *Women* (with sections on women in medicine, midwifery and the regulation of prostitution). The choice between women in medicine and in nursing will be related in this volume. A substantial section gives her correspondence with a wide range of women, family, friends and collaborators. There will be much to upset the common portrayal of Nightingale as "anti-woman."

Her extensive pre-Crimea travels in Europe appear, along with later notes and observations on European politics, in *European Travels.* While Nightingale's letters from a trip to Rome in 1847-48 have been published,[9] those from an earlier trip, later travels in Greece, and very interesting material on northern Europe (notably her visits to Kaiserswerth and other Protestant charitable institutions) have not been.

Two volumes on nursing present, along with the material for which she is well known, the training of nurses at St Thomas' Hospital, the Nightingale School, and the reform of nursing services for the Army, much that has not been published before. The period in which Nightingale lived was one of enormous progress in medical science. Since she was in contact with such a wide range of experts, the correspondence affords interesting glimpses into medical knowledge and practice, on subjects as diverse as germ theory versus miasma, cancer treatments, homeopathy and alternative medicine. The ward observations from her three months' stay at the hospital of the Deaconess Institution in Kaiserswerth, Germany, 1851, which have never been analyzed or commented on, will be published here for the first time. There will be a selection from the vast number of referrals to doctors and hospitals she made for people (family members, employees, former employees, villagers of the Nightingale properties, and even people who knocked on her door unannounced), which will become a rich source for specialists in the history of medicine. There is a full chronology of symptoms and treatment of her own illness.

Nightingale's vision of nursing as an independent, woman-led profession for women was quite different from any in operation anywhere. It would, whether or not women entered the medical profession, include midwifery (and even women's and children's diseases) and be professionally demanding. It would be well paid, at least at the upper levels, with matrons or superintendents having administrative responsibility for the sizable female staffs of hospitals. Only nurses (women) would hire, fire and discipline nurses (women). The material on nursing will explore these themes of the development of the

---

9 Mary Keele, ed., *Florence Nightingale in Rome: Letters Written by Florence Nightingale in Rome in the Winter of 1847-1848.*

nursing profession and its relations with medicine. There is, moreover, much new material on Nightingale's views on women in medicine (discussed below). There is new material, drawing on many non-British archives, on the export of the Nightingale method around the world. The Australian material, notably, has never before been published.

Nightingale began to give advice on hospital plans soon after her return from the Crimean War. She was widely consulted on county hospitals, convalescent facilities and workhouse infirmaries, not only in her own country but around the world. She made donations to new hospitals contingent on their being of good design and kept in touch with the best experts. Her papers, later published together as *Notes on Hospitals*, and selections from this substantial correspondence appear in *Hospital Reform*.

Two volumes relate Nightingale's more than forty years' work on India. The well-being of the people of India, rather than the establishment of the profession of nursing, may be said to have been the greatest cause of her life. She took up the issue of public health in India as early as 1857; she was writing seriously on health promotion and famine prevention, agitating and encouraging Indian nationals to become "sanitarians" into the late 1890s. She could not understand why Lord Stanley (1826-93) would give up the India Office, which he had created, for the Foreign Office, which, for its greater prestige, most people would consider a *promotion*. "We are watching the birth of a new nationality in the oldest civilization in the world,"[10] she declared. Her expertise on India included, as well as public health and the prevention of disease, measures to prevent famine through better irrigation and transportation systems. Her writings include analysis of the role of local government, taxation, land tenure, education and caste system, religion and the status of women.

Nightingale brought to bear all her social-science skills and knowledge in her work on India: her gift for systemic thinking, her care to obtain the best knowledge possible on any issue before proceeding, her cultivation of experts and her vigorous writing. A letter of 1862 shows her regretting that she was "too old to learn Hindustani" (thanking her correspondent for five "precious" Hindustani books); she would "have thought nothing of it ten years ago."[11]

---

10 Typed copy of letter to William Wedderburn 27 November 1885, Add Mss 45807 f190.
11 Letter to Sir Charles Trevelyan 22 November 1862, Wellcome Ms 5482/48.

Nightingale was also caught up with the romance of the East. On reading the "young Bartle Frere"[12] she remarked that "I always feel like a galley slave dreaming of heaven when I read letters which carry one into the East." She was bemused by cultural misunderstandings between the British and Indians, remarking in the same letter that she had received a letter "from a Hindu who is coming to England as an 'articled clerk,' asking me 'to be his mother'!!"[13]

Various experts in her day as well as now argue that Nightingale was wrong on particular points about India, from her insistence on open windows in excessive heat there to her advocacy of major irrigation projects. Generally speaking, however, her analyses have survived the test of time and some, like her early warnings about the perils of deforestation,[14] seem only more remarkable with the benefit of hindsight. She was exceptional for her time in supporting Indian nationalists, indeed breaking with British experts on India who did not. The material to be published in the India volumes includes a substantial number of previously published, but difficult to obtain, essays and letters to the editor as well as her material for the Royal Commission on the Sanitary State of the Army in India and a major, strongly worded, unpublished paper on the injustices of the land tenure system ("zemindary system"), from which Nightingale published parts. There is also a vast correspondence with viceroys, governors and experts on India, almost none of which has been published before. Moreover, Indian issues appear often in Nightingale's private journal notes (and prayers), and in correspondence with other people on other subjects. These have been extracted for incorporation here and show the depth of her commitment to working for reform in India.

Two volumes relate Nightingale's work on war and the military, beginning with the Crimean War and her insistence on Britain's learning from it so that its horrors would not be repeated, the subject of her first royal commission. The second war volume then moves on to her work on other wars (British incursions in China, the American Civil War, Franco-Prussian War, the Egyptian and Sudan campaigns and the Zulu War). Nightingale's role in the foundation of the Red Cross will be related in this volume, along with her critical view of its emphasis on voluntary efforts and its potential, consequently, "to

---

12 Sir Henry Bartle Frere (1815-84), Governor of Bombay.
13 Letter to Harry Verney 14 March 1873, Wellcome (Claydon copy) Ms 9006/30.
14 Nightingale, "A Missionary Health Office in India," in *Good Words* Pt 2:638.

make war cheap." Nightingale's more general views of war and its causes, particularly the role of militarism, are also included here.

Electronic and Print Publication

Publication will be comprehensive in electronic form, that is, all published and unpublished works will be included. The first treatment of manuscript texts is called "I-texts," or texts input to follow as closely as possible the original writing. Thus all abbreviations are kept as they were, as are aberrant punctuation and spelling, enabling those who machine search this body of material by subject of interest to know that they are reading exactly what Nightingale (or her correspondent) said. Faithful reproduction of the original texts permits considerable subsequent latitude in editing. The edited texts have modern spellings and punctuation and have been made as accessible as possible.

Nightingale collections include substantial amounts of correspondence *to* as well as by her. The policy of the *Collected Works* project is to include selected letters from her correspondents. Electronic publication will permit scholars for the first time ever to consult the entire Nightingale oeuvre and to search throughout it for material in their own areas of expertise.

The scale of the *Collected Works* is something to ponder, roughly 15,000 extant letters in more than 150 archives and private collections worldwide. The Nightingale Collection is one of the largest single collections at the British Library. There are also substantial collections in other British archives and libraries, notably the Wellcome Trust for the History of Medicine (formerly the Wellcome Institute for the History of Medicine), with copies of the massive (and still very inaccessible) private collection at Claydon House and the London Metropolitan Archives (formerly the Greater London Record Office). Many city and county archives have substantial collections and there are numerous university, college and hospital collections (a complete list appears in Appendix E). Significant holdings exist in the United States and Canada as well as some material in Europe (notably at Kaiserswerth), Ireland, New Zealand, Australia, India, Japan and South Africa. Great efforts have been made to find and publish material still in small private collections.

Each of the various volumes in the *Collected Works* will begin with a substantial introduction by the volume editor. This will be followed by completed, mainly published, works, each text thoroughly edited and annotated. Finally unpublished notes, draft essays and correspondence relating to the subject matter in question will be presented, again with annotations.

This introduction to the *Collected Works of Florence Nightingale* cannot, of course, contain a full biography, but only an outline of the significant events in her life. Space limitations permit only brief accounts of events and issues and even briefer introductions to major collaborators and other participants. The editorial introductions in each volume will provide historical context and fuller information on collaborators and other participants in the events in question. As well, a full chronology of events, publications and unpublished correspondence will be provided in the electronic edition, which will enable scholars to pursue their particular interests in the material.

I here wish to acknowledge my considerable reliance on what is still the best biography of Nightingale, Edward Cook's two-volume *Life of Florence Nightingale*, 1913, commissioned by the family shortly after her death, and for which Cook was paid £1000.[15] It is a "commissioned biography," maintains a polite tone and avoids mention of such indelicate matters as the perennial money problems of the Verneys. Some strains within the Nightingale family are recognized but others not, notably the exclusion of W.E. Nightingale's parents from the wedding ceremony and William Shore's rejection of Benjamin Smith as a husband for "Aunt Mai." Neither Cook nor any later biographers mention the scandal of Harry Verney's son Edmund, then an MP, later the third baronet, who served a year in prison for attempting to procure a minor for immoral purposes, although Nightingale played a significant role in effecting reconciliation between father and son.

Cook's *Life* yet remains the most comprehensive, dealing with everything from spirituality to politics. It gives by far the most excerpts of her own material, and in my view its judgments are sound as far as they go. (There are some, unimportant, errors in dating and a few other lapses, which will be noted where they are pertinent.) Nearly a century later, and with more material available, there is little with which I disagree. The Cook *Life*, however, is seldom cited here, for any sources to which it led me have been used directly. I also brought in more material than Cook or later biographers had on early family origins (Shores, Smiths and Nightingales). I occasionally used Cecil

---

15 Edward T. Cook, *Life of Florence Nightingale*; there is also a one-volume abridged edition, 1914.

Woodham-Smith's award-winning biography, *Florence Nightingale*, first published in 1950 and reprinted in 1986, although it contains numerous and sometimes flagrant errors. Other biographies are listed in the full electronic bibliography.

After the overview of Nightingale's life there will be an introduction to the major *themes* or *causes* on which Nightingale worked, her "business," as she called it, recalling Jesus' "I must be about my Father's business" of Luke 2:49. This will serve also to lead into the substance of the *Collected Works* proper.

The Dramatis Personae (see p ix above) lists the main family members to appear in this volume. See Appendix A (below) for biographical sketches of most of them and of the Nightingale, Shore and Smith families generally. Family relations are complicated by the fact that Nightingale's Aunt Mai (her father's sister) married her mother's brother, Uncle Sam, the two becoming the "Shore Smiths." Their son, William Shore Smith, Nightingale's (double) cousin, is normally called "Shore." The heir to the Nightingale fortune, he and his wife, Louisa, later took the name "Shore Nightingale" but continue to be referred to here by their old name, as Nightingale did. Other aunts, uncles, cousins, honorary nieces, nephews, great nieces and great nephews, etc. are identified as they appear. Subsequent volumes will similarly have a Dramatis Personae and biographical sketches on significant collaborators in their respective areas.

An Outline of Florence Nightingale's Life

Nightingale's parents were married on 1 June 1818 by an evangelical priest, Dr William Dealtrey,[1] rector of the parish church of Clapham Common, at St Margaret's Church, Westminster (next door to Westminster Abbey), then and now a favourite venue for fashionable weddings. They honeymooned at the Smiths' estate, Parndon Hall, Essex. There was evidently some unpleasantness between the families, for the groom's parents were not invited to the wedding. WEN's father, William Shore, went to London hoping to see the couple the day after the wedding, but they had already left on their honeymoon. He wrote his son: "Don't you think your mother and I ought to have been at the wedding? I have heard it strongly insisted on by people who are correct judges."[2] The young couple left soon after on a lengthy European trip. Their first daughter, Frances Parthenope, was born in Naples in 1819 and named after the Greek name of that city.

Florence Nightingale was born 12 May 1820 in Florence, Italy, and also named after the city of her birth. The large and elegant house the Nightingales rented there, Villa Colombaia (at via Santa Maria a Marignolle 2), is now a school (Beata Maria de Mattias) and convent of the Adoratrici del Sangue de Christo (Adorers of the Precious Blood of Christ). It is situated near the Porta Romana, on a hill where the air is healthier than in the city proper. There is a splendid park and view of the Duomo and Allee of the Boboli Gardens. The Nightingale family was English gentry taking a leisurely continental tour; they stayed at Villa Colombaia nearly three years. The young Florence was nursed there by a wet nurse, Umiliana Pistelli. A three-clause contract

---

1 Letter to Frances Nightingale 31 August 1864, Wellcome (Claydon copy) Ms 9001/57.
2 Letter to W.E. Nightingale 1 June 1818, Claydon House Bundle 12.

was signed 1 July 1820 by W.E. Nightingale for her services.[3] Nightingale was baptized by Dr Trevor, Prebendary of Chester on 4 July 1820 (Cook, *Life* 1:4).

When Nightingale's parents brought their two children home from Florence to Derbyshire they had the charming family house, Lea Hall,[4] replaced by a larger establishment, Lea Hurst, now a residence for the aged.[5] In 1825 Nightingale's father purchased Embley Park, on the edge of the New Forest, Hampshire, now a grammar school. Hence from when Nightingale was five the family had two chief homes: Lea Hurst from July to October, Embley for most of the year; some time was also spent in rented quarters in London. W.E. Nightingale had inherited a sizable fortune and the family lived in great luxury. Socially they were upwardly mobile on both sides, the money having been made in the early eighteenth century in lead mining, quarrying and smelting.

Their father supervised the two daughters' exceptional education. While there was a governess, notably for the early years, he himself provided much of the later instruction. The curriculum included modern languages (French, German and Italian), classical languages (Latin and Greek), mathematics and constitutional history as well as the more conventional grammar, composition, English literature and music. Florence Nightingale was able to translate Homer by age sixteen. Indeed throughout her life she repeatedly compared Greek wars with those in which she was involved, for example Thermopylae (in the Greek wars against the Persians) with Balaclava in the Crimean War. A letter to her sister describes the nurses as the Thermopylae of "this desperate struggle," while Lord Raglan,[6] cold and famine were the "Persians, our own destroyers."[7] She was familiar with the classics of her own language, read contemporary novels and kept up with the latest poets.

There were numerous relatives on both sides and cousins visited for weeks at a time. Outings, picnics, musical performances and amateur theatre were enjoyed (the young Florence was apparently a bossy

---

3 Claydon House Bundle 20.
4 Norman Keen, *Florence Nightingale*.
5 Lea Hurst RSAS AgeCare.
6 Lord Raglan (1788-1855), Commander-in-Chief of the British forces in Crimea.
7 Letter to Parthenope Nightingale 8 March 1855, Wellcome (Claydon copy) Ms 8995/9.

stage manager for Shakespeare's *Merchant of Venice*) (see p 463 below). When Embley was undergoing a major renovation in 1837-39 the family took another extended, eighteen-month continental tour to France, Italy, Germany and Switzerland. The stay in Florence included lessons in Italian, "perspective," piano and singing. The family attended balls at the Duke of Tuscany's; the teenaged Florence loved to dance. She went to the opera three times a week and would have gone every night; Mozart was her favourite composer. The extensive notes and letters from her travels, with trips in her young womanhood to Ireland, Scotland and northern England, are reported in *European Travels*.

In Geneva the tone changed completely as the family met Italian political refugees (much of Italy was then under Austrian rule and the resistance had begun). The contrast between the luxury and pleasure of Florence, which had its freedom, and the rest of the occupied country, came home to her. In Geneva she met refugees suffering poverty for their beliefs. Sismondi,[8] whose *History of the Italian Republics* she knew, took her on long walks during which they discussed politics and economics. The family returned to England in 1839 and the two sisters were formally presented at court in May. Normal life resumed, but Florence Nightingale had had her first taste of political struggle and would be a partisan of independence movements thereafter.

Her interest in nursing emerged in early childhood. She nursed her dolls and accompanied her mother on visits to the sick poor. While still a girl she began to nurse sick relatives, servants and villagers. In 1845 she sought to learn nursing at nearby Salisbury Hospital, which skills she could then apply back home in her village work. Her mother and sister were vehemently opposed to this project.[9] Nursing was then an unskilled occupation, poorly paid and taken up mainly by working-class women who had few other job opportunities. The stereotype has them drinking too much and using coarse language, although Nightingale herself refuted the latter, but not the former: her mother was afraid of her hearing "indecencies," but "I had heard more indecencies from girls [who are] the daughters of her evangelical friends when I had to do hostess in the nursery than I ever

---

8 Jean-Charles Simonde de Sismondi (1773-1842).
9 See Cecil Woodham-Smith, *Florence Nightingale* 74-116, for detailed coverage of the histrionics and the protracted interventions required by sympathetic relatives and friends before Nightingale was permitted to nurse.

did in all my hospital life."[10] The years of lost opportunity continued to rankle in old age. As late as 1900 she recorded that she "never had a happy moment till I went into hospital life" and then "never had an unhappy moment" (f207).

Nightingale's "call to service" is described in detail in the introduction to *Spiritual Journey*. Briefly, she experienced a "call" at age sixteen, although the precise nature of the service to which she was called was not then clear. She in time identified it as nursing, but was frustrated for over sixteen years by her family's refusal to permit her even to study nursing, let alone work at it. In the meantime she was permitted to travel, and she took advantage of those trips to visit hospitals and to meet and question medical experts and nurses (mainly religious nursing sisters). In 1852, two years before the Crimean War, she also experienced a call to be "a saviour."

If the 1837-39 travels sparked Nightingale's political interests, another stay in Rome in 1847-48, and travels in Greece and Egypt in 1849-50 (all reported in *European Travels*), were formative for her intellectual development. Both were taken with family friends, Charles and Selina Bracebridge, an older, childless couple, who later accompanied her to Scutari in the Crimean War. In Rome Nightingale not only visited art museums and churches, she did detailed sketches that developed skills she later applied to hospital architecture. She was especially moved by the beauty of the Sistine Chapel, at a time when she herself was considering conversion to Roman Catholicism. Seeing it, she recounted to her sister, was like seeing heaven. This was a dramatic time for the Italian Risorgimento, or national independence movement. Nightingale attended a great rally in the Roman Colosseum; she cheered the hoisting of the tricolour flag at the Capitol. Moved by the struggles of the Italian cities for liberty she praised Pius IX (1792-1878) for giving up the papacy's temporal powers.

Nightingale had the knack of being in the place of action at the right time. She arrived in Paris shortly after Louis Philippe was sent into exile in 1848. She was in Athens when Britain took over Corfu from Venetian administration in 1850.

Nightingale's trip to Egypt is discussed fully in the introduction to her theology and spirituality in *Spiritual Journey*, where its significance in her own spiritual development and comparative religion is analyzed. At the end of this trip Nightingale succeeded in spending two

---

10 Note c1901, ADD Mss 45844 f208.

weeks at the Deaconess Institution[11] at Kaiserswerth, near Düsseldorf, which gave her a start in realizing her nursing vocation. She returned for three months in 1851. She herself never described the experience as good *training*, and even acknowledged how rudimentary the nursing standards were. But the atmosphere was serious and devout and she learned discipline and order in a health care environment that was excellent for its day, if unsatisfactory by later standards. None of the nurses there were gentlewomen and some were of peasant background, which firmed up her meritocratic inclinations.

Faith and Church

Florence Nightingale was raised in the Church of England; she was baptized while an infant in Florence, and attended church (or chapel) regularly as a child. The family had been Unitarian on both sides and some relatives maintained that adherence; but it seems that neither of her parents did after their marriage in the Church of England. Her vocation for nursing was experienced literally as a voice. This "call to service" 5 February 1837 was preceded by an experience of "conversion" in 1836, prompted by reading Jacob Abbott's *Corner-stone*.[12]

The next two volumes in this series report Nightingale's spirituality and theology, for that is key to understanding all her work as a nurse, social researcher (discovering God's laws) and reformer (acting on that knowledge). Thus *Spiritual Journey*, as well as giving a detailed overview of her spiritual journey, reports her biblical annotations (publication for the first time), sermons (never given in her lifetime) and private journal notes (only a small fraction of which have appeared before in biographies). *Theology* reports, along with her two published essays, her unpublished essays on religion, further journal notes and correspondence.

That Nightingale's beliefs were heterodox is apparent wherever they appear. Yet Nightingale remained in the Church of England faute de mieux. As a young woman she considered conversion to Roman Catholi-

---

11 The Deaconess Institution was founded by Pastor Theodor Fliedner (1800-64) and his first wife, Friederike (1800-42), in 1836. By Nightingale's time the co-leader was Fliedner's second wife, Caroline (1811-92). The institution revived a tradition of women's service in the church dating back to biblical times.

12 The only reference to the conversion occurs late in life in a letter to Maude Verney 10 December 1895, ADD Mss 68888 f138.

cism, but did not convert. Indeed she became increasingly critical of Catholicism over the years, identifying as a liberal, broad church member of the Church of England, and, more significantly, simply as a (Protestant) Christian. She drew on a wide range of sources for spiritual nourishment, including Roman Catholic (from the Church Fathers through the medieval mystics to the French, liberal Dominicans of her own age). Protestant sources also range widely, from the German critical, historical school, Puritans, the seventeenth-century "metaphysical" poets, to contemporary sermons. Influences can be seen that are clearly Lutheran (from her stay at the Deaconess Institution at Kaiserswerth) and Wesleyan (from her own chapel attendance early in life, and an enduring respect for reformer John Wesley [1703-91]), as well as her own Church of England.

Early Writing: *Suggestions for Thought* (1852-60)

The first writing Nightingale ever published, and that anonymously, was a short essay, "The Institution of Kaiserswerth" (1851), after her first visit there in 1850 (see *European Travels*). Her first substantial writing dates from 1852, a sixty-five-page draft of *Suggestions for Thought*, which she expanded into an 829-page, three-volume work in the late 1850s, and had printed in 1860 for circulation to a small group of men, but which she never published.[13] It is published in full in the *Collected Works* for the first time. That this was missionary outreach to the unchurched working class can be seen in the succession of titles she used: *To the Artizans of England* for the first draft, the full *Suggestions for Thought to the Searchers after Truth among the Artizans of England* for the first volume of the three-volume set, falling off to *Suggestions for Thought to the Searchers after Religious Truth* for the second and third volumes.

At the very least Nightingale had reason not to publish *Suggestions for Thought* for the brutally critical treatment of her family—it would have hurt them—and less harsh but decidedly unfavourable remarks about a book co-authored by Harriet Martineau (1802-76),[14] who was

---

13 Three very partial editions are available: Mary Poovey, ed., *Florence Nightingale: Cassandra and Other Selections from* Suggestions for Thought; Michael D. Calabria and Janet A. Macrae, eds., Suggestions for Thought *by Florence Nightingale*; Rosemary Hartil, ed., *Florence Nightingale: Letters and Reflections*.

14 Henry G. Atkinson and Harriet Martineau, *Letters on the Laws of Man's Nature and Development*.

then a valued partner in several causes. More fundamentally, *Suggestions for Thought* represents Nightingale's thoughts on religion when she was still developing them. The material reflects her approach to life before she had seen war or known illness. She is a confident, perhaps arrogant, analyst, much imbued with secular positivism as a philosophy, and hurting from the lack of serious roles for women in her church (that, of course, remained, but she found other outlets). The second and much longer draft dates from 1859, but still includes views she later abandoned.

Suggestions for Thought is here treated as a major source of Nightingale's early views on religion, philosophy and society, but one to be considered with great care. The first draft of *Suggestions for Thought*, which includes the highly autobiographical "Cassandra" (twenty-five pages), dates from the period of frustration and depression that immediately succeeded the Egyptian trip, when Nightingale was still forbidden to nurse. There is a fierce determinism in *Suggestions for Thought*, with Nightingale insisting on a doctrine of "necessity" too rigorous even for J.S. Mill (1806-73). Again, a simple look at her own life at the time serves to explain it, for, forbidden to nurse or prepare to, Nightingale's life was highly determined by forces beyond her control, the conventions of an upper-class Victorian family. Later she was able not only to shape her own life but to affect the lives of millions. Her views on determinism/necessity evolved accordingly.

The emotional, stream-of-consciousness "Cassandra" essay coincides with Nightingale's second "call," this time to be "a saviour," a term which also implies a *healer*. (The *Oxford English Dictionary* gives as its first definition of healer "one who heals or saves; in early use, Saviour.") Yet Nightingale was still not able to realize her first calling. She was suffering from her family's angry reaction to the Kaiserswerth visit, for which she had to compensate by indulging her sister's whims. The Cassandra of her title was a figure in Greek mythology, the daughter of Priam, King of Troy, who was correct in her unhappy prophecy and accordingly martyred. The essay is an impassioned lament for the narrowness of women's lives, interspersed with observations on the opportunities men enjoy. Christian feminist insights are juxtaposed with gender role analysis.

> "[Men] are irritated with women for not being happy. They take it as a personal offence. To God alone may women complain without insulting Him!"[15]

Women were forced to become hypocritical. Yet, in Nightingale's view, "suffering" would be better than "indifferentism," *pain* better than *paralysis*. Better to die struggling in the breakers seeking a new world than to stand idly on the shore. Yet the actual life of a woman of Nightingale's genteel class was spent not on "high ideas and generous feelings" but in sympathy given and received for a dinner, a piece of furniture, a house built in a well-laid-out garden and occasional acts of charity, such as taking soup to the poor. She suggested that "the next Christ will perhaps be a female Christ," immediately to ask, rhetorically: "But do we see one woman who looks like a female Christ? Or even like 'the messenger before her face,' to go before her and prepare the hearts and minds for her?"[16] The essay opened with a paraphrase on John the Baptist, "the voice of one crying in the crowd." She described, using the third person, her own plight as "one alone, awake and prematurely alive" to the "evil and suffering" unseen by the rest of the race. Such a one "has rejected the companionship of the race, unlinked to any human being. Such a one sees the evil they do not see, and yet has no power to discover the remedy for it" (2:374).

There is no doubt that Nightingale was referring to her own self and family when she contrasted the imitation of Christ permitted in "little trifling formal things" like foot washing or saying the Lord's Prayer with the utter failure to follow him seriously. There is much discussion of the family and thoroughly transparent biblical references to "who is my father and mother and . . . ?" (2:409). The reasons Nightingale did not publish the work are obvious; it was not published until 1928, as an appendix to Ray Strachey's classic on the English suffrage movement.[17] Only recently has it begun to be treated as a classic in the history of the women's movement.

---

15 *Suggestions for Thought* 2:374.
16 *Suggestions for Thought* 2:408.
17 Ray Strachey, *"The Cause." A Short History of the Women's Movement in Great Britain* 395-418. Now available also in Myra Stark, ed., *Cassandra*.

Celibacy and Suitors

Nightingale's decision not to marry was a logical consequence of the call to service. At that time of course there were no effective means of contraception, so that the very life and health of a wife were entirely subject to forces beyond her control. Wives were legally obliged to obey their husbands, whose conjugal rights were unlimited. Nightingale, however, was apparently heterosexual and seems to have regretted that her life would be without a husband and physical love. She declined her first proposal, from her cousin, George Henry Nicholson (who died in 1851), at least for the reason that he was a first cousin. This caused a rift in the family, for the Nicholsons believed that she had "led him on." Correspondence later in this volume, however, will show nothing more than a friendly relationship. Another tale of unrequited love also involves a cousin, William Shore, who moved to the United States as a "remittance man."[18]

There is a legend that Nightingale declined another "cousin," John Smithurst (1802-67), encouraging him to become a missionary in Canada since they could not marry. There is no evidence for this one way or the other, nor any evidence that they were cousins (if so it must have been through an illegitimate relationship). The Smithurst family lived very close to Lea Hurst and Nightingale must have known them. John Smithurst was clerk of the closest Church of England church to Lea Hurst, St John the Baptist, at Dethick, from 1819 to 1831. He worked as a warehouseman and built houses before becoming a missionary to the Red River Settlement, where he served with distinction between 1839 and 1851.[19]

---

18 Eric R. Griffin, "Victims of Fiction: Research Notes on 'The Love Story of Florence Nightingale and John Smithurst.' "

19 Smithurst notably translated the communion service and was the mentor to the first aboriginal priest in the Anglican Church of Canada, Henry Budd. From 1852 Smithurst was rector in St John's Anglican Church, Elora, Ontario, where there are stained glass windows of him and Nightingale, and a communion service said to have been given by Nightingale to him. On Smithurst's life see T.C.B. Boon, "John Smithurst," *Church Messenger* [n.d.] 16, Manitoba Provincial Archives PRL 84.3. The original records of his missionary work are at the Church Missionary Society Archives, Birmingham, copies at the Manitoba Provincial Archives, Winnipeg. On the legend see the original article by G.H. Gunn, "The Love Story of Florence Nightingale and John Smithurst," *Toronto Sunday World* 16 October 1921, and John R. Connon, "When Florence Nightingale's Lover Lived and

The available information shows that Smithurst was a fine missionary and a "manly man," characteristics Nightingale would have greatly admired. His politics were Tory, however, which would have counted against him. The age difference also poses difficulties, for he was eighteen years older than Nightingale, who was only sixteen when the supposed heart-to-heart conversation took place which sent him off to the mission field. Moreover it predates her own "call to service" in 1837. Smithurst's case to the Church Missionary Society cites a calling experienced at a Wesleyan meeting the Monday before Easter, 1836,[20] the same year as Nightingale's conversion.

Nightingale's most suitable suitor was Richard Monckton Milnes (1809-85), poet, MP and philanthropist, later Lord Houghton. She refused him in 1849, when she was age twenty-nine, when he finally required a definite answer. The two remained friends and he served for years on the Nightingale Trust, as did his son on his death.

A passing remark to her mother in 1853 refers to "this man who wants to marry me," who knew only "as much of my views and feelings as I do of his," a sarcastic statement, for she "really did not know whether *he* was alive or his brother, and when he talked of his child, I did not know he had one" (see p 138 below). We do not know who this might be. Sir Harry Verney may have been a suitor in 1857, when he was widowed and approached her, as a Liberal MP, to discuss reform issues. Nightingale then introduced him to her sister and the two married in 1858. Nightingale biographer Woodham-Smith believed that Benjamin Jowett proposed to her, but this is doubted by Jowett's biographer, Faber.[21] The evidence, albeit second-hand, comes from a reputable source, Cornelia Sorabji (1867-1954), a former student of Jowett. In her book she said he confided this to her late in his life.[22] Nightingale to her cousin and friend, Hilary Bonham Carter, quoted Schiller, that she had loved and lived: "Ich habe geliebt und gelebt ... and I mourned my "habe" with silent tears the rest of the journey." It is not

Preached in Elora, Ont.," Manitoba Provincial Archives. For critical assessments see Griffin, "Victims of Fiction" 45-52; Virginia Wilson, "Evidence Won't Support Elora Church's Romantic Legend," *Guelph Mercury* 18 March 1988.

20 Excerpts from Church Missionary Society records, Manitoba Provincial Archives.

21 Geoffrey Faber, *Jowett: A Portrait with Background* 312; Woodham-Smith, *Florence Nightingale* 352.

22 Cornelia Sorabji, *India Calling: The Memories of Cornelia Sorabji* 32.

clear if this is a reference to Richard Monckton Milnes or someone else, for this letter seems to have been written in March 1847.[23]

There are joking references in correspondence to two other possible suitors. George Dawson (1821-76) was a Baptist minister, a popular lecturer and social activist in Birmingham. Nightingale and her mother possibly attended his lecture on Christianity and democracy in 1848, price threepence. He was described by her friends as her "futur."[24] One wonders if the two ever met and pondered what might have been (Dawson was then newly married). The question would hardly be asked except for the fact that he kept the letter Nightingale sent him ordering tickets for his lecture although she was not then at all famous.[25] Another clergyman, rector of a church in the East End of London was Rev William Warrington Quekett, who showed Nightingale how he worked his parish and schools for the poor. She described him as "the prince of angels," quipping that there was a Mrs Quekett: "How I hate her" (see p 312 below). Both these men would have been attractive to Nightingale, in the way that none of her other suitors were, in terms both of their social and religious ideals and actions.

At age thirty Nightingale recorded the recognition that *all* her suitors had married (although possibly two or more subsequently presented themselves). With the benefit of hindsight Nightingale much later said that not marrying was one decision she never regretted.[26] She described the problem of marriage as the narrowness of *family* life, explaining that a woman, even more than a man, must remain single if she has "a work of God to do in the world." God will find no woman able to be a help-*meet*, because her "*family life* is expressly fashioned to waste her time for any great object of God's."[27]

> "For joy that a *man* is born into the world," Christ says.[28] And that *is* a subject of joy. But a woman must be born into the *family*. If she were born into the *world*, that would be joy too. But what joy is there in her being born into the smallest of all possible spheres, which will exercise perhaps no single one of her faculties? (f15)

---

23 Letter to Hilary Bonham Carter [March 1847], Add Mss 45794 f117.
24 Letter to Parthenope Nightingale 6 October 1848, Wellcome (Claydon copy) Ms 8993/1.
25 Letter, Columbia University, Presbyterian Hospital School of Nursing C60.
26 See Elizabeth Abbott, *A History of Celibacy* 279-83.
27 Note, Add Mss 45843 f10.
28 John 16:21.

On her sister's marriage Nightingale considered that she had done well, on balance, but her words fall short of being a ringing endorsement. Remarking that her sister was:

> Very fond of Sir Harry Verney, which is the next best thing. He is old and rich, which is a disadvantage. He is active, has a will of his own and four children, ready-made, which is an advantage. Unmarried life, at least in our class, takes everything and gives nothing back to this poor earth. It owns no risk—it gives no pledge to life. So, on the whole, I think these reflections tend to approbation.[29]

First Work in Nursing: Harley Street (1853-54)

Nightingale made a visit to the Daughters (often called Sisters) of Charity of St-Vincent-de-Paul in Paris just prior to her taking up her first, and only civilian, appointment as a nurse in August 1853. The Kaiserswerth and Paris experiences led to this appointment as superintendent of the "Institution for Ill Gentlewomen," as she called it,[30] 1 Upper Harley Street.[31] Nightingale's father made the appointment possible by providing her with an annual income of £500, paid quarterly, in advance, thus permitting her to establish a separate residence. (The amount was raised on her sister's marriage in 1858, when her father undertook to pay all Nightingale's maintenance costs, so that the allowance could go entirely for her causes.) She herself received no salary, nor did she for her later work in Crimea, or anywhere else for that matter (she did make some money on book royalties).

Nightingale's friend Elizabeth Herbert (1822-1911) was on the management committee of the Institution for Ill Gentlewomen and supported her innovations in the only administrative experience Nightingale had before going to the Crimea. Nightingale learned fast and, while in the position only for slightly more than a year, was already looking for a greater challenge. She instituted practical reforms that made the work of the nurses physically easier. At the same time she raised the standards for care. The institution gave her her first experience of sectarian religious strife, the prelude to much worse in the Crimea. Also during this

---

29 Letter to Lady McNeill 17 July 1858, London Metropolitan Archives H1/ST/NC3/SU104.

30 Printed letterhead gives the name Establishment for Gentlewomen during Illness. Private Collection of Tyndale Bisco.

31 The location is now 73 Harley Street, where a plaque notes that Nightingale left for the Crimean War from it.

period there was a cholera outbreak in London. Nightingale nursed women patients at the Middlesex Hospital, notably "Soho outcasts."

The Crimean War (1854-56)

The Crimean War was fought between Russia and Turkey, with Britain, France and, later, Sardinians from the emerging Italian republic joining Turkey against Russia. British and French troops invaded the Crimea 14 September 1854 and the Battle of Alma was fought on 20 September. Wounded men from the Battle of Balaclava, a great but costly victory for the British, were arriving at the Scutari Barrack Hospital (across the strait from Constantinople) just as the Nightingale group did. The Crimean War was the first war for British troops other than colonial expeditions in forty years and the Army was ill-prepared. Large numbers died, although probably not more proportionately than in the Napoleonic Wars. This war, however, was the first one with specialized "war correspondents," with photographers as well as war artists. The London *Times* correspondent drew the unsavoury comparison of the lack of women nurses aiding British war efforts compared with their French allies and their Russian enemy. The French had fifty Sisters of Charity and the Russians, about whom less was known, also had nursing sisters. The War Office, in its preparations for the war, had considered sending women nurses but rejected this as radical. *Times* coverage asked why Britain had no Sisters of Charity. A wealthy, evangelical philanthropist, Lady Maria Forester (1819-94), asked Nightingale to lead a small group of nurses to the Crimea, and offered to supply funding for them. By coincidence Elizabeth Herbert, from whom Nightingale had to seek release from her appointment at Harley Street, was the wife of the Secretary of State at War, Sidney Herbert (1810-61), also Nightingale's friend from the Rome visit. Nightingale's letter to Mrs Herbert crossed with Sidney Herbert's official letter asking her to take a team of nurses to the war. Nightingale made her arrangements within days, her friends interviewing applicants while she organized supplies.

Although she was assured that the Army was well supplied, Nightingale took the precaution of acquiring food, medical supplies, linen, clothing and other basic items in Marseilles en route to Scutari. She often used her own money, which was sometimes reimbursed by the War Office; the *Times* collected £7000, which it put to her disposal. Nightingale's first appointment was at Scutari, in Turkey, some distance from the front; she only went to the Crimea itself some months later. She was, after much skirmishing with the War Office, given charge of nursing services in the hospitals in both places. On arrival in Scutari the nurses found the Army atrociously underequipped medically and lacking in all kinds of essentials, including food and bedding. The wounded were brought by ship from the battlefields in the Crimea, the journey itself taking days. The ships were also ill-equipped so that many men died during transport or on arrival. The barracks given the British by the Turkish government for their hospital in Scutari had been built over a huge sewer. There was no system of ventilation and the space available to each patient was one quarter the normal. At the General Hospital at Balaclava Nightingale reported killing a rat while caring for an ill nursing sister.[32]

Nightingale herself did heroic work; she knelt in the dirt and bound up the soldiers' wounds, nursed the ill (there were outbreaks of cholera and typhus) and assisted at amputations. At night she visited the wards, giving rise to the image of "the lady with the lamp." She provided clean bedding and clothing, good food (and brandy) to the sick and wounded. She wrote letters for the soldiers to their families and advised families of deaths. She instituted a banking system whereby the soldiers could send their earnings home to their families. She established the first healthy leisure outlets for ordinary soldiers, "reading rooms" with cards and magazines, when alcohol was otherwise the only option. She set up the "Inkermann Café," a coffee house for the soldiers. She enlisted the assistance of a priest and his wife to help the women camp followers, who were outside her jurisdiction.

Nightingale's nursing establishment began with the thirty-eight nurses who travelled together to Scutari. A further contingent of forty-seven arrived in December, sent without Nightingale's knowledge, which caused a row over her authority. Nightingale won and her authority was extended to nursing in the Crimea proper.

Some of the doctors never accepted the presence of Nightingale and her nurses; others soon learned that going to "the bird," as she was jokingly called, was the way to get things done. She had supplies that the Army either did not have, or did not know that it had because its record keeping was so bad. This would be the pattern throughout her long career of reorganizing society: there were supporters and

---

32 Letter to Parthenope Nightingale 2 June 1856, Wellcome (Claydon copy) Ms 8996/63.

collaborators, enemies and upholders of the status quo. The nurses themselves, at Nightingale's insistence, worked solely under the direction of the doctors, the only way to get the doctors' co-operation.

The Nightingale method eventually worked in that the sanitary reforms she instituted helped to lower the high mortality rate. Most men died from disease, not bullets, a point she and her team would stress in all their reform work after the war: 19,000 from illness (mainly infectious diseases), 4000 from wounds. Nightingale regarded the deaths from illness as unnecessary—anything above the "normal death rate" was. In the first months of the war Army losses were 60 percent. By the end, the mortality rate from illness was no greater than that of a comparable population in England, men in the industrial city of Manchester.

In his *Florence Nightingale: Avenging Angel*, Hugh Small argues that Nightingale was initially mistaken about the causes of the high mortality rate and that her superficial reforms (better diet, clean laundry, washing patients, etc.) were ineffective. It is a fact that the Scutari Barracks Hospital, where Nightingale was, had a considerably higher mortality rate than the hospitals in the Crimea. It remained high her first winter there, despite the institution of her better practices and the work of the nurses. The killer was infectious disease, the result of the hospital's location over running sewage and its terribly inadequate ventilation. Small further suggests, and marshals considerable evidence to support his interpretation, that Nightingale experienced guilt over this excessive mortality, even to the point of its causing her to have a nervous breakdown in the immediate post-Crimea period, when she had the opportunity to review the mortality statistics.[33]

Nightingale, of course, was not responsible for the decision to establish a military hospital at the Scutari Barracks. It had been taken earlier in the war, indeed by her friend Sidney Herbert, and locating a hospital there was not his only mistake. Nor was it her responsibility to report mortality data, analyze causes of death or institute appropriate reforms (she had neither the mandate nor the status to do any of these things). Yet she at least was capable of analyzing mortality statistics and she might well have felt guilty for not understanding earlier how much worse they were for her hospital than others.

Paradoxically, while Nightingale had originally gone to the Crimea to "emulate" the French Sisters of Charity, then considered the model, she came to consider their standards of nursing abominable.

---

33 Hugh Small, *Florence Nightingale: Avenging Angel*; see especially chapters 3-5.

The fifty French sisters were "semi-literate drudges" who shared "the insanitary habits of their patients." While the British mortality rates declined, "the death rates in the French hospitals continued high and finally topped the worst British rates."[34] From her initially high opinion of Catholic religious orders Nightingale would from then on be more critical, carefully distinguishing good intentions and willingness for self-sacrifice from actual good results.

Nightingale herself nearly died during the war. She came down with "Crimean fever," thought to be a form of typhus, from nursing ill soldiers; some of her nurses died of it. Nightingale of course recovered, but it is now suggested that she returned to England with chronic brucellosis, a subject to which we will return shortly.

A peace treaty was signed in Paris 30 March 1856 and Nightingale left Scutari for England 28 July. She sailed with her Aunt Mai Smith via Athens and Marseilles, declining the offer of a man-o'-war to bring her home. They stayed overnight in Paris and took a train to London. The incognito return shows her extreme abhorrence of personal publicity—she travelled as "Miss Smith" with her aunt. In London she called on the Sisters of Mercy with whom she had worked in Scutari and the Crimea, at their convent in Bermondsey. She then took the train to Derby and arrived on foot at Lea Hurst late on 7 August 1856.

Nightingale returned to England a national heroine. Her soldiers and their families would be ever grateful; her feats were widely reported in the press. A Nightingale Fund had been established while she was in the East; it began operations with £45,000 (worth $3 million U.S. today). A trust was established to run it, Nightingale eventually settling on two projects: the establishment of the first non-sectarian training school for nurses, at St Thomas' Hospital, and a "lying-in institution" for the training of midwives, affiliated with King's College Hospital. Not many doctors from Crimea and Scutari subscribed to the fund, but the troops and ordinary citizens did. A concert given by the popular singer Jenny Lind (1820-87) raised £2000.[35] Nightingale was inundated with "begging letters," which her sister answered on her behalf. Yet she never received a request for money from a soldier. A celebrity, she declined the numerous invitations of the rich, noble and famous.

---

34 F.B. Smith, *Florence Nightingale: Reputation and Power* 67. Smith, who found so much to deprecate in Nightingale's personality and working style, nonetheless gave her full marks for her effective contribution.

35 Cook, *Life* 1:273. See a letter/copy by Nightingale to her from Balaclava, 19 April 1856, Wellcome (Claydon copy) Ms 8996/49.

She decided to ask for nothing for herself although some friends thought that this was the time to line up a good nursing appointment. This decision to forego anything for herself gave her great power in the negotiations to follow, when she asked for a royal commission to investigate the sanitary condition of the British Army in the East.

First Royal Commission, on the Army (1856-59)

Nightingale was the key player on all the stages of the royal commission from its establishment, choice of membership and terms of reference, through the conduct of its work. She undertook such particular tasks as rehearsing intervenors, largely got the recommendations she and her team sought and then went on to work on their implementation. The record of achievement is quite astounding and of interest as well for the modus operandi developed by the Nightingale team, which was then used in all their subsequent reform activities. The "inner Cabinet" or "little War Office" met at Nightingale's rented rooms in Burlington Street, chosen for their proximity to the War Office. The initial group consisted of Sidney Herbert, Dr John Sutherland (1808-91), Sir John McNeill (1797-1883), Sir James Clark (1788-1870), Colonel Alexander Tulloch (1803-64), Colonel John Henry Lefroy (1817-90) and Dr William Farr (1807-83).

It was agreed that the Queen's expected invitation to Balmoral Castle would be the opportunity for Nightingale to persuade her and the Prince Consort to press for a royal commission. The team also briefed Nightingale on the best method to convince Lord Panmure (1801-74), Secretary of State for War. Opposing them were the officials who ran the Army Medical Department, whose lack of preparation and poor administration would be the chief subjects of investigation. Nightingale spent a month at Birk Hall, the home near Balmoral of the Queen's physician, Sir James Clark, after several days in Edinburgh en route for briefing by Sir John McNeill. The strategy worked, a royal commission was agreed on, the members were almost all to their liking and the terms of reference most satisfactory. Then there were delays. Panmure, "the bison," required months more lobbying before the royal commission was actually announced.[36] The team used this

---

36 Small credits Panmure with political astuteness in the delay, to permit development of support in Parliament to overcome opposition in the Army and War Office (*Florence Nightingale* 74).

delay to prepare their own material. The commission was then able to work quickly, issuing its report several months after appointment.

This was the last work Nightingale undertook with any enjoyment of good health, but she became seriously ill part way through. She worked prodigiously, assembling statistics, developing her "cox-combs" or pie charts to portray the data graphically. She worked with the statistician William Farr on the data. She personally interviewed witnesses to prepare them. She declined to give evidence in person but did the next best thing by submitting a written document with her answers to the questions put to her (which questions of course she and her team had formulated). This question-and-answer report is remarkable for its pithiness.

Question: To what do you mainly ascribe the mortality in the
hospitals?

Answer: To sanitary defects.

She showed that there had been a mortality rate of 60 percent in the first seven months of the war from disease alone, worse than any cholera epidemic. The reforms brought the mortality rate down below that of troops stationed in England. This revealed the excessive rate of mortality of troops in peacetime conditions, a problem that would soon be addressed. All these points were fleshed out by detailed tables and coloured pie charts.

Nightingale's material was contained in a report, which, though "confidential," she circulated to a large number of people (asking them to treat it as confidential). It is Hugh Small's contention that she wanted people to know the worst, and that, as a result, many people knew that she was not really a heroine at all (197-98). Certainly we will see many instances later of her insisting on the inadequacy of good intentions, of the need for evaluating, with carefully gathered statistics, the actual results of reform programs.

The royal commission recommendations were directed to putting into place a thoroughly different system. Nightingale then recruited Harriet Martineau to write leaders for the *Daily News* featuring their reform line. Martineau was also persuaded to write a book, *England and Her Soldiers*, published in 1859, to popularize the analysis and recommendations of the royal commission.

For decades after the Crimean War, Nightingale worked to ensure the lowest possible mortality rate in war by the provision of good sanitary conditions and adequate medical and nursing services. She joked about her years of "service" at the War Office, variously describing herself as a long-term inhabitant of it or even as running it. She routinely drew up plans, rules, regulations, lists of supplies, procedures, training requirements, etc. for the War Office. She furnished them to any and all who needed them, and even took the initiative to send them out when no one thought to ask.

The first practical application from the royal commission occurred with Britain's incursions in China in 1857. Nightingale was pleased to conclude that the new methods reduced the overall mortality of the troops in China to one tenth of what it had been, mortality from disease to one in seven.[37] At Harriet Martineau's instigation, she sent material, including actual forms as well as findings from the royal commission and her own advice, for use in the American Civil War. (Martineau, a long-time and staunch opponent of slavery, also sent material.)

Nightingale prepared extensively for an expected British expedition in Canada arising from the "Trent Affair." Britain actually sent reinforcements to Canada in 1861 but a possible war was averted thanks, according to informed opinion generally and Nightingale in particular, to the moderating counsel of Prince Albert (1819-61). Her detailed preparation included estimating distances to be covered by sleds and the comparative weights and warmth of blankets and buffalo robes. Her extensive work during the Franco-Prussian War, 1870-71, will be discussed shortly. She continued to be involved during the Egyptian campaign of 1882 and the Zulu War, updating and refining the preparation process. By the Boer War of 1899-1902 she was no longer involved, although her forms and procedures were used. Indeed the Army Medical Corps was using her forms well into the twentieth century.

Illness and Invalidism

Neither Nightingale nor her contemporaries ever knew the name or the medical details of the disease, brucellosis, that, to the best of our knowledge today, nearly killed her in the Crimean War, and which returned in its chronic phase while she was working on her first royal commission. It is commonly transmitted from cows, sheep and goats, food animals in the Crimea and presumably the source of infection.

---

37 Cook, *Life* 1:398.

There is now a growing body of information on brucellosis[38] to suggest that Nightingale did in fact suffer from a serious, organic disease and was not an "intentional invalid," neurotic or malingerer, as has been commonly charged. Even the *Encyclopedia Britannica* article on Nightingale, as late as 1989, claimed that it had "never been shown that Florence Nightingale had any organic illness; her invalidism may have been partly neurotic and partly intentional."[39] Elaine Showalter referred to Nightingale's "strategic invalidism," showing how she used it, but nonetheless denying its physical causes.[40] Elizabeth Burton would concede only that her health was "undermined" by work in the Crimea to stress the "vague maladies" that occurred whenever Nightingale was "emotionally disturbed."[41] F.B. Smith, Nightingale's most hostile analyst, considered that she "feigned" weakness. The fact that the only evidence of a medical prescription he found in her papers was for an "appetizing tonic" was for him suspicious.[42] He further suggested that "whenever Nightingale announced herself to be ill she was busy" (92) as if this were a matter of choice. Yet the correspondence below will show that she refused to see people she was very keen to: Gladstone, General Gordon, William Rathbone, Jowett, etc., as well as old and dear friends like Mme Mohl and Louisa Ashburton, not to speak of her mother.

Pickering's *Creative Malady*, 1974, gives excellent coverage of Nightingale's work and writing as well as considerable detail of her medical symptoms, all the while insisting that there was "no organic basis" for the latter. Pickering qualified Cook's charitable description of her illness, "dilation of the heart and neurasthenia," as having "no precise meaning," and neurasthenia as something which would now be taken as a sign of "psychoneurosis."[43] Consistent with this, he

---

38 D.A.B. Young, "Florence Nightingale's Fever"; Barbara M. Dossey, *Florence Nightingale: Mystic, Visionary and Healer*, appendix "The Case for Brucellosis" 426-27; and Barbara M. Dossey, "Florence Nightingale and Her Crimean Fever and Invalidism."

39 *Encyclopedia Britannica* 15th ed. (1989) 8:706.

40 Elaine Showalter, "Florence Nightingale's Feminist Complaint: Women, Religion, and *Suggestions for Thought*" 396.

41 Elizabeth Burton, *The Early Victorians at Home 1837-1861* 198.

42 Smith, *Florence Nightingale: Reputation and Power* 92. Of course he did not consult the main sources of her personal correspondence. In any event the lack of medical prescriptions is entirely consistent with the lack of knowledge of the disease and the then lack of effective means of treatment.

43 George Pickering, *Creative Malady* 165.

offered as the most likely explanation of a later change in her condition the declining intensity of "the conflict which caused her psychoneurosis" (174).

A psychoanalytic interpretation naturally features "a strong masochistic strain,"[44] a "psychoneurotic" defence mechanism tied to "vexed relations with her family" and "her consuming struggle for professional success" (41), "the total blocking of her natural sex drives," which prevented her from reaching "true interpersonal intimacy" (36) and, finally, "a severely vulnerable narcissism" (44). Nightingale is said to have "manipulated 'illness'" to banish her mother and sister (37), also to obtain "their solicitous attention and thus to overcome her childhood feeling of rejection" (41).

Even Keen, who suggested lead poisoning as the source of Nightingale's many illnesses and weakness in childhood (there were lead remains from the family's smelter in Lea), attributed her post-Crimea illness to "nervous breakdown" and called her a "professional invalid."[45] More recently there has been speculation that Nightingale suffered from "chronic fatigue syndrome" or myalgic encephalomyelitis.[46]

The symptoms of brucellosis include headache, poor appetite, backache, weakness and depression,[47] from all of which Nightingale suffered. Patients may also enjoy significant periods of remission, which Nightingale did. The disease was only identified in 1887,[48] when she began to be free of its symptoms. There was then *no* cure for it and only some relief, for example with opium, for the pain. There is still no effective vaccine for brucellosis, which is now a rare disease in industrialized countries (veterinarians and farmers are most vulnerable). It is still common in the Mediterranean and in nomadic areas where people keep camels, goats and sheep. Antibiotics are effective in treatment, but these of course only came into use in the 1950s. For some years Nightingale took the water cure at Malvern spa, but later abandoned even that. She also tried, on doctor's orders, a visit to the

---

44 Donald R. Allen, "Florence Nightingale: Toward a Psychohistorical Interpretation" 32.

45 Norman Keen, *Florence Nightingale* 25.

46 A Canadian ME/CFS institute is named the Nightingale Research Foundation.

47 Canadian Medical Association, *Home Medical Encyclopedia* (Montreal: Readers' Digest 1992) 214.

48 By Sir David Bruce (1855-1931), an Australian-born microbiologist who worked for the Royal Army Medical Corps, notably in Malta.

seaside, which did not help. To cope with the disease she harboured her physical resources, working as much as she could every day.

Her illness of course very much affected Nightingale's working style. She used whatever hours of the day she could for writing. She saw few people, preferably only one a day (when more than one she spaced them). She normally saw people only one at a time. Even her parents she saw separately because of the strain.[49]

Second Royal Commission, on India (1858-63)

Nightingale's first involvement with India was prompted by the Bengali mutiny of 1857, or the First War of Independence, as Indian nationalists would later call it. She offered to go to nurse the injured soldiers, but her services were not needed and she herself quickly learned that the murders by the Bengalis were inconsequential compared with the deaths caused by English neglect and mismanagement. Later analysis would indicate that the death rate of Indian women and children from poor sanitary conditions in stations, the responsibility of the British, was as bad as the death rate from the mutiny: "This massacre killed as many as it is supposed fell by the hands of the mutineers."[50] In 1858 Britain took over the administration of India from the East India Company. Nightingale's good friend Lord Stanley (1826-93) was transferred from the Colonial Office to the India Office also in 1858, which gave her the opportunity for action. She lobbied for and succeeded in getting the appointment of a second royal commission, in 1859, with terms of reference on paper confined to the health of the Army in India, but quickly broadened to include surrounding communities. An inveterate newspaper clipper, Nightingale reported her joy on the commission's appointment to her friend Harriet Martineau. To the official announcement in the *Gazette* she attached the following:

Parable: The unjust judge and the importunate widow
Dramatis Personae:
Lord Stanley Unjust Judge
F.N. Importunate Widow
Result of 8 months' importunacy [the royal commission].

---

49 Letter to Emily Verney 10 August 1870, Wellcome (Claydon copy)Ms 9004/65.
50 Nightingale, "Observations by Miss Nightingale on the Evidence Contained in Stational Returns Sent to Her by the Royal Commission on the Sanitary State of the Army in India" 368.

Sidney Herbert chaired the commission until he was transferred back to the War Office, then Lord Stanley took the chair. The other members included Drs Sutherland, Farr and Thomas Alexander (d. 1860), allies from the previous royal commission. Nightingale herself devised the questionnaires that were sent to the Indian stations and analyzed the returned data. Her resulting ninety-two-page paper, with beautiful illustrations given to her by an Indian officer and enhanced by her cousin Hilary Bonham Carter, was published as an appendix to the royal commission report. Nightingale herself paid for the additional expenses arising from the illustrations. The final report, a document of over 2000 pages, was completed in May 1863. She arranged for separate publication of her own analysis and its circulation to influential people.[51] She lined up sympathetic reviewers for the press and generally managed the media campaign. The analysis opened with typical Nightingale invective:

> If there be an exception, that is, if there be a single station in India with a good system of drainage, water supply and cleansing for itself and its bazaars, with properly planned and constructed barracks and hospitals, provided with what is necessary for occupation and health—a station where the men are not encouraged to drink, and where they are provided with rational means for employing their time—to such a station these remarks do not apply. But I have not found it.[52]

Instead, there were "grievous sanitary defects" everywhere, which could lead only to "sickness and loss of life ... cholera, fever, diarrhoea, dysentery and hepatic disease" accordingly. She cited Sir Charles Trevelyan (1807-86), Governor of Madras, on the fundamental point, which provided the raison d'être for the broad scope of the report, that "a good sanitary state of the military force cannot be secured without making similar arrangements for the populations settled in and around the military cantonments; that sanitary reform must be generally introduced into India for the civil as well as the military portion of the community" (368). Moreover, *now* was the time.

---

51 Published as *Observations on the Sanitary State of the Army in India.* The references here are to the longer document.

52 Nightingale, *Observations by Miss Nightingale on the Evidence Contained in Stational Returns Sent to Her by the Royal Commission on the Sanitary State of the Army in India* 347.

> "If the facilities for washing were as great as those for drink, our Indian Army would be the cleanest body of men in the world." (368)

Here also Nightingale dealt, in print for the first time, with the compulsory treatment of prostitutes for syphilis. "Lock hospitals and police regulation are, alas! sometimes recommended, just as if they would do any good" (370). This would become a major item of *business* from 1863 to 1868, and indeed one she would continue to work on sporadically into the 1890s. She noted that admissions to military hospitals for "the disease engendered by vice" (syphilis) were five times as great among British soldiers as among the native troops.

The final section of her observations called for the establishment of a Sanitary Service, for no good would be done, in India any more than at home, "unless it be made some competent person's express business" (370). Since there was no local government, this would have to be done by the Government of India. Specifically there was to be a sanitary commission for each presidency in India (Madras, Calcutta and Bombay), and a Sanitary Department in the India Office. Nightingale would later see a significant role for local governments in public health, but at this point she hoped to achieve significant reforms from above.

From 1858 on Nightingale devoted a major portion of her time and energy to work on India. This makes good sense for a "passionate statistician," for the most elementary acquaintance with the data would show that strategic, well-formulated intervention could save more lives in India than anywhere else she could work; at that time *millions* still died when there were famines. She published frequently, and, until late in life, on a wide range of public health and famine prevention issues. She contributed to famine relief and helped raise funds. She sent short papers and letters to public health congresses and journals in India. She encouraged the introduction of trained nursing in India. She received Indian nationals in her own home who had come to London to lobby for various reforms.

Soon after the Royal Commission on India reported, the then-viceroy, Lord Elgin, died. Nightingale agitated for his replacement by Sir John Lawrence (1811-79), a devoted ally in sanitary reform and a person thoroughly knowledgeable about the country. His appointment in 1863 provided her with an enlightened and sympathetic person to implement the proposed reforms. Nightingale briefed, cajoled and encouraged the next viceroys as well, until it became a ritual for viceroys to call on her before leaving to assume office.

Working Style (1859-99)

There is much of a sameness about Nightingale's life after her second royal commission. She was effectively now an invalid for life. She stayed in her rooms, received visitors, normally only one at a time and by appointment, mainly her inner circle of co-workers. Blue books and other official documents were sent to her. She carried on a massive correspondence with experts of all kinds, exchanging information with them. She kept a substantial library of books, official documents and journals. She did not travel farther than the country homes of her parents, sister and a few friends (within a few hours of London). When her (male) colleagues went on their month's fishing or grouse-shooting holidays Nightingale stayed back in London and worked. There would be no more opera or art museums.

When Nightingale went to Embley to nurse her ailing mother in 1866, she took some time off (her first "holiday" in ten years), but soon involved herself in a new project. She examined the mortality statistics (her friend Dr Farr sent them at her request) for the nearest town, Romsey, and for Winchester, the county seat. She advised them to improve their drains to reduce their above-average mortality rates. Her normal practice on country visits was to take her work with her. She advised government offices and other correspondents where to send the next batch of documents. She bade her co-workers meet with her at her temporary headquarters, and they, of course, complied.

Nightingale did not leave London when the House of Commons was in session so that she could respond to developments. She did not take part in election campaigns, so that she could take a break when an election was called. A letter to her MP brother-in-law remarks that "now my election holidays are over."[53] In July 1866 Nightingale explained to Harry Verney that she could not go to Embley because it was expected that the new minister would bring a Poor Law bill to Cabinet in November.[54] She regretted having to leave London early in

---

53 Letter to Harry Verney 20 July 1865, Wellcome (Claydon copy) Ms 9001/43.
54 Letter 28 July 1866, Wellcome (Claydon copy) Ms 9002/44.

1875, which she did only to assist her mother, thus interrupting negotiations with the India office on irrigation data. For nineteen years she
had never been a "lagger," but was one then and "the chariot rolls by,
and the lagger is justly crushed under the wheels."[55]

As a result of her severe ill health Nightingale's considerable work
on the reform of Army medical and nursing services, the War Office,
the development of trained nursing in Britain and abroad and all her
other causes from roughly 1860 on was all carried out from her sickroom. Her unsuccessful work opposing the Contagious Diseases Acts
was similarly conducted largely by correspondence. So was her pioneering work in the establishment of district nursing in Liverpool, a
project for which philanthropist William Rathbone (1819-1902) first
approached her by letter. Most of Nightingale's work—on the proposal itself and then on finding staff—was confined to writing. The
establishment of trained nursing in the Liverpool Workhouse Infirmary, again at Rathbone's initiative and with his financial support, was
yet another sickroom activity.

The extension of trained nursing into workhouses in London had
some resemblance to the early, heady days post Crimea. There was legislation to see through Parliament, questions to organize and committees to cajole. Yet except for the first royal commission, when Nightingale herself traversed London briefing witnesses, this was done virtu-
ally entirely from her sickroom. The prodigious amount of organiza-
tional work she did during the Franco-Prussian War she did from her
sickroom, by correspondence. So also were the years of research and
writing on India work at a distance. She would have liked to have visited India, and certainly was invited, but illness made it impossible.

A remission in her illness in the early 1880s resulted in a few public
appearances. Nightingale went to Victoria Station to meet the Foot
Guards returning from the Egyptian campaign in 1882, for which she
had helped prepare the medical/nursing services. She attended a royal
review of the Horse Guards, and accepted an invitation of Queen Victoria (1819-1901) to join her at the opening of the new Law Courts also
in 1882.

After her return from the Crimean War nursing was for Nightingale only *one* subject of her ongoing daily business, sharing her time
and energy with other health care issues and other matters of social

---

55 Letter to Harry Verney 16 November 1877, Wellcome (Claydon copy)
   Ms 9007/119.

reform. After establishing the first secular training school for nurses at St Thomas' Hospital she then worked to extend nursing schools to cities in other parts of Britain, to India, the United States, the dominions and colonies. She maintained contact with the trained nurses she placed in various posts. In recent decades nurse historians have been quite critical about Nightingale's personal role in establishing what was called the "Nightingale system of education." Her training institution at St Thomas' Hospital of course was not the first, but was preceded by the Institute of Nursing in 1840, founded by Elizabeth Fry (1780-1845) and St John's House, 1848, both religious institutions. St Thomas' established the benchmarks of organized, secular nursing even if it did not succeed in making training as much a part of its work as some would have wanted.

In addition to the main *business* Nightingale conducted, there were numerous other causes to which she contributed in a minor way (recounted in *Society and Politics*). Friends enlisted her support for *their* campaigns, and she often obliged with an introduction to a book or a letter to the editor. For example, in 1876 she sent a letter to the *Times* on Bosnian refugees, consisting of a lengthy excerpt from a letter she had received from a friend, A. Paulina Irby, then in Slovenia providing aid.[56] Nightingale sometimes started work on a worthy project, but gave it up when it met with too much resistance. For example, she gave many years' attention, unsuccessfully, to projected schemes to promote savings, home and land ownership among the working class (see *Society and Politics*).

Probably because of her illness, Nightingale felt old before her time. She called herself middle-aged in her thirties, just after the Crimean War, and described herself as *old* at fifty-seven.[57] Yet, for all this early self-identification as old, Nightingale continued to work well into her seventies. She was giving extensive and detailed advice on Irish workhouse infirmaries, and the introduction of professional nursing to them, in 1896.[58] She continued to produce serious work on India into the late 1890s.

There is a curious division between the public and private in Nightingale's thinking and practice. On the one hand she was dedicated to the *public good*, believing in a strong role for the public sector,

---

56 "Bosnian Fugitives," *Times* 13 March 1876:10.
57 Diary entry 29-30 October 1877, Add Mss 45847 f2.
58 See correspondence with Lord Monteagle, Add Mss 45787, in *Public Health Care*.

variously at the national, regional and local levels. Living in a democracy (at least for tax-paying men), she was well aware of the need for public support for her projects. Neither her own mission to the Crimea nor sanitary reform there would ever have happened without a great public outcry, prompted and fed by the mass media. Nightingale, consequently, was careful always to have a media strategy for any serious undertaking. She was astute at getting publicity for her causes. She knew when to cajole ministers or officials privately, and when to threaten publicity. She knew how to plant questions in the House of Commons, and get maximum press coverage for them afterwards. She lined up sympathetic reviewers for her reports and organized the sending of advance copies to influential politicians as well as the media.

Yet this paragon of publicity was also intensely private, seeking press for her *causes* but not herself. Nightingale did many good deeds anonymously, avoiding use of her name except when it was necessary for the cause. When a proposal was made to name the street she lived on in her honour she objected strenuously, indeed that she would have to "remove at once and go to quite another street."[59] Her satisfaction came from solving the problem or intervening correctly, in line with the laws of social science. However much she sought to serve the common good, she saw herself as a servant of God, and her accountability was, accordingly, to God, not to any public body. God was the "Commander-in-Chief." To a nursing superintendent she affirmed: "We serve not a committee but the Lord."[60] This accounts both for how often Nightingale took the initiative in the causes for which she worked and declined to let her name be used wherever possible (a list is provided in the electronic publication). Although she was often sought after to take on various projects, what she worked on was overwhelmingly what she thought most needed to be done. She then sought the necessary experts and expertise to proceed.

---

59 Letter to Harry Verney 15 December 1884, Wellcome (Claydon copy) Ms 9010/50.
60 Letter to Maria Machin 22 October 1877, University of Toronto, Thomas Fisher Rare Book Library.

Opposition to Registration of Nurses (1887-94)

Nightingale lost the concerted battle she waged late in her life on the registration of nurses. Nursing for her was an art *as well as* a science, a calling more than a profession. In a paper she sent to the Congress on Women's Work in Chicago 1893,[61] she referred to nursing in all of these terms. Statements she made to the effect that nurses *cannot* be trained should be taken with a grain of salt for she also insisted on the teaching of a scientific component and frequently gave books on medical science to nurses. Yet Nightingale believed from the core of her being that nursing required gifts and devotion not amenable to ordinary teaching and examination. She was sceptical that three years of training necessarily made someone a good nurse. Nurses were, as she once described to Benjamin Jowett, "handmaids of the Lord."[62] Rural public health nurses were "health missioners."[63] These qualities could not be certified by external examiners.

As well, and a point now more sympathetically received, Nightingale understood that nursing practice was still evolving and would always be evolving. Whatever certification might mean after three years of training, it could not guarantee competence years later. She was appalled that registration could be for life and suggested instead that nurses needed certificates from *recent* experience, an idea now fashionable as "continuous education" or "lifelong learning." Nursing professors in the late twentieth century were more prone than in the early years of the profession to consider that Nightingale might have been right to resist registration. Registration resulted in locking nursing into a three-year hospital apprenticeship. By waiting—and Nightingale did not argue that registration would never be desirable—nursing might have developed academic links earlier and/or given greater prominence to community health.

Domestic Arrangements and Expenditures

Nightingale was a gentlewoman: that is, she never worked for pay, cooked her own meals, shopped, cleaned or did her own laundry; from girlhood she had her own maid. Her death certificate described her

---

61 Nightingale, "Sick-Nursing and Health-Nursing."
62 Note to Jowett 1 June 1867, Add Mss 45783 f112, and undated notes, Add Mss 45785 ff102 and 109.
63 Nightingale, "Rural Hygiene," 1894, in *Society and Politics*.

occupation as "of Independent Means." Her family socialized with the great landowners and nobility of her country, and when they travelled (with multiple servants) they were received by ambassadors and dukes. F.B. Smith correctly reminds us that her family was *nouveau riche* (a mere great-great-uncle made the original fortune), although she had "patrician" values.[64] Nightingale dressed as per her class, although as an invalid this meant a plain black silk dress and fine lace to cover her hair. The income her father gave her was adequate for a comfortable style of life and the management of her "business," which required a fair outlay for books and documents, messengers, transportation and printing, and for modest donations to her various causes. A long-term lease her father arranged in 1866 permitted her to settle down in one place. Yet she, like Jesus, never owned any property and always lived, after she left home, in rented, borrowed or leased accommodation. Unlike Jesus, she inherited money and invested it, so that she left £36,000 in her will.

While Nightingale lived comfortably on South St., the house was not large and faced a pub with an insalubrious pubkeeper and patrons whose conduct was "disgraceful," screaming late into the night. The street itself is quite narrow and has no view. By sticking her head out the window she could see a slice of Hyde Park (hence her comments on demonstrations and processions). Nightingale's landlord on South St. was the immensely wealthy Duke of Westminster, a member of the Nightingale Fund Council and supporter of nursing reform. She declined his "munificent offer" of a low rent (see p 593 below). She would, however, have been pleased if he had not renewed the lease of the unruly pub across the street.

It seems there were times when Nightingale was short of money, for she had to borrow money from her lawyer.[65] In 1900 she had to let a nurse go, although it caused her pain to part with her, but "I am compelled to retrench."[66] Yet she did have money to leave at the end of her life. Her sister left her £500/year on her death in 1890, a time when Nightingale's expenditures on work and causes were declining as her faculties failed. Possibly the accumulation of this additional money explains the anomaly.

Her only form of asceticism was her utter devotion to work, keeping it up despite illness and fatigue. Otherwise she enjoyed the crea-

---

64 Smith, *Florence Nightingale: Reputation and Power* 166.
65 She paid back £200 of the £400 borrowed in a letter 19 April 1901 to Janson and Cobb, Boston University 3/9/2.
66 Copy of letter to Miss Walker 4 December 1900, Add Mss 45815 ff152-53.

ture comforts of her class and age, and did not begrudge them to others. To ailing friends and colleagues she sent nourishing, tempting food and drink (a dying nun was sent not only fresh eggs, jelly and beef juice, but port and champagne[67]). She maintained a staff of five or six, a considerable responsibility as her diary of 1877 makes clear (*Spiritual Journey*). Her rooms were well furnished and with unusually little clutter for her era. Consistent with her fanaticism for ventilation, her windows were curtainless. Visitors and biographers commented on the overall light and pleasant result. The food she ate and served was similarly of good quality, but simple. Recipes in her own hand are included later in this volume to make this point. She went to some pains in instructions to her employees.

Nightingale was a believer in moderation in drink. Soldiers, she thought, should drink less and nuns more. She frequently sent bottles of wine to convents, for an ailing nun "an enormously expensive very old brandy."[68] How much she and her guests drank is not clear, but there are routine expenditures for beer and brandy recorded in her account books. She supported cafés for soldiers, to give them options for socializing without recourse to alcohol. Alcoholism was abhorrent. Nightingale struck an old colleague from St Thomas' out of her will for being "in habits of intoxication" for seven years.[69]

Nightingale was fastidious about housekeeping standards. A letter to engage someone to conduct a thorough cleaning notes: "The floor, I am sorry to say, *always* has a close, musty smell, as if they wanted washing. Whether it is our fault I cannot say. Above all, I want freshness."[70] She noticed and loved flowers. A steady stream of greenery flowed into London from Embley, much of which she relayed to hospitals. She thought that flowers had a "civilizing" effect and urged their use in hospitals, workhouse infirmaries and nursing residences as well. When she sent rhododendrons to be planted at a Belfast workhouse infirmary she urged "flowers, plants, a canary or a singing bird in a cage, a tame cat which will not hurt the canary."[71]

---

67 Letter to Sister Frances Wylde 19 April 1887, London Metropolitan Archives H1/ST/NC1/87/15.
68 Letter to Sister Frances Wylde 15 May 1887, London Metropolitan Archives H1/ST/NC1/87/25.
69 Letter to Henry Bonham Carter 15 October 1872, London Metropolitan Archives H1/ST/NC1/72/22.
70 Letter to Mr Thomas 2 August 1884, Archives of Ontario.
71 Letter to Miss Pirrie 14 October 1885, London Metropolitan Archives H1/ST/NC1/85/10.

Friends

The question is frequently asked how one can like such a paragon of virtue or such a dedicated maniac for work, or the assertion is simply made that "you cannot really *like* her, however much you might admire her." True, Nightingale was a formidable genius, heroine, intellectual, workaholic perfectionist; she was utterly faithful in her service and a brilliant writer to boot. She also had more normal human qualities: a temper, a wicked sense of humour and considerable style. She had few friends in the normal sense, or her friends were also her collaborators in some cause or other. But these were real friends. They shared confidences and jokes as well as government documents and reference works. To Sidney Herbert Nightingale once sent some material Dr Sutherland had "stolen . . . for your benefit, a practice I learnt from the Army and taught him."[72] Greetings, condolences, prayers and gifts were sent back and forth. Nightingale was glad of the Turkish towels; she sent pheasant and partridge. William Rathbone sent her flowers weekly for years. Her team, at least the inner circle who were welcomed to her home, were well fed while they were at work. Others were kept at a distance, with careful, often affectionate, correspondence—gifts, too—but not everyone was invited into her home. Harriet Martineau, notably, was never allowed to call, although she offered to when visiting London, and this despite the fact that she had worked assiduously and effectively for years on Nightingale causes.

Nightingale supported her friends' causes as they did hers. There are numerous letters with money or a cheque, usually small amounts, for the cause, with a supportive letter and the wish she could send more. For example, Nightingale sent a guinea to Mrs Fellowes (wishing it were ten times more) toward a harmonium for a ward at St Thomas' Hospital.[73] For the Gordon Boys' Home she sent £5 for books and magazines.[74] She sent money to hospital matrons for use at their discretion—don't consult any committee—for particularly needy patients, for example £5.5 "to supply any wants of patients you

---

72 Letter to Sidney Herbert 5 June 1858, Wilshire County Archives, Pembroke Collection 2057/F4/67.
73 Letter to Mrs Fellowes 7 July 1881, London Metropolitan Archives H1/ST/NC1/81/15.
74 Letter to Amy Hawthorn 24 June 1886, Add Mss 45776 f197.

thought pressing, any little amusements."[75] She gave £30 to Herbert's memorial convalescent cottages, and also worked on the plans for the buildings.[76] Serious disasters, like famine in India and the siege of Paris in the Franco-Prussian War, got larger donations, indeed concerted fund-raising efforts which will be described in the India and war volumes respectively. See pp 742-54 below for the list to date of donations.

Nightingale was fiercely loyal to old friends and villagers around Lea Hurst. For example to Martha Sheldon, who had been in her class of adult mill girls in the 1840s, she sent food and clothing in her old age, obtained medical care and mourned at her death in 1888.[77] She corresponded with former tenants and employees, and had them visit her on later occasional stays at Lea Hurst. In a letter to her brother-in-law on his asking her to invite her friends to Claydon while she was staying there she said: "I could not bring all Lea and Holloway here."[78] A selection from the vast caseload of needy people she assisted is reported later in this volume, "Waifs and Strays."

The Arts

Nightingale's privileged upbringing included a rich introduction to the arts. As a girl she was given music and art lessons, she attended concerts and was taken to the greatest art museums in the Western world. She was "music mad" for opera, especially Mozart. To a friend she recounted hearing Jenny Lind in London in 1847, "but it really requires a new language to define her . . . she must be felt, not talked about."[79] After she became an invalid of course she could not attend concerts. The singer Clara Novello, a fellow Garibaldian, came to her rooms to sing for her privately in 1860, a rare treat (Cook, *Life* 1:500). On another occasion arrangements were made for Nightingale to hear music at home, but she was less keen for she found listening to piano music, even Mendelssohn, nerve-wracking.[80]

---

75 Letter to Miss Pirrie 1 January 1887, London Metropolitan Archives H1/ST/NC1/87/1.
76 Letter to W.E. Nightingale 23 November 1854, ADD Mss 45790 f322.
77 Letter to Bratby 11 October 1888, Columbia University, Presbyterian Hospital School of Nursing C190.
78 Letter 7 September 1881, Wellcome (Claydon copy) Ms 9008/174.
79 Letter to Mary Clarke 10 July 1847, ADD Mss 43397 f292.
80 Letter to F.K. Harford 15 July 1891, Columbia University, Presbyterian Hospital School of Nursing C203.

In her Lebenslauf, her Curriculum Vitae written in English for Kaiserswerth, Nightingale recognized that she had "the strongest taste for music," but that God, in mercy, took away her voice by constant sore throats. Otherwise, if she could have sung, she would have "wished for no other satisfaction. Music excited my imagination and my passionate nature so much" (see p 90 below). In *Notes on Nursing* she observed that the music of wind instruments, including the human voice, had a soothing effect on invalids, but the piano did not.

Nightingale loved architecture and had the opportunity to visit great churches, palaces, abbeys, temples and mosques. Indeed the practice she gained in sketching ecclesiastical buildings she duly transmuted to hospital drawings. Seeing Michelangelo's painting in the Sistine Chapel was a high point in Nightingale's young life. Nor, one feels, were the ironies lost on her, for Michelangelo (1475-1564), a fellow Florentine, a Savonarolian republican in spirit and an advocate of church reform, was forced to glorify the Medicis and paint for the pope. The subject of the Sistine fresco, the last judgment, is a gloomy one. It would never have been Michelangelo's choice (this was commissioned art) and Nightingale herself did not believe in it. Yet she bought engravings of the ceiling in Rome and kept them in her rooms for the rest of her life.

It was possible for an invalid to keep up with literature, and this Nightingale did. Although her reading was overwhelmingly of business—official documents, statistics and texts—she enjoyed novels and poetry. She knew the writers Elizabeth Gaskell, George Eliot, Robert Browning and Elizabeth Barrett Browning as well as their work. She read Martineau's novels as well as her social science. She liked George Sand. She gave novels as well as medical and religious books to nurses. Her tastes ranged from the classics (often in the original) to earnest religious novels, lowbrow, action-packed adventure stories and rhyming poems of great piety. In her great old age Nightingale found enjoyment in the poetry she had learned as a child. She recited Shakespeare, Milton and Shelley, and sang French and Italian songs. Nightingale's views of great writers are included in *Society and Politics*.

Love of Nature and Companion Animals

Nightingale was always fond of animals—there were birds and squirrels at her country homes—and she always had pets, especially cats. Her first "patient" as a child was an injured sheepdog, "Captain," and she took the precaution to boil the water before dressing his wounds.[81] She took her owl "Athena," which she had rescued at the Parthenon, along with three chameleons (two were named after missionaries) and a cicada, "Plato," on her Egyptian/European trip, but Athena ate Plato in Prague.

Nightingale owned cats throughout her life. If she gave them unlikely names—Bismark and Muff stand out—there are examples of this in classical literature. Plutarch recounted the story of a general learning that his household cat "Perseus" had died, which he took to be a good omen that his own general Perseus had not been killed. Nightingale abhorred Otto von Bismarck (1815-98) as responsible for the Franco-Prussian War; she called the incompetents in the War Office "muffs." A Persian tomcat was, appropriately enough, named "Darius."[82] She also had cats named after hospitals: "Tom" and "Barts." It seems that there was a cat "Dr Pusey," named after the Anglo-Catholic leader, adversary of her friend Jowett.[83] She could not understand how her sister could have a cat die in a fictional work, *Avonhoe*, which Nightingale thought had the "true literary ring," but "how could you let little Quick die? I never could have let poor Bismark die."[84] Numerous letters have survived about her cats, finding homes for kittens, the perils of tomcats in rural areas, etc. (see Cat Care below).

There is correspondence showing Nightingale's concern about the poor quality of veterinary care, the "brutelike ignorance of veterinary surgeons in treating brutes." Although Nightingale had been prompted to write because of mistreatment of her own cats, she sought to get the situation corrected "not only for the sake of valuable pets but for the sake of all animals" (see p 764 below).

A letter at age nine to her grandmother recounts the funeral of a bird which died, complete with the epitaph she and Parthe composed.[85] Living in London after the Crimean War Nightingale fed the birds from her window. A letter records her utter delight in birds: "The voice of the birds is like the angels calling us with their songs . . . nothing makes my

---

81 Arthur W. Moss, *Valiant Crusade: The History of the R.S.P.C.A.* 46.

82 Letter to Eleanor Martin 13 October 1879, Leicester Record Office DG6/D/225.

83 Letter to Parthenope and Harry Verney 9/10 September 1874, Wellcome (Claydon copy) Ms 9006/122.

84 Letter [1868], Wellcome (Claydon copy) Ms 9003/134.

85 Letter 30 March 1830, Wellcome (Claydon copy) Ms 8991/6.

heart thrill like the voice of birds."[86] Birds, indeed, prayed along with people: "The wind is northeast—the birds did not sing their morning prayers."[87] When the war in Egypt was over she exclaimed what cause for joy there was: "considering what it might have been. . . . Every little bird seems to sing its praise for this great mercy."[88] Other examples of a spirituality akin to that of Francis of Assisi appear in *Theology*.

Late in life Nightingale became interested in animal welfare and species preservation. There is a draft letter or copy of a letter to the secretary of the Royal Society for the Prevention of Cruelty to Animals enquiring about *legislation*, which she had sought in vain, for the preservation of wild birds. She decried the slaughter of birds by members of clubs, so great that there was only one single wild bird where there used to be hundreds.[89] Yet there is no evidence that Nightingale pursued this subject, although her MP grandfather had been a staunch supporter of animal welfare during his forty-six years in Parliament, and she had two friends who were currently involved: Lord Shaftesbury, president of an anti-vivisection society, and J.S. Mill, a director of the RSPCA. One can only speculate what might have happened in the animal welfare cause if Nightingale had seriously taken it up!

Death Rituals

In the Victorian period death was openly discussed and people took leave of each other when the time was approaching. Some of Nightingale's letters at impending death are deeply moving (see *Theology*). She gave a great deal of attention to her friends' and nursing colleagues' last illnesses. There is much correspondence with inquiries as to their condition and prayers for them[90] (never that death was a bad thing, but regretting their loss). There are letters to the dying person expressing appreciation for his or her life, reminiscing over mutual

---

86 Letter to Hannah Nicholson 22 May 1846, ADD Mss 45794 f36.
87 Letter to Sir Harry Verney 4 June 1886, Wellcome (Claydon copy) Ms 9011/28.
88 Letter to Harry Verney 17 September 1882, Wellcome (Claydon copy) Ms 9009/91.
89 Letter 25 October 1891, Lothian Health Authority Archives, Edinburgh University. It is not clear whether the letter was ever actually sent and, if so, how it was answered (in *Society and Politics*).
90 For example asking about Priscilla Lydia Sellon, in a letter to Mary Jones 22 December 1876, London Metropolitan Archives H1/ST/NC1/76/3.

struggles.[91] She sent delicacies and drink to revive fading appetites. To a nurse dying of cancer she sent jelly ("I don't know what nourishment is given") and a nosegay ("It sometimes gives a moment's pleasure to a great sufferer to see how God was thinking of *her* when He made those beautiful flowers"[92]).

Nightingale attended the funeral of her grandmother Shore in 1853 but few others. Housebound, she found other ways to mourn the loss of those close to her. She sent wreaths with handwritten notes. Naturally she wrote letters of condolence to the deceased's close family or colleagues, often to a servant, and sometimes to the attending doctor. For her own parents she paid considerable attention to the wording of memorial cards and the monument inscriptions (the right verses to quote). She sent flowers at Easter to the grave of her father and later both parents when her mother died, and then also for her sister. Emily Verney she remembered not only with flowers at her grave on the anniversary of her death, but visits to her room.

Nightingale wanted to know who nursed a colleague, Nurse Owen, particulars about the last days, what was being done about the funeral, and could she help?[93] A later letter offers £2 towards the gravestone.[94] She appreciated being sent a copy of the litany used at the funeral of her friend Mary Jones (1812-87).[95] Her concern that nurses be properly buried and recognized is evident in many places in her correspondence. On Nurse Owen's death there are four letters concerning the wreath and gravestone.[96]

Nightingale remembered the dates of the demise of key friends/collaborators, and often remarked on the anniversaries of their deaths in later correspondence and private notes. She also gave considerable attention to ways to remember these people, writing eulogies and obituaries and contributing to projects in their name, notably the

91 A good example is that to a co-worker on India, Sir Henry Yule, 16 December 1889, Woodward Biomedical Library A70, in *Theology*.
92 Letter to Miss Gordon 2 January 1897, Wellcome Ms 5476/90.
93 Letter to Miss Mackenzie 14 April 1879, London Metropolitan Archives H1/ST/NC1/79/2.
94 Letter to Miss Mackenzie 11 September 1879, London Metropolitan Archives H1/ST/NC1/79/7.
95 Letter to Sister Frances Wylde 8 June 1887, London Metropolitan Archives H1/ST/NC1/87/39.
96 Letters to Miss Mackenzie 14 April, 10 May, 11 September and 23 September 1879, London Metropolitan Archives H1/ST/NC1/79/2, H1/ST/NC1/79/4, H1/ST/NC1/79/7 and H1/ST/NC1/79/8.

Herbert Hospital, named after Sidney Herbert and the Gordon Boys' Home, named after (General) Charles Gordon (1833-85). She stopped the newspapers after Sidney Herbert's death for she could not bear to read the articles on him. There is considerable correspondence on Jowett's death as to suitable inscriptions (see *Theology*).

Last Days, Will and Death

Nightingale made her first will while ill and close to death in the Crimea. On return but again ill in 1857 she wanted to be buried in the Crimea, with the dead soldiers, those *who weren't there*. She expected to die in 1859 (there is much discussion with Martineau, each expecting her own imminent death). Nightingale left instructions that "all that comes to me" on her father and mother's death should go to her friend and the husband of her cousin Blanche, Arthur Hugh Clough, who in fact predeceased her in 1861.[97] Also at this time she determined to leave her body to science, or, as she expressed this flippantly to a friend, she wished to "go down to posterity in a bottle of spirits."[98] In 1861, when again she thought death was close, she sorted her papers and eliminated some. Seriously ill again in 1864 she gave instructions that Mrs Bracebridge (or, failing her, Mrs Sutherland) should place her, for her last days, in a *general ward* at St Thomas' Hospital, but in fact she did not need to go into hospital at all. The intention, however, tells us much about her belief in the broad availability of good care and her dislike of privileged care for those who could afford it. (St Thomas' was a fee-paying hospital, of course, not a workhouse infirmary, but neither was it an institution for gentlewomen.) She made another will in 1887. If some of this sounds macabre, it should be remembered that depression is one of the manifestations of chronic brucellosis and that her recurring attacks of pain likely had an emotional toll.

A will Nightingale made in 1896 gave instructions that her papers be destroyed, with the telling exception of her India material. A codicil the following year left the papers to her cousin Henry Bonham Carter, secretary of the Nightingale Fund Trust. Detailed instructions divided up her various possessions among family and friends; alas, her

97 Note, Add Mss45795 f9.
98 Letter to Lady McNeill 22 April 1857, London Metropolitan Archives H1/ST/NC3/SU77.

library was dispersed after her death. The final will, with codicils, is published in Appendix D.

"Begging letters" continued to arrive even in the last year of her life. Captain Scott in preparing for his unhappy expedition to the South Pole asked her for financial support, large or small, to maintain "British exploration in the Far South."[99]

Nightingale died at age ninety after a long decline. The last decades saw the deaths of the rest of her friends and collaborators: Mary Clarke Mohl ("Clarkey"), William Farr and John McNeill in 1883; Bartle Frere in 1884; Aunt Mai in 1889; Dr Sutherland in 1891; Benjamin Jowett in 1893, her beloved "Shore" and brother-in-law Harry Verney in 1894; Mrs Sutherland in 1895; Robert Rawlinson in 1898; Douglas Galton in 1899; William Rathbone in 1902. Some of the last letters she sent were to Sister Mary Stanislaus Jones, one of the last of the surviving Sisters of Mercy from the Crimean War (there are touching letters as late as 1895, 1896, 1897 and 1899.[100] Sister Stanislaus sent Nightingale birthday greetings as late as 1906[101]).

There is very little writing from her last ten years, only short pieces. Her handwriting became increasingly unsteady; she became effectively blind in 1901. Her memory failed so that she had to be briefed on the particulars of any visitors. After 1896, when Embley was sold out of the Nightingale family, she did not leave her rooms in London; her last visit to the Verneys' home in Buckinghamshire, Claydon House, took place in 1895. In 1901 she was persuaded to accept the services of a companion, called a "lady housekeeper" to mollify her, but effectively a private secretary (Cook, *Life* 2:416). In 1906 the India Office was instructed to stop sending her papers; she could neither read nor understand them. In 1907 she was awarded the Order of Merit, the first woman to be so honoured, but too late for her to appreciate it. In 1908 she became the second woman to have the Freedom of the City of London conferred on her. We do not know if she would have accepted other honours if offered, but one must note that many of her male collaborators were made Fellows of the Royal Soci-

---

99 Letter from R. Scott 4 November 1909, Columbia University, Presbyterian Hospital School of Nursing O.23. He and four others died in 1912, after reaching the South Pole, to discover that Amundsen had preceded them.

100 Letters 24 December 1895, 21 October 1896, 26 April 1897, 7 March 1899, Archive, Convent of Mercy, Birmingham.

101 Letter from Sister Stanislaus Jones 15 May 1906, London Metropolitan Archives H1/ST/NC2/V1/06.

ety, Privy Councillors, knights, and even peers, not to speak of their honorary doctorates.

Obviously Nightingale did not achieve her desire for "the grace" of martyrdom but died in her sleep in her own bed. Characteristically she left instructions that her body should be used for medical research, which it was not. The family, consistent with her wishes, declined burial at Westminster Abbey. She was buried with her parents in the churchyard of her parish church in East Wellow. She was carried to her grave by six sergeants (four more than she had stipulated). There is no special marker, but inscriptions on each side of a square monument for each of her parents and her sister (who was buried with the Verney family at Claydon). The inscription for Nightingale, as per her instructions, says only: "F.N. Born 12 May 1820, Died 13 August 1910."

In Nightingale's theodicy death was "going home." She often described it as entering into a new period of service or process of perfection. A letter to her cousin, Shore, on Aunt Mai's death, argued that "nothing will ever make me believe that one whose whole life was an aspiration, such as was hers, ends in a lame and impotent conclusion such as absorption whatever that may mean." She added that God's plan entailed "multiplying Himself, not absorbing into Himself," which of course entailed strengthening God's moral government by law.[102] For further on her views of death and the afterlife see *Theology*.

---

102 Draft letter or copy, March 1889, ADD Mss 45795 f141.

THEMES

Law, Probability and Application

F undamental to Nightingale's philosophy and informing *all* her major writing is a notion of a created world run by laws, natural and social. This she described, briefly, as early as her *Letters from Egypt*, 1849-50, and developed the theme at length in *Suggestions for Thought*, 1852-60. It appears as well in her *Fraser's Magazine* articles of 1873 and her unpublished essays; these are published in *Theology*.

Nightingale's main source for this conceptualization of law was the Belgian astronomer and statistician, L.A.J. Quetelet (1796-1874). Nightingale extensively annotated her copy of his major work, *Physique sociale*, copied out lengthy extracts from it and wrote her own comments and paraphrases (published in *Society and Politics*).[1] She praised him for approaching "more nearly than anyone to Plato's highest sense in dialectic."[2] Like Isaac Newton (1642-1727), Quetelet had a sense of the immensity of the world to study and the modesty of the results to date; echoing Newton he had said, "These are only a few pebbles picked up on the vast seashore of statistics."[3] Yet Quetelet was no less than the "founder of the most important science in the whole world, for upon it depends the practical application of every other *and* of every other art, the one science essential to all political *and* social administration, all education and all organization based on experience." Without it government would otherwise be "guesswork, or as the Germans would say, 'intuition.'"[4]

---

1 Marion Diamond and Mervyn Stone, "Nightingale on Quetelet." The annotated *Physique sociale* is held in the Archives of University College, London.
2 Note, ADD Mss 45785 f35.
3 Draft letter to Francis Galton c1891, ADD Mss 45810 f177.
4 Letter to Dr Farr ca. 23 February 1874, Wellcome Ms 5474/123.

More positively, laws told people (God's co-workers) how to intervene: modify the causes of a problem and you modify human behaviour, "free will and all."[5] God governs by His laws, but so do we, when we have discovered them (f188). For Nightingale as well as Quetelet "free will" was a red herring and she resented the loss of time and energy in debating it. Her/their understanding of law did not immobilize people but, on the contrary, enabled people to act. Laws were *descriptive*, so that it was better to designate their discovery as "registering" them; "We will not say [laws] subject man's action in the plan of God's moral government" (f144).

Any laws discovered were only *probabilistic*. Quetelet, himself an expert in probability theory, she commended for being "always on his guard against confounding probability with truth" (f164). A "Sub 'Note of Interrogation'" stated that "everything, down to the minutest particular, is so governed by laws, which can be seen in their effects, that not the most trifling action or feeling is left to chance" (reproduced in *Theology* 3:29). Yet, while nothing occurred by chance, *unintended consequences* were frequent and serious. She often gave as examples the establishment of foundling hospitals for abandoned babies, and almsgiving to the indigent, which only increased pauperism. (This was not to accept the political economists' approach of non-intervention; the goal was to intervene constructively and effectively.)

Nightingale quite specifically abhorred the "political economy" school, especially of Thomas Malthus (1766-1834), then the reigning doctrine.

> The laws of political economy, if really discovered, are of course as immutable as the laws of nature, but at present there is scarcely any extravagance which political economy is not made to father, for example the workhouse test which probably has made more paupers than anything else—the theory that supply and demand will always, under all circumstances, in all countries, answer to each other—which made the Orissa famine possible under our "enlightened rule."[6]

---

5 Notes on Quetelet, Add Mss 45842 f168.
6 Note, Add Mss 45843 f34.

Positivism and Idealism

Nightingale's philosophy of science is clearly in the positivist tradition, understood as the acquisition of knowledge through research in the real world, as opposed to intuition, introspection or reliance on authority. Yet Nightingale in some of her writing made rude remarks about positivists and positivism, for their atheism or their espousal of a new "religion of humanity." J.S. Mill was the "tenderest" of the positivists. More often she sought to integrate a methodologically tough positivism with idealism in objectives. In *Notes from Devotional Authors of the Middle Ages*, objecting to an article which treated the two as "opposite philosophies," she called the one "a necessary precursor and foundation of the other." She asked: "Are not the two one? ... [for] positivism lays down that all things, moral as well as physical, are subject to law." Moreover, "is not positivism, rightly understood, the only way to idealism—the only way by which we can alter or improve anything?" She disagreed with the view that positivism led necessarily to the substitution of law for the idea of a personal God. Rather positivism provided idealists with the tools to learn where and how to intervene for good:

> A perfect God cannot change His mind. Positivism says the latter half of this, idealism the former half, that is, positivism says that universal law, or the mind of God, is never altered. Idealism says that *He* would not be a perfect God who could alter His mind and that we should expect to see God working as the only way a *perfect* Being could work by universal law.[7]

Consistent with her views on social science Nightingale supported the organizations that promoted it. For many years she sent papers to meetings of the British Association for the Promotion of Social Science, founded in 1857 with a strong applied emphasis. She submitted two papers on hospital construction to its first Social Science Congress in 1858 in Liverpool; one to Dublin in 1861 on hospital statistics; two to Edinburgh in 1863 on aboriginal races and Indian sanitation; one to York in 1864, again on aboriginal races; and one to Norwich in 1873 on Indian sanitation. Dr Farr proposed her for membership in the London Statistical Society (later the Royal Statistical Society) in 1858; she was its first woman member.

As a British empiricist philosophically, Nightingale could be expected to have favourable views of John Locke (1632-1704) and Francis

---

7 ADD Mss 45841 f23.

Bacon (1561-1626), and negative views about the competing "intuitionist" school of German idealism. Bacon was a great inductive philosopher, "much greater than Mill."[8] She had carefully read and drew extracts from Benedict Spinoza (1632-77), reported in *Theology*.

Theology/Theodikè

It will be clear throughout this *Collected Works* that Nightingale's enormously positive understanding of God (a God of law) underlay all her theoretical and practical work. It is indeed for this reason that the next two volumes in this series are on her spiritual journey and theological views and that there will be four volumes in all on religion. This conceptualization of a powerful and benevolent Creator holds all her work together. That she could conceive of health care as a system owes much to her conceptualization of God as the All-good Creator who runs the world by laws capable of discovery by research. All her work in health care and social reform derived from her own call to serve this God humbly as handmaid or confidently as co-worker.

Nightingale believed that to understand the world people needed to understand the "character of God," and that this required our best intellectual and all other faculties (a familiar theme in *Theology*). She herself gave her best efforts to this study, with wide reading on religion throughout her life of Roman Catholic as well as Protestant authors, and at various stages of her life of Middle Eastern religions and Hinduism.

Natural Science

For Nightingale the laws of natural and social science were fundamentally similar: both were the work of God and both were open to human discovery through use of the scientific method, induction from research results. She held, further, that the two sorts of law, social and physical, acted and reacted on each other. Prediction was possible from each. One important difference between the two was that, while we cannot modify the solar system, we can modify the social system. We can predict an eclipse, and predict social events, too. She compared the two kinds of prediction in her second *Fraser's Magazine* article, "A Sub 'Note of Interrogation.' I: What Will Be Our Religion in 1999?"

---

8 Letter to W.E. Nightingale 23 January 1864, Add Mss 45790 f323.

Nightingale's education included little natural science and she had had to plead for some mathematics to be added to her instruction, a subject not considered necessary for girls, and perhaps outside her classically educated father's areas of expertise in any event. Her father took her to a meeting of the British Association for the Advancement of Science at Oxford University in 1847 shortly after the discovery of the planet Neptune. The subject of the meeting was astronomy, and participants included the discoverers. (Her impressions from the Oxford visit appear in *Society and Politics*.) Nightingale was interested in the history of science and had a reasonable lay person's acquaintance with the scientific issues of her time. She made frequent references to scientists in her unpublished notes, especially Newton and Michael Faraday (1791-1867). She knew Ada Lovelace (1815-52), with Charles Babbage (1792-1871), co-inventor of the first calculating machine, the prototype computer. Her disapproval of Charles Darwin (1809-82), whose *Origin of Species* was published in 1859, was not based on any conventional belief antithetical to the theory of evolution but on a disagreement as to the *facts*: "Darwin has got no true principle because he had only one true fact and one hundred false ones."[9]

Naturally she disapproved of *social Darwinism*, the application of the "survival of the fittest" thesis of Darwin to social organization, which justified the *laissez-faire* approach of the political economists. Arguing with Mill she denied that Darwinism was based on careful observation. "They have constructed a circle on two or three points in the circumference and all the points which would not come in to that circumference, they have put out of court."[10] Still, Darwinism was not the "sin against the Holy Ghost" or the sin against hope: that sin was using past mistakes as an excuse for not doing *anything*, effectively the position of the political economy school.

Nightingale's interest in natural science, and her optimism that knowledge can be applied for good, led her to be one of the first people to appreciate the pioneering work on acid rain done by Robert Angus Smith in the 1860s.[11] Dealing with him on Indian water issues in 1865 she sent her congratulations on his first report, under the Alkali Act, on what was probably the world's first legislated pollution abatement: "I cannot forbear wishing you joy, and wishing England joy, of

---

9 Notes for Jowett, ADD Mss 45785 f36.
10 Note, ADD Mss 45842 f17.
11 Robert Angus Smith, *Air and Rain: The Beginnings of a Chemical Climatology.*

your first report on the condensation of gases from alkali works. . . .
You have clearly shown how advantageous it is to employ scientific men
on scientific work like this, and in the end there is every prospect that
you will be able to rid the country of a great nuisance."[12]

The Italian Connection

It is well to bear the "Italian connection" in mind when trying to
make sense of Nightingale, especially her politics. Not only did she
continue to identify with the city of her birth, she read and was influenced by its great authors and loved to use the Italian language. She
was clearly influenced by Dante, whom she cited in various places,
notably on her conception of an active afterlife. Nightingale threw
Italian expressions into letters to friends and relatives who would recognize them. Thus a confusion is a "scompiglio," a fight a "baruffa"
and a mix-up a "garbuglio." Even late in life, in 1880, there are notes
to the Verneys in Italian (see pp 350-51 below).

A book on the Florentine monk Savonarola (1452-98) was published in 1847, which she probably read on her second trip to Italy,
1847-48. Savonarola was hanged and burned at the stake in 1498 for
instituting a radically different form of government, a republican
theocracy. Florence, as a "city of God," was democratic in certain
respects, puritanical in others (in the four years of the experiment
"pagan" paintings were burned). An unpublished note (now in *Theology*) excerpts his poetry and reveals Nightingale's identification with
his martyrdom (Nightingale's emphasis in italics):

> Above all things, love God with all your heart; *seek his honour more
> than the salvation of your own souls.* . . . Lord, I ask you the grace not to
> die in my bed, but that of shedding my blood as you did for me.[13]

This expression of Nightingale's willingness, even desire, to die sacrifi-
cially gives context to her service in Crimea.

The Italian Risorgimento was the primordial independence movement for Nightingale. Her passion aroused by her trip of 1837-38, she
read the prison accounts of the captured independence fighters,

---

12 Letter 15 June 1865 to Robert Angus Smith, Private Collection of Hugh
Small.
13 Loose note, Convent of Mercy, Bermondsey, from *Poesie di Ierolamo
Savonarola* 21. The extract is not dated but was likely made when Nightingale was in Rome the winter of 1847-48.

notably Silvio Pellico (1789-1854). Sardinians, in the newly emerging independent state of Italy, joined Britain and France in the Crimean War, so that there was further contact with Italians from that period.

Nightingale then followed Italian politics the rest of her life, commenting on such leading members of the Risorgimento as Cavour[14] and Garibaldi[15] (reported in *European Travels*). The tri-colour flag (red, white and green) of the Risorgimento was itself based on Dante's[16] vision (red for blood, green for olive trees and white for the Holy Spirit—also the colours of the duomo, in due course the flag of Italy). Garibaldi himself called on Nightingale in London in 1864; she hoped to recruit him to the cause of sanitary reform but found him too caught up with "ideals" and hopeless for administration. Mazzini[17] later supported the struggle of Nightingale and many others for the repeal of the Contagious Diseases Acts.

The partisans of the Risorgimento knew their intellectual heritage. They drew on the Greek classics and knew Savonarola. They were anti-clerical (for good reason), but fervent in faith, and Christian imagery figures strongly in their inspiration. All of this would have resonated with Nightingale. Women, incidentally, were part of the Italian independence movement and some died for the cause. Garibaldi's pregnant wife lost her young child and died herself fleeing from the French Army.

Government and Politics

Nightingale lived at a time when the reigning political orthodoxy was classical *laissez-faire liberalism*, or what would, by the late twentieth century, be called *conservatism* for its denial of a significant role for government. She rejected that approach in principle, apart from rejecting it in the particular examples given above. Never a socialist, she was a left-leaning, pragmatic liberal, who would leave the running of the economy largely to the private sector, in line with laissez-faire principles. Government, however, should be used to solve great social problems that cannot be solved otherwise. Whether or not government should be called on, and what level of government, were matters to be

---

14 Count Camillo di Cavour (1810-61).
15 Giuseppe de Garibaldi (1807-82).
16 Dante Alighieri (1265-1321).
17 Giuseppe Mazzini (1805-1872).

determined from study of the causes of the problem. "Above all it is governments which dispose of life. Is it not then the first, the most essential step to have a political science, to raise it, if it is a science at all, into an *exact* science?"[18]

Ever practical and cost-conscious, Nightingale recommended that *all* government programs be subjected to evaluation. A note she made in Quetelet's *Physique sociale* specifies:

> A government in modifying its laws, especially its financial laws, should collect with care documents to prove, at a future state, whether the results obtained have answered their expectation. Laws are made and repealed with such precipitation that it is most frequently impossible to study their influence. (1:89)

To Francis Galton (1822-1911) she complained that government collected "splendid" statistics, which it then did not use. This was one of the reasons she sought, in one of the last projects of her life, to have a chair or readership in social physics established at Oxford University, the chief place of education of the senior civil service. This would teach Quetelet's method to the people who most needed to know it, those actually administering social programs. Correspondence on this, as for all matters statistical, appears in *Society and Politics*.

Because of the important scope for government action in her system, legislators had a particularly important, even *holy* role to play. Legislators had a "noble mission," she explained in her essay on Quetelet, because they could alter the atmosphere in which we live.[19] Politics was the administration of God's world, "in the particular time and place of the nation," bringing down "God's government from heaven to earth."[20]

Unpublished essays show how much Nightingale was imbued with the spirit of Savonarola's "city of God" ideal:

> If we were really under a theocracy, if we, in serving under the government, were serving God's government, in pleasing God, were really pleasing the Cabinet, the War Office, the Poor Law Board, how easy our work would be! But now, if we are to please our rulers, we must displease God, for the House of Commons does not like at all what God likes! Oh dear how I wish the Lord *was* King or at least Prince of Wales.[21]

---

18 Essay on Quetelet, ADD Mss 45842 f197.
19 Essay on Quetelet, ADD Mss 45842 f183.
20 Note for Jowett, ADD Mss 45783 f203.
21 Proposal for revision of the *School and Children's Bible*, ADD Mss 45842 f3 (in *Theology* 3:553).

Yet people believed God to be quite inadequate to carrying on the business of a great nation:

> A nation would fall to pieces if its business were done according to His will. And no wonder, it certainly would, if done according to what we conceive *now* to be His will. . . . No wonder we exclude Him from our Cabinet, our House of Commons, our politics, our political economy and think that Sunday is *His* day . . . the weekdays are ours—"Monday and Thursday" are "government nights" in the House of Commons; God's evening is another evening in the week.

In Savonarola's time Jesus Christ was proclaimed King of Florence. Nor did Nightingale object to the expression *theocracy*, in the same draft essay noting: "the government of the Jews was called a theocracy—but what a God was theirs! And what a God is ours!"[22] One hastens to add that Nightingale's theocracy would have a strong place for individual rights and artistic expression: no burning of paintings or books.

Nightingale's role as a social reformer required her to work with whatever party was in power. There is no doubt, however, as to her Liberal preferences, especially in her later years when she worked closely with her brother-in-law, Sir Harry Verney, MP, an active Liberal. Socialists and conservatives alike may be dismayed by Nightingale's insistence that God was a Liberal. She told the wife of Verney's son Edmund (who was then running to succeed him as MP), that in helping him she was "working for eternity, to raise the ground the Liberal cause—that *is* the 'saving' of men's minds, bodies and soul, that *is* being fellow workers with God. . . . God is a 'Liberal,' we may say that without irreverence" (see pp 653-54 below).

The Family and Individuals

Nightingale never did any scholarly work on the family so her observations, including a full essay and the autobiographical "Cassandra," are very much a pouring out of her frustrations with the limitations her own family imposed, which were typical for a woman of her time and class. Her early writing on the family is *all* negative, beginning with "Cassandra," discussed above. She believed women should have access to the professions and understood the importance of economic independence. She supported matrimonial property rights for women.

---

22 Draft essay, ADD Mss 45843 f209.

Nightingale's resentment of her family's opposition to her nursing for a time coloured her views on the family as an institution. She (early) even favoured the use of crêches for children of all classes, including the rich. Yet she came around to strong advocacy of the family as an institution, including the creation of "artificial families" for orphaned children. Strongly negative views of the family appear in the one full essay on the family, her *Fraser's Magazine* articles and numerous of her other unpublished essays in *Theology*. They permeate her autobiographical essay, "Cassandra," in *Suggestions for Thought*. In the essay on the family in *Theology* she held:

> People take for granted (1) that "family" *is* to be a *state of war*. And then (2) they talk of its "healing influences" just as we talk of a war hospital. That it is most frequently alas! a state of war, though carefully concealed, is, we fear, little doubt. (3:143)

Yet Nightingale acknowledged that the family was from God, "the essential groundwork of His social system." She observed, from data, that taking a child away from even "the poorest labouring family" and placing it into "the most carefully managed asylum" did not generally have good results (3:143-44). Hence she came to recommend "boarding out," or foster homes, rather than institutions for the care of orphaned children; the family had to be reconstructed (see also *Society and Politics*).

In Nightingale's theology God intended the perfection of all human beings, if gradually and through the recognition of mistakes and their correction. The *individual* then was of greater importance than the family, however much the family was recognized as "the essential ground" of the social system. It was indeed because of the family's capacity to thwart individual expression that she was so bitter about it as an institution.

Social Class and Caste

From early in life Nightingale was appalled by the enormous disparities in wealth between people such as her family and the great mass of people, when the large majority owned no property and enjoyed few comforts, and nearly one third of the population lived in absolute misery. She performed the usual acts of charity for the poor but realized how inadequate they were. She developed more than a social conscience, more than a commitment to systemic, political change, but came to see "the face of God" in the poor, sick and imprisoned. The gospel was her source:

We should consider that the same tie really connects us to every one of our fellows as the tie which connects us with God. That to neglect or ill use the imbecile old woman, the dirty child, is the same crime of *lèse-majesté* against the Almighty that blasphemy of God is.[23]

Nightingale was still young when she became aware of class differences in treatment by the police. In a letter to an American friend she recounted an old lady telling her that the police were attentive "in taking up *everybody that was round*," i.e., taking them to the station to examine them. "And here they have not taken even me," she added.[24]

She made a point of talking to people from all classes and referred to workers as "friends." She identified with the poor people on the family estate at Embley: "I feel my sympathies all with ignorance and poverty; the things which interest me interest them; we are alike in expecting little from life, much from God."[25] Throughout her life she was sensitive to the humiliations to which people of lower status were frequently subjected. In drafting a letter for the chair of the house committee of the Glasgow Royal Infirmary, she advised, "(he is a shoemaker) please write very respectfully."[26] She was concerned that her colleague, Robert Rawlinson, son of a private soldier and known for "murdering the Queen's English," would be sent to eat with the servants when at Lea Hurst to assist with sanitary measures, although "he is just as much a gentleman as you or I" (see p 244 below). A letter as a young woman to an honorary aunt notes Nightingale's support of legislation to limit factory work for women to ten hours a day.[27]

Nightingale's sensibilities on class differences and discomfort with her own family's wealth emerged early and caused difficulties at home. A family friend recalled, post-Crimea, the young Nightingale dwelling on the "painful" social differences that existed and "the trap that a luxurious life laid for the affluent." The friend had laughed at the time at a conversation between father and daughter, "the contrast was so striking," but later took this as a sign of Nightingale's call.[28]

---

23 Letter/draft/copy to W.E. Nightingale 12 October 1867, ADD Mss 45790 f358.
24 Letter to Julia Ward Howe 23 July 1845, in Laura E. Richards, ed., "Letters of Florence Nightingale" 329.
25 Letter to Hannah Nicholson, 24 September [1846], ADD Mss 45794 f39.
26 Letter to Samuel Smith 1 August 1861, ADD Mss 45792 f213.
27 Letter to Hannah Nicholson [spring 1847], ADD Mss 45794 f61.
28 Note by Fanny Allen 15 April [1847], in Henrietta Litchfield, ed., *Emma Darwin: A Century of Letters 1792-1896* 2:160.

This identification with ordinary people remained throughout Nightingale's working life. In the Crimean War she laboured to save the lives of ordinary soldiers. Her promise that lives would never again be lost from such neglect was made with these young men in mind. Her work on sanitary reform was always sensitive to class issues. She realized that the poor could not avail themselves of clean air and water as the rich could, which meant that *public* measures had to be instituted. She recommended sending convalescent poor to the seaside: "For the rich the good of change of air, nay, even its necessity, is never doubted. It is *ten times more* necessary for the poor." Further, "every large town" ought to have a convalescent institution for the poor by the seaside or in the country.[29]

Gentlewoman that she was, Nightingale was nonetheless strongly meritocratic in her approach to organization. Thus she opposed the use of "lady superintendents" in nursing—that is, giving authority on the basis of birth rather than ability. Rather she insisted that they be trained like anyone else. Few of the original Crimea recruits were ladies, apart from her (a few of the Bermondsey sisters were "well born"). She is often credited with opening up the profession of nursing to middle-class women, which she did, but seldom for making it the first, and still the most amenable, profession for working-class women. Nightingale even considered provision for girls who had grown up in workhouses to enter nursing (they would be too young to enter training directly, so she proposed employment in a hospital as an intermediate stage). In her day there were *no* educational prerequisites for admission to a training school and student nurses, "probationers," were given free room and board and a small stipend.

Yet one critic went so far as to claim that "Nightingale spent much energy booting working-class women out of the nursing profession in order to create good jobs for ladies wanting to make a living by helping the imperial Army."[30] In fact, before Nightingale, working-class women did *not* nurse in Britain. Rather they worked as hospital *cleaners*, although they were called nurses and had some duties as patient "watchers."[31] Nightingale's reform was to separate cleaning jobs from

---

29 Nightingale, "Introduction," *Organization of Nursing* 12.
30 Mariana Valverde, review of *Early Origins of the Social Sciences, Canadian Journal of Sociology* 21,4 (1996):581.
31 On the roles of "female domestics," "menials" and "nurses" see Carol Helmstadter, "Passing of the Night Watch: Night Nursing Reform in the London Teaching Hospitals, 1856-90."

patient care, according the title *nurse* only to the latter, and making it a decent, well-paying job, open on the basis of merit, regardless of class origins. There is evidence, moreover, that Nightingale tried to recruit women otherwise headed for domestic service into trained nursing.

When Elizabeth Garrett Anderson (1836-1917) wanted to restrict access by class Nightingale insisted that *all* nurses be highly paid because of their special skills—good pay was needed also because of short supply. Working-class women did make it into nursing and its senior positions, the most illustrious if exceptional example being Mary Jones, a good friend of Nightingale and head of St John's House, who was the daughter of a cabinetmaker.[32] "Lady superintendent" became a job title.

For the 1871 Census Nightingale asked an official how she should describe her occupation, and objected to his reply of "none, gentlewoman." She joked that she would deserve to be fined "for false information" if she replied "no occupation" and thought at least she should put "war hospital matron, or hospital matron retired from active service through illness."[33]

In her decades of work on India the same identification held. She routinely castigated the British government for policies that favoured the landlords and worsened the circumstances of the rural poor. The ryot, the Indian peasant, she repeatedly pointed out, was the most industrious person in the world, and should enjoy more of the product of that labour. She opposed the salt tax for its regressivity; the poor had to spend more of their small incomes on salt, an essential item for food preservation, than the rich. She pressed for land tenure reform and restrictions on usury (high interest rates). Her letters and papers to Indian organizations show the fervour along with her pertinent analysis.

Nightingale shared the views of her class on labour unions as being tyrannical and losing workers' jobs by asking for too much. Yet she was pro-labour in many respects. In an article she published in 1869, after working on Poor Law reform in metropolitan London, she favoured better wages and salaries: "It is always cheaper to pay labour its full value. Labour underpaid is more expensive."[34] She also favoured bet-

---

32 On the entry of working-class women into nursing, in Nightingale's and other institutions, see Carol Helmstadter, "Robert Bentley Todd, Saint John's House, and the Origins of the Modern Trained Nurse."

33 Letter to Harry Verney 31 March 1871, Wellcome (Claydon copy) Ms 9005/33 (in *Society and Politics*).

34 Nightingale, "A Note on Pauperism" 282.

ter holidays for workers, especially women workers in high-stress occupations like the needle trades.

Pauperism, or at least people who *could* work but were living off others' labour, was abhorrent to her. Her *Fraser's Magazine* article on the subject opened with a statement of how much was spent annually on Poor Law relief, with the result only "to increase directly and indirectly the pauperism it is meant to relieve" (281). The solution was to remove all the sick and those incapable of work from the workhouses and provide for their care or cure. She was less specific about what to do for those remaining—she evidently did not think there were many who would choose not to work if work were available. She found it impossible to believe that "at least in exceptional times of distress, the state could not provide work at remunerative prices." We should not "punish the hungry" but teach them "to feed themselves" (282). Nightingale hoped to do more research on the subject, collected material to that end and tried, unsuccessfully, to get her friend Dr Sutherland to edit it for publication.[35]

While the ideas of many radical theorists mellow with time this did not happen to Nightingale. A letter late in life (1891) on the treatment of the people who rioted in Hyde Park and Trafalgar Square called it a "horrible and degrading spectacle that we can do nothing for our vagabonds and unemployed but drive them from street to street with our fists—a far sadder spectacle than war."[36] She remarked further on the scarcity of good health nurses, even for royalty, "but royalty can take care of itself and poverty can't." Nightingale always wanted services to be levelled up; when middle-class women took to their beds for a month to recuperate from childbirth, she thought working-class and poor women needed help so that they could, too.

Nightingale also took on, again without any practical effect and without giving the matter her best efforts, the subject of criminality. She had been greatly impressed with Quetelet's early criminological work. There are extensive notations on it in *Physique sociale*, with her own observations on crime statistics and the prediction of criminality. She published several short articles on the treatment of criminals, urging, among other things, that thieves be required to pay restitution. She hoped that the proposed professor or reader of social physics at Oxford would conduct research both on the prevention of pauperism

---

35 Note March 1869, Add Mss 45753 f279.
36 Letter to Amy Hawthorn, 24 October 1887, Add Mss 45776 f244.

and the treatment of delinquent children, subjects dealt with in *Society and Politics*.

Gender Roles and Status of Women

Nightingale held that women had the same rights to develop their abilities, to become perfect, in her terms, as men. She herself seems to have been remarkably free of gender role stereotyping. When she wanted women to become nurses rather than doctors this was not from convention (there were scarcely any trained women nurses outside religious orders) but from her conviction that nursing, which would include midwifery, was more useful than medicine. It must be remembered that medicine at that time offered few cures for disease and that treatments still included leeching and blistering. Nightingale totally rejected the double sexual standard so prevalent in her time. That is, she refused to believe that men and women were fundamentally different in their sexual drives, so that men had to have other women if deprived of their wives, the Army's excuse for condoning prostitution. The two sexes had the same moral responsibilities, she held, and a common moral nature.

Yet Nightingale was often critical of women. She felt that women did not take up the opportunities they had, notably in nursing. She began her post-Crimea work with a dedicated band of male collaborators, but no women. She seems sometimes to have been oblivious to the fact that women were not then *permitted* in the professions. Nightingale complained that women did not know the names of Cabinet ministers, the ranks in the Army or which churches had bishops and which not, all of which information was available in almanacs and other reference books (Cook, *Life* 2:14-15). She decried women's desire for *love*, to be loved that is, but failure at *sympathy*, that is the ability to feel the situation of another.

When Nightingale complained in 1861 that she had left no school behind her, that her work had taken no hold among women, she was speaking too soon. The only particularly worthy women she knew then were not collaborators in the same way Sutherland, Farr, Robert Rawlinson and Edwin Chadwick (1800-90) were; they may have been able, helped and sympathized, but did not strategize: her friends Selina Bracebridge and Mary Clarke Mohl (1793-1882), the "madre," Laure de Ste Colombe (1806-86), her cousin, an artist, Hilary Bonham Carter, Dr Elizabeth Blackwell (1821-1910), "Rev Mother" Mary

Clare Moore (1814-74), nurse Jane Shaw Stewart (d. 1905), and author Harriet Martineau. Yet, though it is true that her early collaborators were exclusively men this would soon change.

In nursing itself there would be many women whom she unequivocally respected: notably Rachel Williams (1840-1908), Jane Styring, Angelique Pringle (1842-1921), Amy Hughes, Mrs Fellowes, as well as others for whom there was enormous respect and fondness, but mixed with frustration: for example, Sarah Wardroper (c1813-92) and Agnes Jones (1832-68). Of course Nightingale's vision of nursing was as a woman-led profession.

Nightingale's exasperation in working with Dr Sutherland appears throughout their lengthy exchange of notes. Not so well known is the close and warm relationship with his wife, "the best of all my wives," as Nightingale described her.[37] A letter late in life from Mrs Sutherland recalls "how deeply and truly I feel all your love and kindnesses from the first hour we met until now. God bless you always and return all your loving thoughtfulnesses a thousandfold onto your own head, blessings in being blessed." It closes with "ever your affectionate and grateful."[38]

In the Franco-Prussian War Nightingale was deeply impressed by the relief work done by Caroline Werckner (to whom she left money in her will). By the Egyptian and African campaigns of the 1880s there were women more like herself, able to take initiatives, expose injustices, demand inquiries, write reports, etc., notably Amy Hawthorn. Later still we will see her advising her friend, historian Alice Stopford Green (1847-1929), on her candidacy to become Mistress of Girton College, Cambridge and generally taking an interest in women's education. She supported the work of Anne Jemima Clough (1820-92) in girls' education and later in the founding of Newnham College, Cambridge. She corresponded with Jane (Mrs Nassau) Senior (1828-77), the first woman Poor Law inspector and a social reformer.

Nightingale's relationship with Adeline Paulina Irby was fraught with frustration (as will be clear in *Society and Politics*), for Irby was not a lover of facts, yet Nightingale had enormous respect for her courage and daring in organizing Bosnian relief (to which she contributed herself; and she left Irby money in her will). Nightingale had great respect

---

37 Letter to Parthenope Verney 14 August 1858, Wellcome (Claydon copy) Ms 8997/72.
38 Letter 30 October 1887, ADD Mss 52427 f101.

also for the philanthropist Octavia Hill (1838-1912), founder of the Charity Organisation Society and co-founder of the National Trust.

As well as Mary Clare Moore, the "dearest reverend mother" of the Convent of Mercy at Bermondsey, there were other nuns Nightingale deeply respected: of the Sisters of Mercy, Mary Gonzaga Barrie (1825-73) and Mary Stanislaus Jones (1822-1913), to whom she left money in her will. Among Anglican nuns there was Mary Jones (also superintendent of the training school for nurse-midwives at King's College Hospital) and Priscilla Lydia Sellon (1821-76). (Nightingale left money to a later mother superior of Sellon's order.)

Within her own family in earlier years she saw talents being wasted (especially in her cousin Hilary Bonham Carter). Later women family members would be dedicated and competent, beginning with Emily Verney (1843-72) in the Franco-Prussian War, Maude Verney in rural health schemes and Rosalind Shore Smith, who went to Girton College and worked with her husband in the co-operative movement. Nightingale's relationships with women show an enormous range not only in emotional tone but practical collaboration (see *Women*).

Nightingale's pro-women work includes consideration for soldiers' wives. She thought that married men should be able to take their wives and children with them on posting, a practice then allowed only for small numbers. She thought that health care provisions for the men should include their wives. In Scutari she saw to it that there was midwifery help for the wives or partners of the soldiers.

Nightingale's non-medical approach to childbirth should seem familiar to modern feminists. Apart from considering childbirth to be an important matter—for we all have to be born—she considered safe childbirth with trained assistance deserving of careful research, experimentation, evaluation and reformulation as the result of lessons learned. The second project to be funded from the Nightingale Fund was a training institution for midwives, a "lying-in" institution. Nightingale then discovered unacceptably high mortality from puerperal fever in the first six years of its operation: twenty-six deaths out of 780 women giving birth, or 33.3 per 1000 woman/births. By contrast the average mortality of women giving birth at home in 1867 was 5.1 per 1000.[39] More specifically, Nightingale found that mortality was higher where medical students were permitted to attend (48), and she accordingly recommended that medical students not be allowed to

---

39 Nightingale, *Introductory Notes on Lying-in Institutions* 3.

witness births, but only midwives and physician/accoucheurs (69). All midwifery wards connected to general hospitals should be closed at once, she advised (advice not taken). The question as to Nightingale's closing of the lying-in institution, and the statistical basis for making this decision, will be thoroughly examined in *Women*.

Nightingale's *Introductory Notes on Lying-in Institutions* is a pioneering analysis of a subject of great importance to women. It is packed with good advice, arrived at after a careful processing of information. Nightingale herself devised and sent out the questionnaires to obtain comparative mortality data—none were available at the time for Britain.[40] Her statistical analysis showed "a large amount of preventible mortality in midwifery practice" and generally more at maternity hospitals than at home (3). She also examined secondary causes of mortality, especially the influence of age and social condition. Nightingale hoped to continue the research and publish further on the subject but did not. Her most frequent collaborator, Dr Sutherland, helped with the analysis but apparently could not be persuaded to do the work to put out a second edition.

The evidence shows that Nightingale's views on the admission of women to the medical profession were much more nuanced than usually described. For example, she was cautious about Elizabeth Blackwell's sister, Emily Blackwell, becoming the first woman doctor in England, because she understood what pressure the first woman would be under, and what sacrifices she would have to make so as not to harm the cause of women.[41] In 1859 Nightingale arranged an introduction for Elizabeth Blackwell to an eminent doctor to advise her on her career.[42] Later in life Nightingale publicly and actively supported the admission of women. For example, in 1877 she wrote the Dean of the School of Medicine at London University supporting a proposal to facilitate women's access. Still, she would have preferred a different kind of training for women physicians, centred on midwifery institutions and hospitals specializing in the care of women and children, than that contained in the proposal in question. She stressed the need

---

40 She used Lefort's material from France but seems not to have been aware of Semmelweiss's important reforms in Vienna, where he brought down mortality rates by instituting hygienic measures, with lots of soap and scrubbing.
41 Letter 12 May 1856, Radcliffe College, Schlesinger Library, Blackwell Family Collection Box 5:70.
42 Letter to Sir Benjamin Brodie 13 February 1859, Clendening History of Medicine Library, Kansas University Medical Center.

for training "at the bedside" as well as in lectures.[43] Yet she let her name be used. She was aware of the particular need for women doctors in India, where convention forbade women from being examined by a male doctor. In the late 1880s she sought advice from Dr Mary Scharlieb, who had practised in India, and recommended her professional services.[44] Her last doctor was a woman, Dr May Thorne, and her death certificate was signed by another woman doctor, Louisa Garrett Anderson (1873-?).[45] In 1888 Nightingale subscribed £50 to the building fund for a new hospital for women, later named for Elizabeth Garrett Anderson.[46]

Nightingale's views on prostitution and prostitutes were unusual for her time and for ours. She was conventional in regarding prostitution as immoral and she supported "rescue work," that is, the attempt to get women prostitutes out of the business. Yet she did not regard sexual immorality as a serious sin (incompetence and indifference were much worse). She was interested in the factors that prompted women to become prostitutes, including both abuse in the home and economic pressures. In her years of struggle against the compulsory inspection and treatment of prostitutes Nightingale would suggest the alternative of going after the "pimps."

Nightingale became aware of the problem of syphilis reducing effective Army numbers at least by 1860. By 1862 she was aware of moves in the War Office to legislate the inspection and treatment of women prostitutes as the solution. She did the first, behind-the-scenes, work to try to prevent such legislation, which was adopted in 1864 as the Contagious Diseases Act, and subsequently extended. She recruited Harriet Martineau to publicize the anti-CDA position in the more liberal *Daily News*, to counter the favourable coverage in the conservative *Times*. Her name and Martineau's headed a petition published 31 December 1869, in the *Daily News*, which launched the movement for repeal. Josephine Butler (1826-1906) then took on the leadership of the repeal movement, which was successful in 1886, with Nightingale again resuming a behind-the-scenes supportive role. See *Women* for an account of this important step in the development of feminist consciousness and organization.

---

43 Note before July 1877, ADD Mss 45804 f218.
44 For correspondence see ADD Mss 45808.
45 Daughter of Elizabeth Garrett Anderson, Britain's first woman doctor and an adversary on the Contagious Diseases Acts.
46 Louisa Garrett Anderson, *Elizabeth Garrett Anderson 1836-1917* 246.

Empire and Imperialism

Nightingale lived during a period of enormous imperial expansion and consolidation. India came under the direct rule of the British government, from the East India Company, in 1858; Queen Victoria was proclaimed Empress in 1876. The desirability, or not, of British imperialism seems never to have been a consideration for Nightingale, any more than she considered war in the abstract. The empire was a fact. The obligation for government to serve the common good applied no less in its colonies and possessions than at home.

Nightingale began her work on India with optimism about the benefits of British rule. A paper she sent to the National Association for the Promotion of Social Science in 1863 referred to "one of the most important of social questions, namely how the British race is to hold possession of India, and to bestow upon its vast population the benefit of a higher civilization."[47] Ten years later she sent another paper to the same organization's meeting acknowledging that improvements in sanitary conditions had been made. Yet it seems that she never agreed with her friend Edwin Chadwick's "white man's burden" approach; he saw sanitary reform in India as essential so that the British could live there safely. For Nightingale the India Office and the British civil service in India were far too slow in implementing change. By 1878 she was frankly setting out the failures of British rule. An article in the popular journal, *Nineteenth Century*, declared, "We do not care for the people of India."[48] British rule, instead of removing the causes of death that it could remove, took over Indian lands, permitted extortion and usury and let millions die from famine. Nightingale published a number of articles condemning British administration of India. She increasingly sided with Indian nationalists and broke with British officials and experts who failed to take up their cause. She publicly endorsed the election campaign, for the U.K. Parliament, of Dadabhai Naoroji (1825-1917), president of the Indian National Congress (see *Society and Politics*).

Nightingale studied Indian society and its religions. She suspected that caste was often used as an excuse "for not feeding, not cooking for, not cleansing or washing, not housing, not teaching, not amusing, not nursing." It was necessary to establish how far caste was "a reli-

---

47 Nightingale, "How People May Live and Not Die in India," National Association for the Promotion of Social Science, Edinburgh 1863.
48 Nightingale, "The People of India" 193.

gious and how far a social institution," how far it could be overcome or how much one must bow to it.[49] A later letter recounted that she had been told "by an experienced and learned Indian that we [the English] had made the great mistake of encouraging caste, whereas in India the native idea is that military service does away with caste."[50]

Apart from India, a major subject of her life's work, Nightingale took on public health issues in other colonies. In 1863 she prepared a report, "Sanitary State of Native Colonial Schools and Hospitals," for the Colonial Office. She had prepared the forms it sent to the governors of the colonies of Ceylon, Australia, Natal (South Africa), the West Coast of Africa and British North America (Canada). A further "Note on the Aboriginal Races of Australia," 1865, was sent to the National Association for the Promotion of Social Science. Mortality and morbidity data had been sent to her for analysis and advice. Nightingale's observations are exceptionally strained—she was quite out of her element and the data from different regions were not comparable. But even these inadequate statistics showed how badly aboriginal people did in hospital. She suggested they had an instinctive "dread of quiescence in one place."[51] Yet the fate of the aborigines concerned Britain's "national honour" (8). She strongly recommended careful collection of mortality data to enable authorities to take appropriate measures, advice largely ignored. This material will be reported in *Society and Politics*.

War and Militarism

"War brings one back to the Judaic times and quite out of the civilized conventional Anglicisms of the nineteenth century: war makes Deborahs."[52]

It is a great irony that the idealistic Nightingale, who wanted to shed her own blood, identifying with the crucifixion of Christ, should have

---

49 Typed copy of letter to Dr Farr 28 September 1861, Wellcome Ms 5474/44.
50 Typed copy of letter to Dr Farr, 2 October 1861, Add Mss 43399 f54.
51 Nightingale, "Note on the Aboriginal Races of Australia" 3.
52 Letter to Selina Bracebridge 5 November 1855, Wellcome (Claydon copy) Ms 8995/67.

made her name in the Crimean War. This was a shabby war if its
motives are considered. It was a glorious war if acts of personal heroism and gallantry count. That the British, French and Turkish side
won at all is largely attributed to the greater number of crucial errors
made by Russian generals. The infamous "charge of the light brigade"
resulted in the loss of almost the entire British brigade, but the battle
was won when the Russians failed to take advantage of British mistakes.

The British Isles are situated far from the Crimean peninsula in the
Black Sea. The ostensible issues at stake included the status of Orthodox Church members in Muslim Turkey and control over certain
churches in the Holy Land. The underlying motive was, of course,
Russian expansionism. For a time, Russia took over some of the territory of what is now Romania. It seemed to the British and French
likely that they would go farther west and south if not forcibly
stopped. In fact the British, French and Turkish victory resulted in
curtailing Russian expansion, and achieved the neutralization of the
Black Sea and the opening up of the Danube River to international
trade.

Russia at the time was an unmitigated, absolutist tsardom. Serfdom
had not yet been abolished and the rights and liberties enjoyed by
Britons and, to a lesser extent, other Europeans were nowhere in
sight. Nightingale's friend Harriet Martineau justified British partici-
pation in the war on grounds of Russian tyranny,[53] language which
Nightingale also used.[54] Yet Turkey was no more a democracy than
Russia, so that this excuse smacks of the same logic as the United States
defending democracy in Kuwait in the Persian Gulf War. Nightingale
herself, to my knowledge, never said that the Crimean War was a just
one. It seems that she never struggled with the just-war concept or its
application in any particular war. Wars there were, and someone had
to look after the wounded and sick that resulted from them.

In a letter late in life, Nightingale attributed the Crimean War to
"the marching of Russia in to subdue Hungary (in 1848)." This made
the people of England so furious with Russia that they went to war in
1854, not over the ostensible causes, the "holy places—it was our rage
with Russia that brought about the Crimean War." The context here is

53 See especially her leaders in the *Daily News* 5 and 24 May 1854, 8, 14, 22 and
28 August 1854 and 4 October 1854.
54 For example in a letter to Parthenope Nightingale 2 June 1856, Wellcome
(Claydon copy) Ms 8996/63.

that good can come out of evil, as the beatitudes "presuppose evil," and in turn the Crimean War "brought about the reform of nursing."[55]

Among the many wars for which Nightingale's advice was called was the American Civil War, which occurred soon after the Crimean War. There is evidence to indicate that her material was extensively used by the United States Army.[56] The only evidence of her material being used by Southern forces is that the Confederate Surgeon-General reissued her book on field cooking.[57] To what effect her material was used in the Civil War is a matter to be examined in detail in a later volume. There are references in correspondence during the Franco-Prussian War of 1870-71 that "it was the American adaptation of our plans in their war which resulted in a 10 percent death rate instead of 3 percent,"[58] i.e., that the Americans could have done much better if they had followed advice more closely; certainly the Civil War is known for its high mortality.

Nightingale's approach to war often seems technocratic; there were urgent problems to solve, preparations to make. She was acutely aware of the price paid when this was not adequately done, in the Franco-Prussian War no less than the Crimean:

> The organization for war is a matter so essential to national existence that, with the smallest flaw in it, nations are overrun and go to destruction. In war everything is exactly adapted for its end, and the end is carried, for exact obedience is rendered. Where the organization of war is deficient the consequences are so tremendous that there is no need to dwell on the necessity of organization. We see Prussia in possession of France, France prostrate.[59]

Nightingale kept her personal preferences quiet, but was a Francophile.

Correspondence during the Egyptian/Sudan campaigns in the 1880s shows her enthusiasm for trying out new measures for military nursing services, "the great opportunity" to show what a trained, well-administered company could do. Nightingale almost seems keen for a

---

55 Letter to Margaret Verney 27 April 1894, Wellcome (Claydon copy) Ms 9014/161.

56 Frederick Milnes Edge, *A Woman's Example and a Nation's Work: A Tribute to Florence Nightingale* 41.

57 Surgeon-General, *Directions for Cooking by Troops, in Camp and Hospital, Prepared for the Army of Virginia,* Reynolds Historical Library, University of Alabama at Birmingham.

58 Letter to Harry Verney 23 August 1870, Wellcome (Claydon copy) Ms 9004/87.

59 Notes, ADD Mss 45843 f203.

battle to test their preparedness. Regrettable as it was, it "will be worth years of writing and home agitation to forward the true cause. We envy you the noble work. . . . "[60]

Idealism in war was always a theme in Nightingale's writing. She had seen that war drew out great personal courage in men. She had been touched by the daily, uncomplaining sacrifices of ordinary soldiers. Her writing is laced with respect for their stoicism and loyalty to comrades. Late in life she continued to send memorials to anniversary celebrations of the Crimean battles.

Her involvement with the founding and early work of the International Red Cross is complex. Henri Dunant (1828-1910), whose idea it was, credited Nightingale with the inspiration. Dunant happened to be in Solferino on business in 1866 and saw soldiers in large numbers left to die on the battlefield. This war between the rising Italian states and their overlord, Austria, occurred just after the Crimean War and before the Franco-Prussian War. Yet in Nightingale's view the whole premise of the Red Cross was faulty for being based on the *voluntary*, that is, non-governmental, provision of medical and nursing assistance. She derided the approach as one that could only have come from a small state, like Switzerland or Baden, that had not known war. The danger was that voluntary efforts allowed the belligerents to neglect their responsibilities, and thus made war cheap. Indeed this was confirmed by events in the Franco-Prussian War.

Nightingale was decorated by both sides at the end of the Franco-Prussian War for her work in the provision of relief for the sick and wounded. Most of her writing on that war concerns such practical matters as the supplies needed, trained personnel, procedures, etc. She personally gave money for the relief of refugees from the siege of Paris and publicly supported fundraising efforts.[61]

Interspersed among Nightingale's many administrative letters and memoranda of the Franco-Prussian War are enormously interesting observations on the broader issues of militarism, the causes of war and the relative merits of the two sides. Her predicament was that she was pro-French, while the Crown Princess of Prussia (1840-1901), a daughter of Queen Victoria, was the effective and indefatigable organizer of relief operations for the Prussians. Nightingale gave her best

---

60 Letter to Surgeon-Major G.J.H. Evatt 23 February 1885, Florence Nightingale Museum 0543.
61 Nightingale letter, "The Distress In and About Paris," *Times* 1 February 1871:6.

to both sides, was diplomatic in all correspondence with the Crown Princess and never took sides publicly. Privately she abhorred Prussian militarism, blamed Bismarck for the war and thought that Napoleon III (1808-73) got bad press. "The danger of German militarism is not so much the danger of war, though that is not small, as that danger to its own institutions, to its own national progress." A military dictatorship seemed likely, one which would absorb "all the better tendencies" not only of Prussia but it would Prussianize the "far nobler, and better" tendencies of non-Prussian institutions. She joked about "declaiming against" Gladstone, then prime minister of Britain, "but only imagine Mr Gladstone without a Parliament! . . . An honest and industrious bureaucracy, a high standard of national education is not enough to make a great nation. Yet that is all that Prussia has."[62]

None of Nightingale's admiration for heroism and self-sacrifice, however, led her to think of war as a *good* thing. Rather the challenge was how to elicit similar altruism in times of peace. A commemorative letter asks that the soldiers who showed such great virtues in time of war "show the same virtues in times of home life in peace."[63] Even during the Crimean War, when her preoccupations were practical not philosophical, there was some questioning. Notably, on her way to Crimea from Scutari she described her 420 convalescent soldiers as "returning to their regiments to be shot at again." Recalling that Pastor Fliedner of Kaiserswerth had said she was "a mother in Israel," she sardonically added that "a mother in the Coldstreams" would be more appropriate (see p 141 below).

Organization for peace was as important to her as that for war, and she sought to ensure the state properly cared for the sick, poor children, criminals, prostitutes and so forth:

> But *are* the consequences less tremendous when the organization of life is deficient? Can there be anything more appalling in the defeats of war . . . in the collapses of Wörth, Sedan, Metz [battles in the Franco-Prussian War], than there is in the standing defeat of industry and independence in England, one tenth of whose population are paupers, in the standing defeat of her attempts to reclaim criminals . . . in the standing defeat of all her charities and of all her police and of all her Poor Law-ing to reduce pauperism, vice,

---

62 Note 1871, ADD Mss 45845 f34.
63 Nightingale letter on the Balaclava anniversary commemoration, published in the *Times* 25 October 1895:6.

prostitution, crime, if they do not increase it indeed. Are these not failures worse than Sedan and Paris?"[64]

Clearly she did not glamourize war or treat resources for it as being of greater importance than organization for civil life. In many places she stressed the challenge of finding ways to elicit the same kind of sacrifice in times of peace as occurred in war: "Peace hath higher acts of manhood than battle ever knew."[65] On learning that her physician cousin, Samuel Shore Nightingale, had volunteered for Bombay, during an outbreak of plague, she said: "The age of chivalry is come when people *volunteer* NOT to kill but to cure."[66]

Nightingale did not write on advocacy for peace or non-violence as a strategy apart from the occasional brief remark such as those above. Yet the record is clear that this long-serving employee of the War Office, as she jokingly referred to herself, influenced these areas. Specifically she was mentor to Gopal Krishna Gokhale, Gandhi's mentor, who in turn was a significant source for Martin Luther King, Jr., in the American civil rights movement of the mid-twentieth century. King himself opposed American aggression in Vietnam. The civil rights movement generally helped to encourage the non-violent anti-apartheid movement in South Africa. This line of influence all makes more sense when we consider that Nightingale's chief source was Jesus and the cross (to her Good Friday was the most important day in the world). Gandhi, although not a Christian, was also influenced by the teachings of Jesus, as were of course the Rev Martin Luther King, Jr., and Bishop Tutu.

Approach to Health Care

A more holistic approach to health and a concern for health promotion rather than the cure of disease became fashionable in the late twentieth century. These were Nightingale's concerns throughout her life and they permeate her writings from official reports on the health of the Army to advice to mothers running their households. One of her many criticisms of medical practice in the Crimean War was that

---

64 Note, ADD Mss 45843 ff203-04.
65 Letter to Mary Clarke Mohl 26 March 1869, Woodward Biomedical Library A.10.
66 Letter to Margaret Verney 24 February 1898, Wellcome (Claydon copy) Ms 9015/113.

"no provision was made for systematically caring for the soldier's *health*, but only for his sickness. The chief recognized function of the Army medical officer was attending men in hospital, but in no way was it considered his duty to render it unnecessary for men to come into hospital at all."[67]

Notes on Nursing, first published in 1860, was intended for use in the home, not hospital, and is much more focused on health than sickness. Nightingale brought out several editions of this popular work, which was translated into many languages. In 1861 a new edition was published, with a chapter added on infant care, "Minding Baby," and a revised title: *Notes on Nursing for the Labouring Classes*, the edition reproduced in the *Collected Works* in *Public Health Care*. *Notes on Nursing* (in all its many versions) reflects Nightingale's long preference for "miasma theory" over the newer "germ theory," although she accepted germ theory for a small number of diseases. Consistent with miasma theory, *Notes on Nursing* described the general principle of disease as a more or less "reparative process, not necessarily accompanied with suffering, an effort of nature to remedy a process of poisoning or decay." Pain and suffering were symptoms, not of disease, but of the absence of lack of fresh air, light, warmth, quiet, cleanliness, punctuality or diet, "of each or of all" of these, so that the reparative process of Nature had been hindered.[68]

Throughout her writing Nightingale stressed the need for good environmental conditions for good health, beginning with clean air and water. Bad housing was a major cause of poor health. A memorandum to the President of the Poor Law Board in 1865 argued that "the state of the dwellings of the poor, the sanitary or rather unsanitary state of London in general, is not often taken into account in the ill health it produces, for example, consumption, weakness of intellect, rheumatism," not just typhus and cholera.[69] "Those who come from the worst dwellings are always the most sickly" (f65).

Nightingale did not have a good opinion of conventional chemical and drug medicine. God or nature cured and the caregiver's role was rather to provide the right conditions. An unpublished note gives the

---

67 Nightingale, *Army Sanitary Administration and Its Reform under the Late Lord Herbert*.
68 The edition cited here is the critical edition: Nightingale, *Notes on Nursing*, ed. Victor Skretkowicz 15.
69 Draft note after 1 July 1865, ADD Mss 45787 f63.

advice: "Go to God's infirmary and rest awhile."[70] Hence the importance of nursing and, indeed, its greater importance than medicine.

A popular theory from the time of Galen (129-200 CE) was that miasma, or vapours emanating from general filth or decaying matter, caused infectious diseases. It was on this theory that Nightingale based her theory of hygiene, which logically led to sturdy measures for the elimination of dirt, waste and filth of all kinds, which also, of course, got rid of some germs. The germ theory, by contrast, led logically to quarantine as a solution, and this she resisted; good hygiene, rather, was needed. Ultimately Nightingale acceded to the new view.

For most of Nightingale's professional life the "germ theory" was a subject of scientific debate, with respectable experts on both sides. Nightingale was correct, therefore, in her many years of qualifying germ theory as "speculation." In *Subsidiary Notes [on] Female Nursing*, 1858, she argued against the contagion theory as a general explanation for disease, admitting only that a few specific diseases, smallpox, "cow's pox" and syphilis, could be so accounted for. Otherwise the contagion theory was "a superstition."[71] Lest this seem more eccentric than it should, it should be noted that Louis Pasteur's discovery of the "diseases of wine" dates only to 1862, Robert Koch's landmark paper, "The Etiology of Traumatic Infectious Diseases," establishing the germ theory, dates only to 1879, while the discovery of the tuberculosis bacillus dates to 1882, that of cholera to 1883 and of brucellosis to 1887.[72] It is ironical that the illness from which Nightingale probably suffered was itself caused by a specific germ, the *Brucella* bacillus.

Whatever errors Nightingale made in conceptualizing disease, even her most severe critics acknowledge that she was successful in reducing its ravages.[73] Although it took decades, her team's approach to public health was gradually adopted. In the 1890s she was still working on rural health issues, complaining about the inadequacy of enforcement measures. The result of her, her team's and many others' efforts was that mortality rates in Britain fell markedly, a subject to be pursued in detail in *Public Health Care*.

---

70 Note, ADD Mss 45845 f148.
71 Nightingale, *Subsidiary Notes as to the Introduction of Female Nursing into Military Hospitals in Peace and in War* 129.
72 Alfred S. Evans, *Causation and Disease: A Chronological Journey* 9.
73 F.B. Smith acknowledged this unequivocally in his otherwise hostile *Florence Nightingale: Reputation and Power*, also in his *The People's Health: 1830-1910* 414.

Nightingale's extensive work on hospital reform similarly reflects her proclivity to go to the roots of the problem (good hospital design and the right location), based on scientific knowledge, including precise mortality data. She expressed both concern for lasting solutions, in well-designed buildings, and cautioned that not too much be expected from them. Hospital treatment had to fit into the whole scheme of public health care, with its emphasis on health promotion, disease prevention and treatment at home and recourse to a whole range of institutions (see *Hospital Reform*).

Good food was a key ingredient in Nightingale's approach to health promotion. Since the Hippocratics in the fifth century BCE it has been known that invalids cannot eat the same food as healthy people. One of her greatest reforms in the Crimea was the provision of nutritious meals, thanks especially to Alexis Soyer (1809-58), chef of the Reform Club in London, who went at his own initiative to the Crimea to feed the Army. Nightingale later had the Army establish a cooking school and Soyer himself published recipe books for Army use. (Her copies have survived and are housed at the Royal College of Nursing Library in London.) She was appalled by the low standard of nutrition and the Army's insistence on taking its own (preserved) food rather than purchasing local supplies of fresh food. Even a late reminiscence brings this out strongly:

> The troops were living on salt meat, when the finest cattle in the world were swarming on the shores of the Black Sea. . . . Raw coffee was sent out from England when every man, woman and child in Constantinople had his, her or its cup of coffee every morning. And the [soldiers] had [hard] biscuits, when they might have had any quantity of bread. The troops had only salt meat, biscuit and grog.[74]

Nightingale's *Notes on Nursing* gives careful attention to food. The subject was of great interest to her friend Harriet Martineau as well, so that much discussion of food appears in their correspondence (in *Women*).

Conclusion

These are the themes that will appear throughout the *Collected Works*, beginning with the family correspondence below, for Nightingale discussed her ideas, hopes and ongoing work with family members. Collaborators became friends in some sense and close collaborators were invited to her parents' and sister's homes. Messages went back and forth, as did books, letters and documents, between Nightingale herself, family members and her associates. Family members of course shared her interests in politics (they were all Liberals), art, European travel and politics. Correspondence even late in life will reflect back to the Nightingale family travels of the 1830s and 1840s.

The interconnections among the themes will be obvious. Nightingale's work on the foundation of nursing was a lifelong preoccupation, but it was part of a broader concern to reform public health care, prevent disease and promote health. All of this links to her faith, for it was a religious "call" that drew Nightingale to nursing in the first place, and a conception of a Creator God who ran the universe by laws informed her whole approach to health care thereafter. Nurses themselves, as doctors, needed spiritual nourishment to perform their roles. Nursing shared a scientific component with medicine, but it was an art and calling as well.

Nightingale's fame of course came from her role in the Crimean War. She maintained her commitment to save the lives of ordinary soldiers both in the Army at home in peace and in several later wars through decades of work with the War Office. Yet this was only a small part of her life. Even on military matters her interests broadened to the causes of war and the effects of military values and institutions, and she applied the same sort of analysis here as she did on public health care and famine prevention in India.

The very choice of her major work commitments, public health care and India, itself reflects her understanding of God as Ruler by law, with scientific method, especially statistics, providing the means for human intervention for good. The depth and relentless quality of her life's work too can only be understood by its basis in faith. Nightingale saw her efforts as doing what God wanted her to; the call to nursing was only the first stage. She joked about being an "employee" of the War Office, but was perfectly serious about God being the "Commander-in-Chief" whose work she did as "handmaid," servant or co-worker.

KEY TO EDITING

The material in this volume has been carefully transcribed and verified (see the electronic text for a full description of the process). Remaining illegible words and passages are so indicated, with [illeg], or [?] inserted to indicate our best reading of the word or words in question. Dates for material cited or reproduced are given wherever possible, in square brackets if they are estimates only (by an archivist, previous scholar or the editor). Any controversy about date is indicated by a footnote. The type of material, whether a note, actual letter, draft or copy, is given as precisely as possible. Designations of letter/draft/copy signify that the source was Nightingale's own files, given to the British Library or to St Thomas' Hospital and then the London Metropolitan Archives, and are probably drafts or copies kept by her. The designation of "letter" is used only when there is good reason to think that it was actually sent and received (a postmarked envelope, for example, or the archive source being other than Nightingale's own files). In some cases both the original letter is extant and Nightingale's draft or copy, and these show that her drafts/copies are reliable. We do not use the convention of ALS (autograph letter signed), but our "letter" is close to it, bearing in mind that Nightingale often used initials rather than her signature. The electronic I-text gives full information on supporting material (envelopes, postmarks), whether in pen, pencil, dictated, typed, etc.

The practice was naturally to use the best source possible, the original letter where available. Where a draft or copy was also available this is noted (if in another collection). Sometimes the original was no longer available so that a typed or a published copy had to be used.

All sources indicated as "ADD MSS" (Additional Manuscripts) are British Library, the largest source of Nightingale material. The Wellcome Trust History of Medicine Library is abbreviated "Wellcome." Most of those materials are copies of correspondence at Claydon House, indicated as (Claydon copy). If not so indicated they are originals.

To avoid use of "ibid." and "op. cit.," and to reduce the number of footnotes generally, citations are given at the end of a sequence, if the same source is cited more than once. Subsequent citations are noted in the text with the new page or folio number given in parentheses. The term "folio" (abbreviated as f, or ff in the plural) is used for reference to manuscript pages, p and pp for printed pages, where needed, or page numbers are given after the date or volume number without p or pp.

To make the text as accessible as possible spelling, punctuation and capitalization have been modernized and standardized, and most abbreviations replaced with full words. Roman numerals are replaced with Arabic (except for royalty, popes and the citation of classical texts). We have left Nightingale's use of masculine generics as they are, hence "man," "men," "he," etc., referring to human beings generally. Some, but not all, excessive uses of "and," "but" and "the" have been excised. Any words added by the editor to make sense (usually in the case of rough notes or faint writing) are indicated in square brackets.

Italics are used to indicate underlining and small capitals for double (or more) underlining. All indications of emphasis in texts are Nightingale's (or that of her correspondent or source), *never* the editor's. When taking excerpts from written material Nightingale indicated ellipses with x x and we have kept these in. Ellipses for editorial purposes are indicated with ... for skipped material within a sentence .... if to the end of the sentence or more than a sentence has been dropped. Passages that break off abruptly (or folios are missing) are so indicated. For this introduction references are provided only for exact quotations and very specific points. Obviously full documentation from the primary source will be given where the subject is treated, with secondary sources as appropriate. The few uses of (sic) are all Nightingale's.

People who changed their names (usually from marriage or the acquisition of a title, sometimes for purposes of inheritance) are referred to by the more commonly used one, cross-referenced in the index to the other. Dates to identify people are given where that person is discussed (place of identification is indicated in the index), not where there is only passing mention of the person, or the name appears on a list or in a footnote. Of course for many people, notably servants, acquaintances, tenants, villagers and the many people who wrote Nightingale for help of various kinds, identifying information is not available.

Nightingale normally used capital letters in pronoun references to God and we have standardized this. She was less consistent in references to Jesus—we reproduced them as she wrote them.

A bibliography is provided with full information on books and articles cited. Newspaper references are given in footnotes only. References to classical and other works available in many editions (and now often on the Internet) are given by book, chapter, canto, scene, line, etc., as appropriate, and are not repeated in the bibliography.

FAMILY LIFE

The correspondence to, from and about family members selected here represents a small fraction of the extant letters, in each case of representative material. Letters to Nightingale's family also appear in *European Travels* (notably her letters from Greece and Rome, which are newsy and cheerful) and in the volumes on war and militarism (there is much correspondence to her family from the Crimea). Moreover *all* the *Letters from Egypt* were addressed to the family (again full of information and reflections). Those included here have been chosen to portray basic relationships, with all their anxiety and stress, hope and disappointment. They begin with substantial selections of letters to her mother, father and sister and then go on to the extended family and the Verneys.

Most of the items are designated "letter/draft/copy" because it is not possible to distinguish between drafts or copies Nightingale kept herself (often written on stationery with a printed letterhead) and those actually sent and received (both sets were given to the British Library by the family). Nor is pen or pencil any indication of a letter's status, for Nightingale often sent serious letters in pencil. Nor is her signature any guarantee; there are signed drafts and unsigned sent letters, and of course she often used her initials, especially with people to whom she was close. Letters to her parents often close with "your loving child" without any name or initials. Several "letters," at least, one must doubt were ever sent (notably one very hard letter to her father).

Since this *Collected Works* is organized thematically, letters to family members, especially to her father, will appear in other sections as well (notably on religion, politics and Poor Law reform). The letters here deal with personal and family concerns. They are arranged chronologically so that development and change in relationships can be traced. The letters largely speak for themselves so that editorial comments are inserted only occasionally.

The section begins with the "Lebenslauf" or curriculum vitae Nightingale wrote for entrance to the Deaconess Institution in 1851. There are several other notes she wrote around the same time, which reflect her frustration at not being allowed to nurse or study nursing. These notes serve as an introduction to the correspondence to mother, father and sister.

Nightingale's "Lebenslauf" for Kaiserswerth

Source: Lebenslauf, original at Kaiserswerth Diakoniewerk, published in Anna Sticker, ed., "Florence Nightingale: Curriculum Vitae" (Kaiserswerth: Diakoniewerk 1954)

24 July 1851

I had a sickly childhood. The climate of England did not suit me, after that of Italy (Florence) where I was born. I could never like the play of other children. But the happiest time of my life was during a year's illness which I had when I was six years old. I never learnt to write till I was eleven or twelve, owing to a weakness in my hands, and I was shy to misery.

At seven years of age we had a governess, who brought me up most severely. She was just and well intentioned, but she did not understand children and she used to shut me up for six weeks at a time. My sister, on the contrary, she spoilt.

When I was ten my mother would have no more governesses and my father took us himself in hand. He taught me Latin and Greek and mathematics and whatever he knew himself. I had the most enormous desire of acquiring—for seven years of my life, I thought of little else but cultivation of my intellect. And even now when I think what a human intellect may become by industry, ambition comes before me like Circe with her cup to tempt me.

I had also the strongest taste for music. But God was merciful to me, and took away my voice by constant sore throat. Otherwise I think, if I could have sung, I should have wished for no other satisfaction. Music excited my imagination and my passionate nature so much that I recognize this as a real blessing.

God has always led me of Himself. I remember no particular sermon or circumstances which ever made any great impression upon me. But the first idea I can recollect when I was a child was a desire to nurse the sick. My daydreams were all of hospitals and I visited them whenever I could. I never communicated it to anyone—it would have been laughed at—but I thought God had called me to serve Him in that way.

My life was so wholly unpractical that I never did my own hair till I came here. I did not know the difference between rye and barley, between linen and cotton. When I was seventeen (it was the year of the influenza in London) our whole family had it. I had to nurse fifteen servants in bed, my mother and two children of her brother, who were in the house. I had only one assistant, the cook, who was not ill. But soon other nurses were sent for, the influenza passed away and all was at an end with my practical life. Except that, and attending my dear old nurse, who died in our house, I never had any real activity.

The same year I was introduced in London; we were presented at court and our life of society began. There is no part of my life upon which I can look back without pain. I had wandered about in the desert years long, seeking bread and finding none. Then I took stones and ate them, instead of bread,[1] because I was starved. Then I was shown all the glory of the world in the form in which it usually presents itself to women—hearts to be conquered, admiration to be won. And I took it. I worshipped the devil and accepted his gifts. I was much too proud to seek for admiration, but I had pleasure in that which I won, and in those whom the devil made mine. Later, it only remained for me to make the great leap and I should have made it. But God protected me. Marriage had never tempted me. I hated the idea of being tied forever to a life of society, and only such a marriage could I have. I had never given up the idea of reaching at last a better life. But there came a marriage for me which fulfilled all my mother's ambition: intellect, position, connections, everything, not that she ever tried to influence me, I myself was tempted. After several years' resistance—it was such an easy escape out of my difficulties—I could then do pretty much what I liked. An accident prevented it. I will believe that it was God who saved me from casting myself down from the temple.[2]

Meanwhile I had never given up looking about for an opening to serve God. Six years ago I made a desperate attempt to get into an English hospital as nurse. For years I tried all the hospitals in vain. Besides, the very idea terrified my mother and I must confess now that I understand a mother not liking her daughter to go into an English hospital. However that may be, I never could get into one.

---

1 An allusion to Luke 11:11.
2 An allusion to Luke 3:9.

The year before I had tried by going every day for several hours to our village school, to do what I believed to be God's will there. But first my health failed after some months and an illness followed, which my mother fancied came from this cause, and she prevented my going so often. And, secondly, my education had never fitted me for that kind of teaching. I knew that I taught ill. I did not know how to do any better and the very importance of the work, and interest I had in it, and my fear of myself, discouraged me more than if I had taken it merely as a pastime.

Besides, we lived more and more in society. Three months we spent in London in the season, six months at a country house in Hampshire, where the village population was very much scattered and the park so large that no cottages were very near, three months at another country house in Derbyshire. We always had company, from ten to fifteen people, staying in the house in the country and I was always expected to be in the drawing room. Our society consisted of clever intellectual men, all very good society—that I allow. They never talked gossip or foolishly but they took up all our time. Among the many stones I ate, one piece of bread God always granted me: a nephew of my mother's [Shore], whom I almost brought up, and who was the apple of my eye. He was a sickly child. When he went to school, I prepared him. In the holidays I taught him. When he went later to college, I was his instructress. He never had any particular affection for me, otherwise I should have made him my idol, but God kept my affection for him pure. I was ambitious for him and he did not succeed in the way in which I wished. So much the better; God has other views for him.

God has never left me quite alone. What I have suffered in the way of remorse my whole life I can never describe, but it was not repentance unto life,[3] but unto death. I really think it made me worse—I had not found the true way. Once, twice, three times I can remember I thought He had called me but I was not faithful and I fell off again. Then I suffered ten times more. It seemed to me that the greatest temptation always came soon after I had fancied my calling and election sure like Christ's temptation after his baptism. Lately, I have lived a tolerably even kind of life, a great deal in society, going into the village, and to the village school, or the evening school, as often as I could, but that was not often.

---

3 An allusion to Acts 11:18.

For the last two years it seems to me that God has led me into peace, or rather is leading me into it, often troubled, by sin and remorse and old habits, craving for food which He has not given me, but still there is something like His strength under it. Two years ago, to my great surprise, my mother consented to my going into Egypt with two friends. On my return, I was enabled by ways which I could hardly expect, to go to Kaiserswerth. Had I been with any other friend, I could not have done it. Six years before, I had obtained a report of Kaiserswerth. Since then, I had always been wishing to go there and sometimes when the opportunity was in my *very* hand, it was taken from me. This time I had never expected to go; my sister declared I never should, but the way was opened for me by a curious chain of circumstances which I could never have expected, and which I am not at liberty to tell. My sister has always had delicate health and her being ordered to Karlsbad was one reason. A great disappointment which befell me was another—my kind mother was willing to make me amends by allowing me to go. The Sisterhood of Deaconesses at Paris I had seen on my way back from Rome three years ago, but I had not been able to remain.

I had always been in the habit of visiting the poor at home, but it was so unsatisfactory. For me to preach patience to them, when they saw me with what they thought every blessing (ah how little they knew) seemed to me such an impertinence and always checked me. I longed to live like them and with them, and then I thought I could really help them. But to visit them in a carriage and give them money is so little like following Christ, who made himself like his brethren.[4] God has led me by ways which I have not known.[5] He has never cast me off for all I have done against Him. What I owe Him I can never tell in these few minutes, BUT I CAN BLESS HIM NOW, FOR BRINGING ME HERE.

---

4 An allusion to Heb 2:17.
5 An allusion to Isa 42:16.

Notes on Her Parents and Sister

Source: Note on her sister, Wellcome (Claydon copy) Ms 8992/141

[1840s]

A most difficult character to do, and its difficulty arises from its very simplicity. To be all made up of impulse and no calculation, "to be all made of faith and service, to be all made of phantasy, all humbleness, all patience and impatience"—will anyone tell me how I am to describe this? For in the first place, there is no leading feature, no starting projection to lay hold of. There is the most perfect grace, arising more from the most perfect unconsciousness, than from its usual source (facility in doing everything one undertakes, i.e., moving in one's world with ease). There is the most perfect absence of vanity, of self-love. I doubt whether it ever entered her head that she can be this, or that, or the other. Such pure *existence*, without question, without introspection, without consciousness I never saw in anyone. It does not matter what she is as to beauty, for the question never seems to have entered her own mind.

Unselfishness is her characteristic; code she has none; enjoyment of the present is her charm, the shadows of these great qualities are (for every light must have its shadow, only of God could Plato say, that *light* is His shadow) want of self-control, and weighing the relative importance of duties. But how few of us with our best reflection can reach the unconscious unselfishness of impulse, and what a pity therefore to disturb so priceless a gift. All that is necessary is to have self-control enough for two with her and very happy too, to enjoy her fresh and fertile mind, her passionate self-devotion, the constant pleasure of such a society at that price. Oh what is self-command, how easy, how little respectable (anything so artificial) though necessary in a world where one *must* wear clothes, in comparison with her childlike existence. Oh do not disturb it, cherish it, let nothing of darkness or anxiety approach it, to muddy its pure waters.

Of course this character is a most happy one, and therefore a most interesting one. Nothing is so interesting as happiness. Her spirits are unvarying. She is like the Bird of Paradise, who floats over this world without touching it, or sullying its bright feathers with it, rather than the nightingale, which makes its nest in it and sings. Must I find another shadow to all this bright light? It is part of the same, an exaggeration of the present moment, which for a time kills the reality of all beside, a passionate precipitation towards some aim, which for the instant seems the very goal of life, a want of sense of responsibility. But there must be flowers as well as fruits on this earth, all need not have the same object in life. It may be difficult to determine what hers is, but may it not be to make life charming by her charm, interesting by her intelligence?

It seems that her aim in life is meant to be art and literature; there will be always people enough to fulfill its dog duties, and make themselves disagreeable with the pride of duty, et estimez-vous bien heureuse, vous, sa soeur [consider yourself happy, you, her sister], to fulfill that part, and let her be the flower, the whole flower and nothing but the flower. The character of her mind is very difficult to describe. It is certainly not for the abstract sciences. It would be quite impossible to make her understand why, because the square of 2 is 2 x 2, 2 x 3 is not the square of 3; neither did a demonstration give her the least pleasure. And yet, strange to say, her mind, imaginative as it was, was not the least metaphysical or speculative, though her ready sympathy was such that she would enter into anything to please you. But all the arts of imitation, poetry, painting, description were her forte. No sort of literature, except scientific, came *un-kin* to her mind. She had attention so ready that it was really a more fixed attention than that of people who set up for having a pursuit. She would have written well, if she would have given herself time. Her drawing was the type of her character, the expression of it, her language. She felt for truth more than she commanded it: her aspirations were ever higher than her execution.

But if her mind is difficult to define, how much more her soul! which was full of those "nuances" which one knows in the people with whom one lives, more than one can say them, which one perceives only for oneself and not for others and which one feels, but does not seize enough to reflect upon and express. Perhaps they are too delicate to be seized.

She is the true type of woman. She has not the smallest ambition— it is almost incredible, but so it is—not the smallest. The love of distinction or of power would not make her raise her hand to grasp them, if they were within her reach. She would be called remarkably frank, but she had nothing more to tell to her sister than to her fortnight's acquaintance. She talked as openly to the one as the other. She seemed to say everything, but tell her a secret and it was in a tomb, perhaps because she had no vanity, and so did not wear the secret as an ornament.

She was remarkably easily deceived—she always believed you—an agreeable and *very* rare quality, and one you were so grateful for, that you were always full of remorse for having unconsciously deceived her. She had not much knowledge of character, at least it was more intuitive than she could put it into words. It did not interest her though, if she were applied to, she could, by a flash, give light to questions, among which you were all darkly groping. She had the widest sympathies and the fewest friendships. She liked everybody and cared for scarcely any. And, inconsistent as it may seem with her eager soul, she never took fancies for people—a friend to all, she interested herself particularly in none. She could say too sharp things of people, and it made no difference in her conduct to them. She would be just as kind to them when she saw them again.

She was so perfectly happy at home and in the present that she had none of that restless longing for the future, that wanting *something*, but what one does not exactly know, that living in hope, which is the characteristic and the curse of the present day. One can scarcely believe it, but she would have been satisfied to have been stereotyped forever, she never lived in the future. The organization of her moral being was so healthy, so in harmony with the exterior order, that it was almost like that of the ancients, among whom there were scarcely any uneasy souls, any traces of melancholy. Her thoughts never recoiled on herself, nor, working and subtilizing on her own impressions, reflected them back on the general world, as do our sad and restless souls, in the absence of happiness, which always forgets itself.

She had that perfect disposition which masters or accommodates itself at once and easily, not from reflection, but from natural and unsought power, to the circumstances of its world. It is a gift of God, like genius, as unattainable and as precious. She hated the sight of sorrow— it did not even interest her. To admire was her passion and jealousy she could not understand. She was excited by the smallest trifle [breaks off]

Source: Incomplete, undated letter or note, Wellcome (Claydon copy) Ms 8992/146

[before February 1845]
Some unhappy people can have their angels only in heaven but mine are here already on earth. I wish for no others. You are all my angels. I shall never know the pleasure of being admired, [illeg] looked up to and depended upon, but I can believe it to be a very great one, but I think the pleasure of admiration must be greater. At all events, it is the greatest I can fancy, and I would not give it up for the world. So all

of you who will be at Waverley[6] on Sunday, lay your account to be
haunted by my spirit at your feet. . . .

Source: Notes on unhappiness in the family, part in Nightingale's hand, part
copy, ADD Mss 43402 ff64-65 and 79-83

7 January 1851

What is to become of me? I can hardly open my mouth without giving
my dear Parthe vexation, everything I say or do is a subject of annoyance to her. And I, oh how am I to get through this day is the thought
of every morning, how am I to talk through all this day and now, I
feel, as if I should not have strength ever to do anything else. My God,
I love Thee, I do indeed, I do not say it in open rebellion, but in
anguish and utter hopelessness.

Why didst [Thou] make me what I am? A little later, oh my God, a
little later, when I should have been alone in the world or in the next
stage, not now, not yet, not here. I have never known a happy time,
except at Rome and that fortnight at Kaiserswerth. It is not the unhappiness I mind, it is not indeed, but people can't be unhappy without
making those about them so. Oh, if we could but have been alike,
either I like her or she like me. . . .

My father is a man who has never known what struggle is. Good
impulses from his childhood up and always remaining perfectly in a
natural state, acting always from impulse and having never by circumstances been forced to look into a thing, to carry it out. Effleurez,
n'appuyez pas [touch lightly, don't push] has been not the rule but
the habit of his life.[7] Liberal by instinct, not by reflection, but not
happy. Why not? He has not enough to do; he has not enough to fill
his faculties. When I see him eating his breakfast, as if the destinies of
a nation depended upon his getting done, carrying his plate about
the room, delighting in being in a hurry, pretending to himself week
after week that he is going to Buxton or elsewhere in order to be in
legitimate haste. I say to myself how happy that man would be with a
factory under his superintendence with the interests of 200 or 300
men to look after.

---

6 Nightingale's Aunt Anne Smith married George Nicholson, whose country
  home was Waverley, famous for its abbey ruins, thought to have been the
  inspiration for the Waverley novels of Sir Walter Scott (1771-1832).
7 Nightingale used a similar expression, "glissez, n'appuyez pas," in describing
  the boring life of women in society, in "Cassandra," in *Suggestions for Thought*
  2:384.

My mother is a genius. She has the genius of mater [mother], to make a place, to organize a parish, to form society. She has obtained by her own exertions the best society in England; she goes into a school and can put this little thing right which is wrong; she has a genius for doing all she wants to do and has never felt the absence of power. She is not happy. She has too much fatigue and too much anxiety, anxiety about Papa, about Parthe's health, my duties, about the servants, the parish. Oh dear good woman, when I feel her disappointment in me, it is as if I was becoming insane when she has organized the nicest society in England for us, and I cannot take it as she wishes.

Parthe, she is in her element if she had but health, and if she had but not me she is in her element. It is her vocation to make holiday to hardworking men out of London, to all manners of people who come to enjoy this beautiful place. And a very good vocation it is. No one less than I want her to do one single thing different from what she does; she wants no other religion, no other occupation, no other training than what she has. She is in unison with her age, her position, her country. She has never had a difficulty, except with me. She is a child playing in God's garden and delighting in the happiness of all His works, knowing nothing of human life but the English drawing room, nothing of struggle in her own unselfish nature, nothing of want of power in her own element. And I, what a murderer I am to disturb this happiness. It is all that reason, divine reason, can do to prevent me repeating this even now and I repeat it in my heart, while I no longer repeat it in my conscience.

I, what am I that I am not in harmony with all this, that their life is not good enough for me? Oh God, what am I? The thoughts and feelings that I have now I can remember since I was six years old. It was not I that made them. Oh God, how did they come? Are they the natural cross of my father and mother? What are they? A profession, a trade, a necessary occupation, something to fill and employ all my faculties, I have always felt essential to me, I have always longed for, consciously or not. During a middle portion of my life, college education, acquirement I longed for, but that was temporary, the first thought I can remember and the last was nursing work and in the absence of this, education work, but more the education of the bad than of the young.

But for this, I had had no education myself and when I began to try, I was disgusted with my utter impotence. I made no improvement,

I learnt no ways, I obtained no influence. This nobody could understand. You teach better than other people, was the desperate answer
always made me; they had never wanted instruction, why should I?
The only help I ever got was a week with my madre at Rome, which I
made use of directly and taught my girls at Holloway always on that
foundation and my fortnight at Kaiserswerth. Still education I know is
not my genius though I could do it if I was taught, because it is my
duty here.

But why, oh my God, cannot I be satisfied with the life which satisfies so many people? I am told that the conversation of all these good
clever men ought to be enough for me. Why am I starving, desperate,
diseased upon it? Why has it all run to vanity in me, to what impression am I making upon them when it comes to wholesome fruit in
others? The cancer of my life I have recorded; what is the cause of it?
Is it enough to say that rice disagrees with one man and agrees with
another? that, as (Channing[8] says) the ground of sincerity lies in talking of what you are interested about, so none of the subjects of society
interest me enough to draw me out of vanity.

Oh what do books know of the real troubles of life? It is all Hebrew
and Chinese—death—why it's a happiness. Oh how I have longed for
a trial to give me food, to be something real, a nourishing life, that is
the happiness—whatever it be—a starving life, that is the real trial. My
God, what am I to do? Teach me, tell me. I cannot go on any longer
waiting till my situation should change, dreaming what the change
shall be to give me a better food. Thou hast been teaching me all
these thirty-one years—what I am to do in this. Where is the lesson?
Let me read it—oh where, where is it? All that you want, will come, in
one stage or another you (and all the rest of God's creatures) will
have all food, all training, all occupation necessary to make you one
with God. With this certainty, cannot you wait? You have already
learnt something; you say yourself what do they know who have never
suffered?

8 William Ellery Channing (1780-1842), American transcendentalist minister.

LETTERS TO, FROM AND ABOUT NIGHTINGALE'S IMMEDIATE FAMILY

Mother, Frances "Fanny" Nightingale

The letters to her mother begin when Nightingale was aged seven (the first ones are printed). They reveal a happy child reporting to her mother on practical matters of health, church, reading, games, exercise and the well-being and comings or goings of other family members, friends and employees. Since the Nightingales owned two manor houses in the country, stayed periodically in London and had numerous relatives with whom they stayed, as well as entertaining aunts, uncles and cousins at their places, there was much occasion for correspondence. The letters also show at an early age an exceptional child (a letter at age nine about a sermon was written in French!) (see p 108 below). There are comments about nature (caterpillars, shells, birds) and remarkably sophisticated observations from museum and other cultural visits. The letters reveal an earnest, morally engaged girl, keen to do good in the world, especially for the poor, even before her "call to service." There is detailed reporting about church attendance (or reason for not attending) and Bible reading. Clearly the relationship with her mother was such that she could confide such thoughts to her.

By her teen years Nightingale was cajoling her mother for permission to pursue her nursing vocation. Her efforts at teaching (when she was not allowed to nurse) are described. There are two letters from Kaiserswerth begging understanding and acceptance. Later letters, after Nightingale established her independent existence, show her recruiting her mother for practical services and favours. Greeneries, fresh produce, pheasant and grouse, etc. were shipped regularly from Embley to London (mainly for the benefit of nurses and colleagues Nightingale was trying to cultivate). She and her mother shared an interest in cats, indeed there was a traffic in kittens between town and country. At her daughter's request Frances Nightingale invited sick colleagues to stay in the country to recuperate. A much smaller proportion of letters, compared with those to her father, were on "business," but there are some with interesting political and social commentary as well as observations on books and much good humour.

There seem to be no surviving letters from Nightingale to her mother after the death of her father in 1874, few even after 1870. Nightingale stayed with her mother for extended periods during this time so there may have been less occasion for writing. Her mother's loss of mental capacity and declining eyesight may also have made writing futile. There is much *about* her mother during this period, in correspondence not only with her sister but also friends and colleagues. Hence the last period is covered by correspondence written to other people, especially her sister, about Frances Nightingale's last years and death. In 1871 Nightingale wrote a letter to her father on her mother's behalf (see p 269 below). By the next year Nightingale was reading letters to her mother.[1] In December of that year Nightingale told her sister, in a letter not reproduced here, that she was staying on at Embley until Parthenope Verney's arrival because it was "impossible" to leave either parent.[2]

The letters from late in life show a return to a shared faith with her mother largely missing in the many years of Nightingale's adult life. Clearly Nightingale prayed with her mother (as did Harry Verney, at Nightingale's request). She recited her mother's favourite hymns and poems to her: her mother's memory never failing entirely, so that she remembered some hymns, Milton's sonnets certainly and the Lord's Prayer. Nightingale herself was fascinated with the fact of her mother's failing mental capacity being accompanied by enhanced spiritual qualities and appreciation for life.

---

1 For example a letter to Margaret Verney 27 August 1872, Wellcome (Claydon copy) Ms 9005/157.
2 Letter to Parthenope Verney 13 December 1872, Wellcome (Claydon copy) Ms 9005/168.

Source: Letter in child's printing, Wellcome (Claydon copy) Ms 8991/3

Embley

Monday, 22 October [1827]

Dear Mama

My journal will come today. I thank you for your letter. My autumnal garden goes on very well. Shall you come back Wednesday or Thursday? Why I ask is that Aunt Julia[3] says she thinks you'll come home on Thursday and Gale[4] and I and Pop [her sister Parthenope] say you come on Wednesday. Tell Papa and Aunt Mai and Uncle Sam that why I do not write to them is that I have got no time.

your affectionate child

Florence Nightingale

Source: Unsigned letter in child's printing, Claydon, Wellcome (Claydon copy) Ms 8991/12

Embley music room

Wednesday [after 11 August 1828] 10:30

Dearest Mama

I think of you every day. The day you went I finished my exercises and took Mr Millengen a walk to the pond. We dined at 1:00, and after dinner we showed him the garden, gave him an apricot, and he set off on Dick, with William Rennell following him with his baggage in a wheelbarrow. Mr Millengen got to the Vine without any accident, but the coach set off at ½ past 6, he kept Rennell with him till ½ past 5 and took a ride round Mr Stanley's park. The day we went to the forest we had Goddard's gig, and Major's qonkey (donkey); we slept this morning till 9:00 o'clock. Miss Christie[5] is well today, Pop in her letter has written about Miss Christie's illness, so I say nothing about it. We have not had much squabbling.

There was a little note from Aunt Julia for you, which Miss C. has sent to Uncle Carter[6] with a letter of Pop's; Miss Christie wishes you to write to Uncle Carter where to send them, too. The music room's carpet is *down* and curtains are *up*. We read our chapter, and said our prayers in the forest, the chapter was the seventh of Luke. After Mr Millengen was gone, I did my music, my flower and my point.

_____

3 Julia Smith (1799-1883), unmarried sister of Frances Nightingale.
4 Nurse to Florence Nightingale.
5 Lydia Christie became the Nightingale governess in 1827.
6 John Carter (1788-1838) changed his name to Bonham Carter in 1830.

Source: Note in child's printing, in margin to another letter, Wellcome (Claydon copy) Ms 8991/13

[12 August 1828]

Dear Mama

I finished my housewife[7] at the forest (that is to say, put on the strings and cassimere[8]) and I began another. We bought a skein of red silk at Southampton, and the day before yesterday, Gale and Kitty went to Romsey and bought us some flannel and some cambric muslin, to make us flannel petticoats and nightgowns for our dolls, and a yard and a half of red ribbon. Give my love to Papa. Miss Christie is going to send him on my letter and sheriff's writ. Good-bye.

ever your affectionate child

Florence Nightingale

P.S. Do you know where my *smallest* Indian cabinet is? What fine days you have had! This morning we read the twelfth chapter of Luke and said our prayers.

F.N.

Ma chère Clémence [the French maid]

J'espère que vous vous portez bien, et que vous aimez vos trois petits livres. Aimez-vous Cowes? Avez-vous ramassé beaucoup de coquilles et de sable? Je vous remercie d'avoir mis mes fleurs dans l'eau. Je crois que vous aur[i]ez beaucoup aimé aller à la forêt avec nous. Nous avons fait des petits ponts très forts sur un ruisseau de pierres. Savez-vous qu'aujourd'hui est l'anniversaire de la naissance de notre roi [George IV], le douze d'août. Vous pouvez dire à maman que nos têtes ont été lavé[es] ce matin par Mme Gale. Adieu.

votre affectionnée petite

Florence Nightingale

Dear Mama

Hilary [Bonham Carter] has sent me some silkworm's eggs, which I intend to educate as Jack[9] has written to Pop, and told her all the particulars of how to bring them up. We cannot find out about the jam, I think it is a follower of the Galatee, or the next that wins the prize. Miss Christie thinks it is a ship that was jammed in with the Galatee. Good-bye.

F.N.

---

7 A pocket case for scissors, pins, needles, thread, etc.
8 An early version of cashmere, fine cloth.
9 John Bonham Carter (1817-84), son of John Bonham Carter (1788-1838), and also later an MP.

I am very sorry I have made a mistake, and written too much on one side so that Miss Christie has only the middle to copy the sheriff's writ.

Source: Letter in child's printing (with postscripts to her sister and Clémence), Wellcome (Claydon copy) Ms 8991/16

Begun Embley
Friday, 16 October [c1828]

Dear Mama

My bag is lost. It must be either left behind or dropt like my cloak. We had such a hunt for it as soon as we got into the gig, that it must be dropt between Bourne, and where the gig stopt, or else William forgot it. I had in it my prayer book, a pair of gloves, one volume of L'Ecolier, backbone of cuttlefish, some of my work, paper, your stockings and habit-shirt and letters (from Pop to Miss Christie and Gale). Will you bring it with you on Tuesday? We saw a kingfisher—it had a blue back and tail, and I thought a pink or red breast, it was flying across some water. We arrived at Embley at ½ past three o'clock. Aunt Mai stopped at the school, and I walked on by myself to Maria Brent, who was better, and downstairs, working. As I was coming home, I met the two Miss Cooks. We bought two buns, three hard biscuits and two little round ones. I gave Maria Brent one of the biscuits; was that wrong? Mrs Staples gave me a glass of her currant wine. We went to see her yesterday.

your affectionate daughter
Florence Nightingale
Bill
d [pence]
Buns two 1 pence each
Biscuits three 1 pence each
Little ditto 1 ½ pence each
6

Friday

Dear Pop [Parthenope Nightingale]

I hope the housekeeping goes on well. Have you lost your keys? Blanchy recollected me. Please to tell Mama that I am very happy.

Florence Nightingale
Chère Clémence, J'ai fait toutes vos commissions.

Source: Letter in child's printing, Wellcome (Claydon copy) Ms 8991/15

[after 17 October 1828]

Dear Mama

My cloak is not lost. Don't you recollect that you picked it up under the wheel of the gig when it stopt? So need Gale cut me out a new one? Gale has put on the green ribbon you mentioned on my bonnet, which had the black ribbon. Before you wrote to me, I was going to write to Grandmama.

Miss Penton[10] told us the day before yesterday that, when our caterpillar turned chrysalis, it plunged into the earth. So yesterday I made it a bed of earth and above that a bed of leaves. This morning I found a leaf half eaten, and the caterpillar gone. Miss Christie sends her love to Aunt Julia, and is very sorry to say she cannot find Mr Gimbernat's letter.

your affectionate child
Florence N.

Source: Letter in child's printing or copy, Wellcome (Claydon copy) Ms 8991/20

Sunday [c1828]

Dear Mama

We have got a most beautiful caterpillar. We caught it at 1:00 o'clock yesterday. We tried everything we could think of but it would not eat. Miss Penton told us it fed on privet. It is alive and well and eats the privet. I am in a hurry. We keep it under a sieve in the garden. The text at church today was "I am the good Shepherd," St John 10:11.

We are very well and happy. Good-bye dear Mama. Believe me,
your affectionate
Florence Nightingale

P.S. Excuse bad writing; letters are going. Mrs Eyre called yesterday, and sent her love general, and Miss Gubbens called, but did not come in.

Source: Letter in child's printing, Wellcome (Claydon copy) Ms 8991/21

Monday [c1828]

Dear Mama

Yesterday we went to Maria Brent with Alice. Maria was worse. She came downstairs. While we were there, two men came in, one of them began to lecture her, but Miss Christie would not go before she had

---

10 Daughter of the clergyman.

given *him* a lecture, which he understood so far as not to say a word more to Maria while we were there. Papa would not have prayers before 10:00 last night. I made a garland for last night of blue cornflowers and red poppies, with a white cornflower in the middle like a diamond, but Betsy threw it away.

This morning I did my exercises, said my poetry and prayers and read the Bible. I am using the powder of the backbone of the cuttlefish to dry my letter. Good-bye.

your affectionate daughter
Flo

Source: Letter in child's printing, Wellcome (Claydon copy) Ms 8991/25

Embley
Sunday [after 19 February 1829]
11 o'clock

Dear Mama

I have got a little cold, but it is so little that I hope it will be well before you come back. I don't go to church today because of that. I did figures very well yesterday. Then we went to poor Mrs Bungy's, she had a bad headache. We dined in the piano drawing room and I did music, Latin, French reading and valzing, and Miss Christie played. This morning I did everything as usual, except that I have not written my copy, and that I have learnt more poetry, and read in the Bible the seventeenth chapter of the 1 Kings (about Elijah being fed by ravens and being supported by the Sareptan woman, and raising her son to life again) and the fourth chapter of the 2 Kings (about Elisha). Yesterday, we went to Mrs Staples (besides Mrs Bungy's) and she *be'es* very well, and *he* (her leg) *be'es* very well too.

Ask poor dear Bon[11] whether he would like anything besides the books that I could give him. Do it secretly, because I want to surprise him with something. Buy the knife for Miss Christie; I asked her to tell me everything she buys, so I shall know if she buys a knife or not, and then I shall prevent it. I play better at battledore and shuttlecock. We are going to have a game now, I and Miss Christie, as we cannot go out. Goodbye.

your affectionate
Flo N.

---

11 Cousin "Bon" Bonham Carter died as a child in June 1829.

Source: Letter, Wellcome (Claydon copy), Ms 8991/33 (correct French is indicated in square brackets)

Embley
Mardi 15 décembre [1829]

Ma chère Maman

Je suis bien triste sans vous aujourd'hui. J'ai couché Blanche, et je l'ai levé[e] ce matin pour la première fois. Elle a été très bonne, elle n'a presque pas pleuré. Après dinêr [dîner], je suis allé[e] avec ma tante Mai et Blanche à [chez] Mme Staples, elle était mieux portante qu'hier. Nous avons porté de la médecine, et de la Aanelle [?] à Pope vis-à-vis. Il est bien malade. Après cela, j'ai dessiné et peint. J'ai écrit mon sermon dans mon livre, et cette lettre. Je n'ai pas querellé avec ma soeur, ni lu dans un livre. Le soir nous avons dansé avec Lucy Whitby, qui danse très bien. Mercredi. Nous avons déjeûné à neuf heures et demi dans le *bon room*. Je suis allé[e] à Onre Lodge à cheval et Clémence aussi. Nous avons porté à Humby un lapin que nous avons ramassé, et le choix d'une robe ou d'une couverture. Elle a choisi une couverture. De là, nous sommes allé[e]s à [chez] Tiller; à la fille, nous avons donné une chemise de Mlle Coape, à la mère, des chiffons pour ses yeux. De là, à Romsey, où j'ai acheté un pain de chocolat pour Maria Brent, et deux *pocket-books*. Un a une vilaine histoire, que nous allons couper et jeter au feu, et que ma soeur va avoir, et un autre qui est plein de vilaines chansons que nous allons changer. Voulez [-vous] avoir la bonté de marquer ce qui est bon dans ma lettre, et quand vous retournez de la rapporter. J'ai dessiné et peint.

Je suis allé[e] à [chez] Mme Staples avec ma tante Marie et ma soeur, et pendant qu'elles étaient à [chez] Pope, je suis entré[e] à [chez] Mme Staples, et je lui ai lu Psaume vingt-troisième. Je lui aurais lu plus, mais ma tante voulait partir. Elle me disait qu'elle me comprenait très bien. Bonsoir, ma chère maman. Je pense à vous bien souvent, et toujours quand je dis mes prières. Je les dis tous les matins et tous les soirs de tout mon coeur. Je [me] suis permis d'être avec Blanche et Lucy, mais de ne pas parler à la dernière beaucoup. Je peux être dans la chambre avec qui que je veux. Mlle Christie me prend plus d'intêret.

J'ai lu le [en] Français avec Clémence jeudi. Nous avons déjeuné à neuf heures et puis, Gale, Kitty, Clémence et moi sont [avons marché] marchées à Romsey. Nous sommes parties à onze heures, et revenues à cinq heures. Nous avons été chez Mme Withers (pauvre femme! elle a l'air si malade et si triste) où Gale a acheté une robe, chez Mr Godfrey, où Kitty et Clémence en ont acheté, et pour changer mon pocket-book. Comment vous portez-vous? Quand je suis revenue, comme c'était bien tard, je ne pouvais pas chercher une [de] fleur, ainsi j'ai dessiné les mouchettes. Nous avons dansé, et j'ai écrit cette lettre, je me suis couché[e], et j'ai dit mes prières. J'ai lu le [en] Français. Vendredi, j'ai lu le Français, j'ai travaillé, nous avons déjeuné à neuf heures et demi, et puis, j'ai travaillé, et levé Blanche jusqu'à dîner, et après dîner mon travail était la robe de Clémence. Je l'ai commencée aujourd'hui, et je l'ai finie aujourd'hui. Nous n'avons [ne sommes] pas sorti[es] aujourd'hui, à cause de la neige.

Mlle Christie m'a dit cet après-midi que Lucy n'avait pas assez de force pour s'empêcher de me parler, et qu'ainsi je ne pouvais pas rester avec elle, excepté à [pour] manger, danser, marcher et jouer. Je ne peux pas envoyer cette lettre aujourd'hui, parce qu'elle n'est pas tout à fait remplie. Quand reviendrez-vous? J'ai joué aux quatres coins.

votre très affectionate enfant
Florence Nightingale

Source: Letter probably to Frances Nightingale, Wellcome (Claydon copy) Ms 8991/42

[ca. 7 January 1830]

I promise to take [a] run before breakfast to gate or to [illeg] people, ½ an hour's walk before dinner, long walk after, or if cold and dark long walk before and ½ an hour's after, to do twenty arms [exercises] before I dress, ten minutes before breakfast and ten after exercises, if ill [illeg] ten more, to practise one hour a day, if you like it, as I shall not have so much to do, 1¼ regularly; to draw ½ an hour regularly, not to lie in bed, to go to bed in proper time, to read the Bible and pray regularly before breakfast and at night, to visit the poor people and take care of those who are sick, to take medicine when I want it, to go regularly after breakfast on Sundays to go to church when there is anyone to go with me, to read, write and do the Bible, to read any book you put out for me, to read to Aunt Mai and save her trouble, to read this paper every day, to write to you. I think I should be much better here than elsewhere—I should have fewer temptations.

F.N.

Source: Letter, Wellcome (Claydon copy) Ms 8991/52

Fair Oak[12]
28 March [1830]

Dear Mama

Is Miss Christie come home? I have pinched my finger. I did not write sooner because of it. Poor Rebecca has got a headache today like to what Gale has. We went last Sunday to Terwick, but, unluckily, we set out so late that we did not get there till just as the sermon began. We do not go on much with our house, now Hilly is gone, except watering our plants, but Miss Wood and I are making a garden of wild plants. Do you think I need wear my steel boots now it is getting so hot, and could you send me a pair of walking-out *shoes*, as my boots are getting so very hot I can scarcely wear them?

your affectionate

Flo

I am just come from church. Mr Green preached from Luke 15:10, "There is joy in heaven over one sinner that repenteth." There are two tulips and several hyacinths out in the garden. I had no pencil with me, but I recollect he said that it is not in the resolve, but in the doing of a thing, that we must rejoice over. And he gave us three examples. First, in the parable of the man having 100 sheep, losing one, leaving the ninety-nine in the wilderness, and going to seek the one he had lost. Then, and not till then, did he send for his neighbours to rejoice with him.

The same with the woman and her ten pieces of silver. She did not call her neighbours to rejoice with her till she had found her silver, not when she was resolving she would sweep her house and look for it. The same with the prodigal son. He says, I will arise and go to my father, and say, I have sinned and am not worthy to come into thy presence, and the scriptures add immediately after, that he did do it. Then, and not till then, did his father come and fall on his neck and kiss him and order the best robe to be brought and the fatted calf to be killed to make him a feast. Good-bye, dear Mama.

your affectionate

Flo

---

12 The country home of Uncle John and Aunt Joanna Bonham Carter at Ditcham, near Petersfield.

Source: Unsigned copy of letter, Wellcome (Claydon copy) Ms 8991/58

Fair Oak
Wednesday [after Easter c1831]

Dear Mama

Have you seen the sand hills? They are so pretty, all different, white, pink, yellow, red, dirty brown and others. The yellow is the colour of rhubarb. Easter Day we got a spade and a trowel and we went and dug some wild primroses in flower (wonderful is not it Mama?), carried them home and in the afternoon I planted them in Hilary's garden and then helped Jack to pull down the old house, clear it away and give him the poles which he hammered down in the ground. We all helped. Jack took up the fish out of the little pond which he has made and showed it to me. It was quite tame. In the morning when we go to Miss C. we go upstairs and paint, read and play. Alf[13] comes to us very often; he is such a merry little fellow and so fat.

Source: Letter, Wellcome (Claydon copy) Ms 8991/64

Sunday [postmarked 19 May 1832]

Dearest Mama

When you went at twelve o'clock, I had your business to do about settling the carriage for Miss Pentons, which took me till 12:30, when Grandmama came into the music room and walked nearly an hour with my arm, then I attended her to her room and read *Robinson Crusoe* till dinner. After dinner I did twenty-five minutes music with Aunt Mai, and then went out till near 5:00, then I finished my music, held Baby while Nurse fetched Blanchy's supper, dressed, and Grandmama came down, and I walked her about. I supped, [illeg] and served her, then Parthe read and we went to bed, I at 8:30; I slept in your room, and Louise in your next room, but I was rather afraid of Messieurs les voleurs [burglars].

Grandmama was very poorly last night, and had a bad night. Baby had a beautiful night and only waked once, when Aunt Mai waked him, for she dreamt he was falling and stretched out her hand to save him, which waked him. Grandmama was very poorly last night and I have not seen her today, Blades says she's weaker than she was at Ditcham. I had not courage to tell her in the morning of Lady Brydge's death, because the best death affects her so very much, but I did tell her in the evening, and she could talk of nothing else all the evening. . . .

---

13 Alfred Bonham Carter (1825-1910), son of Aunt Joanna and John Bonham Carter.

About 4:00 Nurse came downstairs carrying five little mice in her hand, which she found scattered about the blue room, and she saw an old mouse run off. She had been shaking the mattress, and she believes that the old mouse had made her nest there. Anne says she never saw such small ones, and she says they can only be just born. Aunt Mai had heard the mouse making a strange noise for several nights. They are not an inch long, with such tiny paws and a long tail, very large head, and two bits of skin over their eyes. They have no hair at all and look like little bits of raw meat, they are perfect frights. One died directly, and Aunt Mai burnt it. We wrapped them up in wadding and put them in a basket by the fire and now and then put a drop of warm milk to their mouths, which I think they swallowed. They are such queer things, always stretching out their legs. Three died in the night, so only one is left, which revived just as I was going to bury it. The other four were evidently quite dead, and I buried them in my garden by my squirrel. This one I have wrapped up and put by the fire and I have given it some milk, and it moves about, I think it is possible it may live, poor little thing! I should like to rear one, only one, so much. It would be so interesting to watch it.

This morning I did fifty minutes exercises and sundries by eight o'clock. The twenty-five minutes for yesterday, I did not do very well, but the twenty-five minutes for today I did. Then Parthe and I read the Bible and Gilpin and prayed, then we breakfasted, I did a little Latin, looked after Gale, who has a bad sick headache today. It is so bad she can hardly speak, and I have not seen her, she has been to Mr Winter, who said nothing particular to her foot but causticed it. It is very much swelled today, and she has hardly any feeling in it. . . .

Aunt Mai and I went to church. Fine day, though very blowy I thought. The text was Isaiah 12:3, but I find it is not, and Aunt Mai does not recollect it. It was a sort of cholera sermon, I think, talking about the uncertainty of and the only use of life being to prepare for heaven, a very good sermon. When I came home from church I buried my mice, and I have been ever since writing this letter. Mrs Penton is better, she was at church, but we did not go into her house. Love to Papa. Did the goldfish get safe?

your affectionate child

Flo

I can hardly write on this rough paper, I am afraid you can hardly read. It is 6:45—I must go and dress. I will learn some new poetry tonight. Good-bye, dear Mama.

Monday morning. As soon as I was dressed last night, I had to go and walk Grandmama. Then we supped, and then I ran upstairs to learn my poetry, but, as it was so late, I could not learn a new piece, but I learnt three old ones. I said them to Grandmama and played her some hymns, which I have been learning in the week. Then I went to bed. Our only remaining mouse died last night, a good thing for it, poor little dear. It had such pretty little paws. This morning, I have done my exercises, read Bible while Parthe read Gilpin, and prayed. I did my exercises better than usual, I think. Gale is much better. Good-bye.

Source: Letter to Frances and Parthenope Nightingale, Wellcome (Claydon copy) Ms 8991/67, postmarked 8 November 1833

[6 November 1833]

Yesterday, which was the 5th of November,[14] we had a famous bonfire on the brow of the cliff in the field, and guns were fired, and Guy Fawkes, a boy dressed in a sheepskin with a black face and old hat, a frightful figure, went to every door to get halfpence, which were given, of course. The bonfire looked so beautiful against the dark sky, and the boys, looking like devils or witches, standing around.

I read Silvio Pellico[15] to Hilary, when there is time.

Flo

Dear Mama

I think that I am learning something new. Yesterday Aunt Ju and Hilary and I read some Herschel,[16] and now I understand, which I never did before, about how summer and winter and all the seasons together, with day and night are made, and I understand a *little* about the tides, but not much. Will you tell dear Papa this, that he may not think I am very idle. I do a little Latin sometimes. Love to Aunt Mai and babes, and Gale.

Bo

---

14 Guy Fawkes Day.

15 Silvio Pellico, Risorgimento leader imprisoned at Spielburg Prison, published *Le mie prigioni* in 1832; since the English translation, *My Prisons*, appeared only in 1835 Nightingale was evidently translating the Italian edition.

16 Sir John Herschel (1792-1871), probably his *Discourse on the Study of Natural Philosophy*. Nightingale also used his comments on Quetelet; see *Society and Politics*.

Source: Copy of letter, Wellcome (Claydon copy) Ms 8991/68

Seaview

6 November [c1839]

. . . Last Sunday I read the Testament to myself, and I hope I spent it pretty well. Aunt Julia did not wish to go to church. Monday we walked to Rye. . . . I hope I am doing some little good here, Mama, but there are not many trials, I find, except in the way of putting up with such as having tough old lion for a week, as we call our beef—little inconveniences, and resisting temptations to do wrong when there is nobody to tell you not, such as eating apple when one has taken castor oil, which I resisted today.

your affectionate Bo

I have given up signing myself [illeg].

Source: Incomplete, undated letter, Claydon House Bundle 80

[Waverley]

an account Monday

Dear Mama

I am much better in myself, though my cough is not, nor will [be], I think, till I can get home. But I am so much stronger as to be down on Saturday for one hour, and on Sunday for three or four in the schoolroom. But Mr Newnham has just been and entirely scouts my request to go on Saturday. I have had but one wish all the while I've been in, to get home and be quiet. And, if you knew how much I've missed you, you would be well avenged, though nothing can have been kinder than the people here and Miss J. has been in and read Channing to me every morning she has been here. . . . While you are still quite alone and I hear that you are going to have officials on the 26th I do not much care what we do, and you may ask all the Nicholsons, if you please, and I do not mind.

I have written to Papa and so shall not trouble you with the repetition, especially as you would only think it low spirits. Now I am not at all low-spirited, though Parthe writes I am, I dare say, and humours me as such, not seeing at all that it is reasonable for me to like being alone. However I am quite strong enough now to like seeing the girls very much, and above all, to like going into good Miss Nicholson's room every evening, where she receives me. I am very comfortable now I can read to myself again and not at all low-spirited. . . . I believe my inside is standing on its head by the fright everything is in which first goes down there, and its first idea seems to be to beat a violent retreat. I think a few more mustard poultices will put me in condition to come home. . . .

I saw Aunt Anne [Nicholson] yesterday for the first time and drank tea with her. Not a trace of the foe left behind, and tea-ing on apples. Nothing can have been kinder than she has been. . . .

Source: Letter, Wellcome (Claydon copy) Ms 8992/7

Tuesday [1840]

Dear Mama

You will have heard no doubt that poor Miss Martin's sufferings are ended. She died last Thursday. We are a reduced party here, Aunts Mai and Ju, Jack and myself. Aunt Joanna took the boys and Fan up to town today to have their teeth out, with Uncle Sam, who did not seem very well last night and complained of backaches. Jack was not well enough to go and is pinned here for some days, I suppose, as doctor comes every day. I do not know how long he will be before he is able to return. The plan of Fan's staying in town with Ju is put an end to, as Aunt Patty is not well enough to have the racket in the house. The boys go to the play tonight and to *school* tomorrow. . . .

Dear Pop, I am doing German with Aunt Mai. I have not found my black gloves. I find that it is sometimes two days post from Kingston to Embley but they cannot make out the reason why sometimes it is and sometimes not; so I write today though with little to say, except in case you should not have heard of Miss Martin's death. . . .

Your poor account of Gerald[17] is given us; we have not sent it to Aunt Jane.

Source: Postscript to a letter, Wellcome (Claydon copy) Ms 8992/22

My dearest Mum

How thankful you should be that your daughter for the first time in her life is doing some little good in her generation; do not grudge it her. Aunt Jane was not well enough to go out today. I really think Flora [Smith] has improved a little and I trust I feel it a blessing, as I ought, that a creature so nearly spiritualized as Aunt Jane is should cling to such as me as all now in her distress. Goodnight, dear Mum, I shall soon be with you for good again. But, in the meantime, feel I must not see much of you, though Aunt Jane is so much better tonight that you may be quite easy about her. Though you do not see us tomorrow.

---

17 Possibly Gerard (d. 1858), son of Uncle Oc and Aunt Jane Smith.

Source: Letter, Wellcome (Claydon copy) Ms 8992/57

Dearest Mother   Wednesday [September 1844]

If they press you to stay another day, I hope you will, as Gale is certainly better today, has eaten well and is very cheerful. Mr Poyser [the doctor] has seen her and thinks her better and says she may last some time. I send the letters, in case you may stay as I hope you will. Give my best love to Louisa Mackenzie,[18] and remember me to all the people there. Gale and I spent a very agreeable afternoon together yesterday.

ever dear Mum
your affectionate child
I thought you would like to know Mr Poyser's report Wednesday.

Source: Letter, Wellcome (Claydon copy) Ms 8992/93

Dearest Mother   Thursday [1844]

I should have been sorry indeed if you had broken up so nice a party to come back today as Gale continues so much the same, that I feel, as she takes more nourishment, that she may last for some time. I had a visit from Mrs Young yesterday, who came to see you, as you had not been to see her, and from Mrs Poyser. If you should wish to stay till Saturday, do not think that there is any occasion to hurry home.

I have no news to tell you, not having heard from anybody, and not having been able to make up my mind to write to the Rachel won after serving for her for sixteen years.[19] May they live as long as that patriarch, who, few and evil as the years of his pilgrimage were, had I believed an hundred and forty and seven of them. I have not been able to visit the turnips in the garden owing to the diluvial deposits from heaven. That greedy root, I think, even must have had enough of it.

My dear Gale often reminds me of poor Mrs Hogg, though she is much more anxious to get better and still talks of moving. She talks a great deal in a sort of doze. As I was writing to Mrs Bracebridge something about Hagar, *she* began, "Oh what was that about Hagar and Ishmael, you know, how she found the cold water and it cured the

---

18 Louisa Stewart Mackenzie (1827-1903), later Lady Ashburton, lifelong friend.
19 In Gen 29:27 Jacob serves twice seven years for Rachel. It is not clear who the current Rachel was.

boy's fever, you know."[20] Was not that odd? especially as that is the very only time she ever asked me for anything out of the Bible, except once when she asked me if Mary Magdalene was not the Virgin Mary.

What an inducement it would be to keep a sharp lookout on our thoughts, if we found they were capable of doing other people good or harm in this way. She is perhaps less "spiritually minded" than ever but dear old soul! she is truly great in her way and gave me orders last night that two new pillowcases should be made for that bed, "because next year," she said, "whoever sleeps in this bed will want them, I am sure." Is not that the eternal Spirit living after death? She talks a great deal in her sleep about buying hooks and eyes. And did I tell you, one night that she was very suffering, and I was doubting whether I should speak to her, something good about the weary and heavy laden, she said quite distinctly. "Oh I was so well, quite well till now. But I've been sadly off my teas and breakfasties of late."

Oh my dear Mum, life is nothing so much as profoundly ridiculous after all. Is that what the eternal Spirit is talking about, when it is communing in its dreams with the unspeakable presence and perhaps with the other invisible spirits, on the eve of becoming like them and of throwing off the form of ghosthood which it has put on to dress itself, like a ghost, for a moment for this earth, before the cool morning air sends it to its real home? Not that I have any objection to its talking about pillowcases, that seems to me quite as fine as Regulus[21] providing for Rome before he went back to Carthage.

(Give my best love to the people you are with, and tell Louisa Mackenzie she must come to Embley to make amends. I must contrive to see Aunt Evans[22] again somehow or other, but I am afraid tomorrow she will not want me to sleep on the eve of her departure. But do not be alarmed, I am not going there today, nor tomorrow either most likely.)

ever dear Mum

your affectionate child

---

20 In Gen 21:19 the water saves Hagar and her son from dying of thirst; there is no mention of fever.

21 The exploits of Marcus Atilius Regulus, Roman consul, in the First Punic War in North Africa are told in Horace's *Odes*.

22 Elizabeth Evans (1759-1852) great aunt.

Source: Unsigned, incomplete letter, Wellcome (Claydon copy) Ms 8992/59

[November 1844]

Dolce Madre [Sweet Mother]

Everything here is performing its appointed seasons, black tea and new moon inclusive, as usual (to its own satisfaction and that of others) excepting poor Mrs Rose,[23] who is *greatly* discouraged by the obstinate irregularity of the children, both in attendance and as monitors in forming a class out of school hours and their lateness in the morning. She conceived herself however much cheered by the light of my countenance and expects great things from an oratorical display out of the desk, which you are to make on your return. You know I am not great in the desk, but I could take each *individgle* child and beat him about the head and ears, if you liked it. I promised her to devote the first Thursday in every month to discussing virtue as a problem with the children (inwardly hoping that its solution would not be a vice) and pledged myself to bring it to a reductio ad absurdum.

I doggedly denied the books till you come back. Gale is in a great agitation for an answer about Rebecca. I am afraid you felt a pike in your heart on Sunday morning at 10:00, and again yesterday at 4:00. It was me, groping in your entrails, I mean, your commode. I was obliged to do it at twice, as it is only the oldest divers can hold their breath longer than two minutes, but now I have taken out all the drawers and locked them up in the cellar, not thinking them safe enough in their own commode, and have applied for a patent by which a cupboard locks up its own key in itself. Till which patent comes out I keep the key in my own *inside.*

Thanks for your invitation to William. Pray do not mention its purpose even to Aunt Mai, as his father particularly mentioned to me not to speak of it, and warned me that it would make his stay at Sandhurst impossible, if people were to laugh at him about it and there is no one less indulgent than [breaks off]

Source: Letter, Wellcome (Claydon copy) Ms 8992/65

[end 1844]

Dear Mama

We hope to see you on Monday. I have done my duty by Mrs Empson,[24] whom I like very much, very cordial and ladylike, and as to her

---

23 Teacher in the local school.
24 Wife of the vicar of East Wellow, where W.E. Nightingale was patron.

luncheon, what a manager. I wish I ever saw such a luncheon at home, neat but not gaudy, elegant but not expensive. They have made the place look very pretty and to see people so happy in this miserable world is really interesting. We were philosophical, rhapsodical and a most eloquent trio on the physiology of blue carpets and bad characters (in Wellow Wood) and swore eternal friendship over their muddy drinking water.

Mrs Hogg, I think, is much worse since I saw her last. Gale very cheerful, though you must not expect any improvement. I am so glad we have got her home that I do not seem to care for anything else. I was so afraid that, once let her go, and we should never catch her again. Now I cannot fancy that she can ever move more or change again. What a peaceful sound that is and what a welcome one, if we could but say it everyone of us each to himself, that we are not to change, no more—o never more. Mrs Rose is "well and happy" or, as the court circular would say, in excellent health and spirits. No sickness in the parish.

F.N.

I have had a most loving and interesting letter from Mrs Bracebridge. Addio, pia madre [pious mother]. I think your husband decidedly better and more UP, whether Harrogate gratiâ or not, the deponent is not competent to judge. Goodbye, pious Mother.

Source: Incomplete, unsigned letter, Wellcome (Claydon copy) Ms 8992/73

Dear Mother mine   19 January 1845

I do not think I can come before Tuesday or Wednesday, being rather weak and scarcely able to get up and downstairs, but I will write tomorrow and say if it is to be Tuesday. I have employed my evenings in a profitable and amusing manner since you have been gone, going to sleep as soon as it grew dark, and remaining in that state, which to Miss Martineau appears the most intelligent,[25] when to the question, are you asleep? one can answer YES till 10 or 11 o'clock, when I retire to the molli piume [soft feathers]. Mrs Hogg is no better.

I had a very good class of girls this morning, and impressed upon them many good diabolical doctrines with as much bonne foi [good faith] and pious zeal as a father of the church could have done. Indeed, such was our fervour that I believe an image to the devil, that

---

25 A reference to Martineau's (five) articles on "mesmerism" or hypnotism in the *Athenaeum* in 1844.

great dignitary of the Anglicans, might have been introduced among our devotions with startling effect. I just hinted too at a subject, which made poor little Caroline Humby shrink, but which was brought upon me nilly willy.

Tell Papa that my room and I have sworn an eternal friendship and that I have scarcely left it, except to creep down into the garden and to my meals, always to my meals, which I observe with the most startling precision and punctuality, always waking up for *them* with unerring exactitude. The Empsons have not yet unearthed me, which I consider as "partly owing to Providence." Mrs William Minor is quite recovering and her baby "quite nicely," poor little thing. Don't be angry; it's its misfortune, not its fault, that it lives. *Cap*[26] is better and I see him now parcourant his pleasure grounds on three legs. The brown cat occupies the principal suite of apartments here in the absence of the family. I remonstrated with him, but Gale says "if he didn't the rats would run about like donkeys." And now that we have arrived at the highest type of the zoological circle *at present* existing on your feudal tenure on *this the 19th day of January year of grace 1845*, it is time, I [breaks off]

How sorry I am to hear no better an account of my dear child Shore.

Source: Letter, Wellcome (Claydon copy) Ms 8992/108

[c1845]
Dearest Mother

I cannot come till Wednesday, I am afraid, because, even if I were well enough in other ways, I have been obliged to send for Taylor to come tomorrow to take out a tooth, an old sinner, which had been quiet for a long time. But if it is satisfied with taking out the stopping, and being allowed a free range, so shall I. I am the less uneasy about doing this, because I know that you and Papa never urge in cases of illness. We have had such a tremendous N. wind here today, that the hurdles performed a new Pas Fantastique, and I trembled for the last of the Mohicans, I mean, the elms. The noise in the drawing room windows was positively so great that I went down to see if the Lefroy ghost had taken possession. But the shadows are now sleeping as calmly on the lawn as if nothing had happened, and the great traveller's going down to the West as quietly and gloriously, bless him!

---

26 A dog, Nightingale's first patient.

Mr Bourne, you will be sorry to hear, is much the same. I sent over to inquire and should have gone today myself, if it had not been such a day (cold enough for snow) that I could not get over the little bit to poor Mrs Hogg's.

Mr Empson unrooted me today, and says that poor Sydney Smith is really given up at last. I spare you our petites réflexions morales et chrétiennes, and the whole host of proverbs, wise saws, truisms and alligators, which we brought to bear on this question, from the rich caverns of the memories of two such philosophers. I had a thousand and three more ready, when remembering Parthe's example, by which I hope I shall always endeavour to profit through life, I maintained a strict silence, fearing lest he should stay supper. We had already been moral enough to furnish out ten immoral parishes with True Ways of Life and How to spend Time Well.

The Combe[27] account is not flourishing methinks. I scarcely know what to write to Grandmama so have not written, as I ought. . . .

ever, dear Mum

your affectionate child

Source: Letter, Wellcome (Claydon copy) Ms 8992/112

Friday [1845]

Dear Mama

Gale has only this morning produced the enclosed, which she has had by her a fortnight! The lady is known to Dr Beddome. I hope that silence about your tooth means improvement. I am more sorry for Aunt Mai's suspense among the doctors than anything. Gale is more *doing* about the house, I doubt whether she is really better. I sat by her bed an hour this morning, and though when she was up, she seemed better, anyone seeing her in bed, with the perspiration all over her, would have thought she would never get out of it. At this moment she is in your room, as active as ever.

Papa I think is remarkably "well and happy." I have little of anything new to tell you. The fruit of this day's work has been the school, the vicarage, Mrs Southwell, nothing singular, new or surprising about any of them. At the school those of my pupils who are not in jail for assaults are engaged in breaking their school missis' heart. And I suspect that Mrs Porter has something to answer for in the torments of

---

27 Combe Hurst, near Kingston, Surrey, home of Uncle Sam and Aunt Mai Smith.

poor Mrs Rose and that she thinks her Richelieu[28] abilities will work a way for the Queen Mother to return.

But your arrival is to put everything to rights and Emma Porter vacates on Monday. Mrs Rose rarely *opens* school with more than seven children (out of thirty) and cannot induce the monitors to come to her *out* of school hours. But I promised her that *all* should be set right and we will talk of these things when you come. My pupil who is committing assaults is Charles Dawkins and, as Mrs Rose derived such comfort from the light of my countenance (a very reasonable consequence from the above premises), I shone industriously and graciously.

The Empsons thrive, though she looks delicate. Mrs Southwell was so cool about Rebecca's coming that I was on my dignity too, but she will make her appearance tomorrow morning, depend upon it. And I hope she will, for Gale is so anxious, and I was afraid I should spoil Gale's "broth" by seeming too empressée. Parthe's abilities are tremendous in the kitchen line.

ever, dolce madre,
your loving child
F.N.

Source: Incomplete letter to Frances Nightingale, Wellcome (Claydon copy) Ms 8992/125

[Maundy Thursday, 9 April 1846]
Mop and Louisa Mackenzie and Mrs Bracebridge being locked up with Mr Reeve, Miss Dutton[29] and I remained upstairs. It was Mrs Bracebridge's so earnest wish that I should not leave Miss Dutton alone till Monday, that she wrote herself to the chieftainess. I was sorry, but the chieftainess, I hope, will not be spinous, and I had *two* most kind letters from Louisa, to the effect that she hoped I would stay before Mrs B.'s was written.

Miss Dutton went to bed very early, and I had a most delightful talk with Mrs B. about the Holy Land, which she said had been the great wish and prayer of her life to see, and when that was accomplished, she had never prayed for children[30] or anything else, being satisfied and overblessed. Only think what that is to say.

It was a glorious moonlight night. I am just come from church now. I like to have the Thursday night, the most solemn night of the year, a

---

28 An allusion to Cardinal Richelieu (1585-1642), famous for his political manoeuvres.
29 Hon Anne-Constance Dutton (d. 1858), later Lady Dunsany.
30 The Bracebridges remained childless.

fine night, because I always think of what the full moon looked down upon at that hour 1846 years ago and it seems so ungrateful to spend that night in bed which our Saviour spent in such a way (going from examination to examination) for us and it is the same moon that is looking down upon us now.

I must write a word to Louisa in return for a splendid church service and which she has sent me. I may still go tomorrow, if Miss Dutton is better. I saw Parthe today before church, uncommon jolly. I presume [she] does not write.

Mr Chadwick's new statistic is that £20,000 a year is wasted at Bristol in hard water (1d a week being spent in the soap which is supererogatory, i.e., over and above what is wanted for soft water). Now from £3000 to £5000 would bring soft water from a distance and the supererogatory works will then be spared.

Aunt Hannah would come to us when the Nicholsons go to town, I doubt not, and Helen Richardson too, I think. So au revoir, dear Mother and Father. I have just been interrupted by Mrs Bracebridge making me entertain Mr Tremenheere,[31] whom she shovelled into the back room with me, while she was talking to poor Mr Mills.[32]

ever dear Mum

your affectionate child

Source: Letter, Wellcome (Claydon copy) Ms 8993/12

[Wilton[33]]

[1848?]

Dearest Mother

I send you the enclosed, meaning Mariette[34] and Aunt Jenny's note. Mrs Herbert is in bed today, so I am really glad I stayed, as I teach in her school and do her jobs in the village, and she is in such a fidget if they are not done, because she says there is nobody in her family who *likes* doing it. Therefore she feels there is nobody whom she can ASK to do it. I hope there is not much amiss. But she has a good deal of pain. However she is under [Dr] Tatum, which is all right. What a lovely day.

ever dear people

your loving child

---

31 Hugh Seymour Tremenheere (1804-93), member of a commission on children's employment.
32 A relative of Selina Bracebridge's, née Mills.
33 Home of Sidney and Elisabeth Herbert.
34 Nightingale's (French) maid.

I have given Mariette a note for Jackson about the cerate. Everything in my room is locked up, and I have the keys, so there need be no trouble about that. Oh! if you will take my *Gully*[35] *directions*, which are in the first page of *Gully's book*, which is in the bookcase in my room, I may perhaps want them (there is a letter of Mrs Noel's too in the book, don't take that).

I am sorry not to continue Mr Charles' education, whom I like much, but I have great abundance of teaching to do here. . . .

Source: Unsigned letter/draft/copy, ADD Mss 45790 f102

[Lea Hurst]
Tuesday [22 October 1850]

My dearest Mother

I was rather disappointed not to hear from you this morning. I should be very glad if it were so settled that I should stay, both on account of companionizing Aunt Mai and Aunt Evans and also because I might then do something in Holloway, where I have had so little time and so much to do.

Uncle Sam went this morning. Shore and I should, I think, at all events stay till Friday. Boots, shoes, a comb and warm gloves I must myself buy in London.

ever your loving child

Source: Unsigned draft/copy, ADD Mss 45790 ff117-18

Friday [29 November 1850]

My dearest Mother

It's an ill wind that blows nobody good. I shall not be able to make my appearance till Monday (4:23 at Romsey, with Miss Johnson, please) and no mistake.

Susan Horner has a housekeeper she thinks would suit us; she was housemaid with them twenty years ago, then nurse with Mrs Frank Marcet, then married and widowed, and now wants a place—a valuable person. Mrs Marcet would be the person to write to. Susan has written to the person (Mrs Jones) to tell her to write to you *if* she is still out of place. This entails nothing upon you, if you do not like to inquire further. Susan has also a kitchen maid. Do you still want one and shall I do anything about her? I have got Parthe's hot bottle.

I hope that people are now coming to their senses about the ridiculous row the church is making, which I believe tends to nothing else

---

35 Dr James Manby Gully, whose water cures at Malvern Nightingale and her father took.

but enslaving again all our liberties as dissenters. I hope you saw Baring Wall's good letter. I enclose a copy of Uncle Nicholson's to our archdeacon. I am afraid you were very much disappointed not to see us today, dear Mother, but it was not my fault. I was very much grieved about it, but it is very well now it was so and I do feel of much use here. The Horners are so tiresome and it keeps them off. I do wish all these successive shocks (renewing the first) of seeing people could be spared Marianne. . . .

Editor: Family correspondence on Nightingale's first visit to Kaiserswerth in 1850 seems to be limited to a letter to her father (see p 231 below). (Dates have to be attributed by internal evidence as the years were not given for most, and Nightingale was at Kaiserswerth in August in both 1850 and 1851.) Correspondence evidently went astray on that first visit, which occurred at the end of the trip with the Bracebridges to Egypt, Greece, Germany, etc., as can be seen in a letter of Nightingale's to an acquaintance in Berlin, asking her to check at the Post Office for any letters that might have arrived for her, for "I have not heard so long from my people I cannot but imagine some mistake has been made in forwarding them." She asked that they be forwarded to her at Poste Restante, Düsseldorf.[36]

Frances and Parthenope Nightingale were also on the Continent in the summer of 1851, for the latter to take a cure. The letters to her sister (see pp 303-10 below) are tellingly much longer and more pleading than those to her mother.

Source: Letter/draft/copy, ADD Mss 45790 ff133-37

Diakonissen Anstalt
Kaiserswerth am Rhein
Düsseldorf 6
Preussen
16 July 1851

Dearest Mother

It was the greatest possible relief to me to hear from you. I thought the letter long in coming and did not write till I heard from you. I am rather glad you did not consult Killian,[37] as he might have set your

---

36 Letter to Mme Pertz [August 1850], Florence Nightingale Museum LDFNM 0802.

37 Possibly Dr Hermann Friedrich Kilian (1800-63), an eminent German gynecologist with British connections.

minds at sea again and, as the long journey seems really rather to agree than not, I am very glad she has taken to drawing and that Aschaffenburg and Würzburg are so pretty. I hope that you will have seen all the Albert Dürers[38] at Nuremberg and particularly my Crucifixion, which I am so fond of—the forehead has all the intellect of the God, the Jupiter, and the mouth all the tenderness of the woman. Power and sympathy, the two requisites in a friend, are both there.

I shall be very anxious to hear how Karlsbad agrees—you have horrid weather. With regard to me, I am no longer, I am sorry to say, in the room you saw, but I am not at the pastor's house at all, and therefore hardly ever see them except when they make their rounds. I eat now with the sisters in the great dining hall you saw, and sleep in a room in the Orphan Asylum, the same house where my last year's room was.

I am afraid any account of what I do would be very uninteresting to you. On Sunday I took the sick boys a long walk along the Rhine. Two sisters were with me to help me to keep order; they were all in ecstasies with the beauty of the scenery. It was like Africa turned green, but really I thought it very fine too in its way: the broad mass of waters flowing ever on slowly and calmly to their destination and all that unvarying horizon, so like the slow, calm, earnest, meditative German character.

I have not mentioned to anyone where I am and should also be *very* sorry that the old ladies should know. I have not even told the Bracebridges.[39] With regard however to your fear of what people will say, the people whose opinion you most care about—it has been their earnest wish for years that I should come here. The Bunsens[40] (I know he wishes one of his own daughters would come), the Bracebridges, the Sam Smiths, Lady Inglis, the Sidney Herberts, the Plunketts[41]—all wish it. And I know that others, Lady Byron,[42] Caroline Bathurst, Mr

---

38 Albrecht Dürer (1471-1528), German painter and print maker.
39 With whom Nightingale had made her first visit. In fact the Bracebridges visited her again at Kaiserswerth in August.
40 Christian Carl von Bunsen (1791-1860), Egyptologist and Prussian ambassador to England, acquainted Nightingale with Kaiserswerth by giving her a copy of its annual report; his English wife, Frances Bunsen, was also a good friend.
41 Edward Plunkett, later Lord Dunsany, married a friend, Anne Dutton.
42 (Lady) Anne Isabelle Byron (1792-1860), widow of the infamous poet, family friend.

Tremenheere, Mr Rich (whose opinions however I have not asked) would think it a very desirable thing for everybody, also the Bonham Carters. There remain the Nicholsons, whose opinion I don't suppose you much care for, who would not approve, and many others no doubt. The Stanleys I know would approve. With regard to the time chosen, I grant people will think it odd, and I would willingly have stayed with Papa, as you know, and gone another time. But you preferred not. No one can judge of anyone's family circumstances but themselves and you know how much better Parthe is without Papa or me, although she will not think so. One must judge for her. One cannot tell people what are the excitements which make it desirable for her to be alone and without irritation. With regard to telling people the fact (afterwards) of my having been here, I can see no difficulty, knowing as I do that all my friends whose opinion you most value will rejoice in it as a most desirable thing.

The Herberts, as you know, even commissioned me to do something for them here. The fact itself will pain none of them. Uncle Nicholson said directly (when that foolish Marianne proclaimed something about Papa and me going with you), "I think Nightingale and Florence had much better go to the Hurst—if invalids have a good courier and a good maid they are much better alone." I am so glad the travelling suits her.

The world here fills my life with interest and strengthens me body and mind. I succeeded directly to an office and am now in another so that till yesterday I never had time even to send my things to the wash. We have ten minutes for each of our meals, of which we have four. The people here are not saints, as your courier calls them, though that was a good hit, but good flesh-and-blood people, raised and purified by a great object constantly pursued. My particular friends are, however, all on foreign service, which I am very sorry for, all excepting that one precious soul, whom I introduced you to in the penitentiary, but as we are all too busy to visit each other in our respective houses, I have never been able to go to the penitentiary since I took you there, dear Mother. The pastor [Fliedner] sent for me once to give me some of his unexampled instructions; the man's wisdom and knowledge of human nature is wonderful. He has an instinctive acquaintance with every character in his place. Except that once, I have only seen him in his rounds.

We get up at 5:00, breakfast at 5:45, the patients dine at 11:00, the sisters at 12:00. We drink tea (i.e., a drink made of ground rye) between 2:00 and 3:00 and sup at 7:00. We have two ryes and two broths, i.e., ryes at 6:00 and 3:00, broths at 12:00 and 7:00, breads at the two former, vegetables at 12:00. Several evenings in the week we collect in the great hall for a Bible lesson or an account of missions, etc. But I must away.

ever dearest Mother
your loving child
Thank dear Pop for her letter. Athena [the owl] must not make blots and she must have sand and not drink the ink.

Source: Letter/draft/copy, ADD Mss 45790 ff137-38

Kaiserswerth
8 August [1851[43]]

Dearest Mother

I have just received your letter and am glad you are so well content. I don't think you can expect more progress at present. You will be glad to see by the enclosed that Mrs Herbert is safe. The operation to which Mrs Bracebridge alludes was an amputation, at which I was present, but which I did not mention, knowing that she would see no more in my interest in it than the pleasure dirty boys have in playing in the puddles about a butcher's shop.

I find the deepest interest in everything here and am so well, body and mind. This is life—now I know what it is to live and to love life and really I should be sorry now to leave life. I know you will be glad to hear, dearest Mother, this. God has indeed made life rich in interest and blessings and I wish for no other earth, no other world but this.

ever your loving child, dear Mum

Editor: In the letter below Nightingale shared the joy of knowing useful service with her mother. She had wanted to die before, but "now I should be sorry to leave this life," a sentiment she could count on her mother welcoming. In the letter immediately after it Nightingale refers to the "voice" that called her to service, indeed "how long that voice has spoken." When the correspondence picks up again post-Crimea her mother and sister are onside, assisting her projects. This is evident from the first item, a letter of Mrs Nightingale, on behalf of her daughter, to Richard Monckton Milnes, helping to promote the establishment of her first royal commission.

---

43 Nightingale was in Kaiserswerth in August in both years; internal evidence would suggest this came from the earlier trip.

Source: Letter/draft/copy, Add Mss 45790 ff141-42

Kaiserswerth
31 August [1851]

Dearest Mother

I rejoiced to receive your letter this morning. You have not had my last, written to Karlsbad, where, as I received no address in your last, I directed. I suppose your letters have not followed you, as you left no direction. I hope you will follow Mrs Bracebridge's advice and consult the man at Berlin. I rejoice to find that you do not think Bad Franzens as bad as you expected. We were ordered there for Mr Bracebridge. Were not the J.B.C.'s at the wedding, that they are running about here. The weather is here as cold as winter. . . .

The Sidney Herberts are coming here from Hornburg so I have plenty of visitors. I should be as happy here as the day is long and wish I could hope that I had your smile, your blessing, your sympathy upon it, without which I cannot be quite happy. My beloved people, I cannot bear to grieve you. Life, and everything in it that charms you, you would sacrifice for me. But, unknown to you is my thirst; unseen by you are waters which would save me. To save me, I know, would be to bless yourselves, whose love for me passes the love of woman.[44] Oh how shall I show you love and gratitude in return, yet not so perish, that you chiefly will mourn. Give me time, give me faith. Trust me, help me. I feel within me that I could gladden your loving hearts which now I wound. Say to me, "follow the dictates of that spirit within thee."

Oh my beloved people, that spirit shall never lead me to anything unworthy of one who is yours in love. Give me your blessing, speed me on my way to walk in the path which the sense of right in me has been pointing to for years. Have other paths *right for others* been untried by *me?* But, my beloved people, still have I heard this same voice. This may appear to you the passing fancy of a heated imagination, from which your tender care would rescue me. But little do you know how long that voice has spoken, how deep its tones have sunk within me, how I have turned this way and that, trying if there were other path for me than one which might look like estrangement from home and parents, so loving, so loved. It shall not be so. Again I say, give me time, give me faith, give me the help of your blessing. Then will I prove that I love home and parents and sister and friends. It shall not

---

44 An allusion to 2 Sam 1:26.

be necessary for them to conceal where I am and what I am doing, for it shall come home to their hearts that I am doing nothing of which they or you, my pure, my lovely one, will be ashamed. We would be together always in love. How thankfully would I return to my home if it would bless me, when I come and when I go, while in my absence what peace, if I might hope that you were sympathizing with me. When I was six years old, with Miss Johnson, this has been my first thought, for the last seven years, my first and last.

ever my beloved people
your loving child

Editor: The following nine letters, selected from a larger number, are to the Nightingale parents about Parthenope (letters to her father are included here so as not to break the sequence). Florence Nightingale returned early from her trip to Ireland to bring her sister back from Birk Hall, Aberdeenshire, where she had gone to be treated by Sir James Clark[45] for her nervous breakdown. The Nightingale parents did not take the matter seriously, carried on as usual socially and did not act on Clark's recommended follow-up treatment.[46] Nightingale herself kept away from home as much as possible thereafter, on his view that she was the cause of the distress. She then accompanied her father on a water cure, stayed with other relatives and went to Paris to visit Roman Catholic nursing orders.

Source: Letter, Wellcome (Claydon copy) Ms 8993/109

Birk Hall
Monday [13 September 1852]

Dearest Mother

Mariette [her maid] and I are just arrived. I have only time to say that my dear Pop was very glad to see me, that Sir J. Clark thinks very well of her and is quite satisfied with the progress she has made and I will write more at length tomorrow. I am very glad to have come.

ever dear Mum
your loving child
Post going out.

---

45 Sir James Clark, physician to Queen Victoria, later a member of the Nightingale Fund Council. Birk Hall is near Balmoral Castle.
46 See Woodham-Smith, *Florence Nightingale* 102-04.

Source: Letter, Wellcome (Claydon copy) Ms 8993/110

[Birk Hall]

Friday [17 September 1852]

Dearest Mother

This is to announce that we have made our first walk this beautiful day and we come downstairs now at 10 o'clock; we sleep well and eat well and I see no reason why we should not set out homewards, except that the *time* [menstrual period] is the *end* of next week again and Sir James is not quite certain whether we had better go before or after it. He will decide tonight and you shall hear. He says that she is quite able to travel now, but she does not think so herself and so he does not like to urge her. We shall sleep at Aboyne, at Aberdeen, at Perth, at Edinburgh, at Newcastle, as at present advised, and perhaps one night between Newcastle and home. Don't say another word, please, about dreading the journey or stopping long upon the road. Sir James says that she will want to stop too much and that it would be much better, once under weigh, if she would make the exertion to go on. Please write encouragingly about this.

Yesterday, as we were out, we came upon the royal party in a scompiglio [confusion]. The Queen came out into the middle of the road by herself and said, My niece has had an accident. Luckily Sir James was with us and he went to her directly. It was the young Princess Hohenlohe[47] who had been thrown from her horse and we have not seen Sir James since. But we hear she is better.

Thanks for all the things, dearest Mother, and the list, they were all safe. I have written to Miss Birt to ask her to pay us a visit at Lea Hurst or Embley.

ever, dearest Mum

your loving child

Sir James decides that we had better go on Monday during this beautiful weather and before the *time* comes.

Source: Letter, Wellcome (Claydon copy) Ms 8993/112

[Birk Hall]

Monday [20 September 1852]

Dearest Mother

All going on well here, though our fancies are more in number than the sands of the sea. Last night we slept like a top, have had

---

47 Feodora, the daughter of Queen Victoria's older half-sister Princess Feodora (1807-72) of Hohenlohe-Langenburg.

three good meals today and bowels acted; we have been talking of going downstairs today and should have done it, had it not been for company.

Tomorrow I hope we shall do it without fail. Sir James says she is able to move homewards now, but as she does not say anything about it and seems to dread the journey much, we have not said anything about it, especially as today there was a little snow. But we expect fine weather and much warmer after this, so the prophets tell us. Sir James says, if she could but think herself well she would be so, or rather if she could but think of something else.

I was rather amused at the contents of your box though I know she asked for them. It arrived quite safe, though it cost 10/. Lady Clark was very much pleased with the pine, which looked quite handsome. The pears we smuggled out of Parthe's way. She won't wear any of the things, so I wear them. She makes me write every day to Aberdeen for a new gown. So pray don't send anything more if she writes to you, dear Mother.

She walks about the rooms a good deal and not weakly. Sir James and Lady Clark are quite indefatigable in their kindness, as indeed you know, as well as Charlotte. . . .

Source: Letter, Wellcome (Claydon copy) Ms 8993/105

Birk Hall

21 September [1852]

We came *downstairs* today and established ourselves in the drawing room without difficulty, dearest Mother, had jelly and grouse for our dinner and were downstairs as early as 11 o'clock. It is not cold today. I expect, before the close of this week, we shall have begun our journey home. Sir James is gone to Balmoral today, but saw her downstairs before he went and comes back tonight.

ever dear Mum

your loving child

Source: Letter, Wellcome (Claydon copy) Ms 8993/108

[Birk Hall]

[after 21 September 1852]

Dearest Mother

Your affectionate child greets you; we came down today jollily and walked about, had lamb chops for dinner and have been dictating letters. Sir James thinks of our going Monday.

Will you, please, post pay the enclosed, which is the desired letter to Mme de Goulaine?

ever your loving child

F.N.

Wednesday: all guests departed, house luckily empty.

Source: Letter, Wellcome (Claydon copy) Ms 8993/107

Birk Hall
Friday night [24 September 1852]

My dear Father

Sir James Clark seems to be fidgety about our travelling without a man in Parthe's rather weak state, as she may want somebody to look after the luggage, while Mariette and I look after her. He wants us to have Watson [employee at Lea Hurst] to meet us at Aberdeen. I think it an extra precaution and an extra expense, but am willing to be guided. So, if Watson leaves Cromford on Monday by the train 3:5 P.M., he will leave Ambergate by the train which passes Ambergate 4:13 P.M. on Monday (*the day you receive this*), and he will reach Edinburgh at 4:55 the next morning, sleep a few hours there, leave Edinburgh again at 12:15 and reach Aberdeen at 6:13 P.M. on Tuesday night. We leave Birk Hall on Monday and shall be at *Douglas's Hotel*, Market St., Aberdeen, on *Tuesday* night, where we shall sleep, if Watson will meet us there.

I think that I am very sorry to put you to this extra trouble and expense, but Sir James says that he shall be more comfortable if we have this man. He says Mary would have been no use at all and that Parthe may fancy she can't walk, and then a man will be of use. If you think so too, send him, and let him bring an air cushion and two hot bottles; we cannot want anything else. I don't think we shall want *him*, but if you like to send him. . . .

ever, dear Pa

your loving child

F.N.

Source: Unsigned letter, Wellcome (Claydon copy) Ms 8993/111

Aberdeen
Tuesday [28 September 1852]

Dearest Mother

Here we are safely arrived, by the grace of God and Sir James Clark. Is that profane? Not at all. But true. Bab was very much affected by our departure, in fact, I saw her struggling with her feelings in her nurse's arms.

We came a quiet drive of thirteen miles to Aboyne yesterday, slept there and came on here in three hours today, resting half an hour at Banchory. Parthe is now celebrating Sir J. Clark, "who," she says, "is so great a man that he enabled me to do this journey and made the horses do it in 3½ hours." She slept the sleep of the just all night and till 9:30 this morning, I sleeping with her. No end of pillows and hot bottles, besides partridges, plucked and unplucked, cloaks, arrowroot and biscuits, were sent with us by dear Lady Clark's most kind care.

I have not yet heard of Mr Watson. We shall leave Aberdeen tomorrow or next day. We ate the bigger part of two mutton chops after arriving here, had tea and cold partridge at Banchory and I hope shall have as good a night as last.

I have been to pay a bill of Parthe's here at Lyall's and, paying it, had some comfortable conversation over the counter upon ragged schools, whereupon a very Scotch and elderly gentleman, Mr Lyall himself, I opine, appeared from below. Whereupon we embraced over the counter in a long and close embrace, terminating thus, in a very grim voice, "ye canna go by yoursel to the schools. I sall come tomorrow at 11 o'clock in a cab to fetch ye." And this from a canny Scot I never saw.

Source: Letter, Wellcome (Claydon copy) Ms 8993/106

Edinburgh
30 September [1852]

Dearest people

Here we are all right. We left Aberdeen on Wednesday, I conceiving it my duty to adhere strictly to Sir James Clark's written plan. We had an even downpouring all day, which did not contribute to the cheerfulness of my poor patient and when we got to Perth, the Law was there. Now I have a great respect for the Law, which was meant for a terror for evildoers. But whether we were evildoers, in this case it was a terror to me, for when we drove up to the Royal George we found the judges there where I meant to be and two great enormous Highlanders parading sentinel before the door, besides a third performing his national music on that instrument (whose name I scarcely dare mention, as it calls forth tears of a different nature from those which fall from true Scottish eyes at its sound). From the Royal George we drove to the Salutation, but there also the Law was and we were not— in other words, they were full. At last, in desperation, a dear good woman, Mrs Wilson of the Star, may her shadow never be less! seeing the plight we were in, for by this time my poor child was beginning to cry, took us in, turned out her own three children and gave us her own room.

We came on here today and have lodged ourselves at Mackay's. The train was 1½ hour late at Edinbro', which caused great lamentations on the sofa on arriving. I went to the undertaker's to buy her a coffin and when I came back the dog was a laughing. No, but I ran to Dunean and Flockhart's to buy her Sir James Clark's prescriptions, intending to administer all three and the box and when I came back, the dog was sitting up eating tea and mutton chops at the table, an attitude in which I had not seen her since I came to her. We shall stay at Edinbro' tomorrow; she says she means to stay for a week, a thing Sir James charged me by no means to give into. So I hope to go on Saturday to York, give her the Sunday's rest there, if possible get her to the minster and home on Monday, please God. There is no *necessity* for tomorrow's rest. But I thought it best, one day. If I feel "plucky" tomorrow, I will go and call on the Combes.[48]

Mr Watson has not turned up, but it did not much signify. For what has had to be done could not have been done by him nor by anybody but me. When she thought she could not walk, which Sir James *assures* me is a delusion, I summoned a trusty porter, and he carried her bodily into the carriage. I am certain from pulse and appetite and good sleep and colour of face, all which are improving, that she is much better physically. But as yet she does not think herself so.

The express was certainly anything but express from Perth hither. Still we got in soon after 5:00 and the porters—what a noble race the porters are. By dint of blandishments, the superintendents have always given us a carriage to ourselves. They too are a noble race. The master of the inn at Aberdeen took us to the railroad himself and behaved himself like a benevolent genius. The good Clarks came to see us at Aboyne. Linlithgow was looking beautiful, as we drove through today, with the distant blue hills. But we have seen nothing so pretty as Deeside.

We have still a partridge left and some arrowroot from Lady Clark's bountiful stores, which I mention to show that the commissariat has

---

48 George Combe, author of a book on his father Andrew Combe (1797-1847), a doctor whom Nightingale cited with great respect in her *Notes from Devotional Authors of the Middle Ages*.

husbanded its resources. Of course you will see Sir James Clark in London.

I went to the ragged schools, after all, with Mr Lyall, at Aberdeen, greatly to my edification, and he insisted on paying the cab, greatly to my mortification. Edinburgh Friday, a *very* good night; we go to York tomorrow, au revoir, dear people.

Source: Letter, Wellcome (Claydon copy) Ms 8993/113

York
Sunday [3 October 1852]

Dear Papa

Please let the carriage meet Parthe tomorrow (Monday) at *3:25* at *Ambergate*. If there is any difficulty about luggage, of which there is a great deal, I and the luggage can go on to Whatstandwell, but I think it better to avoid the changing of carriages for her. If we do not come, you will know that some incidental interruption has taken place and will not be alarmed. But I fully *expect us*.

ever dear Pa

your loving child

Editor: On the death of Aunt Evans, Frances Nightingale proposed that Nightingale manage a small institution at the house in Cromford made vacant by Evans's death.

Source: Letter to Frances Nightingale, Wellcome (Claydon copy) Ms 8994/2

[January 1853]

I am very anxious to explain to my dear mother so as to avoid even any appearance of being ungrateful for the kind proposal, which I have received, why I cannot accept it *immediately*. I do indeed feel deeply grateful for the sympathy with my wishes which such a proposal shows. I am most anxious that my explanation should not seem ungracious. My dearest Mother, I learn from Uncle Sam that you are kindly thinking of Cromford Bridge for me. Of course I have given your generous thought my most careful consideration. I have also consulted my friends who are interested in this object. The result of which is that I must say what is no new "say" on my part, but what I have said for the last eight years, viz., that the certain failure which would follow, were I to enter upon such a difficult course, so untrained and unprepared as I now am, would ill requite the expense and the kind thought, to which you would then have gone on my account. In short, I am at present too inexperienced.

I paid the long promised visit (to Bristol, which you kindly urged in the summer), to the Shropshire Bunsens, where the Bristol plan is now transferred, merely in order to learn their plans and give what they were pleased to call my advice, as they had asked me to do "many a time and oft." They have sent their one woman to Paris to train. I think *I* shall also be able to get much information there. But I shall best know when I am there.

As to the Cromford Bridge plan *at present*, I see indeed too small chance of success for me to be justified in accepting it *now*. I am arrived at an age where the power of acquiring is generally supposed to be over, having for eight years constantly desired a training for this object, and during that time having had but three months' of that training. An object too so difficult that only one man, Fliedner, has ever succeeded in it. And now that this is offered to me, it is as if, supposing someone to have had in his life only three months' instruction in drawing, it were offered to him to be at the head of a school of design not yet founded. I should feel the failure equally certain in both cases. I do indeed feel that I can do nothing without preparation. This must be my answer for the present to your kind thought of dear old Cromford Bridge.

ever dear Mum

your loving and grateful child

Editor: Letters from Nightingale's Paris trip in 1853 (where she was permitted to go to obtain some nursing experience) are included in *European Travels*. Letters to her mother regarding her grandmother's death (also in 1853) appear later with other correspondence to her grandmother. Only a few letters from the Crimea period are included here, those dealing with personal matters.

Source: Unsigned letter, Wellcome (Claydon copy) Ms 8994/65

1 Upper Harley St.

1 December 1853

Dearest Mother

I really have no time for these fooleries. Leonora [Garnett]'s marriage is just of a piece with them. I am quite sure she had not seen Dr Pertz[49] six times, his wife but "two months" dead. If he had married

---

49 Georg Heinrich Pertz (1795-1876), chief librarian of the Royal Library in Berlin, helpful to Nightingale on her visit there in 1850. The then Mme Pertz was another Englishwoman.

Aunt Julia I should have supposed that his wife had asked it, and it would not have lowered my opinion of either. Now my opinion of both these two is gone. I always considered the Horners one of the few really united families I knew (borné [limited] and tiresome as they are) and here is a woman forsaking those she has known for thirty-five years for a man of fifty-eight whom she has known for six days and her own country into the bargain. Can anything be a greater proof of the want of interest women take in their lives?? That fatal want of interest which leads my governess class into hysterics, the higher (as it is called) class into a marriage = *lottery*. For I suppose nobody pretends that Leonora is in love with him. In these matrimonial speculations I cannot take the slightest interest, farther than a wish that women's lives could have interest enough to make men shy of asking such a sacrifice. But men are so well aware of the fact that a man, *who has enough*, can hardly look at a woman for fear of its being said that he has "trifled with her affections."

That I am alone nobody can know more deeply than I do. That my life is most solitary and friendless, in the midst of friends, is a truism, *how* solitary I and I only can tell, but would marriage diminish that solitude? Certainly none of those marriages I have ever seen. I have seen the husbands of my dearest friends curl their lips with a curious kind of smile at how little their wives understood them, and most men know their wives about as much as they know Abraham.

This man who wants to marry me now knows about as much of my views and feelings as I do of his, which is saying a great deal, for I really did not know whether *he* was alive or his brother and when he talked of his child, I did not know he had one. If I did not know that it was considered a compliment, I should consider his asking me almost an insult. As it is, I can only take it as another proof of the general melancholy truth that marriage is almost the only interest in a woman's [breaks off]

Source: Unsigned letter, Wellcome (Claydon copy) Ms 8994/99

1 Upper Harley St.
12 April 1854

Dearest Mother

Nothing that you can say can ever hurt me. But indeed the words you allude to were, I thought at the time, those of the most perfect kindness, and I have never had any other thought since. I have always the feeling of your perfect love and kindness towards me and, if I am ever hurt, it is not by words of yours but of my poor Pop's

[Parthenope's]. I confess she often pained me when in London, but *never, never* you. And therefore I am sorry that she should have put it into your head that I was so by you. I have the most perfect and entire trust and faith in your love and sympathy and remember mentioning this to her in London. I am sure the time will come when we shall love and sympathize more together instead of less, my dearest Mother. I dwell upon the thought of this love and sympathy with you as among my pleasantest thoughts.

Source: Unsigned letter, Wellcome (Claydon copy) Ms 9023/23

Dearest Mother
[before October 1854]

I have not been out all day and very sorry not to see Parthe when she came this morning. I fear I cannot go out tonight as I have no nurse I can spare to be with the cancer patients at night. If you can go tonight do not put if off for me—I might be able to go on Saturday, if we go on well.

I cannot think who could tell P. I was out.

Source: Letter, Wellcome (Claydon copy) Ms 8994/114

1 Upper Harley St.
15 October 1854

In the hope that I shall see my dearest mother and sister tomorrow, and that they will give me their blessing on our undertaking,[50] I shall leave it to Mrs Bracebridge to explain what that undertaking is.

F. Nightingale

Source: Copy of letter, Wellcome (Claydon copy) Ms 9020/9

Scutari
5 December 1854

Dearest people

Could you but see me, you would not wonder that I have no time to write, when my heart yearns to do so. Could anyone but know the difficulties and heart sinkings of *command,* the constant temptation to throw it up they would not write to me as good Mr Garnier[51] does

---

50 Nightingale left 21 October for the Crimean War.
51 Possibly Thomas Parry Garnier (1807-68), rector of Bishopstoke, near Winchester, then Dean of Winchester.

praying for grace that I may bear the praise lavished upon me—I who have never had time to look at a paper since I came. Praise good God! He knows what a situation He has put upon me. For His sake I bear it willingly, but not for the sake of praise. The cup which my Father hath given me shall I not drink it?[52]

But how few can sympathize with such a position! Most of all was I surprised at Aunt Mai's sanguine and gleeful view of it. But do not suppose that I think without us nothing would have been done here, and I am satisfied. All this is of course *private*. I subjoin a list of small wants. Pray date your letters.

F.N.

I should like to hear about Harley St.

Source: Typed copy of letter of Frances Nightingale to unknown recipient, Columbia University, Presbyterian Hospital School of Nursing O1

Park Lane
26 March [1855?]

My dear Sir

I am glad that you are pleased with that shadow of a portrait of my daughter. Its shadowy nature helps the likeness now that the spirit predominates so much over the frail flesh, not that we believe her to be in any immediate danger, but, weak as she is, any sudden excitement or emotion is to be carefully avoided.

Many thanks for sending us your notice of her in the Derby paper. It is most just and true and evidently from the pen of one who knew her well and appreciated her, which cannot be the case, of course, with the greater part of those which have been published. Believe, dear Sir,

very truly yours
Frances Nightingale

Source: Letter, Wellcome (Claydon copy) Ms 8995/15

Black Sea
5 May 1855

Poor old Flo steaming up the Bosphorus and across the Black Sea with four nurses, two cooks and a boy to Crim Tartary (to overhaul the regimental hospitals) in the "Robert Lowe" or Robert Slow (for an uncommon slow coach she is) taking back 420 of her patients, a

---

52 An allusion to John 18:11.

draught of convalescents returning to their regiments to be shot at again. A "mother in Israel,"[53] old Fliedner called me, a mother in the Coldstreams is the more appropriate appellation.

What suggestions do the above ideas make to you in Embley drawing room? Stranger ones perhaps than to me who, on the 5th May, year of disgrace 1855, year of my age thirty-five, having been at Scutari this day six months, am, in sympathy with God, fulfilling the purpose I came into the world for. What the disappointments of the conclusion of these six months are, no one can tell, but I am not dead, but alive. What the horrors of war are, no one can imagine—they are not wounds and blood and fever, spotted and low, and dysentery, chronic and acute, cold and heat and famine—they are intoxication, *drunken* brutality, demoralization and disorder on the part of the inferior, jealousies, meanness, indifference, *selfish* brutality on the part of the superior.

I believe indeed, and am told by admirable officers in the service, that our depot and barrack at Scutari—in which to live for six months has been death—is a disgrace to the service and our commandant the worst officer in the service (had and solicited for by Lord Stratford,[54] because he would have a man of rank). But our Scutari staff, military and medical, content themselves with saying that the English soldier *must* be drunk and not one thing is done to prevent him. Nothing has been done but by us. We have established a reading room for the convalescents, which is well attended, and the conduct of the soldiers to us is uniformly good.

I believe that we have been *the most efficient*, perhaps the only means there of restoring discipline, instead of destroying it, as I have been accused of. They are much more respectful to me than they are to their own officers. But it makes me cry to think that all these six months we might have had a trained schoolmaster and that I was told it was quite impossible. That, in the Indian Army, effectual and successful measures are taken to prevent intoxication and disorganization and that here, under Lord W. Paulet's[55] very windows, the conva-

---

53 An allusion to Deborah, in Judges 5:7.
54 Stratford Canning, 1st Viscount Stratford de Redcliffe (1786-1880), British ambassador to Turkey.
55 Lord William Paulet, Commander in the Bosphorus, Gallipoli and Dardanelles in the Crimean War.

lescents are brought in emphatically *dead* drunk, for they die of it and he looks on with composure and says to me, "You are spoiling those brutes." The men are so glad to read, so glad to give me their money to keep or to send home to their mothers or wives. But I am obliged to do this in secret.

On the 1st May, by the most extreme exertions, our washing house opened, which might just as well have been done on the 1st November six months ago. I am in hopes of organizing some washing and cooking for the regimental hospitals and am going up with Soyer, dollies and steaming apparatus for this purpose far more than for any other. Mr Bracebridge goes with us, Mrs B. keeps the bear garden at Scutari. Four vessels of Sardinian troops go up with us, one vessel the Argo, with artillery and horses, ditto but went aground in the Bosphorus and could not get her off.

I have more and more reason to believe that this is the kingdom of hell, but I as much believe that it is to be made the kingdom of heaven. Beware of Lady Stratford.

yours ever
F.N.

Source: Letter, Wellcome (Claydon copy) Ms 8995/50

Castle Hospital
Balaclava
24 October 1855

Here have I been three weeks, my dearest Mother, and I wish you could see me in the most poetic spot in the world, looking out upon the old Genoese castle upon peak upon peak in the cold moonlight or in the red glow of the autumnal sunset, for the nights are hard frost, and listening to the everlasting roll of the sea at the foot of the steep cliff, some 490 ft high, upon which our hut is perched, and thinking of the everlasting patience of God (as typified by that eternal roll) which endures for tens of thousands of years, that we may "work out our own salvation,"[56] which is the only way He sees by which we can become like Him, while my patience is wearied at the end of one twelvemonth (which is now completed) by the ill will, incompetence, ignorance and bigotry with which I have to keep up one slow, weary, melancholy round of opposition varied only with occasional flashes of more vehement hatred and active ill doing.

---

56 A paraphrase of Phil 2:12.

Alas! who has not betrayed us in our cause but Rev Mother, Mrs Shaw Stewart and Mrs Roberts?[57] Yet my name is dear to me—it has won the good will of the humble hardworking part of my countrymen. But oh! what a tale I should have to tell of selfishness, conventionalism and malice. Well! I am too busy to attack or to defend, and am in the midst of extra diet kitchens, baths, linen, stores, sheets, reading rooms, stoves, boring for water, fitting huts for winter, etc. What this winter shall bring forth who can tell? . . .

ever your

F.N.

Source: Letter, Wellcome (Claydon copy) Ms 8996/74

14 July 1856

My dearest people

I sent home, by the Rev Mr Hort, on board the Calcutta, a "*Rooshan*" trophy for you, and two pairs bracelets in a small box, of which Lothian[58] is to have the refusal. I sent for them to Sinope on purpose, by medium of my faithful friend, Colonel McMurdo, Director General of the Land Transport Corps, without whom I do not think I should be alive. Pray, if you see Mr Hort, make much of him. He is a good man. Hibernicè. General Codrington has been courteous, Colonel Windham more than courteous, kind, Lord Rokeby and General Barnard, who brought Lord Gough to see me, talk to me as to an old soldier, and brother in the field. But General Storks and Colonel McMurdo have been and will remain my only friends out here.

ever yours

F.N.

Source: Unsigned letter, Wellcome (Claydon copy) Ms 8996/68

[1856]

I cannot remember whether I told you that, by the kindness of Captain Champion of the "Melbourne," I send you home a wild puppy, found in a hole here in the Crim with eleven brothers and sisters. I tried in vain to tame him. The only time he was beaten, for doing

---

57 Nightingale considered her to be one of the best nurses in the Crimea from St Thomas' Hospital; Mrs Roberts nursed Nightingale during her illness.

58 There is correspondence below with cousin Lothian, later General Sir Lothian Nicholson.

something very naughty, he was very quiet at the time, but never would speak again to the person who did it. His name is Roosh, supposed to be an abbreviation of "*Rooshan.*" His mama is about as big as a calf. There are not six dogs of his species gone home, so he is supposed to be valuable.

Editor: On return from the Crimea Nightingale promptly set to work on her first royal commission but soon became seriously ill. From this time on illness and excessive work become constant themes in correspondence.

Source: Letter, Wellcome (Claydon copy) Ms 8997/13

My dear dear Mother
                                                              14 December 1856

My heart was very full at parting with you and my dear loving Parthe. Your ceaseless watchfulness to ease and help me in the time we have been together can never be forgotten by me. Such devoted love is a very precious possession; it cheers me even while absent from you; it surrounds me with a genial atmosphere even when clouds look black and heavy. You will live with me, I know, if I faithfully strive to do our Father's work as far as is in me, even more than if I left it to see your dear faces and hear your voices.

I know your anxious tender thought for me. Be assured that I will not unnecessarily give you cause for anxiety. He who "would have his life shall lose it"[59] and I know you are willing that I should offer my all of life and health to the Father, to serve whom IS life, and to those poor children, remembering whose sufferings. It is a solace to me to strive that those sufferings shall not have been endured in vain,[60] but be assured that I love their cause too well heedlessly or recklessly to risk any means I may possess to serve it. To my dearest father I would add whatever words could best express my tender love, but neither he nor I are apt at using words to express what is deepest within us. God bless you all, my most dear ones, and for the present farewell.

If work prevents my writing often, it will not prevent that the loving remembrance of you will go about with me wherever I am and whatever I do. I shall not forget your desire for our meeting at Christmas, which would be so welcome to me. You know that I am unable to look

59 A paraphrase of Luke 17:33.
60 An allusion to Gal 3:4.

so far beforehand, but you will be assured if we do not, it will be because such meeting would be desertion of my work.

ever, dear people

your loving child

F.N.

Source: Letter/draft/copy by Frances Nightingale, ADD Mss 45796 f236

30 Old Burlington

Sunday [ca. July 1857]

Dear Mr Milnes

Will you come and see Sir John McNeill[61] (who is with us for a couple of days, in order to put the greatest quantity of sting into the tail of that scorpion of F.'s, the commission). Either on Monday night or Tuesday morning we shall be very glad indeed to see you. We are alone (N.B. the word alone does not mean the same thing in Burlington St. and Brook St.). Believe me,

yours sincerely

Frances Nightingale

Source: Letter, Wellcome (Claydon copy) Ms 8997/48

Bury House

Gt Malvern

25 August 1857

Dearest Mother

I am very glad you are gone down to the Hurst. How beautiful it must look. I am resting in the entire quiet here and shall not move this week.

ever dearest Mum

your loving child

F.

I am glad to be alone.

Source: Letter, Wellcome (Claydon copy) Ms 8997/60

Great Malvern

6 January 1858

To my dearest Mother I apply for ease and for help in my present pressing and difficult circumstances. I will explain: my father's letter to Aunt Mai asks "what next?" in reference to plans, and speaks of a

---

61 Sir John McNeill, head of the commission on sanitary reform in the Crimea, member of the Nightingale Fund Council.

"house in London." I ought not, therefore, to delay saying that, if you are so kind as to think of a house on my account, it is a kindness I am unable to accept, though I thank you for the thought. I am obliged now to restrict myself to *one* companion or, rather, I should say that companionship can be no more for me, while my work remains unfinished.

In order to keep up to my work I feel the necessity of having *one* person with me to perform offices which I am sure my dear mother and Parthe would feel, each for the other though not for herself, that health would not permit. And, for myself, I should feel such anxiety in seeing either of you attempt the sort of life I am compelled to require in the one person staying with me through this work (who might not be in full health and strength) that it would overpower, not help, me. I have no other plan, then, but to ask Aunt Mai to stay with me. I know she will do it willingly.

Such power for headwork as I ever had, I have still, and with that remaining power, I feel called upon to do what I can to rescue the children committed to me from death, from disease, from immorality. This work is in such progress that I may have the hope of seeing it completed, if I can sufficiently save my remaining strength. The details are too small to particularize of what is necessary to do this. Yet they are essential and I know not how to do without them. This help I can receive, without much anxiety, from dear Aunt Mai. But I could impose it upon no one else.

The help and the ease then which I ask from *you*, my dear Mother, is not to misinterpret what I am thus compelled either to say or else to give up my work. One person with health for these small but neces-sary offices is essential to me. More than one I have not the strength to see. During the time I have been in London, I have seen literally no one but those whom the necessities of business have compelled me to see. For these I am obliged to reserve such strength as remains to me. If I could give companionship or receive it, I would beg you to come and share it with me.

I enclose a little nasturtium or something else which the good peo-ple here give me for nosegays. It makes the prettiest winter vaseful. I do not remember ever seeing it. You ought to have it.

ever, my dear Mum
your loving child
F.N.

Source: Dictated letter, signed by Nightingale, Wellcome (Claydon copy) Ms 8997/89

Dearest Mother

Wednesday, 12th, 1859

Thank you very much for your long letter with the better report of Parthe and for your long list of game sent. La "reconnaissance n'est qu'un vif sentiment des *faisans* futurs!" [appreciation is but a lively intimation of future pheasants] and I have a remarkably stupid old friend now sick in bed who would like such *faisans* much: W.H. Burrell Esq MD, 37 Hans Place, Sloane Street, London, S.W.

I am glad to hear that Burton was able to go through the Christmassings and I think she will do well to keep on. I am glad too to hear of little Peter[62] so good a report.

We're sitting with the window open at half past four, a beautiful afternoon and no chilliness. I do hope you have the same and that your attack of cold is going quickly away. I hope Papa will come and see me on his way to the Hurst.

ever my dear Mum's loving child

F.N.

P.S. I have had a note from Sir Charles Trevelyan lamenting the necessity of leaving his family, but without any doubt as to his duty in accepting the governorship of Madras. Lady Trevelyan keeps the house in Grosvenor Crescent open for their children. Hamilton the financial secretary succeeds him as permanent secretary and Hamilton's place, as it is *said*, has been offered to Sir Stafford Northcote.[63] I am surprised at Trevelyan's going, but I daresay he will do it well. Sir John McNeill thinks very highly of his powers of organization but he must surely have ulterior views on Bengal or he would not accept Madras.

F.N.

Source: Undated letter with unstamped envelope, Wellcome (Claydon copy) Ms 8998/10

[1859]

Dearest Mother

I am afraid it would not be possible for me to see you on Sunday, for my engagements thicken. I could see you for a few minutes now or tomorrow and be thankful—perhaps *today* better than tomorrow.

---

62 The Russian boy Nightingale brought back from the Crimea, who became an employee of her father.

63 Sir Stafford Henry Northcote (1818-87).

I think you had better come to me at Hampstead for one night than go straight through to Lea Hurst from Ravensbourne.[64]
ever your
F.

Source: Incomplete letter to Frances Nightingale, Wellcome (Claydon copy) Ms 8998/33

[c1860]

I do indeed feel W.B.C.'s [William B. Coltman] marriage the greatest possible blessing. It is the best piece of news I have heard for a long time. You know I have a very high opinion of Bertha's[65] qualifications for happiness in particular, and life in general, and I do think W.B.C. is worthy of her and will appreciate her the more, the more he knows her.

He is infinitely superior to most men and to most women I know. (You know A.H.C. [Arthur Hugh Clough] is an angel and not a man.) But except Spottiswoode, I know no man whom I would as lief they gave their little Buffie to as this one.

ever dearest Mum
your loving child
F.

It is extremely distressing to me to contemplate my own death in the newspapers (always at the age of *five*) so often. In yesterday's there were three.

The little Gwendolen Galton[66] was here for a day or two for her health, a sweet little thing three times the age and a third the size of Prince Arthur. I did so long to put her up in a small parcel and send her back to God to be made up again.

Source: Letter, Wellcome (Claydon copy) Ms 8999/10

21 April 1861

Dearest Mother

I have sent you by post two copies of my new *Notes on Nursing for the Labouring Classes*. Please give one to Miss Daman as a proof of the

---

64 Frances Nightingale's sister, Joanna Bonham Carter, moved to Ravensbourne, Kent, after the death of her husband in 1838.
65 Bertha Smith, daughter of Uncle Sam and Aunt Mai, married William B. Coltman, son of a family friend who in turn became an important and helpful relative to Nightingale.
66 Daughter of Marianne (née Nicholson) Galton; Sir Douglas Galton was a major Nightingale collaborator at the War Office.

pleasure her verses have given, and tell her I hope she will like the new chapter on "Minding Baby," which I was ordered to write by a schoolmaster of Peckham, Mr Shields, who had made my book a textbook for his children and said that the girls went home and removed dung heaps from before their parents' doors and opened their parents' windows at night (to the great discomfiture of the latter), but that the "strongest motive" was to tell the girls to do this for the sake of "baby." And so I must write a chapter about "Minding Baby."

ever dearest Mother

your loving child

F.

A great part of the second chapter, "Health of Houses," and part of the first chapter are also new. And I was thinking of the Lea Hurst cottages all the time I wrote them.

F.N.

Source: Letter, Wellcome (Claydon copy) Ms 8999/26

[printed address] 30 Old Burlington Street, W.

15 June 1861

Dearest Mother

Do you know that Mme Mohl is in town, 40 York Terrace, Regents Park. You will most likely wish to ask her.

Could you send me by next box my little old poetry book, which used to be on the shelf in your bedroom? I will return it to you. There is only one poem I wanted to look at.

Send me forget-me-nots by next box. A beautiful nosegay is forget-me-not, scarlet geranium, white rose or seringa and reminds me of Italy and our hopes. They are her colours, plus the blue, which stands there for eternity.

ever dear Mum

your loving child

F.

Are the water lilies out?

Source: Letter, Wellcome (Claydon copy) Ms 8998/43

Thursday [186?]

Dearest Mum

I never send anything but game, fruit and flowers to Miss [Mary] Jones, nothing in fact except for *her own* eating or pleasure. All the rest is simply making a present to the hospital treasurer. Don't you think it would be better to send your beautiful box to Mrs Wardroper and then send what I have said above to Miss Jones another time?

A parcel of game is coming here for me from Lady Herbert, which has unfortunately gone through London. If you have any tenants to whom you *want* to give game, and would take this and give me game instead of it, it would save it the third journey back to London.

ever your F.

Source: Note presumably to Frances Nightingale, Wellcome (Claydon copy) Ms 8999/51

[printed address] 30 Old Burlington Street, W.

[1861]

Please ask Mrs Watson to send me one of her beautiful bouquets (with long trailing wreaths of leaves) in the box. Dr Sutherland says my nosegays always look as if they were "drunk," partly because M.B. has no knack of making them up and partly because the person who cuts the flowers has no ideal in his head, and there are no leaves proper to set them off, sent with them.

F.

Source: Letter with envelope, ADD Mss 45790 ff253-64

9 Chesterfield St., W.

7 March 1862

Dearest Mother

So far from your letters being a "bore" you are the only person who tells me any news. I have never been able to get over the morbid feeling at seeing my lost two's names [Sidney Herbert and Arthur Hugh Clough] in the paper, so that I see no paper.

I did not know of the deaths you mention (excepting of course Galton's baby), and am very glad to hear of them—yes, really glad. As for poor Galton's baby, it is a deep loss to him and I cannot be glad.[67] All his future he had built on it. He would have made it such a good father. I don't know when I have been so sorry for the dropping of such a little life on earth.

But Laura [Nicholson]'s husband and baby's father and others do not know how much they are spared by having no bitterness mingled with their grief. Such unspeakable bitterness has been connected with each one of my losses—far, far greater than the grief. Then I have lost all. All

---

67 Nightingale was godmother to the boy, named Herbert.

the others have children or some high and inspiring interest to live for, while I have lost husband and children and all and am left to the weary hopeless struggle with Hawes[68] at the War Office and Lord Stanley in the Indian Sanitary Commission, while it is an aggravation to everything to think that I predicted to my poor lost chief exactly what has happened, if he left the War Office *without* an organization and *with* a Hawes.

Sometimes I wonder that I should be so impatient for death. Had I only to stand and wait I think it would be nothing, though the pain is so great that I wonder how anybody can dread an operation. If Paget[69] could amputate my left *forequarter* I am sure I would have sent for him in half an hour. But it is this desperate guerilla warfare, ending in so little, which makes me so impatient of life—I who could once do so much. And that wretched Sir G. Lewis,[70] writing Latin *jeux d'esprit.*

Yes, the Canadian expedition[71] was very well done, but Lord de Grey[72] and I did that together, and we did it by means of the very machinery, constructed by me and Sidney Herbert, which Hawes is now wanting to destroy.

When I hear the street band playing "Auld Lang Syne," and think that these five last years of my life are indeed now *auld lang syne,* it takes a deal of faith to make God's will mine. For indeed I don't see how, in any world, there could be such a combination for good as that which existed between me and my lost ones here. And as it in no way depressed my joy in it to suffer so much as I did even during that time, so it in no way comforts me to think that *I* shall soon be past my sufferings. For the Army will not be better because I am dead.

Beatrice is going to see Miss Clough[73] before she leaves her school at the lakes, which I am very glad of. From the very first moment I ever saw either Miss Clough or her lost brother (the "man of God"), I

---

68 Sir Benjamin Hawes (1797-1862), under secretary for war.
69 Later Sir James Paget (1814-99), surgeon to Queen Victoria.
70 Sir George Cornewell Lewis (1806-63), secretary of state for war, author of *Enquiry into the Credibility of the Early Roman History,* 1855.
71 Nightingale prepared plans for medical and nursing services for the projected deployment of British troops in Canada, which proved not to be necessary.
72 George Frederick Samuel Robinson, Earl de Grey of Wrest, later Earl of Ripon and Governor-General of India.
73 Anne Jemima Clough, sister of Arthur Hugh Clough, started a school in Liverpool in 1841 and moved it to Ambleside in 1852. She later helped found Newnham College (for women) at Cambridge University.

felt "these people are quite of a different clay from ours. They move in quite a different order of ideas and feelings from what we do."

I think what I have felt most (during my last three months of extreme weakness) is the not having one single person to give me one inspiring word or even one correct fact. I am glad to end a day which never can come back, gladder to end a night, gladdest to end a month. I have felt this much more in setting up (for the first time in my life) a fashionable old maid's house in a fashionable quarter (though grateful to Papa's liberality for enabling me to do so) because it is as it were deciding upon a new and independent course in my broken old age, which I never have been called upon to do even in my vigorous youth. Always before my path was so clear to me, what I ought to do, though often not how to do it. But now it was quite doubtful to me whether (when all was broken up) I had better not have left the Army altogether.

The question was decided in my mind by my being so much worse that I *could* do nothing else, and by Lord Stanley throwing all this Indian Commission business upon us. I have now written the biggest part of their report, but I have not begun my own evidence, nor the digest of the reports from our Indian stations, 150 in number. But oh! if I were now able to do what I could do five years ago, or even what mothers can do for their children, how little my griefs would be to me, except to inspire me to do more.

In the *Medea* Jason says "What remains?" and Medea answers, "I."[74] I remember when I came home from the Crimea, 5½ years ago, writing this from Lea Hurst to those who would have deterred me from stopping in the Army: all are now gone. There remains only half "I." I did all (and more than) I intended when I had "I," and got up that commission, having only "I" to begin with. Now what -- "what remains"?

The Queen, poor thing, is more "bowed to the earth" (her own expression) than ever. She is never able to see but one person at a time, never to sit down to dinner with more than one person, which used to be Princess Hohenlohe or Princess Alice.[75] Even her uncle,

---

74 Euripides, *Medea* lines 501-02. This is a desperate statement—Medea had killed her children and her husband's lover.

75 Princess Alice (1843-78), second daughter of Queen Victoria, married to the Duke of Hesse-Darmstadt.

King [Leopold] (1835-1909) of the Belgians, never dined with her when he was here. She told Lord Palmerston[76] that she should not live long. But I hear there is no reason for fearing this. Lord Palmerston says she is half the size she was. She fronts the work gallantly, but there are such serious doubts whether she can even get through the daily routine of work, without Albert, that the Cabinet considered every constitutional possibility of creating an office, to be filled by Lord Clarendon.[77] It was found to be unconstitutional and that she must do the work herself with her private secretaries.

Albert arranged that Princess Alice should stay two years in England after her marriage. People say that time heals the deepest griefs. It is not true. Time makes us feel what *are* the deepest griefs every day only the more by showing of the blank (which nothing now can fill) every day more and more of the evils which there are none now to remedy, every day one more.

Thank you very much for the weekly box. Tell Burton that I ate a piece of her rabbit pie, which was the first real meat I have eaten for three months. The smallest contribution is thankfully received—even a sausage, when you kill a pig. I could not help sending the game, chicken, vegetables and flowers to King's College Hospital.

I never see the spring without thinking of my Clough. He used to tell me how the leaves were coming out, always remembering that, without his eyes, I should never see the spring again. Thank God! my lost two are in brighter springs than ours.

Poor Mrs Herbert told me that her chief comfort was in a little Chinese dog of his, which he was not either very fond of (he always said he liked Christians better than beasts) but which used to come and kiss her eyelids and lick the tears from her cheeks. I remember thinking this childish. Now I don't. My cat does just the same to me. Dumb beasts observe you so much more than talking beings, and know so much better what you are thinking of.

You may send this letter to Lea Hurst if you like it. Papa wanted to know about the Queen, but don't send it anywhere else. If you could send me up some snowdrops, primroses, anemones and other wild spring flowers with roots, I have a fine balcony here looking on

---

76 Henry John Temple (1784-1865), 3rd Viscount Palmerston, then prime minister.
77 George William Frederick Villiers (1800-70), 4th Earl of Clarendon, foreign secretary.

Chesterfield Gardens, where I mean to take out a license for rural sports and kill cats.

ever dear Mum

your loving child

F.

Parthe told me you wanted to know whether the Dresden Raphael[78] had come in its new frame. Yes, it did, seven or eight months ago (for I remember I had it before 2 August, when my dear master died). The frame is beautiful. It is just what that kind of print wants to lighten it, an open-work frame. I always think good prints are spoilt by framing them in solid work and made to look heavy.

I have turned out all Mrs Plumer Ward's performances in her bedroom, which is mine (I had as soon be in the room with bugs and fleas) and hung up your Dresden Raphael and Murillo Virgin,[79] Mrs Bracebridge's Annunciation, from the Papal Chapel, an unframed Guercino Ecce Homo[80] and Sistine Isaiah, and two chromo-lithographs from Roberts and a Norwegian. [Dr] Sutherland said I was "a vain thing to have decorated" my room. There are some people who always say the wrong thing.

Source: Letter with envelope, Wellcome (Claydon copy) Ms 9000/28

From the house of the fever-compelling Erinnys [Furies]
My dearest [Parthenope Verney]

Pray read the enclosed and put it into the post for Mama.

your miserable F.

The Pigsty, 9 C. St.
Easter Eve [19 April 1862]

Dearest Mother

Your weekly box gives pleasure to many little eyes besides mine, viz., in King's College Hospital. I like Sarah Fletcher very much. She is clean and steady. And I have no doubt we shall hang together till she marries or I die.

---

78 Raphael Santi (1483-1520). Nightingale was deeply moved by his "Sistine Madonna," 1516, which she saw in Dresden in 1850 (see *European Travels*). It was evidently significant for her sister also, for it was the focus of their last conversation and shared prayers the week before her death in 1890 (see p 404 below).

79 Bartolomé Esteban Murillo (1618-82).

80 Francesco Guercino (1591-1666) Italian painter.

The "nuisance" was not removed till Wednesday not Tuesday (vide letter which I enclose and which please return). On Wednesday we mustered strong on my side: Uncle Sam, Dr Sutherland, Bratby[81] and my Messenger[82] and the Pig of Pigs' maid, agent and his three or four men on hers. She had written another insolent letter about me to her agent, positively refusing to have the little interior room (called in the letter to Papa "cupboard") cleared. (She has locked up every "cupboard" in the house). Two VANS FULL of dirty bedding, foul linen!!! dirty stuffed furniture and carpets, we got rid of. The men were carrying downstairs the whole of the day. All agreed, even her own maid, that they had never had such a dirty job. And the men said they had never carried anything which "stank so"! Dr Sutherland said, if I had not persisted, we should have had typhus (of which her own husband died through her dirt).

The men would have left the second van load till next day but that I declared, if they did, I would whitewash over all they left. I had the whitewashers ready. And they came in and instantly began whitewashing. But alas! the workmen are still in the house today (Saturday) which day I have been here seven weeks, so that nearly two months of my five are gone, and have been spent not in a house, but a pigsty and workshop. I have been made so ill by the noise and contention of Wednesday that I have been obliged again to suspend work. Nothing but the sake of the servants and my duty to them would have induced me to go through the agony of the last seven weeks. If it had been only me, I should have encamped in this room, never gone out of it. It would have been far better for me to have left the rest of the house as it was than to have gone through what I have in living in a workshop and in struggling with this wicked woman.

It seems as if I never were to be quit of her. Today I have an attorney's letter summoning me to pay *board wages*(!) to the dismissed housemaid (Papa will tell you what this means). Of course I won't. And now I do hope my family will not go about and say that I "make too much of this grievance," that "all London houses are like this," that my "sanitary ideas are exaggerated," etc. *Les absents ont toujours tort* [the absent are always wrong]. And, I have found, les malades ont toujours tort [the sick are always wrong] because they cannot go

81 Correspondence with Bratby and his wife, both long-time Nightingale employees, is reported later in this volume.

82 Messenger was a Nightingale employee, who worked largely as a messenger.

about and tell their own story. And if my family tells my story for me in this way, people, in their idleness, are too glad to believe it. Yet this is the way that (*non*) sanitary destruction to life and health is achieved and *continued*.

Mrs P. Ward is of the sort who destroys armies (as she did her husband;[83] fortunately she had no army to destroy). F.N. is of the sort who saves armies. Europe has thought that F.N. knows a little more about these things than other people. Yet there is nothing on which her own family lectures F.N. so much, as if her experience were some wild delusion. This is not the way to support truth. It *is* the way to encourage such people as this typhus-begetting (Jove) Fury.

ever dear Mum

your F.

Source: Letter with envelope, ADD Mss 45790 ff286-89

Miss Mayo's house
Hampstead N.W.
9 August 1862

Dearest Mother

Thank you for boxes, the account of poor G. Sterndale's death and a little set of Etruscan china, if meant for me. It came in the last box without any letter. I think that it is hardly any use for me to have any more boxes from Embley, thank you, when you are not there. All is grist which comes to my mill, because I have so many poor patients in London, to whom flowers and vegetables are the only heaven they know. But what the Embley gardener sends, when you are not there, costs in carriage more than what I could get it for in London markets.

I was glad that poor G. Sterndale died "*at home.*" He was well taken care of, glad that he did not try Mr Smedley,[84] whose first bath would certainly have killed him, as it does in all kidney disease. Then one would have felt that he had been murdered by a quack. Had there been an inquest it would certainly have been correct to bring it in "manslaughter." That the poor fellow did die in a week would not have told at an inquest in favour of Mr Smedley.

I have been worse since I have been here. This is the first day I have been able to write. Mrs Bracebridge comes to me today (till Monday),

---

83 Presumably a reference to her husband, Robert Plumer Ward.

84 John Smedley (1803-84), manufacturer in Lea who founded and ran a hydropathic hospital there. (The Nightingales took their water cures elsewhere.)

a great blessing to me, this weary week. Six years this week since I came home from the Crimea, a year since Sidney Herbert died.

ever dearest Mother

your loving child

F.N.

It is better always to send an "*invoice*" with your box.

Palgrave and Tennyson[85] are going to the Peak and Matlock for a tour. You know both are great friends of Clough. I don't know whether you know Palgrave well enough to ask them to Lea Hurst.

Mme Mohl is at Cold Overton.[86]

The Prison Chaplain: A Memoir of John Clay[87] is a book well worth getting for Papa. I have read it. It contains a masterly sketch of the progress of prison discipline, memoirs of the Preston jail chaplain (John Clay), of Maconochie,[88] etc. It is a little unfair upon Jebb.[89] But Papa will find there memoirs of the crank and tread wheel, about which *he* too is a little unfair upon Jebb. It completely agrees with "*me.*"

Source: Letter, Wellcome (Claydon copy) Ms 9000/64

6 September 1862

Dearest Mother

I write to thank for many boxes and for many kind letters and to say that the "partridges" you announce have *not* made their appearance, unless as Lord Dundreary[90] would say, they are three brace of grouse, sent me by Mr Calvert.[91]

Yes, surely, I know Mr Whitehead of Gawcott[92] very well—by his books, which he was kind enough to send me and which taught me a great deal for soldiers' clubs, that they were needed for the unsteady

---

85 Francis Turner Palgrave (1824-97) discussed his famous anthology, *Golden Treasury*, 1861, with the poet laureate, Alfred Lord Tennyson (1809-92) on a walk at Land's End, summer 1860.

86 Home of Eleanor Frewen Turner, sister of Mme Mohl and herself a correspondent of Nightingale's.

87 Walter Lowe Clay, *The Prison Chaplain: A Memoir of the Rev John Clay*.

88 Alexander Maconochie (1787-1860), prison reformer, several times dismissed from positions for being too progressive.

89 General Sir Joshua Jebb (1793-1863), prison reformer and member of the Nightingale Fund Council.

90 The buffoonish hero of a comedy by Tom Taylor, *Our American Cousin*.

91 Frederick Calvert (1806-91), younger brother of Harry Verney and himself a friend and colleague on issues.

92 Rev Thomas Clarke Whitehead, of Gawcott, Bucks, former headmaster.

and not for the steady. I wish I could give him a better living. But, as I can't, I hope he will stay on and get a holiday with you. Parthe says, she "holds me up to him as a bugbear of the effect of overwork." Be it so. Anything which will make him take holiday is good. But let us distinguish: (1) for the permanent work of a life a wise man will husband his strength, also for a work which depends only upon himself; (2) for a work which depends upon others, or which must be done within a certain time to be done at all, I don't see how a wise man can husband his strength.

To which of these categories the work of any man belongs, that man only can judge. And I never preach to anyone as people preach to me. I only say when my advice is asked (which it often is) "decide for yourself to which category your work belongs and act accordingly," i.e., manage yourself, as you would an instrument, to get the utmost amount of work out of it. Which, if the work belongs to category 1, is certainly by lasting out your whole life at it.

But I confess I have felt that my people might give me more credit, at least for deliberation, especially when the event has so dreadfully justified me. Never was life and health employed or given up so deliberately as I have mine. Surely my Crimean work comes under category 2. If I had not done that *while* the war was going on, the sick men would all have been dead. Surely my War Office work has been dreadfully justified as being under category 2. It was entirely dependent upon the life of one man, upon his being in the House of Commons, upon his being in the War Office, upon his willingness to work with me. I never thought of his death. I thought of his leaving office, of ministers going out, of his becoming Lord Pembroke; I never thought of his death. But that came beyond all I had expected. Do you know I have felt so much the little justice my family have done to my deliberation (I ask no more) in their own minds that I wrote the enclosed to Parthe (but never gave it her). Please do so now.

I only ask that my people will think themselves and say to others, at least she did deliberately what she thought right. "She is of age: ask her."[93] No woman ever before directed the labour of a government office. She must be the judge as to the when and the how, if a woman chooses to undertake to direct men over whom she can have no legitimate or recognized control, she shall do it. No one else can judge how she shall do it.

---

93 A paraphrase of John 9:21.

In looking back, the things I regret are not there. I regret that I have let visitors talk to me to the last moment before a meal, thereby incapacitating me for food and sleep altogether.

Please when the M. Milnes come, say everything for me to both. I sent a maid every day to inquire after him and I dare say they did not hear of it. I did not like to ask her to write. Bence Jones[94] told me a year ago that he considered his a very bad case. (You need not tell them this, of course.) He was so dreadfully right about S. Herbert.

ever dearest Mum

your loving child

F.

Source: Letter/draft/copy, Add Mss 45790 f299

20 December 1862

Dearest Mother

Don't forget my greeneries. You cannot send me too many—the sooner the better—to dress the hospitals, etc. *by* Christmas Day. It gives such pleasure to people who never see anything but four walls. Many thanks for the boxes and for your own letters still more.

ever your

F.

I congratulate on Shore's daughter [the birth of Rosalind].

Source: Letter, Wellcome (Claydon copy) Ms 9000/75

Christmas Eve 1862

Dearest Mother

I cannot help writing a word of thanks for the beautiful Christmassings which now adorn St Thomas', King's College and dear Rev Mother's schools and a word of congratulation on Christmas Eve, bitterly sad as the season is to me. Still there are feelings of joy in which we can all unite, joy at the good will in heaven towards those poor men for whom we would so gladly give our lives, whose faithful servants Sidney Herbert and I have been, at the good will in heaven towards *all* the sick and *all* the weary. I am sure I do not grudge to my two that they should pass *their* Christmas Eves in heaven.

---

94 Dr Henry Bence Jones (1813-73), attending physician at 1 Upper Harley St. and member of the original Nightingale Fund Council. He was consulted on Sidney Herbert's last illness, on which Nightingale sent him clinical observations.

Two dozen ginger wine are just arrived from Mrs Radford, of which three broken. How shall I pay my bill? And how shall I thank her?

ever dearest Mother

your loving child

F.

Source: Letter with envelope, ADD Mss 45790 f302

12 January 1863

Dearest Mother

I am glad you liked my little tribute to my dear chief [Sidney Herbert[95]], so great in life as in death, as to me, comparing him with other men, he seems more and more every day. I sadly survive him.

Please tell Sir Harry that his servants may certainly come up on the 23rd. I am quite sure to be gone by then. If you have a few sheets to spare for an unfortunate beggar, I send the list of what I want. But, as it will come out of your pocket, either way, don't pinch for me. Also tell Mrs Webb I much want my nightgowns.

ever dearest Mother

your loving child

F.

Source: Letter/draft/copy, ADD Mss 45790 f304

4 Cleveland Row, S.W.

3 February 1863

Dearest Mother

My strength protests against my writing, which I don't wonder at, for I am of the same opinion myself. But I always dearly love to receive letters (not begging ones).

But now I write to beg. Miss [Mary] Jones is in the most miserable state of health. I think God will take her before me.[96] I want you to invite her while you are alone and will nurse her *as you only can.* She could leave town next week, but must go into Devonshire first and I want her to go to Embley afterwards for a few weeks while you are alone, if you will have her.

To be let alone, to feel perfectly at her ease, to have entire rest of body and mind is what she wants. A drive in an open carriage occasionally is all she is fit for and to be sent to bed at 9:00 o'clock. She is

---

95 Nightingale, "Army Sanitary Administration and Its Reform under the Late Lord Herbert" (see *Crimean War*).

96 Mary Jones in fact died in 1887.

often unable to go up and down stairs. I used to invite her when at South Street "*to spend Saturday and Sunday with* me *in bed.*" And she did it. Hers is such a valuable life. I know Webb would wait upon her kindly and take her her meals *cut up*.

Please tell Papa I am looking forward to seeing him on Thursday.
ever dearest Mother
your loving child
F.

Source: Letter/draft/copy, ADD Mss 45790 ff306-07

4 Cleveland Row, S.W.
23 February 1863

Dearest Mother

You are very good to me and to my dear Miss Jones too. She will come to you on Wednesday (I trust) by the 3:00 o'clock train from here, and will bring a nurse, as you so kindly recommend. Will you meet them in the carriage? She intends to stay a fortnight (she has been obliged to give up all her other visit) but I hope you will make her stay longer.

She has incessant flooding—never entirely without it. Of course such a state gives great fear of her valuable life being terminated by jaundice or rheumatic fever or dropsy. But there is no *immediate* danger to make you anxious while with you. All she wants is fresh air and little fatigue—rest of body and mind.

The south room and music room would, as you so kindly propose, suit her exactly. But I thought you used the music room yourself. She will be no *gêne* [embarrassment] upon you, for the best thing for her is to let her be alone and at rest and at ease. . . .

I next ask for a sod and some grass (in a handful) by every box for the cats. Perhaps the Watsons can recommend *what* grass. Is it the clovery grass they like?

I like my nightgown very much. Please thank Webb for it. I should like them better two inches longer and a little more sloped round the throat in Francis Turner, i.e., cut down in the neck. But if they are all cut out, both these emendations are immaterial.
ever dearest Mother
your loving child
F.

Source: Letter, Wellcome (Claydon copy) Ms 9000/102

[printed address] 4 Cleveland Row, S.W.

15 May 1863

Dearest Mother

Yes, the "sanitarians" know quite well what makes a sickly spring. If the winter has been more than usually mild, it seems to affect the national constitution so as to render it less able to resist any causes of disease in the spring. And this although it spares the old and the pulmonary of course more than a severe winter.

If upon this unusually mild winter follow a wet spring, we expect to see the scarlet fever epidemics, such as diphtheria, etc. If upon it follow a dry spring, such as this, we expect to see the severer epidemics, such as smallpox, etc.

2. Ann Clarke's mother has been released at last and today is the funeral. Ann Clarke, who has been nursing her mother *all this year*, and is much broken, will then go with us to Hampstead for Whitsuntide.

3. Do you think you would make up a fine hamper of home produce for Rev Mother of Bermondsey and send it to me by Tuesday? as on Wednesday I go, if I can, to Hampstead and I should like to send her the hamper on Tuesday. I generally buy her a flitch of bacon two or three times a year, a leg of pork, apples, nothing comes amiss. What I buy is not so good as what you send, and plenty of your American flowers to make a show for her children on Whitsunday, please.

ever dearest Mum

your loving child

F.

Your yesterday box went to cheer poor Miss Jones, flowers and all.

Source: Letter, Wellcome (Claydon copy) Ms 9000/105

4 C. Row, S.W.

23 June 1863

Dearest Mother

I heard some days ago that you would be in town "in a week." I don't know whether this means next Saturday, 27th, but, if fortunately for me it does, I have asked Mr Jowett (who will not be in London again for two or three months) to give me the sacrament next Sunday, 28th, at 3:00. I invite you and Papa as I hear something of Papa going to Combe and coming up with you. . . .

Source: Letter, Wellcome (Claydon copy) Ms 9000/121

7 Oakhill Park
Hampstead, N.W.
31 July [1863]

Dearest Mother

I am sorry I did not acknowledge the ginger wine. I did to Papa and asked him to acknowledge it to Mrs Radford and to ask her to begin the manufacture anew directly, and to send it me when ready as this envoi was only of *one* dozen. The next had better be of *two* dozen.

Also I have ordered *Romola*[97] at Papa's request and will send it him as soon as read. Novel though it be, I think it the fairest and most life-like representation of Savonarola that has yet appeared.

I am glad you arrived pretty well and hope poor Pet [a cat] will reconcile herself in time. But Topsy was the pet with me.

ever dearest Mum

your unfortunate child

Two years the day after tomorrow, two years!! is Sidney Herbert's death.

Source: Letter, Wellcome (Claydon copy) Ms 9000/131

Hampstead, N.W.
25 September 1863

Dearest Mother

. . . Would you send me "wuts" once a week while you are at Lea Hurst? I never could eat baker's white bread and now I can't eat baker's brown bread. So the "wuts" are necessary to me. And could you send me one homemade brown loaf every week. Many thanks for a brace of partridges received. . . .

Source: Letter, Woodward Biomedical Library A.4

28 October 1863

Dearest Mother

Thanks for the magnificent game. Please don't forget the oat cake. I am very sorry about poor Wildgoose.[98] But I suppose it was really a release.

Please to let Watson send me a particular personal description of each of the six kittens, you said two threes, now you say five, which is

---

97 George Eliot's novel *Romola,* 1862-63, discussed in Nightingale's *Fraser's Magazine* article (see *Theology*).

98 Robert Wildgoose, schoolmaster in Lea and later agent to Mr Nightingale; since he died in 1900 the reference is presumably to a death in the family.

it? Also whether any is exactly like Pet. Do not put out any to nurse. It will most likely kill the poor little thing, certainly spoil its coat. I promise to send one to Lydia from London. Also say how they are *known* to be thoroughbreds. (Mine turn out not to be so.) N.B. It does not hurt the kittens for Topsy and Pet to suckle them promiscuously. They always do so.

    ever dearest Mum

    your loving child

    F.

Source: Letter, Wellcome (Claydon copy) Ms 9000/150

6 December 1863

Dearest Mother

    I am quite overdone with India business as you may suppose, but so glad to have it to do. I have seen Sir J. Lawrence, God bless him! and Lord Stanley. These are the only two hours I have been up since I came here. I am to see Sir J. Lawrence's private secretary tomorrow. They start [for India] on Wednesday.

    If the four muffs [cats] are really silky muffs, they are to come here. Papa must judge of the difference between these and my ugly but conversible beasts. I am shocked to hear of the old cat being persecuted, because no one has ever had kittens anything like so beautiful as hers. She must be petted in order to produce more. You know you never offered me her last two families. Does she not take to Tom? I suspect that Pet is the vixen. Topsy was always kind. I think Mrs Watson might bring them to be friends by degrees if she and Topsy were to be fed together? Or if Tom and she were to be shut up together occasionally?

    Many thanks for fine boxes. Could a few more grapes and a few better grapes be sent?

    ever your

    F.

Source: Letter, Wellcome (Claydon copy) Ms 9001/18

115 Park St., W.

19 March 1864

Dearest Mother

    Miss Mayo, my good landlady and friend at Hampstead, *snatches* at Pet with rapture, though I told her all Pet's sins. She begs that Pet may be sent up as soon as possible. If you will send her to *me* by rail, *advising me of the day*, I will send for her to the rail. I think I must brush her up here a little, and then I shall send her in a cab and one to Hampstead, the sooner the better. Many thanks for tongue, moss, etc. and Dentzia's beautiful flowers.

I don't think you need subscribe any longer to Harley St., as you have so many calls.

I have seen Papa. As to Burton's letter, I wish *I* ever received *any* with such feeling, intelligence and spirit as hers.

ever dearest Mum

your loving child

I have just seen Parthe dressed for [the Queen's] drawing room.

Source: Letter, Wellcome (Claydon copy) Ms 9001/19

> Good Friday and Lady Day [25 March] 1864
> as it was eleven years ago,
> the day Grandmama Shore died

Dearest Mother

I am sorry to say I have nothing to do with the Margate Infirmary and know no one who has. But why not put the boy into Sidney Herbert's Charmouth Infirmary? Mrs Fowler[99] says (to Papa) that the Salisbury Infirmary has six beds there. He will tell you what she told him.

You ask me about Ann Woollett. Nothing surprises me so much as the epithets mistresses give to servants. The character I had with that "wretched woman," as you justly call her, was that she was charming, which is just what she was *not*. The character I had with Ann Woollett was that she was "valuable," which is just what she is *not*. She is the most obliging, affectionate, grateful, willing creature I ever knew, *and I know no one single thing she can do.*

If I ask her to put a chair for one of my few visitors, she carries about a shovel full of coal in one hand and puts the chair with the other—of course both go to the ground. She has never once succeeded, since Walker went, in giving me my medicine effervescent because she can never remember to draw the cork with a corkscrew. Walker was actually "valuable," *in spite* of drunkenness, *so* "valuable" indeed that I never believed until I saw her myself *frantic drunk*, she could be drunk, because she did everything so well. Ann Clarke *is* becoming "valuable."

Miss Jones's nosegay did not come by the rail to which I sent for Pet, etc. Pet is just gone by Ann Clarke to Miss Mayo's. Pet is handsomer than ever and committed no sin while here.

---

99 Wife of Dr Fowler, physician at the Salisbury Infirmary and family friend of the Nightingales.

Saturday

Please send a little more forest moss for my glass basket. There was not quite enough to fill it. You do not say how Watson boy Jemmy is.[100]

I think you take in *Illustrated News*. You will see a [illeg] very good little map for the course of Sheffield inundation. Please ask Papa to put down on that map the relative points to Tapton, *of road to* Tapton, also of Meersbrook,[101] that I may "orienter" myself. I will return you the sheet. It seems to me that we ought to give for "auld lang syne." If you will authorize me to give £5 in Papa's name, I will add £5 in my own.

I don't like to hear my dearest mother talk of "maintaining a public servant" in London, meaning me, although it is quite true. If you had the expense of having me going through an operation in London, as poor Laura did, you would scarcely put it in that way. Laura's operation lasted 7½ minutes. Mine has lasted 7½ years. And during all that time, I can truly say that there has not been a part of my body not in pain, not a part of my soul not in pain. During the last three years it has been torture. I question, if God had given me the choice, whether I should have been able to choose it. I am very glad He did not give me the choice.

It is quite true that to enable me to live in London, so as to be able to live at all, has been a great expense to you. I have always gratefully acknowledged it. Still, I think my poor Clough used to put things more sympathetically.

ever dearest Mum

your loving child

F.

Source: Unsigned, incomplete letter, Wellcome (Claydon copy) Ms 9001/28

[18 April 1864]

Dearest Mother

The kittens, however pretty, if not thoroughbred, must be distributed by you in your vicinity. As I stated, I cannot undertake to write letters to ask people whether they will take kittens, not thoroughbred, in my present state. I betrayed and deceived eleven of my fellow subjects by giving them *non* thoroughbreds for thoroughbreds. They will

---

100 Nightingale made arrangements for the medical treatment of Jemmy Watson, son of employees at Lea Hurst.

101 Nightingale's Shore grandparents lived at Tapton and other Shore relatives at Meersbrook.

not take any more. I could find good "places" for twice that number of thoroughbreds, but of *non* thoroughbreds, I will none. I would advise you to keep one tom for yourselves, until I can breed you another thoroughbred tom. But this is a matter of choice *for you*, as I would not take even a 3/4 thoroughbred, much less a 1/2.

I sent the *National* and *Edinburgh Review*s by the "empty" [box] (which I had from Willis and Sotheron, all right and paid for). But please tell Papa that a subsequent *Edinburgh, same number*, came directed to me at South St., "for W.E.N.," was taken in, and that I have it without paying for it, and ask him whether that is all right. . . .

You know that I had Garibaldi all to myself for thirty-five minutes yesterday. He poured out the whole history of his wrongs from his government, as an answer to my reasonings that he should keep in good intelligence with his government, and not fight Rome and Venice. I am more impressed with the greatness of the noble heart, full of bitterness, yet not bitter, and with the little administrative capacity which, while it is praying for a representative government, "like ours," cannot take the evils and the good of a representative government (as I have to do) every day of my miserable life than I ever was by his splendid blunder of Aspromonte.[102]

Source: Letter, Wellcome (Claydon copy) Ms 9001/31

13 May 1864

Dearest Mother

Thanks for good birthday wishes, beautiful birthday flowers and all the goods.

The report of Jemmy Watson is very fair. At *his* age we should consider it as giving a very hopeful prospect. We should clothe him well, take great care of no damp or cold, especially to the extremities, give nothing but light diet, no beer, take care against fatigue of any kind, and hope for the best. Doubtless he *has* all these cares. At a later age there is not so much hope.

The two cats assert their claim to being thoroughbred by having hair so long that it would take me and two persons behind me to comb it.

Please tell Papa that I would gladly see the translation of M. Aurelius by Pierron,[103] if he will get it. Mr Jowett (quite casually) mentioned an

---

102 Garibaldi was wounded and taken prisoner at the battle of Aspromonte.
103 Pierre-Alexis Pierron, trans. *Marc-Aurèle.*

excellent translation by *Long*.[104] I know neither, but should prefer the French one.

Our Indian work is wearing and worrying in the extreme. It is just five months since Sir John Lawrence said *it was essential* that the War Office commission should send him out its schemes for the commissions (*which he has created for us*) AT ONCE. I have worked at my part night and day in urging it on. They, the commission, are nearly where they were five months ago. Never, never have I missed Sidney Herbert as now. I myself have thought *he* might have done more. But these people do nothing. I have no strength to write.

ever dearest Mum

your loving child

F.

We want *some more ginger wine*, please. I share the port wine with poor Burton.

Source: Letter, Wellcome (Claydon copy) Ms 9001/30

31 May 1864

a heavy freezing rain—oh for

a little more hot weather!

Dearest Mum

. . . I don't know whether you can help me in this: poor Burton lives on and on, and is by far the most refractory dying patient I ever had. I have no one to help me in providing for her. She can take nothing but asparagus, strawberries and grapes. I have not put one in my mouth this year, but have given her all mine. And I pay 16/0 a lb. for strawberries besides for her. Sometimes she calls them bad (the strawberries she has out of your box, there are never more than a dozen) last her just one night. (And now she can't take asparagus.) Could you send grapes and strawberries bought at Romsey (I to pay) in next box? I may be asking an impossibility.

The doctor, whom I provided for her by her own selection, and whom she does nothing but abuse, because, she says, there is "chloroform"! and "caustic"! in his prescriptions. I then translated the prescriptions for her and showed her there was nothing of the kind. The doctor thinks she may last for weeks. Dear good Sir Harry (how I do love that man) goes actually between the House of Commons sittings

---

104 *The Thoughts of the Emperor M. Aurelius Antoninus*, trans. George Long. An excerpt from this work appears in her Bible (see *Spiritual Journey*) but from neither of these translations.

and reads and prays with her. And she says, "it's better than the clergyman." Indeed I think it is. That, and the lilies which I send her from you, are really the only things she is contented with. She won't drink any port wine but yours. So I send her that.

And this brings me to my next: I shall want some more ginger wine, please *next* (not this) week. Poor Burton desired me to thank you for your letter and say it was quite impossible for her to answer it. . . .

ever dearest Mum

your loving child

F.

Source: Letter, Wellcome (Claydon copy) Ms 9001/32

3 June 1864

Dearest Mum

The Sutherlands are, I hear, coming to you tomorrow (Saturday) by the 3:00 P.M. train. I only mention this in case you like to send for them. They don't expect it. I wish you could keep Mrs Sutherland *after* HE is gone. She is very far from well. He ought to come back, but I offer no opinion to him.

I was delighted with the flannel shawl, its only fault, that it is only 1½ yards square, instead of two yards. The flowers were lovely. The laburnums quite exquisite. If I had no "smell" here *worse* than that of "may," my head would do very well.

ever dearest Mum

your loving child

Source: Letter, Wellcome (Claydon copy) Ms 9001/34

7 June 1864

Dearest Mum

You cannot believe that these flannels are just twice as good for half the price, as what we get here, unless it is just poor Ann Clarke can be persuaded by any shopman that pink is a good match for pea green.

I will take, please, two square shawls of the widest width, the square to be of the whole width. And two shawls of the narrowest width, the square to be of the narrow width.

ever dearest Mum

your loving child

F.

Source: Undated letter, Wellcome (Claydon copy) Ms 9001/40

[c1864]

Dearest Mum

Indeed I was very glad to see Mr Giffard's answer.[105] It did my heart good. "I do not hold it to be my æbounden duty, etc. to make any declaration at all." Please present my admiring thanks to Mrs Webb for flannels, both new and old (to *destroy* my flannels I pay 10/ a week to the Hampstead laundress).

Many thanks for the splendid contents of numerous boxes. The whole of the last, except the port wine, went to Papa's friend, Sister Gonzaga.[106] Otherwise I have been obliged to give to poor Burton, who cannot (or will not) eat anything but asparagus, peas, grapes, strawberries, peaches and *your* port wine. She says none of these things were in the boxes you sent her. In the morning, with myself, everything but grapes excites my vomiting, even a cup of tea, and I am obliged to give Burton grapes. Don't let them send any more rabbits. The last four boxes they have been bad, so bad that they had to be turned into the dust hole directly.

It is thought, by many, that ministers will be out next Monday.

ever dearest Mum

your loving child

F.

Many thanks for all your letters, dearest Mum. You are the most faithful correspondent I have. Bless you.

Source: Letter, Wellcome (Claydon copy) Ms 9001/51

Hampstead, N.W.
20 August 1864

Dearest Mother

1. The purple lama dressing gown arrived resplendent in beauty and I now lie outside the bed, in order to hide *none* of its loveliness. Indeed, were it not that I am afraid it tumbles, spots with clean water and does not wash well, I would never go back to poor creature flannel. I think the colour quite as pretty as lilac and shows the dirt as well.

---

105 Possibly Jervis Trigge Giffard, formerly vicar of East Wellow, who earlier studied medicine in Paris and was a positive influence on Nightingale in her childhood.

106 Georgiana Barrie, Sister Mary Gonzaga, Convent of Mercy, who nursed with Nightingale in the Crimea and became a friend.

2. The woollen skins are come; they are nearly twice as wide across the hips as any I have had before. I can't fancy any woman filling them. But I don't think it worthwhile to change them.

3. Yes, Hill has sent me flowers worth sending, not small flowers, he is not capable; but beautiful wreaths of passion flower, purple leaves, that orange spike I don't know the name of, one or two gladiolus, etc. I can't say as much for his fruit: a few apricots, no grapes.

4. Yes, I think I should like your large black lace shawl, if you don't wear it yourself. But I am afraid I shall make a present of it.

5. It has not been cold here, but very hot, everything dried up, everything so dear—meat enormous, fish consequently too. I think my housekeeping costs nearly £2 a week more. But then that wicked woman was a capital housekeeper. I have no one now with more head than your little stillroom maids.

6. I had poor Miss Jones of K.C.H. [King's College Hospital] here. She never left her bed. I left mine twice to visit her in hers. I do wish she would go away quite somewhere for a time or she will break up altogether. I don't think her coming here does her much good. It is quite too much for me now, the anxiety of such an invalid, and the fear that my household will give her gooseberry pudding for one dinner and bacon and beans for another.

7. I must give Dr Tanner something, who has attended poor Burton for four months at her own request, and has never taken a fee of me. It must not be less than 10 guineas. If you could get a really handsome vase, inkstand or table at Matlock of about that price, and have an inscription scratched on it something like this, "Offered to Dr Tanner by Florence Nightingale in remembrance of kind assistance given." Or do you think one of Colas's imitation bronzes, now to be had in England, would do better, a Génie Adorant? I don't see I need wait for poor Burton's death to do this.

8. I had occasion to write to Miss Clough and asked her to write and tell you how jaded and driven I have been (I am quite sorry I left London) and that I could not write. In addition the Liverpool Workhouse nursing had all to be settled. Miss Agnes Jones, the superintendent elect, to go down twice to Liverpool, Miss [Mary] Jones of K.C.H. not able to help us in the least, Mrs Wardroper, though almost as bad, working like a horse for it. We supply fifteen head nurses from St Thomas' for it; it is the best thing we have done yet, the first workhouse that ever has been nursed. Mr Rathbone gives £1000 *a year*!!! But the trouble of settling has been enormous and is not over yet.

Really, when I see how people will work, people like Mrs Wardroper, and there are thousands who scarce know how to get through their mornings, then how I wish I could divide the labour fairly.

9. Please thank Papa very much for his last letter, which deeply pleased me. I often fancy I hear in my dreams the rushing of the Derwent, which I used to open the casement in the nursery at night to hear. I am going to write to Papa.

ever dearest Mother

your loving child

F.

Source: Letter, Wellcome (Claydon copy) Ms 9001/82

14 November 1864

Dearest Mother

I did not know that you were going tomorrow. But I must write to you, if I can, to thank you for the new coat, which is very beautiful, also for the new shawl, which is very charming. Also for poor little Carl Fliedner's [her godson] desk which will, I am sure, give the highest satisfaction. And to say how sorry I am not to see you again, dearest Mum. Also to ask what I am in debt to you for all your beautiful things.

I have paid £5, which you were so good as to say I might, for you to the poor Hills of Athens,[107] in addition to my own contribution; the desk was, I think, £3.10.0. Has anything been done about the cutlery for the same? Don't trouble about it, if it has not. I shall miss you, dearest Mother.

ever your loving child

F.

I hope you liked Mr Jowett. I think you will like to see this note of Mr Gladstone,[108] but you must return it me immediately please, as I have not answered it.

F.

Also from Sir Henry Storks, about which I must say the same.

---

107 Rev John Henry Hill (1791-1882) and his wife, Episcopalian missionaries in Athens, and founders of a school. See *European Travels*.

108 William Ewart Gladstone (1809-98), many times prime minister. For correspondence with him see *Society and Politics*.

Source: Letter by Frances Nightingale on behalf of Florence Nightingale, Sudeley Castle Private Collection

> Embley Park, Romsey
> Hampshire
> 1 December 1864

Dear Madam [Mrs Emma Dent]

I have been very ill or I would sooner have acknowledged your most kind and welcome thought of my suffering daughter.[109] She is so broken down by her past and present exertions that she is generally unable to answer as she would wish to the tributes of affection which she receives. She feels obliged to devote the little energy she has left to pursuing the great object of her life, and, as a proof that her mind remains as powerful as ever, I have accompanied this note with a pamphlet which she has just published concerning India. Believe me, Madam,

sincerely yours

Frances Nightingale

Source: Letter, Wellcome (Claydon copy) Ms 9001/96

> 12 December 1864

Dearest Mum

Parthe desires me to send you this (unfeeling and thoughtless, F.N.) letter, which I wish she had not sent me.

Sir C. Trevelyan is NOT "out of danger" and will not be while he remains at Calcutta. Much of India's salvation and Sir John Lawrence's depends upon Sir C. Trevelyan being able to remain in India, of which there is not a chance *after* this winter, and *during* this winter there will be constant danger of a relapse. And this foolish unthinking boy writes of his father in this way.

I take this opportunity to thank for magnificent supplies of game, etc., and to beg for Christmas greenery in LARGE quantities for my hospitals. As Christmas Day is on a Sunday, I suppose people will dress up on Christmas Eve, so that if you would send me please the greenery *on the 23rd.* If you will send me mince pies or any other Christmas fooleries, you know I have plenty of poor people, *not* sick.

How glorious Cialdini's speech in today's Times![110] Like Sir J. Lawrence, I read it with tears of joy. "I deplore the injury to Turin, as on the battlefield I mourn the death of the soldier, of the friend. BUT

---

109 Emma Dent had sent Nightingale dried flowers she had gathered at the burial ground at Scutari.

110 General (Senator) Cialdini's speech about the war for Italian independence, *Times* 12 December 1864:7.

THAT THE SOLDIER AND THE FRIEND MAY LIVE, ARE WE NO LONGER TO FIGHT?" (But that we may live, are we no longer to fight? How often I have occasion to say that.) "Sacrifices elevate the character of nations. Prometheus[111] could transform marble into men. Sacrifices alone can make men into heroes." Why, it is the whole doctrine of the cross. Greater words than these have hardly been said since St Paul.

F.N.

Source: Letter, Wellcome (Claydon copy) Ms 9001/89

[printed address] 27 Norfolk St.
Park Lane, W.
21 December 1864

Dearest Mother

I will gladly give a prize of £3 to your Rifles, if you think it proper. I don't like my neighbours to be behind hand in the national race. It does one's heart good to hear the "nesh" London clerks on a dark snowy night with the thermometer 15 degrees below freezing (as last Saturday night) marching past, with their band playing (exceedingly well) a merry march. I did not hear a cough, but whether this was enthusiasm or discipline I don't know. I thought to myself: how this makes *men* of them—the best of these would be drinking rum and water over a greasy novel, and the worst of them—where would *they* be?

I hear from Lord Stanley, besides my own private information, that poor Sir C. Trevelyan is "entirely done up." But, thank God! Sir J. Lawrence is in better health than could have been hoped.

ever dearest Mum
your loving child
F.

Source: Undated letter, Wellcome (Claydon copy) Ms 9001/53

[1864]

Dearest Mother

I was quite overcome to hear this morning that Burton was so near her end. I was very fond of her. She had a heart, and many now have

---

111 In Greek mythology Prometheus was a champion of human beings against the gods. He is credited with bringing fire to earth and teaching the arts and sciences; he was tortured by being chained to a rock where an eagle fed on his liver.

none. You do not give her address. Please forward the enclosed and send me her address besides.

If you have the Ecce Homo of Guercino (which is far the most effective) or the Albert Dürer of Christ on the cross, please send it her, for me, to lose no time, and tell me what you have done, or the Christ on the cross by Guido.[112] It will take me time and strength to get things framed and sent from here.

ever dearest Mum

your loving child

F.

Please tell Hill not to send any more sods for the cats. *Many* thanks for your letter. I hope you save your eyes.

Source: Letter, Wellcome (Claydon copy) Ms 9001/102

New Year's Day 1865

Dearest Mum

My first New year's greeting must be for you.

Miss [Mary] Jones, Rev Mother of Bermondsey and Mrs Wardroper all admired their Christmas greenery so much. All said it was the brightest holly and the most beautiful wreaths of ivy they had ever seen. With all, it remains up till Twelfth Night.

We send our return boxes regularly. I understand the delay is with the Station Master at Waterloo, but at Christmastime everything goes wrong. I did not get my Christmas greenery till late on the Saturday afternoon and all that had to be delivered that night—I had to send by cab. They actually refused prepayment at the Parcels Delivery, saying they would not undertake it.

There is, as I think, a good article in *Good Words* of January on Sir Henry Lawrence ("Our Indian Heroes"[113]). I know I could not read it without tears. I wonder whether Sir John Lawrence would like to see it. Perhaps *he* would not be satisfied with it. We never are, with those we knew best. I could not take in the newspapers for a year after Sidney Herbert's death, for fear of seeing any sketch of *him*. Perhaps you will ask Mr Lawrence, if he is still with you, whether Sir John would like to see it.

---

112 The "divine Guido," Guido Reni (1575-1642), whose Ecce Homo studies in Dresden greatly moved Nightingale (see *European Travels*).

113 John William Kaye, "Our Indian Heroes; I Sir Henry Lawrence." Henry Lawrence (1806-57), killed in the mutiny of 1857, brother of Sir John Lawrence.

Tell Papa that the only danger is of Sir John Lawrence going too fast in granting liberties to India. He is *preparing* to give them municipal institutions everywhere. (At least *I* say there is NO danger, because his wisdom is equal to his courage.)

ever dearest Mum

your loving child

F.

Source: Letter, Wellcome (Claydon copy) Ms 9001/103

2 January 1865

Dearest Mother

Don't forget to read Sir Henry Lawrence. How curious it is—the great men that have sprung out of that small town of Londonderry, the characteristic of all of whom has been *devotedness to duty*, all apparently arising from the crime of James II.[114]

F.

Source: Letter, Wellcome (Claydon copy) Ms 9001/127

[April-May 1865?]

Darling Mum

I thought your dear birthday letter was intended for Parthe, but I kept it for myself. Now I keep them both—dear to me as showing your love for her, dear to me as showing my dearest mum's regard for me. So there was nothing lost, but on the contrary very great pleasure gained, to one who has not many pleasures.

I hope Papa is getting rid of his lingering influenza. I send an envelope for him which I opened, thinking it a bill, but I believe it is only an advertisement. But I send you an envelope which I am afraid is a real beast with a bill. Shall I pay it? If you return it me, I will.

Helen and Joanna Richardson are now at Folkestone. You know they are without a home. I am sure a long visit to Embley would give them pleasure and do them good. Their direction can always be had at Sir T.E. Colebrooke's, 37 South Street here.

ever dearest Mum

your loving child

F.

---

114 James II (1633-1701) besieged Londonderry for 105 days unsuccessfully prior to the Battle of the Boyne, 1 July 1690, when he was defeated by William of Orange. The Lawrence family were Anglo-Irish, from Londonderry.

Source: Undated letter, Wellcome (Claydon copy) Ms 9001/153

[1865]

The accounts of Hilary[115] are so distressing—one can only trust it will soon be over. She was more fit for heaven than earth. My love to Beatrice and Mr Godfrey [Lushington]. I *can* write no more.

ever dearest Mum
your loving child
F.

Source: Letter, Wellcome (Claydon copy) Ms 9001/144

[Oak Hill Park]
Saturday [28 July 1865]

Dearest Mum

I hardly know what to say to your coming tomorrow. Even ten minutes' talk with those I love best secures me a night of agony and a week of feverish exhaustion. I must make some great change, or I shall not be able to go on with the work at all. But, if you could come up, so as to be here about 4:00, and just come in and kiss me, that would be a great delight. But there must be no talk, specially not about anything agitating, nor about my going this year into No. 35, or any of that business, not about maids.

I can just keep my life in me to work and that is all. When you ask me what the prints are in the drawing room here, when you ask me why I don't have Miss Jones (which would be indeed the greatest pleasure I could have) you little know what my life is, without husband, butler, housekeeper or even maid of my own, and how hard it is for me to work at all. As for going downstairs, I never go out of my rooms here from the moment I come till the moment I go.

Please send me some grapes (this is very earthy). And if you come tomorrow, I shall be very glad to have the Lea desk, as you kindly propose, come in the carriage.

ever dearest Mum
your loving child
F.

---

115 Her cousin, Hilary Bonham Carter, was dying of cancer.

Source: Letter, Wellcome (Claydon copy) Ms 9001/147

10 August 1865

Oh dearest Mum, to think that I should not be able to write to you.
 ever your loving child
 F.

Source: Letter, Wellcome (Claydon copy) Ms 9001/148

16 August 1865

Dearest Mum

I want very much to make a most serious proposal with regard to the Sutherlands and, Pop, I want you to back it, *qua* 35 South St. They have found no house—Dr S. has, as usual, worried her almost to death. And they are thinking of taking a lodging for a year. They *must* turn out next month; it is uncertain what week.

I want Papa to write to Dr S. offering him unconditionally No. 35 till May next. It is, I understand, quite unlikely that it will let till January to anybody. Of course I do not intend Papa to be at any additional expense. I will pay him exactly the rent which the agent fixes. If I cannot pay it at once, I will pay it, *with interest*, in time. I particularly wish Papa not to lose a penny. (I imagine the highest rate the agent could fix would be £300 from September till May.) Mrs Sutherland would, *I am sure*, accept it. As for Dr S., his pride is so insane, his vanity so inconceivable that, though he thinks nothing of bringing me to death's door nearly every day now, of neglecting and confusing all the work, he would not, I believe, sacrifice one iota of pride for fear the *world* should think he had accepted anything from us.

If he refuses, I think it might *then* be offered to them on the terms that they should pay what they would have paid for a lodging. Of course this would be about £40 or £50 only, but even this would save his pride (and I would make up the difference). And he would tell everybody that he had "rented Mr Nightingale's nice house of him." This however is only as a reserve to fall back upon. You might (*quite truly*) put it as a favour to me—the anxiety it would save me to have him next door for the business all the autumn and winter (our busiest time), the comfort it would be to me to have her at hand. (People little know the way Dr S. treats me. One little instance, I will give. He told me he was "*dying*" (sic) and could not come to me, *and went to Epsom for the Derby*. Now, if he were next door, these insane tricks would not agitate me, at least not for more than ten minutes.)

I need hardly mention the intense obligations I am under to Mrs S. nor the pleasure it would be to give her a little relief. It would really be a very great thing for me to have his work for a whole winter without the worry of his uncertainties. . . . (I am obliged to part with Mrs Bracebridge's housemaid, *the only perfect housemaid I ever saw*, on account of temper. Temperance declares *she* won't stay otherwise. So does Lady Clarges' maid. It occurred to me that I might put this woman into No. 35, paying her wages myself.) As for housing the Sutherlands' furniture, I am sure I could do that at a pantech [warehouse] and pay for it, with *her* connivance. There is no time to be lost. They may take a lodging at once.

ever dearest Mum

your loving child

F.

It would console me for all my misfortunes if this could be brought about. Remember, it is DR Sutherland who must be written to, if at all. And by *Papa* would be best.

Source: Letter, Wellcome (Claydon copy) Ms 9001/157

Hampstead, N.W.

18 September 1865

Dearest Mum

Mrs Girdlestone[116] (you know who she is, of King's College Hospital) has been dangerously ill and not expected to live. Miss Jones writes me word that she "hopes" to "take" her away "*soon*" "for a week or two" into the country to recover. It occurred to me whether you would like to invite Miss Jones, Mrs Girdlestone and a nurse to Embley for this recruiting, which I am sure must be as necessary to Miss Jones as to Mrs G.

I do not know that they would go (Miss Jones says nothing about *where* they are ordered to go to me). I have not seen her for I have been totally unable to see anyone here, the greatest of disappointments, as I have always so enjoyed being able to give a whiff of country air to Miss Jones, Rev Mother, Mrs Wardroper, etc.

I could say a great deal about Hilary but I cannot bear it now. I can only think with joy of what she is now and of what she would wish us to think. But the details are too painful to be dwelt upon yet, though I

---

116 Widow of Major Girdlestone, became "Sister Laura" of St John's House.

am well aware that, by Elinor's[117] great kindness and consideration, I have been spared the knowledge of the greater part of them, the suffering was so dreadful.

I am going from here every day. I ought to be in London today; I cannot delay here beyond this day week, on account of my business.

ever dearest Mum

your loving child

F.

Indeed I am but too well aware how ill Mrs Bracebridge is. I wish they would go abroad for the winter.

Source: Letter, Wellcome (Claydon copy) Ms 9001/160

[printed address] 34 South Street
Park Lane
London, W.
29 September 1865

Dearest Mum

I think ALL these things are good. I am delighted to see my (printed) opinion so near being carried out, viz., that all counties should have their convalescent home as the best preventive of pauperism, all hospitals their convalescent supplement. But I am not at all delighted to see them all expecting me to subscribe to all. Croesus[118] could not do it. Also, I never subscribe to any building that I have not a voice in the plans of. Not a week elapses that I don't have a paper of this kind from some county or hospital. No, I have not subscribed. If you like to do so, I shall be very glad. Hospitals and convalescent homes bear so very hardly upon me: Winchester £200, Miss Jones £100, Herbert Memorial £50, and now I have promised £25 to Swansea. Besides which, everybody writes to me *to go about* collecting for them. That *is* adding insult to injury. I have just collected £200 for the Fliedners.

About the house, No. 35, and what I wrote to Pa yesterday, in the uncertainty of all my affairs, I have determined to keep Burch, at least for the present. So that she will not be at liberty to keep the house 35 during the interregnum, when it will stand empty before it is let, and before I go in. I explained all this yesterday to you and Pa.

ever dearest Mum

your loving child

F.

---

117 Elinor Bonham Carter (1837-1923), Hilary's younger sister.
118 King Croesus (sixth century BCE) of Lydia, proverbial for his wealth.

Source: Letter, Wellcome (Claydon copy) Ms 9002/9

[printed address] 35 South Street
Park Lane
London, W.

Dearest Mum   6 April 1866

... I always like *your* "letters" (however much I am "pressed") because you are the *only* person who writes to me without requiring an answer. That is the real secret of writing to the sick—write to them things which don't require an answer. Everybody else writes to me questions. ...

Source: Letter, Wellcome (Claydon copy) Ms 9002/16

Dearest Mum   30 May 1866

I was *very* thankful to have your little bit, written by Aunt Mai. Also to hear from Sir Harry of you. You have such beautiful weather at Embley. (Here it is a bitter blighting East) that I hope, as I hear from Sir Harry, that you get out in the garden, it will do you good. It *ought*, by the beautiful azaleas I have had from Embley.

You know that Jack [Bonham Carter] has accepted a Treasury lordship.[119]

I wish, dearest Mum, that you would consult Mr Taylor now and then, to please me. I need not tell you who know him so much better than I, that he is a safe and simple man, and with real genius about some things.

Emily Verney[120] is in London, as you know. She called here yesterday, but I was not able to see her. They say she is looking so well.

ever dearest Mum
your loving child
F.

I have got a dreadful little Swede[121] to look after, come here to learn to be a matron. She ought to have learnt English first.

---

119 Jack Bonham Carter, MP for Winchester, appointed Junior Lord of the Treasury in 1866, but held the post only a matter of days.

120 Emily Verney, daughter of Harry Verney and his first wife. She worked closely with Nightingale during the Franco-Prussian War (see correspondence later in this volume and in *Theology*).

121 Emmy Carolina Rappe (1835-96), trained at St Thomas' Hospital. On her poor English see Bertil Johannson, ed., *"God Bless You, My Dear Miss Nightingale": Letters from Emmy Carolina Rappe to Florence Nightingale 1867-70.*

Source: Letter with envelope, Wellcome (Claydon copy) Ms 9002/17

[printed address] 35 South Street
Park Lane
London, W.
31 May 1866

Dearest Mum

I forgot to say that I sent your "Alexander Scott"[122] and "Monckton Milnes" by Monday's box. I read Alexander Scott with the greatest pleasure and interest and I presumed to mark it, hoping that it would have not the less interest for you, my dearest Mum, if your poor old child had marked it. I know Papa justly dislikes books being scribbled on, but I thought these were for your own especial reading. What a lifetime it seems to me since I knew Alexander Scott, hard upon thirty years. I was glad to see:

The aisles of blessed Peter
Are open all the year.

my old friend, again.

We have the most inveterate east wind and gloom here I ever knew. Rev Mother is better, but I fear that her life, like mine, is a burden to her, that is, each step of the day's work is a burden. I hope I am a help to Sir John Lawrence, for indeed the cool way people speak of his immense difficulties and the intense way in which *he* feels them *himself* make me mad with the desire of helping him.

Should you ever have to spend August and September at Embley, dearest Mum (may the time be long first, I hope you will, for *many* years and *many more* go on spending the autumn at Lea Hurst. God forbid that it should be otherwise) but if you should ever spend August and September at Embley, I might perhaps come and spend them with my dearest mother. [line missing] I shall never go to Hampstead again, now the Sutherlands are gone. I could not leave London before Parliament is up. For all government purposes, Norwood[123] is quite as far as Embley.

Sutherland may be sent to the Mediterranean for inspections in August and September. In that case, it would be just as easy for me to do the government, Indian, work for those two months at Embley, if I only could once get there. But all this is a castle in the air. God only

---

122 Presumably a book of poems by Alexander Scott (c1525-84).
123 The Sutherlands moved to Norwood, Surrey.

knows. And I know that I hope it will be many, many years before you spend your autumns at Embley.

ever, my dearest Mum's
loving child
F.

If I live, I think I shall live somewhat on the principle that the Jew thought Roman Catholicism must be true, on the ground that it had survived the horrors of Rome. So *I* think I *must* live some time longer, because I have survived the sufferings of last winter.

I don't suppose the journey to Embley would kill me, if I had some man to come to Embley. It would have this advantage, that I should get rid of the dirty old prig, Delany, for the time, and bring only Temperance [Hatcher, her maid].

F.N.

Source: Letter, Wellcome (Claydon copy) Ms 9002/39

25 July 1866
Dearest Mum

I hear Parliament will certainly not be up before the 10th August. I, of course, am busier than ever. But there are hopes this most wicked [Austro-Prussian] war is over. I have heard from the Crown Princess of Prussia (Princess Royal).

You know your little favourites, Sam[124] and Rosie, are going to Lea Hurst on Friday. Rosie said to me, "*I* am going on Friday to see *my* Aunt Fanny" (with great emphasis). Surely you will not disappoint her by not going to Lea Hurst. And the bystanders said, "she *is* so fond of her Aunt Fanny." But, wherever my dearest Mum is, I hope to be with her about the middle of August.

The weather here is detestable, constant leaden east wind, fog.

You know the rioters pulled down half a mile of railing here into Park Lane on Monday night. It was the most pathetic, interesting night I have spent for six months, *so* much good energy wasted, so little spite and violence in their struggling. So much less harm done than at sightseeings (like the Duke of Wellington's funeral), where lives are recklessly lost. So much care for the women and children. For

---

124 Samuel Shore Smith (1860-93), later Dr Samuel Shore Nightingale, son of Shore and Louisa.

my part, though I saw stones thrown and three bonfires, I thought it a very instructive spectacle.

ever my dearest Mum's
loving child
F.

I hear that Parthe is better than ever she was in her life.

Source: Letter, Wellcome (Claydon copy) Ms 9002/133

30 March 1867

Dearest Mum

Papa came on Wednesday as you know. I think he is looking very well. The two kits arrived in high health and spirits. Have they any names? The one with a white nose ought to be called Pet, because it is so affectionate. The one with a yellow nose is an immense curiosity; it has more hair than flesh, and there appears to be very little of it inside its coat. It ought to be called Spitfire. Bismark, the big white cat, just arrived from Lea Hurst with Peter, went up like a gentleman to kiss the kits' hands. Spitfire rose up on its hind legs and tried to box *his ears*, who is at least seven times its size. By standing upright on its hind tiptoes, it can just reach his nose, and it tried to fight him. They are thoroughbred and no mistake.

I am so very busy that I cannot write more today.

ever dearest Mum
your loving child
F.

I hear that Emily [Verney] is looking remarkably well. She is, as you know, at thirty-two.

Source: Letter, Wellcome (Claydon copy) Ms 9002/169

[printed address] 35 South Street
Park Lane
London, W.
9 July 1867

Dearest Mum

I hope you know that I mean to come to you *wherever you are*, please God, *for the two months* immediately following the breaking up of Parliament. This is the only time I could answer for. (What day Parliament will break up, no one knows, but I think they think it won't be much later than usual.) I don't think I shall have more than two months *if so much* this year. . . .

The Queen of Prussia was here on Saturday, as I dare say you know. I liked her much better than I expected. I don't think the mixture of pietism and absolutism of the Court of Prussia much better than that of the Court of Rome, but nothing could be better than what I saw of her. She came quite alone (leaving good-natured Lady Ely downstairs). She did her business and went away again, leaving me much less tired than I am with the most ordinary visit (I received her in bed). She brought me, too, a very kind message from our Queen, of whose great difficulties she spoke in a few, feeling, expressive words.

My acquaintance with queens and princesses is not large, but at least it is as large as with the wives of Cabinet ministers. And I have never seen a royal lady who was not as superior for her interest in great objects and for her power of going *correctly* to the root and reason of a thing, to any other lady, as a person who can read is to a person who can't read.

As for *our* Queen's two eldest daughters, they are superior to any girls I know of any class or country. The Princess Royal has genius and Princess Alice has not. But both are interested and really versed in things of administration and moral philosophy, in which the willful ignorance of most young women makes one's hair stand on end. The Grand Duchess of Baden,[125] who is the Queen of Prussia's[126] daughter, writes me letters (she is, I believe, not yet twenty-seven) which I am sure I wish any administrator we had in the Crimean War could have written.

I thought the Queen of Prussia looked old, harassed, worn (she is fifty-six). And no wonder, if what is said is true, viz., that the death of Maximilian[127] has shaken the Emperor Napoleon[128] on his throne more than anything else *could* have done, and that no one knows what may be the consequence to his dynasty. The confidence in his infallibility is gone. It is said that, if Maximilian had only returned to Europe any tale might have been made up to satisfy the French peasantry. But the fact of his having been shot is fatal. The Queen of Prussia went to Paris today.

---

125 Louisa (1838-1923), Grand Duchess of Baden, visitor and correspondent of Nightingale.
126 Augusta Maria (1811-90), Queen of Prussia and German Empress.
127 Archduke Maximilian (1832-67), Emperor of Mexico, whose wife was a distant relative by marriage of Louis Philippe.
128 Napoleon III (1808-73), President of France 1848-53, then Emperor until 1870.

She desired me to make a collection of my books for her, which I have done, though not half, because it is too expensive. As you asked me, dearest Mum, to make you out a list of my little "works" with the publishers, I am making a collection for you. But you must not give them away, when made, as I do. I *never* have a copy of any of my books *by me*, though I am sure I spend not less than £20 a year in replacing copies which I have given away. People, even when they only borrow them, never return them. I am quite ruined, especially by New South Wales and the United States.

I say nothing about Uncle Sam, because I only trust that all cause for anxiety about him is over. But I do most seriously think that absolute rest and ease is most important and that, if these can be had at Embley better than elsewhere, he should stay there for some weeks. I am afraid I shall not have time to write to Papa. My hands are more than full. Perhaps you would send him this.

ever dearest Mum

your loving child

F.

Source: Letter, Hampshire Record Office 94M72/F585/1

[printed address] 35 South Street
Park Lane
London, W.
25 July 1867

Dear Alice[129]

Only this word to say that your account of my mother's feebleness rather makes me anxious to say to you, wherever she stays or goes, I shall come to her. I am most fearful lest the idea of me should modify her wishes as to going or staying.

Sir Harry writes to you today that 32 will be empty on Saturday. But, if she does not feel equal to come or to go on to Lea Hurst, I am anxious that no idea of me should urge her. N.B. I shall certainly not be free till middle of August. I am *very* glad you are with her (in haste).

ever yours

F. Nightingale

---

129 Cousin Alice Bonham Carter (1828-1912).

Source: Letter/draft/copy, Add Mss 45790 ff360-61

[printed address] 35 South Street
Park Lane
London, W.
19 October 1867

Dearest Mum

I hope that you are not much the worse for your journey. A thousand thanks for the beautiful flowers—made more beautiful by the fact that you picked them yourself. They carry me back to the lovely Hurst. I can hardly believe that you were walking on that exquisite terrace the same morning, where I have not been for eleven years. Time makes it seem as far off as Scutari.

Mr Jowett, whom I have not seen for nearly four months, is coming tomorrow (Sunday) to give me the sacrament. I trust that my dearest Mum will feel able to join us. He will sleep *tonight* at 32, "partly in the hope," he says, of finding you there. (I had asked him before.) He will not come till half past ten tonight and will leave tomorrow afternoon. I am afraid he comes up mainly for us, as he is too busy to stay over Sunday night.

ever dearest Mum
your loving child
F.

Editor: The books and pamphlets her mother requested above were duly sent, with suitable inscriptions. The list below notes book size (8vo or 4to, the usual book size or oversize respectively), number of volumes, abridgments or reprints. Some of the books themselves have since made their way into various archives, for example, *Mortality of the British Army*, 1858, is at the Reynolds Historical Library, University of Alabama at Birmingham, with the inscription: "Mrs Nightingale, accept, my dearest Mother, these little (!) works from your ever loving child, Florence Nightingale, 2 November 1867." The last, unnumbered item on the list was added later.

Source: List, Add Mss 45790 f364

London
2 November 1867

List of F.N.'s little works offered to her dearest mother:
1. Royal Indian Sanitary Report (2 Blue Books) 1863
2. Army Mortality Diagrams (lilac folio 1 volume) 1858

3. Contribution to Sanitary History (green folio 1 volume) 1859
4. *Confidential* Report (2 lilac volumes, 1 thick and 1 thin 8vo) 1858 (These are *really* confidential)
5. Native Colonial Schools and Hospitals (1 pamphlet) 1863
6. Lord Herbert's Army Sanitary Administration (1 thin pamphlet) 1862
7. How people may live and not die in India (1 thin pamphlet) 1863
8. International Statistical Congress paper (thin blue 4to pamphlet) 1860
9. the same in French (pink, 4to pamphlet) 1860
10. How people may live and not die in India (the same as 7, reprinted with a preface) 1864
11. *Notes on Hospitals* (1 small 4to) 1863
12. *Notes on Nursing* (1 volume 8vo) 1860
13. Observations (on Sanitary state) India (1 red 8vo volume) 1863
14. Suggestions on Workhouse Nursing (written by desire of Poor Law Board) (1 folio pamphlet) 1867
15. Method of improving Hospital Nursing (an abridgement of above, 1 folio paper) 1867

Una and the Lion, *Good Words* for June 1868

Source: Letter with envelope, Wellcome (Claydon copy) Ms 9003/4

[printed address] 35 South Street
Park Lane
London, W.
23 January 1868

Dearest Mum

We have got back safe as you see. Good Bratby came and took us up famously. You will be glad to hear that Mr Bismark, the white cat who was lost, took the opportunity of coming back too, and appeared here to receive me.

We have had, to be sure, the most horrible alternatives of the most horrible weathers at Malvern, either fog and frost, for which we could not see out for the fog without, or storms for which we could not see out for the smoke within. The stay at Malvern has quite answered to me for the break in my work.

This morning I saw the hills for the first time (like Cauterets in the Pyrenees, as I always think them). But, after all, low hills covered unequally with snow, against an iron grey dirty sky, are nearly the ugliest objects in nature. I have not been to Malvern since A.H.C. took me there.

You will see by this note a deficiency of pens and ink. Sidney Herbert came to see me during that interregnum in Old Burlington St., when I had my sitting room in one house and my bedroom in another, and told his wife that it was the first time in all his life that he had not seen F.N. surrounded with writing. So I must conclude,

ever dearest Mum
your loving child
F.

Source: Letter, Wellcome (Claydon copy) Ms 9003/16

[printed address] 35 South Street
Park Lane
London, W.
27 March 1868

Dearest Mum

I have been intending to write and thank you every successive week for your dear letters, but have never been able. You are almost the only person who ever write to me except to ask me for something. I am very sorry not to hear that you have been free from spasms. I was in hopes that this splendid spring would have exempted you, dearest Mum, from these.

Jenny Dowding [a maid] is going on very well. She is always a little tearful about Embley when I see her, but she is well and active, clever at her work, cheerful and good-tempered. Even Burch has always a good word for her. She has a wistful look about her eyes, which betokens either sensitiveness or delicacy of health. I wish I could see more of her just as I wish I had more time to write to you.

But "you have no idea how I am overworked," the very words dear Agnes Jones, of the Liverpool Workhouse, wrote to me but sixteen days before her death. The whole work of finding her a successor has fallen upon me. And, in addition, as Harry Bonham Carter says, they appear to expect me "to manage the workhouse from my bedroom." I believe we have found a woman at last to take her place, the younger of two sisters, the elder of whom we have been training as matron for Sir W. Heathcote's[130] new Winchester Hospital. But I am not allowed to mention her name yet as she is still in government employment

---

130 Sir William and Lady Heathcote, neighbours of the Bonham Carters at their home, at Fair Oak, near Petersfield.

under Sir Walter Crofton. But she is no more like to Agnes Jones "than I to Hercules."[131]

I don't think anything in the course of my long life has ever struck me so much as the deadlock we have been placed in by the death of one pupil, as combined, you know, with the enormous jaw, the female ink which England pours forth on "woman's work." Dear Hilary used to say that my demand upon my country was a young woman with a head. And that is just what, it appears, does not exist. At least, if she has a head, it all runs to pen and ink. It used to be said that people gave their *blood* to their country. Now they give their *ink*.

It is impossible to describe the heavenly way in which Agnes Jones's mother and sister have behaved to us. But they, Agnes Jones's mother and sister, will not let Mr Rathbone put up Tenerani's statue[132] to her memory. You know, he ought never to have asked them. He wants me to persuade them. I can't. He does not see (few people do) the awful character of the sacrifice they have made to God's work. And, humanely speaking, it might have been avoided—she might have been alive now. They can only say, we gave her for God's work; God keeps her memory. If you say you want a statue to keep her memory, that is your affair, not ours.

People who *can* make such a sacrifice are not those who care for memorials. If it were to be done, it ought to have been done without asking their leave. If they had been people to have given it, they would not have been people to make that awful sacrifice.

ever dearest Mum

your loving child

F.

I have seen Papa, I think him looking remarkably well.

---

131 Hamlet says that his father's brother (who murdered his father) was "no more like my father than I to Hercules" (Shakespeare, *Hamlet* Act 1, scene 2).

132 The statue by Pietro Tenerani was originally placed in the chapel of the workhouse, and later moved to the Oratory, St James's Cemetery. See Terry Cavanagh, *Public Sculpture of Liverpool* xii.

Source: Letter/draft/copy, ADD Mss 45790 ff365-66

[printed address] 35 South Street
Park Lane
London, W.
25 April 1868

Dearest Mum

I meant to write to you a long letter. But, as usual, I have not half got through each day's work before time and strength comes to an end. Rev Mother [Mary Clare Moore] of Bermondsey has been very ill. And though, thank God, she is better—yet she does not at all recover her strength or appetite. She liked some *orange* jelly, which was sent me from Embley two or three weeks ago, better than anything else. Since then I have been supplying her with orange jelly and other things from Gunter's. If, by Tuesday's box, Mrs Watson could send some more *orange* jelly for her, and also are there not nourishing things like *arrowroot blancmange* or *rice blancmange*? we should be very much obliged. She was delighted with some flowers I sent her from Embley.

I should be glad to tell you more about Bunsen's *Life*,[133] but, though it was sent me three weeks ago, I have not had time to look through even, much less to read, more than half a volume. It is interesting to me as an almanac would be to a person who had been present at all the events and dates. But I see no reason to alter, but on the contrary great reason to be confirmed in, the opinion that all these things being published only tend to lower the public's general opinion of the person treated of, and that the publishing of private letters not only is a treachery and a theft but a treachery and a theft which recoils upon the head of the very memory, so sacred, which they are meant to exalt. I have always steadily refused to give up to dear Mme Bunsen, to Lady Richardson, to Mrs Herbert, etc. the letters I have from their husbands. If I thought that letters in my possession were to be given up after my death I would destroy every letter I have at once, and I would never write another. In these days EVERY letter is *private*, because public news is given in the newspapers. It was quite different in Mme de Sévigné's days.[134]

> ever dearest Mum
> your loving child
> F.

I am afraid poor dear Bismark [a cat] has not been heard of.

---

133 Frances von Bunsen, *A Memoir of Baron Bunsen Drawn Chiefly from Family Papers by His Widow.*

134 The letters of the Marquise de Sévigné (1626-96), published posthumously.

Source: Letter, Wellcome (Claydon copy) Ms 9003/22

[printed address] 35 South Street
Park Lane
London, W.
13 May 1868

Dearest Mum

It has been a dreadful disappointment not to hear from you today or yesterday, and not even to have the weekly flowers or things from you. It is the first birthday I have ever had without hearing from my dearest Mum. Indeed I may say that, except one Tuesday, I have heard from you every Tuesday.

I have been so terrified—I don't think I ever was so frightened in all my life. But I have just received Watson's telegraph, for which God be thanked. I can write no more.

ever dearest Mum
your loving child
F.

Source: Letter with envelope, Wellcome (Claydon copy) Ms 9003/28

[printed address] 35 South Street
Park Lane
London, W.
13 June 1868

Dearest Mum

I am always writing to you *in my heart*, but if you knew what the turning of life's heavy wheel of daily business is to me, and so much of it comes to me merely from the laziness or cowardice of men. But now I must write to you to remind you that this is my dearest Mum's golden wedding, either 15 June or 18 June,[135] which is it? 1868. I am going to write more at length. But today it is impossible.

I believe it is better altogether for the country that I should have had my life. Therefore I will thank God and you for it, though I am not quite sure that, if He had asked me, I could have accepted it. But that is cowardly!

ever my dearest Mum's loving child
F.

---

135 In fact the wedding was 1 June 1818.

Source: Letter, Wellcome (Claydon copy) Ms 9003/31

[printed address] 35 South Street
Park Lane W.
17 June 1868

Dearest Mum

Though you have taken no notice of my filial invitation to tell me when your golden wedding day is, yet the day occupies too much of my thoughts for me not to write again. Would that I had something worthy to give my dearest Mum on her golden wedding day, but I have not. I can only give her my life, i.e., the record of my life. So I send the list of my poor little "works" you asked for and took away when last you were here. (Would you believe it, but I have never had time to make out this list before.) And you must please take that, being all my works, and my "Una" in *Good Words* as written for your wedding day by

my dearest Mum's ever loving child
F.

Source: Letter, Wellcome (Claydon copy) Ms 9001/163

Saturday [1868]

Dearest Mother

I shall hope to see you tomorrow (Sunday) about 4:00 P.M. but, I fear, only for ten minutes. (Talking for more than ten minutes is as much as my life is worth.)

I am *very much* obliged to Papa for buying the house for me. It is on the whole a great relief, though I am afraid it is mainly for the relief it will give to my dear and unwearied friend, Mrs Sutherland (in looking for houses for me), that it is a pleasure to me. I am so weary.

ever dearest Mum
your loving child
F.

Source: Letter, Wellcome (Claydon copy) Ms 9004/8

Saturday [January 1870]

Dearest Mother

Tomorrow Mr Jowett comes to give me the sacrament at 3:00. I had asked Mrs Bracebridge who is to be in town (from Saturday till Monday only) to join us, when I had not the least idea that you would stay over Sunday in London. I cannot bear that my dearest mother should be so near and not join us, if she likes it. At the same time, I cannot bear that she should be with me and not speak to her. But the fatigue to me of taking the sacrament is so great that I do not even see Mrs

Bracebridge. I think it is one of the greatest afflictions not to be able to take the sacrament at church, because there you need not speak to anyone. I am obliged to see Mr Jowett afterwards.

ever dearest Mum
your loving child
F.

Perhaps you could take Mr Jowett back to his house after the sacrament.

Editor: Frances Nightingale's mental faculties and vision began to decline seriously in the late 1860s, so that correspondence is to other people regarding her mother, rather than to her mother directly. In May 1869 Nightingale asked her father to empower the housekeeper to write her about her mother. She did not want to write the housekeeper via her mother "for fear of troubling her, body or mind."[136] A letter to her brother-in-law also in 1869 mentions having written a note to her mother, "though I scarcely know whether she opens her letters."[137] Exceptionally, she did get a letter from her mother in May 1869.[138] Nightingale reported to her sister in detail on her mother's altered state, urging her (and Harry Verney) to "save her from having to make the least decision, or from even knowing that there is the most trifling uncertainty" because of "how much worry it costs her if anyone writes to her to do the slightest things."[139] A letter when Nightingale was herself beginning to go blind reflects that "eyes are a great loss, greater even than ears. My dear mother used to ask every day (even long after she used to cry because she could not recognize me as her daughter): 'How is the country? How is England? Is the country improving?'"[140]

---

136 Letter to Parthenope Verney 2 May 1869, Wellcome (Claydon copy) Ms 9003/99.
137 Letter to Harry Verney 4 April 1869, Wellcome (Claydon copy) Ms 9003/93.
138 Letter to Harry Verney 10 May 1869, Wellcome (Claydon copy) Ms 9003/103.
139 Letter to Parthenope Verney 5 August 1869, Wellcome (Claydon copy) Ms 9003/116.
140 Incomplete letter to Miss Crossland December 1901, Wellcome (Claydon copy) Ms 9015/134.

Source: Incomplete, unsigned letter probably to Parthenope Verney, Wellcome (Claydon copy) Ms 9004/49

Embley
Romsey
19 July [1870]

While the Carters were here, I thought you would hear from them, but, now they are gone, I make haste to write. I found my mother altered certainly. Though she was sitting in the hall to meet me, and insisted on walking all over the downstairs rooms with me, I thought her shrunk and bent, though very spirited and lively. But yesterday, which was the first time I saw her again downstairs, when she was "in all her bravery," I had not this impression. She appeared to me just like what she has been for the last ten years, with the exception, which is very marked indeed, that she is so much more cheerful, so much happier really, *this year and last,* than I have ever known her in all my life. She is pleased and satisfied with everybody and everything (except that she very often asks for her "basket carriage," of that more anon). She has been out every day in the carriage, except Sundays, since I came and *every* day in the garden besides. Webb says she sleeps well afterwards, sometimes till almost 10 A.M. She comes upstairs between 10 and 11 P.M. and is always in bed by 1:00. Webb says her eyes are not worse. "She can read much better without her glasses than I can," says Webb. But I hope and believe she never does read by candle light.

The only material difference that I do see is that she gives up the pretence of being up before 5:00 P.M., which I think conduces materially to her equability. I have been to her every day but one between 12:00 and 1:00, and sat in her bedroom. She gives up offering to come to me, which I am glad of, as it was a strain upon her. Yesterday she and I sat in the library in the afternoon and it was [breaks off]

Source: Unsigned letter/draft/copy probably to Parthenope Verney, Wellcome (Claydon copy) Ms 9004/50

[1870]

Private. While my dear mother loses her memory (consciously, alas! to herself) she gains in everything else in truth of view, in real memory of the phases of the past, in appreciation of her great blessings, in happiness, real content and cheerfulness and in lovingness. I am quite sure that, during the nearly half-century in which I have known her, I have never seen her anything like so good, so happy, so wise or so really true as she is now. I hope to remember throughout eternity things she has said to me this year and last, such as "your father has never had a cross. *I have been his cross.* He has been a better husband to me than I deserved. My lot has been the happiest of lots. I did not deserve it." And, with regard to me, her views are so clear, so generous that I do not like to repeat them, because *I* too feel they are not "deserved." But I do not dwell upon these things so much (to mark the great change that has taken place) as upon her constant expressions of appreciation, grateful appreciation, of you.

She has learnt from life. Many, perhaps most, have no more idea of the phases of their past life than if that life were the life of another, a stranger. A memory, not of trivial facts but of appreciation of what life has been, is the only true memory. This is *truth of mind.* How often I remember that "people are such martinets about the truth of their words, but truth *of mind* they never think of." My mother's memory and appreciation of *life,* especially of *her life with you,* is in fact better and truer now than it has been during the whole of her half-century with you.

MOST PRIVATE. One little thing I ought to say which you may, which you *will,* think a matter quite trifling and yet which I see by experience may make the whole difference in her remaining life. *This* sort of conversation only arises when she is lying quite quietly in bed and I am sitting close to her quite quietly, *never* when she is walking about the room, or when she makes me walk about the room looking at things. Then her mind seems utterly to fail her. The most painful confusion of mind arises in which she often makes the most painful mistakes and remarks. This, which I am certain is much more common than people think, is surely worth attending to. It is not the body walking about the room which is the mischief. It is the mind wandering about. It is the mind having the fidgets, which is the painful part, not the body being fidgety. You might just as well give her a blow on the brain as talk to her while you are walking about or as encourage her to conversation while she is walking about. I have observed it now so much as to be quite sure of it.

Source: Postscript to letter, Wellcome (Claydon copy) Ms 9005/89

Lea Hurst
Matlock
31 July 1871

My dear Sir Harry [Verney]

. . . Father vigorous, mother rather feeble but happy and well. I have the great comfort of sitting by her for an hour daily. Will write again.

Source: Letter, Wellcome (Claydon copy) Ms 9005/140

35 South Street
Park Lane, W.
15 May 1872

Dearest, very dearest Mother

I never had and never could have a better birthday present than your dear little letter, which I keep as the apple of my eye. No birthday celebration half so good was ever invented, for my fifty-second. You say there will not be a fifty-third. This is even more likely, I believe, to be true of me, than in the way you mean it, dearest Mother. But what of that? What will be my future life in this world, if there be one for me, I cannot tell any more than what it will be in another.

For the last twenty years my life has been and is as entirely dependent upon circumstances under God's control, not mine, e.g., the Crimean War, Sidney Herbert, Sir John Lawrence, Lord Mayo, as we know the circumstances *must* be under which we shall continue existence at the moment of death. It is literally true of me, that God must direct my life what it is to be just as much whether I am to live as whether I am to die.

For "birds" and "foxes" there is a settled life, but for the "Son of man" or the daughter of man there is none.[141] More than any other then I must say I have in me powers undeveloped, unknown—I only wish for God to make me what *He* wishes, that I may be able to do all He asks of me, whether in this world or in another. And I ever am

my dearest mum's loving child
whether living or dying
F.

Source: Unsigned letter, Wellcome (Claydon copy) Ms 9005/170

Embley
17 December 1872

Dear [Parthenope Verney]

In reply to your question: Aunt Mai told me that she had written *twice* to you telling you the whole melancholy state of affairs here as regards my mother, that since the beginning of July I have been on guard, sleeping in the music room and scarcely ever out of hearing night or day, that I was called up to London on 30 September at ten minutes' notice on urgent business, that I have broken up my own little household in order to give my mother a trustworthy upper house-

---

141 An allusion to Luke 9:58.

maid, who sleeps in the music room when I am not here, that I left the most harassing and pressing business unfinished in London in order to come down here again on 14 November, which nothing else would have justified but Aunt Mai's enforced departure on the 15th and the conviction of every member of the family who knows that it was unsafe to leave my mother for a single day or night, that it has been destruction to my work my having been now eight months on duty with my mother this year and that to stay beyond 11 December is literally finishing the destruction.

Aunt Mai told me that she had written to you that *I had told Sir Harry* this: (I adding, to Sir Harry, that I had what was *very serious* to tell you and him) and that *this was it.* Aunt Mai told me that, not thinking you sufficiently impressed (by your first answer), part of which she sent me, she had written to you again enforcing the urgency. I hope that you will stay at 35 S. St. as you go through. *Please* write to 35 S. St. fixing the day.

You understand that my father knows nothing of the specific cause (told you by Aunt Mai) for our watchfulness. When I came in July it was truly terrible, but it had been so even before.

Measures essential *for my mother's care*:

Morning, 1. That someone should go in to her between 11 and 12 with a rose or flower;

2. That either Mr N. or her daughter should go in to her for a few minutes between 1 and 2, or both, but at different *and uncertain* times, the person always going into Webb's room;

3. That, on days when she does *not* drive out, her daughter should be with her say from 3-5 P.M., reading, repeating and talking to her (at 5 she gets up).

4. That Sir H. should occasionally go to her *bedside* and pray with her. But, of course, no one must go into her room *unexpected* or *without* inquiry.

5. That her daughter should go frequently into the music room unexpected and *unexpected into Webb's room*;

6. That the approaches to her room through music room and through bathroom should ALWAYS *be kept unlocked, night and day*;

7. That either her daughter or Harriet should *always sleep* in *music room*;

8. That Webb should frequently be questioned as to my mother's bed meals and as to how much she has read to her, etc., that Webb should see that her word is not taken as an oracle *without personal*

observation of my mother's state, e.g., if Webb says: "Mrs N. forgets that she has had her breakfast," it should be answered: "Yes, Webb, and Mrs N. also forgets that she has *not* had her breakfast." Also that Webb should see that she cannot keep Mrs N.'s daughters out of Mrs N.'s room at *her own* plotting;

9. It is doubtful whether anything could secure my mother against neglect except what I did, viz., spend twenty out of twenty-four hours in the music room, where I can hear everything *through*. But, if this cannot be done, then Rules 1 to 8 are the more necessary. (These were observed *besides* the mounting guard in music room.)

10. You can scarcely know the extent of the evil as I discovered it in July (though Aunt Mai tells me she "told you *all*"). (The risk of *fire* at night was, *then*, no small one. Webb has *once* locked my mother up, from 11 P.M. to 5 P.M. the next day, without food, and often to an earlier hour in the afternoon.)

N.B. I feel sure that the evil has been reduced to a minimum since August but ONLY by my mounting guard *night and day*, only by the most unremitting vigilance and showing Webb *by deed* and not by word that Mrs N. *has* daughters who *will* look after her.

22 December 1872

Still you understand that, with a proud woman like Webb, the veil must be kept up that we "do not *know*." Or she would revenge herself on my mother.

Source: Unsigned note probably to Parthenope Verney, Wellcome (Claydon copy) Ms 9006/1

10 January 1873

. . . Whenever, or if ever, there is to be a successor to Webb, may I say this: a "sick nurse" is not the description of person which I should give—"sick nursing" is the least of my mother's wants. A "confidential attendant," a "maid to an invalid aged lady," a person of some education is the description I should give, if I were looking out. . . .

Source: Letter to Mary Jones, Add Mss 47744 ff210-13

35 South Street
Park Lane, W.
7 February 1873

. . . And now I write, though fearing that the business will be troublesome to you, because I know that if it is to do good, especially to my dear mother, you will spare no trouble. We are looking out for a person to succeed my dear mother's maid, who has been with her fifteen years, was previously with me as nurse and had a twenty years' character before that as a (domestic) children's head nurse. What my mother really wants is *not* a *nurse* but a first-rate (domestic) upper servant. She is not ill but she is feeble, infirm, eighty-five, has lost her memory, but her wits are as bright as ever. As she nears the other shore, she shows more mental and spiritual insight than ever in all her life before.

I have twenty doubts about the person, *Mrs Epsley*, I am going to write to you about. *Epsley* says she was nurse in King's College Hospital about 1864 for a year, was in "Twinings" (as she calls it) under Sister Laura with a nurse called Burbidge, also in Men's Ward Nos. 4 and 5, also, she thinks, under Sister Laura, with a nurse named Edwards and another (I think she said) Spong, that a nurse named Rogers died while she was there, that Sister Sophia knew her. I confess, though I did not perceive any other signs of want of frankness in her, that I did not believe her account of why she left K.C.H. and that I think she was surprised and rather disconcerted when she found out that I was known to you since she was at K.C.H. She has been recommended by Dr Laurie, has been nearly four years nursing a Rev Dr Blackman till his death 1868, then at a Mrs Johnson's a year, at a Mrs Salwey's a year, Rev Charles Nevill's eight months nursing his mother-in-law, at a Miss Croft's five months, 150 Harley St. All these old people, whom she says she nursed till they died, she gives references to all the survivors.

I am too old to think much of any of these "characters" and five months is such a little time for the *last* "character." Still the woman may be an "angel" and she reads well aloud, which is essential for my mother. I put it in the Lord's hands for I have done my utmost and am in an extremity. God must choose.

The fact is that my father and mother are neither of them in a condition to be without a near relative. Upon me, the only one of the family who has any real work to do, the whole thing is thrown. Last year, I spent at Embley nearly eight months of it, and twenty-two hours out of every twenty-four in the room next my mother's. The consequence was that my London work was almost ruined and I reduced to a trembling sort of corpse. Yet, even so, I could not do half what father and mother wanted. Could you recommend someone quite above all suspicion for my mother's maid, dear friend?

Source: Unsigned letter to Harry Verney, Wellcome (Claydon copy) Ms 9006/18

4 March 1873

We have not made the slightest way to getting my mother to allow "Grace" to *do* anything for her and Friday is near at hand. (This is *not* Webb's fault; she completely understands that she is to go on Friday.) Webb will try and persuade my mother to let "Grace" come in to her this morning and do something for her in bed. And if you would be with my mother *while she has* her *breakfast and talk to Grace* IN *the room* WITH *my mother?*

My mother was very feverish while I was with her yesterday afternoon; she talked half the night, she positively refused to let Grace into the room when Webb asked her. All this I have, not from Webb, but my own observations.

My mother preserves so much grace and self-control that no one who does not see and hear her as I do has the least idea how *she* feels. (I have seen Webb, as always, twice this morning and am sure that she is honestly, though not of course quite disinterestedly, trying to reconcile my mother to "Grace" before Friday.) No one has any idea what the shock may be to my mother on Friday. Twice I was summoned to my mother's bedside at Lea Hurst to find her livid and, as far as my knowledge goes, on the brink of convulsions when she was worried to have "Elliot" instead of Webb.

Source: Letter probably to Parthenope Verney, Wellcome (Claydon copy) Ms 9006/19

5 March 1873

The only thing that has happened awry is that my mother was rather chilled in the bath. Perhaps Grace should be told to note any reaction of heat or cold when she puts her to bed or in the night. And, if cold, my mother is warmed with a hot blanket or flannels in the night and not with making too much fire in her room.

F.

Source: Unsigned letter, Wellcome (Claydon copy) Ms 9006/25

7 March [1873]

Dear P. [Parthenope Verney]

This is a bad beginning indeed, but it is better it should have happened at once that it may never happen again. It was a terrible mistake leaving my mother with two strangers: Miss Pringle and Harriet, yesterday afternoon for nearly two hours, *without telling me*, who was lying here in [the] music room waiting to go in to her. For seven years, no one has given my mother the po[t] but Webb and me. And I *always go* to my mother *from 3:00* or as soon after as she will let me *till she gets up.* My mother has had a very restless night and has hardly slept at all. (Nothing would have induced my mother to ask Miss Pringle or Harriet for the po[t]. And it seems hard that the very day after the person who has never left her for an hour for fifteen years is gone, this should have happened.)

All this I explained to Grace in London. She behaved beautifully when I spoke to her this morning and I thought her less stolid than yesterday. But please tell her—no one can arrange it better than you—this today, from yourself, that we may both be to her slow mind in the same story. Or certainly the last state of my mother will be worse than the first.[142] For nothing of this kind ever happened before.

Editor: The next letters date from just after W.E. Nightingale's death, 5 January 1874. Parthenope Verney was at Embley when he died, Nightingale in London.

Source: Letter, Wellcome (Claydon copy) Ms 9006/69

35 South St.
22 January 1874

Dear Pop [Parthenope Verney]

I wish to do what you think best. I had intended to come down end of next week. I heard that poor mother was continually often asking for me. I think, with you, that it is better not to come when there are or will be so many in the house, and will put off till further advised, this being understood that I could come down at a few hours' notice, if sent for.

About "a companion" let me say one word: poor mother, who is much sharper than people take her for, told me exactly what you tell me now, "that Aunt Julia" and she mentioned someone else (even before the loss of our father) "thought someone would be necessary as a companion, and some lady at Tenby was talked of" (I, F.N., do not know whom) "and some other lady." Poor mother, after talking about it many times with much agitation made me swear that I would "protect" her from it while she, [Aunt] Julia, lived." She said: it "would kill" her. She also said that somebody "would kill" her if I

---

142 An allusion to Luke 11:26.

spoke of it. I do not think even this final, but you would not think me right if I did not mention it, would you?

You can show this to Aunt Ju, or perhaps I had better write to her myself, shall I? No one can possibly have so great an idea as I of the unexampled difficulty of the situation with poor Mother, because *I* cannot even when with her (and though since 1866 I have had her, and for months quite alone, when dear Father has been away) do without someone to go out with her and be with her in the evenings now.

Therefore I say I do not consider even what passed between her and me as final, but I think you should know it. I can see hardly any parallel between giving her "a companion" and changing her maid, for there was always "a companion" to explain that to her.

ever your F.

Source: Unsigned, incomplete letter, Wellcome (Claydon copy) Ms 9006/70

Embley
4 February 1874

My dear Sir Harry and Parthe [Verney]

. . . My poor mother, at first I thought her more altered than I could have supposed possible, not between what she was in *afternoons* three months ago and what she is now, for when up and walking about she has long been as confused in memory, but between the *mornings* when I sat by her in her bed and she used to show more mental and spiritual insight than ever she did in her life in the last years, and now.

On Saturday it was terrible, the wandering, real and painful wandering, *not* merely of memory. I thought, oh I am too late, the mind is gone. But Sunday morning I was by her bed as soon as she spoke. She knew me at once and began at once to speak of our loss. Then I said all that is so true about *him,* and I shall never forget the look of divine happiness which came over her face (it is enough to have lived for) when we repeated, Today shalt thou be with me in paradise.[143] It is natural and comfortable that she should ask, when shall I go after him? . . .

---

143 An allusion to Luke 23:43.

Source: Letter, Wellcome (Claydon copy) Ms 9006/85

Embley
17 March 1874

My dear Sir Harry [Verney]

... My dear mother's welcome of me this morning was inexpressibly touching; she shed tears. In haste.

your affectionate

F. Nightingale

Source: Letter, Wellcome (Claydon copy) Ms 9006/88

Embley
2 May 1874

My dear P[arthenope Verney]

Please telegraph to me on *Monday* morning early that you are coming. It is all but impossible for me to put off my business in London another day and equally impossible in my opinion to leave my mother till I know you are on the road to her.

I will see the "lady companion" in London if you will appoint her, and write to you.

F.

Source: Unsigned letter to Parthenope Verney, Wellcome (Claydon copy) Ms 9006/95

35 South St.
14 May 1874

Miss Parish has spent the afternoon here. She will come to you on *Saturday*: be at *Romsey 5:40.* Please *meet her,* will stay till Tuesday or Wednesday, or longer or shorter as you like, wishes only to do as you like, and will return to Embley, if you like her to do so, or will come to you at Claydon, if she suits Mother, or will stay and take charge of my mother at Embley, if that is any relief to you at Embley while you are winding up affairs. I am *sure* she is a woman of deep feeling, of great kindness and religious purpose, of much accomplishment and a thorough gentlewoman and considerate. But, there is always a "but." She is to me a very fatiguing person: maniérée: though it is the old-fashioned mannerism of good society, like the old Berrys, also old-maidish and fidgety. I should call her intellectual, yet look forward with some dread to giving her my hard-spared moments, if ever we live together.

I am not sure that her manner may not suit my mother. I am sure she is tender, affectionate and helpful. I think she is a little confused in mind: e.g., I could hardly make her understand that *Embley* was not yours (you had said to her that you "wished her to see my mother at her home") or that my mother's companion was not to live *there* with my mother and you. I don't think she will take any charge off me about the housekeeping or anything, men servants or anything, but I am sure she will be most willing to try to amuse and cheer and comfort mother morning, noon or night, as the case may be. I have heard nothing of the German lady. Too pressed to write more.

Source: Letter, Wellcome (Claydon copy) Ms 9006/99

35 South St.

26 May 1874

My dear P. [Parthenope Verney]

Though this day robs me of the last vestige of an earthly home (and instead of people providing a home for one so worn out and helpless as I, we have now to provide a home for dear, dearest mother). Yet I do not forget what this day must be to you in speeding her departure from the home of fifty years. I cannot speak about it.

Please return me THIS *letter* from Claydon with your answer. I will not write now of what I feel. Indeed I cannot. God bless dear mother and you and the Coltmans for taking care of her.

F.

Source: Letter, Wellcome (Claydon copy) Ms 9006/101

35 South St.

1 June 1874

My dear P. [Parthenope Verney]

I was most thankful to have your letter and news of dear mother. Indeed, the beginning a new life at eighty-six was a fearful chance. Tremendous, I thought, but how good God has been to her in preserving her spirit of enjoyment. Some people think it requires faith to pray. *I* think it requires faith *not* to pray: it has required all mine indeed, I know, not to pray that God would take her, *before* she had to be moved, but I know no one who has made such spiritual progress at *any* age as she has at eighty-six and is not this God's highest blessing?

It occurred to me several times to propose that her father's pictures[144] should follow her (out of the music room) wherever she goes, but I knew you would think of this if feasible. She enjoyed them

---

144 William Smith, Mrs Nightingale's father, had been an art collector.

the very last time I took her into the music room. I should not like at all to "empty her tallboy" while she lives. God bless her and you.

F.N.

Source: Letter, Wellcome (Claydon copy) Ms 9006/110

35 South St.
29 July 1874

My dear Sir Harry and Parthe [Verney]

Would it be possible that you should invite my mother to stay at Claydon for a year, that is till next May? In which case she would return from Lea Hurst about the end of October to Claydon and I would, as you have so often so kindly asked me to do, come to Claydon to take charge of her at any subsequent period when you might wish to be away or staying at 32 S. St.? God bless her and you.

ever your affectionate

F. Nightingale

Source: Letter, Wellcome (Claydon copy) Ms 9006/128

Claydon
21 September 1874

Miss Parish

PRIVATE

My dear Sir Harry and Parthe [Verney]

Either she drinks or she has a screw loose. In any case she is totally unfit to take charge of my mother alone and I am totally unfit to take charge of Miss Parish. It was not till last night that she came into my room in a condition which puts it *beyond a doubt* that she is one or other of these things. . . .

Editor: Although Frances Nightingale had to leave Embley when Aunt Mai inherited it she was allowed to live for some time further at Lea Hurst. Shore and Louisa Smith then took her into their home in London.

Source: Letter, Wellcome (Claydon copy) Ms 9006/164

Lea Hurst
Cromford, Derby
12 August 1875

My dear Sir Harry [Verney]

. . . I am sure that you would be delighted to see how keenly, yes, keenly, my mother enjoys this place: enjoys her old seat in the drawing room window, the terrace, her own bedroom and balcony room. She is like a new being—enjoys the children and Shore's wife. As she says, "I do so like having my own people about me again." Sometimes she is just what she was twenty years ago; she says, "oh you have brought me here to be among all the old things which I know so well and the people I love." (Still I do not at all disguise from myself how frail she is.) She sends for me regularly as soon as she has breakfasted. I stay till she gets up, bringing in a child, which delights her. Then she comes to me when she is dressed till she goes out. . . .

Source: Letter, ADD Mss 46176 ff62-63

[before June 1876]

Books for my Mother
My dear Shore [Smith]

Would you (my housemaid at 35 South St. is so helpless) kindly go to 35 and see if there is any parcel from Claydon *since I left* and if that is *Macaulay's Life, volume 2*, bring it here. (I told her to forward all parcels here and she has not.) Would you further look in the bottom shelves of *book-cases against the drawing-room wall*, nearest to *34 side* and *nearest* the *door* for *Jeffrey's Life*, two volumes I think, and any other *books* that you think will do for *my mother* and bring them *here*. I am sorry to give you this trouble but it is quite necessary, as you will agree, for her (and this I do not think Miss Mochler sees at all or even Miss Irby enough) to have contemporary political biography read to her, to hear names of political men that she has known in her youth and some, not too much, newspaper. I give her a *Times* to herself and *Illustrated News*.

Fruit: if it would not trouble you to bring some *grapes*, apricots, oranges and other fruit for my mother, but do not trouble about this. I *have* them from London for her. In great haste.

ever yours
F.N.

Source: Letter, Wellcome (Claydon copy) Ms 9007/34

35 South St.
1 June 1876

My dear Sir Harry and Parthe [Verney]

About the time of going to Lea Hurst, or of my mother leaving London, it must of course depend upon her health. We accept your invitation for her "to Claydon on 1 August" under the same contingency, or we take her to Lea Hurst. There must be some mistake, you say, "we must ask you not to repeat Mother being called upon to support Shore and family for all the Lea Hurst time." Of course Mother will not and did not pay a single item. It all *will* come out of *my* pocket *as it was all paid out of my pocket last year.* (Not a single item was charged to my mother's income but what was charged when no one was there but herself and household of course.) *Her* travelling expenses, etc., not one item of which had anything to do with Shore or family, were charged to her income, nothing else. . . .

yours affectionately

F. Nightingale

Source: Postscript to a letter to Miss Mochler, Boston University 2/2/7

12 November 1879

P.T.O. Please say to Mr Shore Smith Miss Irby writes from Sarajevo: "May *Miss Johnston*[145] go and see *Mrs Nightingale and talk to her about her grandfather, Sir Fowell Buxton and the slave trade, a subject on which I never knew your mother not wake up to. Miss Johnston wants to go* partly I think because she was so devoted for years to her own old grandmother." *Miss Johnston's* address is *10 Ovington Gardens.*

Source: Letter, Wellcome (Claydon copy) Ms 9008/2

[printed address] 10 South Street
Park Lane, W.
6 January 1880

My dear Sir Harry [Verney]

Yesterday my dear father had been gone home six years (according to our reckoning). My mother came to me. I thought her much altered but very peaceful. She took great pleasure four times in looking at the photograph of his monument. . . .

ever yours affectionately

F. Nightingale

---

145 Priscilla Johnston (d. 1912), co-worker with Irby on refugee relief in Bosnia, granddaughter of Sir Thomas Fowell Buxton (1786-1845), who had worked with William Smith, Mrs Nightingale's father, to abolish the slave trade.

Source: Letter, Wellcome (Claydon copy) Ms 9008/6

31 January 1880
the anniversary of Mrs Bracebridge's death

Immediate

My dear Sir Harry [Verney]

I am daily so much "put to" it for messengers since my dear mother's illness that, unless you can kindly help me with an occasional man servant, I must engage a second messenger. I cannot possibly get another today. Could you kindly put a man servant at my disposal from 10.30 *today* till 1:00? It is to go after a nurse for my mother (or Morris will not last out).

I am sure my mother was the better for your prayer yesterday. . . .

yours

F.N.

Editor: Frances Nightingale died the night of 1-2 February 1880. Neither daughter could attend the funeral.

Source: Letter, Wellcome (Claydon copy) Ms 9008/7

2 February 1880

My dear Sir Harry [Verney]

There are many very strong reasons to my feeling why those who should follow my dear mother to the grave should be only *Shore* and *his wife* and *yourself*. I would not *ask* any of the "cousins," not one.

If William Coltman and Harry B.C. like to offer, let them. But pray do not let us do anything to prevent Louisa going with Shore. It is converting a lovely act of love into a farce to ask "the cousins," is it not?

The people *she* would like would be yourself, *Louisa, Shore, coachman* and *Charles* and *Morris*, if she would like it. No one else. . . .

ever yours affectionately

F.N.

Source: Letter, Wellcome (Claydon copy) Ms 9008/8

4 February 1880

If I have not written, my dear Pop, it is because heart and hand and mind have been fuller than I could bear. I will write tomorrow, please God. God bless you ever.

always your F.

An immense magnificent cross and wreath come just now from the trained nurses for her dear memory for Friday.

Source: Note, Wellcome (Claydon copy) Ms 9008/9

5 February 1880

If you would like, dear Pop, to see the beautiful crown and wreath contributed by all the nurses of St Thomas' to my mother's grave, please send in a man to bring you the boxes.

F.

Mr Jowett comes to give me the sacrament at 6:30 tonight.

Source: Letter, Wellcome (Claydon copy) Ms 9008/10

5 February 1880

My dear P. [Parthenope Verney]

I think a card in remembrance of my mother would be valued by some of the Lea Hurst people more than any earthly possession. If you think so, I would send in (as soon as I can get a maid to find it) our memorial card for Miss Hill and another, not of course to be copied but as specimens. We can then settle what we will have.

your F.

Source: Letter, Wellcome (Claydon copy) Ms 9008/11

6 February 1880

The accompanying flowers, dear Pop, taken out of my mother's coffin by dear Louisa's care are for you. I have a long letter to write you about darling mother, which I will today, if only possible.

Enclosed are the two memorial cards. Something like *Miss Hill's*, I think, would be pleasing, but I am not at all wedded to it. I don't think you mean, limit the cards to the "estate houses." Not above two or three of my intimate poor friends with whom I am in daily intercourse at Lea Hurst, Holmes, Broomhead, a woman dying of tumour, Limb, dying also, Shardlow, Henstock, etc. live in the "*estate's*" houses.

ever dear Pop

your F.

Source: Letter with envelope on death of her mother, Royal College of Nursing, Edinburgh RCN/FN1/9

10 South St.
Park Lane, W.
10 February 1880

My dear Sir [William Webb MD]

I should not have waited for your more than kind note to write to you about my dear mother, who went home so peacefully with a smile on her face, as if she saw God, just after midnight on Sunday night,

1-2 February, but that I am so broken down with the last ten days. I know your kindness will wish to hear something about her last illness, for illness it was, followed by inability to eat, which killed her.

She came to me on 5 January, the sixth anniversary of my dear father's death; four times she looked at the photograph of his monument, I repeating the inscription. Her last long look at it I can never forget. (But I think I may have mentioned this before.) On 20 January she went out in the carriage for the last time (with Morris, her maid; Miss Mochler was taking a two months' holiday in Ireland, and did not return till after all was over). She was observed to have a slight cold, and on 21 January she came downstairs (for the last time) but did not go out. Dr Andrew Clark and his assistant, Dr Burnett, attended her. Dr Burnett saw her on that day and prescribed for her and then till the end. (The death certificate was bronchial catarrh and senility, but she never had a *chronic* cough.)

For several nights the cough at night was incessant. She could not expectorate and the noise and difficulty of breathing were painful. It was the fog which killed her. But she was so patient; she always said, "I am quite comfortable." Every day till the last, the Sunday of her death, she was dressed and sat in her great chair in her bedroom or dressing room. Every day the ceremony of bringing up dinner was performed, but appetite quite failed. The dryness of the mouth was distressing. She used to pray to be let alone. For the last week of her life a few drops of beef tea was all she swallowed, except once.

My cousin Shore, whose love and devotion to her (and his wife's too) never failed: he strove for her life as if his own depended on it, though he was suffering and in bed from slight congestion and cough. He would get up, even in the night—she always knew him—because he thought she would take food from *him*. He was so happy when he could get two or three teaspoonsful or a morsel of sponge cake into her mouth. But, after doing this to please him, she would take an opportunity to put it all out again, quite dry.

At the last Dr Burnett thought there was inability to swallow. Still there was so much strength, though she was terribly wasted. Dr Burnett did not think she was dying. Her pulse was good (though the last night but one, which was a foggy night, the trained nurse said she had no pulse; that was the terribly restless night, but the pulse revived).

The bronchial attack had entirely passed away some days before the end; there was little or no cough and she had expectorated quite successfully. She was always better in the daytime. And when she was sitting dressed in her chair, her manner was so courteous and self-possessed, though silent; people did not know how ill she was, and that she was taking nothing.

To herself she used to repeat her favourite hymn, "My God, my Father, while I stray,"[146] and the Lord's Prayer in a clear, strong voice. She knew she was dying and her whole demeanour was, "It's all right; I'm going home." There were three sonnets of Milton,[147] "When Faith and Love" [sonnet 14], the sonnet on his twenty-third year [sonnet 7] and that on his blindness [sonnet 22], which she for years made me repeat to her every day when I was with her. When we came to "They also serve who only stand and wait" [sonnet 19] she always stopped me and repeated it herself. Never, never, never did she fail to respond to these and others of her old favourites. When I repeated the Lord's Prayer and we came to "Forgive us our trespasses," she always stopped me and said, "My dear child, *remind me to forgive*." There were many other hymns and psalms which she always, always re-echoed. Gambold's "O what is death?"[148] I shall never say them to her more.

She knew me without knowing me. The last time but one I ever saw her she said, "Filomena,[149] and so she does the hospitals still. That's quite right. I'm so glad of that." After her death my Crimean hospital belt was found. Shore she always knew, and when she heard he was coming, it was not pleasure, it was joy: "Bless the Lord, O my soul,"[150] she would say. But I could tell so many things of her. She had intense joys and intense sorrows in these last years, which few knew anything of.

On Saturday 31 January (on this day we had one of our own trained nurses to sit up, who was of the greatest use) she had her bath but, after it, was much exhausted, and herself took a whole teacup full of beef tea with a spoonful of brandy in it, holding the cup herself. She was laid on a sofa and was very calm, Rosalind Shore Smith passing the afternoon with her. But the night was restless to a degree. (The fog of Saturday and Saturday night killed her.) She was not still

---

146 In *Hymns Ancient and Modern* 264.
147 John Milton (1608-74), poet and MP.
148 Rev John Gambold, poet and hymn writer.
149 Henry Wadsworth Longfellow's poem on Nightingale, 1857, was entitled "Santa Filomena."
150 Ps 103:1.

for one moment. As the nurse said, "she was all over the bed." Sunday was the first day she did not get up, but the fog had gone off and she appeared better. During those restless nights, which thank God are over now, she would moan and put out her hands uneasily and take off her cap. She seemed to wish to be "going," but so gentle a wish. The last night very gentle rubbing, or rather stroking, of her forehead and hands soothed her. She was allowed to keep her cap off and died so, her noble head and soft white hair looking so beautiful. After she had ceased to speak or swallow, Mrs Shore Smith repeated the Lord's Prayer and she put out her arm and beckoned, seeing something we could not see, and waved her hand over her head in a sort of gentle triumph, as if she would say again, "It's all right. I'm dying."

At 9:00 P.M. on Sunday Dr Burnett saw her: her pulse was good and he thought she had days to live. But immediately after he went she composed herself to death, "decently and in order," as she did all things during her long life. At midnight the change came: a bright light as it were passed over her face. She saw what the others could not see; her face was glorified and the expression remained. Then she closed her own eyes and her own mouth, folded her hands and went home, without a sigh, like a child falling asleep, or rather, as I love to think, like a child passing into the Immediate Presence of the Father. His smile rested on the lovely face, the "rapture of repose" was there. Mr and Mrs Shore Smith, Morris and the nurse were round the bed. Shore was kissing her and would not believe she had left him, but with *her* all was peace, and more than peace, blessedness.

She looked then and afterwards fifty years younger, like a picture there is of her at Embley with us two as children. There was not a redness of skin all over the body, not a wrinkle on the face; the whole body was as pure and calm as a child's, no running at the mouth, no odour about the breath or anywhere. And till the coffin was closed on Thursday night, not the slightest change, as she lay surrounded with all white spring flowers, telling of spring and rising again, the children coming in and kissing her and liking to stay with their mother in the room, as long as the dear old face, or rather the young immortal face, for it was the "mortal coil" of immortality, not of death, that was there.

On Thursday night it was brought down into the dining room; the coffin where she lay, looking so beautiful with all her flowers round her, was closed and a wreath and cross of everlasting and flowers, which our trained nurses had sent, laid upon it like a dead soldier's sword and medals. Shore read a short service, while the servants could not restrain their sobs. (They had all gone up and seen her.) On Friday 6 February it was buried by my dear father at Embley, as she had always said, borne by the labourers whom she wished, Mr and Mrs Shore Smith walking close behind, never giving up the dear charge till it was laid in the earth, with their son and Sir Harry Verney and his son, and the servants, and the nephews and nieces. But better than all, the church and churchyard were crowded with the people and tenants. I do not believe there was one person there who attended as a matter of form, but all could remember some twenty, some thirty, some fifty years of kindness which she had spent upon them. The coffin was quite covered with wreaths and crosses and a large white crown of flowers and violets and rosemary ("that's for remembrance"[151]). It was just what she would have liked herself. Gentle tears rained down.

I have dwelt far more than I intended upon what closes the last chapter of my dear, dear father and mother: "thrice blest to go." But I could fill three times the space with remembrances of her. My intention only was to give you some little medical history, because any medical remarks that you would be so very good as to make would be deeply interesting to me. Previous to the last illness, she had had some attacks of restlessness, though nothing like what she had at Lea Hurst. I understood that Dr Andrew Clark and Dr Burnett said to my cousin Shore that there might supervene "pressure on the brain." Nothing of the kind was however apparent in her last illness. She was rather remarkably gentle and lucid, and even in resisting food she would only cover her face with her hands and pray to be let alone. The nurse said she had never seen so beautiful a deathbed. Morris's care left nothing to be desired.

20 February 1880

I believe I must go away for a little. For six years and six weeks I have not had one day's rest of body or mind, and this time which ought to be peace is such a whirl, people coming and staying four hours when all one longs for is silence. I have been unable to finish this letter till now, its unpardonable length is due to hurry and interruption. Forgive and pray believe me,

ever sincerely yours
Florence Nightingale

―――――

151 Ophelia in Shakespeare's *Hamlet* Act 4, scene 5.

Source: Letter, Wellcome Ms 5483/25

[printed address] 10 South Street
Park Lane, W.
10 February 1880

Dear Mr Buxton [carpenter at Lea]

I send you a cheque for my account, which I am sorry did not come before. I thank you very much for the oak table, which is a very precious recollection to me.

You know that my dear mother is gone home. She rests by my father at Embley. All the people followed her to the grave. I could have wished that you and some others from Lea Hurst, which she loved so well, could have been there. The coffin was quite covered with beautiful white flowers, wreaths, and two crosses and a crown. Our trained nurses sent a beautiful cross and wreath. You and I can remember Lea Hurst almost from the first and go over our recollections together. . . .

sincerely yours
Florence Nightingale

Source: Letter, Wellcome (Claydon copy) Ms 9008/14

11 February 1880

I withdraw my mother's age, my dear P., though it greatly loses in pathos thereby, but my father's age must in that case be also withdrawn [in the memorial note].

But the *place* of death is *always* put and in this case the circumstances are so remarkable that it is quite impossible to omit it. The antithesis of the house in London and "the house not made with hands" is not painful but half the pathos (as in the verse so popular leaving "the cottage on earth to dwell in a palace in heaven"). The poor people would not think it the right card without. I send several that you may patch them as you like.

(I put on my wreath about joining our heavenly and earthly Father.) I *think* I like No. 4 the best [see below], but am not particular, only I feel it *quite* impossible to leave out that she died with Shore, don't you?

your F.

If Sir H. likes the black instead of the gold line, *please* let him have it. But I explained to him that what we did was gold-edged card in *black*-edged *envelope*, and I thought he concurred.

F.

Source: Draft memorial notes, Wellcome (Claydon copy) Ms 9008/25

In loving remembrance of
our Mother
Frances Nightingale
Who, from her nephew's, in London
Mr and Mrs Shore Smith's
went home to God
just after midnight
on February 1-2 1880
in her 92nd year
As well as of our Father
W.E. Nightingale
Who died at Embley
5 January 1874
in his 80th year.
"And he walked with God and he was not, for God
took him." [Gen 5:24]

"I must work the works of Him that sent me while it is day; the
night cometh when no man can work." John 9:4
"Lord, what wilt Thou have me to do?" Acts 9:6

Now the labourer's task is o'er,
Now the battle day is past,
Now upon the farther shore
Lands the voyager at last.
Father, in Thy gracious keeping
Leave we now Thy servant sleeping. . . . [152]

In loving remembrance of
our Mother
Frances Nightingale
who from her nephew's house
in London
tenderly cared for by
William and Louisa Shore Smith
went home humbly trusting
to join our heavenly
and our earthly Father

---

152 In *Hymns Ancient and Modern* 401.

just after midnight
on 1-2 February 1880
having survived six years
our Father
W.E. Nightingale
who died at Embley
5 January 1874
And he was not, for God took him.

The simplicity of my father's inscription is such that I am not sure I do not like this the best:

Frances, for 56 years
wife of William Edward Nightingale
and daughter of William Smith
MP for Norwich
died 2 February 1880
God is love
1 John 4:16

If Parthe wishes for our two names as her daughters, I think they could only be placed in this way: *To our Mother* (*before* the inscription) and (quite at the *bottom*) thus:

Frances Parthenope Verney
Florence Nightingale. . . .

Editor: In fact the inscription is slightly different from all of the above proposed wordings: Devoted to the memory of Frances Nightingale, wife of William Edward Nightingale, died Feb 1st 1880. God is love. 1 John 4:16. Bless the Lord O my soul and forget not all his benefits. Ps 112:2. By F. Parthe Verney and Florence Nightingale. The inscription for their father was simpler still: William Edward Nightingale of Embley in this county and Lea Hurst, Derbyshire, died Jan 5th 1874 in his 80th year. And in Thy light shall we see light. Ps 36:9.

Source: Letter, Wellcome (Claydon copy) Ms 9008/15

My dear Sir H. [Verney]   11 February 1880

These *are* "distressing" indeed. I wish I had never seen them. I had pictured her so different. The only one I could bear to have is the one I enclose.

Parthe asks me if I "remember" "When Faith and Love, etc." [Milton's sonnet 14]. I repeated it not only every Sunday, but almost *every day* to my dear mother and never, never, never, did she *not* respond to it. Then she would always have the two other sonnets. . . . Then another, "And joy shall overtake us as a flood" [sonnet 13, "On Time"].

Parthe asks me if I "remember" "O what is death? Tis life's last shore," etc. I do not know why I left it off this last time at Lea Hurst, but *till* this *last* time we always had it nearly *every day*. And she actually learnt to repeat it after me, at her age!!!

Were not her *card* for the POOR PEOPLE, I should very much have preferred putting in some lines of Milton's sonnet to what I have put. What do you say?

F.N.

Father, W.E. Nightingale

Editor: Nightingale's correspondence with her father here concerns general family matters, especially their own relationship (letters to her father on religion are reported in *Theology*, on politics and housing in *Society and Politics*). It will be immediately clear that this was for Nightingale the easiest of her close family relationships, but yet it too had serious vexations. It was her father who finally relented and allowed her to pursue nursing (giving her the necessary financial support to live independently, and later buying her a long-term lease on a house, paying her taxes, etc.). There is real appreciation of his intelligence and decency, although with regret that he did not make more of these (she would have liked him to have been, if not an MP, President of the Derby Infirmary). Their common intellectual interests get full play. Yet Nightingale felt that her father never accepted her as a competent expert in her field (already seen in the notes above). We do not have his letters to her, but it would seem that in some cases he frankly disagreed with her on hospital construction, sanitation and ventilation!

It seems that her father did not always respect her wish to keep her letters confidential. He evidently passed on letters in which Nightingale complained of her sister or made negative remarks about her, and this prompted retaliation. Nightingale was also hurt by the suddenness of his death (he said no goodbyes and left no messages). She continued to mourn his death, sending memorial wreaths at Easter for years thereafter.

Source: Letter, Wellcome (Claydon copy) Ms 8991/5 [correct French in square brackets]

Embley

Mercredi, 18 Decembre 1827

Cher Papa

Je voudrais bien que tu reviendrais [reviennes] aujourd'hui. J'ai apprit [appris] une pièce de poésie: les deux premières lignes sont "O is he gane my good auld man? And am I left forlorn?" Ces lignes m'ont fait penser à toi. Agathe a été à Southampton pour deux jours. Il y avait une église française là. Il a plut [plu] pour deux jours et deux nuits. Les robes de Mme Whitby étaient tout à fait mouillées. Ma tante Marie sera ici avant toi parce qu'elle vient Samedi et toi tu ne vient [viens] que Mardi.

J'ai réglée [rédigé?] ces lignes moi-même. Je crois que tu nous a[s] oublié[es] tout à fait. J'ai oublié tout mon Latin. Mme Whitby s'en va aujourd'hui à deux ou trois heures. Veux-tu m'écrire une lettre aussi en Français? J'écrirais mieux si je n'étais pas dans une hâte terrible. Adieu et crois-moi pour la vie

ton affectionnée fille

Florence Nightingale

Source: Letter, Wellcome (Claydon copy) Ms 8991/25

Embley

Sunday [after 19 February 1829]

11 o'clock

Dear Papa

I played with Miss Christie at battledore and shuttlecock yesterday, and I got once 9, once 8 and several times I got 7. We were very much tempted to send our letters in the Duke's frank, but we thought we might make some mistake. Has Pop had many teeth out at Mr Dumergue's?

Flo

Editor: Her father by 1844 acknowledged that his daughter "astonished me more and more. She is not like other folk of a truth, and I shall be her humble servant in many matters."[153]

---

153 Letter by W.E. Nightingale November 1844, Wellcome (Claydon copy) Ms 9038/29.

Source: Letter Wellcome (Claydon copy) Ms 8992/69

[Lea Hurst]

Wednesday night [1844]

Dear Papa

You know that clever man of Thebes, one Cadmus,[154] is no friend of mine and need never have existed, I think, for any power he gives one of expressing one's thoughts. So I have not taken up the iron pen before, although said thoughts have been much at Harrogate, but words are what always have brushed the dust off the butterfly's wings unless indeed one had a quill taken from the vermilion *"penne"* of Paolo's[155] Angel of the Annunciation. No mortal has yet got in alive into our rest. Some providence has hitherto kept off the Horners, though our exemption cannot last much longer, I am afraid. One of us has been down every afternoon to drink tea with the grandmother and aunt of us (generally more than one), and have done our best to fill your place with them.

Your poor friend Mrs Fern came this day while the rest were out, to pay her *pound* rent, which I took from her, and many tears she shed over her two children dead since she saw us last, and two more supposed to be going the same consumptive road. She that lives, you know, where Phebe Ward used to live and the daughter, whom we saw last year, in such a distressing state, is one of the dead. She was very much discontented not to see you in persona, and I promised that you and I should call on your return. She was a perfect Niobe in her woe.

Our fine weather is all gone, to heaven, I hope, or to an other and better place, and our fine nights too, which is much more pathetic as, if one were asked, looking back, to say what one knows to have been really the greatest pleasure of life, many an one would answer, I suspect, to have spent the night at the casement, watching its solemn procession and hearing the mysterious night wind, which seems to stir no leaf. One listens to it going by, without feeling it touch one's face; it is like the vision of Job, and makes one's flesh creep as if one heard a spirit, as if one perceived in it the Unspeakable Presence. If it were not for the eternal fidget of the day, who would know the deep peace of night, "the welcome, the thrice-prayed for, the most fair, the best-

---

154 According to Greek mythology Cadmus, founder of Thebes, taught the people writing, using Phoenician letters.

155 Possibly Veneziano Paolo (fl. 1350), Italian painter.

beloved Night,"[156] when one feels, what at other times one only repeats to oneself, that the coffin of every hope is the cradle of a good experience and that nobody suffers in vain. Otherwise, when one sees in every cottage a trouble which defies sympathy, and there is all the world putting on its shoes and stockings every morning all the same, one rather wonders at the eternal silence among those cold stars. The nursery casement here is the best place in the world for hearing the night wind, every breath of which our hilltop catches.

We are leading what is called a regular life, which always means that people dine *irr*egularly at 3:00 o'clock instead of dining regularly at 7:00 and read regularly fifty pages of some reading society's library book, with said society's cover on it, in the evening. In this way we are steadily working through *Coningsby*,[157] which seems to me more fitful than inspired, no flights, but some good grasshopper jumps. . . .

I have given up riding and all sports of the field, even my gun, and have subsided into an "excellent plain cook and housekeeper." Walking down the coach road to poor Poyser's, I found an immense field spider finishing his morning's work, walking round and round drawing the thread out of his tail with his right hind leg, and (as cleverly as any Manchester machine, working under the highest degree of excitement) hooking the thread on to each radius with his left hind leg, as he passed them. His morning's work done, he began to catch flies, and meanwhile ants were dragging away large moths and all scales of animals were at the work of destruction. And I, moving grandly on my pivot, stood watching the consumption and wondering whether there were superior intelligences, whom we are equally unconscious of, who in the same grand way are observing on us killing each other to the tune of slow music, and are thinking why we cannot eat each other fair like savages at that rate.

The Carters seem to have lived on sunbeams, and kept company with the spirits of a Rosalind and a Beatrice (meaning the Shakespearean ladies) by Marianne's glowing account of them. She made my old bones shake with laughter and they have been stiff in consequence for twenty-four hours. But Parthe and Mama have taken all the bread out of my mouth in the way of news and have told you too, no doubt, of Miss Martineau's wonderful improvement. They have left me nothing but a picture to make, and as we will *not* say that drawing

---

156 Henry Wadsworth Longfellow, "Hymn to the Night."
157 A novel by Benjamin Disraeli, *Coningsby, or the New Generation*, 1844.

is my forte, I send you a sketch in pen and ink of a friend of ours, whom *perhaps* you will recognize, but you are not obliged/condemned to read it. I only aspire to fill up a sanitary walk, when rivals in the way of conversation are not near for I have made my talk already longer than I thought; in return, I will make one some other time which shall be too short.

A Dieu, then, dear Papa, I hope you will not answer Au Diable.
yours fervently
F.N.

Source: Unsigned letter, Wellcome (Claydon copy) Ms 8992/90

Dear Papa   Wednesday [January or February, 1844 or 1845]

You are curious for my "experience of the sickroom" [at Waverley] so it would be very ungracious of me not to give it (though I have not yet set pen to paper). It is humbling enough. I felt, as the body fell off, so little of any other life in me, that when anybody came into the room, I was obliged to ask them to read something strong, Channing or the Bible, by way of an excitement to make me care to live on, for the mental life was flickering, flickering, as if it would go out. This makes me feel, that if I had been going to die now, when the call came for me to rise up again, I should kick and struggle a little, like a weak chicken in its shell, and that is all that would come of it, because there would be nothing strong enough, when the body was gone, to stand up and live on by itself. Still I do not say povera natura umana [poor human nature], but only povera natura mia [my poor nature], for what *all the* world has sung about the joys of convalescence must be true. Miss Martineau says the more the body falls in pain and weakness, the stronger the conviction of an independent and unchangeable self. She *should* have said, I suppose, "Here lies the difference between strong minds and weak ones." [breaks off]

Source: Letter, Wellcome (Claydon copy) Ms 8992/85

                                                         Tapton
                                              Saturday [July 1845]
Dear Papa

Could you put these poor Levicks into any way of getting their things back? The police are all comatose and, though they *know* the man to whom the cap belongs and though they have found a pair of the Levicks' boots at a pawnbroker, who can swear to the man who brought them, they do *nothing.* The reason why, they say, is that they are not a searching police—they really seem quite stupid, for the man was seen in the evening without his cap and the next day with a new one. . . . In great haste, ever, dear Papa

   your affectionate child

Source: Letter to "young people," Wellcome (Claydon copy) Ms 8992/101

. . . Papa will be glad to hear that the police are on the track of the robbers, whose blood we hope to drink next week, and that his war-like charge at Sheffield was told again to Mrs Levick by the police, with an accompaniment of drums and trumpets, greatly to her delight and gratitude. . . .

Source: Unsigned letter, Wellcome (Claydon copy) Ms 8992/116

[1845 or 1846]

Dear Papa

   Did you ever read a play called Lost and Won, where a gentleman comes to *life* for half an hour, merely, as afterwards appears, for the sake of frightening his son to *death*. Such was the appearance of the Stansfields yesterday morning on me. . . . The Tollets are still here, drawing mad, and I hear of nothing (for they are in raptures with the place) but very clever mountain, good bits of colour, happy sky, and as it is full moon tonight, I hope she will come in for her share, and we shall have very talented moon, happy Jupiter, clever shadow she casts. The Horners and Fowlers are gone to York, Dr Fowler to read some papers of his own, and I am widowed in every thought, till he comes back. Oh what a man it is! we had one delightful rainy day, while he was here, and I read Condillac[158] and D. Stewart[159] to him all day, and before Christmas I hope he will have part of a book out, to which he says the whole remainder of his life is to be devoted, a sort of refutation of Berkeley,[160] i.e., to prove (not that all nature is only the mind cognizant of its own operations, as Berkeley does, and that matter is only the *other end*, as it were) but to prove that it is a perceptive *mind* cognizant of the operations of the *body* and also to prove that our thoughts are really not under our own command, but strictly governed by the laws of association, which he says he can demonstrate.

---

158 Étienne Bonnot de Condillac (1714-80), French theorist on perception.
159 Dugald Stewart (1753-1828), Scottish idealist philosopher.
160 George Berkeley (1685-1753); see especially his *Treatise Concerning the Principles of Human Knowledge*.

So that that collect has a profound sense, "O God, from whom all just works, all good counsels and all holy thoughts do proceed."[161] He believes too that one sense suggests to another, what an interesting thing he may make of it. Of course we talked a great deal of Dr Howe's[162] letters and his blind and deaf mutes. One of his pupils, Julia Brace, who has the care of the linen of the asylum, sorts 160 pairs of stockings, AFTER *they have been to the wash,* by the sense of *smell* alone, and the only mistake she ever makes is when two new patients of the same family come to the asylum, when she makes them a family heap, instead of an individual one, but she soon learns the individuals and gives to each his stocking. So it appears that there is a family effluvia, divided again into individual effluvias, and we shall have it in the Peerage under Arms, rampant lion, etc. Motto che sarà sarà [what will be will be]. Effluvia Roseate [rose-coloured effluvia]. Of course everybody here called Julia Brace a very nasty individual, but I cannot understand that sort of feeling. Che sarà sarà.

Dr Fowler made me read Bell on the hand with him, à propos to Condillac, and brought forward all his physiological facts in support of his metaphysical theories, reminding one so always of the wise householder, who brought forth out of his treasure things new and old. Oh how rich life is, if one did but know how to get at it. What a fullness of life there is—there is the intellectual life, the life of sentiment and the life of art. When he is here, I never want any other life and then one is surprised someday, when one begins the life of enthusiasm and feeling to think how one could have done so long without it.

Mrs Fowler had her head full of schools; she is a real home missionary, and yet has room enough left for one's small matters. She always believes one, too, when one speaks—an agreeable and very rare quality. A friend is to her not only to be confided in but also to be trusted to. She was very much upset by their Reuben's sudden death, the boy, you know, whom they brought up from four years old and have had

---

161 A paraphrase of the second collect at evening prayer, Book of Common Prayer.

162 Dr Samuel Gridley Howe (1801-76), director of the Perkins Institution and Massachusetts School for the Blind, Boston, MA. He and Julia Ward Howe visited the Nightingales in 1844. Julia Brace (1807-41) was a deaf and blind pupil.

twenty-two years. Mr Horner and Dr Fowler do not attach great faith, I see, to Miss Martineau's case.[163]

The Horners were in great force, full of the Bunburys, of Sir Henry Bunbury's[164] 320 allotments at half a guinea's rent each, by which he seems to have made respectable and happy a whole population, of his twelve Sir Joshuas,[165] one of them of Lady Sarah Bunbury, *his* aunt, and his second *wife*'s mother, the beautiful Lady Sarah Bunbury, you know, daughter of the second Duke of Portland, whose history is such a romance. She was the sister of the Lady Louisa Conolly, whose letters to her nephew are in Moore's *Life of Lord Edward Fitzgerald*. She ran away from her first husband, Sir Charles Bunbury, the caricaturist, and the wretch afterwards redeemed herself and married Mr Napier—dusaristotokeia [unhappy mother of the noblest son] indeed, for she was the mother you know, of the three famous Napiers, and of one daughter, who married the present Sir Henry Bunbury, the nephew and heir of *her* first husband, a curious connexion. The Sir Joshua of her is famous, mater pulchra *progenies* pulchrior [beautiful mother of more beautiful offspring[166]]. The Horners found the two Napiers mounted on a chair, looking at their mother's picture. I wish you had been here to hear Mr Horner's interesting account of the allotments, but indeed they all missed you every moment. I hope you will see them at York. Mr Horner took your place with much grace and kindness, he always made Dr Fowler's ball rebound, though not, you know, originally interested in his subjects. He brought here such a book, Wicland, (the German's) view of Horace's character and odes,[167] he said he could not think now, how anybody could ever have understood Horace without it. I shall get it in London, and as there is no translation of it, it will be the proudest moment of my life to translate it to you, if you like to hear it.

Mrs Horner has the rare art of looking at her husband *en plafond*, without breaking the back of her neck. She is very graceful in her sim-

---

163 A reference to Martineau's cure from "mesmerism" or hypnotism, noted above.
164 Henry Edward Bunbury (1778-1860), 7th baronet, a democrat who voted for the Reform Bill in 1832, art collector and promoter of workers' welfare.
165 Portraits by Sir Joshua Reynolds (1723-92).
166 An allusion to Horace, "O mater pulchra filia pulchrior" [daughter lovelier than your lovely mother], ode 16, to Tyndaris, line 1.
167 Horace (65 BCE-8 BCE), Roman poet.

plicity. I never knew her before, one of those people who find words in their hearts which, without the pretension of enlightening, yet are like a clearing up. One never thinks of saying of her mind, that it has talent, but not either that it is without it, for it satisfies all contingencies without making itself remarked in any. She has that goodness, which does instead of lights, because it is real goodness, and therefore never does good when evil might come of it. She might reconcile almost anyone to marriage, from their loverlike attentions to one another. Yet I must say I shall be very glad when we are by ourselves again.

Grandmama will stay here till Wednesday. We see our two young people at Cromford Bridge every day. Poor Gale is no better, but Mama, I dare say, has told you all the news. We never had so much illness in the village and Mr Poyser is gone to York. I am very sorry, dear Papa, to have written you such a stupid letter, but I attended the funeral of my intellects last week, in the new and elegant "Patent Funeral Brougham, combining hearse and mourning coach in one vehicle, and constructed expressly for the interment of *children*," as my intellects were always infantile and am now in half mourning for myself.

I have done *Coningsby*[168] to Mama and do not think there is much in it. It is more fitful than inspired, more languid than pathetic. I do not think it is worthy of Mr Parker or Uncle Sam and, as to the third volume, talk of French novels to see what English ones are! Yet Mama did not seem at all scandalized by it. I suppose it is not improper *enough* for us. Do you remember where the not very unrespectable Mr Ormsby says, that he wanted to bet at White's that Lord Monmouth's marriage could not last two years, but he thought being his oldest friend, it was perhaps as well not to do it. That is English life. I think it is ten thousand times worse than anything that Italian history lets one into for there is none of the enthusiasm of vice in it, the poetry of wickedness, and it has not either even the hommage que le vice rend à la vertu, l'hypocrisie [the hommage vice pays to virtue, hypocrisy].

Farewell, dear Papa, I think I hear you sigh when you open this envelope, Here is another volume, or at least a pamphlet, of hers coming. . . . I know you hate my Reflections on Men and Manners,

---

168 The real Thomas Coningsby was Paymaster under William III and Lord Lieutenant of Ireland, but recalled. The novel makes a case for Tory party policy, with which the liberal Nightingales would have disagreed.

and I have tried to write a letter like a reasonable creature, without any moral sentiments, or immoral, but I am afraid the Ethiopian cannot change his skin[169] at least not at my time of life.

Dr Fowler asked me to come to Salisbury to read with him. He made me feel quite a sensible and agreeable woman while I was with him. Don't you know you sometimes meet with a person, who seems to finish all your half-formed thoughts for you, to be not so much a sympathizing friend, as the real companion of your pre-existence. One becomes sooner intimate than acquainted and one seems to hear not his, but one's own thoughts more definitely arranged and more clearly unfolded. A thousand obscure things seem to receive light, they utter words that make us think forever. He said many strange things, which immediately appeared to be true and seemed to condense in a sentence the secrets of life. And yet this man says, "I have been looking forward all my life to being blind, and laying up my stores for this time and now I find I have nothing to fall back upon."

I used to think it affectation, when people with incomparable memories complained of a bad one—you know Macaulay[170] does it—but I suppose that the nearer they come to the conception of what a memory *might be*, the more they perceive their own falling short of it, just as the peace of a good conscience is never for good people to feel, but only for bad ones. How I should like to be able to create; a writer, an artist of any sort must be well able to dispense with all other pleasures in the delight of creating—what an existence it must be in itself.

Source: Letter, Wellcome (Claydon copy) Ms 8992/122

Embley
27 January [1846]

Dear Papa

Your account of our old ladies was most flourishing; it is so refreshing to me to be with such a woman as Aunt Evans, who never formularized her feelings, nor gave expression to her ideas, in this artistic age, when we find more pleasure in the expression than in the feeling itself. Speaking is more like my dog Teazer, who says, I must evaporate. It works off all our thoughts and feelings. Out of the effervescence, not the "abundance," of the heart the mouth speaketh, now.

---

169 An allusion to Jer 13:23.
170 Thomas Babington Macaulay (1800-59), 1st Baron Macaulay, historian, Liberal MP and family friend.

In this too highly educated, too little active age, the balance between theory and practice seems destroyed, the just connexion between knowledge and action lost sight of, the inspiration unacknowledged, which is to be sought in effort, even more than in thought, the actual addition to our store of *knowledge*, which is supplied by every *deed*, and the positive subtraction from thought, which a life of thinking suffers, not considered.

In the last century it does not appear, at least among women, to have been so. The education of the faculties, and their sphere of action, were in harmony and we hear consequently little, in poetry or fiction, of uneasiness or melancholy. In this century we have advanced the standard of the one (theory) without that of the other (action) for man cannot move both feet at once, except he jump and he now seems to stand askew. May we not hope that, in the next century, without the one retrograding, the other may be brought up to stand alongside and the balance again restored.

But for this, trials must be made, efforts ventured; some bodies must fall in the breach for others to step upon. Failure is one of the most important elements of success, the failure of one to form a guidepost to others till, at last, dog comes who, having smelt all the other roads, and finding them scentless and unfeasible, follows the one which his master has gone before.

Why cannot a woman follow abstractions like a man? has she less imagination, less intellect, less self-devotion, less religion than a man? I think not. Yet she has never produced one single great work of art, or science or literature. She has never, with the exception perhaps of Deborah [in Judges], the Virgin and the Mère Angélique,[171] been deemed a fitting vessel for the Spirit of God. She has never received the spark of inspiration and, though she may have indirectly left the impress of her character on the world, yet nothing she has said or done has had a record in history and the Song of the Virgin Mary [Luke 1:46-55] remains the only expression of female feeling which has found its echo in every heart and every church. And why? Why is her frame never deemed a worthy house for the Spirit of Truth? nor hers a worthy tongue to proclaim the service of the Kingdom of Good, by which I mean the struggle with Evil? Is it not because *the habit* of never interesting herself much in any conversation, printed or

171 Mère Angélique, née Marie Arnauld (1591-1661), Convent of Port Royal; see *Theology*.

spoken, which is not personal, of making herself and her own feelings the subject of speculation (and what is the good of studying our own individuality, save as the reflection of the generality) of making all she says autobiographical, and being always in a moral tête à tête of considering her own experiences as the principal part of her life, renders her powerless to rise to any abstract good or general view. It cuts her wings, it palsies her muscles, and shortens her breath for higher things and for a clearer, but sharper, atmosphere, in which she has no lungs to live. She has fed on sugarplums, her appetite is palled for bread. . . .

ever, dear Papa
your affectionate child

Source: Letter, Wellcome (Claydon copy) Ms 8993/21

Wilton
Thursday [late 1840s]

Dear Papa

So those wretched Storers came out worse and worse. I am glad that the whole thing is to come out, but do not see that it at all follows that a chance ought not to have been given them. In the workings of Providence (which Sir J. Graham[172] says we are *not* to imitate, in which the few will be found to agree with him) chances are always allowed people till the very last. The evil seems to me to be far deeper, in the relations between landlord and tenant of the nineteenth century, not between those of any individual landlord and tenant. But that is too deep a subject for me to go into.

I had my usual quantum of interesting visiting in hospital and training school with Mrs Fowler, of metaphysical talk with the doctor, who is keen as ever and in his ninth decade, seems but to be growing *up* instead of growing *old*. I revert to my original faith that the hundredth year is the true maturity, to which the fiftieth is but the childhood, or rather that it is the time (so purposed by Providence at least) when the child sums up the lessons of today in order to prepare for the lesson of tomorrow. I find here, where I have adjourned today, a different world, not mine in truth, but one full of interest and goodness, not one where my calling could ever be, but which certainly has great callings and great objects in hand.

---

172 Sir James Graham (1792-1861), First Lord of the Admiralty and home secretary.

I find Sidney Herbert occupied in reforming the church, wanting to make all canons resident, to occupy themselves as schoolmasters of a country college, affiliated to Oxford and Cambridge, and to send up its undergraduates to the mother universities for examinations and honours, educating them cheap in country towns.

The dean and one canon [are] to have an ecclesiastical college for breeding young clergymen and training them upon poor people to their duties, whereby the characters of young men going up for ordination could be accurately known and spoken to. This is part of his plan; I will tell the rest anon. Mrs Herbert is charming as usual. The place would enchant you and Parthe. I hope to be home on Monday to welcome you home.

ever dear Papa

your loving child

Source: Letter dated 2 February, Candlemas Day [1849], as I witnessed it last year, I the Quirinal, Claydon House Bundle 124

Dear Papa

Everything here is in statu quo atmosphere like a warm bath, Empsons giving broth and blankets, two services, and if I ask it, to the old people, the sacrament. Farm account enormous, literature at a standstill. I never open a book, nor my mouth, except to victual it.

Oh my fair hopes! where are they? Now that the year is almost past, which began them, three there were, and where are they now? I *hoped* the old accustomed sins, the familiar friends of every man, children of the spirit of the time (Carlyle's definition of the devil) would be uprooted by a new time.

I *hoped* that, in the new ploughed soil, would be sown more easily the new crop of virtues and objects necessary for the nineteenth century's last half. I *hoped* for now or never the new life. Bah!

What's that wretched Sardinia about? What, in the name of wonder, is France about? I wish *1850* were a *political* year of jubilee as well as an *ecclesiastical* one, a year of the remission of all political sins—the acceptable year of the beginning of a new life.

Mama and I read the newspaper and the Bible and my phraseology, as my ideas, are equal parts of both. Very glad shall we be to see you home again, dear Papa.

ever your affectionate child

Editor: While there are several passionate and pleading letters to her mother and sister from Kaiserswerth, there is only one to her father, from the first trip, which makes the case for Kaiserswerth in a straightforward way, and also deals with an errand Nightingale ran for her father consulting an eye specialist near Kaiserswerth. A letter from Selina Bracebridge says that she is glad that Nightingale wrote her father, and hoped that he would answer "a direct *yes* or *no*," not leaving it for her to decide how long to stay; she hoped that Nightingale would see "that amputation case safe through."[173] The correspondence picks up again post-Kaiserswerth.

Source: Unsigned letter, Claydon House Bundle 124

Cologne
15 August [1850]

Dear Papa

I have been to see the oculist at Gräfrath. It is two hours from Düsseldorf, a small village crowded with English and patients from all countries. We had numbers given us to wait our turn. The crowd waiting was so great I began to despair, people having been kept there two days. But whom should I find there but Miss Lonsdale, daughter of the Bishop? She spoke a good word for me and I bolted boldly in when she came out. So interest and audacity succeed in this world. The man's sagacity is evident and his honesty. I know he refused Lady Pembroke's case. He said high spectacles and blue spectacles filled the oculist's patient room. He thinks that yours *is* a case of external, not internal inflammation, but he cannot judge without seeing the eyes.

He says that, if you chose to come, he does not think he need detain you more than a couple of days. He said with regard to delay, if it were internal mischief, delay would signify extremely, if it be external, as he suspects, it would not signify so much if you did not come till the spring. He thinks much can be done for it. I acknowledge that I don't think you could bear Gräfrath. It is on the road to Elberfeld, but you might stay at Düsseldorf or Elberfeld and go over via railroad and minibus, as I did.

I have had a delightful time at Kaiserswerth, spending two or three days in each department, so as to make myself as much acquainted with them as I could in that time. Trout took me there and brought me back. I stayed in the pastor's house. He is a man of a thousand, not agreeable, not interesting, but if you can fancy a Napoleon who has dedicated all his gifts to God, without a Napoleon's vanity, that is

---

173 Undated letter, Claydon House Bundle 40.

Fliedner's character. He directs this vast establishment with a most wonderful power of organization. I cannot tell you how much I thought of many of the sisters with whom I was in the closest contact, almost all out of the lower classes, and when I contrasted them with the seminarists, i.e., that normal school, though these were out of a higher class, I saw what power the having devoted all to God has in refining the intellect and giving grace to the character.

I am convinced now there *can* be Protestant charity as beautiful, as sensible, i.e., as well prepared and educated for its ends as Catholic. The infant school mistress is also a woman of first-rate talents and gifts. I did not think so much of the normal school, though Fliedner takes the most extraordinary personal pains with them. But the hospital, though poor and ugly and by no means a pattern of cleanliness, is with regard to all essential points, the Christian school it is for the patients, the humanizing, refining, propriety-teaching school, and the tender care of the nurses, it is indeed a model for England.

The "Frau Pastorin" [pastor's wife] has as singularly the gift of direction as her husband, which is so rarely the case. I met my dear people [the Bracebridges] again at half an hour from Kaiserswerth. I do not think him so much better as I expected but at Pyrmont he was so unwell that we found it impossible for both of us to leave him. We are going to Bourne [?] today to see if he would like it for the winter, but I hope we shall not be long now. I think before the end of next week I shall really be at home. I got all your letters at Düsseldorf, dearest people. Write to me at Ostende.

Source: Note on back of envelope addressed to W.E. Nightingale

I think Kaiserswerth quite all that I expected and a few months there would teach an Englishwoman all that is necessary if she had sense to apply it with the modifications necessary for England.

Source: Incomplete letter/draft/copy to W.E. Nightingale, Add Mss 45790 ff107-11

26 October [1850]

[begins abruptly] zealous to do good I would say, "Don't I advise you not, the higher your notion of what teaching is, the more you will be disgusted by what you do, unless you take pains to qualify yourself beforehand." When, on the one hand, I see the numbers of my kind who have gone mad for the want of something to do, people who might have been so happy, Miss Edmunds, Aunt Evans, Aunt Patty and, on the other hand, I see the tribes of unmarried women whose whole life is set upon doing good (with which the neighbourhood of Tapton particularly abounds) and who are actually doing harm, I remain in mute astonishment before so practical a nation, who has made a science of everything but the science of doing good, who has provided a training for every other profession but that of education. And my heart, to use David's language, longeth, nay thirsteth,[174] my flesh crieth out for the day when we shall all have the means given us for fulfilling that very *home* vocation, which people are so often wrongfully accused of wishing to neglect, when the fact is that they have so high an opinion of it that they cannot bear to rush blindfold into the mistakes which they see committed by their neighbours.

We have twice been up to see the dear little Hurst. It was looking beautiful, and I felt so sorry to leave it. I can fancy you now at home, glad to have left the house of mourning, indeed I should have felt the same, not knowing what on earth to do, say or look in such a crowd, because the ordinary life of servants waiting at dinner, people processioning two and two along the passage, is no preparation for seeing the truth, the whole truth of grief. You must either see the whole truth, or turn away your eyes from it altogether. I am so glad to be here in quiet, where I can think of the whole truth of the case, where it ceases to be mournful, in any sense that God can put upon the word mournful, where one sees more as God sees, instead of in a bustle where that becomes impossible.

I quite agree that with the poor Nicholsons, "grief must have its course." Indeed I pray that all may feel it deeply, for in feeling it deeply is the only comfort, the only truth. "My mission" there would be *not to distract* their thoughts, but to *help* them to dwell upon it, which is the only way in which you can feel *all*, and not the *mere* loss, which, in ten or, at most, twenty years, will be indifferent to all. "Time is the best comforter" is to me one of those most nauseous untruths, which I cannot imagine how people's common sense accepts. To dwell upon a thing, which you know will perish, which you hope will perish, namely the mere grief for a loss, is the most halfway measure, the most unsatisfactory thing. "Daughter of God and man, *immortal* Eve,"[175] let her look the whole case in the face, the facts that will not perish through all eternity.

Dear good Aunt sends you her best love and thanks for letting me be here, for which indeed I too am most thankful.

---

174 An allusion to Ps 42:2.
175 Milton, *Paradise Lost* 9 line 290.

Aunt Mai and I went last Sunday to Ebenezer Enlarged in Cromford[176] and we heard a better sermon, we both agreed, than we have heard for the last twenty years, very interesting, not at all exciting, very reasoning. Indeed I don't believe I have been able to listen to a sermon before for nearly that space of time. The Wesleyans have been progressing for the last thirty years, I imagine, if they have come to such doctrine as that. The church, I should think, has not. The singing was good and the prayer very good.

ever dear Papa

your loving and grateful child

Source: Unsigned, incomplete letter, Wellcome (Claydon copy) Ms 8993/35

Cromford Bridge

30 October [1850]

Very many thanks, dear Father mine, for the thought of *my* saint. When I shall see them all hanging up round my room, in their original glory, I shall say Sancte Michael Angele, ora pro me [Holy Angel Michael, pray for me] and think of you. My idea about such things is that, if they are what art is meant to be, they encourage, not incapacitate for "workaday life" and I have come so much to try art by this test that many who are set down as the highest artists by the world in general (such as Shakespeare, Titian,[177] Cimarosa,[178] Walter Scott) seem to me to have been mere artisans by the side of men whose *genius* bears no comparison with theirs.

Aunt Evans is quite joyous. I really believe that she has at this moment the spirits of a girl of sixteen, the pleasure of the change, of having the care of our dinners, of feeling that we are "comfortable" and like to be with her, and that Miss Hall has a rest, makes her quite frolicsome. I am sorry that you think my "telescope wants turning inwards." If anyone could see my heart, they would find written upon it, not "Calais," and not "Kaiserswerth" but "Qualify, qualify." My great ambition is to see before I die the means within the reach of every poor young woman for qualifying herself for the vocation of "home," for "ordinary habitation at home." In that eminently practical mind, the English, there seems to me here an extraordinary want of practicalness. She brings up her cler-

---

176 A Methodist chapel renowned for a woman preacher, Elizabeth Evans, who was the model for George Eliot's Dinah Morris in *Adam Bede*.

177 Vecellio Tiziano (c1485-1576), Venetian painter.

178 Domenico Cimarosa (1749-1801), composer.

gymen on Aristotle[179] and Aristophanes;[180] it is not perhaps extraordinary that she considers no training necessary for her Lady Bountifuls, her Sunday School teachers, but music and reading, yet she would resent the being thought to deal in this way with *other* pursuits.

A sister nation, most unpractical in politics, yet shows common sense in this. She supposes that, except a few heaven-born geniuses, people must learn to teach, be taught how to do good or they will, like ignoramuses in *other* things, do harm. I declare, if I had a daughter [breaks off]

Source: Letter, Wellcome (Claydon copy) Ms 8993/50

Dear Papa   1 December 1851

I doubt whether it is possible for even a water cure to produce any difference whatever at the end of one week. Is [Dr] Gully satisfied that you should try only a week and then come away? I stayed seven weeks and found little difference till after I came away. If it is the noise which you dislike, I think it would do me a great deal of good to have a little water cure after my measles, and I should like to come and take a little lodging with you very much, dear Papa, Mr Taylor having given his consent yesterday week that I should do everything as usual (except see Parthe).

We could also combine the conference to be held at Birmingham, on Wednesday week, on the best way of managing juvenile delinquency, and moving government to do something. All the practical and well-known men are to be there. Mr Bracebridge writes that it must have weight and is going himself. It is on the 10th in the morning. After this exploit, we might either come home or remain a little longer at Malvern, I being rather sure that less than three weeks is no trial at all.

ever dear Papa

your loving child

It is so cold that I can hardly move my fingers. Gladstone, Sydney Turner,[181] Hill,[182] Tufnell,[183] etc. are to be at the conference. I am quite in travelling order.

---

179 Aristotle (384-322 BCE), Greek philosopher.
180 Aristophanes (c445-c385 BCE), Athenian comic poet.
181 Sydney Turner (1814-79), Dean of Ripon and expert on young offenders.
182 Frederic Hill (1803-96), Inspector of Prisons.
183 Henry Tufnell (1805-54), Whig Cabinet minister.

Source: Copy of letter, Wellcome (Claydon copy) Ms 8993/85

Private   12 May 1852

My dear Father

On my thirty-second birthday I think I must write a word of acknowledgment to you. I am glad to think that my youth is past and rejoice that it never never can return, that time of follies and of bondage, of unfulfilled hopes and disappointed *in*experience when a man possesses nothing, not even himself. I am glad to have lived, though it has been a life which, except as the necessary preparation for another, few would accept. I hope now that I have made into possession of myself. I hope that I have escaped from that bondage which knows not how to distinguish between "bad habits" and "duties," terms often used synonymously by all the world. It is too soon to hallo before you are out of the wood. I like the Magdalen in Correggio's[184] picture, I see the dark wood behind, the sharp stones in front only with too much clearness, of clearness however there cannot be *too* much. But, as in that picture there is light. I hope that I may live, a thing which I have not often been able to say, because I think I have learnt something which it would be a pity to waste. I am ever yours, dear Father, in struggle as in peace, with thanks for all your kind care.

F.N.

When I speak of the disappointed inexperience of youth, of course I accept that not only as inevitable but as the beautiful arrangement of infinite Wisdom, which cannot create us gods, but which will not create us animals and therefore wills mankind to create mankind by their own experience, a disposition of perfect Goodness which no one can quarrel with. I shall be very ready to read you, when I come home, any of my "works" in your own room before breakfast, if you have any desire to hear them.

Au revoir, dear Papa.

Editor: Nightingale's father in 1853 arranged an annuity of £500 for her to permit her to become superintendent at the Institution for Ill Gentlewomen, 1 Upper Harley St., and live independently without the ignominy of salary.

---

184 Allegri Antonio Correggio (1494-1534), northern Italian painter.

Source: Letter/draft/copy, ADD Mss 45790 ff152-55

1 Upper Harley St.
3 December 1853

Dear Papa

You ask for my observations upon *my* time of statesmanship. I have been so very busy that I have scarcely made any résumé in my own mind. But, upon doing so now for your benefit, I perceive (1) when I entered into service here I determined that, happen what would, I *never* would intrigue among the committee. Now I perceive that I do all my business by intrigue. I propose in private to A., B. or C. the resolution I think A., B. or C. most capable of carrying in committee and then leave it to them. And I always win.

I am now in the heyday of my power. At the last general committee they proposed and carried (without my knowing anything about it) a resolution that I should have £50 per month to spend for the house, and wrote to the treasurer to advance it me. Whereupon I wrote to the treasurer to refuse it me.

Lady Cranworth,[185] who was my greatest enemy, is now, I understand, trumpeting my fame through London. And all because I have reduced their expenditure from 1/10 per head per day to 1/. The opinions of others concerning you depend not at all or very little upon what *you* are but upon what *they* are. Praise and blame are alike indifferent to me, as constituting an indication of what myself is, though very precious as the indication of the other's feeling. My popularity is too great to last. At present I find my committee only too easy to manage, but if they could be so taken in by my predecessor!

Last general committee, I executed a series of resolutions on five subjects and presented them as coming from the medical men: (1) that the successor to our house surgeon (resigned) should be a dispenser and dispense the medicines *in* the house, saving our bill at the druggist's of £150 per annum; (2) a series of house rules, of which I sent you the rough copy; (3) a series of resolutions about not *keeping* patients, of which I send the foul copy;[186] (4) a complete revolution as to diet which is shamefully abused at present; (5) an advertisement for the institution, of which I send the foul copy. All these I proposed and carried in committee, without telling them that they came from *me*

---

185 Lady Laura Rolfe Cranworth, member of the management committee.
186 In the years before photocopiers, or even typewriters and carbon paper, people used to write out a clean "fair copy" as the final document, so that a "foul" copy is an earlier draft.

and not from the medical men. Then, and not till then, I showed them to the medical men, without telling *them* that they were already passed *in committee*. It was a bold stroke, but success is said to make an insurrection into a revolution.

The medical men have had two meetings upon them, and approved them all, nem. con. [no one contrary], and thought they were their own. I came off with flying colours, no one suspecting my intrigue which, of course, would ruin me, were it known, as there is as much jealousy of the committee of one another and of the medical men of one another, as ever Napoleon had of Wellington, or what's his name of Marlboro?[187]

I have also carried my point of having good harmless Mr Garnier, our parish clergyman, as chaplain and no young curate as chaplain to have spiritual flirtations with my young ladies. So much for the earthquakes in this little molehill of ours.

Lady Monteagle,[188] Lady C. Murry and Lady C. Russell are my standing committee for this month. The S. Herberts are gone to Wilton.

ever dear Pa

your loving child

Source: Unsigned, incomplete letter/draft/copy, ADD Mss 45790 f157

1 Upper Harley St.
22 February 1854

Dear Papa

I am sorry to say that the information I have concerning the morals and manners of the Gray's Inn Hospital is so bad (among the bad this the worst) that I should not feel inclined to assist it, if it were I. Of the Westminster, which I have always considered one of the best, though the poorest, I had a head nurse with me last night (a very admirable woman) and she told me that, in the course of her long life's experience at the *Westminster* Hospital she had never known a nurse who was not drunken, and that there was *immoral* conduct practised within the very walls of the ward, of which she gave me some awful instances. So much for our moral boards. That this impinges the *principle* of hospitals I cannot think. Without hospitals, where would be our surgical sci-

---

187 John Churchill, 1st Duke of Marlborough (1650-1722), who won many battles for England on the Continent and in Ireland, was involved in many intrigues, dismissed from office and charged with various offences.

188 Baroness Elizabeth Monteagle, a family friend and member of the management committee.

ence? If you do away with hospitals you must, of course, do away with lunatic asylums, union houses and all the rest of the machinery of overpopulated civilization. [breaks off]

Source: Letter, ADD Mss 45790 ff158-59

[ca. April 1854]

I remember you were struck with Strauss's[189] comment on the tendency of some "to soar into the skies," instead of "mending" what is at hand. Man, says he, will never improve as he might, till he ceases to believe in a future state. But I believe there is, within and without human nature, a revelation of eternal existence, eternal progress for human nature. At the same time, I believe that to do that part of this world's work which harmonizes, accords with the idiosyncrasy of each of us, *is* the means by which we may *at once* render this world the habitation of the divine Spirit in man, and prepare for other such work in other of the worlds which surround us. The kingdom of heaven is within us.[190] Those words seem to me the most of a revelation, of a New Testament, of a gospel (of any that are recorded to have been spoken by our Saviour). Whether here, or elsewhere, then, *are not the conditions of a heavenly kingdom the same?*

I can only add that you misread me, if you thought by "crazy old place" I meant this world. I meant simply this poor little institution, No. 1 Upper Harley St. This world is not an old place, but a very young one.

ever, dear Pa

your loving child

F.N.

We have had an awful disappointment in a couching for a cataract,[191] which has failed. The eye is lost (through *no* fault of Bowman's[192]) and I am left, after a most anxious watching, with a poor blind woman on my hands, whom we have blinded, and with a prospect of insanity. I had rather, ten times, have killed her. These are the cases, not those like the poor German thing who died, which make *our* lives so anxious.[193]

---

189 David Friedrich Strauss (1808-74), German theologian. See *Theology*.

190 A paraphrase of Luke 17:21.

191 A procedure to remove a cataract by depressing the lens with a needle until it lies below the axis of vision.

192 William Bowman (1816-92), later Professor Sir, a distinguished ophthalmic surgeon, Nightingale ally and member of the Nightingale Fund Council.

193 Mathilde von Raven; for more on whom see p 809 below.

Source: Letter to W.E. Nightingale, Wellcome (Claydon copy) Ms 8995/30

Scutari
19 August 1855

"Oh that I had wings like a dove[194] and could look at your western skies for a night," I may well re-echo, Father dear. Our eastern skies, diversified as they are by the red glare of a fire at Constantinople, bringing painfully before one's imagination the fiery glare of our destroying war, which lights up our political night and the too-real fire of a night at near Sebastopol, our eastern skies are far less beautiful physically and morally.

If my name and my having done what I could for God and mankind has given my dearest father pleasure, that is real pleasure to me. The reputation (fashionableness I should call it) which has unexpectedly followed me has not been a boon to me in my work. But if *he* has been pleased, that is enough, I shall love my foolish name now and shall feel it to be my best reward that he can have satisfaction in hearing the name of the child he has educated repeated by others, drawing, I do believe, often sympathies together. If my work does that, I am sure he will feel *that* some return for what he has done for me.

If ever I live to see England again, the western breezes of my hilltop home will be my first longing, though Olympus, with its snowy cap, looks fair over our blue eastern sea. Who could believe less than I that I have been living for nine months within sight of it? Pray tell all my friends in Lea and Holloway who remember me that I often remember them amid the bustle and strife, less wearing *that* of landing 500 sick, as we did yesterday than of fighting, conciliating, persuading purveyors and commandants—Oh Gladstone and Herbert!

I have had a very kind letter from Lord Panmure.

F.N.

Source: Postscript to letter, Wellcome (Claydon copy) Ms 8995/74

Castle Hospital
Balaclava
14 November 1855

PRIVATE

Lord Raglan, in his last visit to me, asked me "if my father liked my coming out." I said with pride "my father is not as other men are—he thinks that daughters should serve their country as well as sons; he

---

194 Ps 55:6.

brought me up to think so—he has no sons and therefore he has sacrificed me to my country and told me to come home with my shield or upon it. He does not think (as I once heard a father and a very good and clever father say) "the girls are all I could wish, very happy, very attentive to me and very amusing." He thinks that God sent women, as well as men, into the world to be something more than "happy," "attentive" and "amusing." "Happy and *dull*" *religion* is said to make us "happy and *amusing*" . . . but my father's religious and social ethics make us strive to be the pioneers of the human race and let "happiness" and "amusement" take care of themselves.

Source: Letter, Wellcome (Claydon copy) Ms 8996/75

Scutari
17 July 1856

My dearest people

I cannot yet fix the day for coming home. It depends upon many things, not dependable upon myself. I am just working as hard as I can to get home. All I want is to get home quietly, without anybody knowing it. I shall take out my passport under the name of Smith. Lord Lyons has offered me passage to any port I like. Aunt Mai and Co. gone over to Stamboul [Istanbul] to the bazaar.

ever yours
F.N.

Source: End of letter and continuation on inside flap of envelope to W.E. Nightingale, Wellcome (Claydon copy) Ms 8997/7

Edinburgh
13 October 1856

With regard to the Derby Infirmary, I doubt much whether I could do anything at it for the next four months. Just starting for Balmoral.[195] Dear Papa, I hope you are better.

ever yours
F.N.

I wish you would be President of the Derby Infirmary.

---

195 To see Queen Victoria, the Prince Consort and Lord Panmure to urge the establishment of a royal commission on the errors of Crimea.

Source: Letter, Wellcome (Claydon copy) Ms 8997/32

30 Old Burlington St.
20 March 1857

Dearest Pa

I am sorry that you will not enter the House of Commons in this world, but I am very sure that there is a House of Commons in the next, I hope one upon sounder principles. If *that* world is in advance of *this*, it must be. If not, we must go and "prepare a place" for them.[196] Do you believe that God's word is *not* "pray" but "work." Do you believe that He stops the fever, in answer not to "from plague, pestilence and famine, good Lord, deliver us,"[197] but to His word and thought being carried out in a drain, a pipe tile, a wash house? Do you believe that mortality, morality, health and education are the results of certain conditions which He has imposed? Then you must believe that Houses of Commons, or similar institutions, are far more certain than churches to exist in all worlds till we become like God.

I will write again, but I can now only ask whether you are likely to be in town soon, as the election is contested in Derbyshire, as I am going to Chatham to see the hospitals there and would put it off till you came, if you do.

ever dear Pa
your loving child
F.N.

Source: Incomplete draft/copy to W.E. Nightingale, ADD Mss 45790 ff177-79

30 Old Burlington St., W.
23 March 1857

When I left England for Scutari, little expecting ever to see my dear father again, I left for him words true then and true now, that I loved him as I never loved any but him. I need not say more to express how deeply I must feel the affection and the confidence of the letter before me. It would have been dear to me to see you where truth and honesty, such as yours, are desperately wanted, in an English House of Commons.[198] But let us not waste regret on the impossible.

With regard to health, let me say that I do not always agree with you as to the desirableness, even for health's sake, of giving up one

---

196 An allusion to John 14:2.
197 From the litany, Book of Common Prayer.
198 W.E. Nightingale ran once for Parliament, in 1835. See *Society and Politics*.

and another object of interest, because there might, in pursuing it, be some bodily suffering, some temporary loss of health.

I rather think health *gains*, on the whole, from following up true and good interests, even when it loses at times and for a time. But, unless at an age when habits of life have to be formed, it would be clearly unwise to enter upon a *course of life*, destructive of the health necessary to pursue it well. So we will not give a regretful look to the House of Commons *in this world*. Yes, in futurity there will be a House of Commons in the real sense of the phrase. Of this I think I could bring moral evidence, as well as evidence that, in this futurity, the experience learnt *here* may be available.

But, before this futurity opens upon us, let us work while it is called today.[199] To my father's active spirit two populations afford scope *for* work. To his sincere desire after what is true and wise, a world full of error and confusion (which it is for mankind, progressively, to clear up and enlighten) affords much to be borne in the spirit of a true philosophy. As I receive, amidst cares and difficulties all but appalling, soothing and comfort from the confidence and affection of my father, may he find, in my true love and sympathy, something of that peace and hope which, with my whole heart, I, F.N., desire for him.

Source: Letter/draft/copy, Wellcome (Claydon copy) Ms 8997/75

30 Old Burlington St.
8 October 1858

Dear Papa

I think this school affair such a brilliant opportunity of introducing civilization instead of brutality that I have done a daring thing—I wrote to Rawlinson[200] yesterday (he who sanitarized the Crimea and Scutari), the first water engineer of the age and saw him this morning. He was going down to the Liverpool meeting on Monday and said directly that he would sleep at Lea Hurst on Monday and do your business for you. He is quite the first authority in sanitary water appliances and has an enthusiasm for all these things. Any fee *I* will settle with him afterwards. Pray forgive him for murdering the Queen's

---

199 An allusion to John 9:4.

200 Robert Rawlinson (1810-98), later Sir, civil engineer and member of the sanitary commission which made the extensive renovations to the Barrack Hospital at Scutari, and with whom Nightingale worked for decades. See *Hospital Reform* for their correspondence.

English. I think it is so creditable to him; he was the son of a private soldier.

Let Beatrice ask him how it is possible to give boys and women an enthusiasm for keeping their own out-offices clean and he will tell her. Let him tell her about Alnwick. He will go down on Monday by the train which reaches Ambergate at 2:30. I promised he should be met there. I thought Mama would do it in her daily drive—it saves strength and health. His is bad and he must go on to Liverpool on Tuesday. Nevertheless, if you do not like it, could you send a message to the Ambergate Station Master to tell Mr Rawlinson to go on to Cromford and that he will be fetched there?

Not having time for a reply from you, I have settled these things with him. He is a man whom I like and respect far more than anyone I met in the Crimea except Sir J. McNeill—far, far more than Sutherland. He has a passion for art and the country, so will be very easy for Mama to talk to. He would like very much to see the country.

With regard to the appliances, please tell Beatrice that I do not think expense must be considered. From a long experience of large bodies of men, I know that the best things are the cheapest in the end. And I should be very glad to take my share in the expense of proper appliances.

ever dear Pa

your loving child

F.

Source: Letter, Wellcome (Claydon copy) Ms 8997/76

30 Old Burlington St
9 October 1858

Dear Papa

A fear came over me that I had expressed myself as if Rawlinson were a kind of foreman and that you would not know where he was to dine or sleep. (*He sleeps with you on Monday night.*) He is just as much a gentleman as you or I. And I know I shall have all kinds of difficulties in making him take a fee, although I expressly told him that I could only consult him professionally and that no pay, no advice.

He has ruined himself forever with the War Department by standing up for the pay of the workmen and foremen who were sent out to the Crimea under the orders of the Sanitary Commission, although Sutherland, who was at the head of that commission, ought to have taken this upon himself. I do not blame Sutherland. He has it not in him to do that kind of thing. But no one, who has not been so much mixed up with professional life as I have, can know *how few* have it in them, *how few* will, for the sake of right, lay themselves open to being called what Lord Panmure called me, a "turbulent fellow."

I commend Mr Rawlinson to your utmost kindness. I also assure you that his authority in all water matters is quite the first in the United Kingdom and may be safely depended upon.

ever dear Pa

your loving child

F.

Source: Letter, Wellcome (Claydon copy) Ms 8998/28

> 30 Old Burlington St.
> London, W.
> 12 July 1860

Dear Pa

The "International Statistical Congress" (of which I am a member and for which I write papers) meets in London today and for the next ten days. Delegates from every civilized country come. QUETELET is the Belgian one. They meet at my rooms a good deal for business (I, of course, not seeing them) under Dr Farr's presidency, and I am obliged to give them to eat. Lord Mayors, H.M.'s ministers, Prince Albert and all the institutions of the country also give them to eat (but *not*, I suspect, for business).

Now I want you to send me all your flowers, all your fruit, all your vegetables, in fact *all* you have got, for this great occasion, which is to "cement the peace of Europe"!!!! Also, oatcake or anything you think, of our savage productions will do to show our "distinguished" foreigners. If you did not dislike travelling, I should almost have thought it worth your while to run up and chatter French and Italian to them here, and take a brace of them back with you.

ever dear Pa

your loving child

F.

Editor: It is not known whether the following letter was sent (the source is Nightingale's own files).

Source: Letter/draft/copy, ADD Mss 45790 ff196-98

[printed address] 30 Old Burlington Street, W.

4 April 1861

Dear Papa

I was obliged to see Saunders (the dentist) today for myself. So I asked him about things in general. He says it is of the utmost importance, if people intend to have false teeth at all, to have them AS SOON *as possible* after the last tooth has fallen out. Otherwise the *muscles* of the jaw contract and there is no end to the trouble caused. The muscles do not contract *after* they are accustomed to the false teeth which support them. This is according to common sense.

You compare art and hospitals (justly): their present low ebb, the prospect of a future. Dearest, *no one* has a right to speak of "the future" who has done nothing to prepare it. What I could, with quite moderate talents, I have done, with regard to hospital construction. As far as that is concerned, I can lie down and confidently see a future for the germ I have sown, though I shall not live to know it. But what have you, with far greater talents, done for art? In what way have you prepared anything of a future? Unless I am to believe M Jeanron[201] a fool or a knave, I must believe that you could, *that you can now*, do much for that future. Have you even begun "to *walk*"? This is an allusion to a speech of Dr Walter's. I asked him whether I should ever be able to go to India. He said, had you not better first be able to walk?

I have never seen *you* even try "to walk." Had you not better begin now? There is still time.

F.N.

Editor: The next few letters deal with a proposal for Nightingale to move to an apartment in Kensington Palace, at the invitation of Queen Victoria, a subject of vexed correspondence also with the Verneys (below).

Source: Letter/draft/copy, ADD Mss 45790 ff199-200

[printed address] 30 Old Burlington Street, W.

20 April 1861

Dear Papa

If I must answer the offer you mention, it would be thus: that I have to see a great variety of people on a great variety of subjects, and that no *residence* could be of any use to me which was not near enough to

---

201 Philippe-Auguste Jeanron, art historian, a Paris acquaintance.

the official centre of London to enable me *during the business season* to see these people at a moment's notice and without deranging them from their avocations, they being all business people. Such sun, quiet and air as are consistent with this condition, of course I must have.

The worst that could come of this answer would be the repetition of the offer of Kensington. But I should never accept it, *except for the autumn* and early winter months. (They have royal residences nearer than Kensington but I am sure I should not ask for them.) I may as well mention as an accessory which would tell with you more perhaps than with me that Sir James Clark, Drs Williams and Sutherland all said that experience had proved that I must never spend another winter at Hampstead or be there later than the beginning of December (I agree with them). Now Kensington Palace is certainly *worse* than Hampstead. I think W. Cowper[202] thinks that I have retired from business or am in the bankrupt line.

ever your child

F.

Source: Letter/draft/copy, ADD Mss 45790 ff201-04

[printed address] 30 Old Burlington Street, W.

22 April 1861

Dear Papa

It requires only an explanation of my work for anyone to see (without farther talk) that I may as well give it up at once as go to a place different by eight miles nearly (to and fro) from this, *qua* Whitehall. The proposition made, as I learn from the Board of Trade, was to find me an apartment *which would suit me* in one of the royal residences. Without the slightest communication with me, the Verneys pitch upon Kensington. When once Mrs Herbert was setting forth to me her views upon hospital nursing I exclaimed, quite involuntarily, What *can* you know about it? Does Parthe know more about my work than Mrs H. about hospitals? Where should I have been now in any part of my life's work, had I followed any part of her life's advice? It would not appear to me so extraordinary, had they disposed of me in marriage, as their disposing of me in my habitation. No more than man is made for the sabbath[203] am I made for the *house*.

---

202 William Francis Cowper (1811-88), later Baron Mount-Temple, held many Cabinet posts.

203 A paraphrase of Mark 2:27.

The "sanitarians," though this is a secondary matter, persist in saying that Kensington Palace is very unhealthy, that it is as little fitted for my change of air, in comparison with Hampstead, as I say it is little fitted for my business residence. I have consulted one or two of my collaborators, under the strictest seal of secrecy and, contrary to my expectation, which was that they would shilly-shally, they said at once it would "shelve my work altogether" to go to Kensington.

Believe me, dear Papa, what success in life I have had is due to my not seeing double with my eyes as so many do. Remember that Sir H. bought me a horse at the very time he was assured that my ever riding again on horseback was just as possible as that a man's leg which had been cut off should grow again.

ever dear Pa

your loving child

F.

I cannot see how Sir H. having been Colonel Phipps's[204] school fellow makes him competent as my advisor.

Source: Letter/draft/copy, Add Mss 45790 ff217-21

Hampstead NW

21 August 1861

Dear Papa

Indeed your sympathy is very dear to me. So few people know in the least what I have lost in my dear master. Indeed I know no one but myself who had it to lose. For no two people pursue together the same object as I did with him and when they lose their companion by death, they have in fact lost no companionship. Now he takes my life with him. My work, the object of my life, the means to do it, all in one depart with him.

"Grief fills the room up of my absent" master.[205] I cannot say it "walks up and down" with me. For I don't walk up and down. But it "eats" and sleeps and wakes with me. Yet I can truly say that I see it is better that God should not work a miracle to save Sidney Herbert, although his death involves the misfortune, moral and physical, of five hundred thousand men, and although it would have been but to set aside a few trifling physical laws to save him. . . .

---

204 Sir Charles Beaumont Phipps (1801-66), secretary to Queen Victoria.

205 Sidney Herbert died 2 August; paraphrase from Shakespeare, *King John* Act 3, scene 4.

"The righteous perisheth and no man layeth it to heart." The scripture goes on, "none considering that he is taken away from the evil to come."[206] *I* say "none considering that he is taken away from the good he might have done." Now, not one man remains (that I can call a man) of all those whom I began work with, five years ago. I alone, of all men "most deject[ed] and wretched," survive them all. I am sure I meant to have died.

Pray be careful how you write this heavy news. For Bertha has not been very well and they keep it from her. The news was only received at Combe this morning.

ever dear Pa

your loving child

F.

Parthe has found time and strength to write me eight closely written pages of worry, worry, worry, because I said that *her* house was "devoted" to "talk." I cannot think who could have told her that I said so. I hope, dear Papa, that it is quite understood between us that my letters to you are *for you alone.* I always thought that you desired this as much as I do. It is indeed quite necessary. This is the reason why I was so unwilling to come into any house of Parthe's, to accept any obligation from her. This is the *third* time this fatal year that she has chosen my time of deepest misery and distress to give me a scold eight pages long.

Source: Incomplete unsigned letter, Wellcome (Claydon copy) Ms 8999/48

32 South St.

22 December 1861

Dear Papa

Would you kindly send up a box of Christmassy hollies, with berries (if there are any), evergreens and what flowers you can, to dress a Christmas tree for the child patients at King's College Hospital? Mrs Watson has so much taste that she would choose them. I think if Mrs Burton would send up some mince pies I could find some clients whom they would not hurt. The box had better come here and then I will send it on. It ought to set out on Tuesday the 24th. Nothing will come amiss. (The tortoiseshell kitten is gone to this hospital.) I should like *somebody* to enjoy this sad, sad Christmas of this miserable year, which has broken so many hearts, already too heavy laden.

---

206 An allusion to Isa 57:1.

My dear Clough![207] I should like you to know that he said to me with regard to you (he who so seldom used strong expressions): "we ought to *pray* for your father's life"! He said this in allusion to the management of the people of Lea Hurst and Embley. He felt so strongly the shortcomings of all the Sam Smiths, except Beatrice, though he had a very high opinion of Shore's *nature*. . . .

Source: Undated letter, Wellcome (Claydon copy) Ms 8999/53

[c1861]

Dear Papa

I say nothing about myself. It would have done me so much good to have had one drop of sympathy. I, who for four years have never heard one word of feeling from my own family, though I am sure they have never seen anyone strained to the utmost pitch of endurance of body and mind as I am.

Adieu.

F.N.

Source: Dictated, unsigned letter to W.E. Nightingale, ADD Mss 45790 ff271-72

Sunday, 23 March 1862

"Father to me thou art, and brother dear, and mother too, kind husband of my heart" (Andromache's parting address to Hector in the sixth book of the Iliad).[208] The poet[209] then goes on to draw the parallel between this and our relation to God, and ends with:

Thou art as much His care, as if than thee
Nor man nor angel lived upon this earth.

Dear Papa, I wanted to have sent you the whole of these lines, but I can't find the book, because I think they are an accurately true description of God's "tendresse à mon égard," but then I would not say "au lieu de" but "together with" his bienfaisance universelle [universal goodness]. The eternal laws are as much constructed in the view of and for the good of every one of us as if every one of us were the sole being upon this earth, but then you see that is nonsense

---

207 Who died in November.

208 Homer, *Iliad* 6.450. Andromache asked Hector to have pity on her and their child, in effect to take fewer risks (she had lost seven brothers in a battle before, in which also her mother was killed). Hector declined, realizing the possibility of her being taken slave; he died a hero.

209 The poet is not Homer but John Keble (1792-1866), who began his poem by quoting the *Iliad*. Entry for the Monday before Easter, *Christian Year*.

because the public good is the good of each one of us or, as Plato said: "Common sense is the sense of the common interest," and the common interest is the interest of each one of us. It all turns to the same thing.

I send you the great man's "Hey diddle diddle" because I was too weary to get up and look for the trash last time. Please return to me. It is a great thing to have trash sent us by a secretary of state.[210]

I think you would like an article on "La Suisse chrétienne," including Rousseau, by your old friend Taillandier, in the *Revue des deux mondes* of 15 March.[211]

Please send me back my letter to you upon this house, for I mean to send it to Mrs Bracebridge, who knows Mrs Plumer Ward and is so sharp that she'll find some way of letting her see it. Also, if I live to write another edition of my *Notes on Nursing* I mean to put it in there. I was very glad to hear from Mr Brench [?] that my description of a nuisance [garbage] at the Burlington in my first *Notes on Nursing* had been recognized and had very much injured the Burlington.

Source: Partial draft/copy to W.E. Nightingale, ADD Mss 45790 ff280-81

9 C. Street
23 May 1862

Private

I must tell you the first joy I have had since poor Sidney Herbert's death. Lord Palmerston has forced upon Sir G. Lewis the reorganization of the War Office, which follows from the non-filling up of Hawes's place as deputy secretary, and the appointment of Galton in his other place (modified) called ASSISTANT under secretary. Sir George Lewis has this day written it to the Queen, Galton resigning the Army of course.

F.N.

. . . Tell Kingsley[212] that the Protestant doctrine, namely that to be disappointed in love or in search of a love is THE qualification for a good nurse or "sister" (advocated by him[213] and triumphantly vindicated in

---

210 Presumably the "Latin jeux d'esprit" of the secretary of state for war in a letter to her mother 7 March above.

211 Saint-René Taillandier, "La suisse chrétienne et le dix-huitième siècle" 420-67.

212 Charles Kingsley (1819-75), priest, Christian socialist and novelist.

213 In his novel, *Two Years Ago*, the heroine goes to nurse in the Crimea hoping to find the doctor she loves; for an excerpt see *Society and Politics*.

practice by Mrs Teresa Longworth[214]) has been for the first time, as far as I know, in *Roman Catholic* literature, stated in a Roman Catholic novel, AD 1861, but it is by an English pervert [convert].

Kingsley's doctrine that the *highest* life is two in one and one in God, I should think, is denied by no Protestant but Miss Sellon.[215] It is incalculable the mischief his other doctrine does, as I can *practically* testify. You would not expect a man to accept or value a woman's love very highly on the *rejected* plan, yet it is thought such a good reason for God to accept it. Yet He does NOT. These women make infamous nurses.

F.N.

Source: Letter/draft/copy to W.E. Nightingale, ADD Mss 45790 ff282-85

9 C. St., W
Poor Queen's birthday
[24 May 1862]

Lord Palmerston has forced Sir G. Lewis to carry out Sidney Herbert's and my plan for the reorganization of the War Office *in some measure*, that is, by "taking in" Sir G. Lewis's ignorance and idleness. Hawes's place is not to be filled up. Galton is to do his work as "assistant under secretary." This brings with it some other reforms. Lord de Grey says that he can reorganize the War Office with Captain Galton, *because* Sir G.L. will know nothing about it and never inquires. Sir G.L. wrote it (innocently) to the Queen yesterday. . . .

No, Sir C. Trevelyan would not have done at all. It would have been perpetuating the principle (which I have been fighting against in all my office life, i.e., eight years) of having a dictator, an autocrat, irresponsible to Parliament, quite unassailable from any quarter, irremovable, in the middle of a (so-called) constitutional government and under a secretary of state who *is* responsible to Parliament. Inasmuch as Trevelyan is a better and abler man than Hawes, it would have been *worse* (for any reform of principle).

---

214 Maria Theresa Longworth (1832-81), who nursed with the Soeurs de la Charité in the Crimean War, became engaged to William Yelverton (later Viscount Avonmore) at Galata Hospital. The two were later married but Yelverton subsequently claimed that the marriage was not valid and married another woman. Longworth lost her lengthy court battles to have the marriage declared legal, exhausting her financial resources.

215 Priscilla Lydia Sellon (1821-76), founder of the Anglican order, Sisters of Mercy of Devonport.

I don't mean to say that I am the first person who have laid down this. But I do believe I am the first person who have felt it so bitterly, keenly, constantly, as to give up life, health, joy, congenial occupation, for a thankless work like this. Nunc dimittis servam tuam, Domine [Now let thy servant[216] depart, Lord].

No "reform" was to be expected from Trevelyan. On the contrary, he would have confirmed the dictatorship. And, with an idle master like Lewis, he would have been an absolute (though wise) despot. It has come too late to give happiness to Galton, as it has come too late for me. He seems more depressed than pleased. And, I do believe, if he feels any pleasure, it is that now he can carry out Sidney Herbert's plans in some measure.

"Poor Florence, our work unfinished" was his last prayer, his last εὐχή [wish]. How often I have said to God, "O remember his prayer, his last prayer, O God." In this sense (as εὐχή) prayer is no doubt true. I do not mean that God alters His mind, but I HAD done all I could to bring about the εὐχή.

It may seem to you some compensation for the enormous expense I cause you that, if I had not been here, it would not have been done. Would that Sidney Herbert could have lived to do it himself. Would that poor Clough could have lived to see it. He wished for it so much, for my sake. Had Hawes, that worthless profligate, died but one twelvemonth sooner, I do believe it would have saved Sidney Herbert's life, as it would certainly have saved the most fatal error Sidney Herbert ever committed.

Poor Mrs Herbert spent the afternoon here yesterday. She had only come home the day before. The poor little great nobleman[217] is at Eton, eleven years old, £60,000 a year. The old scamp [the previous Lord Pembroke] left £100,000 to that woman at Paris. There is not a farthing of ready money anywhere, but a great debt, which Mrs Herbert has to pay. Her six younger children are almost without a provision. It is not quite certain yet whether Wilton falls into chancery. I trust they will, if it does, give her [Elizabeth Herbert] a large allowance and that she will have courage to save for the younger children. I cannot help repeating that there is a great "*fond*" of justice and magnanimity in her.

---

216 A paraphrase of Luke 2:29. Nightingale has put the usual masculine form for "thy servant," servum tuum, into the feminine.

217 Sidney Herbert's son succeeded to the title Earl of Pembroke on his uncle's death, only shortly after his father's death.

I am always first with her because I was first with him. My claim to be consulted, to be informed, is always recognized. It is this which I think our family so singularly deficient in. They recognize NO claim. Had I never known poor Clough I could not have been treated more as a stranger in his death.

Hampden is come, not Savonarola yet. My admiration of Savonarola is mainly this: that he was the ONLY religious teacher I know of who distinctly recognized the duty, as a religious duty and claim, of every citizen to aid in forming a free government. It is most extraordinary that England, the most political nation in the world, has never recognized this in any form as a part of religion. God is an old woman who does not understand much about politics and has nothing to do with the House of Commons.

If Hookham [a book dealer] gets the right edition (and I have told him to write to Florence for it—he says he can't get it in London) I will show you in Savonarola's *Trattato circa il governo di Firenze*[218] (which *is* in the edition of Audin di Rians), a passage which I think beats all statesmanship and moral philosophy of the present day. It is to the effect that God has expressly left imperfection for men to work out perfection *for themselves* (by His laws) in *government of states* as in other things. . . .

ever dear Pa

your loving child

Please send this to Mrs Bracebridge at Atherstone, by next post. I have no power to write (what it is her right to know) and my joy to tell her.

Source: Letter, Wellcome (Claydon copy) Ms 9000/71

26 October 1862

Dear Papa

. . . As to the "soft water" at South St., boiling will always get rid of a certain amount of hardness and chemists *distil.* During my illness at South St. I always got my soft water (distilled) from Savory and Moore's, but distilled water, you see, costs money. (Sir James Clark never lets the Queen use any other nor would I, if I had the ordering of home boilers.)

As to your hypotheses, you see I don't know that one of them exists. A "tank for rain water," I conclude, does *not* exist. For, although Parthe's Mrs Williamson (the charwoman) would tell any amount of

---

218 Probably *Poesie di Ierolamo Savonarola,* illustrate e pubblicate per cura di Audin de Rians. For excerpts see *Theology.*

lies to save herself trouble, I don't know why she should tell us that. So I suppose it will end, as most things do, by my seeing Humphrey myself, when I go into South St., and having a rain waterpipe put in, also in having Mrs Walker's sitting room whitewashed where, she tells me, the rain has come in and spoilt the ceiling.

Yes, I have always thought the Hindu philosophers have done just what I would *not* do, viz., speculated about the nature, neglected the character, of God. I believe M Mohl would tell you that the Hindu metaphysics are the first in the world, their moral philosophy the last, or rather none at all. Brahmanism appears to me the most monstrous of all the despot priesthoods, with no God at all, Buddhism a beautiful social reform, but also without any idea of a perfect God. I see your Dr Perfitt[219] still preaches in Newman St.

ever your loving child

F.

Source: Letter/draft/copy, ADD Mss 45790 ff310-11

4 C. Row, S.W.

19 March 1863

Dear Papa

A thousand and more thanks for your willingness to buy me a permanent house to myself. But it was only a raid of Parthe's such as she ran two years ago to make me accept the Queen's offer of apartments, such as she runs about every two years. However, she has yielded to my reasons with good humour, and I am grateful to my friends, in my humbled state, even for ceasing to trouble with good humour.

I have often said the Christ of the present day is not efficiency in good—it is good humour. I believe I am beginning to be thankful for it myself, and to be glad when I get no worse. I wish I could say all's well that ends well. But these raids take a terrible deal out of me. Everybody seems to think me a convenient subject to make a raid on. Do not (a burnt child fears the fire and I have been so burnt that I have ceased to trust my nearest friend), do not let Parthe suppose that I speak of her well-meant efforts thus.

ever dear Pa

your loving child

F.

219 Philip William Perfitt, Theists' Free Church, Newman St.

To me it seems simple madness to talk about buying a house in town for *me*, unless it were something which was such a catch it would be worth having anyhow.

Source: Letter, Wellcome (Claydon copy) Ms 9000/107

30 June 1863

Dear Papa

What a loss is Sir J. Jebb. To me he was the true cast of hero, saint and martyr. He was the last of our set. There are none like him, no, not one,[220] left behind to take his place. . . . I have written to poor Lady Amelia [Jebb], for I think none but myself can know what her loss is. I have lost in less than two years the two chairmen and the secretary of my little Nightingale Fund. Would that that were all the loss in them! But Sir J. Jebb looked on the criminals as an ill-used race, whose salvation he was to work out.[221] Where shall we find that generous confidence now. . . .

Would you send me up my *Sylvia's Lovers*, by Mrs Gaskell,[222] which Parthe took to Embley?

ever dear Pa

your loving child

F.

Source: Letter, Wellcome (Claydon copy) Ms 9001/39

28 June 1864

Dear Papa

I was greatly disappointed not to hear from you, either today or yesterday, the smallest hint as to what you would like to do if I failed in getting you a room in this street. There is not a room to be had either in hotel or lodging house, in Park St., for love or money. And as I could not now hear from you in answer to this, till Thursday (besides which you never do answer by return of post) and on Thursday there would not be the slightest chance of getting you a room by Saturday—I have empowered the mistress of the Grosvenor Hotel to get you a room in Coburg Hotel, Charles St. or in a lodging house near, Peter [his servant] to have a room near you, you to have your meals here from the Grosvenor, Peter at the Grosvenor.

---

220 An allusion to Rom 3:12.
221 An allusion to Phil 2:12.
222 Elizabeth Gaskell (1810-65), family friend and author of *Sylvia's Lovers*.

But this might be arranged otherwise, if you like it, and if you will only write. I could have got you a room in Portman Square, but I did not know whether you would like to go so far. And you do not give me the least hint *how* far you would like to go, if I failed in Park St. If the worst comes to the worst, there is always Ann Clarke's room here to fall back upon. But the partitions are so thin that this house is exactly like only one room to live in. I hear all Ann C. does, as if she were sleeping in my room, though it is on another floor.

London is crowded on account of this great debate. Since I have been in public life, I have heard nothing so sickening as the run in favour of Denmark—that a free, strong country like England should unite to crush out/wrest all freedom from those two wretched little duchies [Schleswig-Holstein]! And all from the frivolity of Palmerston. A more masterly exposition in favour of *wrong* than his last night surely never was.

ever dear Pa
your loving child
F.

Source: Incomplete letter, Wellcome (Claydon copy) Ms 9001/68

Hampstead, N.W.
12 October 1864

Oh dear Papa, you are come south and you never told me. Oh how could you? I have not heard one word from you for upwards of a month. Do you mean to come and see me? Do you not? Not one word.

But, what is worse, Mrs Sutherland has been in all the agonies of finding me a house. I have been daily waiting to hear from you, and yesterday we ought to have decided. As I mentioned to you, I am quite too feeble now for the move in January, and therefore have given up going to the dear South St., if another could be found. Besides which *against* South St. is the great difficulty of finding a house in the third week of January. You know, two out of the three times I have been there, once I had to go to a hotel for six weeks and to have a second move in March, once I had to go to a hotel and could not move again at all. If then I could find a suitable house now it seemed madness to give up the chance, knowing I should not have it again in January.

Poor Mrs Sutherland has, as usual, literally turned herself into a cab and house agent for me. There is to be had 27 Norfolk St., which is beautiful and noisy, 1 Bolton Row, which is stabley and quiet. 27 Norfolk St. from 1 November to 1 May for 300 guineas, afterwards the price is so enormous that I should not think of it. And in the prospect of a dissolution [I] should probably come down here for from May till November. Still you see I only have my two moves a year. It would be too provoking if you were giving an enormous price for a house in town for me when (if) there is a general election.

Source: Letter/draft/copy, ADD Mss 45790 ff320-21

27 Norfolk St.
Park Lane, W.
5 November 1864

Dear Papa

Do PRAY send me back John Stuart Mill's letters by post, without delay. The letterweight, book weigher and British and foreign postal guide not yet arrived. Could you tell Watson to send me, *by next box*, a small silver cup with my initials, F.N. (forty years ago, Uncle Ben[223] gave us each one, F.N. and F.P.N.) I want mine, please, for a sacrament cup.[224]

ever dear Pa
your loving child
F.

Source: Undated, incomplete letter/draft/copy, ADD Mss 45790 ff334-35

Dear Papa

I have sent for Müller[225] according to Parthe's desire. It shall come to you by the next "empty" [box]. Horace Mansfield's *original* remark about the myth of Prometheus reminds me of "Mr Puff": "Perdition catch my soul, but I do love thee."[226] "*I think I have heard that line before.*" I shall not keep Müller, for I think we have got a good deal farther (indeed I think Aeschylus had, perhaps you may remember that I read Aeschylus's *Prometheus* with you) than Müller or Mr Horace Mansfield either. Indeed I did not know that the "myth of Prometheus" had ever been taken for anything else. The Christian myth of Christ

---

223 Uncle Benjamin Smith (1783-60).
224 Nightingale's friend Benjamin Jowett began celebrating a communion service for her at home in 1862. A photograph of the communion set actually used appears on the dust jacket of *Theology*.
225 Friedrich Max Müller (1823-1900) published extensively on Eastern religions, including a fifty-one volume edition of *Sacred Books of the East*, 1888-92.
226 From Shakespeare's *Othello* Act 3, scene 3.

obtaining "gifts for men" *against* God's will is not finer than that of Prometheus. But the finest of all would be that of Christ, of *man*, obtaining "gifts for men" *with*, not against, God's will, which is not a myth but the real fact.

There is a most interesting chapter (far better than Müller) in Grote's *History*[227] on Grecian mythology. That, and his inestimable chapter on Socrates, volume 8, constitute the main merit, I think, of his *History of Greece* [breaks off]

Source: Letter/draft/copy, ADD Mss 45790 ff336-41

Hampstead, N.W.
15 September 1865

Dear Papa

I have not written because I could not. I thank you very much for your letter, which touched me deeply. The "golden bowl is broken"—those words keep running in my ears, with reference to *her*[228] because it was the purest gold, the most *unworked* gold I have ever known. But she is gone to a higher and more perfect service. If God had asked me (which I assure you He did not) I should have said rather take her now than leave her here thirty years more. That is, for *her* specially, you understand. (There *are* those whom I would have given my salvation for, if they could have been kept but one year more here.)

But better for *her* to go, that is, if it had not been for this dreadful, this agonizing illness, which even now one can scarcely think of with resignation. No, I don't think she is looking down upon us now (this in answer to Mama's dear letter). I am sure I don't wish it. It would rack those who are gone and do us no good. It would break Sidney Herbert's heart to see what is doing here now, if he could look and see. I think they go to an ever higher and more perfect service.

I no more believe in heaven than I do in hell, that is, in the sense of a permanent unprogressive state. This *is* hell, but not a permanent one. And probably there is no state, called heaven, to which there is not a higher heaven. "Which way I fly is hell—myself am hell"[229] is a truer line than Milton ever wrote elsewhere. And "the kingdom of heaven is *within*," but we must make it *without*, too, *as he did*, is one of the divinest of Christ's sayings.

---

227 George Grote, *History of Greece*, 1846-56.
228 The recent death of her cousin, Hilary Bonham Carter.
229 Milton, *Paradise Lost* Book 4 line 75.

You ask me what is to be done with 35 South Street, for which (house) I am deeply grateful to you. The Sutherlands have no house yet (they have seen sixty-nine houses). I think they may still fall back on 35 South Street. As it can't let at Michaelmas it makes no difference to leave it open for them. I don't think they will settle nearer London than Dulwich. But, even there, is nothing yet to be taken at once. No, I could make no use of 35 (this in answer to Parthe) till I go into it. I have never been dressed (here) more than I am, to sit up in bed.

Even to go into a dressing room, if I have to go out upon a staircase, is often impossible to me. To go out into the street from one house to the next would be absolutely and always impossible to me. I never go out of my front door from the moment I enter my house to the moment I leave it. Here I have not once left my bedroom floor, often not my bedroom. The house must be kept, therefore, quite irrespectively of me, from the moment it becomes yours. You will put someone in to keep it. . . .

I stay on here from day to day, from sheer inability to get out of bed. But I am most anxious to get back to London (this in answer to Mama's kind wish that I should stay here). I had made an appointment with an Indian in London for next Monday, 18th. Longer than *Monday week*, 25th, I am quite determined not to stay here. Besides which I cannot bear the expense of three houses going on at once.

So much for the present. Please God I will write again. Let this letter be for you and yours only. I assure you I treasure yours as the greatest of my treasures. Please tell Mama that I have had partridges and grapes from Embley, for which many thanks—that I have had "no grouse from Scotland," nor any "grouse" at all this year. I merely mention this, because she desires me. For the same reason I mention that the "four *Lancets*" have never been found.

ever dear Pa

your loving child

F.

Have you read Grote's three volumes of *Plato and the Companions of Socrates*? I should much like to have them to look over again, if you have them.

F.N.

Let me just say—I who am much given, too much given, to be, instead of the "lamb of God," God's *wild beast*,[230] how nobly Elinor [Bonham

---

230 An allusion to Hos 13:8.

Carter] has gone through the "agonizing" attendance of the last four months, and been a sister to *her* in death.

Source: Letter, Wellcome (Claydon copy) Ms 9001/170

[printed address] 34 South Street
Park Lane
London, W.
27 October 1865

Dear Papa

A little line only to say that a van full of furniture was returned last night (with four drunken men) from Mr Fortescue's to 35. My good Mrs Sutherland received it, my housemaid being in hospital. Glass, china, kitchen utensils are in great quantities. A good deal is very bad, but I am happy to hear that there is plenty to enable me to give the largest dinner parties, and the largest of my evening routs. Mrs S. says £30 would not replace the kitchen utensils alone, now restored. *No inventory came.* The furniture (strictly speaking) is irrecoverable, being gone to Mr Fortescue's country house, of which I regret most two small bookcases. I only hope he will be made to pay for it.

Mrs [William] Cowper's letter was so *asking* for sympathy for Lady Palmerston[231] and them all, that I have written to them a long letter (please tell Sir Harry), though with some small hesitation.

ever dear Pa
your loving child
F.

Au revoir when more of this.

Source: Incomplete letter to W.E. Nightingale, Wellcome (Claydon copy) Ms 9023/58

[1865 or later]

... An architect) has done the same, so has Mrs Sutherland. I don't say this to throw dirt at the house, which is in the best situation in London, but only to show you what I have had to pay. I know but too well what you have had to pay. And it has cost me more sorrow than you think to know that I am standing at a higher rent than I have stood since I left the Burlington (which rent I deeply regret). At least I have not cost you the rent of a Hampstead house this year. I meant

---

231 Lord Palmerston had just died. The Palmerstons were friends and neighbours of the Nightingales in Hampshire.

(but I have no time) to send you, as you ask me (today) the list of my expenses during my absence at Embley, besides the repairs bill.

The housekeeping expenses for housemaid and cook were 28/ a week, when cook came down to Embley 21/ a week (as I could not leave the housemaid alone in the house). I will write again. In haste.

ever dear Pa

your loving child F.

Source: Note, Wellcome (Claydon copy) Ms 9001/181

Dear Papa   Saturday [1865?]

A half hour between 12:00 and 1:00 or between 2:00 and 5:00 would suit me. Pray say when. And I hope you will like to take the sacrament with me from Mr Jowett tomorrow (Sunday) at 3:00.

But I shall hope to see you in the morning too tomorrow.

F.

Source: Incomplete letter to W.E. Nightingale, Wellcome (Claydon copy) Ms 9023/60

[1867?]

I kept this letter a day to write more, but will put this off a day or two. Oh dear Papa, my soul is sometimes exceeding sorrowful, even unto death.[232] Surely I have borne the sorrows[233] (of many hundreds of thousands and those of my own family too). A little sympathy would have done me so much good. You have given it me, but nobody else. I have been scolded at, on the contrary, none knowing how many have laid their sorrows upon me and how none have tried to bear mine. *I* must not scold, but *everyone* may scold me. PRIVATE.

F.N.

Source: Letter, Wellcome (Claydon copy) Ms 9002/122

[printed address] 35 South Street
Park Lane
London, W.
13 March 1867

Dear Papa

I am looking forward to seeing you next week.

---

232 An allusion to Mark 14:34.
233 An allusion to Isa 53:4.

Thank you for writing about Count Bismark [a cat]. To my surprise and joy it is that he is alive. *Of course he must come back with you.* By that time I shall have found him a comfortable home in a suburban retreat. I would not leave him by himself at Lea Hurst on any account.

Now mark the progress of a myth, in the idea of the schoolchildren that Bismark was my Russian cat, brought home by me thus: *Peter* was a Russian, brought home by me. They have in their lessons a *white* Russian bear. Therefore Miss N's *white* cat, under *Peter*'s care, must have been brought from Russia by Miss N.

As usual I have no time to write though much to write about. How we must mourn the good Dean Dawes.[234] I mind, as if it were yesterday, seventeen years ago, staying with them at King's Somborne and seeing his tears, sacred tears, at leaving his people.[235] Now King's Somborne school is all ruined. He was nearly the last of my oldest friends.

ever dear Pa

your loving child

F.

The east wind here beats every winter I have ever seen in London.

Source: Unsigned, dictated letter, Wellcome (Claydon copy) Ms 9001/182

Thursday [26 December 1867]

Dear Papa

The splendid evergreens arrived quite safe on Tuesday night, so late however, consequence of its being Christmas eve, that I couldn't send them that night. I sent them the first thing on Christmas morning and they were received with acclamation at King's College Hospital, at Rev Mother's and at Sister Gonzaga's. I don't think the mince pies would be disdained even if they were to come now.

The letter which you had on Tuesday morning was posted on Sunday night. Ought not you to have had it on Monday afternoon? Now I do assure you for once the postmaster was wrong. I weighed that letter twice in two weighers and it was only 1 ounce.

Our information looks *more* like war instead of less like it, but we've already spent half a million in sending out this expedition. And, whether there is war or not, it is all up with our getting our improvements into the estimates next year.

---

234 Richard Dawes (1793-1867), founder of a model school, King's Somborne, Hampshire, near Embley, later Dean of Hereford.

235 In 1850, when he left to become Dean of Hereford.

I had a long and dismal letter from poor Mrs Herbert at Mentone. She appears only to live on my letters because they are the only ones which tell her about her husband's work in the War Office and yet how can I write to her when I can scarcely do my own work? . . .

"There is Sutherland," just think what the difference of the moral atmosphere is! living in the society of Dr Sutherland and Dr Williams, to me who can seek no other society, and living with Sidney Herbert and A.H. Clough! But I care so much for this poor world that, even now I assure you, with these and all my friends gone, I could gladly, if I had only the health that I had when I came back from the Crimea, go forth and pursue my own work, leaving that which their death has rendered impossible. But in this lies the very sting of my fate, that I have sacrificed my means to work in order to carry out work with others, which their loss renders impossible, and have left myself none to work alone. I need hardly say how different it would have been if it had pleased God to take me and let Sidney Herbert survive.

Farther, about my health, I don't think it is exactly possible for anyone to appreciate, who has not felt it, the impossibility of any faith *taking the place* of physical capability. Mind I am not here speaking of physical suffering, but of physical want of power. When I read of Jacob Bell, in the midst of the acutest suffering being able to go on with his work till up to one hour before his death,[236] I think what a happy man! I am quite sure, on the other hand, that my dear Clough suffered more from being unable to do anything for fourteen months before his death than from any other cause, and I can truly say that I pitied him more than myself and that I could rejoice at *his* gain when he died more than I grieved for my own loss. . . .

Source: Letter, Wellcome (Claydon copy) Ms 9003/29

[printed address] 35 South Street
Park Lane
London, W.
13 June 1868

Dear Papa

I write to you to remind you that this is your golden wedding year. On 15 June or 18, 1868 (which is it?) you will have been married fifty years [1 June, see p 192 above].

---

236 Possibly the Jacob Bell on whom "Riches in Death: A Discourse on Death" was given 25 July 1852.

There is a letter of Bunsen's to his wife, on the anniversary of *his* wedding day, which I think is worth all the rest of the book put together: "our pilgrimage is now in the *downward vale* of life; let us try to secure *frequent moments of solemn consecration,* of taste for the higher consciousness, which presupposes leisure and repose x x. With you I desire ever more and more to share the highest reach of spirituality x x to find the response to my better self x x. I pray to be enabled to see more clearly and that the way may be shown me x x think over our life." I wish I could copy for you the whole letter, which ought, I think, to form part of an anniversary wedding service.

The tragedy of *my* life is so deep that I must put off writing to you about this. I hope to see you on the 26th, 27th, 28th as you propose, you and "the boy."

Oh dear Papa, "the gentlemen" and ladies "of England who sit at home at ease"—does it appear to you that *that* was the moment (when my "Una" was hardly cold in her grave[237]) to say that she was gone to "harder work"? What I had to say to the women of England was, why did she die? *Because you would not help her.* If I mistake not, the passage you object to was this: "Let her not merely 'rest in peace' but let hers be the life to stir us up to fight the good fight against,[238] etc." That sentence I would repeat, if I could, like a street preacher to all those lazy, selfish women in carriages, whom I see blocking up the park at this moment before my eyes, *who killed her,* not tell them that *she* is gone to "harder work."[239] As for myself, I am so weary and heavy laden[240] that, if the next existence for me were that of an owl, so that I could live for 100 years at rest, without any men throwing their business upon me which they ought to do themselves, I should be glad. At this moment I am days and weeks in arrears. So must close, but shall be ever, dear Pa

your loving child

F.

I will write, if I can, so that you shall have it on your golden wedding.

---

237 Agnes Jones, first superintendent of nursing at the Liverpool Workhouse Infirmary, who died of typhus on the job.

238 An allusion to 1 Tim 6:12.

239 Nightingale's memorial article on Jones, "Una and the Lion" ends: "Oh, daughters of God, are there so few to answer?"

240 An allusion to Matt 11:28.

Source: Letter, Wellcome (Claydon copy) Ms 9003/32

Dear Papa   17 June 1868

Though you have not vouchsafed me any communication as to what day is your golden wedding, yet I resume mine. My life is and always has been such a tragedy, if by tragedy you mean the combat of the man's soul with destiny. Of course I don't believe in destiny but have no objection to say the powers of evil, only that *we* believe the gods are with us. The ancients and a great many moderns believe the gods are against us in the struggle with powers of evil. But I have not borne a high part in this tragedy. I have been and am so dragged to pieces with small conflicting claims, which obscure and fritter away the great end and story of the tragedy. And the power of resistance, which I was always sadly deficient in, is you can't think, how much diminished by illness.

Mr Jowett's life is a tragedy in the highest sense. But then he takes so much nobler a part in it. Then I am a wreck, stranded, oh these many years on the rocks and at short intervals there comes a storm, and my ship is driven again with a great bump upon the rocks, parting amidships a little more than before. I have always lost my main friend or fellow worker just when his or her presence seemed most essential to carry on the work.

Mr Jowett's life is a tragedy, a perpetual struggle with destiny. But then there is so much of the heroic element in it. I often wonder that people don't look more at Christ's life from that side, as the grandest tragedy and heroic life that ever was. (But all *that* is spoilt by the muz and maze they are in about the atonement.) I think what is discouraging in the world as it is is the absolute want of the tragic or the heroic element in most lives, especially in our family and class. I do not believe there is the least struggle or the least consciousness of the need of any struggle, *for the world*—there may be a little for themselves to be good-tempered, etc. There is not either the least consciousness of the struggle when they see it in others. I have heard Mr Jowett and Dean Stanley likened to one another. Now, in the life of the first, there *is* the tragedy, the heroic element. In the life of the second there is not the faintest trace of the heroic side. He is incapable of bearing the slightest part in a tragedy. His own comfort—to be comfortable in this world *and the next*—is the moving principle of most men.

A thousand thanks for the payment of the rates for this year up to Lady Day and July, and also for the last year. This is truly a beautiful house.

ever dear Pa

your loving child

F.

Source: Note, Wellcome (Claydon copy) Ms 9003/68

[printed address] 35 South Street
Park Lane
4 January 1869

Dear Papa

Many thanks for the payment of the rates, etc. About your "response and objections" to my "political economy," I am afraid that you have not read my letter (as Aunt Mai says). I have a long letter to write you about theological matters, but no time now.

ever dear Pa

your loving child

F.

Source: Letter to W.E. Nightingale, Wellcome (Claydon copy) Ms 9003/118

Embley
Romsey
1 October 1869

I think my mother "carefully" understands that you will not be back here til Saturday week (9th) (I am sure *I* do). I do not see that she has any reluctance (after a "careful" inquiry) to "Bertha and her husband and children" coming here on "Monday week 11th." She is very fond of Bertha. What disturbs her is any uncertainty, any confusion, having to make any decision, having the power to recall a decision she has made, being asked to reconsider a decision, be it of the most trifling nature. When this happens from a person walking about the room, to herself walking about the room, the confusion of mind is so painful that, though I have mentioned this before, it is so impressed upon my mind that I mention it once more. (She has come into my room almost hysterical to know if she could not put off a person whom she had made me write to accept, against my own advice to her the moment before.) *Burn.* . . .

Source: Unsigned, incomplete letter probably to W.E. and Frances Nightingale, Wellcome (Claydon copy) Ms 9004/11

[printed address] 35 South Street
Park Lane
13 February 1870

I am afraid that you are very cold up o'th top o'th nob, not that I think snow and east wind disagreeable or ugly at Lea Hurst. The last winter I spent at home I spent with you there in a deep snow and liked it very much. Here there is a tremendous northeasterly gale— too much of a gale to leave fog—hard frost and driving snow. But this is not nearly so trying as the dense dark London fogs of January, darkness all the twenty-four hours.

Sir John McNeill has been through London on his way to Italy, for health I am sorry to say. He came to see me last Sunday. He is seventy-five. I cannot see the least difference in the vigour of his mind, the excellence of his judgment, the accuracy of his memory and attention. As I told him, to see him is at once to me the highest hope and the deepest pain. It reminds me of the days when a great career was just begun (Sidney Herbert's) when we were full of the highest purposes and the most successful plans. Since then, all our hopes seem blasted, and all our plans destroyed.

Still when we look at India and what it was fifteen years ago, when we look at the Army and what it was fifteen years ago, we must hail a great progress. And who am I that I should complain if we have not had more? (I will send you a letter that I have had since, from Sir J. McNeill, if you will return it me.)

Mrs Bracebridge is in London on their way back to Atherstone. She says she has had a good winter at Hastings. I cannot think her less lame. Sir Harry looks better.

I read Bishop Temple's recantation, poor wretch! I suppose there is joy among the devils over one more bishop that degradeth himself. At least there is among the Puseys and Denisons.

Source: Letter probably to W.E. Nightingale, Wellcome (Claydon copy) Ms 9004/37

7 May 1870

Dear

What was I going to say? I find, from the banking people, that you were good enough to pay in my quarter's allowance here in London. I thought that you would subtract from it the £50 which, you will remember, you kindly gave me *in cash* at Embley. Finding this not to be the case, I enclose a cheque to your order for £50. Please acknowledge.

ever your loving child

F.

Source: Letter to W.E. Nightingale, Wellcome (Claydon copy) Ms 9004/40

10 May 1870

You will see by the two enclosed that I had anticipated you. But alas! not one moment of strength ever have I to send off any but the most pressing business. I am sure that Sir Bartle Frere would gladly give you a copy of the "Indian missions" if he had one. But he has not. It is not yet printed separately for sale, though I have begged and prayed him to do so.

You say my mother "thinks only *too much* of - -. Alas the thinking *too little* in men and women has oftener left me mourning. Surely the devil invented the plan of letting the thoughts drift away from anything hard or sorrowful. O how are we [to] learn the lessons of life, hard enough to read anyhow, if we are to pass them by "railroad speed"? as I have heard M Mohl express it too truly. To me this disposition, which destroys all experience, all reality, all wisdom, all knowledge, seems increasing in men.

The friends of my younger age *are not.* Those who laid things to heart are not, are no longer now. "She pondered all these things in her heart."[241] Does that man or woman exist now who *ponders* things in the heart?

ever your loving child

F.

Sir Harry just come looking very well. . . .

F.N.

Source: Letter, Wellcome (Claydon copy) Ms 9005/95

my mother's bedside
8 October 1871

My dear Father

My mother has desired me to write to you at once that she has quite made up her mind that it is right that *Watson should go,* that you should tell him that you accept his warning. She thinks it better not to

---

241 A paraphrase of Luke 2:19.

enter into incriminations. Consistently with justice, the earliest time at which he can go she thinks will be the best. She is quite determined not to part with Peter.

ever your loving child
Florence Nightingale
(for Frances Nightingale)
Turn Over
My dear Father

My mother unprompted by me (who have *never once* mentioned the subject to her) made me write down what is on the other side. She has said all this to me *every* day, only *more strongly* and clearly. And Aunt Julia can testify, if needs be, that I told her what my mother's (repeated) words were at the time, so that this is not a mistake as to my mother's *considered* opinion.

F.

Source: Letter, Wellcome (Claydon copy) Ms 9005/96

9 October 1871
My dear Father

After I had written the enclosed, I found that my mother had taken time by the forelock and had sent down to tell Peter that *she could not spare him* and he must stay *as long as she lived*, that Peter answered (very properly) that he had the best master and mistress that ever lived, that he would try to put up with disagreeables for their sakes and that *he withdrew his warning* IF YOU APPROVED and (he added) if I did. Will you enable me today to tell Peter that you accept?

Source: Letter, Wellcome (Claydon copy) Ms 9005/117

[printed address] 35 South Street
Park Lane
4 March 1872
My dear Sir Harry [Verney]

You are so good in thinking about my dear father's "readers aloud," that I will tell you what has passed, in order for you to judge for yourself if anything can be done. In November, when Watson left, I was quite uneasy about the "reading" and set myself steadily to find a boy who would read *well* enough. None could be found in our school. But I actually chose, through the medium of kind friends, and all but engaged a most eligible (lame) boy, weak in his legs but not in his other qualifications. The particulars were all arranged without giving my father the least trouble, which would have set him against it.

But when it came to the point my father would have none of him, not even, as proposed, for a short time, though Shore, who was here, strenuously advocated it.

During my father's absence this last month my mother has had Peter in to read every night, correcting him whenever he was wrong. The result is that Peter now reads quite well enough to please my father. And together with Webb's reading, whose voice he likes, there is now quantity enough as well as quality. I am sure that I could not interfere farther without worrying my father. He is very cheerful, went to church yesterday at an amazing pace. But I think how weak and rather altered and he does not lose his cough. . . .

ever yours
F.N.

Source: Letter, Wellcome (Claydon copy) Ms 9005/150

35 South St.
26 June 1872

My dear Sir Harry [Verney]
. . . My father comes on *Thursday* about 3:00, sees Sir James Paget here for his throat at 3:30. Will you not *breakfast* with him at 10:00 (or dine with him at 7:00) here whenever you can? He would so much like to see you at breakfast. God bless you.

ever yours
F.N.

Source: Letter, Wellcome (Claydon copy) Ms 9006/2

35 South St., W.
26 January 1873

My dear Father
Can you send me by Tuesday's box volumes (*1* and *7*) of *Middlemarch*.[242] They are at Embley. I believe they are mine, but, if they are yours, I think you will be glad to be rid of them. They are to make up a set I have been asked to lend—odious reading, *I* think (*I have* volumes 2, 3, 4, 5, 6, 8).

----

242 George Eliot's *Middlemarch*; for comments on see *Theology*.

Also, would you kindly send me Gladstone's *Faraday*[243] (one of the last books which Emily Verney read) which I lent you. I sent you Butler's *Great Lone Land*.[244]

ever your loving child

F.

Source: Letter, Wellcome (Claydon copy) Ms 9006/61

35 South St.

29 November 1873

My dear Father

I am afraid you will think me very fidgety but I think I shall look in upon you on Tuesday for a fortnight. As that dear little Miss Pringle said of my mother: she wants some one to *warm* her. You know that I could come for the whole month of January, which is almost the only month in the year when I can well leave my work and that from February till August I cannot leave London except at the risk of destruction. But January is the month when everybody else can come and so I will try to come in February. But I dare not put off seeing my mother till February.

I will write again however. I may not be able to come on Tuesday. Let Mrs Crook send me the weekly box on Tuesday, unless you hear to the contrary.

ever your loving child

F.

Editor: The next letters date from after her father's death, 5 January 1874.

Source: Letter to Parthenope Verney, Wellcome (Claydon copy) Ms 9006/64

35 South St.

6 January 1874

All for *him* is best as it is. He has "another morn than ours."[245] How much he must know now! What great things he will do hereafter, freed from death, called life, which us from life doth sever.[246]

---

243 John Hall Gladstone, *Michael Faraday*.

244 William Francis Butler, *Great Lone Land: A Narrative of Travel and Adventure in the North-West of America*.

245 T. Hood, "The Death Bed."

246 Milton, sonnet 14.

One's soul reaches forward to strive to see behind the veil. O that we could *see* him in God, what he is feeling. But all we know is God knows, the infinite Goodness knows, what He has done with him. And we think that little!!

I am glad that my mother has been told. I shall come exactly as is thought best for her by you. It was quite a new idea to me that I should survive *her*. The idea that *I* should survive *him* never once (really) crossed my mind. I thought he had ten years' of life, I not one. I am thankful that you were all there—his last days were not alone. I will write as soon as I hear what you all think. I cannot write now, much. (I have written to Mrs Bracebridge, for fear she should hear suddenly.) Aunt Mai will be very much overcome; she did so love him.

ever your loving F.

Source: Letter, Wellcome (Claydon copy) Ms 9006/65

35 South Street
Park Lane, W.
7 January 1874

My dear Sir Harry [Verney]

Thanks to you and Parthe for letters. Please write again. Have you written to the people at *Pleasley* [near Lea Hurst]? I know no one there now but Miss Fox (who is gone). Or I should willingly have written. I wish I knew the Lea Hurst people now to write to those who loved *him*.

ever yours affectionately
F.N.

Mr Jowett has telegraphed to ask whether he can be of any use at Embley. I think I shall write to him, not yet, but if you think otherwise, will you write him at *Belgrave Road, Torquay*?

Source: Letter to Parthenope Verney, Wellcome (Claydon copy) Ms 9006/66

35 South St.
8 January 1874

I do not think his death awful for *him*. His was the purest mind and I think the most single heart I have ever known. It is *his* New Year; he was quite ready to part with his life. He always wished to go out of the world quietly—it was a part of his single-minded character to do so— he was as shy as a bird.

For us it is sad and dreary to have no last word or farewell, but he would have had it just so, if he could, I believe. And I believe what he said to dear Blanche was meant as a farewell to us. It was not in his character, you know, even had he been perfectly aware of what was coming, to set any form of speech to say. I suppose we shall never know how he spent that last night. No doubt you have questioned Mellar whether he slept, whether he was asleep when Mellar took him his broth at 3:30 A.M., whether he said anything in the morning.

His going up to fetch his watch himself was so like himself that I can't find it in me to regret it. He never could have borne to be waited upon; *he* would not have it other than it is. I think he was in some respects the truest father to his places, people and cottagers, which he so loved and cared for, never pauperizing by indulgence, wise and careful, always helping them to help themselves, even to seeing himself how the wives kept the rooms tidy. I don't suppose he ever made a single pauper. And his being with the party carving for them to the last was so like him. I hope that cottage will be seen after which I believe he was building something to.

The walking funeral is what he would have liked, but poor Shore will not be able to walk. Have you asked Henry Coape Smith?[247] He was so fond of those children and of her. I never saw anyone who hated the smallest "demonstration" or show so much; he would not have liked us even to wear mourning. But no one knows what a breakup it is to us, and to have had no last word; I never once thought that *I* should survive *him.*

I wrote as soon as I possibly could. Dear William Coltman was not here till past 4:00. I had a St Thomas' sister going to Edinburgh actually in the house wanting to see me. I saw him first, then her, then dear William again. It was 6:00 o'clock before the two were gone, too late for that post. And when they were gone, I could neither eat nor sleep nor sit up in bed. I had business letters ready to Miss Pringle at Edinburgh but, though the dear soul loved father and mother, I did not add the news. I wrote only (by William Coltman) a few lines to Aunt Mai.

I have written to Louisa. I do not like to suggest, but would you write, too? Not didactically, of course, cannot you fancy *him* writing *himself* to say he was gone? I shall try to do my work as much as possible as usual and as soon as possible, as *he* would have had me. You know *he* would not have wished his own death to disarrange a single day. I must go on for a few months or years longer and try to "finish

---

247 Frances Nightingale's mother was Frances Coape Smith.

the work God has given me to do,"[248] and then we will all lie down and be at rest.

It is the greatest possible comfort that dear mother grieves but so gently. It is a comfort, too, that the nights, which are the hardest part to others, are the least so to her and the mornings the same. If mother prays "to go after him," so does many another.

On Monday morning early I marked Prosper Mérimée's *Lettres*,[249] recommended by Mme Mohl, not very good, volume 2 best, see end, for *him*. And he was dying then, and sent it by linen box. I look at my arum and think it is the last plant of *his* I shall ever have. And so with all. Oh where is he? Where is he in this his new year?

ever your loving F.

[Note on envelope] I have answered your question in another envelope. I want a bookcase very much; I had far rather have one of old recollections, the one which stood in my room, afterwards Papa's, perhaps it is now in Grace's room. I hope it has three shelves. If you could send it up to me—no one can want it now.—I should be very glad (when you are packing up). I should like too to have Michelangelo's Notte, the last thing I gave him, now in his room.

Have you put up his monument? In great haste. God bless you. I am just getting up for an appointment. . . .

Source: Letter to J.J. Frederick regarding her father's death, London Metropolitan Archives H1/ST/NC1/74/1

[8 January 1874]

. . . My dear father was taken from us quite suddenly on Monday morning at 8 o'clock. He had got up at this usual early hour. There was a large family party in the house, but when they ran in to him he was quite gone. For *him* it is best so. He was quite ready to go. . . .

yours sincerely

F. Nightingale

Editor: Nightingale's "spiritual mother," Selina Bracebridge, died 31 January 1874. The next letters deal with her as well as her father's death.

---

248 An allusion to John 5:36.

249 Probably Prosper Mérimée's two-volume *Lettres à une Inconnue*, 1874, described by a translator as "love letters of a genius."

Source: Unsigned, incomplete letter Wellcome (Claydon copy) Ms 9006/70

Embley
4 February 1874

My dear Sir Harry and Parthe [Verney]

... You know that Mrs Bracebridge passed away on Saturday morning at ¼ past 5:00. She was taken ill on the Sunday with cough, difficulty of swallowing and of breathing. On Thursday at noon was the last time she took notice; she tried to say something and failed. She was more than mother to me, and oh that I could not be a daughter to her in her last sad months. What should I have been without her? And what would many have been without her? ...

I am glad to keep my father's watch as it was, just where it stopped, at least for a year. Had he been a younger man, had he had a young son, it had been different. But now it seems to me appropriate to him, who saw 9:00 o'clock in heaven, and to the place, which is such a breakup since his life below was broken up, to let it stand as he and it stopped at 25 minutes to 9:00.

I take the greatest care lest some shake should set it going again. It is soothing to me to let it lie by my bed just so, and to remember that he became past pain at that hour. ...

For me the place "all withered when my father died." For me it is different from what it is for anyone else. I lie in the same rooms I did, not his, hear the same laughing [breaks off]

Source: Letter regarding death of W.E. Nightingale, Clendening History of Medicine Library, Kansas University Medical Center, Paget 3

35 South St.
Park Lane, W.
27 April 1874

Dear Sir James Paget

I was about to write and thank you for your kind advice (for Mr Jowett) to consult Sir William Jenner (Mr Jowett followed it in every respect). Also I was going to write to you about my dear father, who, you may perhaps have forgotten, consulted you at my house, and about whose ailment you were so very good as to write to me, when that very morning my dear father was taken from us quite suddenly, a great blow, to me especially, whose mind it had never once crossed that *I* should survive *him*. In the same month my best old friend, Mrs Bracebridge, without whom my life and Scutari would have been impossible, we lost. And Quetelet and Livingstone,[250] nearly all my heroes, whose great heroic life gave wings to me, something to do and die for, in the base perplexities of lesser life, are gone.

I only hope that you are pretty well. Pray believe me
ever yours faithfully
Florence Nightingale

Source: Unsigned letter, Wellcome (Claydon copy) Ms 9006/144

35 South St.
28 December 1874

My dear Sir Harry and Parthe [Verney]

My father's epitaph, you ask me. (You know what we should have liked but if you do not, I think my father's characteristic was) seeking after wisdom.

It comforts me daily to know that my dear father is now on the direct way to feeling that sympathy with perfect Wisdom, the desire after which was really the thread of and key to his whole life, to its failures as well as to its high search after truth. God bless him. The blessing from perfect Goodness *will* be his through his feeling real sympathy with, almighty Wisdom. Any words expressing the search after light and wisdom would be appropriate to him, but it is difficult to find these words in one text. He was very fond of Job:

Where is the way where light dwelleth? (Job 38:19)

God is light (1 John 1:5).

Or God is light and in His/Thy light shall I/he see light (Ps 36:9).[251]

Or simply: He shall seek me and find me (Jer 29:13)

Or, He shall search for me with all his heart, and I will be found of him (Jer 29:13-14).

Or, He hath called him out of darkness into His marvelous light (1 Pet 2:9).

Or, He will bring me forth to the light and I shall behold His righteousness (Micah 7:9).

Or that God may give him the Spirit of Wisdom (Eph 1:17).

Or simply, Blessed are the pure in heart, for they shall see God (Matt 5:8).

Or, Arise, shine, for thy light is come (Isa 60:1).

---

250 Dr David Livingstone (1813-73), missionary and explorer.
251 In fact the memorial stone is engraved "And In Thy Light Shall We See Light." Ps 36:9. Most of the verses are slightly paraphrased to be more personal.

Or, He sought the Lord if haply he might feel after Him and find Him (Acts 17:27).

Or, The Lord shall be thine everlasting light (Isa 60:20).

Or simply, I would seek unto God (Job 5:8).

Or (two different texts), He gave his heart to seek and to search out wisdom, and in Thy light shall he see light. . . .

Or, One thing I have desired of the Lord: that will I seek after (Ps 27:4).

Or, My heart said unto Thee: Thy face, Lord, will I seek (Ps 27:8).

Or, I communed with mine own heart: and my spirit made diligent search (Ps 77:6).

Source: Letter to Sir Harry Verney, Wellcome (Claydon copy) Ms 9013/3

4 January 1890

. . . Tomorrow my father will have been dead sixteen years.

ever yours and P.'s

Sister, Parthenope, Lady Verney

Editor: The ill feeling between Nightingale and her sister Parthenope is so well known that what might be interesting in this correspondence is the extent of good will, attempts at understanding, offers of love and, later, actual reconciliation. The surviving correspondence is immense, for the Verneys kept letters, even the briefest of notes. Much of this concerns practical matters, coming and going between London and Claydon, arrangements to see mutual friends, servants and servant problems, orders of food and other household items. When illness prevented Nightingale from going out Parthenope Verney assisted her in the purchase of clothing. Some of these domestic arrangements are covered in the third section of this volume, but only a very little has been kept in the letters selected here since there is a good deal of repetition, especially concerning their domestic employees (hiring, training, supervision, medical and dental needs, illnesses in their families, excursions, Christmas presents, parties and holidays).

The Verneys entertained nurses at Claydon, notably at summer garden parties that were much appreciated. After Embley was no longer available for Christmas greens the Verneys sent them (to decorate hospital wards). Nightingale often asked them to put up visitors at their place, and she in turn had Verney relatives to sleep at her house when that was needed.

A vast number of notes shows that her sister continued to want to have much more frequent social contact than Nightingale was willing or able to give. Nightingale's commitment, we know, was to her work, and she reserved her best hours for writing letters and briefs and seeing experts and officials. Many notes simply explain that she cannot see her sister because of pressure of work, sometimes explaining with whom she had appointments that day. Year after year she turned down offers of meetings on India mail day. Other misunderstandings were also protracted. There is vexed correspondence over Queen Victoria's offer of an apartment at Kensington Palace to Nightingale (raised also p 255 in a letter to her father). There are disagreements about the care of their mother after their father died, where it is also clear that it was Nightingale who made the practical arrangements. There are quibbles over the wording of the memorial note at her mother's death and differences over the disposal of her mother's furniture. Parthenope Verney evidently chided her sister for working Sir Harry too hard, which prompted anguished explanations to the contrary.

Yet there are also some gems. Quite apart from some of the letters from Italy (in *European Travels*) and some of the correspondence from the Crimea (in *The Crimean War*) there are a number of letters where Nightingale explains her philosophy/theodikè, a subject more often discussed with her father. (One of these letters, from her period of extreme determinism, is quite chilling.) So also is Nightingale's letter to her sister on medical education for women. Yet when her sister began to publish articles[252] and books Nightingale read them, complimented her on (some of) them (and purchased the books for distribution to nurses and workers' reading rooms). She asked her sister's advice on "Una," a non-technical article. She asked her sister and Harry Verney for advice on her "pauperism" article. There are wry observations on friends, politics and the arts. There is even a sisterly risqué reference to a young woman who wanted to "get her bread" by her "passion" for soldiers: "In profane English, how would you construe this?" (see p 328 below).

The correspondence shows how much of the work on family matters Nightingale took care of. It was she who advised her sister on the

---

252 The articles posed more of a problem, for they made her sister one of the "magazine-y" writers Nightingale so decried, offering opinions without serious expertise on a subject.

illnesses and approaching deaths of other relatives. Nightingale over-whelmingly made the arrangements for the care of her mother in old age, hiring servants, maids and companions and visiting for months at Lea Hurst to run the household, pay the bills, etc. Parthenope Verney was apprised of these various matters, and consulted on some. It was Nightingale who sent, in both their names, memorial wreaths to their parents' grave.

The late correspondence shows real tenderness and admiration for Parthenope Verney's courage in her last illness. Nightingale told her sister that she prayed for her hourly. She asked for prayers for herself and admitted her faults. Parthenope Verney asked for her prayers, a touching moment Nightingale had never expected to experience. On their last meeting Nightingale was able to comfort her sister through their shared faith.

Parthenope Verney on her death left a lengthy but incomplete manuscript of a history of the Verney family, which Margaret Verney finished and published, Nightingale supporting with practical advice all the way. It seems that when her sister did things Nightingale approved of, like serious writing, she wanted her to get full credit. Some of the nicest moments of this correspondence are as author to author. When Parthenope Verney was writing about peasant propri-etors, Nightingale fed her Franco-Swiss material and an official report on Bulgarian peasant proprietors.[253] There are also disagreements, but Nightingale clearly asked her sister's advice at least on style, for example to look over draft letters for Lady Dufferin, to ensure that they were not "too didactic."[254] The correspondence with Harry Ver-ney, later in this volume, will similarly show Nightingale's concern that her sister be appropriately remembered after her death.

Source: Letter in child's printing, Wellcome (Claydon copy) Ms 8991/8

Dear Parthe [Nightingale]   4 April [1828]

You have not sent *God is Good.* Here is a new game for you. Take any word, and see how many words you can make out of the letters. The best way to do those words I told you is to cut out the letters. There is a box of letters at Embley, so you need not take that trouble. I took "breath," and I made forty words. You need not take all the

---

253 Letter 1 July 1885, Wellcome (Claydon copy) Ms 9010/85.
254 Letter to Harry Verney 29 April 1889, Wellcome (Claydon copy) Ms 9012/187.

letters, you know, but as many as you please. You must not double a letter, that is, putting in two of the same kind in one word. Is it not a nice game?

Here are two words for you to make two words out of them, of the same quantity of letters but changing the places of them: GAY ONES and GREAT HELP. The first is very easy. I have found it out, the last I have not.

your sister

Source: Note appended to letter to Frances Nightingale, in child's printing, Wellcome (Claydon copy) Ms 8991/15

Tuesday [after 17 October 1828]

Dear Pop [Parthenope Nightingale]

I am going to polish my shells with oxalic acid. We have nearly taken out an ink mark on the leather tablecloth in the music room with it. I have drawn the caterpillar, and Miss Christie lent me paints for it. Last night, I slept with Miss Christie in the great bed in the nursery bedroom, Martha slept in Clémence's bed, and Blanche in another.

F.N.

Source: Letter, Wellcome (Claydon copy) Ms 8991/52

Fair Oak
28 March [1830]

Dear Pop [Parthenope Nightingale]

Why don't you write? I should think you had plenty of time and I write you such long letters, and you, but very seldom, write me two or three lines. I shall not write to you if you don't write for me. I am making a bag for Gale but pray don't tell her, for it is such a nice large patchwork one that I want to surprise her. I have written all this immense letter today. My hands are quite tired. Tell Mama she owes me 5 shillings and three pence today for my weeks. I have been here six weeks and two days. Is not tape very cheap here? I bought 9 yards the other day at Rogate for three half-pence. Good-bye.

your affectionate sister
Florence Nightingale.
All this [have] I written in one day!

Source: Letter, Wellcome (Claydon copy) Ms 8991/67

Dear Pop [Parthenope Nightingale]   [postmarked 8 November 1833]

We went to Ryde on Monday, and I took your staircase Trochus to change it. We walked up and down the street five [?] times, looking for the shop, could not find it—at last we turned into a bakery shop which looked like it and asked for it. The man said that had been the shop, but it was only set up for the season and the woman was gone to Portsmouth. We asked at another shop if they would take it, but they would not. We found some of the Buccinum turris, the two-penny shell. We asked the price. It was 6 pence and the woman would not lower it, so we have done no business for you, my poor Pop.

I bought a 4-pence operculum,[255] and 2-pence Bulla because I did not like to go into the shop without buying something. You may have them if you like it, if not, I will keep them myself. We could not buy the great operculum either, as the woman was gone. We could find nothing at Ryde for you, so Hilary will spend your shilling for you at Portsmouth and buy the [illeg B.U. Buccinum undatum?].

We found such a beautiful and perfect sea-jelly on the shore Sunday. Aunt Julia said she never saw such a beautiful creature. It was large as half a tea tray. (N.B. this account is without exaggeration, taken from Aunt Julia's observations and mine) of a beautiful light sea-blue, something like an immense mushroom, the plate, table, or whatever you choose to call the top, fringed with purple, mounted upon a sort of column with three large valves, into which you could put your hand, at the end of which were six legs, spreading out all round, long, and three-sided like a prism, and fringed with a puckered fringe, just like a Savoy cabbage, the edge of which was deep blue. Each leg had a flap of the same colour, etc. at the top. It was very heavy and elastic; we carried it into the sea. In the plate, which was quite transparent, you could see a mark, just like on starfish, perhaps it was one, which it had swallowed, but we could find no mouth, it was so very beautiful, such a. . . .

Flo

---

255 Plate which closes the opening of a mollusc.

Source: Letter, Wellcome (Claydon copy) Ms 8991/81

My dear Pop [Parthenope Nightingale] [postmarked 17 January 1837]

Disappointment and dolour [pain] are still my lot, which were perhaps greater when I saw them return without *you* than when I saw them depart without *me*. Shore is expelling the nine lives out of my body one by one yet he and I are great friends, but I grow thin under his discipline, particularly when I have the whole responsibility of his mental health and parts of that of his bodily upon me. But he has been very good these two last days, dear boy! so I must not complain of him. I have been working like ten dogs while you have been away at literature and the children, so that although I have been always up before 6:00 and sometimes before 5:00, I have not allowed myself five minutes play since you went away, either in needlework or books of "entertainment combined with instruction." Oh! what a good boy am I! Friday will therefore be a day of jubilate for me from the prospect of a little mental relaxation and of seeing you and your friends. I am desired to write to ask Hilary and Jack [Bonham Carter]!!!

Papa desires me to say that you are to go on where you left off in Dante, and that he will be anxious to see the translation you will produce of Canto I revised and corrected by Miss J., to whom remember me as well as to the rest of la noblesse. Thank Marianne and Lolly [Nicholson] very much for their documents, which are of great use in expelling the blue devil. As I hope to see them all so soon, I do not bore them with my lack of news. Poor George Renhill has had a relapse and is as bad as ever. Betsy S. has not been to bed since Monday week. I saw her today. She is really quite admirable in her composure and indefatigable exertions. As old Mary says, he would kick up a terrible to-do if anybody were to do anything for him but her. Gale and I rejoice in your convalescence. She thought you would be left behind but I had no idea of our parents' hard-heartedness. Jervis is come back to Southton. I have heard from E.E. all the parish here is ill of influenza and 300 people ditto at Romsey. They have used up all the leeches and cannot get any in the country for love or money.

your Bo

I have had a letter from Hilary, enclosing your letter from Aunt Jane and a small billet-doux for you from herself. Edith [Bonham Carter] quite well. She will not come here for it was an epistle of condolence for staying at home. . . .

Source: Letter, Wellcome (Claydon copy Ms 8991/82

[ca. January 1837]

Dear Pop [Parthenope Nightingale]

My manifold businesses curtail my promised epistle and at ½ past 9:00 I sit down to this wee bit. I sleep now with Shore, whose extraordinary snortings, groanings and grumblings à la walrus mingle agreeably with my dreams. He is however astonishingly well, alone in the house he keeps so! I shall be dolorous till you come home now Papa leaves me. I have had a nice letter from Hil[ary Bonham Carter], her father's indignation which had reached an awful summit at her prolonged stay here, burst before her arrival and left her unscathed. Little harm was done to her she tells me. . . .

Source: Letter, Wellcome (Claydon copy) Ms 8991/83

[2 February 1837]

Dear Pop [Parthenope Nightingale]

Notwithstanding your ungracious silence towards me after the two propitiatory notes I had sent imploring forgiveness, and the title of music which I was to send, I write to tell you that Gale continues improving. Her cough is still troublesome and her pulse high, but she had a good night and gets up today. Mr B. gives good hopes of her. Shore was in bed yesterday but today is up again and Mr B. says there is little the matter with him. I sleep with him in the yellow room; he tries to persuade me he is very bad but this affectionate solicitude is in vain. He is very good, and Bertha, without anyone to set her on to mischievous actions as Shore, is confined to the nursery, is angelic and reigns sole mistress of my heart.

Gale inquires minutely after you every day and did so when at the worst, whenever she was able to speak. She is as obstinate as ever about taking her medicine. In the middle of her woes she insisted on explaining to me about the sending and airing of your shifts by Papa. I am very glad you have seen him. He was poorly and low on account of his late solitude and nursing cures him. But that will vanish as soon as he gets away from home!

So Uncle Carter is gone to town! Hilary sends me a letter of Aunt Pat's which is to wait your return, which to all appearance will now be protracted till years have laid their heavy hands on both our heads. Mama and I seem doomed to solitude and anxiety in February but we sing a duet of our own composition every evening to the tune of nod, nod, nodding and Mama actually went to bed last night *before* 10

O'CLOCK!! Shore talked to me this morn for two hours before I woke and my sleeping answers sound ludicrously in my ears e'en now. I could not send your music by Pa—he was so full and as you have no evening gown there was no use in sending the long black mitts duly brought by Mrs Collins. Love to Thérèse.

your affectionate Bo

Mama is pretty well. G. Rennell is out again. We have had two nice warm days here. Mr and Mrs Donne are gone to a living of £60 a year near Shaftesbury which suits them very well. Mrs D. has a good fortune and went in her own carriage! says gossiping Mr B.!!!

Source: Letter, Wellcome (Claydon copy) Ms 8991/86

[ca. 12 February 1837]

Dear Pop [Parthenope Nightingale] and Marianne [Nicholson]

Aware that your excellence in the epistolary line did not meet with a suitable return from us, I have been wishing to write for these three days, but Mama would not let me write till she could write herself, always saying she would do so the next day, and so it has not been done at all. All our people are going on well. Gale [is] downstairs again in the housekeeper's room and resisting Mama's exhortations, menaces, warnings and entreaties to make her sit in one of the rooms upstairs, where she will not be exposed to a constant draught from the back door and to the entrées and sorties of all the servants referring to her for everything. In consequence of this, her determination, your return will again be delayed for some time, as while Gale sits downstairs, an increased household would bring increased care upon her.

Kitty is recovering from a sharp attack of ague (dreadful headache) which she had for three or four days, so that Gale and she used to sit up in the two beds opposite each other looking rueful, but now, Kitty declares herself quite well. I thought that I was going to be left sole wielder of the bottle and administrator of the reins of the household by Mama's violent headache and chills one evening, which she thought promised ague of the same nature as Kitty's. But a drive next day in pouring rain restored her to her pristine vigour. We have had such hurricanes of wind and pelting rain for two days and nights as have laid fields under water, filled the pond, and yesterday, when we went to West Wellow, the *new causeway* was the only thing visible in a sea of floods which almost reached the level of the grand work.

Three unhappy ponies were standing on a little bit of land just big enough to hold them, without other land near, where some naughty boys were supposed to have driven them, but Mr Alsop [?], who was applied to on behalf of his own ponies, said that they would come to no harm. Today is a beautiful day and the floods have fallen, I saw on my way to the school, but the water is lying in all the hollows of the park and common.

We hear this morning that Uncle Ben is again in marching order but not coming to the House till he is wanted, that Uncle C. is not very well, having had slight influenza, but all others prosper at Ditcham. Aunt Joan is detained in her room by a cold, but Baby flourishes wonderful[ly] and sucks and grows and grows and sucks continually.

Very good accounts from Combe, Uncle Sam and all well, and nothing stands between them and perfect happiness but the mutability of human affairs, says Ju [Aunt Julia Smith]. Aunt Mai says that Baby knows all her letters but four!!! which bright example I hold up to un-book-loving Puff [Bertha], but I fear in vain. Aunt Mai says that all she hopes for from the little dunce, who loves nought but play, is that she and Baby will be able to pursue their learning together, difference of ag[e] making no difference in their acquirements. They are very good indeed but Shore's nightly confession contains sometimes strange things.

One day Puff secreted some apple in her hand at dinner in her little hand and, her deep depravity not appearing in her hypocritical face, succeeded in making her exit from the room and giving it to Shore. She seldom steals for self. I saw them going lovingly upstairs together and suspect some'at whenever they seem particularly amiable hand in hand. Shore comes into my bed now i' the morning and makes me tell him stories before I am awake.

It is incredible what some people's industry will perform, e.g., the piles of manuscripts which have arisen like mushrooms under my pen during this last month, [during] which I have been nurse, governess, assistant curate and doctor in the absence of Mr G. At all events I have killed no patients, though I have cured few. But the lives of British worthies, the histories, the analyses which I have achieved, enough to smother Papa when he returns. I feel rather awed and subdued by your boasted acquirements, ma chère soeur, and hope you will communicate them gently and by degrees to me at your return and not stifle me at once. I wish to put the best by foremost and boast of my own doings, too, as much as possible. The solitude which you speak as about to be your lot is dissipation compared to ours, but we will endeavour to relieve it by our epistolary sympathy during the absence of your relatives. We have finished the Talisman: it is so harmless that no doubt you may read it to yourself when you come home, Pop. We have not yet begun anything new.

Dear Marianne and Pop, accept my heartfelt thanks for your letters, which are merry companions at my solitary breakfast. I read them every morning to Gale who likes them much. I have had a charming letter from Papa speaking of the universal influenza, but he is uncommon merry. Little Renshaw no better. Yeomans' man had a hurt at the quarry. Woman pretty well. George [?] Flint dead. A sharp frost has totally cut off the bud of my hopes of going to Waverley. It is impossible.

your affectionate
Bo

Source: Letter, Wellcome (Claydon copy) Ms 8991/88

[postmarked 19 February 1837]
Dear and exemplary Pop [Parthenope Nightingale]

Gale sends you her love. Daily and hourly are the praises bestowed on your epistolary merits in this house devoted to calomel and castor oil, having only a glimpse of the external world from your letters. You will be happy to hear that our labours in the above line have recommenced from the internal *exhibition* (medical term) of a small ivory ball swallowed by Puff on Thursday last and which has not yet made its reappearance, notwithstanding the remedies aforementioned, but Mr B. bids us not be uneasy as in such convenient rotundular bodies he has known the reception of a halfpenny produce no inconvenience.

Yesterday was celebrated Miss Bertha's birthday, which was solemnized by a ride to Romsey, the first of which was a couple of magnetic swans as a present from myself, and which have produced great satisfaction, the little tea things, a kettle holder cross-stitched by himself from her brother, a bag from Gale and, which perhaps caused the greatest satisfaction of all, bread sauce for dinner and a Twelfth cake of jelly crowned with bay leaves, which were duly sucked by the delinquents and, lastly, exemption from exercises, the only profit which accrued to me from the day, which otherwise only caused impoverishment of pocket. I must not, however, omit an old apron of Mama's conferred upon me by the bountiful Puff, as my own was hanging in rags.

She looked beautiful in the evening, in a crown of camellias and roses. She is however, notwithstanding her exuberance of colour and spirits, a good deal pulled down by the *flenzie*. Her rotundity we discover is produced by her fashionable dress, which stands out from her on all sides. She is really rather thin and long, of the Shore make, and is often flushed. Shore is very well but we take them out now in the carriage as both are rather relaxed by weather and confinement indoors, not to say the absorption of sundry morsels of cheese, apple, butter and sugar, ivory glass, etc., which have taken place as you know during the last five weeks—the former from the nursery cupboard, the others notwithstanding our vigilance, owing to their unexampled depraved appetites and hypocrisy. All these things come round to me however in auricular confession at night. But, these iniquities apart, they are much improved.

Puff Oh! miraculous triumph! knows *all* her letters *great and small*. I always thought she knew them but either her good will or her knowledge have sprouted so wonderfully that now she will say them all and even the invincible D. has been conquered by being D. for dunce. Yet even now, so is she mistress of her art, that if a fit of perverseness comes over her for a few minutes anyone would declare she did not know them. She often *asks* now however to say her letters.

Gale is still better, but her recovery is so very slow that without any actual disease she often relapses into her former lying in bed all the morning weakness, and bad nights, though the day before she seemed rapidly recovering. Such is the case today but her spirits are now as good as usual. Her weakness is very great, as she will exert her strength some days to the utmost and then you find her after dressing *herself*, trembling with exhaustion, and after a few minutes being with the children obliged to go and lie down. She has not been downstairs yet as, although she intends to do it every day, and although she declares herself quite well, we feel that a very slight exertion of cold would quite upset her. She looks so thin and ill. Mr B. however thinks very well of her recovery, and I only give you this account of her weakness, which is her *only* bad symptom, to show you that it is impossible for us to come to you, much as your secluded servants desire it, or for you to come to us till you are summoned which, I joyfully expect will be next week, when Baby comes home.

We have had another nice letter from him. Uncle Ben better and in town, Aunt Joan better and going out. You hear of the misfortune of the failure of the Strafford[256] question. I should think Uncle C. would

---

256 Strafford was a constituency where voters were known to take bribes for their votes. The vote in the House on a new writ was 152/151 (*Hansard* 13 February 1837: 445-53).

annoy himself terribly, as his one vote would have turned it the other way, and that spiteful Buckingham has voted against his former would-be principles, a grand exhibition before his going to America. Mr Giffard [vicar of East Wellow] as usual croaks and grumbles about the possibility of ministers going out and of a revolution following the introduction of Tory ministers, till I believe he almost persuades himself that the said event has already taken place, and the bad state of affairs begun. His disappointment at not going to Ditcham, which visit was to have taken place this week, has probably produced this gloomy turn.

Mama and all the maids are gone to church this morning in a storm of wind and rain, leaving me to cudgel the brats and read to, as Gale. But as she is in bed I cannot do both arduous offices ipso ipsimus tempore [at the exact same time]. The little sense and learning is rapidly leaving me to the darkness of idiocy and so farewell my beloved sister. I look forward to rebeholding you and your adopted family in a few days.

Editor: The Nightingale house at Embley was extensively renovated 1837-39, the family travelling in Europe to avoid the inconvenience (see *European Travels*). Evidently Parthenope was with the Bonham Carters when her sister and parents first saw the house on their return.

Source: Unsigned letter, Wellcome (Claydon copy) Ms 8991/105

[ca. October 1839]
Dearest Pop [Parthenope Nightingale] and Hil [Hilary Bonham Carter]

I read your letters this morning while we were *still* in bed somewhere in the attics, with great improvement and edification.... You have been very good in writing. I have been very bad, but the enclosed volumes were all put up to be sent yesterday and then there was no one to take them to the post, we being all in a scrummage between moving and not moving, so they have been reopened to receive this second outpouring, which I fear me will not be so acceptable as if it came in two.

We came down to the house last night, Papa going in the morning to act the housemaid, we following in the afternoon as we could, the road being considerably under water and the coach and one, alias cart, going to and fro upon the earth, or rather upon the water all day, the last importation not having been made, which also was to bring the household, who stayed to have their tea, till near 9 o'clock. We three therefore remained in undisputed possession of the empty house till that time and sat by the fire in the servants' hall, no candles or other lights being procurable, Mr George having forgotten to send down all the groceries ordered.

Hogg was the only being who came to see whether we were dead or alive and, in an affecting voice which I had never heard from his guttural tones before, murmured, almost with tears in his eyes, that I should see your mam wandering about in the passage in the dark and the master sitting by the servants' hall, it's *very* strange! The water by this time had come into the passage but the mattresses by the fire were almost dry, when it was discovered that . . . the coachman had got a wan light. One was forthwith procured from the carriage lanterns. We got on such dry things as were forthcoming and began our search, the most important thing to be done as soon as we had light, in the larder. Some raw meat was visible, and also at last some bread, which was brought out to be dried by the fire and we took up our station in the passage to open the back door to passengers. At last Major appeared in a great cloak, bearing, poor comfort! a looking glass. But soon the last journey of the coach and one was accomplished—why so delayed we could not discover—and food was procured, not having had any for twenty-four hours. . . .

At 11:00 we were housed, Mama in the late spare nursery bedroom, now, by the bye, a very nice room and ought to be a state room. Nursery with two chairs and the two white and gold drawing-room bookcases our sitting room. What a nice room it is, the adjoining bedroom with all the grand furniture of the house ranged round it. Papa's dressing room, and the right-angled room now transferred to the east side of the house. . . . Last night was a favourable change of the moon. This morning, but Master Noah's hazy weather was a fool to it and where the floods are to go next is doubtful.

We were to have gone today to the Sherfield sale, including "seven odd volumes of les Aventures d'une Jolie Femme" and "twelve sundry Dutch *or* German books" and Mr and Mrs Lockhart's full-length portraits, but poor Mr Lockhart's things will be bought for nothing in this weather. Mary Roberts is to be our kitchen maid, the young Curtis's were to have been groom boys but do not think themselves "*polite* enough." The mezzanine does not look so dark as it did and has a bed in it. The house does not strike us as very large though there are so many new rooms. No foreign boxes shall be unpacked till you come home. We have had a *very* nice entertaining letter from Miss Clarke beginning "dear Madam and all of you." Old Noyce is still alive and very glad to see us. I have seen her twice and she hopes to see you before she dies.

The rain is getting into our ceilings a little, I am sorry to say, but then the fishes are beginning to stick in the elms, Vide Hilly, and all portents becoming natural.

Source: Unsigned letter, Wellcome (Claydon copy) Ms 8991/106

[ca. October 1839]

My dearie [Parthenope Nightingale]

Life is going on very quietly here, I hope it is the same with you [in Harrogate]. We are going into the [illeg] today or rather into the nursery flat, the nursery being our sitting room. You are probably in haste to know your fate so I will begin at the beginning. We arrived here at ½ [past] 4 on Friday and posted down to the house immediately. The drawing room is the admiration of all beholders and well it deserves it for, to put you out of your pain at once, it *is* superb. I might distend at length on the harmony and unity of the colouring, the richness of the moulding and the beauty of the conception, without at all too much raising your expectations. The oak ceiling and pendant is beautiful and the paper quite the thing and the cornices over looking glasses not objectionable, now that the whole thing is coloured. But there are sundry pink roses got there nobody knows how, which have so singular an effect that Mama thinks of sending for someone from Winchester to repaint them.

As we approached the house and looked in at the window, our bosoms to palpitate began and Papa ran round the corner and hid himself. But, though the room is by no means *now* a *light* one and looks smaller as well as darker, the whole could not be better. The dining room is much lighter. All the workmen went out on Saturday and we began putting up the beds immediately. Mama does not at all like the light green papers in the music room, our two bedrooms and hers, and thinks the walls of bow room and ante room painted green very inharmonious, for which the unhappy Herbert has received manifold animadversions. The green is cheerful however and the state bedrooms for the Duke and Duchess and the Contessine are beautifully papered. *The bookcases, my dear, are a failure,* resign thyself. The cupboards under them are shabby and on the shelves, silence is the best comment.

292 / FLORENCE NIGHTINGALE: HER LIFE AND FAMILY

The garden room is one of the prettiest in the house, both as to paper and everything. The green was certainly a pity and they have painted all the window shutters and woodwork of *our* rooms off the bottle and decidedly on the grass to match. Aunt Mai's, the yellow room, is as *light* as out of doors and there are some nice rooms upstairs. But the drawing room is a consolation for all failures: it is all one colour and the warmth and richness of the same is impossible to depict in half as glowing colours as those upon the wall.

The new terrace also looks well. Of flowers there are few, of fruits none, not a grape or a plum to be seen and apples have failed everywhere. Rain has been almost incessant ever since we came. Our mattresses, on which we are to sleep, have just gone down and will probably soon have become the pool of Siloam. We ought to have ridden down atop of them to protect them from the deluge.

Shall I now retrace our adventures? By my unparallelled exertions and with astonishment bordering on insanity, I mounted the carriage at half past and we reached the door at the same time as Miss Strutt and all sat together. . . .

But of Thalberg[257] how I can ever say enough, of that beautiful andante, and of the *Don Giovanni*,[258] the last variation of which was vociferously encored, in which he is playing "Meco tu dei ballure" [You must dance with me] with his left hand with a mighty noise as of many trumpets, while the right is making long swimming scales up to the highest note and down again like a musical box. He is so immensely improved and is really now a Malibran[259] on the piano; he is voice, instrument, orchestra and all together. His singing of Deh vieni alla finestra e scendi nel piccol lagno ["Oh, come to the window" in *The Lady of the Woods*] was quite an illusion, but it is impossible to give any description of it. We agreed that he played those studies which we heard at Bridge Hill *too fast* so that one could not follow the modulation. Miss Strutt thought that, with the exception of the one famous run, Mr Schulz played the andante with as much execution and with *more* expression than Thalberg. The former worthy I did not see much as Thalberg carried him off to Manchester with him. Thalberg is a remarkably agreeable man, but of him more anon.

The evening at Derby was lugubrious, one's spirits fall after the immense excitement of music, but we had a pleasant journey up to

---

257 Sigismond Fortune François Thalberg (1812-71), pianist and composer.
258 Mozart's *Don Giovanni*, Nightingale's favourite opera.
259 Maria Malibran (1808-36), renowned mezzo.

town the next day with Colonel Buckley, full of the Queen's virtues and Lord Melbourne's[260] easy and good term with her. He calls her dog a frightful little beast and sometimes contradicts her flat, all which she takes in good part. She reads all the newspapers and knows all that the Tories say of her and makes up her mind to it, but hates 'em cordial. . . .

Saw Jack [Bonham Carter], who arrived the morning after we and, by dint of many good whips spoiled, consented to go down to Harrogate, we hope. Came down to Basingstoke in two hours and posted on in 4½. Jervis [Giffard] goes on the 23rd so that next Sunday is his farewell sermon. I never saw him so agreeable as when he dined on Sunday with us. Baby very miserable but well. Choice of Bishop of Wellow now reduced to two.[261]

Went to the Sunday School i'th morn, babies reduced to twenty. We are waiting to go down to the house till a moment when wrapping our petticoats round our heads in a way which Hilly alone can appreciate we can rush down without being consigned to be the inhabitants of a watery deep. The floods are up, the rain falling like Switzerland. Our *own* great bedroom looks beautiful. I shall be very glad when you come home, my dear. I have been absorbed quite in the reading of something of George Sand's[262] which I want to talk to you about. Mme Tastu[263] has written you a very affectionate letter. I do not feel that I have said half enough about the drawing room. Mama and I went all over the house last night with two expiring candles while we were waiting for our supper, and it struck us that the house lighted uncommonly well, even the green window shutters and woodwork, which look queer when seen against the scarlet outside, look well by candlelight.

We live in a nonchalant, peaceable way and I find my task pretty easy, except indeed when I was with Aunt Julia, when it sufficed for one to enounce an opinion for the other, who had none, before to take up the cudgels and fight for the dear life for the contrary opinion. I was getting tired of this way of life when we came here. . . .

---

260 Lord Melbourne (1779-1848), prime minister.
261 Presumably for a successor to Jervis Giffard.
262 George Sand (1804-76), novelist.
263 Amable Tastu (1795-1885), poet and translator.

Source: Unsigned, incomplete letter, Wellcome (Claydon copy) Ms 8991/107

[ca. October 1839]

Thanks for the epistle just received, dear Pop, you can have nothing to do but writing to us so you must keep it up with spirit. Yesterday morn our friends departed, very early, i.e., as soon as Uncle Oc could be embarked. Gerard had been in bed all the day before with a bilious attack so we hardly expected them to go at all, and very disconsolate were we without them till a mighty irruption arrived to lunch on the drawing-room floor, first Mr Duckworth then Mr and Mrs. . . .

You ask if we received Mrs Davenport? We refused her *two* offers for where she was to sleep unless in the new grates, and where she was to hang her clothes, unless as I do, my whole wardrobe over the top of my door, left open for that purpose. And she, Mama says, a particular delicate woman I do not know. We were very merry with the Waverley party, which Aunt Anne was so good as to send us because, as she said, "she liked to see other people on the *gad* when she was not so herself."

Henry [Nicholson] desired me to make his excuses to Jack for not coming to shoot. It seems they got one hired quadruped with which they set forth one morn, and which fell lame at the end of ten miles. Then the skies fell so outflooding the flood; it was then 10 o'clock and, calculating that the beast would not get them to Ditcham till near 1:00 o'clock, they most unwillingly turned back. This is their story—let Jack digest it. Henry was in high spirits at having had a magnificent day and some very good shooting here to compensate for the partial failure of the first. For, though they persevered till 6:00 o'clock (I saw them as they came back from gathering sour apples in the garden after the day), without shoes or coats and their shirt-sleeves sticking to their arms, after which they dawdled about for awhile as I told you. Then Uncle Oc took a cold bath and went to bed while he dried his trousers at the fire and the braces. Not accomplishing the same process in time, he came down, the clothes frequently parting company during the evening and he walking about with the indispensables in one hand and the waistcoat in the other.

They killed fifteen brace one day, I forget what the other. Sam went away after the bad day, always good-natured as usual and we were so merry which I think I told you before. But, though you know I do not dislike solitude at all, yet the process of stupefaction had become some time. They are very anxious to come again to shoot pheasants, but Henry says Sam will not move again, being a regular fixture. They give hopes of a *to-do* this winter but Ma says it will not be till the last extremity if we do not give one. Eliza G. sends you her particular love and Jervis has left a sacred book for your profane moeurs. . . .

Aunt Jane was in a hurry to get back to her tot at Waverley. We sent off in the little carriage—they were going to stop at Alresford a few hours, to see poor Mrs Hopkins who, we are afraid, is in a very melancholy way from what Aunt Jane says. "I cannot but lament my childless condition still," and the morbid misery is still her tone and poor Mr H. says with bitterness in his voice "she is pretty well but you saw her letter," though he keeps up pretty well. . . . Jane Elsey [?] and old Betsy are both sinking but not rapidly. I go today to read Mr G.'s farewell sermon to them. Poor Major cried like a child and ditto any others when we talked about him.

We hear from the Duck[worth]s of a Mr and Mrs *Shore* of *our* family, a great windfall of a liberal literary and enlightened clergyman and admirable wife. If they were not now at Madeira, but perhaps the matter will not drop here. He has beautiful daughters, too, and it would be a great thing if we could get some such companions, but I set up my little back because he takes four pupils and if we are to have that sort of animal coursing about the common, and setting fire occasionally to the vicarage, as Aunt Jane says is the common practice of pupils, we shall not be able to walk about by ourselves in freedom. He is cousin to Lord Teynmouth[264] and a most agreeable man, with information flowing like oil. So much.

The day before yesterday was the only fine day we have had since the deluge, now fine mornings and rain again. Tomorrow they are to go to Southton to dine at Admiral Giffard's and see Baby Jervis or Johnny as he is called (of whose virtues and graces by the bye I do not think I have told you half enough) and a butler and sweet Mary Jane, whom I hope we shall not lose because the Giffards are gone, and who has bestirred herself to get us but. . . .

Source: Unsigned letter, Wellcome (Claydon copy) Ms 8992/78

20 February [1844/45]

My dearest child [Parthenope Nightingale]

. . . I am very sorry, my dear, that I led you to think by some letter that it was a very gloomy way of taking the world's ways, a record of mere melancholy moods and feelings and morbid discontents. I did

---

264 Sir Hugh Aglionby Shore, English baronet and Irish peer, Baron Teignmouth.

not know it was anything but very stale old truths, universally acknowledged, and no new expression of them. Was it that between the discerning of the new knowledge and the despair at the disappointment, the soul sometimes dies. Never mind, if it *is* so; what does it signify? for is there not one who has said, he that believeth on me, though he were dead, yet shall he live?[265] That shows too that two thousand years ago, it was acknowledged that the soul could die. Was it that the tree of knowledge of good and of evil[266] shall not console us for the loss of our tree of life? No, but the knowledge of God shall.

I think it is a mistake to say that the end of life is to know ourselves and what we can do, as Carlyle does, because misery may become so miserable, that it loses all interest in itself, and often we do not feel ourselves of sufficient importance to ourselves or to anybody, to care much about the dear self at all, so that it seems to me a discouraging and desperate mistake, to propose self-knowledge, as all books do, as the end of our experience. Oftenest we wish to forget ourselves—we are too tired of ourselves. But to know God and all his ways and all His intercourse with us, and the most favourable circumstances for seeking Him, surely that is a good so far surpassing all other good, that whoever acknowledges it as possible at all, must think it the chief aim of life. Why it did not please Him to reveal Himself directly to us is what really makes that which people call the "dark mystery" of life and its desolate emptiness. We cannot solve it; we cannot even guess at it except by the old thing, Wer dem Satan, etc.—the proverb is somewhat musty. The first sin of each of us had thrown a shadow over the face of the High and Holy, to *us*, and thus has perpetuated itself. It has not been isolated, this consequence has been its worst part . . . as the first impulse given to each of the planets sent them on their eternal round, and they went on, henceforth generating their own motion, so the first sin had done, separating us forever from the worship of Goodness: oh let no one misprize the blessing of a pure heart for it only can "see God."[267]

We have just had such a beautiful walk through the woods about Shootash, the air so balmy and springlike, and the woods so full of flowers, Hugh rushing about like a lunatic, picking daffodils and violets, cutting lances, throwing them at me, and exclaiming every minute

---

265 An allusion to John 11:25.
266 An allusion to Gen 2:17.
267 An allusion to Matt 5:8.

on the beauty of everything, like one possessed. We wouldn't ride, he said, because we couldn't enjoy the beauty of the day so much. I think our subgeneration has the very strong feeling of nature—he was so delighted with the *view* from Shootash. . . .

One of the ways of God I think is to teach us how the springs of sorrow and of joy wait upon His word. David knew at least as much of human nature as we do and when he writes, There be many that say, *Who* will show us any good? *Lord,* lift *thou* up the light of thy countenance upon us. Thou hast put gladness in my heart, more than in the time when their corn and their wine increased,[268] he seems to be recording the experience of a world before and after him. When we think too under what circumstances that was written (circumstances of all others likely to excite reasonable gloominess) driven from his throne by his nearest and dearest friend, his own child, and his suffering probably exasperated by that *most* intolerable feeling, if I had but done this or that, he might never have been what he is. Under such circumstances his experience is worth having. . . .

Source: Incomplete, unsigned letter, Wellcome (Claydon copy) Ms 8992/76

Saturday 8 February 1845

My dearest [Parthenope Nightingale]

. . . I do not like what you say, my dear, about our youth. I do assure you I find old age has its pleasures, indeed I believe that many a one could say the bitterness of *youth* is past and be thankful for it. You cannot think that heaven has a mother's breast only for twenty-five years, and then changes her tone and disposition towards us. I never read of "good will towards men" only till they are five and twenty, five and twenty, five and twenty" (bis) set to a catch and after that *ill* will and a grudge but perhaps you think, though the angels sang the first part aloud, one certain eve, they were singing the reserved clause to themselves, and the baby nodded assent in his manger to this plan. I think this is very likely and that probably the everlasting Treasury means that you may draw your cheque upon it for a quarter of a century's happiness, and that it is a sinking fund, where capitals are received, for that number of years' income.

The only art I know, my dear, to make men happy or to keep them so, is to shun the future and avoid the past (à part this is impossible). But one thing I do say, this, à la *Waterpark,* I do not think this is to be

---

268 A paraphrase of Ps 4:6-7.

our art from any distrust of heaven's powers of liberality, but only because I believe it is His intention to teach, "individual, take what the day finds for you, mind the temper of the day and never look forward more than a month, if you can help it."

I went down yesterday to take the sacrament with Mrs Hogg—it was so like the upper chamber, my dear, where the doors were shut, and all at once he stood in the midst of them.[269] We five shall never meet there again, but one or perhaps more of us shall most likely have heard the wings of the messenger, and gone forth on that invisible journey, before we take that supper again. How solemn life feels at these moments and even the heavy frozen air and the perfectly still iron nights seem to enter into the feeling. What a reverence one has for the being who is waiting her wondrous change. This moment there, so low, so agonized and now beyond the stars.[270] Oh my dear how I did feel, as we were all kneeling there, that the most real thing in the room was Him, and that *we* were only ghosts, shaped into a body, into apparitions, for a few moments, and that fade away again into invisibility, and the illusion of time is over, and eternity has begun with us as with ghosts. We *are* real and authentic spectres, for we too put on form for a moment and put it off again, almost before we have had time to wind up our watch. A few sighs, the ghosthood taking shape and time costs us, a few stormy visions, and then the morning air sends us to our real home. I would we could take the advice of dear old Horace—how could he be so wise without the idea of immortality? How much stronger *they* must have been than we poor Christians, those calm and *healthy* heroes, who did without the compensation = future, and yet were never melancholy. Alas! poor ghosts, for us:

Tis immortality, tis that alone
That midst life's pains, abasement, emptiness
The soul can comfort, elevate and fill.[271]

My best love to all my dear ones. There *are* realities and remembrances which raise one above even this heavy sultry life, but it is not philosophy, as *you* say, it is a cup of cold water, in the form of a letter, a remembrance like the sacrament, a child's arm round one's neck, and sometimes, my dear [breaks off]

---

269 An allusion to Luke 24:36.
270 An allusion to "The Pauper's Deathbed" by Caroline Bowles Southey.
271 Poem attributed to Horace.

Source: Unsigned, incomplete letter, Wellcome (Claydon copy) Ms 8992/89

[1845]

Thanks so many, my well beloved [Parthenope Nightingale] for your scrap. . . . We are settled into our quiet life again, I am happy to say, and I hope it will last for the *next* two months at least. I could see every piece of furniture in my room at Broadlands grinning at me to think, when we five separated for the night, we five perfectly well-dressed and well-behaved ladies, and betook ourselves to our respective fenders there to talk to them, what were our respective reflections and how far we had each of us been imposing on one another and on ourselves. How I should have liked to have been the several fender of each. I wonder how far the mocking Geist [spirit] of society is desirable and whether all that fire of persiflage and raillery is necessary.

I must say though for all the Palmerston family that not one of them do it and I was thinking more of Mrs Fox, who poor soul, I am sure is full of feeling underneath, and Mr Wall. It really would seem as if company was intent on working out the proposition the mind is its own place for fun (as Lizzy always says, when she is particularly *out of her mind* with spirits. My mind is its own place) and desired to live *there* and live there alone too and nowhere else. . . .

Source: Letter, Wellcome (Claydon copy) Ms 8992/123

Saturday [7 February 1846]

My dear child [Parthenope Nightingale]

I send your frock, etc., the book, I suppose will arrive, but has not yet. There is talk of the Bishop of Norwich's house in Brook St. for us till Easter. Tom Phillips, Esq. has written to Mama about it. I should be glad to be in town then, because I think Shore might come to us for his Sundays, and, in a place where *so* little attention is paid to the boys out of school hours, *why* they do not get into all sorts of scrapes, I think is partly owing to Providence, and not to Mr King certainly.

This day last year I took the sacrament with poor Mrs Hogg. How tomorrow, and tomorrow and tomorrow creeps in this petty pace from day to day[272] to the end of our lives. There never was a word spoken more felt than that. Here we are again at the 7th of February,[273]

---

272 Shakespeare, *Macbeth* Act 5, scene 5. The next line is "To the last syllable of recorded time."

273 This date is also the anniversary of Nightingale's first call to service, 7 February 1837.

Mama and Shore and I together again exactly in the same way as we were this day last year, but two of the people, in whom we were most interested this time last year, have been lighted the way to dusty death, and their little world goes on just as if *they* had never been in it.

Aunt Mai writes that B. is no better. Shore and I rode to Anfield the other day to look at Anne, the niece of Mary, the niece of Patience (Patience of Combe) for them, and ask Anne whether she were sober, steady, modest and pious, all which she was sure she was. We found the most melancholy history going on, the husband thrown out of work by Sir W. Heathcote[274] (for having stolen a stick) and this having gone on for two years, no other work to be had, and none for his thoughts but this idée fixe, he went mad, *a thing* came every night to tell him to destroy himself, and he is now in confinement. How all this world reminds one of the parable of the gold and silver shield; God is sometimes all that books represent Him, but sometimes he is a consuming fire—He has said so himself and we feel it and it eats out our souls.

O dull heart of man—how do thy hopes make thee ashamed. What was not "this time next year" to have done for thee and all thy neighbours and when it comes . . . but this moment is to bring the Empsons to luncheon, so I must leave off and with best love to all six young female girls, not forgetting my best and dearest friends, Aunt Hannah and Miss Johnson, am ever

thy affectionate F.

Thank dear Fan for her note. Have you heard that poor Mrs Ferrand is *dying* at Paris, of rapid consumption I believe, following the exhaustion and loss of blood of the operation. I hope it is not a return of the cancer.

Source: Incomplete letter, Wellcome (Claydon copy) Ms 8992/132

My dearest [Parthenope Nightingale]   18 April [1847]

I must write thee one word of greeting on thy birthday, being very glad that that day had its existence in this poor young world of ours. And mayst thou always be the lark singing in the bright sunny atmosphere of art and never descend, like the rest of us, to the busy scratching rabbit warren, where the inhabitants are digging and burrowing and making a dust for the bare life.

---

274 Neighbours of the Bonham Carters. See also p 189 above.

Me and my dove go on well together, though I cannot reconcile my dove's energy in coming to England with what I see. But man is a patchwork quilt. I am obliged to keep myself to a strict regimen of milk and manna, in order to purify for intercourse with her innocence. She never heard of brandy or heterodoxy and Strauss and exertion are alike unknown to her.

We have had Miss Bathurst here to sleep and the Empsons once to dine. Last night I had tea company; all the monitors drank tea with me in the still room, looked at pictures, listened to my magnificent stories and discourses, and spoke not.

Schiller's[275] progress, which made him unrecognizable after a week's absence, is not hereabouts discernible. The flowers and parish being exactly in the same state as in December. Don't fidget yourself about [breaks off]

Source: Unsigned letter, Wellcome (Claydon copy) Ms 8993/2

Great Malvern
7 October [1848]

My dear [Parthenope Nightingale]

I sent you yesterday Miss French's letter in a fit of generosity, because of the Frankfurt account in it. Please send it back as I have to answer it. M[arianne] N[icholson]'s was the one you were to "read and burn." I told you yesterday (that Dr Gully did not agree with me) in order to inspire you with confidence in him, which I hope had the desired effect. Mama's pounds of admiration are twofold, first because he doesn't agree with me, second, because he does agree with her.

This morning the operation began; a young woman roused me out of bed, set me down, with only a small girdle about my loins, like John the Baptist, before a great tub, and seizing a dripping towel out of it, began a violent assault on my back, while, in order I believe to divert my attention, she gave me another dripping heap of linen, counselling me to do the same to my chest, which of course, I carefully avoided doing. She then popped my feet into cold water, and proceeded with the same operation on my legs and said she'd come again at 12 o'clock.

Mama is to have a very mild infusion of the same process. Then I ran up to the top of the hill before breakfast. The weather here is like summer; we are going out on another campaign after lodgings. . . .

yours ever

275 Friedrich von Schiller (1759-1805), German poet (see also *Theology*).

I have heard again a nice account from Aunt Mai, which I will send you; she thanks for your letter to her.

Source: Unsigned letter to Parthenope Nightingale, Wellcome (Claydon copy) Ms 8993/19

[1848]

I have made the acquaintance of a poor little Estonian exile here of three and twenty, from the island of Oesel (where's that, *stoopid*?) who is living, or rather dying, here by giving lessons. I made it in such a curious way. Thinking, in my black darkness, that the Estonians spoke Polish, I went to her to translate the Minsk pamphlet,[276] which I have, and to take lessons from her (i.e., under that excuse). But she knew nothing of the language. She has very bad health (I have just been sitting by her bedside) and is a great admirer of the Russian system (to which Oesel belongs) of serfdom! She is a little woman of a great soul, and has gone through a *course* to "taking up the cross" such as our luxurious young ladies little dream of. *How* little one half the world knows (or cares) of what the other half is doing.

Has Mama told you of the poor "marchioness" in our kitchen here? Best love to my dear Pa.

ever my dear thine

Source: Unsigned letter, Wellcome (Claydon copy) Ms 8993/4

Malvern
22 October [1848-50]

My dearest [Parthenope Nightingale]

I was very glad to hear of Mary F.'s marriage, though I thought she was married to Sarah. How often an attack of Terror of Old Maidenhood comes over a woman about forty. If she can weather it, the mad dog goes off, and she does very well. Otherwise, I think that is a very common age for people who have been Sisters of Charity all their lives to take fright and become wives.

I have thought of a motto for my ring seal.[277] *From home to home*, the wish that is wished to Grecian brides. I think it would be very pretty (for intimate friends) if you could but invent a symbol for it. I have

---

276 Nightingale met Makrena Mirazyslawki, Abbess of Minsk, at the Sacré-Coeur convent in Rome (see *European Travels*). She gave Charles Dickens an account of the abbess's cruel treatment by the Russian government and Orthodox church, which he published in 1854 (see *Society and Politics*).

277 Nightingale attached this ring to her "chatelaine," which she left in her will to her cousin Bertha (Smith) Coltman.

propounded it to Mr Bracebridge and he can think of only a rainbow or an arrow. Perhaps you will be more astute. . . .

Editor: Nightingale's five letters to her sister from Kaiserswerth in 1851 attempt to get her acquiescence to her plans to become a nurse. The first makes the case positively, of how happy she was at Kaiserswerth. It and the next one also give travel tips, for Parthenope and Mrs Nightingale were travelling on the Continent that same summer. The third, long, letter pleads that Nightingale be allowed to pursue her own different course of life, asking her sister's blessing on "my sense of right in my path of life."

Source: Letter, Wellcome (Claydon copy) Ms 8993/44

> Kaiserswerth-am-Rhein
> bei Düsseldorf
> 4 August [1851]

My dear child [Parthenope Nightingale]

I was delighted to hear of Charlotte Coltman's marriage, which news had already reached me through Σ [Selina Bracebridge]. The sooner the better, I thought, for both their healths. Also Mrs Curzon has a son.

I wish you could have given me a better account of yourself. I go on most prosperously; I have everything here that I want. Yesterday the sisters mounted an old tower, eight storeys high, which stands between us and the Rhine, and sang their sweetest songs; I was just crossing the garden and knew not whence it came. The trees hid the top of the tower and through the still hot midday summer air across the blue sky, it came like the voice of the angels in heaven, or of Elijah ascending in the chariot of fire.[278] And when they ended with Home, Sweet Home, which we are not afraid here to sing on Sundays, and I thought of the *home* of happy exertion, of peaceful labour which awaits us all, my old tears flowed. Everybody sings here so beautifully and the cook practises her voice at the piano.

My wants are all supplied, I can truly say, with Addison.[279] Last night we had the most lovely soft warm moonlight and a steamer with lights came up from Rotterdam, steadily through the dark river. I thought of Christ's footsteps on the lake. Luise Fliedner is gone to the

---

278 An allusion to 2 Kings 2:11.
279 Joseph Addison (1672-1719), essayist.

sea for her health. I was sorry, but I saw but little of her or of any of them.

As to anyone knowing where I am, you know *I* do not care about it. I certainly don't want Louisa here. On Wednesday we have the consecration of a new deaconess here, which I am so very glad to see. We have now above 100 deaconesses. Yesterday there came a princess of the Prussian family, I thought a very vulgar one, but a good-natured sort of thing. I had to entertain her part of the time, so you see we are anything but out of the world. On the contrary, I thought it a great bore to have to leave my work to entertain company.

The weather is intensely hot, too hot I am afraid for you. I like it and am perfectly well, body and mind (though I am afraid you would much rather hear that I was not), therefore I refrain. The Bracebridges come here about the 11th and I have offered Papa to go home with them. He writes me very happy letters.

Farewell, my dear Pop and farewell, my dear Mother.

ever your loving child

Get well as soon as you can.

Source: Letter, Claydon Bundle 124

Kaiserswerth
6 August [1851]

My dearest [Parthenope Nightingale]

I am very sorry to learn that you hate Franzensbad so much, but I trust, as we have had some return of fine weather, that you will have had it too. It would be a thousand pities for you not to see Prague when you are so near and the journey on the Elbe is so easy and pretty, if not very cold. We made 3½ hours from Prague to Lobositz by rail and six hours from Lobositz to Dresden by Elbe, but I believe it is often less. I am sure you will regret not having seen Prague, Wallenstein's house, the Hradschin and everything on it you must see, but the lovely position is the thing.

In Dresden I never troubled myself about the china, which I hate, or the armour, which reminds me of times which I abominate, in order to see the pictures better, but the collection of armour is the finest in the world.

The Sidney Herberts (she writes me word) are not able to come before the last week this month and she begs and entreats that I will be here—I suppose to assist them in choosing a deaconess, as that was their object the first time I was to have come here. You will perhaps meet them at Dresden. He is now unwell at Hornburg. I don't know that anybody else knows where I am, so I shall not write to anybody.

I hope you will both of you, dear people, benefit by your troubles afterwards. It is a very easy six hours from Dresden to Berlin. I can tell you nothing of the road from Berlin to Cologne as we went to Hamburg to see a "Kaiserswerth" there,[280] then to Pyrmont, from whence I made the journey to Kaiserswerth in a day. But it is a most dull traget [trajet/journey], unless you go to Magdeburg. I don't think there is much to repay you.

I believe that as soon as you have left that unfriendly place you will feel the good of it and I am, dearest people,

ever your loving child

Yesterday morning died the flower of all our sisters.

Source: Unsigned letter, Wellcome (Claydon copy) Ms 8993/45

Kaiserswerth
bei Düsseldorf
19 August [1851]

My dearest child [Parthenope Nightingale]

I am very glad to hear that you like people to be happy in their own way and hope that that means that you mean to let me be happy in my own way. Indeed I know of no other in which people can be so. "Do unto others as you would be done by" is not the question; "as *they* would be done by" is the only true reading. I am most thankful to hear that you take this view of the subject.

The Bracebridges were here last Wednesday and carried me off for a night with them to Düsseldorf, bringing me back early the next morning, which I enjoyed exceedingly, but they will probably give you their own account of the place. I certainly do not want the Nicholsons here, but there are a great many of my friends whom I should like to see here exceedingly.

I am very sorry to hear that Mama has been so poorly and that you, my dear, are not making more rapid progress, but it must come afterwards. You don't think I don't know that you love me, my dear. I have had too many proofs of it. I am perfectly happy here, which I *know* you will be glad to hear, but I never knew what happiness was before—but we have no suffering which deteriorates, which is the only true suffering.

---

280 Presumably a reference to a visit to the Bethanien Hospital (see *European Travels*).

The King came here the other day and the whole sisterhood turned out to meet him. I did not go, ostensibly because all the sisters off my station went and someone must stay, but really because I can have no sympathy with the man and therefore would not go to stare at the King. It was however a pretty sight, all the children in a cart with flowers and flags. Here he is idolized and he certainly makes himself very agreeable to these people.

The Bracebridges do not return to England immediately; they are gone to a place (Blankenburg) near Ostende. We have had tremendous storms and floods. I have heard from Aunt Mai and Papa, very nice letters, recommending me not to return with the Bracebridges. Adieu, my dearest, and au revoir, I hope much better and stronger. You do not give me the least idea of your plans. I suppose you have none as yet.

ever yours

Source: Letter, Claydon Bundle 124

Kaiserswerth
9 September [1851]

My dearest [Parthenope Nightingale]

In answer to what I know you are saying and thinking, first I want to say that fears concerning the future prevent my gaining all good and strength that is possible from the present. I look again and again if there be any light to rescue those who so dearly prize each other from the sad sorrow of grieving or injuring each other. I see a satisfaction even in the rapid deterioration which has taken place of late years in my own character. It was natural that my people should wish—it was right in them to wish—my full trial of the ordinary life of those in my position (and which I can have of the best) and which, bringing so much of interest and enjoyment to them, in all love they desired for me. It would have been unreasonable if I had not tried this, for we have to learn what our own nature is by trying it in various circumstances. I feel a satisfaction in thinking that you will feel I have had experience of the best of England's life in our class.

You know how earnestly I desired to try a way, which would have satisfied the whole world and you, and saved me the misery of doing a new thing, of trying an untried path—misery to me, because it is so to you. I desired it because I thought I could live to a considerable degree the ordinary life of home, so as to gratify in some measure the wishes of my home, at the same time following the pursuits which would satisfy my own nature and sense of right to any *effective* degree, leaving it free to fulfill what is my sense of its appropriate work in the thought of God. I do not forget that these do not always go together, that, in SOME cases, during this life, the appropriate work is never found, in others, *cannot rightly* be pursued, and that the present improvement of the nature is to be patience under this trial. Many are unconscious of any fitness for one work rather than another.

Whether food for me and peace for those who are devoted to me are incompatible is a question which I should not have thought so important if I did not see another question. Do not they care too much for me ever to be happy if I am starving? Perhaps some can go on through life without food, or find it where others cannot, but some, however much from love they might wish it, cannot live without food. Can I, if I would, give up my food for the peace of those I love? *For,* can they in possibility have peace or happiness if I have not food? To render them unhappy is paralysis to me, but would my (moral) death be life to them, devoted as they are to me? If I could tell how I appreciate their love, how strong is the wish in me to return it in their happiness, how the experience of years proves this could not be by renewing past attempts (but *that* being granted which would fulfill the call of the divine voice within me, which summons me to work, body and heart would be with them), how I am not unmindful of their feelings in regard to the world's voice, but might I not remind them that those they, as well as I, most value as friends, would *most* sympathize with my purpose, would see me with more pleasure a part of the year, if the other part were spent as I should think right, than if all were given to life like the past which, however excellent, however full of interest for some, experience proves to me is not that to which I am summoned.

I am not surprised at your letter. You look upon my life here as a passing fancy which it is not impossible I shall give up when gratified. A. was a person of most lovely and tender character devoted to B. At the time in question, it was the custom in their line of life to live on vegetables and fruit or meat so modified that it had not on the human constitution the effect of meat. This diet was in general most palatable. Some to whom it was not satisfactory unresistingly conformed to it, knowing no other, but with B. it entirely disagreed. While, having for some weeks in A.'s absence adopted animal food, she knew that it supplied her with health and vigour and enabled her to take a part in the world's work and God's purpose, which, when sickened by the ordinary diet, was impossible to her. But A. was possessed by an undoubting feeling that the ordinary diet was alone right, was terrified at the imagination of the evils which would, she felt, result to B. from any other. She was miserable when she thought of B.'s partaking of any other. B. was deeply sensible of A.'s affection, which would indeed have sacrificed life or any of its gratifications for her. To render A. unhappy paralyzed B., rendered her incapable of benefiting by the food adapted to her constitution, even when a casual opportunity occurred of partaking of it. As life went on B. became disheartened, unable to find relief in that which was not natural to her. Had it been in her nature to become simply inactive the evil would have been less. She might have patiently awaited another existence. Or could she, like many, have derived nourishment from what was not peculiarly adapted to her nature, she might have lived well, while waiting to live better.

But there was a work for her to do and nature spoke plain when this work was not doing. Thus went on two [illeg] of God's souls, love and the fear of inflicting pain, two of the elements to which nature most trusts to direct mankind aright, being their destruction. The life of A., formed for love and sunshine was one of disappointment in seeing the idol of her imagination pass through life as through a prison from which she was conscious B. wished to escape, and in which she exhibited the effects of life in fetters. Yet to the last A. was never conscious that this sad result was from the want of the food natural to B. She only felt that B. had vain longings for unnatural food and had not enough of that which was natural and right. Their position, which afforded the most abundant and beautiful vegetables and fruits of the country and which, to the taste of A., were delicious, increased the difficulty. Peace to you, suffering and noble spirits in some other world, if here it is not to be found. God is and it is all well in His eternity.

How many have had a call within them which, in the beginning, gave pain to those they loved, but ended in their joy? From Christ, whose mother sought him sorrowing,[281] but who lived to see him rise to heaven, to Mrs Somerville,[282] who sat up by night working in blankets, to indulge an appetite for science disapproved by her parents.

When I was in Egypt, I heard it was your life to tell what would give pleasure to others, or increase their interest in me. You would find as much sympathy from various friends in this case. . . . The parched and

---

281 An allusion to Luke 2:41-52.
282 Mary Somerville (1780-1872), distinguished mathematician, after whom Somerville College, Oxford, was named.

swollen tongue, the gurgling throat she said are sharp but short agony, but this thirst, if less severe is more protracted, how shall I bear it? *Ought* I to bear it when I see water within reach?

My earnest affection, my heartfelt gratitude are yours, but I have also thirst for what I believe to be my right work. If you could, through love and imagination, become my champion, I and my home would be a blessed one and you, seeing me so happy, would be happy, too. If you were with me, who is there against me? (that I should fear). Thirst for what I believe to be my right work, alike from experience when I have had it and when I have not had it, this thirst and affection and gratitude are now at war. If you could so look at the case that your smile, your blessing might help me, that through you might arise the greatest of boons, peace of mind to us each and all! Your blessing on my following my sense of right in my path of life is what I most desire.

Auf Wiedersehen, my beloved

Source: Unsigned letter, Wellcome (Claydon copy) Ms 8993/47

[Kaiserswerth]
14 September [1851]

I am very glad to hear that you are going to Prague, dearest people; we travelled so rapidly through Germany that we did not know a soul till we got to Berlin. I told you to ask Ju for the direction of her German master at Dresden, I not knowing him and not knowing whether you would like Ju's friends, did not do it without your leave. But he has very pretty pictures (copies) which is all I know of him. If you go to Berlin, which I am afraid you will not, Mme Pertz is very unlike her sisters (the Garnetts) and was so kind to us and introduced us to all the best people in Berlin in the learned way and she lives close to Unter den Linden, where you will also live. But I know no soul at Prague nor Dresden and we took no pains to do so, I hating to be gallivanted about at pictures and Σ too.

I don't think you saw our lost sister; she was only thirty-six. By "the doctor" do you mean Dr Springer? I believe you ought to know him at Prague, though he is on a very different side from your baronne. I can perfectly understand the two stories. Is it not the old story of the slaves? And can you expect anything else? It will be very nice to visit the baronne.

You can buy old lace and pretty things at Dresden in the old shops, if you have a mind. Thank you for your letter, ever dearest Pop. Au revoir at the end of the month, when we shall all join company again together.

ever yours dear people

Have you written to Papa about the printer's bill? The man has written to him about it. (St Ann's St.)[283] he writes me word.

Source: Unsigned letter, Wellcome (Claydon copy) Ms 8993/54

[1851]

My dearest [Parthenope Nightingale]

When I left you, I adjourned to the Stanleys where I had a long talk with Mary[284] (very nice), a little one with Arthur and a little one with Mrs Stanley. They undressed me, because Mrs S. said, if I hadn't my bonnet off, she couldn't cut leaves. That queer Lady Stanley, who tells one all her husband's torments about the horses, came in. I couldn't help liking the queerity. They were much disappoint[ed] because Kingsley did not come, and asked me to come on Monday, but I didn't confess to being in London.

Thence I went for my body to Mme [illeg] then to the ragged dormitory, where I saw a new boy, promising, I thought, then to the Burlington, to gather up traps and news of you, then to your shop, for crochet and then here, where we had a nice pleasant quiet evening. Sunday we went to a charity sermon at the lock hospital[285] and after it, all over the lock. Both the matrons I liked exceedingly. It was really the first institution of the kind I had ever seen in England which I could at all liken to Kaiserswerth. The matrons were really matrons and not wooden guardians and the girls looked happy.

Mrs Chadwick, who went with us, had never been in a hospital nor seen any kind of suffering whatever. Oh ye gods, how one half the human race hides its head in the sand, depriving itself of the means of discovering remedies for the other half. She was so much affected she could not go over the hospital. I thought to myself, I'd rather be a patient than you.

(The day we went down the river I happened to say to Quekett before Lord Ashburton[286] that the conditions of the existence of the agricultural female were such that she could not but be low, mean,

283 The printing of Nightingale's pamphlet on Kaiserswerth.
284 Mary Stanley (1813-79), daughter of a bishop and sister of Arthur Stanley, who took a group of nurses to the Crimea.
285 For the (compulsory) treatment of people with sexually transmitted diseases, especially syphilis.
286 Presumably the son of Lord Ashburton, husband of Nightingale's friend Louisa Stewart Mackenzie.

degraded. Lord A. went off in a fine rhapsody about devotion to her children the finest existence, the domestic hearth and all that. How people talk and don't take what is before their eyes.)

In the afternoon Σ sent me to Miss Blackwell's[287] to ask her to go with us to Quekett's and to make a long day of it. Accordingly she came the next morning. (We had a Cook, a New Zealander to breakfast with us, told us a great deal that was interesting.) Quekett has built himself a nice little parsonage. We went to his savings bank to find him, where we *did* find him, despatching (with the help of all his staff, pupil teachers, schoolmasters, all pressed into the service, what an education for them), 2000 people in an hour. Oh how I envy him. Afterwards he took us to seven of his schools, examined the children before us, delighted in everything he did, with a wholesome appetite for praise, no false humility, no "miserable sinners."[288] Everybody's face cheered up to see him. Everywhere we saw the little gardens he had given the seeds for, the little glass boxes he had fitted up the cottages with for their ferns, making a horrid row into something Christian and cheerful.

But I don't think you'll like him—his voice is loud, his manner is hearty. Subordination, respect and gratitude don't appear to occupy any large place in his thoughts; he is ungraceful, the *strong* element is predominant in him, the healthy more than the beautiful. His morale is in such robust health, indeed, that a little scrofula would make it more interesting to many. This made me rather shy of asking my friend to Embley. With regard to his religion, I am *sure* that's safe enough; there is no lack of that in the schools, but it is a working, not a talking religion. *And* he has actually managed to bring the raggeds! to a *service* in the schoolroom, the first clergyman who ever did this.

Source: Unsigned letter, Wellcome (Claydon copy) Ms 8993/55

[1851]

Dearest [Parthenope Nightingale]

I was most thankful to hear that you had accomplished your journey pretty well and that you had seen [illeg]. I have done all your behests body and all and have got Mudie's books. I have talked to Mr Bracebridge about consecration. Quekett is the prince of angels. I will go by Great Northern. Thank Papa for note and thank all for letters. I will send Dr Howe as soon as Mr B. has read it.

---

287 Dr. Elizabeth Blackwell (1821-1910).
288 An allusion to the confession in the Book of Common Prayer.

I went to ragged school printing—not yet done—they have got a perfect godsend in an incense boy of Cardinal Wiseman's,[289] who has been three times in prison and has turned a perfect Protestant, the man told me, in the dormitory. I told the man it was a special Providence, worth £3.15 to them, advised him to put it in the papers, told him it would bring them more subscriptions, turning one incense boy into Protestant than fifty ruffians into good men, and pressed him to make much of it at the meeting.

I have got your silks. Had a very pleasant morning with dear Mary Stanley though Kingsley did not come.

> Hyde Park S.
> Tuesday

Quekett kept us the whole day, fed us, showed us everything, has nothing on earth to do but saunter about with us and as I never go away under a present, gave me lots of things, and will come and see us. But oh! there's another *Mrs Quekett* on the tapis; how I hate her. Nobody here knows that I am here. A scratch for Athena [her owl]. I hope Mama has settled Futcher [schoolmaster]. I saw Mr Ellis yesterday and got another present. Will you look in the *pocket* of that carpetbag you so magnificently offered to lend me, whether the key of my little portfolio is there and send it me. If not in that fascinating pocket, I am undone.

Source: Letter, Claydon Bundle 123

[February 1852]

My dear child [Parthenope Nightingale]

Papa will have told you that we came with J[ohn] P[arker][290] and his wife from Masbro' to Sheffield on Saturday. I think you were mild and merciful. O Lord! O Lord, how could he? But it is a painful subject and I don't mean to "relude" to it any more, unless I speak to Athena [her owl] about it. So I hereby liberate my soul and no more speak on the matter.

Alice Parker came with them and I am sure she sees it (poor girl). I think you must acquit Sarah now for her dry bone. We shall be with you, dearest people, tomorrow—we long to see you, but don't stay at home to see Aunt Mai if you have anything to do. I believe she will be

---

289 Nicholas Patrick Wiseman (1802-65), the first English cardinal since the Reformation.
290 John Parker, MP for Sheffield and son of grandfather Shore's senior partner in Parker and Shore's Bank.

up again on Sunday to hear Mr Martineau, who preaches that day at Essex St. I tell you this in case it should be inconvenient to stay at home.

Otherwise, let all I have to say wait till tomorrow, only my most true gratitude for your kind letters, dearest people, cannot wait till then, with which I am yours, while this machine is to him, most dear lady.

F.N.

Editor: Much of the material on Parthenope Nightingale's psychiatric difficulties in 1852 is recounted in Nightingale's correspondence with their mother above. What follows here are excerpts from a 72-line poem Parthenope wrote while working her way through her dependence on her sister.

Source: Poem by Parthenope Nightingale c1852, Wellcome (Claydon copy) Ms 9050/6-8

I have passed a dim and dreary season;
Grief and pain were mingled in my life;
Hardly could I tell wherein the right lay,
Could not tell my own way mid the strife. . . .
God has broken down my idol for me,
That I might to His raise up *my* will,
Ta'en away from me the busy nothings,
Filling my life, and said, Peace, wait, be still. . . .
Now be thou sure that thou has learnt the lesson,
The storm and trouble come to thee to show,
The plant twixt barren rock and rushing river
Learns what to choose and where it may not grow.

Editor: Nightingale appreciated her sister's good will in approving of their parents' offer of Aunt Evans's house in Cromford to become some kind of nursing institution she would manage. See her letter to her mother (p 136 above) for her reasons for declining.

Source: Draft/copy, ADD Mss 45791 f274

Tapton
[January 1853]

Oh my dearest Pop [Parthenope Nightingale], I wish I could tell you how I love you and thank you for your kind thoughts as received in your letter today. If you did but know how genial it is to me, when my dear people give me a hope of their blessing and that they would speed me on my way, as the kind thought of Cromford seems to say they are ready to do. I will write to Mama about Paris and Cromford. My Pop, whether at one or the other, my heart will be with thee. Now, if these seem mere words, because bodily I shall be leaving you, have patience with me, my dearest. I hope that you and I shall live to prove a true love to each other.

I cannot, during the year's round, go the way which (for my sake, I know) you have wished. There have been times when, for your dear sake, I have tried to stifle the thoughts which I feel ingrained in my nature. But, if that may not be, I hope that something better shall be. If I ask your blessing on a part of my time for my absence, I hope to be all the happier.

Editor: Nightingale gave up the hard determinism described in the following letter when she read Quetelet. J.S. Mill's critique of these views appears in correspondence in *Society and Politics*.

Source: Unsigned letter, Wellcome (Claydon copy) Ms 8994/69

[summer 1853]

My dearest [Parthenope Nightingale]

Your moral philosophy question I would so gladly answer but that I feel it as impossible to do so in a letter, as it would be to explain the path of the moon in a letter, without entering into the whole subject of astronomy. Without entering into the whole immense subject of God's government (a *far* more difficult and unexplored one than astronomy) it is indeed impossible to answer so important a question as "how are our mistakes ordained of God as well as our misfortunes? How can we bear what we have done ourselves?"

The heads of my (attempted) answer would be: it was not your fault—it was God's fault or rather it was His wisdom; you could not help it, you could not do otherwise. To blame yourself is as untrue as to blame others. Everything happens by law, by *God's* law. If the laws of God had been different, which made you what you are, imperfection would not have been on the way to perfection. Your mistakes are part of God's plan. If the plan of God had been different from what it is, everybody would not have had perfect happiness, which everybody *will* have some day. Then when people come to see this, all that energy which is expended on wishing "we had done otherwise" will be turned to considering the laws of God, and how we can further His purpose, for which they are constructed, perfection for each and for all.

If that unfortunate Miss Ryder, the superior of the Good Shepherd at Bristol, who has just poisoned one of her penitents by mistake[291] (I know her) could see that that mistake was in the plan of God, that she and the penitent and all the world would not attain to perfect happiness, if it were not for those laws by which she made that mistake, she would, instead of being miserable for the rest of her life, resign herself nobly to the laws of God as the greatest sufferer which they could have made, and suffer in accordance with God's will.

Will this creed make us negligent, careless? make us say, "we could not help it, we may do what we like"? If we do, the laws of God will so bang us about that we shall see it is part of His purpose that we should learn His plan by our sufferings and our mistakes and we shall not commit them (merely *because* we were not to be blamed for them) any more than we shall put ourselves in the way of toothache and sciatica *because* we are not to be "blamed" for having the toothache and sciatica. This is all the answer I can make in a letter. But the subject of the moral laws of God is at least as interesting, and a far more unstudied one, than that of His physical laws.

Either God governs all or nothing. If He governs *anything*, He has surely not left the most important kingdom of all without His laws, plan and superintendence. It is much nobler to bear one's own mistakes *in accordance* with the will and plan of God than merely to bear one's physical sufferings. Oh! God in the flesh, know Thyself, unite Thyself as one with all-comprehending thought, accept Thy high office to work out, to manifest that thought, phase after phase, now and forever, that thought that we shall, *by the exercise of our own nature*, by the learning of Thy laws which cannot be learned *without our mistakes*, rise to Thy perfection, to be one with Thee. I am very glad you are better, my dearest, I hope to meet on Saturday.

farewell now, my love

Editor: From the following letter it would appear that Nightingale had actually given notice to leave the institution on Upper Harley St., presumably to accept one at King's College Hospital. Of course she went to the Crimean War instead. The reference to Heliopolis concerns

---

291 By giving the woman the wrong medicine. See the *Times* 17 January 1853 on the inquest.

Nightingale's *Letters from Egypt*, which Parthenope Verney had printed as a book, although it was never distributed (see *Mysticism and Eastern Religions*).

Source: Unsigned letter, Wellcome (Claydon copy) Ms 8994/110

1 Upper Harley St.
25 August 1854

My dearest [Parthenope Nightingale]

My notice to quit is of course a secret. I do not see that you are "redevable" [beholden] to anyone of "timely information" about my intentions, except the Bracebridges and the S[hore] S[mith]s[292] and these I have told, as you see K.C. has expressly stipulated for secrecy and oh! what a tragico-comico vaudeville I might write (if I had but the time) of the interviews I have had with the leading men who have come to look at me—how frightened they are at what they have done, how many compliments they think it necessary to pay, without in the least understanding what I would be at and how I sit by like Agrippa's broomstick.[293] If I don't turn up in one hospital, I shall in another.

I will send the books directly. Rolandi has sent no parcel, so I went to him and he said he had none to send. Yesterday I just scampered through Bunsen and have marked the passages which struck me particularly that we might feel as if we were reading it together. But please rub out my marks. I don't agree with all, but I think it a great step.

Dear Mr Hallam[294] came here during his one morning in town. I thought him much broken. But I do not agree with you about old age. To me it is a time to which I *look forward*, when I shall be very glad to lay down my oars, and gather up the fragments of all my experience, and wind up those most important matters of reflection and thought which a too busy life prevents my speaking of [cut off] to myself and to God, which a too practical life prevents my speaking of to others. But then I shall be beyond the reach of fear or of favour and my practical life cannot then be spoiled by it. I shall speak my thoughts openly to the world, as Bunsen, after forty years of silence, has done at length. So I, after forty, perhaps fifty years, shall say to the Church of England, your religion is extinct, your men are unbelieving, your women are superstitious. Your litany makes us laugh, your sermons

---

292 Presumably Uncle Sam and Aunt Mai Smith.
293 Heinrich Cornelius Agrippa von Nettesheim (1486-1535), writer on magic and the occult.
294 Henry Hallam (1777-1859), eminent English historian.

make us cry. You become every day more impertinent to God. You pray against "plague, pestilence and famine," when God has been saying more loudly every day this week that those who live ten feet above a pestilential river will die, and those who live forty feet will live. And you want *Him* to alter *His* plans and you won't do a thing to alter yours. You pray against "battle, murder and sudden death,"[295] when God has said every year that, if the present state of education in Great Britain continues, there *will* be 999 murders in Great Britain annually. And you won't do a thing to educate the people. You will only pray, i.e., you will only continue a superstitious service, which excites [line cut off]

I have only had time to look over the enclosed this morning. I very much approve of all you have done and have scratched two lines through Heliopolis as directed. But I have not had time to do much to it, nor to put anything into ink.

I don't accede to your theory of looking back and be thankful. I can look forward and be thankful. I can admire and sympathize with God's grand plan of infinity and eternity and perfect good to be worked out in both. But if I am to be thankful for this world, in which (could we for a moment realize the misery which takes place *today* during one *half hour* in it, in the lunatic asylums, the gin palaces, the houses of vice, the hospitals, in war and slavery, etc.), we should go mad, I must decline being thankful at all.

Have you read Hill on crime,[296] especially what he says about female employment in it, which has long been a favourite idea of mine? Printing, gilding, cabinet making, *clerkships*, etc. to be done by women. Prostitution is now the most lucrative female employment. You demoralize women by shutting them out of all employments but governessing and needlework. This is the most fruitful source of female crime. Needlewomen always help themselves out by prostitution and don't blame the shop [?] masters. They ought to be praised, not blamed, for affording women occupation at all.

Editor: The only letters by Nightingale to her sister to appear here from the Crimea period are a message with a gift and a birthday greeting; there are then several by Parthenope Nightingale about her sister

---

295 "From lightning and tempest; from plague, pestilence, and famine; from battle and murder, and from sudden death, Good Lord, deliver us" (Litany, Book of Common Prayer).

296 Frederic Hill, *Crime: Its Amount, Causes and Remedies.*

at the war. Many other letters both to and by Parthenope will be published in *Crimean War*.

Source: Letter to family, Wellcome (Claydon copy) Ms 8995/25

28 July 1855

. . . I send you by Σ a bridal scarf for Parthe, the meaning of which is that the *new* "me" she has wedded, which is really the old original "me" now thirty-five years old, acknowledges the eternal union with a wedding garment. Also a jug and basin, wherein rose water is here poured over the hands, of which festivities we do not know much. . . .

Source: Note appended to a letter to Samuel Smith, Wellcome (Claydon copy) Ms 8996/48

General Hospital
Balaclava
19 April 1856

My dearest [Parthenope Nightingale]

As I sit in my den opposite the surgery door, watching the extra diets from my window, and the thick forest of masts over the Extra Diet Kitchen's felted and whitewashed roof in Balaclava Harbour, with a beautiful tuft of primroses on my table gathered for me by a man of the 39th, I think of thee on this thy birthday and think how likely it is that the birthday may soon come which will see both of us pursuing the work of God in another of His worlds. Some natural tears I drop, but there is nothing to me melancholy in the thought—I think of all the real love there has been between us which is eternal and how curiously your aspirations for me have been realized, even to the roc's egg.

The last tug of war has been the worst, the last four weeks in the Crimea, but we have now *five* hospitals under our care in this Crim Tartary in beautiful order (Castle Hospital under Sister Bertha [Turnbull], Monastery Hospital under Miss Wear, two land transports under Mrs Shaw Stewart, two land transports, Karanji, under Sister Helen, R.C., and General Hospital, Balaclava, under me. Is it not curious that we should begin to be acknowledged now at the eleventh hour, so that now they cannot form a new or a miserable hospital without sending for us and extending what Mrs Shaw Stewart calls my "sad but noble domain" or servitude—it matters not which—all at once so much, for this was before the general order.) And if I could think that the tug of war would continue, that would be the best hearing for me, for that alone would bring reform.

ever yours faithfully
in war and in peace
in the active and the passive
F.N.

Source: Letter by Parthenope Nightingale on her marriage, Columbia University, Presbyterian Hospital School of Nursing O6

Embley
19 June [1858]

My dear Lady Monteagle

Your kind letter was a great pleasure to me, and a comfort, too, for it went to the *heart* of the matter, which has made me very anxious. I doubted my own power of undertaking such work.

I ought to have thanked you before, but I find great difficulty in writing at all. My sister has so entirely occupied my life that I can hardly realize any other, and my dear two [parents] here with whom I have lived so intimately and to whom I owe so much, make the parting from home a sore struggle, even though I know to how excellent a man I have given my future, caring so truly for the best things in the best way, and what a tender and affectionate helpmate he will be.

I am sorry to say that Florence is suffering a great deal. This hot weather aggravates her symptoms, while the work goes on as ever. (We hear a bit of success now in the end of that incubus, Andrew Smith, head of the [Army] Medical Department, which will do her good!)

Dr Williams was anxious that she should drive, but the motion of the carriage increases the action of the heart, and much as she wants air she has been obliged to give it up. My aunt says that she neither sleeps nor eats in this weather. Dr Williams is very strenuous about quiet and not a word more talking than is absolutely necessary with the commissioners, as her only chance of getting through at all, and this is our comfort for not being with her.

With all our kindest regards to you and Lord Monteagle, believe me,
yours affectionately and gratefully
Parthe Nightingale

Source: Letter, Wellcome (Claydon copy) Ms 8997/68

My dearest [Parthenope Verney]

28 June 1858

This is only to say that Lady Dunsany[297] is dead, not because I think it a misfortune but that you might not hear it first from the newspaper. She died very gently yesterday (Sunday) morning. She was unconscious and quite without pain. Almost her last conscious words were "to give her love to all her friends and wish that they might have the same comfort of their faith in death as she had," something to this effect.

I think if you were to write a few words to Lord Dunsany (I wish I could) it would relieve his sad hours. She was very fond of you.

ever yours

F.

Source: Unsigned incomplete letter by Parthenope Nightingale, Columbia University, Presbyterian Hospital School of Nursing O7

Lea Hurst

24 September [1858]

My dear Lady Monteagle

We are grieved not to see you again and not to be able to profit by your kind invitations, but the fact was that my poor sister was so exceedingly unwell that she could only just see those absolutely necessary for business. During that last month she scarcely either slept or ate, the last week (though she went on working fourteen and fifteen hours a day) she could hardly stand and her lips were quite blue with exhaustion, Sir James Clark said. At length she could work no longer and went off to Malvern and we returned home, for my poor mother was very unwell too, with the heat of London and the anxiety about F. Our good Scutari aunt, who is with her, sends us but a bad account of her state. She never left her room or her sofa for a month and now only comes into a room downstairs for half an hour in the evening, to see a commissioner on business. She still continues grievously feeble and feverish, does not sleep above two hours in the twenty-four, and has no appetite—a very precarious state they call it, though there is no disease the doctors declare, only the utter exhaustion from overwork of every part of her. Rest is the only thing for her, may it only be . . . we comfort ourselves as best we may.

---

297 A friend from adolescence, née (Hon.) Anne-Constance Dutton, married to an Irish peer, Lord Dunsany.

[That] we see a person living so absolutely as she does for the highest objects, without one thought of self, ever seeming to come up even for a moment, is so beautiful that it ought to comfort us, but we the weak, lagging, to her, mourn sadly as the privations and the bodily suffering [illeg] entails and which no one can imagine without seeing. . . .

F.'s "spoils of war" may amuse some of your numerous children. We go on having the same curious letters about her from all parts of the world. The last batch was an address from South Australia; a poem from America; a request that she would sit for a stasioscope, the proceeds to be given to the India Fund, and the man said he should make £10,000; a letter from an Arab interpreter to the French Army saying the effect of her example among the Arab and Turkish ladies was such that they gave themselves value in their husbands' eyes by saying, see what a woman can do, and had risen in consequence; a request from America that she would let them have her "work on the Crimea" (everybody is determined that she is writing one) and they will give the proceeds to construct an institution for nurses in America, under her auspices. They shall be able to sell 50,000 copies. . . .

Source: Letter, Wellcome (Claydon copy) Ms 8997/69

[c1858-59]

My dear [Parthenope Nightingale]

I do not think I ever said to Papa what you report him to have written to you, because real love never hurt anybody. But there is so much ἀπέρωτος ἔρως, unloving love, as friend Aeschylus has it, l'amour de ce qui n'est pas, as somebody else has it [in *Choëphoroi, or the Libation-Pourers*]. If, for instance, I found myself loving gardens or houses or woods more than the wish of my husband in these things, more than pleasing him in these things, I should say to myself, you had better run away, I had much rather you ran away at once, it is doing less damage in the long run. Oh my dear, do always like to please your husband first, do like this always better than anything else or never marry.

I had much rather hear that you gave up covering the chair, as you say, for 7/6 than all the fine words about "woman's love" and so on.

ever yours

F.N.

Source: Letter, Wellcome (Claydon copy) Ms 8998/1

Highgate
26 May 1859

Dearest [Parthenope Verney]

Would you order two copies, one for Claydon and one for Embley, of Harriet Martineau's *England and Her Soldiers*, Smith and Elder. Would you also create a run upon Mudie [book lender] for it, by writing yourself and making everyone else write to Mudie for it. We are told this is the way to make a book known—through that "great fact," Mudie.

Also, any provincial libraries or reading rooms, at Romsey or Claydon, should have it by your means. It is not at all infidel.

Sir Harry was so good as to call here yesterday.

yours ever
F.N.

Source: Unsigned, undated note, Wellcome (Claydon copy) Ms 8998/15

[1859]

Dearie [Parthenope Verney]

Could you send me one, two or three, or even six, bottles of sherry, to pay for, of course? And, if you have a *homemade* pot of strawberry or raspberry jam, to spare? Many thanks for the beautiful flowers and plants.

Dearie, could you order the shop where Mama bought that beautiful photograph of the head of Guido's Bologna Christ (which she gave me) to send me facsimiles from which to select *two*. It is for India. I don't know where she got it, but I have never seen anything at all like it.

Source: Letter, Wellcome (Claydon copy) Ms 8998/6

Hampstead
30 September 1859

My dearest [Parthenope Verney]

I think Sir Harry's plan [for a hospital in Buckinghamshire] an exceedingly ingenious one and the architect's an exceedingly abominable one. I should fight for his with all my might. But I have suggested a few modifications which I should think an architect would adopt and a committee vote. I hardly know whether it would strengthen your hands or not to show the enclosed paper. I should say:

1. Get Sir Harry's plan voted;
2. Get these modifications adopted, if you can;

3. I should be very glad to criticize any plans you send me, before they are finally adopted by the committee.

yours ever

F.N.

If I had a distinct ground plan *of what is built already*, which I do not quite understand, I should know which of my suggestions in the enclosed paper are impracticable and which would require modifying. It appears to me rather doubtful whether, with £6000, you could not build a very nice hospital from the foundation. I would furnish you with a plan.

Source: Letter, Wellcome (Claydon copy) Ms 8998/23

29 May 1860

My dear [Parthenope Verney]

It is about the worst case I ever heard.[298] I never was so "shocked" in my life, except at King's College Hospital being built over old St Clement Dane's churchyard. You come clearly under the "Burials Act." (I hope you will be tried and transported for the terms of your natural lives, Freddy and all.)

The only thing to be done is for Sir Harry to write at once to Cornwelle Lewis [home secretary] (the slowest oaf, though learned, I know) and say he wants an inspector to be sent down to Claydon immediately, stating the circumstances. (The Home Office works the "Burials Act," as of course you know.) Grainger or Holland will be sent down and will say what is to be done.

I have consulted Dr Sutherland and he says *this*: (you have no alternative. For, if you don't, I shall lay an information against you myself. I know the Burials Act Office very well. And Dr Holland is my devoted.) In my old age I take just the contrary course from what I did in my youth. I "protest" on every occasion and with all my might. Dr Tait at Carlisle[299] lost all his children (but one) of an epidemic disease by placing them over an old churchyard. The Bishop of London grants a license (as no one protested on the first occasion) for placing that unfortunate King's College Hospital over an old churchyard *forever*. Such are the effects of non-protesting.

F.N.

_____

298 The unsanitary state of the church graveyard at Claydon, so close to the house.
299 Archibald Campbell Tait (1811-82), Dean of Carlisle 1850-56, Bishop of London 1856-69 and later Archbishop of Canterbury. See *Theology* for Jowett's correspondence with him regarding Jowett's taking communion to Nightingale at home.

The purport of Sir Harry's note to Sir George Lewis should be "the churchyard at the Claydons has become overcrowded and nuisances arise from it. Would you be so good as to direct an inquiry to be made with the view of precautionary measures being adopted?" The Home Office takes all the responsibility and directions are sent [bit missing] at Claydon is closed, you shall have £25 for the infirmary. If not, not. Not a penny of my money shall you touch.

 F.N.

Source: Letter, Wellcome Claydon copy Ms 8998/24

10 June 1860

My dear [Parthenope Verney]

 I send Hallam (£5) because you ask me. Nothing can prove, certainly not £5, my respect for dear old Hallam [who died in 1859]. I would rather give to the living than the dead. Also I send £1.6 as you ask for the Ladies' Sanitary Association, £1.1 for them, and 5/ for their tracts, of which I never saw one that I would not give 5/ to be without.

 This £1.6 I send for "la raison contraire," because nothing can prove my disrespect for the Ladies' Association, and so they may as well have this, as you ask it. They can't do much harm with it.

 I am going to answer all your questions without waiting for the reports. Gas spoils enough air for eleven (not six) men. I have put this in my little book.

 ever yours
 F.

Source: Letter, Wellcome (Claydon copy) Ms 8998/35

Mr A. Jackson's
Upper Terrace
Hampstead, N.W.
12 October 1860

My dear [Parthenope Verney]

 Did you ever think of Mrs Sutherland as your secretary to the "Ladies' Sanitary Association"? You might "comb out" the world and not find a better. But you know Dr Sutherland is so extraordinary (in selfishness) that it is quite impossible to say whether he will consent. If you think well, the best way would be for *you* to write to *him* (you who are a great favourite with him). *I* would explain to Mrs S. (politely) why *she* is not written to.

If you have time and if it is good for Emily, would you drive down with her here some day? And would you tell me first what day, if any, that I may not tire myself too much to see you? and would you spend £5 for me on something she would like to take with her? It is not a very sentimental present (a fipun note) but I dare say she has "no end" of "church services." And when I was a girl, I know I should have liked to have been "tipped" a "fipun" to spend on a writing case or little clock or travelling bag and to have chosen it myself.

ever yours
F.

You know all I think about W.B.C. [William Coltman] and Bertha [Smith]. I QUITE approve. But I wish she were not to live with Lady C[oltman].

Source: Letter, Wellcome (Claydon copy) Ms 8998/49

[1860]

My dear [Parthenope Verney]

An excellent second tract (in orange) has been sent me by Douitt, "The Health of the Parish" which tells people what to do, how to do it, whom to go to, in favour of which I recall my abusive language against the "Ladies' Sanitary tracts."

F.N.

Source: Letter to Parthenope Verney, Wellcome (Claydon copy) Ms 8998/53

[1861]

I *am* having a new gown made precisely like the old one, an event which occurs once in eighteen months. But if you should see a black *skirt* suitable to me, without any trying on to do, and would buy it for me, I am quite agreeable and grateful.

F.N.

I am told that the new chapter "Minding Baby" in my sixpence *Notes on Nursing for the Labouring Classes* is very successful. I think myself it is the best thing I have done.

Source: Letter, Wellcome (Claydon copy) Ms 8998/51

30 Old Burlington St.
Sunday 14th [July 1861]

My dear [Parthenope Verney]

I am quite agreeable to try the Cleopatra, if Mama is so good as to wish to pay for it, and if I may reject it, when tried, if found unsuitable. I have been so pestered with "treasures" of invalid chairs, into which I could not get and out of which I could not get when I was in. People seldom understand that when I am incapable of doing anything I am in bed, and that what I want, when up, is an easy sofa, NOT on which to loll but on which *to do something*. No chair or sofa I ever had answers this requirement. The consequence is that I spend more time in bed than I otherwise should, because it is at once the place where only I am easy enough to do something and where only I can lie when I can do nothing.

Please go and do the civil to Mr Floris, the toothbrush [merchant] in Jermyn St, and thank him for his (really) beautiful flowers, which he will keep on sending me every week. They are many of them out-of-doors flowers, I think, because they have a scent.

I shall be GLAD to criticize Bishop Potter's[300] hospital if not too late. I never think I am too ill to do anything which comes in the way of business, though I am much too unable to consent to people wasting my time in what someone else might do just as well.

I believe it to be the rarest (though by no means the highest) talent, to be able to gather all the threads of a *new* subject and put the knot on. In nothing has this struck me so much as in hospital construction. I have now received some hundreds of plans, chiefly by architects, said to be "founded on the principles of my book," or to be "on the pavilion or Lariboisière system." The last but one (which was Bishop Potter's) was a cathedral church, complete wards forty feet high, beds where the altars are in a Roman Catholic church, warranted perfect!!!!

I don't think it safe to take a maid from the old chieftainess, but I am still on the lookout and shall be glad to hear of anyone *safe*. For many reasons, I don't think it will do to go on as we are now.

ever yours

F.N.

---

300 Probably Henry Codman Potter (1835-1908), Episcopalian Bishop of New York and a social reformer.

Source: Letter, Wellcome (Claydon copy) Ms 8999/33

Hampstead
London, N.W.
7 August 1861

My dear [Parthenope Verney]

You see I am come here.[301] It is very pretty and sunny and quiet. It is five years today since I began the work which my dear master's death has ended. Oh my dear master, my dear master, that he should have been taken and I left, he who could do so much with me, and I who can do nothing without him. His last articulate words were for me. He said more than once, "Poor Florence and *our* *un*finished work." Oh he was better than us all. His was a great simplicity. His family have been very kind, writing me all the particulars, several times. And SHE telegraphed to Williams (the very day) to come and tell me. But no one understood and knew him but me, no one loved and served him like me.

He did not die happy as they said. He knew that he could not say, it is finished.[302] He died with a cheerful resignation to God, which was heroic, because he knew that he had no more work in him. If he had died as they said it would have been only selfish to go to heaven himself and leave us in the storm. But his was the purest ambition I ever knew, the purest heart. I don't think anyone understood this like me.

Up to the day fortnight of his death he struggled on, oh he was dying then, to do his work. His last official acts were to write the instructions I had written for him. I did not see them till after his death. He tried at the last to do what I asked him and it was too late. But he never said, as they say he did, that he had "reorganized the War Office and a child could complete it." On the contrary, disappointment that it was not done, nor even begun, hastened his end.

I have written an article on him at Gladstone's request. I don't know where it appeared. I have stopped all the newspapers and not seen one since his death. *I* knew him so much better than anyone else did. I cannot bear to see his qualities and his faults travestied. And nothing would distress *him* so much as to take credit for things which were *not* done. Oh what have these two years not ravaged in my life. Unless Dr Sutherland were to turn into an orangutan, I don't know

---

301 On the death of Sidney Herbert, 2 August.
302 An allusion to John 19:30.

what there is left to happen to me. Send this to Papa but don't copy it. You will see that it must not come round to his family in any way.

F.

Do not ask about the article; Gladstone and I have been corresponding about him and this must not be known. I dare say it will come back to me and then I will send it you.

I have closed my paper for the Dublin "Social Science" meeting with a little tribute to him[303]—oh how much more he deserved than all we could say. But I don't think that I could have finished my paper except to do this (at Dublin where he was so known and so well loved). Also, at my request, the new magnificent Woolwich Hospital is to be called after him. "Exegi monumentum aere perennius" [I have raised a monument more durable than bronze][304] *he* may say; I don't believe any man ever was so loved.

Source: Letter/draft/copy, ADD Mss 45791 f336

22 August 1862

My dear [Parthenope Verney]

I send tomorrow by Dr Sutherland a packet of choice Indian seeds sent me from the Madras Presidency. I offered them honourably to Mama, but she says her gardener has no idea of gardening and yours has. If *you* don't think so please return them *faithful* and I will send them to Wilton or to the Belpers.[305] I suppose they want stove heat(?)

ever your F.

Thanks for the grouse. I write now because Dr Sutherland is quite sure to forget the seeds. You must ask for them.

I had a letter from Major Powys Keck's niece, asking me to help a young lady who has had *a "passion" for "soldiers"* all her life and wants to *"get her bread by it."* In profane English, how would you construe this?

---

303 Nightingale, "Hospital Statistics and Hospital Plans" (in *Hospital Reform*) and "Army Sanitary Administration and Its Reform under the Late Lord Herbert.

304 Horace, ode 30 line 1.

305 Family friends in Derby; Edward Strutt (1801-80), created Lord Belper in 1856.

Source: Letter, Wellcome (Claydon copy) Ms 9000/72

12 November 1862

My dear [Parthenope Verney]

I have been too ill to write since I came here. There is a fine healthy breeze in both drawing rooms. I think I shall enjoy it a little longer, and then I have no doubt I shall be obliged to "give in" and accept your curtains. I think the view from my bed out of the W. bay on an autumn afternoon cannot be prettier anywhere, except in a mountainous country, when you can see it.

We have had very bad weather, as perhaps you know, and twice were obliged to burn candles till 1:00 o'clock, even in the drawing room. Today and yesterday are sunny. I don't think even royalty can have such a princely bedroom as mine.

It seems impertinent to ask Sir Harry to his own house. But I HOPE if he comes to town, he will sleep here, if he prefers it to his brother's.

Today poor Clough has been dead a year.

ever yours

F.N.

Source: Unsigned letter, Wellcome (Claydon copy) Ms 9000/82

[1862]

My dear [Parthenope Verney]

Your red lily which came from Claydon is quite gorgeous—two stems, five flowers on one. I am glad to hear from an indifferent bystander that the Fletcher women have made your house quite beautifully clean. Sarah Fletcher came to me here and asked me, by your desire, what carpets she should put down before Mama came. I said the carpet in the big bedroom, of which the floor is splintery and does not do to scour too often.

About my going there, I had intended, when I left this house on 1 November, to be guided entirely by what is best for the War Office work, when you were so good as to offer me your house. But I am afraid I shall never be able again to live *except on one floor*, with a little room *alongside* where I could see a man, or sit (without dressing) while my own room is being done. I have not once been downstairs (*to sit*) here, even with these easy stairs. I spend my *afternoons* in bed in a beautiful south bedroom on the bedroom floor. On fine days I go out for five or six minutes in the garden, often without dressing, and just have my coffee to rest on the ground floor.

I am afraid I should never get up the stairs at South St., for what makes the drawing room so good is the noble height of the room, or if I did I should never get down again. And I should not like to turn your *drawing-room floor* into an invalid's bedroom. I am much weaker than I was at C. St.

Source: Letter to Parthenope Verney, Wellcome (Claydon copy) Ms 9000/76

Christmas Day [1862]

Pray let Freddy [Verney] dine and sleep here on Monday. It will not make me "nervous" at all. It would make me very "nervous" if he did not. I am so busy, so behind hand with my work, that I am afraid there would not be a chance for my seeing you, dear, *except* on Sunday.

I am not what I was this time last year. Sir John Lawrence says that we ought to have been at least five months' forwarder with our work. And Dr Sutherland has scarcely done a stroke since 8 July. I have had Lord de Grey here and we have concerted a plan for helping Sir J. Lawrence.

ever your F.

The India military authorities are coming round, i.e., the blow is struck; they declare themselves vastly "ill used," but they do what we want. Sir C. Trevelyan has just sent me a printed paper from a Colonel Crommelin, R.E., who has the supervision of barracks in Bengal, which has adopted nearly all our principles. Now I saw a few weeks ago a private letter from this Colonel C. full of foul-mouthed violent abuse against us. We ought to be and I hope are very thankful. For this adoption of our principles, without thanking us, is all we want.

Source: Note to Parthenope Verney, Wellcome (Claydon copy) Ms 9023/41

115 Park St.

[1862?]

Please come tomorrow (Saturday) at 10:30 for a quarter of an hour. And please take the sacrament with us on Sunday at 3:00. Tomorrow I hope to fix an additional hour to see you.

F.N.

Source: Letter, Wellcome (Claydon copy) Ms 9000/132

26 September 1863

Dear [Parthenope Verney]

I cannot tell you how glad I am to hear (which sounds very inhuman) that Sir James Hope is to have the North American and West

Indian station.[306] It will do so much good. I should like very well to go to the West Indies, if I were Emily, and should the climate do. Pray give my respectful regards to Sir James.

I suppose there is not the least chance of Sir Harry going to the Edinburgh meeting. I only wrote for the chance, as I must send my papers.

ever yours

F.

Source: Unsigned, undated letter, Wellcome (Claydon copy) Ms 8999/55

[c1863]

Dearie [Parthenope Verney]

It is *quite* impossible to me, I am sorry to say, to see anyone whatever today, which is besides Indian mail day. Sir J. Lawrence is seriously angry, though not nearly so much as we deserve, at the unwarrantable delay of the War Office and India Office in sending out his plans. I am exceedingly glad that he is angry, though it all falls upon me.

I am very sorry for Mlle v. Zechau's loss, but glad of the Princess Royal's gain. We owe that princess something and she is so lonely, now Stockmar[307] is going. If Mlle v. Z. has time to spare on the 18th, write me word. But I cannot sacrifice the bird in the hand, Sir J. Lawrence, for a bird not even in the bush.

I shall hope to see Emily for ten minutes before she goes anywhere for the winter, to judge for myself of her, though small good will that do her to hear when Dr W. has given *his* opinion. Who "has *not* had low fever" this last year? It is universal. Little Mary Herbert is now, they fear, dying of it at Constantinople. George and Maud[308] have been sent home. I have not been a day without an attack. . . .

Source: Letter, Wellcome (Claydon copy) Ms 9001/63

28 September 1864

Dear Pop [Parthenope Verney]

I gladly give £5, and am quite agreeable to giving £10 (if you like it) to your volunteers, whether in pots or in cash, as you like it, of course— I not knowing the convenances. I presume it is to be annual.

---

306 Admiral Sir James Hope (1808-81), brother of Harry Verney's first wife.

307 Baron Stockmar (1787-1863) came to England with Prince Albert and was considered to have influenced him unduly; the reference is probably to his death.

308 Children of Elizabeth and Sidney Herbert.

If you have Mill on representative government[309] or Newman's *Apologia*,[310] could you send them me by post?

ever your F.

Source: Letter, Wellcome (Claydon copy) Ms 9001/109

Dearie [Parthenope Verney]   22 February 1865

Would you like to come—Mr Jowett is to give the sacrament next Sunday at 3:00. Would you like to ask him to luncheon before? not that there is the least occasion. You know he has his £500 a year at last.[311]

I thanked Miss Coutts[312] for her £20 to the Fliedners, for which I am truly grateful, to Sir Harry. I was truly sorry not to see him last Sunday. Mrs Sutherland came down to me upon a quite unexpected matter, regarding the India Office.

I have got 7 millions for India barracks—how well it looks— £7,000,000. But Sir J. Lawrence says it must be 10 millions. And it shall. The baby has had dysentery since it got there. And Lady Lawrence is gone to Barrackpore with it.

ever your

F.

Source: Unsigned letter, Wellcome (Claydon copy) Ms 9001/123

Dearie [Parthenope Verney]   19 April [1865?]

I stayed up tonight till 7:00 o'clock because the maids told me you were "coming back" here "from Eaton Sq." to "fetch my answer" and I wanted to kiss you on your birthday. (They do make such careless mistakes in their messages.) I send my answer. Perhaps it had better not be forwarded in *my* handwriting.

I am not at all surprised at Miss Vernon's letter. I sometimes think that my whole business in life is to defend charitable funds from people who want to use them "for the poor," whose "*chief inducement*" is to be sent somewhere.

---

309 J.S. Mill, *Considerations on Representative Government,* 1861.
310 John Henry (later Cardinal) Newman (1801-90), *Apologia pro sua Vita,* on which see a letter to W.E. Nightingale in *Theology.*
311 Jowett's salary had been kept down on account of his suspected heresy; liberals, including Queen Victoria, were incensed at this treatment of him.
312 Perhaps Angela Georgina Burdett-Coutts (1814-1906), Baroness, philanthropist.

Also, it is past praying for that ladies shall ever understand the difference between monthly nurses[313] for the rich and midwifery nurses for the poor. I am quite certain Sir J. Lawrence will never appropriate any part of Indian funds to pay for the passage out of the *former*. Indian ladies are rich enough. Let them do it.

2. I return Emily's letter, what a nice letter.

3. I wanted to know whether Sir Harry wishes the inquiry into the French poor relief system pursued and what course he means to take in opposition to the Unions Chargeability Bill.

4. Mr Jowett comes next Sunday to give me the sacrament at 3:00. Will you come? Would you like?

5. Could you take this poor Italian's music back to him, with this message from me, that it goes to my heart not to acknowledge it, but that I am an entire prisoner to my bed, overwhelmed with business. I see no one. He might just as well ask a nurse in a hospital or a patient in a hospital to recommend him. (It goes to my heart to refuse him because other beggars will call at my house two or three times *and actually send up their photographs to me,* as if I were a woman of bad character.) But this man has never called once.

Source: Undated note by Parthenope Verney with Nightingale reply, Wellcome (Claydon copy) Ms 9001/189

My dear [Florence Nightingale]

I have written this for the Sanitarys who wanted a tract on the Whibock child murder. I half thought of sending it to *Good Words* or *Chambers* in order for a wider circulation, but it bears its "tract" origin too strongly on its face I believe? I meant it for the poor to read. *Good Words* is too literary I suppose?

FN: Dearie I think this should be a tract, but I am the poorest judge possible. I don't think *Good Words* or *Chambers* are at all read by what we call "the poor." And their style is so different. But I am a bad judge.

Source: Incomplete letter to Parthenope Verney, Wellcome (Claydon copy) Ms 9001/199

[1865]

I could see you today at 3:00 or at 4:00, please. But if you would go to the opening of the S. London Working Men's Exhibition, I should be

---

313 A monthly nurse attended a woman for the month after birth, thus permitting her to rest.

better pleased still. Sir Harry was so good as to say he would go. They want "sponsible people" and I am very glad even that the little half-crowns should be put in their pockets.

The whole was set on foot and practically worked by a common clerk in the War Office, Mr Frederick,[314] now, I am happy to say, a commission secretary. He scraped together upwards of £1000 from guarantors, of whom I am one. The men, when my name was given out, all cheered, though they did not cheer the Prince of Wales. I could not help shedding tears. . . .

ever yours
F.

Source: Letter, Wellcome (Claydon copy) Ms 9001/110

[printed address] 27 Norfolk Street
Park Lane, W.
[c1866]

Darling [Parthenope Verney]

There is not the remotest chance of my EVER wanting a carriage in this life again, except when I am *compelled* to move.

Would Sir Harry come in sometime this afternoon to see me sign the agreement? Would you tell him that I have written to Paris for more information about the relief system of the poor as the imperial policy has meddled with everything since my day, thirteen years ago. But it appears to me that the only real opposition which could be got up in the House of Commons to Mr Villiers' bill would be *by having witnesses from Paris*. And there is no time now for this. I do not myself think that *anything* could make the French system do in England.

ever yours
F.N.

Source: Letter, Wellcome (Claydon copy) Ms 9002/10

19 April 1866

Dear Pop [Parthenope Verney]

I send you a Turner [reproduction] for your birthday. But I think I shall change it for one which is coming from Colnaghi, but not come. So this is only a stand-in-its-place, to mark the day.

---

314 J.J. Frederick, a close colleague to whom Nightingale left £300 in her will, and her India blue books.

For that scrimpit dud of a lock of hair sent to Sabilla Novello,[315] I have a sonnet from her sister. (I should have had two, had you let me send the whole lock.) I suppose Mama must see the sonnet, and then let it come back to me, please, for I have not read it yet.

I am sending back the two azaleas. They have *behaved nobly*. And I would not send them back now but that I think they want "a course." I am so sorry to part with them, as if they were human creatures. Please let them be well done by.

ever thy

F.

Source: Letter, Wellcome (Claydon copy) Ms 9002/11

[printed address] 35 South Street
Park Lane
London, W.
4 May 1866

Dearest [Parthenope Verney]

Sir Harry is so good as to offer me your carriage for the next fort-night, but it would not be worthwhile. I might not be able to use it more than once.

On the days the "Thorn in the Flesh" [Dr Sutherland] is here, I can do nothing else. Indeed I am always worked up to more than my full strength. This is the reason why I can *never* do anything *unexpectedly* as to day.

F.

Source: Incomplete letter to Parthenope Verney, Wellcome (Claydon copy) Ms 9003/21

[before Whitsun 1866]

Rev Mother of Bermondsey has been dangerously ill with pleurisy and fistula. (Mrs Bracebridge says Manning[316] will kill her.) All my Embley things, including flowers, have recently passed on to her, besides Gunter's turtle soup. She understands that I shall never forgive her unless she becomes as fat as a Lord Mayor with time and soup.

I should much like a box of *flowers* and *strawberries* on Whit Monday (for myself), large quantities of azaleas, yellow and white. (I can't com-plain this time of the red rhododendrons, beauties have been sent me,

---

315 Translator of Nightingale's *Notes on Nursing* into Italian.
316 Henry Edward Manning (1808-92), later Cardinal; see *Theology* for his treatment of the Sisters of Mercy.

lilac ones I hate.) We can't get any strawberries in London; they are either so dear or not to be had at all.

I have got the Turner *Orvieto* photograph from Colnaghi, which is what I wanted to give you, dear Pop, on your birthday. It is the finest specimen of a Turner I know. It is not mounted, but, if you like it, I will have it mounted. And the *provisional* Turner I sent you I would just as lief [soon] keep for myself.

I always have *peculiar* reminiscences of Embley on Whitsunday. I hardly know why, but I believe it is the azaleas.

ever your F.

Source: Unsigned letter, Wellcome (Claydon copy) Ms 9002/92

Dearie [Parthenope Verney]   [1866-67]

It is very good of you to offer to come tomorrow but I could not see anyone, not if it were to save my life. I thought you knew that I worked every day from 7:30 to 5:30, and that *before* 1:00 I could not see anyone *except* to save the Indian Empire.

Source: Letter, Wellcome (Claydon copy) Ms 9002/200

Dearie [Parthenope Verney]   Sunday [1867]

I should be very glad if Emily liked to come to the sacrament. I fancied she would not (you know, Mr Fremantle, of Claydon,[317] led the seven chiefs against Thebes, Thebes = my big Plato).

F.N.

Source: Letter, Wellcome (Claydon copy) Ms 9003/17

Dearie [Parthenope Verney]   Easter Sunday [1868]

Temperance [her maid] is very much shut up with me and I should much have liked her to go to Westminster Abbey this afternoon. If her brother is going with you, could you take her, too, with the carriage?— to hear the dean [Stanley].

F.

---

317 William Robert Fremantle, Vicar of All Saints, Middle Claydon, the Verneys' church, married to a daughter of Sir Harry Calvert, the 1st baronet. See *Theology* on the treatment of Jowett and the other authors of *Essays and Reviews*.

Source: Exchange of notes with her sister, ADD Mss 45791 f350

[19 April 1868]

My dear [Florence Nightingale]

I hope you will see me today. If so what time? Emily arrived last night all safe I think.

FN: I am so overwhelmed with work but can *not* *not* wish to see thee on thy birthday, at 3:00 please, but not to stay later than 4:00 or at 4:30. Love to Emily.

Editor: Nightingale gave a broad hint to Harry Verney that she had not seen her sister's book *Avonhoe*.[318] A later letter asks him to tell her that she had been "quite cheered and nourished in my heart" from reading it.[319]

Source: Unsigned letter, Wellcome (Claydon copy) Ms 9003/91

12 March 1869

Dearie [Parthenope Verney]

1. Many thanks for Spencer and the corrected "Una." We are just now in the thick of our work and I am afraid I must put off the doing of it till August.

2. Mr Jowett is coming here to give me the sacrament on Sunday at 3:00. Would you or Sir Harry, or both, like to come? *R.S.V.P...* ....

Source: Letter to Parthenope Verney, Wellcome (Claydon copy) Ms 9003/131

17 December 1869

... I sent a copy of *Stone Edge*[320] to Miss Osburn, our superintendent at Sydney. She has read it *aloud* with great satisfaction. She is a Derbyshire woman, a Carr. She has made great friends with Lady Belmore, the governor's and Mrs Lambert, the commodore's wife, the latter a great friend of Jervis Giffard's. ....

---

318 Letter to Harry Verney 25 September 1868, Wellcome (Claydon copy) Ms 9003/46.
319 Letter to Harry Verney 7 November 1868, Wellcome (Claydon copy) Ms 9003/52.
320 Parthenope Verney's novel, *Stone Edge*.

Source: Letter to Parthenope Verney, Wellcome (Claydon copy) Ms 9004/28

> [printed address] 35 South Street
> Park Lane, W.
> [April 1870]

I send you H. Martineau's letter (on *Lettice Lisle*).[321] Please return it to me. With all the drawbacks, I think her one of the best literary judges yet existing.

If you are writing on Bunsen, do you choose to see an unpublished printed fragment of his *Life of Jesus*, which I have? (But I shall not send it you, if you are going to criticize him in that shabby and savage manner.) I have also M. Müller's criticism, cut out of the *Times*, on the *Life*, if you like to look at it again. . . .

Source: Unsigned, incomplete letter, Wellcome (Claydon copy) Ms 9004/39

7-8 May 1870

Female Medical Education

Dearie [Parthenope Verney]

I am afraid that I think it would take at least a month to work out anything for this difficult question. I am afraid that my opinions are so essentially different that all I could do would be, like the critic on M Grandperret, the Public Prosecutor, to suggest doubts which I could not solve without questioning you, the Public Prosecutor *at almost every sentence* (of what I have marked in red).

For example, *do* you wish "lady doctors" to have the same "training" and "examinations" as men? Certainly not. (I have expressed my opinion so often in answer to questions and appeals from Mrs Butler[322] and all the "tall-talk" ladies—and from Dr Acland,[323] Mr John Stuart Mill and other men that it is almost a public one. I have looked in vain for a note I possess of these correspondences, but am quite unable to undertake such a search thoroughly at present. Otherwise I would have sent it you.)

Briefly, my opinion is this: (1) *Do* you wish to make women men doctors? Certainly not. Do you not wish to make women something

---

321 Nightingale sent Martineau a copy of her sister's novel, *Lettice Lisle*, inscribed: "Offered . . . as a tiny token of ever-living love and remembrance . . . 29 March 1870 (Harvard University, Houghton Library).

322 Josephine E. Butler, leader of the movement for repeal of the Contagious Diseases Acts (see *Women*).

323 Henry Acland (1815-1900), later Sir, Professor of Medicine at Oxford and a good ally on many issues.

higher than men doctors? namely to make women women doctors? The "training" and "examination" of *men* is, as is acknowledged by all true doctors, almost as bad as it can possibly be.

If I am asked whether I should vote for women to participate in these, I should say certainly not. (2) The province of *midwifery* (including the diseases of women and children) is undeniably women's province. So far as I know this is denied by no one—except on the ground that women cannot get the education for it. France, as usual, has seen this—and for sixty-nine years there has been in France as perfect an education, *practical* and *scientific*, for midwives, as well can be. It includes a two years' course, during which they (the pupil midwives) deliver the lying-in women at a hospital of 200 beds where no pupils but the midwives are received. A first-class certificate is not given under a two-years' course, a second-class certificate under one year. Without a certificate, no midwife can practise in France.

The lady professors of this institution have always held a rank, both *scientific* and *practical*, quite equal to that of Simpson,[324] Locock[325] or any great accoucheurs. They attend the highest classes and even royalty in their confinements. They are physician accoucheuses, not merely midwives. (I do not see how you can make anything of the "small Napoleon" here. The fact, I believe, was simply this: the Empress Eugénie wished to be attended in her confinement by the "sage-femme en chef" of that time (physician accoucheuse). The Emperor insisted on her having a man. The entrance of the man (and the fright and "*émotion*" consequent, by no means an uncommon occurrence) interrupted the natural labour and, it is said, risked her life. But I don't see how you can make anything [breaks off]

Source: Letter to Parthenope Verney, Wellcome (Claydon copy) Ms 9005/48

Tuesday [18 April 1871]
About Miss Wedgwood's *Wesley*,[326] I have so dog's-eared and docketed it, I have so mauled and marked it that I *can't* return it. (I thought it was meant for me.) The subject is always to me of such absorbing interest that a man in quite recent times should have far surpassed *in fact* the *legends* of the saints of the first and Middle Ages in the num-

---

324 Sir James Simpson (1811-70), Professor of Midwifery at Edinburgh.
325 Sir Charles Locock (1799-1875), physician accoucheur to Queen Victoria.
326 Julia Wedgwood, *John Wesley and the Evangelical Reaction of the 18th Century.*

bers of his real converts during his lifetime. Part of the book is so well done that I have read it again and again.

But there is a constant strain after the point and manner and wit of Sir James Stephen,[327] forcing upon one that *she* is the raw pupil, *he* the master. There is the constant use and curious misuse of the word "logical." There is the obtrusive putting forward of rather poor philosophical explanations of theologies, always the "you see *I* am not taken in" lurking behind, which makes the book tiresome. Still much is well done and I gratefully accept it, if you will give it me.

I return Mr Bret Harte. Is that a "nom de guerre"? It is disappointing. There is nothing in it at all like "the Luck of Roaring Camp"[328] by him, have you read that? Shall I lend it you?

F.

With dearest love and holiest wishes on the best of days, 19 April 1871.

Source: Unsigned letter, Wellcome (Claydon copy) Ms 9005/93

Tear this up   26 September 1871
Dearie [Parthenope Verney]

I meant to have come into your room yesterday to have talked over, as you desired, the affair of your house, 32, for Mama. But I find seeing her after (and Papa before) luncheon quite as much as I can manage. I do not think you need give thought to the matter, i.e., of the *date* of letting 32. My father wants to go to Embley early, though, when *he* asked me I answered that I *could* stay here till 20 October, he settled that as our day for going. He did propose that Mama and I should stay here till that date, he going to Embley sooner. But this I should not think it right to undertake. It *is* a charge to me being with Mama at Embley by myself. But then she is *there* and would be there by herself, where here she is here (although she speaks now quite differently, of wishing to "live *and die* here") and with a journey before her. I could not think it right to take this sort of charge, that at Embley being heavy enough. Add to this, I *might* be obliged to go up to 35 myself any day after the 1st (though it is not likely).

I think, as at present settled, that Mama will go up to your house about the 12th, as you let on the 19th. In that case I should go (to 35) on the 10th (by Papa's desire, because of the horses). I think too this

---

327 Sir James Fitzjames Stephen (1829-94); for Nightingale's criticism of him as a "magazine-y" writer see *Theology.*
328 Bret Harte, "The Luck of Roaring Camp."

place is too cold—much colder than last year—*I* think for Mama's drives late in October.

I am glad you have written a Welsh story.[329] I hope it is a *"poor"* one. Many thanks for the beautiful gladiolus, etc. I had from Claydon when you went to Rhianva (there *were* no "grapes"). I hope to see you before you go. I shall come someday into your room.

Source: Letter, Wellcome (Claydon copy) Ms 9005/112

[1871]

Dearie [Parthenope Verney]

Mr Jowett comes today at 3:00, I believe, to give me the sacrament, with Beatrice. I have not asked any of the maids because I am so poorly. Of course I shall be delighted if you or Sir Harry or both would come. R.S.V.P.

I am afraid it will be such a scramble, else I should dearly like the music, but I don't think I shall be up.

F.

Source: Letter, Wellcome (Claydon copy) Ms 9006/33

Sunday 30 March 1873

My dear P. [Parthenope Verney]

It does take out of me so very much seeing anyone in the morning. It makes the whole of the rest of the day useless. I can do nothing afterwards but lie and pant. It takes in fact so many half days out of my life, which I can ill afford. People have no idea how weak I am. (I have been writing ever since it was light, letters on a recent "Tenant Rights" Bill at Calcutta, which ought to have been written days ago.)

Will it not do this afternoon? at 6:00? But, if it will not, then at 1, please, for ten minutes. I dare say Andrews told you that Miss Drummond, sister of her mistress, will be in London tomorrow for a few days, and would *see* any lady about her, if desired.

yours

F.

Editor: Correspondence to Parthenope Verney on their father's death has been related above. The next letter deals with his will and Nightingale's annuity from him.

---

329 Possibly "Old Welsh Legends and Poetry."

Source: Letter, Wellcome (Claydon copy) Ms 9006/67

> 35 South Street
> Park Lane, W.
> 15 January 1874

My dear Sir Harry and Parthe [Verney]

You kindly desire me to tell you my bankers and the periods of payment of my income most convenient to me. The London Joint Stock Bank, 69 Pall Mall is the bank, and the four Quarter Days of the year the times when payment suits me best.

If you feel, as you most kindly said, and as William Coltman told me that Parthe strongly said to him, that my dear Father would have wished my income to be made up to £2000 a year, I cannot refuse your kindness, but thankfully accept it, the more as expenses arising from my work become every year greater.

You were so good as to *say* that I was to *say* what was due to me from my dear Father. I find it is £275, viz., the quarter due at Christmas 1873. (The deduction, £10 a week, which he always made for my stays at Lea Hurst and Embley, had been already made from the previous quarter.) I like to think that he had been very eager latterly to give a standing order to Arkwrights to pay my quarter whole at quarter days into my bankers, I to repay deductions to him. He rode to Wirksworth on a pouring wet day to do this. He afterwards wrote to Aunt Mai and to me that it *was* done. He had often previously said to me so eagerly: I *promise* you that it shall be done. I cannot at all account for its not having been done. He wrote to me not two months ago: "I feel as if I had been keeping back another person's money" because the payments had been not made, sometimes. But it is much more to me that he should have wished and said these things than that they should actually have been done 100 times over.

Ah dear Father, I do not ask: where is he? for he might better ask, *where* are *we?* For *him* 'tis Death is dead, not he, he hath passed from death into life.

ever your loving
Florence Nightingale

Source: Letter, Wellcome (Claydon copy) Ms 9006/72

Embley
7 February 1874

My dear Sir Harry and Parthe [Verney]

Our defeat looks unpleasantly like a rout. Mr Lowe,[330] who has certainly had more to do with dragging down Mr Gladstone's government than any man, said chucklingly on the day the dissolution was announced, "this next Parliament will be *pluto*cratic and the one after it will be revolutionary."

I shall go back to London soon after you come because I have pressing business there, and in order to be able to come here again when you are obliged to leave my mother. I could stay here till the beginning or end of the week beginning 16 February. Therefore, if it is any convenience to you to put off your coming for a few days, you may possibly wish to know this.

ever yours
F.N.

Source: Letter, Wellcome (Claydon copy) Ms 9006/98

35 S. St.
Whitsun Eve
23 May [1874]

My dear P. [Parthenope Verney]

How many *Whitsun Eves* I have passed in the Embley rhododendrons, but this is the last.

You ask me whether I should like more of the furniture besides the one bookcase. I should be very glad of *three bookcases, provided* they will not be missed . . . *the one I mentioned* out of my own old (Papa's) room and *two out of the music room, provided* that does not strip the music room too much, or (what I should like better) . . . and *one out of Papa's study*, which, besides having been his, would be very convenient to me, from the closet below, but I don't want to disturb his room too much. . . . What I *should* like would be *for his sake* the *table* in the *middle of his study* (which I remember so well when I used to go to him for my Greek lessons at 7:30 A.M. when I was sixteen). . . . I particularly wish not to be instrumental in dismantling the house. Often and often during my seven weeks with dear Mother she said in her bright moments even that she *wished* "dear Mary—why, she's my *dearest friend*" to enjoy the house. "And, if it *oughtn't* to be mine, why I don't *wish* it to be

---

330 Robert Lowe (1811-92), later 1st Viscount Sherbrooke, home secretary.

mine any longer." With such an emphasis, what gift of places could God make to her like the gift of giving up a place in such an angel way. Any request I make is therefore subject to NOT making the house look *dismantled*. Were it not for this, I should make many more.

I shall of course consider anything I receive as *(my mother's) furniture* and make a list of it accordingly.

I have been offered repeatedly these past years 100 volumes (to choose) from Embley. These I never took though I feel a constant want of reference books here. I *should* like the *two volumes* [of] *Johnson's Dictionary*; in *three volumes Dante* (Bow room); and perhaps Donnegan's [Greek-English] *Lexicon* and *Kaltschmidt's* German Dictionary and two or three novels, *subject* to the above "*provided*"s. Now of course I should *like* the *Biographie Universelle* but that would be making too great a gap. I cannot write any more. May God bless you and her!
F.

Source: Unsigned letter, Wellcome (Claydon copy) Ms 9006/100

35 South St.
30 May [1874]
6:00 A.M.

My dear P. [Parthenope Verney]

It is an unspeakable blessing that dear mother has been got safely so far on her journey downhill. None but God can know how I dreaded for her mind the being let down at a rapid run that hill up which none climb again. I write now to say that it is quite impossible alas! for me to see you today, that you may not be troubled on your last day to come.

Also, please take back the *Correggio* (I send it); it is a particular horror of mine—so profane, so indecent, like frogs—I *could not* keep it. I should have liked the *other Correggio*, as sublime as this is the reverse, *St John, framed*, in the music room, but did not like to ask for it. I had it once. *May I write for it?* St John.

Also, the only pleasure the *Sistine Chapel* can be of to me is *mounted* on its *purple cloth* with its *two screens* (I thought I said this) as poor mother gave it me and I returned it. *May I write for it now?* Also, Mrs Crook writes to me that you only told her "several things" were to go to me but gave her "no list," said nothing about the *Sophocles*, only mentioned *(1) table, (2) bookcases* in music room and *Papa's table*, did not say WHEN *they were to come. Had I not better write to Mrs Crook* myself for them and save you the trouble? She *asks* me to do so. (I do not ask for an answer to this in your hurry of today of course.) I am in the most urgent need of *bookcases: my own books* are *on the ground*. And now comes this fresh lot of mother's, also of course ON GROUND.

I see with much pleasure the *Biographie Universelle*, the *Dante* and *Johnson*. But, had I known that all the books in library were to be packed away, I should have asked for more *books of reference: Cruden's Concordance, French Dictionary* two volumes, *folio Latin Dictioner, Italian* [Dictionary] two volumes, *Petrarch*,[331] *Alfieri*[332] and many others.

Kaltschmidt's German Dictionary is not come, but only a very, very inferior and useless one. *One* volume of *Tancred*,[333] the 2nd ed., is come *alone*, some duplicates of *Byron, Virgil* (small print),[334] etc., which I have, *not Shelley* which I have not (and numbers of *magazines* which I shall send to pantech [warehouse]). Don't trouble about this now. I will not write more, indeed I cannot. This is a mere *business* letter.

Of course I shall be guided by authority: if the *bookcase* and *table* in Papa's room (which I should dearly have liked to have had—I wished much for the deep *drawers* and *cupboards* in them) are "too old and heavy" to move, is there anything else *with drawers* I could have? If so, *can* I have *three bookcases* (two out of music room and my own)?

Source: Letter, Wellcome (Claydon copy) Ms 9006/114

35 South St.
18 August 1874

My dear Sir Harry and Parthe [Verney]

I gratefully acknowledge the receipt of the half-year's annuity, due under my father's will and from Parthe's voluntary addition.

yours affectionately

F. Nightingale

The accounts from Lea Hurst are good this morning. Thanks for the beautiful Tritomias.

---

331 Francesco Petrarch (1304-74), Italian poet.
332 Vittorio Alfieri (1749-1803), poet and playwright.
333 Benjamin Disraeli, *Tancred, or, The New Crusade*. The character Mr Vavasour is said to have been modelled on Richard Monckton Milnes.
334 Virgil (70-19 BCE), Roman poet.

Source: Letter, Wellcome (Claydon copy) Ms 9006/132

Lea Hurst
Matlock
2 November 1874

My dear Parthe [Verney]

I did not know that you were come home or I would have written before to tell you of the following: I observed that the cupboard in the cedar room on the left-hand side of the door leading towards my mother's room was fastened with paper bands and sealing wax. And I would not even go near it to look at it till one day as, returning from my mother's room, I opened that door into the cedar room, the upper door of the cupboard blew wide open and I approached to shut it. In doing so, it was impossible not to see the portfolio of my Roman letters, which my father had so often asked for. I took it out. I also saw the portfolio of my Egypt letters. I took it out. I would not even examine the other contents of the cupboard although I should very much have liked to have found my *Greek* letters. I will keep the Roman and Egyptian letters to read during the winter, very dear to me now on Mrs Bracebridge's account. Could you send me the Greek letters?

I have ventured to borrow your St Augustine, G. Sand's *Contes Ville-gois*, *Demolition of Port Royal*, *Pensées* de Pascal, *Histoire de Port-Royal*, my father's Greek Testament (all from the cedar room), my mother's [Thomas] Adams's *Private Thoughts*, one volume of Robertson's Sermons[335] . . . one volume of Hookham Frere, *Memoirs* of Rev Haldane Stewart. I will return all these at once if you wish it. . . .

ever yours affectionately
F.N.

Source: Letter, Wellcome (Claydon copy) Ms 9007/171

Lea Hurst
Cromford, Derby
28 October 1878

My dear P. (Parthenope Verney)

Shore has settled with Yeomans and me that all the things as regards whitewashing and colouring, that is, nearly throughout the house, shall be done when I leave. Remains the new servants' hall, proposed.

---

335 Frederick W. Robertson (1816-53); there are numerous editions of his sermons, which Nightingale cited in *Notes from Devotional Authors* (see *Mysticism and Eastern Religions*).

The brew house requires nothing but flooring, clearing out the utensils, cleaning up, etc. and a window putting in in place of the door. It is of course the same size as the present servants' hall.

I have seen both Buxton and Yeomans as to menservants' rooms in place of *present* servants' hall, etc., very convenient and agreeable prospect. I enclose for your criticism a plan which Messrs Buxton and Yeomans have made. (1) I objected to a bedroom over larder for many reasons. They say that it would only be proposed to raise the larder side walls *3 ft 6"* (and to have dormers), that it would not at all interfere with larder's *ventilation*, and that it is not proposed to have a fireplace in it. For all that, I do not like the plan as interfering with East room. But you will be the better judge.

(2) With regard to the two bedrooms instead of one where present servants' hall is: the most important part. I proposed to have the *two*, because you cannot put a butler and footman together, and indeed two bedrooms are better than a two-bedded room anyhow. (3) Anybody who ever inhabits this house will find it an immense relief to be able to put the maids (without cramming) part into the attics, and part into the present three bedrooms to be entered *at this end* by my mother's bedroom (two of which three are now always occupied by men) and for the men's and women's *staircases* to be entirely separate and apart, so that, if you see a man going up the women's staircase, you know it is a mistake.

(4) Anybody inhabiting this house would find it a great convenience to have the nursery floor entirely at liberty, if it can be so without cramming up the maids. (5) The present menservants' rooms are most inconvenient: the doors of the butler's and cook housekeeper's room (the Watsons') open absolutely opposite each other and *upon* the butler's bed, then the large room (the only one which has a fireplace), *over* the present servants' hall, is too large for one footman, the present (my mother's coachman being married and lodging with his wife at the gardener's. To put two maids in this good room instead of in the long room (nursery floor) and to banish the men would be a good arrangement for whoever inhabits this house.

(6) For myself, if I come here again—hardly perhaps likely—under the same circumstances, I could not think it right to decline to undertake the immense responsibility with a NEW housekeeper or butler or BOTH, every year, and both the last under thirty, of such very anxious arrangements as I have had to undergo this year and especially last year, unless the men and women were on separate staircases. . . .

Please give these plans your best consideration, return them to me with your remarks, and I will then refer them to Shore. Have you done anything about the carpets for drawing room and balcony room? . . .

Quite dark with tremendous thunderstorm. Mrs Wildgoose is just coming to see me. In great haste.

ever yours

F.N.

My best love to dear Mary, daughter of Louisa, I wish I had time to write to her.

F.N.

Source: Letter, Wellcome (Claydon copy) Ms 9007/256

Lea Hurst
14 October 1879

My dear P. [Parthenope Verney]

The mother of those *Adams*, of Adamshurst, in *Natal*, interested in the kaffirs' wrongs, whose papers you have, is in England, only for a visit. She is the mother of the wife, has lived with them since their marriage and works to the full as much as they do on behalf of the kaffir.

Her name is Brooks, her address: *Mrs H. Brooks*, care of J. Rider Brooks Esq, Garthlands, Arkley, *near Barnet*. I have written to her asking how long she will stay in England, and asking her to see me when I return to London. I have not mentioned you, but you may possibly like to ask her to Claydon.

I am afraid, from what Mrs Adams says in her letter to me, that Mrs Brooks's *stay in England* is to be *short*. Mrs Adams's is a most interesting letter (about the kaffirs). I will send it you. When I come back to London, will you kindly send me all the Natal papers you have with anything you have written on them? Mrs Adams also sends me more papers. I wish I were a more efficient helper.

We were extraordinarily disappointed not to see Sir Harry. I had expended a whole coalmine in warming the house and sent all round the country for tender meat, etc. and all but sent out my invitations to Wildgoose, Haywood, etc. Tomorrow is the school examination. This week is the grand bazaar! "tea," etc. of the Methodist community, of which last Sunday the children came to sing here, really beautifully. Alas! I am such a poor representative.

This week I earnestly hope that the institute (reading room) will be taken over into the committee's (Wildgoose's) own hands. But all this wants a man's word to urge on. When Sir Harry offered himself, I hoped he would give that word.

I return your letters with thanks by next post.

ever yours and his affectionately

F. Nightingale

Editor: Frances Nightingale, who died 2 February 1880, left legacies to both daughters, naming Nightingale as executor (see p. 351 below). Letters regarding her last years, illness and death have been reported above.

Source: Wellcome (Claydon copy) Ms 9008/24

29 February 1880

My dear P. [Parthenope Verney]

I have not been getting better for Ramsgate,[336] and I do not return because I cannot. I am the less disappointed, because we expected me to feel even much worse than I do, when the immense strain of the last six years and six weeks was taken off. All last year the doctors were telling me that I must go away at once and altogether for three months at least.

I want to have now a few days of entire silence and then I must return. I want to see you, my dear Pop. Even here beggars have found me out. I do not know whether you would care to enclose the two notes about Miss St John (which I enclose) to Miss Thornton, who and not I is the heir to Sir Robert Inglis. But I always feel it a great liberty when it is done to me and therefore I do not press it. She knows what to do better than anyone with claims.

Her beautiful letter, beautiful in thought and feeling, the very poetry of religion, I will return. My mother's fifty years of active, kind intelligence has been forgotten in so many notes of condolence that they jar upon one. But Miss Thornton's is the very genius of friendship. I must read it over once more.

Thanks very many for books and flowers and letters. I am afraid Shore has been very poorly, very, and Louisa too, but less so. I am so glad the watch, etc. is come. So no more at present from,

ever your F.

---

336 A seaside town to which Nightingale had gone to recuperate after her mother's death.

Editor: Nightingale sent her sister and brother-in-law postcards in Italian from Ramsgate, where she had gone to recuperate.

Source: Postcard notes, Wellcome (Claydon copy) Ms 9008/27

2 Marzo 1880

Grazie tante e ben sentite a voi ambedue per il gentilissimo invito a Claydon. Udir cantare gli uccelletti e veder spuntare le primevere mi sorride. Forse più tardi, se voi rinnovate l'invito caro. Adesso bisogna ritonere da quà: e sarà piu facile per la vista telescopica di Claydon. Non mi pento io di aver veduto un mare procelloso. [Many heartfelt thanks to you both for the very kind invitation to Claydon. To hear the little birds sing and to see the spring blossom would please me. Maybe later on you will renew the kind invitation. Now we must return from here and it will be easier for the telescopic view of Claydon. I do not repent having seen a tempestuous sea.]

F.N.

Avete il numero di Marzo del *XIX Century*? [Do you have the March issue of *Nineteenth Century*?]

F.N.

Source: Postcards in Italian, Wellcome (Claydon copy) Ms 9008/27

8 March 1880

Dove è (a Embley?) quel glorioso Correggio?) delpadr Madre: "Ego dormio sed cor meum vigilat," cisè Christo bambino dormente e la Vergine vigilante. In questi ultimi 6 anni eccoti lo stato di nostra Madre: l'anima infantile vigilata dallo Spirito vegliante creativo, di Dio. La memoria non era più, l'anima viveva. "Mia mente forse dorme ma il mio core veglioa," ecco quid che andava dicendo. Come mi sarebbe caro avere quel litografo adesso.

C'é permesso di domandare la grazia della carrozza domani (*Martedi*) alle tre/3 pomeridiane, cioè *2.50*, P.M. a Victoria Station? E de il servitore potrebbe (colui che viene colla vettura) tornare cogl' impedimenti, molto gravi, e cosaccie in un cab, sarebbe per me risparmio di molta fatica.

[trans. from Italian] Where (at Embley?) [is] that glorious Correggio of the father and the mother? [trans. from Latin] I sleep but my heart is vigilant, [trans. from Italian resumes] that is, the child Christ sleeping and the vigilant Virgin. During these last six years that has been the state of our mother, the childlike soul protected by the vigilant creative Spirit of God. The memory was gone but the soul lived.

"My mind may be asleep but my heart is awake," here is what she was saying. How I would love to have that lithograph now.

Are we allowed to request the favour of the carriage tomorrow (Tuesday) at 3:00 in the afternoon, that is 2:50 P.M. at Victoria Station? And if the servant could (the one that comes with the carriage) return with the impedimenta [luggage] many thanks, and little things [in English] in a *cab*, [trans. from Italian resumes] it would save me a great deal of hardship.

Source: Postcard in Italian to Parthenope Verney, Wellcome (Claydon copy) Ms 9008/31

12 March 1880

Vorrei sapere come sta Sir H. Felicissimo augurio una carta postale, ti prego, sorella "pia." [I would like to know how Sir H. is. Best wishes, a postcard, please, "pious" sister.]
    F.

Source: Letter to Parthenope Verney, Wellcome (Claydon copy) Ms 9008/37

26 March 1880

Mother's affairs

I have hurried on Henry Bonham Carter, as you so wanted the money, my dear P., and he has been very kind about it. He writes to me, "this is in train, waiting for an Act of Parliament, which somewhat reduces duties. In the meantime it may be arranged to pay you over some money. How much do you require? I am going to open an account at Smith's Bank in your name and mine for your mother's administration. Some of her little fund of stock will be sold to pay debts and what Parthe and you now require. It will be convenient that you should give an order to the Bank to honour my sole cheques. I should think there will be £800 to £1000 coming to you." Henry B.C.

I answered this by giving the "order" and saying that you would like to have £500 *at once*, that you really wanted it. I have since heard that it was *paid to your account* YESTERDAY, that I should be glad of the same: but that, *if you could have yours*, I could do with half the sum. I believe however that the same will be paid in to my account tomorrow.

Sir Harry said to me on Monday: "your mother has left us a legacy of £1000. As you are the administratix, please let it be paid at once." I merely answered that I had done all I could to hurry on Henry B.C. (I did not mention what Sir H. had said to Henry B.C.) I did not know that my mother had left a will.
    F.N.

Source: Letter, Wellcome (Claydon copy) Ms 9008/46

Seaforth Lodge[337]
Seaton
19 April 1880

My dearest P. [Parthenope Verney]

On your birthday I wish I could send you a flowery tribute from this glorious place, or rather a whiff from the noble sea horses, which come charging in, without ceasing, in tremendous squadrons from the wide and far Atlantic, but the whistling of the winds covers the thunder of the waves and sometimes one seems to hear the cries of the poor Atalanta. A blackbird tried to sing two days ago, but was instantly silenced.

The wide-winged sea birds overhead chuckle in their flight and say, None but us, none but us can sit on the cliffs. Perhaps they are going up the channel as far as Dover and I will entrust one with a billet, under his wings, of love to thee, my dearest Pop, which, as he says he cannot carry a serenade, shall take a more prosaic fipun note, with best earthly birthday blessings and heavenly.

I feel that I have nothing now to do but to work the work of Him that sent me[338] while it is called today, and so prepare for the Immediate Presence of God. Pray for me that I may do it less badly. I have made no progress yet. The sea gulls send word that no winged thing can breast the gale or sea today up channel. So this must go by vulgar post.

I would I could send you and pick as of yore an Embley nosegay of lilacs from the American garden, always out on thy birthday. Rebecca Buxton is dead, the carpenter's daughter, at Lea. And old Hannah Allen,[339] the prophetess, is failing. I wish you would send and inquire how Gwendolen Galton is *for me*. I wrote a long letter to Marianne to inquire and sent it by hand before I left, but received no answer. I am afraid she may be very ill.

Mr Rathbone's failure [to be re-elected] very disturbing. Liverpool ought to insist upon having him her own again and find another seat for Lord Ramsay. *Very* anxious to hear about Bucks and North Der-

---

337 Home of Louisa Ashburton.
338 A paraphrase of John 4:34.
339 A former governess at Lea Hurst (there is much correspondence about her below).

byshire and Lord Hartington, but more so still about Mr Gladstone being in ministry. Pray tell anything you hear to

ever your

F.

Source: Letter, Wellcome (Claydon copy) Ms 9008/71

10 S. St.

14 July 1880

My dearest Pop [Parthenope Verney]

You ask me, "will you allow me to have the China at the old valuation made by Alsop?" It *never was* valued separately from the "plate, etc.," but all valued in a lump. The books and "pictures," etc. valued in a lump in the same way. This was made a great difficulty of by the Executor and a new valuation was made absolutely necessary. I have *no power* to stop the valuation of that or of the "pictures" and "prints," etc. or of anything else. But I do not see how that need affect the division.

As to the "books," I earnestly wish that they may be *left at Embley* and "not divided" for the present. It is absolutely impossible for me to attend to it at present. And I would have (and did offer the sacrifice of almost any money) staved everything off for the present.

You shall have my "half of the bust" and welcome, *not* "to buy" it but for you to *leave* it to Shore or his successor.

My dear P., I should have thought you would have felt that my mother's one wish during these latter years was to give to and to bless and to do for *Shore*. And I am carrying out her mind, which I am sure will be yours also. Had she said *that* to me about "mother of F.P.V. and F.N.," I am sure it would have been "of Shore." As for my part, I was made to swear upon the Bible "so help me God" that I would do my best as administratrix. That oath I must carry out to the best of my power, as you, I am sure, will agree. Would to God I had never accepted the office which was to rend my heartstrings. Or would to God I could have had my offers accepted to put the whole thing off. I am quite bowed and broken. God bless you, my poor Pop, and give us all peace.

your old Flo

Source: Letter, Wellcome (Claydon copy) Ms 9008/162

1 July 1881

I do not wonder that you are uneasy, my dear P., about Sir Harry's inveterate activity. But *I* have nothing to do with it, except a constant effort to restrain it, almost at the peril of my own.

With regard to the "military *orphans* on Friday" in last week, I *could not* have "said something about it," for I did not know he was thinking of orphans. I did not even know of their existence. He told me he was going to Claydon. If he means the "military *widows* the day before (Thursday)" I certainly did "say something about it," and a great deal, to persuade him *not* to go, two days running (seeing him on purpose, when I was half dead). I told him all the harm I knew of the institution, which is a great deal.

About the opening of the St Marylebone Infirmary (which we nurse) the day before yesterday, I was so careful that I did not even answer his question. He then wrote to me to ascertain the hour, which I did by telegram (4:00 P.M. on Wednesday) thinking then he had an invitation and that he was "*in*" for it. To my horror I found out that he had none, that he expected me to get him one (which I did) and that he meant to go down to Nottingham the next morning, *i.e.*, the *same* morning as the college opening by P. Leopold.[340] There is perhaps no one so fearful of his overdoing himself as I am.

Many thanks for the lovely roses. As Rover says, *do it again*, and for the strawberries and dear Margaret's letter. I thank God about the railway. Am very sorry about dear little Ellin.

ever your F.

I saw Sir Frederick Roberts[341] yesterday going to Madras. I scarcely ever saw a more manly man, not in appearance but in essence.

---

340 Prince Leopold (1853-84), son of Queen Victoria, Duke of Albany, opened University College, Nottingham, 1 July 1881.

341 Sir Frederick Roberts (1832-1914), Field Marshal, later Baron Roberts of Kandahar.

Source: Unsigned letter, Wellcome (Claydon copy) Ms 9009/2

> [printed address] 10 South Street
> Park Lane, W.
> 2 January 1882

Every good and perfect gift[342] for the New Year, and many New Years, to you and Sir Harry my dear P. . . .

Source: Letter to Parthenope Verney, Wellcome (Claydon copy) Ms 9009/8

> 2 February 1882

Dear mother went home this last night two years, my dear P. I have been reading again your article in the *Contemporary*.[343] It is very graphic and agreeable reading. But still I want more about Hamlet ("peasant proprietors") in the play of Hamlet. Thanks for your magnificent rabbit.

I am glad Sir Harry is gone out of this fog. Sir Harry was so good as to offer me a share of a truck of little woods from Claydon with Mr Fred and George [Verney], and desired me to answer. I would accept if he would let me pay.

Thanks for the lovely snowdrops. I have two books more of yours to restore. When am I to have the Peasant Proprietor books? If you are so kind as to have the "little woman" at my expense for Julie to superintend and make my black skirt (when shall I pay the bill?), I shall be very much obliged and will send in a skirt for a pattern with variations. God bless you.

ever your F.

Source: Note to Parthenope Verney written on an envelope, Wellcome (Claydon copy) Ms 9009/51

> 16 June 1882

Sir Harry permitted me to open this letter, take out the prescription and send it to Squire's to be made up. It shall come by him. I will write to Sister Bertha about Katie Perkins. I was obliged to give £20 for the bed, or I could not have had it at all under the circumstances which I wrote to you. If they keep the poor child on, it will not therefore cost you anything. May she improve!!

---

342 An allusion to James 1:17.
343 F.P. Verney, "Peasant Proprietors: Jottings in France in September and October."

I will write to the Devonport Penitentiary (Home of Hope)[344] about the frightful case you tell me of at Steeple Claydon. But if the girl is "shameless," will she go? They only take VOLUNTARY penitents. Is she a case where the magistrate has interfered to place her in a penitentiary? May God convert her, for man cannot!

Source: Exchange of notes between F. Nightingale and her sister, Wellcome (Claydon copy) Ms 9009/83

Friday, 9 August 1882

My dear [Florence Nightingale]

I should be very glad if you could see me for a few minutes. Smallpox is in the neighbourhood and we have had a very slight case and I want good advice. I am afraid you are very unwell.

F.P.V.

FN: I would gladly see you for a few minutes at 5 or at 6. But the sanitary authority of your "neighbourhood" is the person to ask. If I gave "advice" contrary to the law of the land you could not follow it.

Source: Letter, Wellcome (Claydon copy) Ms 9009/96

30 October 1882

Dearest Pop [Parthenope Verney]

I send you (to look at) the photograph of the Titian's Assumption in the Accademia at Venice. I never understood the picture before, a miracle of fore-shortening, and a parcel of people worshipping a lady-god was all that I saw, more stupid me. But what an ideal this is, the "pure in heart," *they* shall "see God."[345] She has so entirely left the world behind her, herself behind her, that *is* "rapt" devotion. I think it ranks *with*, though unlike, the very finest heads of Christ (of which I still think Guido's crowned with thorns one of the greatest) and Michelangelo's greatest Sistine prophets and Raphael's baby Christ in the Dresden [Sistine Madonna].

How unlike Murillo is *this* Virgin! and indeed how unlike Titian in general! It is an inspiration, like Mozart's *Don Giovanni*. Please let me have it again tonight or tomorrow morning. I also send (for you) a very different thing, Whatstandwell Coffee Room—don't despise it—108 members already, where we were told we should not have forty.

---

344 An institution of the (Anglican) Sellonites, the Sisters of Mercy of the Holy Trinity at Devonport.
345 An allusion to Matt 5:8.

My love to Maude, and tell her we regretted not having her and children two at Lea Hurst with Mr Fred. I left the Holloway Reading Room wringing 200 hands at not hearing her violin this year and Mr Fred's songs. Lea Hurst was a sheet of gold when we left. How *ugly* London is, black leaves instead of golden, an oleograph instead of a sun. We came away through such a storm as I have not been out in since Crimea. All the country below Derby under water, men climbing up trees and not rescued till next morning. I don't mean I saw the men in the trees but in the newspapers.

We had a disastrous foot trudge through the slush and snow to Belper Station. I had been quite knocked up, as you may suppose, before I left Lea Hurst. And since I came have been unable through illness to see any of the many men waiting to see me on account of this (more) disastrous inquiry into the Egypt Army Medical Service. But one is coming today who always stays till 9.30 P.M. Also, about India (Bengal land, rent law question).

But, more disastrous than all, is your illness, my dear Pop.

Source: Letter, Wellcome (Claydon copy) Ms 9009/103

2 November 1882

Dear Pop [Parthenope Verney]

I am very sorry you want a night nurse and it is a very risky thing to recommend a private nurse, but I should send to Miss Pyne, Westminster Hospital, who I know has several private nurses at liberty now, and who would be "proud to serve" you. I should tell her exactly what I wanted: not a crack surgical nurse to dress a man's broken bones, but a nice, clever, quiet nurse, as near a good domestic maid to a lady as possible, who will not talk and keep you awake, but will do her work tenderly and silently.

You know Miss Pyne was trained by us, was years with Miss Pringle at Edinburgh. . . . She would take pains to send you what you asked for. I am afraid there should be no delay for it is quite an accident that she has several nurses at home now.

ever my dear Pop

your F.

Source: Letter, Wellcome (Claydon copy) Ms 9009/104

10 South Street
Park Lane
6 November 1882

My dear Sir Harry [Verney]

I share deeply your sorrow at Parthe's suffering. But, thank God, there is not, so far as I know, one dangerous, much less "fatal" symptom. The danger is exactly the reverse of what you fear and is, as Dr Acland told you, that this might become chronic or confirmed. As Parthe has herself written to me, "and I may have twenty years of this!" There is no symptom of rheumatic fever, or of suppressed gout or of anything dangerous. Those would be doing all they could to induce or confirm this state into becoming chronic, if they were to "suggest" "fresh remedies," "further advice," or be always "proposing" something else.

She has had ten doctors in little more than five months! Nothing could be worse hardly for her. I will gladly see Dr [William] Ogle or Dr Acland if you like, if a time can be found when I *can* see him and give him a fee. He will certainly tell me the truth.

yours
F.N.

Source: Letter, Wellcome (Claydon copy) Ms 9023/103

Saturday [18 November 1882]

Dearest [Parthenope Verney]

I trust you had a quieter night last night. God bless you. Pray don't think of getting up this wintry day; it is so very cold and nasty. It would retard your getting better.

May God be always with you. He loves you, my dear Pop.

ever your F.

God speed your week's festivities. I am going to write to Captain George's oldest boy about a kitten.

Please look at Louisa's Ardnagashel sketches.[346] More than anyone, she gives the sea in motion: the resistless rush and fury of the sea coming in, I think. She has the *genius* of colour, like Mrs Bracebridge. Neither could ever sketch from except when inspired. God bless you all.

ever yours and Sir Harry's
F.

---

346 Shore's wife Louisa came from Ardnagashel, County Cork.

Source: Letter, Wellcome (Claydon copy) Ms 9009/123

8 December 1882

Dearest [Parthenope Verney]

Dr Ogle will come tomorrow, if wanted, to give you the subcutaneous. He hopes you will have a better night tonight. God be with you. For so He giveth His beloved sleep.[347]

ever thy

Flo

Source: Letter, Wellcome (Claydon copy) Ms 9009/125

11 December [1882]

My dear Sir Harry [Verney]

For several days the introduction of a day nurse has been inevitable. Julie is overworked. The night nurse ought always to be off duty *by 10* A.M. or she cannot go on. On Friday I tried to persuade Parthe, but she only said "I am not ill enough yet." Nor is she, but still it is necessary. Can you persuade her without frightening her? If so, I would recommend another nurse from Miss Pyne's, and would write another note to her, Miss P., if you wish it, and will send it.

Dr Ogle desires me to write to him *before 4* an account of Parthe's state. I am sure he does not realize the extent of her wandering. I should avoid telling her that he thinks her better. It annoys her. I should wish to have now the night nurse's report and later on a bulletin, with *all* particulars about 1:00 or 2:00 o'clock, before I write to Dr Ogle. God bless our dear invalid.

yours and hers

F.N.

I have a blister behind each ear, a mustard poultice on my chest, and have been so for several days, or I would come in and see her, whatever the weather, I need scarcely say. I hope you have no cold.

Source: Letter, Wellcome (Claydon copy) Ms 9009/133

10 South St.

15 December 1882

Dearest Margaret [Verney]

My letter to Dr Ogle yesterday afternoon was merely to introduce him to you as an angel from heaven who had come (unawares)[348] to

---

347 An allusion to Ps 127:2.
348 An allusion to Heb 13:2.

feed the patient, as angels do, you know, sometimes now as they did in the O. Testament, and to soothe and calm and comfort the sufferer, as also is their calling. I told him that exact records of the sleep and food taken would be given to him now by *you* and that you would take charge of the carrying out of his orders. I am sure you have done a great deal already to do her good.

I did not post that, my old note, but I have now written another, which perhaps you would have kindly (immediately) sent. And he will be sure to come this afternoon. I believe she is now taking no day medicine, waiting for him. I return the record of food (liquid and solid) you so kindly sent to enable you to make out the record for him. Would you kindly add to it the *brandy* taken? I await with anxiety the bulletin of the night. I fear I shall not be able to see you this morning (and it is not fit for you to come out) for linseed disputes my possession. I am obliged to get up this afternoon to see a W.O. man, on business, but I hope to see the nurse or you or Julie some part of the day, if the weather improves. With love to Sir Harry,

ever my dear angel's
grateful F.N.

Source: Letter, Wellcome (Claydon copy) Ms 9009/166

11 February 1883
Dearest Pop [Parthenope Verney]

I am with you in the weary nights. What is more, the loving Father is with you: "Come unto me, all ye that are weary and heavy laden,"[349] as dear Mrs Wass[350] had in her bed hanging up. This is the bad time of year for you; when drier weather comes, you will find the good. Dr Acland does not say there will be a "stiff knee."

They missed you so at Buckingham. All the people did. And Margaret said the house at Claydon seemed like an empty frame without your presence. She said she could not bear the rooms without you. I must find the letter—her letters are not empty frames—and send it you. God bless you, my dear Pop.

ever your F.
Do the thrushes sing before it is light in your trees?

---

349 A paraphrase of Matt 11:28.
350 The Wass family owned the lead smelting works at Lea.

Source: Letter, Wellcome (Claydon copy) Ms 9009/183

25 June 1883

My dearest Pop [Parthenope Verney]

God bless your silver wedding and He *has* blessed it, though there is a sad, sad time now. Yet I know you would not have it otherwise: the twenty-five years have been blessed. I fear to say more for fear I should not be sufficiently patient of *your* suffering. You are more patient than I am of what, dear Pop, you suffer.

May God bless you very much, bless you infinitely, according to Himself.

ever your and Sir Harry's
loving F.

Source: Letter, Wellcome (Claydon copy) Ms 9009/191

[printed address] 10 South Street
Park Lane, W.
6 August 1883

How I mourn, dearest Pop, for your great sufferings. To the Father whose love is tenderer even than ours I commend you almost hourly.

I shall hope to be with you soon, dearest.

ever your
F.

Source: Letter, Wellcome (Claydon copy) Ms 9009/196

[printed address] 10 South Street
Park Lane, W.
13 August 1883

Dearest Pop [Parthenope Verney]

I trust to see you on Wednesday. I often think of what you said, that God was working out in you that patience[351] might have her perfect work. I think you must have written what is on the other side. *Dr Payson, when racked with pain and illness,* "God has used a strange method to make me happy. I could not have believed a little while ago that in order to make me happy, He would deprive me of the use of my limbs and fill my body with pain. But he has taken away everything else, that he might give me *Himself.*" So too says St Paul, "As the *suffer-*

---

351 An allusion to James 1:4.

ings of Christ abound in us, so our *consolation* also abounded by Christ."[352] Shall we see whether God can make us happy?

ever your F.

Source: Letter, Wellcome (Claydon copy) Ms 9010/18

27 May 1884

Dearest [Parthenope Verney]

May my strawberries find favour in your mouth—heard you had none. I could almost wish you were not going in this east wind. How grieved not to see thee. I will write.

your loving
F.

Source: Letter, Wellcome (Claydon copy) Ms 9010/20

10 South St., W.
7 June 1884

My dear Sir Harry and Parthe [Verney]

I had been hoping that fine weather would bring relief to both and that Sir Harry would not write too much.

I am so glad that Maude is with you, would that *I* could be, but it is quite, quite impossible. I have scarcely been out of bed since Thursday fortnight. Quiet in my own room is what is ordered. Even were I able to come, I should not be able to leave my room. I should be of no use to Parthe and only an anxiety, and scarcely able to see you more than once a day and only you, dear Sir Harry. You *must* believe indeed that it is *impossible* if I cannot come to Claydon when Parthe prefers. At present I am unable to do anything. I can hardly stand or write and it will in all probability be eight or ten weeks before I can do so well. And as soon as I can, I *must* see people. I have done none of my usual work this year and June and July will be my last months to do it in, if indeed it should please God that I do it at all.

Pray believe me—and with what regret I tell you at all about myself. It is when you are quite alone that I wish to be with you, as you know. God speed you both. I cannot tell you how sorry I am that Margaret cannot come this month.

---

352 2 Cor 1:5.

I have not written to the Freres[353] yet! How solemn and tragic, after the way of thinking of this world, his death, how glorious after the fashion of another:

Martirio in terra appellari [Called a martyr on earth]
Gloria si appella in cielo. [In heaven called glory]

I am sorry I have nothing to do with the ophthalmic hospital nor with any other special hospital. I stick to St Thomas' and its special branches. I cannot tell you how much I think of you. God bless you again and again.

ever dearest people
yours
F.N.

Source: Letter, Wellcome (Claydon copy) Ms 9010/36

10 South St., W.
19 October 1884

Dearest Pop [Parthenope Verney]

I miss the singing birds, the pomp of autumn tints. (The trees fade away in London like eternal death, in the country they put on all their most glorious show like eternal life.) I miss the clouds and blue sky, the beautiful scenery of the heavens. But more than all I miss what eye doth not see, nor ear, hear, but only the heart of man conceives and understands.[354]

I cannot but think and believe that there might be a future of much ease and some bodily activity before you, to utilize the mental activity which there is sure to be, if a multitude of small details, small in themselves, but of untold importance for the future which we do so desire and pray for, were carefully attended to, e.g., (1) never to get tired, for nerve capital when trenched upon cannot be replaced at our age; (2) to keep strictly from exposure to damp and cold in carriage drive and within stated hours when out, not more than 1¼ hours out; (3) never to talk when it has brought on the cough; (4) to see no one except Sir Harry but by appointment or at least to have your "pleasure" taken first whether you will see him, her or it or not; (5) in short, to avoid all fatigue; (6) an open fire and a window open *at the top* is always the safest atmosphere. In fair weather in London to have the windows always open at the top *till* you occupy the room, but to

353 Sir Bartle Frere died in 1884.
354 An allusion to Isa 64:4.

keep the room warm by open fire. I could multiply these, but I fear there is a chance not only of your not observing, but of your not even reading them.

May the heavenly Father grant what the earthly friends would give their lives to secure, that is, that everything may be done which He has appointed as the means of recovery of my dearest Pop.

ever your old Flo

If I might, I would fain add never read anything which simply makes you angry or tell a story which makes you simply angry. The Italians, wiser than we, used to avoid anger or have themselves bled after being unavoidably angry, because it made "sangue *nero*" [black blood] a literal fact. Always read what inspires you enough to make you overlook Byron's "thumb."

F.N.

P. turn over. I have found [devotional author] Lady C. Long which you lent me here. I am so distressed that I did not find it before, but I hope it will be in time to occupy its old place in your room. I return three delightful letters.

Source: Unsigned letter, Wellcome (Claydon copy) Ms 9010/61

10 South St.
15 March 1885

My dearest Pop [Parthenope Verney]

You will know without words how grieved I am not to be able to come and see thee and I am afraid it will continue a long time. Sir Harry is always saying that you would be so good as to come and see me, but I think the being carried along from door to door in this weather quite wrong and impossible. God bless you both.

ever thy F.

Today I am unable to see Sir Harry or anyone besides those I *must* see on business which will not wait. I have had to give up so much, but God can take care of His great empire, His great souls and His little ones.

Source: Letter, Wellcome (Claydon copy) Ms 9010/67

27 March 1885

Dearest Pop [Parthenope Verney]

You know how I long to see you. I had not the least idea that you could or ever did go out at 1 or at 1:30, which is Sir Harry's hour, and so "take turns with him." Any day, *every* day that you could would be happiness to me.

You know how my afternoons have been filled and I have been obliged to give "carte blanche" to people to come without appointment. I am done for, trying for the last many months to lead two lives. Major Young is now gone. The ladies must take their chance.

Would you, dear, begin now coming at 1:00 or at 1:30? Or would you name any hour, except between 2:00 and 3:00, when I *must* rest, *today* for me to have the joy of seeing you?

I do not know who could have thought that I saw Sir Harry *instead of* other people. I have always seen him over and above my work, as I would gladly see you. But I have had to see *any*one, morning or afternoon, in connection with the war work or, what is infinitely more trying to me, give them "carte blanche" to come or not. The war would admit no delay. In the morning I have also had to write up for them (my head and eyes are now nothing but shooting pains). I have refused Mr Jowett and all friends on *other* business *because* the war admitted no excuse.

Hoping to see you today, a verbal answer, please.

ever thy F.

Sir Harry has often seen me in bed. That is when I have had one or even two people as early as 9:00 or 10:00 o'clock.

Source: Unsigned letter, Wellcome (Claydon copy) Ms 9010/71

Easter Day [c1885]

If you are good enough to send the carriage *after* you are gone to Westminster Abbey and let it take me by the Abbey, along the Embankment and back by the Abbey home for ¾ hour, as Sir H. proposes, I should be very much obliged.

Do your maids go to the Crystal Palace tomorrow?

Could I see you at 6:45? (you kindly ask). I see Sir H. at 6:00. With best Easter blessings.

Source: Letter, Wellcome (Claydon copy) Ms 9010/73

Ravensbourne
Keston, Beckenham
9 April 1885

I am afraid, my dearest Pop, that you have been more suffering this bitter northeaster and even fear that Sir Harry may be giving you more uneasiness, but I hope not.

I hear that Sir Harry has a spirited letter in the *Times* about the Volunteers. Pray tell Mr Morey to look out for you in the mass of papers in your dining room my copy of the *Oxford Magazine* which I lent Sir Harry for you with Mr Jowett's sermon on Gordon in it. (You said you would like to see it.) It is in small 4to shape, this *Oxford Magazine*, light yellow cover, my name in pencil on it. And when you have done with it, please tell Morey to send it on to me.

Miss Becker died quite suddenly at Stuttgart, on Thursday, found dead in her bed, a great shock to poor Alice. Lady Belper writes to me that she, Miss Becker, was "the best friend" she ever had. That *is* a tribute.

Colonel Primrose is dead on the Nile.

I shall not be able to return on Monday. God bless you. The Bonham Carters have been so kind.

ever yours

F.

Source: Letter, Wellcome (Claydon copy) Ms 9010/76

19 April 1885

My dearest Pop [Parthenope Verney]

This is thy birthday. Dost know I often think that God wishes thee many happy returns of the day, both in this world and the future ones, NOW more than ever?

And so do I, thou well mayst know. God bless thee. IF it is wise for you to go out, and IF Miss Williams does not come, would you come and see me today?

ever thy F.

Source: Unsigned letter, Wellcome (Claydon copy) Ms 9010/80

[printed address] 10 South St.
Park Lane, W.
7 June 1885

My dearest Pop [Parthenope Verney]

How gladly would I have obeyed your kind summons to come to Claydon. But alas! it is impossible. How lovely the place must be looking, how the birds must be whispering at dawn their prayers to God.

You seem vigorous, thank God, but your pain I fear at times is great. I hope if you do not do too much, and if you admit sun into the library to prepare the room for you when you are not there, that as the steady summer increases, the pain will decrease.

I send you an article on "peasant proprietorship" in France by Roth (*Statistical Journal*) and also on dairy farming, Franco-Swiss (*Agri-*

cultural Journal). *He* is a growing authority. I will get you any others by him I can. Please return them to me when *quite* done with, also the volume of *Port Royal*[355] when *quite* done with. God bless you, my dear Pop.

ever yours

The Sutherlands were so delighted with your article in *Contemp[orary Review]*.[356]

Source: Letter, Wellcome (Claydon copy) Ms 9010/92

10 South St.

13 July 1885

My dearest Pop [Parthenope Verney]

... Have you read, by "Jackanapes" (you know she[357] is dead), "The Story of a Short Life," Jackanapes is a gem, unapproachable, but I think I like this almost better. The V.C. singing; with 300 "men at his back," to the child at the moment of death. Heber's hymn seems to me unapproachable too in its pathos, of a different kind. "Laetus sorte mea" [Happy at my sort]. (O why did she die?) I also send another book of hers, "Brothers of Pity" at the beginning is so lovely. And a very different little book, Runciman's "School Board Idylls," heart-rending but stirring.

Fare you well. I trust you will have some fine hot weather soon without east wind to do you good, my Pop.

ever your F.

I hope you like the P.C. [postcard].

Source: Letter, Wellcome (Claydon copy) Ms 9010/97

23 July 1885

I have seen Bryant, Mrs Richmond's maid, and think her a very nice woman indeed, but talk-y. She did not however *gabble* but talked because she was so interested. I feel, however, if you were to think of her, we must ask Mrs Richmond whether she *can* give "silent service" or talks all the year round. She is thirty-four but looks twenty-four, is not, I should be afraid, very strong in the back and perhaps lifting

---

355 Mary Anne Schimmelpenninck, *Narrative of the Demolition of the Monastery of Port Royal des Champs*, which Nightingale extensively annotated. See *Theology*.

356 F.P. Verney, " 'Little Takes' in England versus Peasant Properties in France and Germany."

357 Author of religious books for children, Mrs Ewing, née Juliana Horatia Gatty (1841-85).

may be a difficulty. She went out at eighteen as nursery governess and stayed six years, then three years at ladies whom she nursed till they died, then home, then two years at Mrs Richmond's, whom she left to come to St Thomas', then with us seven weeks. We liked her exceedingly, but her back was quite unequal to a heavy male surgical ward. We were sorry to part with her. Then she took a nurse's place with a poor young burnt lady, Sir G. Eliot's granddaughter, where the work was much harder for, whereas our women are only twelve hours on, with recreation, she is twenty-four hours on, and only "bed" for two or three hours. In consequence of strong remonstrance, they have given her several hours "off" today and yesterday. I advised her to try staying on (till end of week, and then to let me know her decision). I told her that, if her decision then was to leave, you must see her before anything could be decided on your part. So it stands. I will let you know as soon as she lets me know. I think she would be attentive, careful, sensible, kind, conscientious and not conceited. In great haste.

ever thy F.

She is nice looking and pleasing. She can't be *very* delicate or she could not stand her present place a week. God guide us.

Source: Letter, Wellcome (Claydon copy) Ms 9010/98

10 South St.
28 July 1885

My dearest Pop [Parthenope Verney]

Bryant has been with me. I am glad to tell you that Nurse Bryant has decided to leave her present place, which she does on Tuesday, after Sir James Paget's visit to her patient on Monday. She will come to Claydon to see you by the 11:00 train, I *hope* she will get off. Will you have her met at Claydon Station by that train and send her back the same evening? She will have to sit up that night. Mrs Richmond has kindly asked her to stay with her to rest till Saturday next. She then meant to go for a week's rest to some friends at Hitchin, which it is obvious she sorely needs.

I told her that you *might* want her on the Saturday, that your maid was leaving on the Friday. God grant that this woman may succeed. The lifting must be a difficulty, as Mrs Richmond told her, from her weak back, I told her that as a patient you were, alas! comparatively easy to lift, and that she would have the help of another person. She appears to me nervous and excited from want of sleep, and no wonder.

I of course asked her when I *first* saw her to go down to see you at once. She said she could not without deciding to leave her place, which I could not say you would replace. Their unhandsomeness has now released her. I find from her that you have telegraphed to Mrs Richmond. Good speed.

ever your F.

Source: Letter, Wellcome (Claydon copy) Ms 9010/113

10 South St.
18 October 1885

My dearest Pop [Parthenope Verney]

You spoke of writing an article for *Macmillan* on the *relief march* from Kosti to the Nile (below Khartoum). I ought to have written long ago (you asked) to say that Mrs Hawthorn looks forward to this, as excellent. I returned and you kept your scrap for the purpose. Sir Harry wrote me a deplorable imploring letter *not* to ask you to write a *Life of Gordon*. This was quite unnecessary. You probably did not show him my letter, exhorting you merely to answer and offering to convey the answer, "Blow me if I do!"

I cannot help sending you for Ellin, though I think it is more for a boy above twelve, because the pictures of "The Roman Sentinel at Pompeii" and that of "Casabianca standing at his Post" to his father's orders and burning with his father's burning ship are so very serious. Mrs Ewing's "Convalescence," it is so very pretty, the old Captain, "when you are my age, little chap, you won't think what you would like to have, but what you ought to do, what you have to do or to bear, and how you can do or bear it best, that is the *point* to make for." And "if a man is confined to his bed and wants to be in battle, he is as much a coward as a man who is in battle and wants to be in bed."

I heard today of Dr Acland being "summoned to Claydon." I hope this does not mean that you or Sir Harry are worse.

ever, my dearest Pop, yours

F.

Thanks for lovely flowers. Are you so good as to remember to write to Mrs Trevelyan in favour of Robert Robinson, who has now taken Reddings Farm on the estate of her father, Mr Phillips, at Claverdon in Warwickshire?

F.N.

Source: Letter, Wellcome (Claydon copy) Ms 9010/116

10 South St.
26 October 1885

My dearest Pop [Parthenope Verney]

I hope you were pleased with the tribute in the *Times* of this morning. I am sending copies about to some old friends and retainers. It is "tastefully" done. Sir Harry says he will be so good as to lunch here on Wednesday. I really fear his going to this Mansion House meeting, on account of the shin. But should he do it, would you ask Mr Morey to send me a postcard to say *when* the luncheon should be ready, *1:00* or *2:00* o'clock? or when? God speed.

ever your F.

Source: Letter, Wellcome (Claydon copy) Ms 9010/118

10 South St.
13 November 1885

My dearest Pop [Parthenope Verney]

I hailed the arrival of the *Nineteenth Century* with delight. Your article[358] is very weighty and the extracts from foreign sources telling. Sometimes there is rather an abrupt transition from these to your own experience, as if the editor had been *piecing* it. "The maimed women x x whom we saw." *Where?* But this is only a hypercriticism—I think the article *says* a great deal.

Mr Jowett, who was at Lord Rosebery's[359] with Sir Harry told me that he, Sir H., had addressed "wise words" to the party "which came very well from him," especially impressive words on the subject of racing to Lord Rosebery, which he took very well.

We have had nearly a week of almost darkness in London. I hope you have had better weather, but I fear you have been suffering. Is Sir Harry able to ride and walk?

Miss Georgiana Hurt writes to me of the "very beautiful daughter" of Sir Jos. Lee "at Lea Hurst." "I hope she has a mind to receive the beauties of that dear place." She adds she also writes about you. Lord Edward Cavendish has been staying at Lea Hurst. He held a meeting in Lea School. They say he will win.

---

358 F.P. Verney, "Foreign Opinions on Peasant Properties."
359 Archibald Philip Primrose (1847-1929), 5th Earl Primrose, Liberal leader, later prime minister.

I hope that the Greigs are gone. Poor woman, she wrote to me of your kindness in her last letter. So did he, and I hope that Mr Robertson does well.

Your short "Peasant Proprietors" will doubtless soon be out. I return Margaret's charming letter.

ever your F.

Source: Letter, Wellcome (Claydon copy) Ms 9010/121

10 South St.
28 November 1885

My dearest Pop [Parthenope Verney]

Thank you for your jolly little volume.[360] At this moment the tide of copies which is coming in and upstairs and the tide of copies going out and downstairs forbid the ingress or egress of any other persons or goods. I order them for our divers reading rooms, for which I also order Green's *Short History of the English People*,[361] *Gordon in Central Africa* and the like as standard books.

I send back the lines on Sir Harry, which are charming, pathetic and true (I did not receive them till *after* the day Sir Harry desired me to send them back). I hope, if you put them into *Aylesbury News* you will send me a copy.

Sir Harry said, looking at my kitten, "he has his life before him," as if he, Sir Harry, had *not*. I feel, for *him*, he has his life before him, this the mere episode of an early morning hour. But, as Zoroaster[362] takes care to remind us, one part of eternity is of as much importance as any other part, and no part can we have again; if we have not got its good out of it, *that* good is gone forever. But this life, as a part of eternity, is fully as interesting and important as what we generally call eternity.

Yes, the elections have gone cruelly against us, against me especially, for all the representative men pledged to support India's interests and Lord Ripon, except Mr Bright,[363] are unseated. Our greatest loss is Sir Roper Lethbridge,[364] a man "whom I would not touch with

---

360 F.P. Verney, *Peasant Properties and Other Selected Essays*.
361 Nightingale'a friend, Alice Stopford Green, published a revised edition of a history by her late husband, John Richard Green, as *Short History of the English People*.
362 Zoroaster (6th cen BCE), Persian prophet.
363 John Bright (1811-89), Liberal MP.
364 Sir Roper Lethbridge (1840-1919), press commissioner for the Government of India and opponent on the Bengal tenancy bill.

a pair of tongs," who has won his seat, and is now our representative for India, knighted by the "Boy with the Drum." (An Indian Conservative is to an English one as a mad dog to a gentlemanly racehorse.)

But I still look to the counties to redeem us and "Onward Comes the Great Commander,"[365] who we know is on the Liberal side. When is Captain Verney's polling day? I hope, with you, Margaret will not kill herself, but she is too grounded on the Rock to do that. Tell her to give me a telegram on the polling day.

Thanks many for your most kind invitation. I am afraid I cannot stir till the week after next, I am so busy. And then I shall have to work up the nurses before Christmas. But it is most tempting and I will see and write. Thanks again, and thanks for beautiful flowers.

ever your

F.

Did you see in Friday's *Times* a short letter from Sir Louis Mallet on "fair rents" and allotments?[366] Sir L.M. is my "economical priest" and authority, especially on land questions. What a tragedy, what a Greek drama, the King of Spain's death and life! Aristotle's *Politics* are out, Mr Jowett's, and he has sent them me, two volumes.

But if you had such a thing about you as a foolish book or a rabbit in the pocket of your best gown, the smallest would be thankfully received.

Do you know that Gordon, when he saved China in the great Taeping rebellion, always said it was Sir James Hope "as done it" and wrote it at the end of his diary. Tell Sir Harry this.

I think I shall go in for *patronage*. The elective principle is faulty. And the Paddington Board of Guardians have *elected* the wrong Medical Officer for our nursing staff!

---

365 An allusion to a hymn by Philip B. Bliss, "Hold the Fort," 1870, inspired by General Sherman's signalling to his forces holding the fort near Atlanta in the Civil War, with such lines as: "Hold the fort, I am coming," Jesus signals still;/Wave the answer back to heaven, "By Thy grace we will." In the hymn Jesus is identified with the Northern General Sherman: "Onward comes our great Commander, cheer, my comrades, cheer!" (www.cyberhyman.org).

366 Sir Louis Mallet (1823-90), free trade advocate and former permanent under secretary for India: "Fair Trade and Fair Rents," *Times* 27 November 1885:7.

Source: Letter, Wellcome (Claydon copy) Ms 9010/124

10 South St.
9 December 1885

My dearest Pop [Parthenope Verney]

Many thanks but I am afraid there is not the slightest chance of my being able to get to Claydon before you come to London. I have more than one engagement next week which I cannot possibly put off, people coming up from the country on purpose and from the India Office.

Lord Salisbury seems determined to stick. And, if he can reform the procedure of the House of Commons, which he certainly will not let *us* do, and settle the Irish affair, which ditto ditto, perhaps it is the best for us. Randolph[367] is the real terror of the situation. There is a beautiful hymn:

The devil and me
We can't agree,

altered to

Lord Randolph and me
We can't agree,

by F.N.

People say you should never give two good reasons where one will do. My other good reason is I am quite unfit for the journey, short as it is. I have scarcely been out of bed, except to see people, since I left Claydon. I wish I could hear a better report of you. But you seem, as dear Papa used to say, spry and active.

Do you remember Sophie Voidel? She writes the enclosed. I hope Sir Harry is riding the white horse.

ever yours and his

Source: Letter, Wellcome (Claydon copy) Ms 9011/11

12 March 1886

I grieve so very much, my dearest Pop, over your suffering and that I am not able to see you for such a long time.

Have you read the book I send of G. Sand's? *Le Château de Pictordu* and *Les Ailes de Courage* are such gems. . . .

You are so good as to send me a pudding many a night. Might I ask for, instead, a little bit of meat from Sir Harry's dinner? Anything that

---

367 Known as Lord Randolph, Randolph Henry Spencer Churchill (1849-94), secretary of state for India 1885-86 and a rabid Tory.

will do for him will do for me, so it be tender. They, the doctors, tell me to eat meat. And oh for not to know what is coming.

ever thy F.

Source: Letter, Wellcome (Claydon copy) Ms 9011/15

19 April 1886

Again, my dearest Pop [Parthenope Verney], we thank God for this day, and for the wonderful, most wonderful mental activity, above all, with which He conquers pain so severe, and illness, such as would conquer and many a hero too. How much we have to thank Him for, while we pray Him to soothe and to soften and to bless body and mind.

Fare you very well, very, very well and He does make you fare well, in spite of pain. Bless God and God bless you.

ever thy F.

Here comes the unsentimental bit of paper and Fauriel's posthumous book.[368]

Source: Letter, Wellcome (Claydon copy) Ms 9011/16

10 South St.
23 April 1886
Good Friday

My dearest Pop [Parthenope Verney]

Would you be so very good as to send me the photograph of Sir Harry you so kindly promised, price £1.1 enclosed, for me to frame. (Don't send me the one *framed* you intended for Captain Verney. I hope he has it.) Also to send me the address of the photographer that I may procure another from him.

ever thy F.

I sent a wreath and cross, of immortelles and corn, to Wellow church-yard for Easter Sunday as always, in your name and mine.   .

F.

---

368 Claude-Charles Fauriel (1772-1844). Mme Mohl was his literary executor. His lectures were published posthumously, *Histoire de la poésie provençale.*

Source: Letter, Wellcome (Claydon copy) Ms 9011/20

Claydon
1 May 1886

My dearest Pop [Parthenope Verney]

When I found you were alone in the library, and we might have had such a nice talk (for me) it required all my promise to my doctor, who came this morning to give leave or veto, and who would only let me go on parole that I would not put my feet to the ground or sit or stand for some days, not to break all bounds and come straight in to library. So praise my self-denial.

Poor Shore has been very bad again with pleurisy. Today is his birthday. I had had such a nice letter from Ellen Tollet—*very* pathetic.

Carlo will, I think, come to grief. He was barking after two of those white-faced cows or bullocks, each of which tried to toss him. *But*, he said, I *will* drive. The park is my own.

The thrushes sang a little evening prayer to God and I even thought I heard a young nightingale, but faint. Then there was the murderous cuckoo, and only inability prevented my rushing out and murdering him, as he will murder the innocent young hedge sparrows, and toss them out on the ground. What does Darwin say to that?

God bless thee. Au revoir.

ever thy F.

Source: Letter, Wellcome (Claydon copy) Ms 9011/32

10 South St.
21 June 1886

Dearest Pop [Parthenope Verney]

I am always thinking of you and longing to hear how you are and longing still more to think that you are somewhat better and taking care of your dear self. I left my heart behind me, and oh how I pray Our Father, the God of the "refiner's fire"[369] to make us His children.

I send the paper you wished for, the beautiful testimony to Sir Harry, as you said. It is, as you will guess, by Captain [Edmund] Verney. I send also £10.10 for Dr Acland, which I meant to have put into your hand. Fare you very well, fare well, fare well and au revoir, I hope.

ever, dearest Pop
your loving
F.

---

369 An allusion to Mal 3:2.

Source: Letter, Wellcome (Claydon copy) Ms 9011/37

10 South St.
9 July 1886

My dearest Pop [Parthenope Verney]

I would fain hope that with this steady dry weather you are somewhat less suffering. Miss Octavia Hill's letter, so full of sense and conviction, I now return. I have had a charming letter (M.S.) from her. I did not know she was so genial. I also return with thanks your letter from Bonjean, the worthy son of a great father, and a number of others, lent me kindly by you. I hope my friends Ralph and Gwendolen[370] are now quite flourishing.

General Chamberlain has been here (Sir Neville), delightful as ever. He says he goes about in his "small way," as he hopes others are doing, and talks to the people, and when they have grievances, he says, trying to educate them, if they are new voters, "Now, you have to send good members to Parliament, who will make good laws. Your grievances will be now, more or less, your own fault. And, mind you, they will always fall on the poorest. I and others have a little money at the bank. But I shall button up my trousers pocket and money will not fructify, if you don't send good men to Parliament. Now, let's talk about what are good men and laws."

I have had the Vice-Chancellor of Oxford [Benjamin Jowett] here twice and taken the sacrament. I asked him, of course without mentioning names, your question: had he said that Mr Gladstone was "crazy with vanity"? He said, so far from *having* said it, he *could* never have said anything like it, as, though he was not a Gladstonian, his opinion of him was quite the reverse.

I meant to write you an account of your "young man" being so tired on the Wednesday and going to a long hot big banquet, so that I sent to inquire after him at peep o' dawn on Thursday. And your "young man" was gone!! gone to Esher and came back like a lark. But I was so angry with his taking up my time with the photos, when there was so much to do and to say, that I won't.

I have had a Mr Baring here, first cousin of Lord Northbrook (when I heard Francis Baring announced, I did so think of old Sir Francis[371]) who is going out to India with his newly married wife "for

---

370 Children of Frederick Verney.
371 Francis Thornhill Baring (1796-1866), 1st Baron Northbrook; his daughter Mary was the second wife of Jack Bonham Carter.

twenty or thirty years," to arrange for cheap good literature (not Christian only), a sort of penny library or rather *anna* library, an anna is half a farthing—in all the vernaculars for the people, comprising sanitary, agricultural little stories, etc. The Hindu vernacular literature is, as you know, generally stories of successful cheats (as Macaulay said of Italians, *they* would all be on the side of *Iago*). He came that we might talk over their sanitary, etc. wants, so different from those of the English poor.

Thanks many for the splendid little rug and for the *berries* and flowers.

I am going to have a man just come from Russia. He writes and says how deplorable now the state of the peasants, how unlike 1863, when he was there, just what you say.

Your *Painters Five*, by Lady Eastlake,[372] was left by cruel mistake the morning we started on the drawers under the bookshelves in Captain Verney's dressing room. I was so afraid it (the two volumes) would lodge itself there I made Lizzie write to housemaid. Pray, if it has not returned to you, send Mr Morey for it. I am so glad Mr Ager is better. À Dieu, à Dieu, à Dieu and au revoir.

ever thy F.

Source: Letter, Wellcome (Claydon copy) Ms 9011/49

10 South St.
28 August 1886

My dearest Pop [Parthenope Verney]

I fear I shall not be able to come so early in the week as next Tuesday. I am so exceedingly busy, but you may be sure I shall come as soon as I can. But, dearest, it is as much out of the possibility of human things as anything I know of that I shall ever be able to sit in the saloon and listen to "the music." Sir Harry must not come, offering me his dear arm, and saying: "you *must* come down, because I ask you, into the saloon." I shall probably never be able to come downstairs at all, except to doddle out quite alone and unseen into the garden occasionally. (But it is almost as impossible to get out and in of Claydon House unseen as in and out of Windsor Castle.) I am very sorry that I could not come this week. I shall hope that you will be able to spend part of your afternoons in the blue room, if I am there, as we did before. Lady Dufferin's work[373] is very heavy in hand.

---

372 Elizabeth Eastlake, *Five Great Painters: Essays Reprinted from the Edinburgh and Quarterly Reviews.*
373 Wife of the Marquess of Dufferin, Viceroy of India 1884-88, who started the Lady Dufferin Fund for work in India.

I do trust that this weather is at all events doing you some good. It must be charming in the country. You are very good about the nurses/probationers. Mrs Wardroper is ill and gone away and I *hope* her letters do not follow her. Miss Crossland is so busy and the probationers doing so much extra work in the hospital that I fear their longed-for jaunt cannot come off just now. I shall see Miss Crossland today.

ever your loving

F.

"Quarterly Review: London Library: Russia" If it was that one you kindly lent me in the blue room, I sent or carried down *all* the books you lent me the day before I left, 18 June. I certainly have not got it.

F.N.

Source: Letter, Wellcome (Claydon copy) Ms 9011/69

10 South St.
30 December 1886

My dearest Pop [Parthenope Verney]

My heart is always with you. If I have not written, it is because I really have not been able—the arranging of Christmas distributions, besides my other work. I think I shall do no more Christmases.

Margaret's dear letter has been a Christmas gift indeed, but don't you think there is a vein of sadness about her now? as if we had made too much of it, and there was not really such an improvement in Lettice.[374] It was the most beautiful letter. It shall be returned to you next week.

I wish you, oh such a good New Year, in spite of all. For in many an effort for good, you can still find happiness. But still I hope for diminished pain, and believe in it, and to Sir Harry the same good New Year.

Abominable [Lord] Randolph's prank is disastrous, just as we have got the secretaries of state to do something for us. The only thing for us now is for Goschen (who *is* a Conservative) to take Randolph's place and let the Cabinet members stay as they are. Administration is now utterly sacrificed to party politics. They chop and change the offices among the ministers (Cabinet) as if we were at a pantomime. The life, terrestrial and eternal, of 250 millions, or of the whole forces, of course signifies nothing, a mere Christmas card to play. If

---

374 Letters appear below on Lettice Verney's serious illness (see pp 656-58 below).

they are going to do that chopping and changing now (as they chop and change poor ryots' land in India) why God save us, for He alone can.

My best Christmas and New Year's love to Sir Harry and remember me kindly to Mrs Davidson. I enclose a little note from Ellen Tollet, but a little scrap. A few feeling lines in pencil, asking us to pray for her, I liked much better.

You know perhaps that Lady Belper has moved poor Freddy to her own house near Kingston. But the account is very bad—no real recovery of consciousness. Sometimes, she says, "I can scarcely bear it."

ever dearest Pop

your old Flo

Source: Letter, Wellcome (Claydon copy) Ms 9011/95

4 March 1887

Dearest Pop [Parthenope Verney]

Accompanying are outdoor flowers from Monte Carlo. Be not alarmed; they do not gamble among themselves, at least not in Lent. Please do me the favour of taking what you like and send me back the rest. They smell like Lea Hurst.

ever your F.

Source: Incomplete letter, Wellcome (Claydon copy) 9011/100

8 March 1887

Dearest Pop [Parthenope Verney]

I am afraid you are still very bad. I give you joy about Sir Harry: I thought we were "in for" it, not that he is at all out of the wood. You did quite right to put him under Sir A. Clark's orders. It is a pity when a good man is so naughty.

Old Widow Barton died yesterday at Holloway, a happy release, a loss to me. Papa used to go nearly every Sunday afternoon when she and her husband and charming daughter (both died long before her) kept the Leashaw Lodge. And, sitting on the three-legged table before the fire, how often she has described to me the scene: say: "Barton, read me a bit of a chapter." How like Papa that was, not reading or preaching himself. "Sometimes the squire used to choose it, but much more often he used to say, 'Barton, you choose.'"

When I first went to Lea Hurst after Papa's death, Widow Barton was living a forlorn but patient life in a tumbledown room of Sims in Holloway, quite alone, supporting herself, with almost sightless eyes, by Smedley's work. She was a most interesting woman. I telegraphed to her when she was dying, through Bratby, and even then she noticed it and said, "I do pray for her," but "I am sure *Miss Nightingale* would let me get up." She had been ill and suffering for more than a year and for several days before her death could take nothing, not even water, yet resolutely sat on the sofa or hard settle till last Friday, saying "she had never been lazy" (which was quite true) and was with the utmost difficulty by the united exertions of doctor and friends got to bed. . . .

Source: Letter, Wellcome (Claydon copy) 9011/125

28 April 1887

My dearest Pop [Parthenope Verney]

A good journey to you and as easy and pleasant a return to Claydon as our loving Father and the beautiful place can give you. "Il est si bon et Il s'entend si bien à nos affaires" [He is so good and He looks after our concerns so well]. Would I could make it easier to you. I commend you to Him, who is Love.

    ever thy F.

I send £1 for the 18/6 carpet. Do you remember in Dante he says:

Did we know everything, the Son of Mary
(Son of Man) need not have come.
State contenti, umana gente, al quia,
Che, se potuto averte veder tutto,
Mestier no era partoris Maria.[375]

Source: Letter, Wellcome (Claydon copy) 9011/131

10 South St.
12 May 1887

My dearest Pop [Parthenope Verney]

How can I thank you for your letter, your birthday letter, and for the splendour, in perfect harmony, of screen which lights up my room like a flood of sunshine. I am so fond of birds. If only these could sing! I am so careful of them that they are shrouded in clean sheets from bedtime till about 5:00 P.M. the next day. I wish I *could* "come, come," but am chained like a galley slave to the oar.

---

375 Dante, *Purgatorio*, canto 3 lines 37-39.

Mrs Scharlieb[376] of Madras spent the afternoon with me yesterday. She has quite given up Madras and the poor, poor R. Victoria Hospital on account of health and has set up making a home for her children in Park St. and supporting them by private practice, of which I have no doubt she will have more than enough. But poor Madras—I never was so disappointed. O these children—she sacrifices thousands for one son. No one can fill her place at Madras; hundreds could do so in England. Her work was immense, unique. She was "facile princeps" [easily the leader] and now it is all over.

I had a visit from dear Sister Airy,[377] rescued from the Tasmania. She thanks you for your invitation, but *must* remain at home *this* month. Her account of the rescue, of the hospitality of the poor Corsicans, was the most touching, the most simple and lovely, in the midst of overwhelming seas and the thunder of waves and wind, with the soft spring wildflowers where they landed, the glorious scenery of the snowy mountains of Corsica down to the very cliff under which they struggled ashore when their boat was swamped, and their final conveyance in about thirty carts, two days after, to the fashionable chef-lieu of Sartene, a town clinging to the sides and top of a rock like the Peak of Teneriffe, surrounded by similar peaks covered with snow. And all for others and nothing for herself. *She* seemed lost, in helping the shipwrecked and children. I must write you the whole account. God bless you.

ever my dearest P.
your F.

Source: Letter, Wellcome (Claydon copy) Ms 9011/135

10 South St.
Whitsun week, 31 May 1887

My dearest Pop [Parthenope Verney]

I am afraid you have been very bad. As the Holy Spirit made of those cowardly quarrelling disciples, at Whitsuntide, so may He make of us brave and right-judging men and women, but you are brave already.

Mr Jowett has been ill. He is now in London for rest, staying incog[nito].

---

376 Mary Ann Dacomb (Bird) Scharlieb (1845-1930), later Dame.
377 Sybil Airy nursed in the Egyptian campaigns and was shipwrecked on return. She was later matron at the Royal Victoria Hospital, Bournemouth.

Miss [Mary] Jones, formerly of King's College Hospital, and who now for twenty years has had two houses in Kensington Square, one of which she made into an incurables hospital, and a sisterhood of her own, doing temperance work, publishing a temperance newspaper, district and workhouse visiting, etc. has had typhoid fever for nine weeks, during which much has passed between us, and cannot live over the day. Of all women I have ever known, she has had the most unbounded influence over women, for she had nothing to offer them, nothing but herself, her love and duty.

I have seen Mr Henry Cunningham.[378] He talked much and well, and much of you.

This is the coldest May weather I ever remember. Mrs Scharlieb has been with you, I think. She defrauded me of an appointment last Sunday week, to the very great detriment of India, for it was not for amusement but for Lady Dufferin's Fund, whose senior aide de camp, Major Cooper, who came home by the wrecked Tasmania, had been with me. I don't know when I shall be able to offer her another appointment.

I am sure you will like Justice Windeyer[379] very much. Pray give him my kindest regards, and Mrs Windeyer is a most active person among the East Enders. I believe. God bless you, my dear Pop.

ever your old

F.N.

My kind regards to Mrs Davidson and Mrs Broadhurst. I hope Sir Harry takes his coffee at 6:30 A.M., *before* he leaves his bed, as ordered by Sir A. Clark and Mr Savory.

Source: Letter, ADD Mss 52427 ff73-74

10 South St.
3 June 1887

My dearest Pop [Parthenope Verney]

The account from Embley is much better today.

Miss Jones died yesterday morning. She is my oldest friend in the nursing cause. When dying and apparently speechless she said, all at once, in a distinct voice to her two oldest "sisters," kneeling by her,

---

378 Henry Cuningham, later Sir (1832-1920), an India expert and also a survivor of the Tasmanian wreck.

379 William Charles Windeyer (1834-97), later Sir, a progressive politician in Australian, appointed judge in 1879.

"Little children, keep yourselves from idols,[380] little children, love one another." What would one give to know what she is feeling now! . . .

Source: Letter, Wellcome (Claydon copy) Ms 9011/174

10 South St.
10 September 1887

My dearest Pop [Parthenope Verney]

Many thanks, I am as well as "could be expected" after leaving Claydon. It looked so transcendently lovely with the sun breaking out after the rain as I stood and saw and listened out of my east window for the last time and all the birds were singing a low song of love and joy. I blew two kisses in at your dear door as I passed downstairs.

We came into the dusty foliage of London in a N.E. wind, but the leaves are still thick. But I have been seized, bound hand and foot and immersed in Indian business ever since the moment of my return.

I am so pleased that you are pleased with Mr Richmond's picture[381]— I was so afraid—and that there would be "Love's Labour Lost." Then people do so ask for photographs. I had a letter from Mr Peacock of Whatstandwell, full of gratitude to you and Sir Harry, as well they might be. I am sure you have put new life into them.

Some splendid Tritomias now adorn my room and I did not tell you, I forgot, that I bought a brisket, and Mrs Broadhouse cooked it for me, this as a pattern for here.

We are in all sorts of breathlessnesses here. You would see that Sir John Gorst[382] moved the budget last night of a fifth part of the population of the globe, and this trifling matter attracted a house which was all but counted out. What must India think of us? Sir J. Gorst is ill and our business hangs fire. Indian finance is in a desperate condition, aggravated by the capture of Burma, of course, an awful expenditure. Lord Dufferin is "disappointing," so say people. . . .

Mrs Robertson. I could not feel satisfied without writing to Dr Benson the morning I left Claydon. He replied with what I thought a very sensible view of her case, but one cannot judge without more inquiry. And you think she ought to see someone in London, in which I dare say you are right. Mr Croft,[383] to whom I would gladly have sent her, is

380 1 John 5:21.
381 William Blake Richmond (1842-1921), later Sir, painted a portrait of Nightingale for the Verneys.
382 Sir John Eldon Gorst (1835-1916), under secretary of state for India.
383 John Croft (1833-1905), resident surgeon at St Thomas'.

out of London till end of month. But there are two men, both in London, who take the places of the great men at St Thomas' when away on holiday, in whom we have the most implicit confidence. Both are good. She will probably like the married man the best.

I could not send her as an out-patient to St Thomas' in any case, "them's my sentiments." But I would gladly send her to either of these men she likes—both live near here, and pay the fee. Either will of course order her a truss with pad and she will go to Spratt's and be fitted. It is not a difficult case, I believe. I wish I had some woman to send with her, but I have no one who is knowledgeable. However all three men are entirely to be trusted, as much so as Mr Croft. Only I am fond of his excessive carefulness. Spratt has a sister who fits women.

Mrs Robertson is exceedingly obliged to you for your kind offer of a bed at No. 4. She will come up on the 19th, if you will kindly give orders, and she will have her meals here. The two men we recommend are (I have inquired at St Thomas') Mr Pitts and Mr Makins (Mr M. married Mrs Fellowes[384]) if she would say which she would like best. Mr Pitts is perhaps rather the cleverer, but both are safe men. If she would also say what train she comes by on the 19th. . . . My dearest love to all your people dear. God bless you. I never forget to pray Him with all my heart for my Pop.

ever my Pop

your F.

Source: Letter, Wellcome (Claydon copy) Ms 9011/181

10 South St.
16 October 1887

My dearest Pop [Parthenope Verney]

It is indeed a loss, dear Mr Greene.[385] How I wish I had had the opportunity of taking the sacrament with you from him once more! But oh what a gain to him! He said to me *so* simply one day: "When I was a young man, I was nearly lost in a fishing boat in a storm off the coast of Portugal" (or Spain, I forget). "Then I was not ready. Now," and he said something that made it evident he was alluding to this as his last illness, "I *am* ready."

---

384 Widow of a general, Mrs Fellowes trained at St Thomas', nursed in the Zulu War and became a key collaborator of Nightingale's; see *War and Militarism*.

385 Thomas Huntley Greene (d. 1887), vicar at Middle Claydon.

Yes, he was really in Christ's kingdom *here* as much as he is *now*. Sir Harry read me one of his last sermons at Claydon. There was this sentence: "Our place in Christ's kingdom is being determined *now*." O God, give us three places in Christ's kingdom *now*! And He says He *will*, if we choose lovingness—Mr Greene was so full of lovingness. That is Christ's kingdom. "God is love and he that dwelleth in love dwelleth in God and He in us."[386] *Can* God dwell in *me*? Colonel Fordyce, when he fell shot dead in the Caffre [Kaffir] War, had just time to cry out, like a soldier at his post, "Ready, my God" and died.

I must stop I am so driven. May I send this very unsentimental offering now, £25 and another at Christmas. Kindest regards to Mrs Davidson.

ever dearest Pop

your loving F.

Source: Letter, Wellcome (Claydon copy) Ms 9011/199

> 10 South St.
> Park Lane, W.
> 18 November 1887

My dearest Pop [Parthenope Verney]

How grievous has your cough been and how thankful I am that you are, I mean that *it* is somewhat better. I have done as you bade me, [said a] prayer for love and wisdom, dearest Pop.

Mobs and fogs in London—dreadful—grand display tomorrow in Hyde Park, Special constables, mobs.

You have heard, I dare say, that Aunt Mai has had a relapse these last three weeks. She now never leaves her bed, only is moved into south room most days from music room. She has suffered much pain. She writes to me: "for myself, though I have made a step downwards *towards the end*, I am really more comfortable than I have been since I left off being downstairs on 24 May. I now spend my days in bed between two rooms, and so *I shall remain while in this world*." She has two trained nurses always; one night, one day. "What I could do before, I can do now in my new *and easier* way of life." How sweet that is!

My doctor and oculist attends Lady Hatherton and Georgina Hurt, and talks of them. He says, of Miss Hurt, she is now blind of both eyes with cataract, but the eyes are so bad he should not operate, only that she is *so* deaf that she would be in total darkness and almost total

---

386 A paraphrase of 1 John 4:8 and 12.

silence if he did not give her back a little sight. He admires them both very much. He says Lady Hatherton is making a good recovery from her operation (cataract in both eyes) only she caught a little cold, because she *would* see a missionary. She is so active she did not like being kept in bed at all. He says *he* can make Miss Hurt hear, speaking very slowly, one word at a time, but very few can now.

Have you heard anything of Ellen Tollet? I have not. I have no eyes, no brain, no time, no strength, to do anything but my own work, and by no means always that.

We have had dense fog for days. This is rather a sad letter. Times *are* sad; I hope my next will be cheerier. God bless you, dearest Pop.

ever your F.

Robins and thrushes, starlings and crows, feeding at the window, so hard.

Source: Letter, Wellcome (Claydon copy) Ms 9011/204

> 10 South St.
> 9 December 1887

Thank you for your article in the *National*,[387] dearest Pop. But why favour the *National*? I send you a beautiful letter from Otto Goldschmidt, which please return, also 10/ for poor old Moss, with many thanks.

I am very feeble and my doctor wants to send me away for two or three months altogether. I trust your cough at least is better.

ever your F.

Source: Letter, Wellcome (Claydon copy) Ms 9012/20

> [printed address] 10 South Street
> Park Lane, W.
> 19 April 1888

My dearest Pop [Parthenope Verney]

This is the day that gave you to this world. I have not lilacs and laburnums to lay upon your altar, as we always had at Embley. Excuse a prosaic £25.

I pray God that, in the midst of an intense trial of pain and suffering, heroically borne, you have still, dearest Pop, much happiness.

How hard it must be to the German Emperor to feel, "Thy will be done, for it is righteous love." Yet I believe He does.

ever thy loving F.

---

387 "Peasant Properties in France, 1787-1887."

Source: Letter, Wellcome (Claydon copy) Ms 9012/24

10 South St.
28 April 1888

My dearest Pop [Parthenope Verney]

I do hope you will give Sir Andrew Clark [a physician] a trial. I rejoice to see the west wind. I am afraid you were very tired yesterday with people. All dressed was I, all but my gown, to gallop down if you had come, but I was glad you did not. It was not fit for you. I meet you in the arms of the eternal Father: "A child must have but a poor opinion of a father's love who never comes to him (or uses his privilege of conversing with him at all hours) except he wants to get something out of him."

I don't know whether you read my poor remarks on Bismarck. Those curious cynical confessions, but very interesting. Your books all very acceptable (all returned). I like the *Life of Emerson*[388] better than I liked his essays.

Droz is very pretty. "Chez Paddy" very good. You have kindly sent in Mme Mohl;[389] I don't think I can read it. Do you mean me to return it to *Beatrice*? I have only been out of bed once these two months long enough to have my room "done." And I have never repeated the experiment, or I should have come to see you, my dearest Pop. Good speed to Claydon.

I am very sorry that you have been able to take that excellent remedy for a cough (Unionist dinners) so seldom.

ever my dear Pop
your loving F.

The account of Aunt Mai is failing. Shore is there.

Source: Letter, Wellcome (Claydon copy) Ms 9012/40

10 South St.
4 July 1888

My dear Sir Harry and Parthe

God bless you both. Our probationers will have a happy day, even if the weather is not quite propitious. I hope you will not be overtired.

---

388 Ralph Waldo Emerson (1803-82), poet and essayist. Probably Amos Bronson Alcott, *R.W. Emerson: Philosopher and Seer.*
389 Presumably her book, *Letters and Recollections of Julius and Mary Mohl*, ed. by Mary Charlotte Simpson.

To you Lady Ashburton would have come today, but cannot. She will come over tomorrow for "a few hours" to see Parthe, if possible. She goes to Marienbad on Tuesday.

My poor prayers—*rich*, if Christ prays in us—are with you.

F.N.

Source: Letter to Parthenope Verney, Wellcome (Claydon copy) Ms 9012/58; draft in ADD Mss 45791 ff355-56

10 South St.

21 October 1888

I do pray indeed, my dearest Pop, that, as you said, you "be not dismayed."[390] But God says to you, as He did to Joshua, after Moses' death: "Be strong and of a good courage, for I am with thee"[391] and thy spirit is heroic. I have a great reverence for Moses and Joshua. It seems to me that Moses was the greatest statesman that ever lived and the most devoted man. Others have legislated. He alone led. It was as if Cavour had left Turin and Rome and had given himself to lead, civilize and form into a nation the miserable superstitious creatures of the Abruzzi, whose name is "abrutissement." That Moses, brought up as a king's son, nursed in luxury, educated, versed "in all the learning of the Egyptians,"[392] should leave all this to head and go back to a parcel of wretched slaves from whom he had sprung and from whom he had been saved—to lead them about for the whole term of his natural life to extreme old age in the desert, without a country, because he saw that they would be totally unfit without this discipline to become a people at all beats everything we read of in history. The result is as unparallelled as the preparation: a nation *without a country*, which has survived every species of degradation and is still the strongest and most abiding element though scattered over the whole world in the world.

Out of it has come our religion. It still holds the purse of Europe. Money and spiritual life. To Joshua having, without Moses, to put the keystone to the organization of this great work, comes a spirit which, happily for us, is very fully described: "as I was with Moses, so I will be with thee: I will not fail thee, nor forsake thee. Be strong and of a good courage: Only be thou strong and very courageous." (And so you are, my Pop, "As thy

---

390 A paraphrase of Josh 1:9.
391 A paraphrase of Deut 31:6.
392 A paraphrase of Acts 7:22.

day, so shall thy strength be,"[393] as you said) "very courageous, that thou mayest observe to do according to all the law"[394] (and how little they had then to go by, compared to what we have! They scarcely knew that God is the loving Father). "Turn not from it to the right hand or to the left, that thou mayest prosper whithersoever thou goest. This book of the law shall not depart out of thy mouth: but thou shalt meditate therein day *and night.*"[395] (How little they had to "meditate" on, how very little, at night, compared to what we have, and yet how very, very few, even of the saints and philosophers, think out the plan of the almighty Father, the plan of His moral government, or how to manifest it or "observe to do" it), "that thou mayest observe to do according to all that is written therein: for then thou shalt make thy way prosperous, and then thou shalt have good success. Have not I commanded thee. Be strong and of a good courage; be not afraid, neither be thou dismayed: *dismayed: for the Lord thy God is with thee whithersoever thou goest.*"[396]

I was reading in a little *nursing* book, which was sent me for my "opinion": "Still there is something that never can be conquered, unless we choose, and that is our will, our spirit. If we choose we can make the most abject slave of the disease that is killing our body. x x So suffering produces heroes, when acted on by will. x x So is personal disease and misery reproduced under other forms for *higher service.* Pain, which we naturally shrink from x x becomes, when once will is mixed with it, a medium for the rapid acquirement of new force, which shows itself in varied aspects, as courage, endurance, steadfastness, intensity of purpose, insight, unselfishness. We learn many things in days of health but not x x. Here is the grand opportunity. Make pain and disease and death yield to you their inner core and transmute you into a hero, one who takes his spirit in his own hands, and gives it back to God who gave it." So are you, my Pop, a hero.

We have had outrageous fogs here, but I comforted myself in that there would be still, sunshiny, autumnal days at Claydon, so lovely. My kindest regards to Mr Calvert. I sent Sir Harry six copies of the Queen's Jubilee Atlas, and Sir Morell Mackenzie on the Emperor,[397] because he

---

393 A paraphrase of Deut 33:25.
394 Josh 1:7.
395 Josh 1:7-8.
396 Josh 1:8-9.
397 Morrell Mackenzie, *The Fatal Illness of Frederick the Noble.*

asked for them. It is equally impossible to believe that Mackenzie could have published this book without her, the Empress Frederick's leave, or that she could have had the unwisdom to give her leave. Everything that has happened must make her position more intolerable. In reading the few pages I did, I thought: how can M. Mackenzie expose himself to be given the lie to by these exact Germans, who of course have an attested copy of the post mortem? This apparently is just what they have done, confuted him. But this heartless fight over the Emperor's remains is agonizing. Never was there anything so horrible. How *can* she bear it? And the German papers: "The Liberals would soon have found out the Emperor Frederick was wrong. And so would he!! etc."

I took away my scrappy three lots written for you of Indian notes, intending to add to and arrange them, at least to read them over, and have not even looked at them! Shall I send them back as they are? Remember me most kindly to Mrs Davidson and Miss Beart.

My love to Lettice, Aunt Florence's love. Thanks many for your beautiful grapes and flowers. I went away with a heavy heart. Good-bye; good-bye.

Henry Bonham Carter's third son, Norman, from Balliol, sails on Thursday for Calcutta (civil service). Alfred has been laid up for two months with breaking the sinew to his knee tendon. A little girl is just born to him. God bless you.

ever your F.

Source: Letter, Wellcome (Claydon copy) Ms 9012/70

[printed address] 10 South Street
Park Lane, W.
Christmas Day 1888

My dearest Pop [Parthenope Verney]

I am so grieved you are so bad and with your anxiety and my own. I do think of Sir Harry, and commend you both, with my whole heart, to our Father, who *is* almighty *Love*.

I don't like the Ten Commandments: it is all, "you shall *not*, you shall *not*," till Christ explained them. Negatives never gave love, love to each other and to God. And I don't like the (perpetual) perfection of telling us of the having *no* other will but His. That is only another negative. A *strong* will, to *second* His, that is the real end and aim and perfection. And I think you *do*. Let *that* be our Christmas blessing. Alas! how far I am from it! Fare you very well my dearest.

ever thy F.

Louisa Ashburton has just been here, full of you.

Source: Letter, Wellcome (Claydon copy) Ms 9012/77

30 December 1888

Dearest [Parthenope Verney]

How blessed is the news! I heard from Dr Acland last night after the visit. But he insists on the absolute necessity of Sir Harry being careful, not "doing too much, body or mind, *not getting up*, reading overmuch, *talking*," all that you know and he *must* obey for your sake and God's.

I am sorry Dr Acland goes on Tuesday. God bless you both.

ever your F.

. . . Miss Shalders sent me a sermon in verse (supposed to have been preached by Ugo Bapi in Santo Spirito Hospital, which I know so well, dreary place, at Rome) which has such lovely things in it.

I think, when God looks down the ranks of heaven x x
He doth behold the Angel of the Earth,
Stretched like Prometheus on the promontory x x
Bound to a perpetuity of pain,
Willing and strong, and finding in his pain
God and his one unbroken note of praise
In the full rush of cosmic harmony x x.
As children might, impatient of the school,
Despise the letters, longing for the songs
And stories that they catch the echoes of.
The songs are written, but first learn to spell!
The books will keep, but if we will not learn,
We shall not read them when the right time comes,
Or read them wrongly and confusedly,
And *each hour* has its lesson, and each life.
And if we *miss* one life, *we shall not find*
Its lesson in another; rather go
So much the less complete for evermore x x.
For must we not believe
A soul, bred up in perfect rule of growth,
And of obedience to the Will Divine
Through all its stages, would be born in each
In physical and spiritual harmony
With that world's order as conceived by God? x x

Editor: By 1889 her sister was so crippled that she had to be carried for visits. A letter to a close colleague and kindred spirit declined a visit on a Sunday because "I always reserve Sunday afternoon for my sister, who likes to be carried in and spend that afternoon here." [398]

Source: Letter, Wellcome (Claydon copy) Ms 9012/80

10 South St.
5 January 1889

My dearest Pop [Parthenope Verney]

I was so thankful for your letters, you cannot think. Praised be God. Today is the anniversary of our dear father's death. Sam will put "rosemary that's for remembrance,"[399] and bay, and violets on his grave. Shore was here last night. I believe Aunt Mai's life may now be counted by days. He goes back to her tomorrow (Sunday). My love to "Morfy"[400] and the boys—dear Morfy—if I may say so.

The fogs here are terrible. You know that Louisa Ashburton is threatened with cataract in one eye. She goes to Power, of Bartholomew's, today for his verdict.

You will be greatly relieved that Sir H. Acland is prospering. He was so cut up with anxiety, the sudden cold and irregular food that he was quite ill on Sunday and Monday last. But they broke their journey at Lucerne. He "quite enjoyed his journey" (Miss Acland to whom I telegraphed writes) "and slept better than he had for some time and looks so well and vigorous as to delight our friends the Heathcotes. In spite of the cold, he has just gone to Altnach by steamer (two hours) with Miss Heathcote. We go on to Milan tomorrow and to Genoa on Monday. I will send a card to you or Lady Verney from Pegli. We much long for good news of Sir Harry."

Dearest, may God bless you both and He does bless you.
ever thy F.

My kind regards to Mr Calvert, please.

---

398 Letter to A. Hawthorn 3 July 1889, ADD Mss 45776 f265.
399 Ophelia in Shakespeare, *Hamlet* Act 4, scene 5.
400 Harriet Julia Morforwyn Hinde, wife of George Verney; or one of their daughters, Catherine Morforwyn or Morforwyn Mary; sons James Hope, Harry Lloyd and Edward Vortigern.

Source: Letter, Wellcome (Claydon copy) Ms 9012/82

10 South St.
7 January 1889

Dearest [Parthenope Verney]

You will know what I felt (and indeed every maid here too) about the fire—I will not describe it. We thank God, we bless God for this great unspeakable deliverance; and more, yet more for His wonderful calm, God's own peace keeping your minds and hearts during the storm of danger. We cannot be thankful enough. Sir Harry writes: "We are under God's hand, and where else could we be so well?"

The frost and fog here have been so severe that we still tremble at the thought of that night. I should like to thank Mr Morey and John Webb and the Fire Brigade, but where did it get water enough in such a frost?

I'm like the "sluggard" telling my dreams. But I, wakeful during the greater part of the night, kept thinking of fire, and that "Macbeth should sleep no more." I think it possible, though the superstition should not be pushed so as to destroy our peace, that two sisters or brothers may communicate with each other by other means than words.

Pray tell Sir Harry how touched I was by his letter and that I will write. God bless him and you, dearest. Is "Morfy" gone? and who have you now?

ever thy F.

Source: Letter, Wellcome (Claydon copy) Ms 9012/87

10 South St.
17 January 1889

My dearest Pop [Parthenope Verney]

I was so thankful for your note this morning. I do trust those rigours are keeping off. We don't like them at all.

You will have been prepared, dearest, by what I told you, to hear that, since last Friday, dear Aunt Mai's life has been only a question of hours and, alas! of more or less suffering. She went home at 1:00 this morning, home to her God after whom she had longed, whom she had sought more than anyone I know, except perhaps M Mohl. To know Him, to understand in some measure His moral government in everything and everybody she saw was the object of her life. Now she knows, now she understands, now she will make eternal progress: Him, the Almighty Love, she has found. They will all miss her dreadfully, Shore most of all. They were all there.

ever thy F.

I will write tomorrow.

Source: Letter, Wellcome (Claydon copy) Ms 9012/93

10 South St.
27 January 1889

Dearest [Parthenope Verney]

I fear you are *very* suffering. Louisa Ashburton was here last night, inquiring after you. You know that she has cataract in both eyes. But, alas! She has gone to an American female quack who promises to cure her!! I am bound to say she looks better and sees better. But oh! the risk.

I was so thankful for Morey's telegram last night. If there is anything else I can do, you are bound to tell me. But would you not let Dr Benson write a report to good Sir Andrew Clark, who has taken such an interest?

Aunt Mai's funeral was very, very touching. The schoolchildren and many of the poor people made nosegays and posies and wreaths of wild flowers, "very nice and rather pretty." The children lined the path we know so well. The poor young ones—I mean her grandchildren—hardly know how to bear losing her. She was such a centre to their love.

Do you ever hear of Ellen Tollet? I like to think of Miss Pringle with you for a little. You have been so good in writing. I hope to hear tomorrow morning. God speed you.

Our affairs at War Office and India Office are very desperate. To save £800 or £1000 they will destroy everything, millions of lives in India. To get £800 or £1000 they would eat their fathers.

ever, dearest, yours
F.

Source: Letter, Wellcome (Claydon copy) Ms 9012/100

10 South St.
3 February 1889

Dearest, very dearest [Parthenope Verney]

I trust that Sir Harry is observing good Sir Andrew Clark's directions, staying in bed for a few days, taking his food still, but not depressed. I try to do, as I know you do, "hang on God's unknown will from moment to moment," the will of almighty Love.

Pauline Irby says that when he was getting better there were some nice notices about him in the *Manchester Guardians* before 16 January. She writes most anxiously, and Shore is so sympathetic (in his own trouble). He is at Embley now. Barbarina[401] has had the measles—eyes suffering. They have taken her into the country for a bit.

How sad and terrible is the suicide and death of this Austrian Crown Prince.[402] There is no sorrow like unto that sorrow.[403]

Wildgoose, at Lea Hurst, has lost his wife quite suddenly. It reminded me of Ezekiel: Behold, I will take away the desire of thine eyes at a stroke. Yet shalt thou neither strive nor cry. So He spake in the morning. And at even my wife died. And I did in the morning as I was commanded.[404]

Thanks, thanks for the lovely flowers last night and still more for the telegram. Wildgoose's memorial card to his wife said: "who passed *through* death," I like that word.

ever, dearest, always with you

yours and his

F.

Source: Letter, Wellcome (Claydon copy) Ms 9012/102

10 South St.
4 February 1889
P.M.

Dearest, ever dearest [Parthenope Verney]

I learn at your courage, but indeed it is a privilege, as you say, to watch and see and know the last years of such a life. The last years of such a life are even the most valuable. Hail to thee, happy soul, the soul of sweetness and of faith. Would I were with you, but God is with you, the Almighty Strength and Wisdom. Now we feel Him.

ever yours and his

F.

Source: Letter, Wellcome (Claydon copy) Ms 9012/111

10 South St.
7 February 1889 P.M.

Dearest, very dearest [Parthenope Verney]

I have this moment had your letter of yesterday. Nobody shall come till you think it quite right and wise to admit them. But indeed I don't

---

401 Margaret Thyra Barbara Smith, later Lady Stephen (1872-1945), daughter of Shore and Louisa.

402 Crown Prince Rudolf of Austria (1858-89), had recently shot himself and his lover, Baroness Maria Vetsera, in a suicide pact at Schloss Mayerling.

403 An allusion to Lam 1:12.

404 A paraphrase of Ezek 24:16-18.

think they want to come unduly. Margaret says: I do so respect and understand her wish (meaning yours). Fred says: we only wait our (that is your) orders from the sickroom. They all long to be with you as much as I do, but really their spirit is obedient as much as their legs. Nobody shall stir an inch till you give the signal and they shall be content, which is what you want.

We are so thankful that there is anything of real improvement that we would not mar it even by a thought or a wish. He wrote to me in happy faith. He said you had made such a beautiful prayer for him, which strengthened him so much. I did not understand whether you had spoken it or written it for him.

We all pray unceasingly, our life is a prayer for him and for you. John and Charlotte Clark came yesterday and begged me to give you their deepest sympathy. Mrs Hawthorn writes, whatever you decide upon as best shall be done, and willingly, do not fear.

ever dearest your and his

F.

Source: Letter, Wellcome (Claydon copy) Ms 9012/184

> [printed address] 10 South Street
> Park Lane, W.
> 18 April 1889

My dearest Pop [Parthenope Verney]

My heart and thoughts and prayers are always with you in the terrible strain you have borne so gallantly and so devoutly for the last four months, but they will be especially with you tomorrow which is your dear birthday, and in spite of all we may praise God that you were born and live. Tomorrow is Good Friday, the type of suffering and progress, divine progress. I send a prosaic little present to your feet.

ever yours and Sir Harry's

your F.

I sent today to Embley in *both* our names, with an inscription, a really heavenly cross and wreath to be laid on my father's and mother's grave on Easter Sunday.

F.N.

Weather here perfectly detestable. Miss Irby is come: 20 Hyde Park Gardens.

Source: Letter, Wellcome (Claydon copy) Ms 9012/219

10 South St.
18 July 1889

My dearest [Parthenope Verney]

I answered Miss Farrer's letter to you (which you sent me this morning) today to her. I accepted her terms [to work as Nightingale's secretary]. I asked her to come tomorrow; I begged her to go "Tuesday and Wednesday next to another engagement," as she wished. I apologized to her, and indeed I do to *you*, for my dereliction these two mornings. (This morning I had a man with me.) I hope to use her several mornings, though indeed I hardly know how. I ought to dictate letters to her, but that involves her being in the room with me. A Dieu.

ever your F.

Monday she copied a letter for me. Have you kindly had her two mornings or three?

Source: Letter to Parthenope Verney, Wellcome (Claydon copy) Ms 9012/244

Claydon
20 October 1889

Many thanks, my dearest, for your most kind note. I am indeed sorry if anything has passed in which you have been the sufferer from me. I need scarcely express again how sorry I was for that unlucky event on the day of the declaration. It is grievous to me to have to say in answer to your kind wish that I could not put off my going to London now. In the last two or three days I have sent my business papers and my business replies to the men I have to deal with for immediate consultation with me and I have told them that I shall be in London tomorrow.

I was also told that I might have to see the secretary of state "in October." The death of my Gordon (Mr Hewlett[405]) greatly increases the pressure and difficulty. We have also some very anxious St Thomas' business which will, I believe, be decided this week. I have said I shall be in South St. tomorrow.

I do not think that Margaret [Verney] can feel "hurt" at my going. I have always gone away when she could come. And one year I went away on the morning of the afternoon she came, as now exactly. We are supposed to be due in London in the first week in October. I would I could say what I cannot, and what all this explanation but mystifies, how real

---

405 Thomas Gilham Hewlett (1832-89), Sanitary Commissioner, Bombay Presidency. The allusion is to General Gordon.

and deep is the love which I feel reigns and rules between us, although obscured sometimes by the "dense and tainted air" which we try to escape from and from which God's love will deliver us.

Shall I come down to you this evening, if thou art too tired to come to me?

ever thine, with love which will be infinite as God's

F.N.

Editor: There are many brief notes to Nightingale's sister (below) in the last weeks of her life. During this time also Nightingale inquired from the butler and relatives concerning her condition. The sisters last met, in London, roughly a week before Parthenope Verney's death. She then made her last trip to Claydon to die. It seems that Nightingale was aware that the end was near although her brother-in-law may not have been (he was away when his wife actually died). Some further correspondence follows regarding Nightingale's own remembrance of her sister and tributes to her.

Source: Letter, Wellcome (Claydon copy) Ms 9013/8

[printed address] 10 South Street
Park Lane, W.
21 January 1890

Accept this bit of paper, dear Pop, pray. Affecting letter from Gerard Sellar[406] about his father's death, his mother's "endless courage and unselfishness—was there ever anyone like her?" And Edith's care . . . to keep little Rosalind "cheerful" [the two younger daughters]. The funeral is today.

Our affairs at St Thomas' and Edinburgh the deepest tragedy I know.

your F.

Source: Letter, Wellcome (Claydon copy) Ms 9013/11

9 February 1890

Dearest [Parthenope Verney]

I should be very sorry not to see you, if you think it worthwhile to be carried through an east wind! Upstairs!! For half an hour!!! At ¼ before 3!!! I have heavy business later, and I must give up Sir Harry before.

your F.

---

406 Son of Gertrude Smith and A. Craig Sellar, grandson of Uncle Octavius and Aunt Jane Smith.

Source: Unsigned letter, Wellcome (Claydon copy) Ms 9013/34

15 April 1890

My dearest Pop [Parthenope Verney]

I wish you would have Sir A. Clark again and tell him all about yourself. I think he should see what you call your bumpuses and recommend for the dressing of them.

ever your F.

There is a curious fad among some of the best doctors now, which I for one believe in, NOT that I ever heard this applied to the dressing of sore places like yours, alas! viz., that animal and not mineral unguents should be applied to the living body, which immediately assimilates, for example lanolin, which is animal, and not vaseline, which is mineral. I know it made a great difference to me to be rubbed with Neat's foot oil, though it makes one smell like a fish, of *not* recent extraction, instead of vaseline.

You have not got Lecky's *England* in the - - century (which Sir Harry is reading) at Claydon, have you?

Source: Letter, Wellcome (Claydon copy) Ms 9013/36

10 South St.
19 April 1890

My dearest Pop [Parthenope Verney]

Blessed be this day that brought you into this world. Blessed be God who has given you such heroism as to make even joy out of His sorrows and His beauty, to draw pearls from His depths: "de profundis." "Grace sufficient" for you as for St Paul, His strength made perfect in our weakness. It is not when we are strong that we are strong, nor when we are weak that we are weak.[407]

To a very young lady who undertook one of the largest workhouse infirmaries in the United Kingdom, single-handed, has persevered since for seven or it may be eight years, I had to send this morning a small subsidy, to hope that she would condescend to use it as intended, because the greatest gift she could give her infirmary was her own health. I don't say that to you, but I think we are bound to use all means we can. May God bless you! And He does bless you!

ever dearest Pop
your loving F.

---

407 An allusion to 2 Cor 12:9.

Do you think there is any "remission of sins" for those who destroy the primroses today to throw them on Lord Beaconsfield?

F.N.

Source: Letter, Wellcome (Claydon copy) Ms 9013/37

24 April 1890

My dearest Pop [Parthenope Verney]

Thanks for the magnificent cherry branch, which has already received adulation enough to turn a stronger head.

I wish you would have Sir A. Clark or Mrs Scharlieb, not that I expect miracles, but I cannot and do not believe that *nothing* can be done for the cough. And I am so sorry that you should go out of London without a little ploy.

Do you know the eldest daughter of Lord Cottesloe, who married a Cartwright? What sort of woman? She recommends strongly the widow of one of their farmers as a good cook housekeeper to me. And that naughty Miss Farrer, who has been so good to me, says the only objection is that they have all such robust stomachs that they don't know what good cooking means.

What do you say about a recommendation from them?

ever yours

F.

Source: Letter to Harry Verney, Wellcome (Claydon copy) Ms 9013/42

30 April 1890

... I have telegraphed to Mrs Hawthorne: *today* lunch at *1:45*. She will not ask to see Parthe, or keep her in. I am so very anxious to know how P. is and what Sir J. Paget said.

ever yours and hers

F.N.

Source: Letter, Harvard University, Countway Medical Library

3 May 1890

Dear Mr Morey

I hope you will be so good as to let me have a telegram or at least a postcard to say how Lady Verney is this evening, and by and bye to say whether her night nurse is come. God speed you.

yours sincerely

F. Nightingale

Source: Letter, Wellcome (Claydon copy) Ms 9013/44

My dearest Pop [Parthenope Verney]   Sunday 4 May [1890]

I have thought of you night and day during this last week. I have kept today quite free, but yet I don't like your coming out on such a dirty day and I am unluckily quite unable to leave my room.

It was quite a mistake the message you had yesterday. I was obliged to answer by telegraph an appointment and wished to know what you wished: that was all.

5 May 1890

God bless you, ever, dearest, on your way. He *will* bless you with love that cannot be spoken.

ever your F.

I hope your night nurse is coming directly.

Source: Letter, Harvard University, Countway Medical Library

[printed address] 10 South Street
Park Lane, W.
7 May 1890

Dear Mr Morey

Thank you very much for your letter and two telegrams. I was very anxious to hear. I dare say you will be kind enough to write me another note or two and to tell me when the night nurse arrives.

I enjoyed the primroses and wildflowers which you were so good as to send by John Webb. And will you kindly thank the Jackson children for them?

Sir Harry is, I think, even more busy than usual. He is now at the opening of the Military Exhibition by the Prince and Princess of Wales. And the streets are quite crowded towards the Embankment, they say.

ever sincerely yours
F. Nightingale

Source: Letter, Wellcome (Claydon copy) Ms 9013/46

10 South St.
8 May 1890

Dearest, ever dearest [Parthenope Verney]

I think of you and what you suffer night and day. Sir Harry was talking a great deal about you this morning. He had been speaking a little about the "papers" and "the book." But, he said, it is "all nothing to her health. She must not do anything which she does not like. I shall like everything that prevents a moment's hurry to her or bother. She must not do anything to bother or fatigue her. Nothing will vex me but her doing that."

Then came the few tears. He went to see poor Turnham, as he will have told you. Max Müller called upon me on Monday. I never saw him before. What a lovely man and manner he is. We talked India of course. I rather doubt his being very practical. But he told me an extraordinary story about the persecution of Christian converts in India which I shall tell you. O why can't we be, all those who call themselves Christians, of one mind? God bless you.

ever your
old Flo

Source: Note, Wellcome (Claydon copy) Ms 9013/47

10 May 1890 (9:00 P.M.)

Telegram from Morey: Parthe *not* better. Blessed Margaret is going on from Marsh Gibbon tonight to Claydon. My letter did not find her at Onslow G[ardens]. They were at Marsh G. till Monday but clever good little Lettice opened my letter and telegraphed my request to her mother at Marsh G., and I have a telegram from Marsh that she is going on to Claydon tonight. Blessed Margaret.

Source: Letter, Wellcome (Claydon copy) Ms 9013/48

10 South St.
10 May 1890

Dearest blessed Margaret [Verney]

The account of my sister has been getting worse and worse every day since she went to Claydon. I have just had a letter from Morey saying she is worse than he had ever known her and in a "very serious" condition. The difficulty is to know what to do. (1) It would be worse than vain to send down Andrew Clark—she attributes her "worse"ness to him. She is corresponding, I know, with Dr Harper, the homeopathic quack; I would gladly send him down, quack as I know him to be, and believe it is the only thing to do in the *doctor* way. (2) Her only wish is to be "quiet" and for Sir Harry not to be disturbed or to come. He will be here in ¼ hour, but I know not what he knows. I believe he dines at Lady Burdett Coutts to meet Stanley. Her cough is spasmodic and I fear to excite her.

Sir J. Paget told Sir Harry the disease was gaining on her. (3) *Nurses*: they telegraphed to me (without her knowledge) to send down a night nurse (hers having failed). I did, and the night nurse sat up with her last night. Account this morning: "not ten minutes rest all night." (4) The only thing I can think of is whether blessed Margaret would go down with or without Sir Harry. You are the only person (who has judgment) that she would tolerate. Perhaps you might even not see her, but tell us what to do. I think Sir Harry far from well. His foot is very bad. He himself is alarmed at it, but curiously unalarmed about her.

Forgive me for adding to your anxieties. God bless you.

yours ever

F.N.

Editor: Parthenope Verney died aged seventy-one 12 May 1890, Nightingale's birthday, and was buried 15 May, Ascension Day.

Source: Telegram, Wellcome (Claydon copy) Ms 9013/51

[Si]r Harry Verney

[M]y thoughts and prayers are yours, but Christ is closer still. I write by post.

[F.] Nightingale

Her suffering was over sooner than she expected. Can we grudge it her? Though we shall miss her till we see her again.

F.N.

Source: Letter on death of Parthenope, Wellcome (Claydon copy) Ms 9013/50

[printed address] 10 South Street
Park Lane, W.
12 May 1890

My dear Sir Harry [Verney]

She has "a better morn than ours."[408] The last day I saw her, yesterday week (Sunday afternoon) she who talked so little about her religious feelings even to me said: "I do know that God does everything for the best, though sometimes" (with a little laugh) "this last London time I did think Him rather hard not to let me see people." Then she said (after saying, Frederick wants you to put down the last week of Christ's life). "Tell me some of the beautiful things He said those last days." I am unready, you know; but I told her some as well as I could. Then she said: "pray, pray that I may have done what I ought in

---

408 An allusion to T. Hood's poem, "On Death," which ends, "she had/ Another morn than ours."

London, now that I am going to Claydon I may do what I ought there." It was only one week more suffering but that she did not know.

Then (I could not think whom she was talking to, but) she was looking at my print of the Dresden Raphael and she said, "do you believe that that infant [words missing] was the Saviour of the *Universe*? It seems such a long time for those other worlds to wait." And then "O God send that infant Saviour to me who need him so much in my pain." I repeated those few lines of the dying child:

> I see the beautiful child Jesus a coming down to me.
> And in His hands he beareth flowers so rich and rare.
> And those were love and life.

She echoed this, said two lines I did not know, the last of which was that the mother of the dying child gave her up to Jesus "and asked her not again." *That is what* PARTHE SAYS TO YOU *now.*

Then I repeated to her some lines of Emily Taylor: "When summer suns their radiance fling,"[409] which she almost always asked for. And though she was coughing violently she echoed every line she particularly liked.

Today is my birthday, but the better birthday is *hers.* You will have blessed Margaret with you. God bless you.

ever yours and Parthe's

F.N.

Source: Inscription for gift, enclosed in a letter to Edmund Verney 13 August 1890, Wellcome (Claydon copy) Ms 9013/69

Claydon House
12 May 1890

In loving remembrance of Parthe Lady Verney
To William J. Morey
With Florence Nightingale's grateful regards
on behalf of her for whom
he did so much
as servant and friend
to the last

---

409 Unidentified passage, perhaps by Emily Howson Taylor.

Source: Letter, University of Liverpool Archives, Rathbone Papers IX7.184

Ascension Day [15 May] 1890

Dear Mr Rathbone

How can I thank you enough for your most lovely token of remembrance! And so kind of you to bring it yourself. It is doubly welcome, for today is my sister's birthday, her burial day, and it is Ascension Day, too. Sir Harry's grief is lost in her joy.

ever yours gratefully

F. Nightingale

Source: Letter, Add Mss 45810 ff6-7

[15 May] 1890
Ascension Day
12:00 o'clock

I am very much obliged to you, dear Mrs Neild, for kindly offering to stay with me over Sunday, in order to save me from having a stranger just at this time of grief, which I own I dreaded very much. But on thinking it over, I should be so sorry to make any change in your arrangement with Mrs Grey, because I was so glad that you were going back to her, even if only for a time. And I *have* engaged a cook housekeeper to come to me on Saturday, though I suppose she will not come till evening. The wrench *must* come, and it may as well come Saturday as Monday—thank you all the same.

Let us rather try that our "*hearts* and *minds*" may "ascend up" where my dear sister and your dear son are gone. As I try to do what my sister would have liked, so I am sure you will try to do *in everything* what your son would have liked. Almost the last words she said that last time I saw her were: "pray, pray that I may have done what is right in London, and now that I am going to Claydon, that I may do what is right there." So I pray for you that you may do what is right now that you are going to leave me. And do you pray for me. This is the hour of my sister's burial, or rather not her burial, for she is now alive with God, as your dear son is.

Florence Nightingale

Source: Letter, Wellcome (Claydon copy) Ms 9013/195

Inscription

Thank you for sending me this, dearest blessed Margaret. It does one good, I think. It makes one look forward to the unchanging love of God. Don't attend to what I am going to say. It is really hypercriticism and I like everything you do—I only put because you invite.

Does it not look as if she were "laid to rest" (slept) "until the day-break"? Whereas is not death merely a "shuffling off of the mortal coil," the reality, the soul living on without a moment's cessation? On the other hand, *time* itself ceases.

I like so much the bringing in "Ascension Day" but "*laid to rest* on Ascension Day" seems at first sight rather a paradox? On the other hand, the New Testament is full of such beautiful paradoxes and it may even seem as if it were "laying to rest" the controversy which afflicts so many. I shall be quite satisfied with it. We are going to put something up to her on my father and mother's monument.

ever dearest yours

F.N.

[The monument reads: In memory of Frances Parthenope, Elder Daughter of William Edward Nightingale & Frances Nightingale, & Second Wife of the Rt Hon Sir Harry Verney, Bt., of Claydon House, Buckinghamshire. Born at Naples April 19 1819, Died at Claydon May 12 1890. Buried at Middle Claydon. "Oh all ye works of the Lord, bless ye the Lord."]

Source: Letter, Harvard University, Countway Medical Library

[printed address] 10 South Street
Park Lane, W.
5 June 1890

Dear Mr Morey

. . . Thank you very much about the thirty newspapers for St Thomas' nurses and for sending me one, the only one I have had the courage to read about *her*. The "In Memoriam" was beautiful. And thank you for not forgetting Lizzie Coleman, who valued it greatly.

I will take charge of the distribution of the thirty for St Thomas' if you will give them to Messenger. The nurses will be much touched and I will say, if I find that there are not enough, that you will kindly send more. I will find out those who interested themselves in sending the "wreath."

My dear sister and Sir Harry looked upon you as a faithful friend, as well they might. And I am sure Sir Harry's gift was just the sincere gratitude from him *and her* as to a faithful friend, so trustworthy and kind. And I hope you will accept the same feeling from me who always say God bless you and believe me,

ever yours sincerely

Florence Nightingale

Source: Letter, Harvard University, Countway Medical Library

[printed address] 10 South Street
Park Lane, W.
10 June 1890

Dear Mr Morey

I inquired about Lady Verney's little debt to Miss Farrer and have paid it. I do not think this need go into the Executor's accounts at all. It has been done in the most delicate way, thanks to you. And Miss Farrer thinks that my sister herself commissioned me to pay it. Miss Crossland and the nurses will be delighted with the copies of the newspaper, so kindly sent. . . .

sincerely yours
F. Nightingale

Source: Letter, Harvard University, Countway Medical Library

[printed address] 10 South Street
Park Lane, W.
5 July 1890

Dear Mr Morey

I send acknowledgments for your two cheques with my earnest thanks to all those who hold my dear sister in loving remembrance and to yourself in particular. Those wreaths were a great pleasure and comfort to me (I have paid the account). Please remember me gratefully to all who remember her and me with her. . . . With kind regards to Mrs Morey, pray believe me,

yours ever sincerely
F. Nightingale

Source: Letter, Harvard University, Countway Medical Library

Claydon
19 November 1890

Dear Mr Morey

I think it is usual under the circumstances of this family that the livery servants should be in mourning for twelve months. Perhaps Sir Harry has some other reason for what he says. But I do not see myself, as you say new clothes are wanted, that this should be any reason for their not being mourning. Perhaps Sir Harry does not remember the month, though I am sure he misses her every day of his life. (I was surprised at his saying to me he should not want any more black-edged paper a month or two ago.) He has not said anything to me on the subject of the clothes and I naturally should not speak to him, unless he did. . . .

yours sincerely

F. Nightingale

Editor: Nightingale sent copies of the Verney Memoirs to her sister's friends in 1892.[410] She gave another volume to a nursing colleague, in the name of her sister, "her last, but unfinished work."[411]

Source: Memorial note, Wellcome (Claydon copy) Ms 9014/83

In loving remembrance
of my dear sister
Parthenope Verney
who is gone home to God
this cross is offered
by Florence Nightingale
(undivided by death)
on the anniversary of death, 12 May 1892
"O God! Thou hast created us for Thyself;
And our souls are restless till they find rest in Thee."[412]

---

410 Letter to Harry Verney [1892], Wellcome (Claydon copy) Ms 9014/86.
411 Note to Miss Crossland May 1892, Add Mss 47740 f209.
412 Augustine, *Confessions* 1.1.

LETTERS TO, FROM AND ABOUT NIGHTINGALE'S EXTENDED FAMILY

Grandmother, Mary Shore

Nightingale frequently visited her paternal grandmother, Mary (Evans) Shore, who lived at Tapton Grove, in the pleasant, rural outskirts of Sheffield. She nursed her grandmother Shore several times in serious illness and came back from Paris to attend to her in her last days. She held her hand when she died and made the funeral arrangements.

The correspondence ranges from childhood letters to her grandmother to letters to her parents and a friend on her grandmother's last illness and death. It seems that Nightingale took the initiative to get to know her grandmother and her grandmother's unmarried sister, Nightingale's (great) Aunt Elizabeth Evans. The first, undated item, suggests that Parthenope Nightingale hardly knew either. The rest of the correspondence is reported chronologically.

In a much-later conversation with Benjamin Jowett Nightingale described her grandmother as having "died at the age of ninety-five of a broken heart, because her sister had died three months previously at the age of ninety-three." Grandmother Shore was "violent, but with a depth of affection which assured you that she was the same, however long she might have been absent."[1]

Source: Incomplete, unsigned letter, Wellcome (Claydon copy) Ms 9013/107

... My "Aunt Mai" as we used to call her was the very first in afterlife to say to me how unfair she was to her mother ... a woman into whose mind no meanness ever entered, nor any gossip or ill-natured pettiness ever passed out of her mouth. Of how few great town ladies could one say that?

---

1 Jowett commonplace book, for October 1873, Balliol College Archives 1 H 24 f63.

My father and sister were, as perhaps you know, singularly subject to the "caprice des yeux." If St Paul himself had been ungraceful, he would have found no favour in their sight. But he and I have often talked in afterlife of a certain greatness there was about his mother. My dear sister never really knew her.

Source: Letter in child's printing, Wellcome (Claydon copy) Ms 8991/1

Embley
14 October 1827

My dear Grandmama [Mary Shore]

After we went from Tapton we went to Buxton [Derbyshire] then to Betley Hall, where Mr and Mrs Tollet live, then to Downton Castle [both in Herefordshire] and Boultibrooke [in an adjacent county in Wales]. I wish you would give us a cure for the rats for I think they will make a hole in the drawing room.

Papa and Mamma, Uncle Sam, Aunt Mai and Miss Johnson are going to Petersfield. Aunt Julia [Smith] will teach us our lessons when they are gone. They will remain there a few days then Miss Johnson, Uncle Sam and Aunt Mai will go to London and Papa and Mama return here 15 October. Mr Beber, a German teacher, came here. He told Susan Cromwell, the mistress of our school at Wellow, how to teach the children. Pray answer me my letter. I teach Agathe, the French girl, English. Goodbye and believe

your affectionate granddaughter
Florence Nightingale
P.S. Give my love to Street, a goodbye to the great dog Nelson.

Source: Letter in child's printing, Wellcome (Claydon copy) Ms 8991/63

Ditcham

My dear Grandmama [Mary Shore]

Papa sent for us to meet him here and we came here on Friday. We left Aunt Mary and Baby and Blanche quite well. Mrs Coltman has been confined with a boy, and she has been in imminent danger, though she is now rather better, but still in danger. She is in a high fever, and may not see anybody, but her nurse and doctor, not even her baby, who is suckled [by] another person.

This house is a delightful place, on the top of a high hill, with downs all round. Goodbye, and believe me, dear Grandmama,

your affectionate
Flo N.

Source: Letter in child's printing, Wellcome (Claydon copy) Ms 8991/9

Wednesday, 2 July [1828]

Dear Grandmama [Mary Shore]

. . . I have been to the Zoological Society twice. There are two leopards, two bears, two parrots, two emus (which are very large birds), two rabbits, one lion, two cockatoos, three squirrels, four kangaroos, six monkeys (three in a cage, three chained to a pole with a little house at the top), one rattel (a very fierce creature), several Esquimaux dogs, Captain Parry's Esquimaux dog, one guinea pig, one Costi Monti, three lamas (one brown one, one white one and a small brown one), and other creatures that I forget the name of. . . . I have been to Grandmama's twice and I have been to Mrs Hibbert's twice.

Goodbye

Florence

Source: Letter in child's printing, Wellcome (Claydon copy) Lea Hurst, Ms 8991/11

[ca. July 1828]

Dear Grandmama [Mary Shore]

Aunt Mai calls her baby [Blanche], the thing. Is not that very disrespectful? I've been to see Aunt Mai three times. I've had the baby on my knee. It's very small and its head is quite round and it sleeps a good part of the day. It cries very little and it has got lots of hair. Besides the baby, I've heard the Tyrolese sing—there are four men and one woman. The men are dressed with green coats and hats with blue or green feathers, the woman has got a red handkerchief round her neck, a green gown with flowers.

Does it blow and rain as much at Tapton as it does here? for we can scarcely get round the drawing room windows. Thank you for your invitation to Tapton. Aunt Mai's coming here we hope. Our carriage is going to Derby and she should come back in it. Goodbye.

your affectionate granddaughter

Flo

Source: Letter in child's printing, Wellcome (Claydon copy) Ms 8991/6

Embley

30 March 1830 [1828?]

Dear Grandmama [Mary Shore]

Mrs Sydney Shore and Miss Lydia Shore[2] are here. Miss Lydia plays with us. Mrs Sydney is better here. She draws. She takes her luncheon with us. She walks better. She is merrier. She paints. She plays on the piano. She does not look much better. She goes to bed early. She sleeps better. She was not very well yesterday. She does not go out on cold days. She eats shrimps. She goes on Tuesday, because other people are coming. I am very sorry for it. . . .

I found a tom-tit dead and I've buried him on the lawn. I invited Mama, Miss Shore, Pop, Aunt Patty,[3] Gale and Mrs Mahon, but Gale and Mrs Mahon couldn*'t come*. Miss *Christie* came *instead* of Aunt Patty to the burial. I picked a primrose out of my own garden, put it on the grave, took a stick, tied a piece of paper to it, and wrote this: Here lies tom-tit, caught in a greenhouse and killed by Luke. I don't know what age it is. Died Sunday March. Buried Monday.

> Tom-titty bird! why art thou dead?
> Thou who dost bear upon thy head
> A crown! but now thou art on thy deathbed
> My tom-tit.

Epitaph on a tom-tit. Pop made the two first lines of the verse but I made all the rest. Papa has been a-hunting the fox. Is Nelson [the "great dog"] alive? Answer me my letter if you please. I am
    your affectionate
    F.N.

Source: Copy of letter, Wellcome (Claydon copy) Ms 8991/59

Embley

8 January 1832

Dear Grandmama [Mary Shore]

We have a tame pigeon and squirrel. We found in the garden the pigeon; it was wounded and nearly starved, and now it eats out of our hands and flies upon our knees. We think it must be a tame pigeon

---

2 Wife of a cousin Sydney Shore (1790-1827) of Norton Hall and his sister, Urith Lydia Shore (1800-64), a favourite cousin.

3 Martha Frances Smith (1782-1870), unmarried sister of Frances Nightingale.

that has escaped. Our squirrel comes every day to be fed, which we do with nuts. Mr Knyvett, our music master, with his wife and little boy, are here. The little boy has had a bad cold and cough, and Baby [Shore] and Blanche have caught it. Baby is such a sweet little thing, he laughs a great deal. Blanche is very fond of him. . . .

We have had a great deal of company this Christmas, and Mama is quite tired and not very well. We had a little ball last night and we sat up till past twelve. We had a little supper then and went to bed, but Parthe is telling Aunt Evans about it, so goodbye, dear Grandmamma, and believe me

your affectionate granddaughter

Flo

Source: Letter, Wellcome (Claydon copy) Ms 8991/102

[postmarked Sheffield]
18 Upper Southwick St.
10 May [1839]

My dear Grandmama [Mary Shore]

You will be glad to hear that Uncle Sam has been moved from Thames Bank to a lodging in Hyde Park, which they are both very much pleased with. They are nice cheerful rooms, within a pleasant walk from us, and we see them several times a day. It was by Sir Benjamin Brodie's[4] advice that he was moved, who is attending him now, greatly to Aunt Mai's satisfaction, as all the family have such an opinion of Brodie that it takes any anxiety off her mind. She herself is very well and very glad to be near the best advice in London and in such a good situation. We have very nice weather again now, and shall stay in London through May. Parthe has been enjoying herself very much and does not seem at all the worse for it. We are going tonight to the play with the Miss Shores, whom we have seen several times. They are looking very well, but have been mostly busy in buying furniture.

. . . Aunt Octavius has weaned her baby and both are much the better for it. Nothing could have been kinder than they were all the while Uncle Sam was at Thames Bank. . . .

I believe Mama and I are going to the Queen's birthday drawing room on the 19th. I was presented at the last drawing room and was not nearly so much frightened as I expected. Mr [John] Parker went with us, greatly to our satisfaction. The Queen looked flushed and

---

4 Sir Benjamin Collins Brodie (1783-1862), surgeon, well known for his diagnostic skills.

tired, but the whole sight was very pretty. . . . With all our best loves, believe me, dear Grandmama,

ever your affectionate grandchild
Florence

Source: Letter to Mary Shore, Wellcome (Claydon copy) Ms 8991/103

[postmarked 23 May 1839]

Aunt Joanna's two youngest children seem so delicate that we do not reckon upon their promised visit at Lea Hurst with the whole family as at all certain. The Nicholsons are with us here and Marianne and I are working hard at our music. We have been to the opera once, which we enjoyed exceedingly. We dined at Mrs William Evans's the other day and met all the family, the Babingtons, the Macaulays[5] and the Gisbornes. They have a very nice house at Kensington Gore. We have seen Lady Sitwell and Mrs Gaskell several times.

London is very full. The Queen is very gay and goes almost every opera night to the opera. Tonight there is a grand illumination all over London in honour of her birthday and the lamps are putting up now in front of our hotel. Goodbye my dear Grandmama and with all our best loves to you and dear Aunt Evans, believe me

ever your affectionate grandchild
Florence

We shall leave London about the first week in June as there is still carpeting and curtains to be bought and are all looking forward to seeing you, dear Grandmama, and Aunt Evans. Papa desires his particular love.

Source: Letter, Wellcome (Claydon copy) Ms 8992/99

Embley
1 March [1845]

My dear Grandmama [Mary Shore]

We were so glad to hear from Papa so good an account of you and how little you thought of cold and winter. Papa came home last Tuesday after attending the Assizes at Winchester and, except some toothache, has been very well since. Laura Nicholson and Miss Johnson, who had been with us nearly a month, left us soon after he returned and we shall be very quiet this next month, after which we

---

5 Presumably including Thomas Babington Macaulay, whose work Nightingale often cited.

go to London, most likely. I have had a very nice letter from Blanche at Liverpool, seeming much interested in her employments and in Mr Martineau's discourses[6] and Beatrice seems to have been very popular and very happy at Ditcham.

I have been riding with Papa, but today the rain has been incessant. Shore wrote me a very good letter in a fine round hand while his Mama was away. No doubt you have heard from her all about her journey with Papa and that the Octaviuses are pretty comfortable now at Thames Bank, where Aunt Julia [Smith] is staying with them. We kept up our reading with Miss Johnson till the last day she stayed and she told us a great deal, for she is full of information. She was governess to some of the Coape family and now lives near Waverley. With all our best loves, believe me, dear Grandmama,

ever your truly affectionate and obliged granddaughter
Florence

Source: Unsigned letter, Claydon Bundle 122

Tapton
7 February 1852
Dearest Mother

I find no difference in Grandmama, except a great difficulty in making herself understood. I don't know that I ever saw anyone, except a paralytic person, with so much difficulty, and it vexes her not to be understood. But I believe it is mainly hurry. She is most affectionate. She sends her most affectionate love to you (this she repeated twice), my *most* affectionate love and tell her how much I enjoyed the sea kale. I lost no time in beginning upon it and that I sent the pheasant to Mrs Sutton and the partridges to Meersbrook, and the other pheasant to Mr Goodman and the rest to my sister. They are all very kind to me, and tell her, when the newspapers come, I always put the direction to my mouth by way of a kiss, do you understand me? Remember you tell her that. She asked a hundred questions about you and Parthe, how you were.

There are many (to me) more painful contemplations than her in her decline. She seems to me a giant among pygmies. There is nothing mean, nothing worldly, nothing humbuggy or hypocritical about her. I shall never be ashamed of her. Her affections are colossal, her

---

6 The Unitarian minister, James Martineau (1805-1900), gave lectures at the girls' school run by his sister, Rachel Ann Martineau (1800-78), in Liverpool.

ways are impetuous, straightforward, simple. When she and Aunt Evans are gone, I shall feel that there are two great Ichthyosauri[7] become extinct. She may be often ridiculous but she is never small, base, thinking of opinion. Compare them with the Coape blood and it is like comparing the generous, magnanimous, untamed elephant with the grinning, clever, imitative ape. When I say this, it is not to blame either—if the world were all elephants there would be nothing left for us to eat. If the world were all apes, there would be no independent action. The world might as well be a world of mirrors. . . .

Editor: Nightingale returned from Paris in March 1853, where she was nursing with French sisters, to be with her grandmother in her dying days. Most of these letters had only a day of the week on them, so that exact dates had to be estimated by internal evidence. Nightingale evidently had some difficulty in making the funeral arrangements for a letter, not reproduced here (see the electronic version), reports that she had been refused "permission to bury my dead in Ecclesall Church." In fact her grandmother was buried there, where her grandfather had earlier been buried. There is a plaque in the church with their names and dates.[8]

Source: Unsigned letter, Wellcome (Claydon copy) Ms 8994/16

Tapton
Monday [14 March 1853]

Dearest people

Just arrived and only in time to write a word to tell you that I am safe here and all right, and so glad I came. I have seen her twice—the first attempt I made she did not know me. I thought it would be a satisfaction to her as she lay thinking to think that we were all about her. So I made a bold attempt, went in again. Hannah let in the light quite wide and I said, it's Florence. She pulled me down and kissed me with immense vigour and said quite distinctly, goodbye, goodbye. I don't think she will ever speak again. She takes hardly anything now.

I shall go back again and try if she would like to be read to. I think she slightly wanders at times. She is very restless, but, should she sleep again, she may live some little time. I am most thankful I came. I think it was quite too much for Aunt Mai. Tomorrow I will write full particulars of journey and everything, all accomplished. Senza intoppo [with-

---

7 An extinct genus combining the features of reptiles, fishes and whales.
8 Letter to family 26 March 1853, Wellcome (Claydon copy) Ms 9010/7.

out hesitation] I am glad to be quiet. The place here looks so wintry. The first snowdrops are come, but she will not live to see them. On Monday she was ninety-five and she will see her snowdrops in another land. Soon it will be spring to her, sooner perhaps than to us.

ever, dearest yours

Source: Unsigned letter, Wellcome (Claydon copy) Ms 8994/71

Tapton
Tuesday [15 March 1853]

Dearest people

Our dear old soul upstairs is still alive, but she has taken nothing for twenty-four hours, not even tea, has had two very restless nights though now she is sleeping. She knew me quite last night again, said Kiss me, thank you, quite recognized my having come to her.

My mind is so full of this that I cannot bring it to consider the offer, which I asked Mrs Bracebridge to write to you, which Lady Canning has made me.[9] I had considered the matter as quite off and only learnt this offer, on arriving in London, from a very urgent note, which I found from Mrs Herbert, awaiting me in Victoria Sq., and asking me to come to her that very night, as she could not come to me, which I unwillingly did. I slept in Victoria Sq. with Beatrice, who stayed in town to receive me. Mrs Bracebridge left a letter telling me that I must come to the Atherstone Station to speak to her, where she would be waiting to tell me this affair, and that I could go on to Tapton that night. However I could not, so I came on to Tapton Monday morning. I did not know the end was so near here.

I am quite well now, thank you, and was quite well again before I set off, which we did on Friday. Mrs Mohl had got a governess of Mme de la Rochefoucauld's, a very stupid old Englishwoman, for my escort. We had a very beautiful day for crossing, and were in London by 6:00 o'clock, where I found Beatrice, drank tea with Mrs Herbert (he had a great man dinner in the House) and left London by the 10:00 o'clock mail train the next morning, taking Beatrice to Bedford Sq. I had no hurry nor fatigue and have quite regained my strength, thank you. I shall wait for your answer before I take the Canning matter into consideration, dearest Mum.

---

9 To become superintendent at the Establishment for Ill Gentlewomen, Upper Harley St.

Source: Unsigned letter, Wellcome (Claydon copy) Ms 8994/21

[March 1853]

But she lay quiet beneath the folds and never stirred. I suppose she was not there. Anyhow her stormy days are over and her foundations will be laid with sapphires, for I saw a little bit of the blue sky peep out. I asked Grandmama whether you should write to her. She said, thank them, tell them I cannot see, tell them it will not be long. But I think she would like to hear all the same, she always says, tell them they are very good. . . .

ever thine

Source: Unsigned letter, Wellcome (Claydon copy) Ms 8994/19

Tapton
Friday [18 March 1853]

Dearest Mother

Your most kind and touching letters did our hearts good, as you intended. I am *very* glad to leave the Canning affair as you say. Our dear one still lingers here, like the icicle which I see hanging from the rose tree at her window, but I think the morning's sun will melt her away. Her being here from day to day seems a miracle, for forty hours not even a teaspoonful of water passed her lips. Today she has taken one or two of milk. I fear she suffers from the thrush,[10] which is over-spreading her mouth and throat and sometimes her inarticulate cries are distressing. One of us never leaves her. She is always conscious and gives us sometimes such touching proofs of it, though she rarely speaks. She always knows me from *Hannah* in that dark room and when I give her anything says, thank you, bless you, goodnight, farewell. Today she said hope and peace and I am so glad. She had a very restless morning, but this afternoon has been calm. Her muscular strength is still great and all her faculties vigorous. Dearest mother,

ever your affectionate and grateful child

Her truth and religious feeling, which never expresses itself as feeling more than it does, and always feels truly, genuinely and warmly is very touching at this time. The snow has been lying deep on the ground, but it is melting away not more surely than she is doing. The poor little crocuses she was fond of were covered up to their heads. We should have liked to have seen Papa but I think it impossible that she can live till he comes, even were he to set off directly. We feared to send for him, lest we should snap the feeble thread of life.

---

10 A fungal disease of the mouth.

Source: Unsigned letter, Wellcome (Claydon copy) Ms 8994/18

Tapton
Saturday [19 March 1853]

Dearest Father

Aunt Mai has "laid her down" and commissioned me to answer your note. The truth is, dear Papa, that you could not have come; she could not see you and she would not know you and it would be only a distress to yourself without being a pleasure to her. The fact is that she is so restless that she often gets up three times in a quarter of an hour and she requires three people to get her up.

Neither Aunt Mai nor I have had our clothes off since yesterday morning. All through the night we could not conceive that she could live ten minutes and here she is still at 6:00 o'clock in the evening. She *may* live through another night, she cannot longer. As it is impossible for us to keep anything on her at times she looks like Domenichino's St Jerome,[11] that grand old head, struggling for life. Yet all that we have told you is true. In the intervals she always recognizes us, gives the most touching little proofs of hope and trust. I am so thankful we are here. She constantly appeals to us. When wearied out last night with suffering, not from pain but restlessness, she said, the Almighty; I said, will bless and keep you; she said, *love, love, love*. Three times we thought she was gone. She said, when she recovered, pray the Lord to have pity on me. I *am* dead. Amen, Amen, she says continually.

I am willing to think she has no pain, but she labours hard for breath. That she lives from hour to hour is inconceivable. Since 9:00 o'clock on Friday night, this struggle with death has begun. Yet she goes down to her grave like a hero and has never given up the reins till the last. Even now, we can do nothing but what she orders.

ever, dearest people, yours

Source: Unsigned letter, Wellcome (Claydon copy) Ms 8994/13

Tapton
21 March [1853]

Dearest Mother

She is still alive and the worst symptoms are passed. I mean the most distressing restlessness. She has not moved since 9:00 o'clock last

---

11 Domenichino Zampieri (1581-1641), Italian painter. The Communion of St Jerome, 1614, is at the Pinacoteca, Vatican.

night, she is too weak. The cries are the only symptom of restlessness which remain. We have done very well with Papa and I am very glad he came. He has seen her twice and I am sure she recognized him and if it lighted her path with one ray of pleasure, it was well worthwhile. The difficulty was to know what to do with him as the front room is the only bedroom in the house where her cries cannot be heard. Aunt Mai was already in bed in that (she lies down from 6:00 to 12:00 and I from 12:00 to 6:00, dividing the night). But he kindly stayed up till 12:00, when I called her, and then I put him into that room where he still sleeps.

Meanwhile I watched for a quiet moment when she should be still long enough to permit him to see her. Then I took him in on my own responsibility about 11:00 o'clock at night. She certainly tried to smile. The next morning again the same, but he has not seen her since; it has been impossible, he is out all day, so it does not matter. His being here has pleased her without distressing him. The cries are not painful now, but unconscious. What with frequent vomiting, having been now since Friday night without one drop of even water passing her lips, and with an exertion of voice which would kill a healthy person, that she is still alive is miraculous. Aunt Evans's nineteen hours talking were nothing to this. Still her mind is clear, she recognizes us and what she says is full of love and trust. I think she bears it like a hero.

Many thanks for all your love and kindness. We are well and very careful of ourselves.

ever, dearest Mother, yours

Source: Letter by F. Nightingale and Mai Smith, Wellcome (Claydon copy) Ms 8994/12

[24 March 1853]
Good Friday eve

Dearest people

It is just the same. No difference except that we have to keep perpetually painting with nitrate of silver to prevent the sores from spreading. The restlessness continues and must wear her out at last. The mind is clear. Mr Chalmer[12] came yesterday and prayed by her and she recognized him. She has taken nothing.

---

12 Edward Boteler Chalmer, vicar of Christ Church, Fulwood.

I suppose you opened Aunt Mai's and my letter to Papa, dated Saturday. Pray destroy it that it may not be sent on to him. I mean the letter discouraging his coming.

ever yours, dearest people

F. and M.

Source: Letter, Wellcome (Claydon copy) Ms 8994/14

[25 March 1853]
Good Friday
the day of her release

Dear Papa

It is over at last. The springtime is come for her at last and the valiant old spirit is gone to renew its strength. About 8:00 this morning she passed away, so calmly that, though I had hold of her, I could not mark the exact moment. Between 1:00 and 2:00 this morning we had her out of bed for the last time, and renewed everything about her, painted all her poor sores, and made her comfortable for death. We had an awful difficulty in getting her into bed again, but she appeared soothed by the change. She never moved again, except a little uneasy motion of the head, nor spoke. About 4:00 the cry ceased and her breathing became very short and hurried.

How conscious she was I am quite uncertain, but her eyes were open, and the expression of her face solemn and earnest in the extreme. I should say she was waiting for death. Two hours before it came, she became quite composed. There was a stoppage in her throat which you could see externally, and there was an occasional little cough to get rid of it, not of irritation or impatience but of a little surprise: "What is this?" The end was like the dropping of water, slower and more gently came each breath like the drops out of an empty vessel till the time when the last came was imperceptible. There was not the slightest change in the face.

Forty-eight hours ago the rapid spread of the sores was appalling. Now all is peace and such a rest. Wonderful restorative power there was in that nature; when she died the sores were almost well. The funeral will be on Friday, if possible. We found, after her death, her papers all put by most orderly in a drawer, among them a packet directed to you in her own hand. We opened this and found the missing list of bearers. We have done what we could today in the way of orders. With the other papers we have nothing to do till after the funeral. The cold was so intense last night that the nitrate of silver froze in her room.

The servants have done everything very well. I cannot express the unspeakable relief that all is over, and so painlessly, and no long waiting before her, as we thought in January, and this awful week at a close. It is just a week today since she has tasted neither food nor sleep. Will you tell Beatrice that her mother or I would have written, but that she will hear all from you and that I thought of her when I closed her eyes? Aunt Mai is asleep or she would write. Love to all. I hope the sun shines on you, dear Papa.

The full moon shone on the waste of snow last night, as the face grew beautiful in the light of death and young in the hope of life. I almost wish you could have seen her as she is NOW. There is no trace of suffering or decay. She might be fifty. It is impossible to believe she is all but a century. I have never seen her so before. Such power, such sweetness and such a "rapture of repose." All her agitations have ended there. There is a look of satisfied expectation about her. I never admired before the noble cast of her features; it is a face which might have done anything. There is not a wrinkle, not a semblance of old age.

ever, dear Pa

your loving child

Source: Letter with envelope, Columbia University, Presbyterian Hospital School of Nursing C4

Tapton
Easter Eve [26 March 1853]

My dear Mrs Sutton

You will rejoice with us, I am sure, that my dear grandmother fell asleep yesterday morning with words full of trust and love. She appeared to wait for the sacred day for her own release. After a week of great suffering, which had made us think that every hour must be her last, she became quite calm on Good Friday morning, and went to rest like a child. Throughout her illness her mind was clear, her affections strong. She repeated every psalm or prayer I ever said to her after me, adding to "The Lord is my shepherd," a *kind* shepherd, and saying no fear, I hope, pardon, with God. Mrs Henry Greaves and Mr Chalmer both saw her and prayed with her and she responded fervently.

We were distressed to hear that you had been ill after your visit to her, but I am sure that you will be glad to have seen her so religiously calm and to know that your visit was such a great pleasure to her for the last time.

My aunt, Mrs S[amuel] Smith, desires her kindest regards. She begged me to write to you, as she is somewhat worn out, and believe me, dear Mrs Sutton,

yours most truly

Florence Nightingale

Source: Letter with envelope, Columbia University, Presbyterian Hospital School of Nursing C3

Tapton

29 March [1853]

My dear Mrs Sutton

I am very much obliged to you for the little book which you have so kindly sent me, which I shall value both for its own sake and for yours, and also because it was the last book which I ever read to my dear grandmother. It was your gift, I believe.

I shall never forget the earnest manner in which she responded to and repeated after me the most striking passages. After that she was unable to listen to anything consecutively. Passages out of the scriptures and especially out of the psalms (the twenty-third was her favourite), she would re-echo, as I repeated them to her from time to time in the quiet nights. But your little book was the last which she was able to hear before her worst suffering began.

Believe me, dear Madam, with my aunt's kindest regards,

yours most truly

Florence Nightingale

Source: Letter, Wellcome (Claydon copy) Ms 8994/70

Tapton

Wednesday [30 March? 1853]

Dearest Mother

As Fletcher is off, we shall come up to town by the Great Northern on Friday. We shall be at the Burlington about ½ past 4, if trains are punctual. So that, if you want to see Aunt Mai, you will perhaps like to be in at that hour. She will leave London by the ¼ to 6 from Waterloo.

All that I have to say I put off till then. A great snowstorm this morn, these northern climes! We saw a whole neighbourhood full of her old friends yesterday. They all came. We went to church at Fulwood on Sunday and old Chalmer preached the first sermon I have listened to these ten years. I will do Rodgers on Friday morning.

Thank you, dearest people, for all your kind letters. Love to Athena [the owl].

F.N.

Source: Incomplete, unsigned letter, Wellcome (Claydon copy) Ms 8994/17

Tapton
Friday [1 April 1853]

My dearest Mother

The day is over, the house is empty and deserted, now that mighty presence no longer fills it. The dear old place is to be let or sold and I feel that the years, which were little short of a century, are past and gone, never to return. I have a clinging tenderness for the poor old place and for the forlorn and deserted room upstairs.

The day was very striking to me, from its utter contrast to Bonsal, and from its striking characteristic of her. From the moment we closed the coffin last night, after I had filled it with beautiful flowers, sent from Banner Cross, which had strewn all her bed, and we had brought it downstairs to rest its last night in the little breakfast room below, the wind kept rising till it blew a perfect hurricane. We had had a fortnight so perfectly calm with the still falling snow, that this melancholy sough was the first sound we had heard. All night it blew, and it rained, and this morning ushered in mild and dark and stormy (so unlike the night, this day week, on which she died) till by the time we reached Ecclesall [Parish Church], the sun shone out hard and bright. The wind was so high in the steep road, up through the churchyard, that the bearers had the greatest difficulty in keeping their footing with their burden, and I expected to see the whole blown down. The pall was torn hither and thither. (It was where my poor aunt was once blown down and much hurt.) As for us, the mourners, instead of keeping any sort of procession or order, we were blown all manner of ways, into the gutter, on to the tombstones, and Beatrice, who was with us, could hardly be dragged on. All this was so like *her*, and her storm which blew down my poor aunt's mind.

At last we reached the church, where we found a number of people, true mourners, already assembled—some I saw crying bitterly and none that were there I am sure but had had their hearts warmed by "Mrs Shore," and had gone out of true respect and love. We took our places beside the deep vault, under Grandpapa's monument and dear old Chalmer read the service.

The wind blew down the glass of the carriage as we came home, then came more clear bright sun and then a violent storm of rain.

What I meant is that the whole thing was so characteristic of her, the *vehement* storms, the bright daylight, without a moment's pause or interval, forgetting all the past and clearing up without a shadow of a cloud upon her brow and then the gust of true, deep feeling—it was so like her. Now she is gone, the house deserted and all is over, soon to go into the hands of strangers and I shall not ever see the Ribes blossom. Somebody else will mark the tender green of the larch against the dark yew tree, as we did, with her, last spring.

Now about our plans, dearest mother. Papa goes back to the Hurst on Monday. He will not stay any longer and, as it seems lonely for him by himself, we have determined (though there is still much to be done here) to go with him. . . .

Source: Letter, Wellcome (Claydon copy) Ms 8994/20

3 April [1853]

My dearest [Parthenope Verney]

I shall not forget your plants, nor, Mama, your covers. Uncle Sam went to town this morning. We, with the servants and bearers, went to Ecclesall Church, where the hymns were chosen for us and the homely kindness of the people touched us much. On Friday the church was full of people, all in mourning, many sobbing, and all there out of the sincerest respect and love for her, I am sure.

We have had inquiries without end. We go to Lea Hurst tomorrow as Papa will not stay any longer. Aunt Mai returns here on Friday. She is obliged to return for business and to see her mother's old friends. Whether I return with her (for a week or ten days) depends much upon you.

ever dearest people
your loving child
The place is to be sold.

The Bonham Carter Family

Editor: The first two letters are to a cousin who died in childhood only a few months after the second one.

Source: Letter in child's printing, Balliol College

[watermark 1828]

My dear cousin and friend Bon [Bonham Carter]

I have been reading the 121st psalm. We think it very beautiful and we think you would like it. Mama is gone to pay a visit at Mrs Whitby's at Lymington. She will be home Saturday 11 April. Aunt Mai is coming here on the 10th.

This is a story that Miss Christie, my governess, told me. In France there are people who have stalls in the street to clean and black people's shoes. There was one man who was of that trade—sometimes he had not many customers so his dog, Barker, would go and wet himself in a puddle and splash the people who passed by, and then his master got customers. Here is another story. There was a swallow who made a nest. One day she went out, and while she was out a sparrow took possession of her nest. When she came back she found the wicked intruder. Not being able to get him out by herself she made a great noise and called all her companions to her assistance. They came. After looking some time and thinking of some way to give their poor companion assistance, they all flew away, but soon came back bearing in their mouths a bit of mud, which they placed at the door of the nest, so that they completely shut up the sparrow and starved him. He found his tomb in his usurped house.

your affectionate cousin
Florence Nightingale

Source: Letter in child's printing, Hampshire Record Office 94M72/F587/1

April [1829?]

Dear Bon [Bonham Carter]
Here is a list of my books:
1. Goody Two Shoes
2. Tales of the Vicarage
3. The Promised Visit
4. Juvenile Biography
5. Fruits of Enterprise
6. Bird Catching
7. Maria's Visit to London
8. Irish Legends
9. Sunday Evening Conversations
10. An Abstract of the History of the Bible.
These are all.

I forgot to tell you that I have got [the] first and third volume of Berquin,[13] Pop the second and fourth, and I have Sandford and Merton. Which would you like?

_____

13 All four volumes of Berquin's *L'Ami des Enfans* are in the Balliol College Library. Inscriptions show that they were given to Mary Shore (Aunt Mai) in 1807, then to Florence Nightingale in 1827.

Here is a beautiful hymn of Montgomery's called Prayer. I have learnt it.

1

Prayer is the soul's sincere desire,
Uttered, or unexpress'd,
The motion of a hidden fire,
That trembles in the breast.

2

Prayer is the burden of a sigh,
The falling of a tear,
The upward glancing of an eye,
When none but God is near.

3

Prayer is the simplest form of speech,
That infant lips can cry,
Prayer, the sublimest strains that reach
The majesty on high.

4

Prayer is the Christian's vital breath,
The Christian's native air,
His watchword in the hour of death
He enters heaven with prayer!

5

Prayer is the *sinner's contrite* voice
Returning from his ways,
While angels in their song rejoice
And say, "behold he prays."

6

In prayer, on earth the saints are one,
In word, in deed, in mind
When with the Father and the Son
Sweet fellowship they find.

7

Nor prayer is made on earth alone,
The Holy Spirit pleads,
And Jesus, on the eternal throne,
For sinners intercedes!

8

O Thou! by whom we come to God,
The Life, the Truth, the Way!
The path of prayer thyself hast trod;
Lord! teach us how to pray![14]

Goodbye, dear Bon, believe me,
 your affectionate cousin
 Florence Nightingale

Source: Letter in child's printing, Wellcome (Claydon copy) Ms 8991/30

Dear Miss Brydges [Boultibrooke, Herefordshire]   [ca. June 1829]

Do you know poor Bonny Carter, my cousin? Such a dear, kind boy! He has been very ill for six or seven months, and 7 June (Sunday) between 6:00 and 7:00 o'clock, he died. He was kind to everybody to the last, and so very patient, he was never cross. Half an hour before his death he asked to see Aunt Patty, and he was looking about the room for a sofa for her. We left Gale in London to help to take care of him, but nothing would do. His complaint had got so much the better of medicine, doctors, nursing and all, that all hope was given up. He had a great deal of pain throughout his illness.

Mama saw him once, he talked to her a great deal, and was so anxious to give her everything she liked. Gale slept by his side. One night, she got up to do something for him and he said to her, "Come, it will do very well—there's a good creature, go to bed, now, go to sleep." One day, he said to his Papa, when in great pain, "I will bear it as well as I can, but if I were strong, I think I should leap about the room with this pain." Give my love to your Papa and Mama, and believe me,
 your affectionate
 Florence Nightingale

P.S. How do the handkerchiefs go on, which you were doing at Embley? How are your Papa and Mama? Good-bye.

---

14 James Montgomery, *A Collection of Hymns* No. 823.

Source: Letter, Hampshire Record Office 94M72/F587/3

Burlington St.
Friday [185?]

Dearest Aunt Joanna [Bonham Carter]

What will you say to me if I came down with Alf [Bonham Carter] tomorrow night till Monday? I do so long for a sight of all your faces. And it was not proved till today that I could go, which gives you no time for an answer to stop me.

Pardon me and let me sleep in a drawer, dear Aunt Joanna,

yours lovingly, gratefully, repentantly

F.N.

Though these ex post facto repentances are unsatisfactory things.

Cousin Hilary Bonham Carter

Editor: Hilary Bonham Carter was a kindred spirit to Nightingale, her junior by only a year. Nightingale admired her cousin's artistic ability, but felt she did not do enough to develop it. Hilary Bonham Carter lived with Nightingale after Aunt Mai returned home but, feeling that her cousin was too self-sacrificing and neglected her art as a result, Nightingale then made Hilary leave. The undated letters immediately following would seem to be from their teen years.

Source: Letter, Hampshire Record Office 94M72/F587/6

Embley
Tuesday

Dearly beloved [Hilary Bonham Carter]

With exquisite *yawnings* of the heart do I sob out the cruel fact that you and I shall not *continny* our studies together, at least not just now. That my prospect is removed afar off and that the prospective delight of taking many rides on three quadrupedated animals, instead of a solitary one, is blotted from my view. Under these afflicting dispensations, I can find few words to express other than that Papa shall bring Sam's watch and the naval military gazette and that I hope that worthy is recovering his elasticity of mind and limb. I heard from Miss Parker this morning, enclosing a pair of *mitts* worked in red chenille, as there were none left like yours. . . .

I suppose Sam has recommenced hunting upon the strength of Mrs Lyford's recommendation. Give my love to the Horners. I do not know which of them, besides Susan, is with you. I cease, for we are all in a state of cold which beggars description and are going to *play about*.

ever my dear little pog's

disconsolate viddined [?]

F.N.

Source: Letter to Hilary Bonham Carter, ADD Mss 45794 ff76-78

23 January

One word, my dear dear one, on this thy birthday, though I am not given to the above "*mother*," in respect to people's entrance into this poor dear young world; all psalms and prayers begin with praise for the light of another day, but often, of the morning's light, behold us very weary. You, however, who have exchanged the, *I* want to do *something*, for, to do *the* thing which *is wanted* (conjugating the active and passive verb so as to correspond exactly and making the article the definite one, defined, i.e., by a call from without). You cease, I do indeed believe, to feel the weariness of life, for such naturally inherit the blessing given to that divine "poverty of spirit."[15] And such too *receive* the promise, that they shall hunger no more,[16] for they are fed with the same meat (which Christ found all-sufficient for him) to do the will of Him that sent them,[17] for what is duty or conscience but the will of God for the particular dutist? Therefore, my dearest, I can truly and sincerely say joy, joy, on thy birthday.

Aunt Julia [Smith] is here, Jack [Bonham Carter] just gone. To me his visits are one of the greatest pleasures and helps.

I have just discovered your library done up in a small parcel which, by the system of exhaustions, only was determined to be yours. Till Blanche was gone, I always thought it had been hers. It consists of Taylor and Thiodolf, and shall be sent by Shore. . . . Best love to Fan[18] and to Miss Becker, with thanks for her letter, which I will answer, when I am not, as ever, thine hastily in word but not in thoughts.

F.N.

Source: Incomplete, undated letter/draft to Hilary Bonham Carter, ADD Mss 45794 ff81-86

[before 1853]

How often do we say to children, both of larger and smaller growth, how you do fret yourself about such trifles; it really is beneath you, when we should say, your trifles are not my trifles. As I once heard dear J.P. say, "his prejudices are not my prejudices." One person thinks it very absurd that another should vex himself about a railroad,

---

15 An allusion to Matt 5:3.
16 An allusion to Matt 5:6.
17 An allusion to John 4:34.
18 Frances Marie Bonham Carter (1822-70).

and the other answers, but you don't consider it makes the whole face of nature, whom I love so dearly, ugly to me. Another thinks it quite ridiculous that a third faches himself about someone having taken "some trifling offence," but doesn't that make the whole face of *his* friend ugly to *him?* "Since trifles make the sum of human things," and everything human is sacred, I think one should never approach even a child's tears for the loss of its pet rabbit without reverence.

The immeasurableness of the bitterness of sorrow contained in that little heart, we cannot, with our limited understanding, comprehend, nor dare to say whether it does not equal Napoleon's for the loss of his empire. For the heart is infinite, while the intellect is bounded, and the least of sorrows should therefore be to us of awful and mighty import, for they are of an eternal significance, which we cannot see, and before which we veil our faces.

I think I would never either try to persuade myself or my friend to get over a sorrow, *because* it is a "trifle." Chacun à son goût [each to his own taste]. And the secret of the love, which *understandeth* all things,[19] for giving happiness, is to serve everyone according to that goût [taste]. What is trifling to us is not trifling to them, and vice versa, if it is something, which *must* be a stumbling block if not removed. Let our wisdom be instead of bearing, to overcome, instead of forgetting, to cure, instead of resigning ourselves, to conquer. The Epicurean's wisdom of "taking things as they come" is impossible of attainment. One might as well "go stand upon the bench" as go telling people to "bend to circumstances" because that's common sense, and we never shall have common sense. Besides, advice can be of no use which requires us to destroy our own identity. Common sense accommodates itself to circumstances, but the better wisdom accommodates circumstances to itself. The obstacle which it cannot get rid of, it mounts upon, as a step upwards. I always long to cry, "That's a lie," when I hear people saying, "It is *such* a trifle, he's a fool to care about it."

But I didn't mean to give you all this intolerable deal of sack, I didn't. And now I must leave off, having no time for more. Will you ask Aunt Patty, when you see her, if she has received a £5 note in two letters, from me? If I write, it looks as if I wanted an answer, and I only

---

19 An allusion to 1 Cor 13:2.

wished to know, because if the letters *were* stolen, she would think that I had been so unpardonably forgetful. Farewell my best beloved.

ever thine

F.N.

My best love to Fan, if she is with thee again. Aunt Evans pretty well, but all but blind, very patient though, always remembers thee. . . .

Source: Letter/draft, ADD Mss 45794 ff95-96

Dearest child [Hilary Bonham Carter]   [ca. 10 February 1845]

You did not happen to see a little book of Abbott's called *The Way to Do Good*[20] when you were here, did you? I was reading some of it to Shore once and cannot find it now. My young people are not yet come home, you see.

Mrs Hogg died yesterday morning and the face which was just before so convulsed is now so calm. I have so much to tell you of her when we see each other. When that weary head rolled upon my shoulder, it seemed to me as if "many things were becoming clear to me." Now we go to life and she to death—which of us for the better part, the gods only know.

I am sure patience had its perfect [words cut out], as long as she was sensible, last week her sufferings were too great. She had her prayer at last that she might see before she died—she saw us all and a few hours before asked me why I had my bonnet on and where I was going. Now she can speak truth and be understood. Now she knows even as she is known,[21] she has awakened from the dream of life and left us behind to envy her rest. . . .

I took the sacrament with Mrs Hogg a few days before she died. One feels such a reverence before the spirit that is waiting to put on incorruption[22] and being tried in its painful, painful passage to the grave, whether it is capable of infinite endurance and able to the weight of immortality. How one feels then that the most real presence in the

---

20 By Jacob Abbott (1803-79), American Congregational minister. *The Way to Do Good: or The Christian Character Mature* was published in 1836, the year of Nightingale's conversion and the year before her "call to service." It describes faith in Jesus' atoning sacrifice as the "cornerstone" and a life of doing good as the "superstructure" built on it. It, and Abbott's *The Cornerstone*, 1834, evidently both informed her "call."

21 An allusion to 1 Cor 13:12.

22 An allusion to 1 Cor 15:42.

room is the invisible presence which hovers round the deathbed and that we are only ghosts, that have put on form for a moment, and shall put it off almost before we have had time to wind up our watch. *We* are the apparitions. But I must have done, my dear. Best love to Ju [Aunt Julia Smith]. I shall hope to see you soon.

Do you recollect your last visit to poor Mrs Hogg? She always knew my voice, and sometimes when she was in convulsions, she would answer and then the tears would come and she was still. I never saw such sufferings. I wish I had gone every day before she became so very ill. I was thinking only of myself then and shall always repent it.

ever yours [lines cut off]

Source: Incomplete, unsigned, undated letter to Hilary Bonham Carter, ADD Mss 45794 ff98-103 [first sheet missing, presumably because of Nightingale's request that it be burned]

[ca. 25 April 1846]

. . . Is it possible that it is six months, though sometimes it seems to me more like six years, so much has passed in my inner life since then. Oh that tadpole whirl of "restless activity," which swims round and round under the glassy surface of our civilized life. We talk and we dine and we dress, as if the tadpoles, our hopes, were not breeding in thousands in silence, and abandoned in despair, as if the struggle between fear, the Dweller of the Threshold, and the Spirit of Light, with his sunbeam wing, was not going on fiercely, ceaselessly. As if the cup, which we have filled with the deep fountains of the soul (where, "by strong convulsions rent apart"[23] we have garnered them up in this, as in a lachrymatory, that they might not all run to waste, or be dried up) was not often dashed to the ground, and its waters lost, as if the deepest passions of our hearts were not roused in all of us and those hovering hopes and plans (which, though so unsubstantial, are not unreal—oh no, for they make up our whole real life) were not struck by an arrow and fallen. As if we did not all feel that we are always standing on the edge of an abyss, so dark that we see not the bottom, and so deep that our head swims round, and we are afraid to speak or to move for fear of the next step.

---

23 From Longfellow, "Voices of the Night," about a goblet:
   . . . filled with waters, that upstart,
   When the deep fountains of the heart,
   By strong convulsions rent apart,
   Are running all to waste.

How truly you say that all seems unreal and that all actors are not on the theatre. Everything reminds me of the Indian in the fable, who sitting in the tree, with terror, under the shape of a tiger, climbing up, is only engaged in fighting with the fly (*care*) which is whizzing in his face. All is like a dream, you say, yes, the world, and the pink satin ghosts in it, and ourselves most of all. If we could always be true to ourselves, have a sacred trust in our intentions, we should need no other truth. But we lie to ourselves first; the lying to others follows of itself.

That the sufferings of Christ's life were intense, who doubts? But the happiness must have been intenser—only think of the happiness of working and working successfully, too, and with no doubt as to his path, and with no alloy of vanity or love of display or glory but with the ecstasy of single-heartedness. All that I do is always poisoned by the fear that I am not doing it in simplicity and singleness of heart. Everything I do always seems to me false without being a lie. But God has been very gracious to me, dearest. *My* helplessness has been the same to the last; unseconded by any effort of mine, he helps me and leads me by a way which I have not known, by a way sometimes agonizing and crushing, and afterwards raising and consoling. And if the miserable feelings are not mine, which I have known, it is his unsolicited doing. I trusted *not* in thee and thou hast sought me, I could write in a new psalm.

I think we shall be quite quiet at present. Helen is not coming yet. The Nicholsons were asked for today, but none of them come. Aunt Anne, I am afraid, far from well. If I *ever* said to myself, I wish or I do not wish, I should be sorry now that our time in London were not coming with yours, but I am quite sure it is best that it should be over and done and as it is. I do not like writing to you, dearest, because I feel as if I never should stop, the more pity for me I cannot see you and I have not told you a word yet of my friends at Richmond and London. Miss Clarke [Mme Mohl] we heard from yesterday. She will not come to us till Lea Hurst. I had such a walk before breakfast, everything in a blaze of beauty, "as if a God had been abroad and left His impress on the world."

There is nothing makes my heart thrill like the voice of the birds. Much more than the human voice, it is "the angels calling us with their songs" and the fleecy clouds look like the white walls of our home. Then one falls back from the ideal world into one's own apothecary's shop, where one is perpetually pouring from one bottle to the other of one's own recollections, which sit like snakes upon their bottom rings behind every azalea and making the mixture still muddier and nastier of one's own ideas. If Providence hadn't put Adam to sleep in a hurry, he would have been crazed before Eve arrived, with all his boasted paradise.

Dearest, I must go, it was *because* I was going down alone that I felt myself compelled to go home, *not* because I was going with anybody. If there had been anybody else going home I should not have minded being away a little longer, but as they were quite alone, I thought, that I should be *less in the way* at that time at home than at any other time. This is to apologize for my impudence in supposing myself wanted here. The more I write, the more I want to see you: the "daughter of the voice is so much better than the son of the ink" and so I must stop after one word about my visits.

Mrs Keith M[ackenzie], Miss Dutton, and Louisa Mackenzie, may be shortly described as the respective representatives of the Soul, the Mind and the Heart. The first has one's whole *worship*, the second one's greatest *admiration* and the third one's most lively *interest*. Mrs Bracebridge as all three, the human Trinity in one. Never do I see her without feeling that she is eyes to the blind and feet to the lame. Many a plan, which disappointment has thinned off into a phantom in my mind, takes form and shape and fair reality when touched by her Ithuriel's spear, for there is an Ithuriel's spear for good as well as for evil.[24] And till that touch I never know whether my plans are mere shadows, which the removal of the light, which gave them birth, will send to their real home, the house of nothingness, or are capable of being moulded into form. *She* is not the light, which originates plans in anyone's mind, but she is the bright and true mirror, which reflects faithfully all and every impression brought to her by those desirous of the clearing glass of her sympathy.

I hope you will see Louisa in London. I cannot talk to you about her in a letter, etc. Are one's earthly friends not too often Atalanta's apple? thrown in each other's way, to hinder that course,[25] at the end of which is laid up the crown of *righteousness*.[26] And so, dearest, it is

---

24 In Milton's *Paradise Lost* "no falsehood can endure" the touch of Ithuriel's spear (book 4 lines 810-11).

25 In Greek mythology Atalanta was a huntress who refused to marry any man who could not defeat her in a race. Aphrodite gave a suitor three apples to drop in the race, thus slowing Atalanta down.

26 An allusion to 2 Tim 4:8.

well that *we* should not eat too much of one another. That word righteousness always strikes me more than anything in the Bible. Strange that not happiness, not rest, not forgiveness, not glory, not success, should have been the thought of that glorious man's mind (when at the eve of the last and greatest of his labours), but all desires so swallowed up in the one great craving after *righteousness* that, at the end of all his struggles, it was mightier within him than ever, mightier than even the desire of peace. How can people tell one to dwell within a good conscience, when the chief of all the apostles so panted after righteousness that he considered it the last best gift, unattainable on earth, to be bestowed in heaven.

Farewell à regret, my beloved one. Best love to dear Fan, to whom pray give this letter, if you like it. I think of her constant[ly]. Lea Hurst this year?? I hope so.

Source: Incomplete letter, ADD Mss 45794 ff106-07

Embley
Friday [June 1846]

Dearest child [Hilary Bonham Carter]

I am very glad to hear that you have been at Kempstone, where you would hear all that could be told about our dear old friend and I hope we shall hear it in due time. I do not know how long Ju is going to stay in London, nor whether she is likely to see Mrs Jameson,[27] who, I am afraid, is abroad, but I should be very glad if she could get any particulars from her (Mrs Jameson) of the German lady she, Mrs J., knew, who, not being a Catholic, could not take upon herself the vows of a Sister of Charity, but who obtained permission from the physician of the hospital of her town to attend the sick there, and perform all the duties which the Soeurs do at Dublin and the Hôtel-Dieu, and who had been there fifteen years when Mrs Jameson knew her. I do not want to know her name if it is a secret, but only if she has extended it further into anything like a Protestant sisterhood, if she had any plans of that sort which should embrace women of an educated class, and not, as in England, merely women who would be servants if they were not nurses.

How she disposed of the difficulties of surgeons making love to her, and of living with the women of indifferent character, who generally

---

27 Author Anna Brownell Jameson (1794-1860); see her lecture, "Sisters of Charity" in 1855. See Dale Spender, *Women of Ideas and What Men Have Done to Them* 157.

make the nurses of hospitals, as it appears she was quite a young woman when she began. These are the difficulties which vows remove and one sees nothing else that can. If Mrs Jameson would tell Aunt Ju all she knows about this German lady, and Aunt Ju would ask her, I should be truly obliged to her.

I am glad you are with Aunt Jane, dearest, who I am afraid, is sadly *wored* out. I hope we shall see you here before the rows begin. . . .

Source: Unsigned letter with envelope, ADD Mss 45794 ff110-16

[Lea Hurst]

Thursday [14 August 1846]

My dearest [Hilary Bonham Carter]

Your letter is very dear to me, though I cannot quite enter into all you say about the sufficiency of good intentions. The kingdom of God is come, I know; Jesus Christ says so,[28] and we feel it. But my life is so full of anxieties, of eager fears about things which are inextricable, things about which I really don't know *which* I wish, that I kneel down when the sun rises in the morning, and only say, Behold the hand-maid of the Lord,[29] give me this day my work, no, not my work but Thine to do. I ask no other blessing. For the things which I ask for I do not wish, and the things I do wish, I know I shan't have. In a world into which we are come under so many disadvantages, how can we help anxieties and morbid responsibilities?

Well I know that it was God who created the good, and man the evil, which was not the will of God, but the necessary consequence of His leaving free will to man. I know that misery is the alphabet of fire, as you say, in which experience with her warning hand writes, in flaming letters, the consequences of evil (the kingdom of man) and that without its glaring light we should never see the turn back into the kingdom of God, or heed the directing guidepost. But the judgments of nature (the law of God) as she goes her mighty, solemn, inflexible walk, sweep sometimes so fearfully over men that, though it is the triumph, not the defeat of God's truth and of these laws, that falsehood against them must work misery, and misery is perhaps here the strongest proof that His *loving* hand is present. Yet still all our powers, our hopes and fears must be engrossed by it. We cannot lay down our anxiety that, even with good intentions, we may not have conscientiously improved our judgments, that we may have sinned against the Holy

28 An allusion to Mark 1:15.
29 Luke 1:38.

Ghost[30] by voluntary ignorance, by thinking truth nothing more than what one "troweth" by letting light in only in one way, by seeking to illustrate, not enlarge our minds.

With Shore, for instance, when I see how no things are trifles, how a vizier got out of prison by a black beetle with a bit of butter on its head, how a wave propagates itself over the whole lake, I am sometimes almost mad with anxiety and feel that I could say, Thy will be done, to anything except his turning out ill or a mere sporting man. When we trace back some of our own strongest associations, for good or for bad, to some casual word dropt by a person in a temper, or under a false impression, and feel how a whole existence depends on a beetle's having a bit of butter on its head *or not*, the county of Yorkshire must be given up for a lunatic asylum, if we had not the liberty of carrying all these eager anxieties to the Father of spirits. But in the night He always shines a brighter fire, while in the prosperous day he appears to us often only as a cloud, *now* as He did of old.

Pray believe, dearest, that I never think that *you* are affronted knowing, as I do, that while others judge us by the consequences of our actions upon themselves, or by whether we do what they think right, you judge by whether we do what we think right. But I hope you will not misunderstand now, I mean that suffering as we do from a great many faults that are not our own, as Cain came into the world under much greater disadvantages for Adam having been not quite good, and so ad infinitum, proving that the fable of original sin has, like all fables, oh *how much* truth in it. We must not be angry with ourselves for making of this life a fièvre douloureuse [painful fever], for I doubt whether even those happy ones who are able to have the most sacred trust in their own intentions can do otherwise. We cannot sit above the stars and say, I did my best: advienne que pourra [come what may]. We cry, Life is a fever, where shall I find repose? But let us resign ourselves to it, for if we were not in fevers perhaps we should do absolutely nothing. The best tonic is an uneasy mind. And as long as evil has its reign in this world, I want no other heaven. I can desire no further benefits than to be allowed to return and return with renewed and better powers from the fountain of power till the kingdom of God is really come here.

Your news was most welcome for I had heard none of it, my dearest. I had not heard from Ma since Aunt Anne came up to London. I

---

30 An allusion to Mark 3:29.

should have written to her and you, but while my man was here, I really had no time. I wish, dearest, that Fan could have come here. I should have liked it so much (and Jack has not been here since in or about the Year of Grace 2 or 3) but Mama said that, if Fan went out taking long rides, as she did last year, she would kill herself, and we could not help it. I am *not* sure that I agreed with her, but if Mama thought so it was the same as if it was so. I wish you could all have come, but I hope for Embley.

Louisa Mackenzie writes from *Brahan*, Miss Dutton comes here next week. I have no news for, excepting jaunting up to Derby with my lad on his way south, I have not crossed my threshold. . . . When I think, as you say, that the influence of each of us is *end*less and *bound*less, being perpetuated to the "last syllable of recorded time,"[31] and (like the voltaic current) running along from link to link of the infinite chain, we might well sink for fear, if it were not for the feeling that we have really no work of our own to do, and that God knows his vessels, and made an ass into Balaam's best friend[32] and a gourd into Jonah's.[33]

But you will be tired, and I must stop. Excuse the wanderings of a bad pen—thy verse is beautiful, and as poets are the true prophets, is doubtless true, not in the next world, but in the next world but two (or three). In this I doubt if duty will bring beauty yet, except in a sketchy outline or two here and there, but for the whole group, must we not wait? What was that sublime selfishness which made Addison say, Come and see how a good man can die.[34] Was that beauty, when there were numbers of miseries about him dying like dogs, to whom no possibility had ever been given of living but as dogs. What if the first hour of our living again in what we believe will be a clearer atmosphere, will also be the first hour of our seeing, not darkly, but revealed to us face to face,[35] a multitude of duties unseen, undone, unlooked for till then, as the going out of a candle reveals to us the moonlight without. Alas, this class of God's schoolroom has fallen (or risen, I don't care which) into such a state, that, *whatever* we do, we may see clearly all

---

31 From Shakespeare's *Macbeth* Act 5, scene 5.
32 The story of Balaam and his ass is told in Num 22.
33 An allusion to Jonah 4:6.
34 Addison on his deathbed was visited by his dissolute son and told him: "See in what peace a Christian can die," in James Sutherland, ed., *Oxford Book of Literary Anecdotes.*
35 An allusion to 1 Cor 13:12.

the evil which *may* arise from either course, whichever we take, so that your interpretation of, O Lord, forgive, occurs to me at every step. (The worst of having once sinned is, not that we shall suffer next day, but that, whatever we do next day, however right, must drag after it some bad consequence, so that experience is but an earth-born flower after all, and seldom bears angels but crabs here, until, grafted with a more heavenly wisdom hereafter, it opens into St Paul's apple of hope.) Bless thee, my dearest, and believe me,

thine ever and always

I should dearly have liked to see Hughie [Bonham Carter] before the holidays were over but I believe it was thought as well by all the mothers that the few remaining days of holiday should be passed in strict penitence, seclusion, optics and catoptrics.[36] Will you tell Fan, dearest, *how* very sorry I was not to see her here and that I would have written, but for the reason which prevented my writing any letters, but will. And give her my best love. I forgot to say how Blanche made me love and respect her while she was here. Her soul is heavy with stuff as a rose is weighed down with dew. But in a few hours the sun will rise, and fecondes the dew, and the rose will lift up its head the brighter for having been so laden. Pray excuse this dirty letter—a bad pen always will spell wrong.

[on inside envelope flap] Once more thanks for all thy news and once more fare thee well. You say, dearest, how hollow words are. True, unless the *word* is merely the trail of light left by the *thought* passing into the *action* it is hollow. I never feel that thy words are hollow because of this very thing.

Source: Letter, ADD Mss 45794 fff134-35

[1846-47]

Dearest heart [Hilary Bonham Carter]

Many thanks for all thy information, rich and rare. My young people are so dazel'd with the pomps and vanities of the world, the wild beasts of that evil forest, whose very robins are birds of prey, that they stay over the ball and me and my children must spend another long day in a lovely bunny pie, for love of the contents thereof shot by Uncle Oc and Willy. B. and I walked into Herder [?] this morning, and then on to Romsey, to provide ourselves with pocketbooks to record the "great thoughts" in. . . .

36 Optics dealing with reflection.

The Umgang [association] with children is very sweet—there is not that perpetual strain of appearing what we are not. It is very purifying too because one is so quite sure that all one does with them *is* single-hearted, for they do not appreciate one's "poetry," one's "learning," one's "singular good sense," one's "vast research," but think we were born so. They never say how good, or how clever, but take all or nothing as making or not making impression upon them. But they are singular good judges of *character* and nothing which is not single-hearted does make impression upon them.

With what pleasure too I lay aside the reins with Shore—there never was anyone less fitted to manage and drive than "me." I drove him sometimes too hard, always fearing that I did not drive hard enough. But now he is old enough not to be driven any more, but to drive me. He must come to me now and ask me to help him (for which I would read law, my morning star, if thou wert to put on a chancery wig), not *me* whip *him* to his dictionary any more. And I do exchange my office with such joy. There is much about him that makes me more hopeful. I think his religious thoughts are strengthening into feelings, and that growing older, instead of making him more "sauvage" in intimate intercourse as I expected, is making him more affectionate and more holy. But I must go (not however because I think that thou wilt reject this). Thine how much thine—canst thou read this?

F.N.

Source: Unsigned letter, ADD Mss 45794 ff117-20

dingy old Burlington [St.]
Tuesday [March 1847?]

My dearest [Hilary Bonham Carter]

The principal object of this speedy invocation is to entreat that my sponge be sent me in a small parcel per post, as it, like my dressing gown, has been the charm of my youth, and is now the solace of my declining years. The secondary object is to say how happy was the time I spent with you. Ich habe genossen das irdische Glück, ich habe geliebt und gelebt, as you once said, and I mourned my "habe" with silent tears the rest of the journey. . . . [37]

---

37 A quotation from Schiller's epic poem, *Wallenstein*, or Coleridge's translation of it:
   Thou Holy one, call thy child away!
   I've lived and loved, and that was today;
   Make ready my grave-clothes tomorrow.

Source: Unsigned letter to Hilary Bonham Carter, ADD Mss 45794 ff117-20

[March 1847?]

... I thought Shore looking rather bad the last day. In all other respects he charmed me, all that he told me was good, excepting, my dear, the absolute want of all intercourse (about the things which, after all, old and young find the most interesting), in that school.[38] It is no worse than other schools but I was in hopes it would be better, but the absence of it is complete.

This thing I must testify to, in the atmosphere of your house, which is that, in *any* other, even in Bedford Sq., my boy, if I were to approach him, much less to run at him, except when we two were quite alone, would be so overcome with confusion, that it would be quite impossible for me to have any intercourse with him in public. I always renounce it. But at No. 82, he actually sat with astonishing coolness on the arm of my chair—I may say stroked my velvet with a composure amounting to audacity— and I felt at once that, in that atmosphere, he might be spoken to without bringing all his mauvaise honte [awful shame] into his English cheeks. I had not the least idea that he would have dared before his schoolfellows to have come within the hundredth part of an inch towards showing us the schoolroom or that he wouldn't have turned blue at all such jokes as calling me his grandmother.

With best love to Aunt Joanna and many thanks to her for all her kindness.

ever thine

Source: Unsigned letter, ADD Mss 45794 ff125-29

Lea Hurst
10 September [1847]

Dearest [Hilary Bonham Carter]

How long it is since I have written, and yet how much I have had to say. There is no danger of my ever forgetting you a single day. The first thing in the morning I read one of your Schefers. Then I think how much I should like to sit down and write to you and then the "material interests" come and consume all my article, meaning time. Still I always feel as if that made no difference, as if there were no

---

Coleridge found it "not in my power to translate this song with literal fidelity" so reproduced the German passage. Nightingale saw the original manuscript in the Royal Library in Berlin (see *European Travels*).

38 In 1847 Shore was studying at Edinburgh Academy.

silence in our sympathy, because there were no words, and as if between us many words were not wanted. May God make thee like the ain [own], as the Ostiaks say, that is, incapable of suffering. But happiness, eternal happiness, what do we think it to be? Not to be without (what the "idle and inconsiderate at their festivals" call) suffering unchangeably lucky. The next state will probably have greater trials, greater temptations, greater events of good and evil change, than this miniature world.

That the mind makes its own happiness and its own suffering we see already here. It makes its own "extract of joy" and "extract of sorrow" out of the things which are assigned to each man's lot, and out of which every suffering can come to one and every joy to another, each one moulds his fate. What then is eternal peace? It is a peace (as we see in the great type of the Man of Action), which springs up out of the deepest depth of human misery, our Saviour's peace. This must be what we should expect in another state: peace, "his peace," as he emphatically acknowledged it to be in the most dreadful moment of his life. What can we ask for more? What can we desire so much? His must be our eternal happiness, *his* must be what *we* are to hope for. He says it is for us and in the expectation of the greatest trials and disappointments (such as he perhaps is even now not exempt from) and in their eternal happiness, such as he said he had, we may take courage and go on.

Laura, Lothian and Blanche are with us. Aunt Mai and Beatrice come today. Selfishly, I am overwhelmed with disappointment that you are not going back to Brighton for the winter. Your presence there was such a godsend to the boys, especially to mine. The King school is too enormous a subject to enter upon now, as also Shore's obligations to you. And with regard to the spirit of the school (I don't say the spirit of *our boys*) I have long since drawn my conclusions, as I dare say you have yours.

But the subject—ever fresh, ever new, ever beautiful, ever wonderful of Mrs Mohl: how seldom Providence manages so well. Although He has clearly marked out some (as I always declare) to be old maids, yet I think He had as clearly marked her to be a wife. In single life, to her class of mind, the stage of the present and the outward world is so filled with phantoms, the phantoms, not unreal though intangible, of vague remorse, fears dwelling on the threshold of everything we undertake, alone, dissatisfaction with what is, and restless yearnings for what is not, cravings after a world of wonders, which is, but is like the chariots and horses of fire (which Elisha's frightened servant could not see till his eyes were opened[39]).

The stage of actual life gets so filled with these that we are almost pushed off the boards and are conscious of only just holding on to the footlights by our chins. Yet even in that very inconvenient position love still precedes joy, as in St Paul's list, for love, laying to sleep these phantoms (by assuring us of a love so great that we may lay aside all care for our own happiness, not because it is of no consequence to us, whether we are happy or not, as Carlyle says, but because it is of so much consequence to another) gives that leisure frame to our mind, which opens it at once to joy. I have so much to say about her marriage, but I am writing before breakfast and I must stop. Tell Ju, with my love, that I will write, and that she may be very glad to hear of Mrs Plunkett's confinement,[40] as they were *very* anxious about her and that it is a little girl, which is very inconvenient, as the family were very anxious for her "to do" the heir. But when Ju has lived as long in the world as I have, she will be more surprised at getting anything that she wants than at not getting all that she wants. . . . Farewell, an enforced farewell.

thine now as ever

Source: Letter, Add Mss 45794 ff130-31

Embley
20 October [1847]

My dearest [Hilary Bonham Carter]

You will not be more surprised than I am to hear that I am going to Rome with Mrs Bracebridge and Mr for three months and going next Tuesday. Poor old me, who certainly never expected nor intended to leave England again. It's very disgusting, isn't it? when I flattered myself that I couldn't be spared, but hopes presumptuous fade and fall. I have great satisfaction in reflecting that some things will go to the bad while I am away.[41] I make no apology for uttering this sentiment, having always observed that selfishness here is in infinitely better odour than want of judgment and that—see the popular dictionary—the last accomplishment of the unfolding angel, self-forgetfulness, is synonymous with folly in our dialect.

---

39 An allusion to 2 Kings 6:17.
40 Mrs Plunkett, later Lady Dunsany, Nightingale's friend, née Anne-Constance Dutton.
41 Nightingale was then teaching at a ragged school.

Why do I go? All my friends think it such a fine thing for me to see Rome, and three month's communion with my Ithuriel truly are not to be despised, and Pius IX's toe is worth kissing. All that I want to do in life depends upon my health, which I am told a winter in Rome will "establish forever." A.P.F [?] I go. I have put out *Faust*,[42] Guizot,[43] Vico[44] and Euclid for thee to go by Mrs Empson. I should like to have accomplished my visit to you first, but it is impossible. Write me thy commands for Rome and Pius IX.

I had just taken lessons of a Pio Nono [Pius IX] of a Nottingham Infant Schools master, which will, alas! be thrown away now. The commercial spirit of Great Britain is strong in me. It was all settled only today, so that I must be thine ever though in haste and bustle.

F.N.

Best love to Miss Becker, Fan, Aunt Joanne, all. I send the letter which thou didst want to copy.

I had a nocturnal walk with Adam the night before we left L.H. and gave him thy greetings. They were very glad to see him at home. . . . Write to me sometimes at Rome, my dear, as well as here. I am so glad that Jack is gone to Ireland. Keep the enclosed for me till I return in January or February. A thousand thanks for all thy kind offers of conveyances.

Won't some of you come and see my poor solitary lark while I am away? I am very sorry that her officiating vergership and my pontifical visitation should have happened exactly the same year. The parent birds will be quite alone for a little.

We go by sea from Marseille to Civita Vecchia. . . . Is Mrs Mohl/ Clarke returned to Paris? We stay there two days.

Source: Unsigned letter, Hampshire Record Office, 94M72/F587/4

Wednesday [after 1848]

Dearest [Hilary Bonham Carter]

Aunt Evans desires me to write and thank you and say all that is kind in answer to your dear little note, which indeed I can for I am sure, out of your many sympathizers, there was no heart which responded more warmly to your appeal than the old lady's, or wished the young pair joy with such a youthful trust in their happiness and flutter of cheerful life for them. She was exceedingly pleased with your kind

---

42 J.W. von Goethe, *Faust, a Tragedy*. See *Society and Politics*.
43 François P.G. Guizot (1787-1874), Huguenot historian.
44 Giambattista Vico (1668-1744), Italian philosopher.

thought of her. She is deafer and thinner, but more lively than ever, and younger, i.e., as Aunt Mai says of real youth, [illeg] more energetic, more really alive. . . .

Source: Incomplete letter to Hilary Bonham Carter, ADD Mss 45794 ff153-54

[25 March 1853]

. . . I am able to give but a very confused account of what has passed [death of their grandmother Shore], having been so much occupied, as you will believe, and indeed hardly having had my clothes off for six nights. The fact is that the Canning thing[45] has been on, then off again and why do you think? through Marianne [Galton]'s tongue. I am loth to write this in the shadow of the awful calm upstairs and in the light of her own sacred baby. But it came into the wise head of one of the geniuses of the committee to consult her, as my cousin, and *she* could not resist the making a good story (I hardly know what). But the committee wrote to me that they were off, because *she* said it was cruel to take me from my family. Then Mrs Herbert and some others were furious and made me write a letter to the committee saying that I should submit it to my family. In short the sapient committee is on again and I have hardly any heart left for it. If my family like to refuse it for me, why, they are welcome.

Part of the committee's terms are that I shall come in *directly* (and not go back to Paris at all), even into the old house, as they are at their wits' end. I don't know how it will turn out except that I am to go up to town as soon after the funeral as possible, talk to the committee and meet my people in town. I am weary, very weary and don't much care for it and am loth to give up my St Vincent de Paul's.[46] The reason why I tell *you* this long story, my dearest (there is no secret about it any more, M.G. having made a joke of it everywhere, NOT *Laura*, bless her!) . . .

---

45 The arrangements for Nightingale to manage the institution at 1 Upper Harley were made with Lady Canning.

46 The Sisters of Charity in Paris, where Nightingale was nursing for a few months; the order was founded by Louise de Marillac (1591-1660) and Vincent de Paul (1581-1660).

Source: Unsigned note, Wellcome (Claydon copy) Ms 8999/50

[1861]

No dear Hilary [Bonham Carter]

I told you expressly that I would not go to the expense of *buying* silk for a bedroom curtain. I only fancied a breadth of our old drawing room curtains because I was so fond of them. If that won't do, I will have calico, which is much cleaner, white, with a Vitruvian border,[47] which might be sewn on, or pink, covered with white (curtain) muslin. But I will not trouble you to buy these.

Source: Letter/draft, ADD Mss 45794 f174

London
January 1862

Dearest Hilary [Bonham Carter]

I have left you £1000 in the earnest hope that, though not in possession, it may enable you, at some present sacrifice, to provide yourself with an atelier or other means of pursuing your art.

ever yours
F. Nightingale

Source: Letter, Add Mss 45794 f211

[printed address] 4 Cleveland Row, S.W.
25 June 1863

Dearest [Hilary Bonham Carter]

I asked Mr Jowett to give me the sacrament next Sunday at 3:00, because he is going to be absent for two or three months. Would you like to join me and *would you ask* Miss Clough if she would like it too?

ever yours
F.N

Source: Letter, ADD Mss 45794 f214

13 July 1863

Dearie [Hilary Bonham Carter]

I accept with favour your situation for two of the little cats, in preference to situations offered, four deep, in families of the highest rank and political influence, for the following reason: it is good for the health and spirits of little cats when they first leave their mothers to go two together for a time—they wash each other. Therefore, if *on the 21st* you will call for the two little cats, you shall have them, if they can

47 Convoluted scroll pattern.

lap by that time. Also for your beautiful Florentine pictures. I like to see them, but not to keep them. I am not worthy of them, for I like them better *without* the colour. . . .

ever yours

F.

Source: Letter, Add Mss 45794 ff216-20

Hampstead, N.W.

11 August 1863

Dearie et Mme ma parente [Hilary Bonham Carter]

. . . They *are* so ignorant about us. I dare say they think I have only to hold up my finger and hundreds of pounds will flow in. And I should not be surprised (but of this I know nothing) if Sister Cordero[48] does not think, for she knows that I am mixed up somehow with government that I can get ministers to interfere for them. Miss Burt actually wrote to me that it was my *duty* to interfere with *Lord Palmerston* for *Poland,* seeing that my opinion was much taken by government (sic).

If this is the opinion of woman's duty by a very highly educated, VERY sensible Englishwoman, what may not be the vain fantasy of an Italian nun?

F.N.

Editor: Hilary Bonham Carter died in 1865, after having assisted Nightingale with the production of graphics for the Indian royal commission report. The following excerpts show Nightingale reporting on Hilary's last, painful, illness to a colleague, Dr Farr, with whom they both worked on the royal commission material.

Source: Letter to Dr Farr, Wellcome Ms 5474/90

9 June 1864

. . . My dear friend Hilary is less suffering, [there is] more quiescence in the disease, more prospect of its being prolonged—no hope of recovery. God will decide. I cannot join the cry of satisfaction at prolonged life, but, as I say, that is for God. Neither she nor I have any prospect but that of increasing suffering until death. But how much more I dread it for her than for myself. . . .

---

48 Superior of the Sardinian sisters Nightingale knew in the Crimean War.

Source: Letter to Dr Farr, Wellcome Ms 5474/92

2 September 1865

... Our dear friend Hilary [Bonham Carter] is dying painfully. The only wonder is how she lives through each twenty-four hours. But the suffering is much less acute and the wandering of mind much less painful. ...

Source: Letter to Dr Farr, Wellcome Ms 5474/93

6 September 1865

... I cannot say the gratitude to God with which I write that "our dear friend," as you have often called Hilary Carter, was released this morning early. The end was peace, but the suffering had been cruel. I know scarcely a human being of whom one feels so sure that she is gone to a higher and more perfect service. My thoughts turn to you in this, as they have done in many previous sorrows. ...

Cousin Alice Bonham Carter

Source: Letter, Hampshire Record Office 94M72/F585/3

[printed address] 35 South Street
Park Lane
London, W.
10 November 1867

Dear Alice [Bonham Carter]

I must thank you for the beautiful stuffs for screens. The Indian embroidery on a dark ground, which I suppose belonged to dear Hilary, I think you would hardly like to see returned to you after my time is out, tarnished and spoiled. The very pretty gold and red stripe, which I suppose is the one Elinor [Bonham Carter] brought from Cannes, fits my wretched old screen exactly and makes it look quite sublime. I *idle* for the sake of looking at it. I have still dear Hilary's beautiful lioness, which I look at hourly.

I am so glad that Elinor is able to go to Liverpool to work with Miss Clough.[49]

ever, dear Alice
your affectionate
Flo

---

49 Anne Jemima Clough directed a girls' school in Liverpool before becoming the first principal of Newnham College, Cambridge.

Source: Letter, Hampshire Record Office 94M72/F585/5

Embley
Romsey
15 August 1872

My dearest Alice [Bonham Carter]

I am so stifled in dirty anxious cares and sordid *defensive* business that I know not how fittingly to approach her who, I hope, is *all* happy now and with the best kind of all happiness. I feel—in spirit—don't you know?—like the maid of all work who has to wipe her dirty hands on her dirtier apron before she can shake hands with the radiant bride,[50] whereas I should like to feather my pen out of the wing of the dove and dip it in the brightest Thessalian spring to give her joy.

Seriously, my dear child, my joy has been pouring forth all this time ever since I heard it, and I knew not how to present it to her. *You* must do it, not because I am not too dirty to touch *you* but because you are the dear sister who is almost as glad of her joy as she is herself, and who can give her joy for me much better than *I* can. How joyful is this time compared to what it was last year for her, when all were so anxious about her and when you went to Paris to settle about her going to Cannes. That was so very dreary. Now I hope it is *all* right and that, after a somewhat trying life, she is established, not in the mere pleasure of holiday makers and love makers, but in the really highest happiness, "solid, substantial, never-failing bliss." But I am afraid of her wicked little tongue, so I shall not be sentimental but merely ask you to give her joy for me from the bottom of my heart, aye and from the top, too, with all my soul and with all my strength. Do you know that there is hardly any man whom I should like to know so much as her chosen? And, therefore, I think I may wish him joy, too.

I do not forget, dear Alice, that your life will be in some things more poor for her being a little farther away, but it will also be more rich. I know that you feel it to be all joy in your unselfishness, almost as much as if you were her sister in heaven.

And now, my dear child, my thrifty soul is thinking of furniture. I wish I could afford to give her a good piece, but I can't and I don't know what she would like. What do you think? Shall I send you £25 and ask you to choose? Or shall I be quite prosaic and send her the £25 and ask her to put it in her pocket? If that is not enough to buy a

---

50 Elinor Bonham Carter married Albert Venn Dicey (1835-1922), a distinguished legal scholar.

piece, there is more to come. Advise me, do. Shall it be two stools for the ancient Briton to sit on? God bless them both and He *will* bless them. And believe me,

ever yours and hers lovingly and joyfully

poor old Flo

My mother has doubtless sent her congratulations to yours and to Elinor. She is quite sympathetic and tenderly glad (when one talks to her about it) with intelligent interest (and would send a message if she knew I was writing), often has more affectionate insights than ever in all her life.

F.N.

I, too, feel thankful that I have lived to see this joy, dear Alice.

Source: Letter, Hampshire Record Office 94M72/F585/6

19 August 1872

Dearest Alice [Bonham Carter]

I open my letter because I have just received Elinor's dear letter by afternoon post. Tell her I think it is beautiful, *that* is real love, and I am sure true to the *least-est* little letter. I do so delight in seeing people really in love, that is, you know, with real people—love which makes people heroes (let the devil say what he will).

And I say, God bless her, God bless them both, not only with all my heart and with all my soul and with all my strength but with all my mind.[51] And He *will* bless them.

F.N.

Source: Letter, Hampshire Record Office 94M72/F585/7

Lea Hurst
Cromford, Derby
21 September 1876

Petition of Women

Bulgarian, etc. emancipation

Dear Alice [Bonham Carter]

You ask me if I know anything of Miss Albert—nothing but a rather unwise letter, NOT VERY, I saw of hers. But Mr Lewis Farley, who is, I believe, the president, has a bad name with almost all of us, even with *good Serbians.*

I think it, the petition, is such a good thing to do that I felt tempted to sign it quand même. (She *had* written to Miss Irby.) But all our other

---

51 An allusion to Mark 12:30.

groups of things, for "Sick and Wounded," for "Bulgarian Relief," etc. have been taken up and amalgamated, each group by some great central concern, *as they ought to be*.

And I am not without hopes that women's petitions will also be, so that one can sign without having anything to do with "League" people. I sent it (unsigned) as you directed. God speed the right.

yours affectionately

F.N.

Source: Letter, Hampshire Record Office 94M72/F585/8

[printed address] 10 South Street
Park Lane, W.
21 July 1881

My dear Alice [Bonham Carter]

How good of you to take so much trouble about poor Mme Mohl. The nieces entirely and strongly deprecate my taking lodgings *at all* for her. They do not make the least mien [appearance] of intending to come. I have no doubt they are perfectly right.

At first when I opened your note I was struck with alarm that the "she" who had "written" to you "with addresses of lodgings" was Mme Mohl herself. But I think I understand it is Aunt Julia. I think I would let it now entirely alone. What Mme M. wrote to me was to take her lodgings for herself alone, "without a maid," "in" *my* "*street*." For us to start a fresh plan for her, which she has not herself contemplated, I think would be unwise, even if we could get the niece.

I wrote to her, Mme Mohl, on Tuesday after I had had the various answers that (without saying why) lodgings could not be had as she proposed. And I wrote to Elinor, the same morning, a note which I hope she forwarded to you. I gave Mme M. your kind message about how, thinking she was going to Klagenfurt and not coming to England till September, you had filled up your house till I did not say when.

There is scarcely anyone our hearts bleed for as for her. Her note to me was heart-rending. I shall never be surprised at her arriving at my door without notice. But I pray *not*. What *will* become of her? You are very good to have bestirred yourself so much. I may yet have to claim it all and to make one of the nieces come. But I trust not. With love to Aunt Joanna,

ever yours affectionately

F. Nightingale

I hope she, Mme Mohl, will not come to England at present but go to good Ida[52] in Carinthia.

Dear Alice, I reopen this letter: I have just had a long letter from poor Mme Mohl. She writes *most* affectionately and pathetically, but says, "I wish I could box everybodies (sic) ears successively that has been saying I was going with these poor things" (Ida and Anna) to sprit their journey." Not one word about coming to England. She seems to have quite forgotten it.

Source: Letter, Hampshire Record Office 94M72/F585/9

Lea Hurst
Cromford, Derby
21 November 1881

My dear Alice [Bonham Carter]

I cannot help sending you a line with my dear love to give you joy on, as I believe, Aunt Joanna's ninetieth birthday. I hope she is as well as your care can make her, such tender care.

I have seen such an exceedingly nice woman here, age forty-three, daughter of Joseph Smith, gardener at Cromford Bridge for thirty years, who still lives. If Aunt Julia wanted a maid, I think she would do. *I* should have taken her at once had I wanted one, subject of course to her (twelve years') character from Ireland proving satisfactory (she left this Irish place because they were compelled to diminish their household). As *housekeeper* in a small family (*not* cook) or as *maid to an elderly or invalid lady* she wishes to find service.

I am sorry to say that I shall be wanting a *cook* (in South St.) by the middle of December—the "good" woman proving a failure in almost every way (as cook) and utterly dirty and a muddle. I am sure you will kindly think of me (and mention my wants to "the family") if you hear of anyone.

My best love to Aunt Julia. Oh what a letter of interest to her and to me I could write her from here, had I but strength. But I have scarcely been downstairs at all. Miss Irby goes tomorrow.

ever yours affectionately

F. Nightingale

Excuse (*not* conventionally) this villainous scrawl.

___

52 Ida Zabierow Schmidt, niece of M Mohl.

Source: Letter, Hampshire Record Office 94M72/F585/12

[printed address] 10 South Street
Park Lane, W.
15 February 1885

My dear Alice [Bonham Carter]

I am so glad to hear of you and Edith.[53] What a life you may make for her if she can recover health and work under Miss O[ctavia] Hill. My fervent wishes are hers, and yours yet more, dear Alice.

With regard to our beloved Mme Mohl, I have not time or strength (which is the same thing) even to look out her letters, much less to look them over to see what is *not* private for the purpose you mention. I think (and I thought Mrs S.'s article was evidence of it) that Mrs Simpson had the most surface knowledge of her. She merely knew her picture, the tricks of voice, speech and manner. She did not know the living original mind which made her the life of M Mohl, M Fauriel and many others, which made her the inspiration of the rich as in England many have been of the poor. Yet I am very glad that you are helping Mrs Simpson. How is Elinor?

ever yours
F. Nightingale

Source: Note, Add Mss 45845 f245

5 January 1899

Alice Bonham Carter, very sorry, too poorly to see her just yet. Inquire for Edith, can't see her, hope to see her soon. Malcolm Bonham Carter's £5 towards bicycle, £10 for a boy, write to her. . . .

Cousin Henry Bonham Carter

Editor: There is a massive extant correspondence with Nightingale's cousin, Henry Bonham Carter, who served for many years as secretary of the Nightingale Fund Council, which will be related in *Public Health Care* and the nursing volumes. Here only a few letters are included, those strictly on family matters. Nightingale's fondness for her cousin is clear in many references in early family correspondence, e.g., hunting and shooting, the result in killing rabbits with a ferret was tolerable for Alf and "not very good for Harry, who ran away weeping."[54] A

---

53 Edith Bonham Carter, later a nurse.
54 Letter to Frances Nightingale January-February 1840, Wellcome (Claydon copy) Ms 8992/7.

letter to Aunt Patty in 1845 reported that he was "doing very well" at Cambridge (see p 537 below). To her mother she passed on news: "Harry was at Holmwood several days; he saw Fan at Malta for two hours, he was full of Athens and Constantinople and very entertaining."[55] One published letter to a Bonham Carter son, Charles (1876-1955), is also given here.

Source: Letter, ADD Mss 47717 ff41-42

Embley
Romsey
10 February 1872

My dear Harry B.C.

We are so very glad that Sibella's time of trouble is over.[56] Thank you for writing to us so soon, and that she has all good prospect of being none the worse for it. And we congratulate the little man who has come under your and her tender care. God bless him and her.

We send her a few harmless flowers, wishing they were better, and of course we send a nosegay of snowdrops for the baby, with whom, I am sure, my little friend Joan is delighted. I must write to my love (that is, the baby) a Valentine.

Pardon this hurried note, not hurried in thought, for indeed we give thanks. . . .

ever yours and Sibella's
most affectionately
F. Nightingale

12 February 1872

My mother sends her best love and congratulations to Sibella, that it is "all right." And of course a message of greeting to the new little man, whose complexion you uncivilly reflect upon. If he turns out like the baby with its little paw in its hair (whose photograph you were so good as to send me) he cannot be *more* charming. I am very glad the village nurse has done well.

ever yours
F.N.

---

55 Letter to Frances Nightingale early 1852, Wellcome (Claydon copy) Ms 8993/123.

56 His wife's delivery of Reginald Bonham Carter (1872-1901); Sibella Bonham Carter (1837-1916) bore eleven sons and a daughter.

Source: Letter to Parthenope Verney, Wellcome (Claydon copy) Ms 9008/49

My mother's affairs: Henry Bonham Carter   24 April [1880]

Henry Bonham Carter writes to me, my dear P., this very kind note: "I have been remiss in delaying to respond to your kind proposal that I should accept £100 as an acknowledgment of your and Parthe's appreciation of what I may have done in the way of help in your mother's affairs. To accept this would not, my dear Flo, be agreeable to me, detracting as it would from the pleasure which is afforded by being able to be of some service in matters which could not perhaps have been so conveniently and easily done by another. If you had had a brother, such business affairs would have fallen upon him as a matter of course and I hope that you will both, in this respect, allow me to stand in the position of one. I have not mentioned the subject to Parthe and I should be glad if you would communicate my wish to her."

Henry B.C.

How *very very* kind this is. *How* kind he has been. But do not you think we could get him to "accept" the £100 for one of the *Dicey* (boys[57]). I vote for this.

F.N.

Source: Letter, ADD Mss 47722 ff70-71

Claydon House
Winslow, Bucks
25 September 1889

My dear Harry [Bonham Carter]

We do trust that you are better. We do so grieve for the painful consequences of what was really a very severe accident, but then you cannot think how we thank God for your being safe in life. What should we have done without you? And, to put it in the most prosaic way, what thousands are dependent upon you? For such an escape we have indeed the deepest gratitude to our Almighty Father and we hope that soon all traces of pain will pass away. They have been long enough and too long. When we think what might have been—but it behooves us to be strong on St Michael's Day and we can only feel sympathy that you should have so much suffering, of which you have made so little, and which, I fear, must have been aggravated by the anxious business of this time.

---

57 Sons of Elinor Bonham Carter and Albert Venn Dicey.

Bother the bears! We ought to present you with a golden bear and St Michael for an inkstand in commemoration of your fortitude. I am so glad that Sibella, to whom my best love, is enjoying that lovely spot. In thankfulness to God and to you

ever yours

Florence Nightingale

Source: Note to Henry Bonham Carter, ADD Mss 47725 f200

[15 February 1894]

. . . A quite poor woman, a great sufferer, and one of our friends from Lea Hurst, who cannot spell, wished me this year that it should be the "holiest, happiest and most blessed year I had ever lived." So wish I that this may be not the least fruitful in blessings to others, which is saying a great deal and to you and yours and of all your sixty-seven years.

Source: Victor Bonham Carter, *In a Liberal Tradition* 120

10 South Street
Park Lane, W.
28 January 1897

Dear "Charlie" [Bonham Carter]

I should be very sorry not to see you before you go. Would 5:30 or 5: tomorrow (Saturday) or Sunday suit you?? Or have you twenty-five better engagements?

your affectionate

F. Nightingale

This is you!

Je suis le capitaine de vingt-cinq soldats
Et sans moi, Paris serait pris.

Source: Letter, ADD Mss 47728 ff184-85

[printed address] 10 South Street
Park Lane, W.
27 May 1898

Not Immediate

My dear Harry [Bonham Carter]

I am so very glad that you are going to take a little holiday and so very sorry not to see you.

I am sure you disapprove of my father's daughter accepting *house charity* from my landlord, and another man approves it. But I think I prefer your opinion. However we can talk about that when you come back.

How curious is the conflict of opinion about Mr Gladstone, the furious rage of those who admire him against those who do not, and neither knowing exactly what they are talking about. However, dissent made England. Look at France.

yours ever

F.N.

Thank you very much about the report, N. Fund and for all you do for us. . . .

The Nicholson Family

Editor: Strains in relations between the Nightingale and Nicholson families are evident from early in Nightingale's childhood. Apart from those shared with her parents and sister, Nightingale encountered disapproval in 1843 when she declined the suit of her cousin, Henry Nicholson, someone she evidently liked but for whom there is nothing to suggest any stronger feelings (they felt that she had encouraged him). He, in any event, died in 1851. In 1853 when Nightingale was finally about to get her first opportunity to nurse, the Nicholsons were opposed (other relatives, notably Aunt Mai, approved and assisted). As a letter above shows, Marianne Nicholson even gave her negative views to the management committee, which put the whole project on hold for some months.

"Aunt Hannah" Nicholson

Editor: A much larger number of letters to "Aunt Hannah" is included in *Theology*, for Hannah Nicholson was a significant influence on Nightingale's spiritual sensibilities in her childhood and youth. Only a few letters dealing with family relations appear here. These portray Nightingale as a troubled young woman, still under the thumb of her parents. She was able to confide in Hannah Nicholson in a way she could not with her own mother. Indeed she referred to herself as "your child." Yet it seems that Hannah Nicholson, as the other Nicholsons, opposed Nightingale's desire to nurse. When Nightingale finally was permitted to take up the position at Harley Street, her sister explained that the family had not "chosen or desired such a course for her," but were "honestly and lovingly anxious that she should do what she thinks right."[58] References to Aunt Hannah from the Crimean War suggest that she was then near death.

---

58 Letter by Parthenope Nightingale to Hannah Nicholson c1853, Wellcome (Claydon copy) Ms 9039/9.

Source: Letter/draft/copy to Hannah Nicholson, Add Mss 45794 ff10-15

Wednesday [September 1844?]

I long to thank you for your message, my dear Aunt Hannah, my own self. Though I have nothing worth writing about to you I feel that I saw so very little of you at Waverley that I often wished I had been ill again, in order to be allowed to come and sit quietly again in your place of rest. Truly I may say it was the sweetest hour of the day, for the peace "which passeth all understanding,"[59] which you seem always to be full of, sometimes passes from you to those who are with you. Small peace have I had since, and I cannot think now how I could enjoy so little of it at Waverley, except that I am so infirm of purpose that if anybody asks me to do anything at the time I know I shall never have the courage to say no.

I hope you will not desert your poor old child, my dear Aunt Hannah, and that you will not forget your promise to come and see us here sometime before the spring. You must let me look forward to that, though in general I know you think it is best for us neither to look before nor behind, as far as things here are concerned. . . .

We like our new clergyman and his wife[60] very much. They seem as happy as if, they say themselves, they had picked out their own lot and been allowed to cut it out for their own selves. I am sure their hearts are in the right place and, when that is the case, everything else goes right. I am sure he does not take to his profession merely as a livelihood, but because he has his soul in it. I think he gives us very good sermons too.

The school, I am sorry to say, is not so flourishing, though the schoolmistress is very earnest, but she has had little circumstances against her, which I hope will pass away. Mama has left her two poor infants to themselves all this time, as perhaps you know, but poor Aunt Mary is so much in want of her that she may remain, I think, till it is settled whether Aunt Mary goes to Switzerland, in which case Mama will certainly bring Beatrice home with her (I hope to spend the winter here).

Meanwhile we are a very quiet little quartet, William being the most regular and industrious of human beings, in the prospect of Sandhurst, and a very good boy in all respects, as I need not tell you. How little one ever thinks that one is talking to a handsome young sol-

---

59 Phil 4:7.
60 William Henry and Mrs Empson.

dier when one is with him, he being the very reverse in every respect to that tribe of individual.

Mr Noel is doing great things at Romsey Church, and really renewing it beautifully, having collected a very considerable fund (by his own personal influence, I suppose we must say). . . .

Source: Letter/draft/copy to Hannah Nicholson, ADD Mss 45794 ff57-58

Embley
Christmas eve [1844-46?]

. . . I am afraid you will not come to us now, for, from the day after tomorrow we shall have a crowd of people, and when they will be gone I do not know. Do not let another year pass away without coming to see us. It is now more than a year since I have seen you. Give me your thoughts tomorrow, my dear Aunt Hannah, I want them sadly, and take me with you to the throne of grace. Bless me, too, as poor Esau said. I have so felt with him and cried with a great and exceeding bitter cry: Bless me, even me also, O my father,[61] but He never has yet and I have not deserved that He should. I shall think of you and find no words to say how very earnestly I am

ever your loving and grateful
Florence

Source: Letter/draft/copy. ADD Mss 45794 ff65-66

Embley
16 May [1849]

My dearest Aunt Hannah [Nicholson]

I cannot say what a disappointment it was to me to hear that you were actually determined never to come to us again. *You* will *know* how I grieved when I heard there was no hope of seeing you. I did think you would have come this time, you would have been quite quiet. How am I to see you? Am I hardly ever to see you again? Except that little sight of you at Laura's marriage I have hardly seen you for years. And you know how much your kindness always is to me.

I cannot admit the goodness of your reasons of not going anywhere more except to relations! Are we not relations? related in heart to you, dearest Aunt Hannah, I sometimes hope that I am. Related in life it must be a very long while yet before I can *hope* to be.

---

61 The sad story in Gen 27:34 where Esau asks for his father's blessing, but his brother Jacob, by fraud, gets it first.

I had much to tell you of, which I think would have interested you, because it interests me (you see I always reckon on your sympathy, as if it were impossible to trespass on it). My little thieves in Westminster, my ragged school, which was my greatest joy in London, and many other things which I have never time to write about, but which I always lay by as I will tell Aunt Hannah this when I see her.

I know you never forget me, dearest Aunt Hannah, that you remember me where I best like to be remembered and that you always will. But it would be a sore trouble to me never to be with you again as we *have* been together, except just at flying moments. I have not time to say more as we have a house with divers children, etc. in it. Let me wish you joy, however, over dear William's marriage, and believe me, ever my dear Aunt Hannah's

grateful, loving, longing child
Florence N.

Source: Letter/draft/copy, Add Mss 45794 ff74-75

1 Upper Harley St.
12 March 1854

My dearest Aunt Hannah [Nicholson]

Thank you *very* much for writing. Your deathbed room has scarcely ever been out of my thoughts. But life is a more awful thing than death. My many thoughts you will guess, as I believe I can yours. But I must prevent myself from writing, for I have much to prevent me. Shall I never see you?

ever my dear Aunt Hannah's
grateful and affectionate
F.N.

Aunt Anne, Cousins Henry, Lothian and William Nicholson

Source: Letter in child's printing, Hampshire Record Office 94M72/F587/2

[November 1826?]

My dear Aunt Anne [Nicholson]

I hope you have got safe to your journey's end. I hope you saw the eclipse of the moon the day you went.[62] Papa says that you were blind boobies if you did not watch it for a whole hour as we did. The garden goes on very well.

---

62 There was an eclipse 28 November 1826.

We have got a very little pretty new book called *Sacred Poetry*. Papa has hunted twice this week. My eye is well and I went to church on Sunday. Kate or Laura has left a pinafore here. Gale wants to be remembered by nurse and all the children. I hope Marianne and Laura and Kate do their exercises. Pray give my love to everybody and believe me

your very affectionate niece

Florence Nightingale

Please give me an answer.

Source: Letter, in child's printing, Wellcome Ms 5482/1

Embley

Sunday [after 14 January 1829]

Dear Henry [Nicholson]

Thank you for your picture, and thank Aunt Anne, and all of them for the book and pictures.

Yesterday somebody threw some gunpowder into the fire and Betsy, going to poke it, it flew into her arm and set her gown on fire. Pop [Parthenope] went into the room and she says that it was all in a smoke. Some towels were burnt.

Here is a riddle. What can you add to 9 to make 6? For instance, a gentleman sent 9 ducks to his friend, the man who carried them stole 3. Now you must know the gentleman wrote the number of ducks on the basket. How could the man alter the number 9 into 6 so that there was no blotting out and so that he was not found out? You must recollect that he added something.

We had a play which we acted on Twelfth Night. It was "Alfred, a Drama" in *Evenings at Home*. Freddy, Pop, Clémence (our French maid) and I acted it. Freddy was Alfred; Pop: Gubba; Clémence: Ella; I: Gandelin. He [Freddy] had on a black cap and a smock frock. Pop had a smock frock and a pair of Freddy's shoes. Clémence had Papa's cocked hat and sword and a large camlet cloak. I had a white shirt and a woollen shawl, a calico turban hanging down behind.

Mama went to the ball the 14th of January, came home between 5:00 and 6:00 o'clock and stayed in bed till after our dinner. She had on a dark green gown, white sleeves and diamonds. Goodbye.

your affectionate cousin

Florence Nightingale

P.S. I send Aunt Anne, Laura and all of them my love. It snows here and is warmer today. We had a grand supper Twelfth Night. I drew the sweetpea.

Source: Letter to her grandmother, Mary Shore, Wellcome (Claydon copy) Ms 8992/31

Ditcham

Friday [January 1841]

. . . We shall be glad to find ourselves at home again after being so long away, though we have had an uncommonly gay time at the Nicholsons. They acted a play of Shakespeare's, the *Merchant of Venice*. Parthe painted the scenes with the assistance of a Mr Austen, and her scenery was generally admired. I was manager. Henry Nicholson, who acted the principal character, Shylock, did it really wonderfully well. We danced a great deal, several nights though we were never *very* late, you will be glad to hear, except at a public ball, where Parthe did not go, and where we went to honour Sam Nicholson's stewardship. . . .

Source: Unsigned letter, Wellcome (Claydon copy) Ms 8992/32

[1841]

Henry [Nicholson] is 31st wrangler,[63] my dear . . . he is delighted and everyone more than satisfied. Uncle Nicholson brought the news home from Guildford on Saturday night but would tell no one till Henry came in, who was very much surprised. He has been so jolly ever since that it has been nothing but a succession of what a roll! as every name in the paper of honours was examined.

An extraordinary number of poor creatures have been disappointed . . . all booked for first-class men in classical Tripos and all first-class men in college have been plucked, so that they cannot now enter the classical examination. Henry is on uncommonly good terms therefore with himself for having beaten a many, but I must say he has a great deal of pity to spare at intervals for the pluckt. . . .

Source: Copy of letter to Lothian Nicholson, Wellcome (Claydon copy) Ms 8994/36

1 Upper Harley St.

19 August [1853]

My dear friend [Lothian Nicholson]

The quantity of work for the last week (in settling this new place) and the poor Ocs's sorrow have prevented me from attending to your note sooner.

---

63 Ranking of first-class students in mathematics at Cambridge University.

I think you are perfectly right to defend your sister.[64] And this being my opinion, I should neither have applied to you about this matter, nor will *I* now that you have done so to me, enter into any explanation, which must be painful to you.

On rereading your note I almost wish you could reread it yourself. I cannot but think you would smile to see how, "without inquiry" and, without any possible means of information, you accuse others of "at once *without inquiry* giving credit to a story so improbable." About my affair I will however say no more. But there is another matter, concerning which you have spoken in your letter to Parthe, to which you refer me. Knowing the generous and chivalrous attachment which you feel towards Blanche, I am sure that you will be relieved to hear that you have been *entirely* misinformed and I trust you, dear Lothian, to contradict the report, if ever you hear it. I hope that you will come and see me "in service," when next you have a day to spare in London.

Finally, dear Lothian, one word. Our old, and, I hope, real friendship encourages me to say it: do not engage in any paper wars. You will convince nobody and arrive at no satisfaction yourself. In great haste.

ever your most loving coz

Flo

Editor: The reference to "if she lives" in the next letter probably refers to Hannah Nicholson. Lothian Nicholson, a Royal Engineer, served in the Crimean War; he later rose to be General Sir Lothian Nicholson.

Source: Unsigned letter to "friends," Wellcome (Claydon copy) Ms 8995/26

[Scutari]

7 August 1855

. . . Lothian Nicholson came yesterday and goes to the Crimea today. He looks well and in good spirits, though his face is blistered with heat. I was so very glad to see him. He gave me an account of dear Aunt Hannah's sufferings. If she still lives, ask her to send a message, tell her how I have thought of her and loved her and how I shall miss her being on earth—I should have liked to have seen her again. The old are so much better than the young. . . .

---

64 Presumably a reference to Marianne Nicholson's telling the management committee at 1 Upper Harley St. that Nightingale's becoming superintendent would be harmful to her family.

Source: Copy of letter, Wellcome (Claydon copy) Ms 8995/31

Scutari

19 August [1855]

Dear Uncle Nicholson

I feel I must find time to write one word, though that is unworthy of the subject, to tell you what great happiness it gave me (after my nine months' exile) to see Lothian again, looking so well, so manly, so full of zeal and energy. He is gone up to see what I think every young man ought to see, the most wonderful page I suspect of the history of the nineteenth century—not excluding Waterloo, which was *success-ful*—whereas we are *un*successful and the *why* is the most curious and instructive peep a young man can have under the surface of our brilliant British prosperity. I could scarcely regret his going up to add his still pure and loyal and uncorrupted hand to the few others who redeem the general lukewarmness, corruption or complaining of the authorities out there, stiffened and warped by education and by weariness. The moral deterioration is quicker than the physical.

I was much pleased to hear the way in which Captain Gordon (Engineer), the best man we have here,[65] spoke of Lothian. The earnest prayer of us all must be that he do not have to pay for his experience. But there is such a thing as patriotism still, I suppose, in England and who can regret that Lothian should do something for God and mankind, for which I assure you there is room out here.

I cannot tell you how much I have longed for one twenty-four hours in England to see again my dear Aunt Hannah. Perhaps before this she is where one would not presume to wish her back from. With love to all, ever my dear Uncle,

your affectionate niece

Florence Nightingale

Source: Incomplete letter, Wellcome (Claydon copy) Ms 8995/71

[1855]

Lothian [Nicholson] is just returned from Kinburn and the expedition to the Bug and was to sail yesterday, in command of the troops on board of the "Indian" with the expedition to Kaffa which, if taken, we shall occupy for the winter. He has had dysentery for a month and looks ill but in high spirits. He rode up to see me from Kamiesch Bay.

---

65 This is not Charles Gordon, later General, who was also a Royal Engineer, but still a young subaltern in the Crimean War.

He was the director of the mines for blowing up the dockyards at Sebastopol, will soon be a major and on the highroad to a colonelcy. I glory in his being here and such earnest young blood is the only thing to regenerate us. He, like myself, is worn out with the official conversation, which is entirely limited to two words (as the old barrel organ was to two tunes), viz., "promotion" and "gazette."

General Simpson sailed today leaving not a regret behind. Sir W. Codrington[66] and General Wyndham are very popular appointments, excepting with Sir Colin Campbell who heroically took himself off in consequence. Sir Richard Airey[67] is going home, which I am sorry for, as one did get some business out of him, and General Barnard goes to the Second Division, instead of being Chief of Staff, which I am sorry for.

It was a great thing to be well with the great men, to keep down the insolence of the vulgar underlings. There is nothing that these will not do to annoy you and prick you out of the Crimea, in which they won't succeed, Deo volente [God willing].

Nicholaïeff will probably be the seat of next year's operations. But we must still hold this place.

ever yours dearest people
F.N.

Source: Letter to family, Wellcome (Claydon copy) Ms 8995/74

Castle Hospital
Balaclava
14 November 1855

The expedition to Kaffa is countermanded and Lothian remains here for the winter. I saw him today, looking and calling himself much better and in ten days he blows up the famous dockyards of Sebastopol, to replace all which city, with its fleet, as they were, would cost the Russians £300,000,000, three hundred millions, for fear you should not be able to count my noughts. Yet what is this to have done? after all. Far better have made Sebastopol a free port under our protection.

Lothian is probably Major by this time and is much disappointed not to have Kaffa and a colonelcy. . . .

Editor: Nightingale was proud of her cousin when he was promoted to Colonel: "I feel quite raised in the scale of creation by being the

66 General Codrington became Commander-in-Chief on Lord Raglan's death.
67 Sir Richard, later Lord Airey (1803-81).

cousin of a Colonel in the R[oyal] E[ngineers]."[68] The next Nightingale letter is to another Nicholson cousin, William Nicholson, from much later in life.

Source: Draft/letter/copy, Add Mss 45808 ff196-97

30 August 1888

My dear William [Nicholson]

We have grieved with you and for you all over the sad, sad trial which time cannot cure. Rather one feels it more every day and the sad and trying illness which went before it, but it must be some mournful comfort to you that it happened in your own house and that everything was done that could be done.

For his young wife it must be terrible indeed, and for his sisters. I think his was just the age when a father feels it most—it is not the darling little child snatched away that is the greatest loss, but the young man whose experience of his too-short past gives such promise for the future. Such a promising young officer, so zealous in his duties, so good for his men. But promise here will be fulfilled hereafter and perhaps he is with his mother now. *She* must form a large part to you of that future world, and now you have two there, two parts of your own life. May God bless and comfort you.

I am here now at Claydon with poor Parthe, who perhaps you know has been for the last six years a cruel sufferer and complete cripple from arthritis. I have not seen her so ill since 1883 [and] to this is now added a racking cough. She would have written if she could—she grieves for you. And I would have written before but that since I have been here I have scarcely been able to write even a pencil note.

But our hearts are with you in this sorrow, in which however there can be no bitterness, however deep the sadness. Fare you very well. One may pray that one may fare well in grief as in happiness, nay sometimes even better. Once more God speed you, for auld lang syne

ever your affectionate
Parthe and Florence

Me the sinner
In God's loving hands
O may my hands be loving too
To them.

---

68 Letter to Douglas Galton 31 July 1858, Add Mss 45759 f8.

Cousin Marianne (Nicholson) Galton and Douglas Galton

Editor: The correspondence here begins with adolescent enthusiasm, but the relationship was soured (as noted above) by Marianne Nicholson's opposition to Nightingale's becoming a nurse. Nicholson married Captain (later Sir) Douglas Galton, who became a close collaborator with Nightingale on War Office work, especially hospital construction and such favourite subjects as drainage, sewers and ventilation. The vast correspondence with him appears mainly in the war volumes and *Hospital Reform*, with messages to and about Marianne by the way. The correspondence here, after the early years, picks up again with family concerns, notably the ill health of their daughter, illness of their son-in-law, Cammillo Fenzi, and the death of a Fenzi granddaughter from bad sanitary conditions in their home in Florence. It ends with condolences on the death of and later reminiscences on Douglas Galton.

Source: Letter, Wellcome (Claydon copy) Ms 8991/88

Embley
19 February [1837]

My dear Marianne [Nicholson]

I cannot leave your numerous kind notices of your degenerate cousin without expressing my gratitude, notwithstanding the bewilderment of my brains between the noise of the elements without and the brats within. Alas! that the impossibility of expressing it viva voce at Waverley remains unchanged, as it would really do Mama a deal of good as she is rather worn and languid. But we hope now in a few days to welcome you to this den of past sickness and present iniquity which, although it be but a hut compared with your illustrious abode, is as desirous to be honoured with your presence. I use the language of the Betrothed, which we are now reading on account of its brevity. It is very pretty, however, do you know it? Pray express the same gratitude for their notice to your renowned brothers whom I shall never see again, and to whom I cannot write in terms so eloquent as I know you are capable of employing for me. Alas! for the local concerts, I read the Musical World assiduously. Au revoir my dear.

your affectionate
F.N.

I think the *revoir* so often put off and planned is now *really* coming to pass.

Lea Hurst, the Nightingale home in Derbyshire, as it now is, a nursing home. Photograph courtesy of RSAS Agecare.

Offered to Harriet Martineau, as a tiny token of ever living love & remembrance. from Florence Nightingale. London March 29/70

LETTICE LISLE.

BY

THE AUTHOR OF "STONE EDGE."

Lady Verney

WITH THREE ILLUSTRATIONS.

LONDON:

SMITH, ELDER & CO., 15, WATERLOO PLACE.

1870.

Nightingale's dedication of her sister's book to Harriet Martineau. By permission of the Houghton Library, Harvard University, EC85.M3663.Zz870V.

35 South St.
Park Lane W.   Jan 2/73

My dear Blanch
    I lit upon the Edit: of
Byron (without Don Juan) which
we wished for, both of us, for Arthur.
It was old, of course. — not dirty.
& I hope looks pretty smart,
now it is bound. —   There are
2 Vols. more than in our Edition —
— wh: may be trash.   Please
with draw any Vols: you like. — I
am not a good judge. —
Childe Harold, — the descriptions of
Greece in the Tale. Poems, — Chillon, —
& Manfred but ~~especially~~ above all
Manfred there is nothing like
it in the world. — especially
the last Scene. — The Spirit
there is really a spirit — the
only spirit out of Job &
Saul   The 'ghost' in Hamlet
is surely merely a very gross
unpleasant
dead = alive unburied man,
with the most vulgar full =
bodied sentiments, clamouring
for vengeance on his murderer,
(— not even so spirit- like as a
dying man-) quite unlike what his
Son describes him - a Thief & Impostor. I am sure going to take
Manfred, to my mind, stands   the spoons.
alone — & is the most spiritualized
view of immortality, of what
hell & heaven really are,
of any poetry in the world. —
One only wonders how Byron ever

wrote it —

I send "Edinburgh" for Thena
— but am really not sure that
it is the right book, after all.

I was so very sorry to hear
of your accident. I trust
it is right again —
    My love to children
                ever yours
                    FN.

Please show Arthur enclosed
Envelope   My address is
35 S. St.
    Park Lane   W.

Nightingale's letter to her cousin, Blanche (Smith) Clough. Courtesy of Archives of Balliol College, Oxford.

Nightingale portrait on the UK £10 note circulated in the 1970s.

Pedestal of Nightingale statue, Waterloo Place, London. Photo: Marilyn Greaves.

Nightingale statue, Waterloo Place, London. Photo: Marilyn Greaves.

Gravestone of Arthur Hugh Clough, Protestant Cemetery, Florence.
Photo: Jane Gerrior.

F. N.

BORN 12 MAY 1820.

DIED 13 AUGUST 1910.

Nightingale family gravestone, St Margaret of Antioch churchyard, East Wellow, Hampshire. Photo: Ronald Francis.

Untended grave of Samuel Shore Nightingale, St Margaret of Antioch church-yard, East Wellow, Hampshire. It reads: In memory of Samuel Shore Nightingale MRCS LRCP DPH elder son of William and Louisa Shore Nightingale, born 28 Nov. 1861, died 20th June 1925. It is a singular piece of wisdom to apprehend truly and without passion the work of God. Religio Medici. [Samuel Shore Nightingale and his brother, both unmarried, were the last to bear the Shore Nightingale name.] Photo: Mikhail Francis.

Source: Undated letter to Marianne Nicholson, Wellcome Ms 5483/75/1

I must write our welcome of your return to the natives, my dearest, though I dare say you have had many, and at the same time tell you how sorry I am not to have had the letters you wrote me from Berne, Milan, Frankfurt and especially that from Venice, which told us how you like Tipaldo and his little wife. But I have written to all the Directeurs des Postes to rate them soundly, and have sent lawyer's letters all round threatening rigorous prosecution, if the letters are not given up. It is the more provoking as Joanna Horner and others have had theirs *safe* and I am not sure that my case is not one of war, authorizing England to act immediately on the offensive.

The natural desire of food, interest in the human creature and manifested in your desire for a cook, was the first thing which apprised us of your landing, and again the old cover, lithographed to "Miss Nicholson, Waverley," comes forth from its second thousand.

Miss Clarke [Mme Mohl] left us, alas! at 7:00 A.M. this day, Lady Sitwell and Mr S. Wright ditto. Last week we had Major Jebb, Mr Weld, the Speaker, Sir D. Le Marchant, Baron Rolfe, the Mills, Mr Keith Mackenzie, etc. and much we missed your sweet presence, but you will, we hope, grace our neck this November. Miss Clarke was called off suddenly by a letter from her sister and nothing but the judicious arrangement of Parsons in carrying off the knives from the half past 6:00 o'clock breakfast would have preserved my life another moment after she drew off.

We have not the remotest conception where you have been since Milan and, therefore, I am shooting in the dark, but have a great deal to tell you when we have retied the thread between us. Meanwhile, I am sure, contrasting these pluviose scenes with those left behind you, you must long since have been asleep while I have been talking. The poor natives salute you and all yours. I mean to hold on tight to life till I hear from you, which will immediately transport me to a better world, till which time I am, in haste,

your ever humble slave

F.N.

Source: Letter, Wellcome (Claydon copy) Ms 8992/81

[spring 1845]

I hope my Geliebte [probably Marianne Nicholson] will have written today to say what she wants to come, her best gown, in course [corset?] and her gown à deux jupes [with two skirts], I suppose? and for the evening, the furniture to make her green entre-deux a white one? . . .

You do not want news, do you? Of news I have little, of wits I have none. Diplomacy and I have got off a dinner at Lord P[almerston]'s. Papa is gone to Broadlands[69] to shoot. Turnips is bad and *Cap* is better. Mama is busying herself in the destruction of the man whose dog was the death of our dog, and *beaters* is at supper. Health and wickedness reign in the parish and peace in our interior. Such is the aspect of our shore, should the second line be true, 'tis home but living home no more; it is because thou a merry devil art no longer in it. But wisdom flourishes, indeed is so overgrown, that soon where wisdom is in this house, no one else will be able to get in. And yet we are rather jolly I think too. And so farewell Geliebte. . . .

Source: Letter, ADD Mss 45759 ff58-59

Upper Terrace
Hampstead
8 September 1860

My dear Captain Galton

It occurred to me that perhaps you might like to send Gwendolen and her nurse here for a week. We have but one small room (now the little Cloughs are here) but it is airy. And Marianne might think (for "sanitary" reasons) it was better for her to be here than in town during the week which, I understood you, would elapse before they went to Lady Belper's. We would take care that the "Field Marshal" did not knock her down. If she came on Monday, we should be proud to receive her.

yours most truly

F. Nightingale

There are donkeys on the heath which form the ecstasy of the little Cloughs' existence, to ride on.

Source: Letter to Harry Verney, Wellcome (Claydon copy) Ms 9008/26

Ramsgate
1 March 1880

. . . Would you send to the Douglas Galtons for me and inquire after Gwendolen and say that I have been so entirely beaten down as to be unable to write to Mrs Douglas Galton about my dear mother?

yours affectionately and P.'s

ever F.N.

---

69 The Palmerston country home, near Embley.

Source: Unsigned letter to Douglas Galton, ADD Mss 45765 f52

Lea Hurst
Cromford, Derby
18 October 1881

. . . I hope that you left Evelyne's and the Fenzi affairs settled to your and her satisfaction. One would be sorry to hear that Commillo's energetic efforts on the path of Italian agriculture were to be cut short.

Are they to live henceforth in Florentine affairs? Yet a more lovely sojourn than Florence could hardly be. My heart always turns to her. . . . I hope Marianne and Gwendolen are pretty well. Are they in London? Please give them my best love.

Source: Letter to Douglas Galton, ADD Mss 45765 f160

10 South St.
6 July 1882

How grieved for the loss of the little Cammilla. I have her photograph before me—so robust, like an English child trying sturdily to do her duty in standing for her photograph as in anything else, not as if she were being looked at now laid low. How grieved for her parents, *not* for *her.*

I trust no one else has this dreaded diphtheria. Pray give my tenderest greetings to the parents, for my heart is "greeting" for them, as the Scotch say. Pray tell Marianne how much I feel it. . . .

Source: Letter to Douglas Galton, ADD Mss 45765 f162

Claydon House
12 July 1882

. . . How sad, how *very* sad and painful the dangerous illness of the father, so good a man, so great an improver (in which so much of the future of Tuscany and of Italy is bound up), following on the death of the darling little child, and Evelyne so exhausted with nursing. I trust that you have now good accounts of them both. I have only just heard through a kind, kind letter forwarded to me today from Marianne to Parthe. How terrible has been the anxiety.

There must be, one would think, some defect in the drainage of the house—*where* is their house in Florence? (Beautiful city, how *can* she have defects?) No doubt you will insist on this being looked to. I do indeed grieve with you on this sad and grievous history. My best love to Marianne and Gwendolen. . . .

Source: Letter to Marianne Galton, ADD Mss 45767 ff237-38

4 August 1889

. . . But what I write for now is to know how your dear self is and your precious eyes, and also how Lothian is and what you think of him and what the doctors think of him, and whether he is making, as all his "troops of friends" so earnestly pray, steady progress towards recovery. He must never think of working so hard again. But I trust this does not mean anything at all approaching to an invalid life.

Lady Nicholson has been good enough to write to me several times, but I do not like to trouble her too often. If you would kindly ask Miss Washbourne to give me news of you and of Lothian, and, believe me, with love to Gwendolen,

ever your affectionate

F. Nightingale

Excuse my "paw."

Source: Letter, ADD Mss 45767 ff240-41

[printed address] 10 South St.
Park Lane, W.
9 May 1896

Dearest Marianne [Galton]

I am grieved indeed that Sir Douglas is so poorly. Thank you very much for writing. I will try again in a "few days" as you give me leave. Please thank him very much for his kindness in sending me a copy of his able and interesting report on "Feeble-minded Children."

I have been corresponding with a lady at Manchester who is the leading spirit there of the "Health Visitors" and a Guardian besides (on the way to train our Bucks "Health Missioners"). She says the two great enemies of the poor are (1) overcrowding, (2) *personal* uncleanliness, that it is no use providing 6d baths 1½ miles off for poor mothers. They must have a penny day within a reasonable distance to take themselves and their little children to, at least once a week. The Manchester "Health Visitors" *sell soap.*

Do not say this to Sir Douglas, if you think it will worry him: Sir R. Rawlinson has again written to me on Hong Kong plague. He learns on good authority that in the last plague, two years ago, the corpses were either thrown into or washed into the sea, which produced an abominable nuisance (it was the same in Balaclava Harbour, which Sir R.R. himself put a stop to). . . .

Good health and God speed to you both.

ever your old Flo

Source: Incomplete, unsigned letter, ADD Mss 45767 f242

[1899]

This is a sad birthday, dearest Marianne, but let me send a few poor roses to say what words cannot say. There is so much to live for. I have lost so much, so much, in failures and disappointment as well as in grief. But do you know life is more precious to me now in my old age? I have rarely felt it precious. To do what little I can do to prevent or to attenuate mischief I am glad to be here.

How much you can do. How much for him you have lost in those he has left behind to you. I feel for you in his loss more than for anyone except his Mary, and yet three poor daughters and children. How you will help them.

May God be with you and He *is* with you.

The Smith Family

Uncle Sam and Aunt Mai Shore Smith

Editor: Many more letters to Uncle Sam and Aunt Mai will appear in other sections of this *Collected Works* (on war, nursing, *Theology* and *Suggestions for Thought*) and see the biographical sketch in Appendix A. The correspondence reported here deals with practical family matters. Uncle Sam had looked after the banking for Nightingale during the Crimean War and was involved in setting up the Nightingale Fund. Considerable correspondence on these financial matters is not included here; just enough has been selected to show the sort of reporting Nightingale had to do on the handling of her own personal finances. Samuel Smith was also involved in the preparation of Nightingale's first will (there would be several more).

The surviving correspondence with Aunt Mai, which follows that with Uncle Sam, is scant and does not do justice to the importance of their relationship. In early years the two saw each other frequently so that probably there was little occasion to write. Then, when Aunt Mai returned to her own home after looking after Nightingale in hers, there was ill feeling and few direct letters. There were strains in the relationship in any event, for Aunt Mai inherited the entailed estates from Nightingale's father, according to Peter Nightingale's will, for she had a son, Shore, and the Nightingales had only the two daughters.

The last letters in the set show a re-establishment of the intensity of the early relationship, including a return to discussing the moral government of God (more on which appears in *Suggestions for Thought*).

Source: Incomplete, unsigned letter probably to Parthenope Nightingale, Wellcome (Claydon copy) Ms 8992/5

[1840]

... Uncle Sam has bought me a *Dreissigjähriger Krieg* [Thirty Years War] to go on with here, as our whole German literature at Embley consists in a stage copy of the Fidelio. I thought it would not be unacceptable and I am to report regularly of progress to Bea [Beatrice Smith]. I am brimful of grammar and improve slowly in the herculean task of telling stories, much to the littlies' approbation. ...

Source: Letter, Wellcome (Claydon copy) Ms 8992/66

Wednesday [1844]

Uncle Sam [Smith]

You have the reluctant permission, but the undivided approbation of the Council of Three here sitting, to stop till next week. Parthe shines in macaroni, and I, in the sun's absence, play moon at housekeeping and schoolkeeping with much more brilliancy. I hope to goodness you will save your tooth.

With best love to dear Bab and her Mama, and dear Mother
yours longingly
F.N.

Source: Letter with envelope, ADD Mss 45792 ff68-70

6 November 1857
three years from Inkermann

Dear Uncle Sam [Smith]

I have thought often of what you said that I ought to make a will about that money, that Fund. I am sure I don't know how, and I think it would be much better left to the council. I know no one but Mrs Shaw Stewart who would do any good (or indeed anything but harm) with the money. She, I know, would not take it. I really believe that the way to do least harm would be to leave it to, say, St Thomas' Hospital, where the (very good) matron and the (very sensible) Resident Medical Officer, Mr Whitfield, have a great idea of raising the nurses, but cannot, because the treasurer won't give them the funds. It seems a pity that £40,000 should be going about begging when there are so many old and good institutions in want of funds. Please advise me. I don't see that I am called upon to make *any* will.

I assure you, though I behave like an infidel, that I am not without shame or without gratitude for my possession of your wife [then staying with Nightingale].

ever yours affectionately and gratefully

F. Nightingale

Source: Letter with envelope, ADD Mss 45792 ff71-75

30 Old Burlington St.
London, W.
11 November 1857

Dear Uncle Sam [Smith]

To tell you the truth, my share of the Fund, included in my father and mother's settlement, had slipped my memory. I quite agree that it should not be disposed of by my failure in making a will. I have, however, not the least idea of what it amounts to. If it were anything like £30,000 or £40,000 the thing I have principally at heart, which others could do as well as I, and without doing any harm, would be to build a barrack or to improve an existing one, according to my ideas, i.e., with day rooms for the men, separate places to sleep in, like Jebb's asylum at Fulham, lavatories, gymnastic places, reading rooms, etc., not forgetting the wives, but having a kind of model lodging house for the married men. Sir John McNeill, Mr Herbert and Dr Sutherland would best carry out any plan of this kind, and I would not tie them up in any way, but let them apply it to these purposes, whether in huts, old or new barracks, one or more, or in any place or country belonging to us, as far as the sum would go.

I should like to give a few hundreds to help Beatrice in the Lea Hurst or any other school, a few to Aunt Mai to publish her "Stuff,"[70] and a few to the Cloughs' children, if they have any, merely as a little present, not that it would be any worth to them. It would make no difference to the barrack, £2000 or £3000 more or less. This is really all I have to say. I take for granted that my mother, even if she survived my father, would have the enjoyment of the money till her death.

With regard to the Fund, I *have* in type a few suggestions as to the defects in hospital nursing, as a guide to the Fund supporters. In my evidence before the Herbert Commission there are some more definite hints as to *military* hospital nursing. Mrs Shaw Stewart and Mr

---

70 Nightingale called her own drafts of *Suggestions for Thought*, on which she worked with Aunt Mai, her "Stuff." Is this to suggest that her aunt had her own, distinctive manuscript?

Whitfield would be the best counsellors. Indeed, most of the suggestions (in type) are hers. Clough would be able to produce these at any time. They are entitled "private and confidential" and he superintended the printing of them.

Many, many thanks, dear Uncle Sam, for all you have done for me and believe me,

ever yours gratefully
Florence Nightingale

Source: Letter with envelope, ADD Mss 45792 ff77-78

London
29 June 1858

Dear Uncle Sam [Smith]

I wish you would give Clough and Blanche my £500 *now* and I had rather they should not say thank you.

I have been consulting the sanitary greater and lesser lights about the site for a house. It seems that a few hundred yards often make the difference of health or disease. If £500 would enable them to give £30 a year more for a house, it would be something. That difference in price often makes the difference in health. And for Blanche, who is unable to walk much, and who cannot keep a carriage, it is so peculiarly important.

ever yours gratefully
dear Uncle Sam
Florence Nightingale

Source: Letter/draft/copy, ADD Mss 45792 f80

[July or August 1858]

Dear Uncle Sam [Smith]

Clough really MUST take the £500. I wish I could buy them a house, but, as that can't be, a trifle like £500, dribbled out by £50 or £30 a year as long as it will last, to give themselves a better house, is, for the sake of health, really what they can't refuse. As for Clough being shy, if I could give him £10,000 a year it would be a poor acknowledgment of what he has done for us.

ever yours sincerely
F.N.

Source: Letter not in Nightingale's hand, ending and signature by Nightingale, ADD Mss 45792 f82

Great Malvern
9 February 1859

My dear Uncle Sam [Smith]

Thank you very much for your very kind letter. "Like a reasonable Christian" I have signed and re-enclosed the enclosed, because, first, I am not in a condition to fight and, secondly, if, as I hope, we get forward the soldiers' day-room scheme enough before I die (not that Sutherland has struck a stroke at it since I have been away) and a sum of, say, £1700 is wanted to start a specimen with, I can always repay the enclosed amount into Glyn's to make it up.

ever dear Uncle Sam
gratefully yours
Florence Nightingale

Source: Signed statement by Nightingale in lieu of will, ADD Mss 45795 f9

[ca. 20 April 1859]

I wish that all that comes to me upon my father and mother's death should go to A.H. Clough, with only this proviso that whatever he has had out of the Nightingale Fund should be repaid to it with compound interest.

F. Nightingale

Source: Signed statement written by A.H. Clough, initialed by Nightingale, ADD Mss 45795 ff10-11

Highgate
20 April 1859

I desire that the money which my uncle, Samuel Smith, has paid for the building of the school at Lea may be repaid to him or his heirs out of the money which would become mine at my father's death.

Florence Nightingale
[signed] A.H. Clough

I request my father to make a liberal present to Mary Bratby, to whom I have left something in my will, but desire this to be given in addition.

F.N.

20 April 1859

Written at her request and signed by her in my presence, in the sitting room upstairs at Highgate West Hill Lodge, on the night of the

20th April 1859, when she was suffering from severe illness, her father, aunt and Blanche being in the house.

A.H. Clough

Source: Letter/draft/copy, ADD Mss 45792 ff95-98

30 O. Burlington St.
11 August 1859

Dear Uncle Sam [Smith]

I think it is only fair that the 1/4 of the "entailed estates" which would come to me under the circumstances you mention should go to Shore's children in the way he would apportion it, if he could. And if there were none I think it had better go with the £26,000 under the same conditions and in the same way as the £26,000, namely to Clough, because I don't know anyone else who would be so likely to carry out the objects on which I should have spent it myself, if I had had it. At the same time I don't want *him*, Clough, to spend it *all* on those objects.

I hope and believe the "contingency" you mention is so very remote, speaking like a life insurance, that I don't trouble myself much to think about it. I don't speak about Beatrice's objects because she would have money to spend upon them if the same event which gave me mine gave her hers.

A thing came to my knowledge on Sunday which makes me think that John Sutherland, MD, should have £1000 out of the "£26,000." With all his faults he has worked hardest certainly at the Army matter. And Mr Herbert, like many another great man, has not considered this. At the same time I should like to consult you about this. If there will be much trouble in remaking or unmaking that blessed old will don't do it. (Mr Herbert told me on Sunday that he did not mean to do a thing for Sutherland, which I had *quite* understood was to be done.)

The soldiers' schools have been handed over to the Horse Guards, Lefroy tells me, and he has nothing more to do with them. So the fund at Glyn's, which I want to devote to furnishing soldiers' day rooms, will have to go to Galton and Sutherland alone. But I should like to have the power of handing it over by cheque or in any other feasible way at any moment to Galton and Sutherland.

yours affectionately and gratefully

F.N.

Source: Letter/draft/copy, ADD Mss 45792 ff134-35

[1861]

Dear Uncle Sam [Smith]

I think A.H.C. by no means well enough to return to work in a hurry. I have told him what I think, namely that he wants travelling, amusement, want of thought. I know that Blanche's condition makes difficulties, but they should be got over. It is difficult, without alarming a man too much (as they have done with Mr Herbert) to tell him how serious his case is.

I am certain that he ought to have now six weeks (best only a fortnight at each) at two or three different places with Blanche and the children, and then three months travelling abroad at Paris and in Greece, where he seems to have a fancy to go. I fear Blanche cannot go with him. I wish some man could; he ought not to travel alone. I have written to Blanche, but of course without alarming her. I hardly think she is at all aware that minor considerations must be postponed to his state.

F.N.

Source: Unsigned draft/copy, ADD Mss 45793 ff4-6

Fever-compelling Fury's
3 May 1862

Dear Uncle Sam [Smith]

What *are* missions for? Here have I been applying to the Earl of the "Syrian Missions Aid" Society and to the Baronet of the "Syrian Relief Fund" Society and to all the missions, Christian, Jew and infidel, both the above having had large parties at their own houses in Grosvenor Sq. and St. for the purpose to help poor Fliedner, who is the only person who has done any real good in Syria, and who has just paid £1000 and has immediately to pay [an]other £1500 for *his* mission schools at Beirut and Sidon, upon an income of three pence a year, and I cannot get a halfpenny for him. You don't know of any fishmonger missions do you?

I send him £25, which is all I can, and which he asks me to send him "either in banknotes or in a cheque on my banker." But, as I don't know what is safe, I send *you* the cheque and ask you to be so good as to settle how to send it. An Herrn Pastor Fliedner, Diakonissen Anstalt, Kaiserswerth-am-Rhein, Düsseldorf, via Ostend.

About my own affairs, I believe I must ask you to send me [an]other £60 for housekeeping and another £30 for other things. You must not think the last £60 are all gone in housekeeping: £22 went in six months' wages to two and one-half women. It was paid in quarters, but the first quarter I drew upon myself. Also I have paid the last instalment of whitewashing and cleaning (house) out of the last £60. Also I have had to buy a few things. The Fury (of dirt) had not left out even towels for her own servants! I believe they never used any in this house. Also, my doctor's fees still come very heavy, and these I have often paid out of my own money.

Source: Letter/draft/copy, ADD Mss 45793 ff13-15

18 January 1863

Dear Uncle Sam [Smith]

I have for some time wished to say, could I not relieve you of part of my money matters? Now that you are not well, that Parliamentary business presses, and that of course poor Blanche's affairs fall more heavily upon you [on her husband's death in 1861], it seems more urgent to urge it.

If you could tell me exactly how you do it, what board and lodging you refer (separately) to Papa, and how you draw and pay in the cheques, what items you refer to his yearly allowance to me, what that is, and how you pay in and draw the cheques, I am sure I could do it. Perhaps you would kindly get Glyn's and the joint stock bankbooks for me once more this year, as I have been obliged to draw rather heavily on both this Christmas. I want to see what is left.

Perhaps you would kindly keep on your protection of Robert, as I could not undertake to correspond with him. As for the rest, pray accept my warm thanks for all you have ever done for me and consider that it might be better for you now to let me try and do it (I have no intention of charging Hilary [Bonham Carter] or anyone else with it). I have signed the agreement for 4 Cleveland Row, £432 from 21 January for six months or £150 from 21 January to 7 April. It is a bad bargain, but Mrs Sutherland had seen forty-one houses for me! The house is (completely) newly done up, but it is too small.

ever yours gratefully
F.N.

... Thank you very much for your last "account" and letter, which you wrote here yourself. I was too ill even to reply verbally that day, but I had it on my mind to say this then.

Source: Letter/draft/copy, ADD Mss 45793 f16

4 Cleveland Row, S.W.
27 January 1863

Dear Uncle Sam [Smith]

I am so sorry to be worrying just now, but the account need be looked over, neither now nor never. I am afraid I must ask you for £60. You see the board is not more than usual, but Christmas bills have had to be paid.

yours ever gratefully
F.N.

Source: Letter/draft/copy, ADD Mss 45793 ff49-52

Oak Hill
Hampstead, N.W.
10 October 1864

Dear Uncle Sam [Smith]

I am in perplexity about my houses for a political reason (!), of which houses I have a great choice, thanks to good Mrs Sutherland. Could you tell me what the probabilities are next year of whether ministers will go out and when, and when the general election will be (there *must* be one next year, must there not?)

At our shop many think ministers will be out as soon as [the] session opens. In that case, will the general election probably be then? I can have 1 Bolton Row, (which is *stably* and quiet) for £400 a year for one year from 1 November, which, if I lived in it all the year, would be hardly £8 a week. I can have 27 Norfolk Street for six months (which is beautiful and noisy) from 1 November for 300 guineas, with a chance of staying on, though I suppose at an enormous price. I have made up my mind (almost) not to go to South St., as being too feeble to move in January, with the *additional* chance of being forced to go into a hotel (as two years out of the three I have been there). It is almost impossible, at least it is the very worst week in the year, to get a house for exactly the third week in January.

Please advise me. I should not like to find myself nailed to a whole summer in Bolton Row, when the business season is broken up by a general election, and I might come down here. Still less should I like to find my father nailed to paying an enormous price for Norfolk St., when everybody is out of town for the election.

Suppose the election should take place *after* the Easter recess, I believe Norfolk St. would then be the best thing I could do. For I should have it till 1 May, and then I should come down here (perhaps going to 115 Park St. for a few weeks in July). Each year I have hoped that the nature of the business would allow me to spend the summer out of London. I hope so this next year, but then I have always been disappointed. How long does it take before a Parliament re-assembles after a dissolution?

ever yours

F.N.

Source: Letter/draft/copy, ADD Mss 45793 ff58-59

Dear Uncle Sam [Smith]   3 February 1865

I am overcome with joy at your news of this morning.[71] It was very, very good of you to give it me. (Of course no one will hear of it through me.) No one [is] so capable of leading the single life with advantage to herself and her country as Beatrice. Yet I am glad it is not to be her lot. Glad, at least, that it *is* to be her lot that she can find someone worthy to share the work of God with her. I have the very highest opinion of Godfrey Lushington, chiefly, as you say, from A.H.C. I do believe, if anybody is worthy of Beatrice, he is. Yet it will take a great deal to convince me that any man *is* worthy of *her*.

I deplore the loss to Lea, to my father, to you all (though *you* will probably, and I hope, be nearer to her) to the "preaching" the "stuff," which last grief will make you laugh. But, for all that, though an old maid myself, and never having regretted my old maidenhood for one moment, I rejoice with exceeding great joy.[72] May God bless her, and God will bless her, and him too, and you too—is the wish of

ever yours gratefully

F.N.

I hope there is a little pecunia on his side.

---

71 The forthcoming marriage of Beatrice Smith to Godfrey Lushington.
72 An allusion to Matt 2:10.

Source: Letter, Wellcome (Claydon copy) Ms 9001/177

[printed address] 35 South Street
Park Lane
London, W.
[December 1865]

Dear Uncle Sam [Smith]

A thousand thanks for your kind letter of Thursday. I told Papa (at Lea Hurst) that I estimated the getting into this house at £200 including, of course, Humphrey's bill. I think it will be a little more.

Though I devote my life to getting in tradesmen's bills (having no maid with the least *nous*[73]) I am slow in getting them—I have paid Humphrey £139 odd. I have just got in the ironmonger's bill, £20 odd but I am afraid there will be another for about £30. I have paid a scourer and cleaner's bill. Every article (in the house) of furniture had to be cleaned. Not a coal scuttle would hold coals and so with everything. I suppose it is so with all, in buying a house, where there was absolutely no one to act on our side. But even I could hardly have anticipated that there was but one article in the whole house which has not required something done to it. Every cistern, tap, etc. was out of repair and has had to be done *since* I came in.

This is all I can say with exactitude at present and I don't at all wish to charge it all to Papa, if you think best not. Considering the enormous expense I am of to him, I should be quite satisfied to pay all above Humphrey's great bill, if you think fit. And about that there is no hurry. I have paid Clowser. Could you be so very good as to write a note for a chequebook for me to the London Joint Stock Bank, and send my messenger with it.

ever yours gratefully
F.N.

The replacing those kitchen scales alone cost £1.1.0.

Source: Undated letter to Parthenope Nightingale, Wellcome (Claydon copy) Ms 8992/133

[c1847]

. . . Aunt Mai never interested me so much—she makes more discoveries than Schiller. . . .

---

73 Greek for "mind."

Source: Letter/draft/copy, Add Mss 45793 ff203-04

35 South St., W.

16 April 1868

Private

Dearest Aunt Mai [Smith]

I have had a very kind note from Uncle Sam, telling me about quarterly payments, and asking me up to what date my father had paid the ground rent, etc., which I have answered. There *is* a point which has been in abeyance since I came into this house 2½ years ago, which Uncle Sam has desired me, very kindly, to settle several times, and which I should have settled this last winter, had it not been for his illness. I could not bear to trouble him. Then I felt that the least little worry would bring on his pain. You also said so. Now I ask you, rather than cause him any trouble whatsoever, to put this letter in the fire.

This is the reason why I ask you whether I shall ask him anything at all. The matter is this: when I came into this house (in 1865) he told me that my "father was to pay all the rates and taxes and the ground rent." Later (and indeed nearly every quarter) he (Uncle Sam) has desired me to *estimate* for the rates and taxes, to send *him* in the *estimate* and let him obtain it from my father. I never had the time to do this till I went to Malvern in January, when I made up the account of the rates and taxes for the past year, 1867, which I have now before me (and for that year only, not for 1866). I could not *estimate* for 1868, because this house, previously assessed at £200, was raised lately (from £200) to £300 (the inhabited house tax is 9d in the £). The property tax was raised last session from 4d in the £ to 5d. On paying my Lady Day taxes, I find that my rates and taxes *for 1868* will be more than twice as much what they were when I first came into this house.

Last autumn, when Uncle Sam was here, he again wrote me a very kind note (from the dining room) which I now have before me, saying: "W.E.N. must pay rates and taxes and the ground rent (£50 per annum). I will ask him for it thereafter." (Uncle Sam's illness was the reason why I did not send him in the account in January.)

I have paid all the rates and taxes since I came into this house, and everything, except one year's ground rent (£50) from Lady Day 1866 to Lady Day 1867, which my father paid himself, and which, when he was here two or three weeks ago, he reproached me rather severely with, as if wishing me to refund to *him*. I do not wish (or ask) to be repaid the rates and taxes I have paid (although I was promised them) *ever* since I came into the house, viz., for 1866 and part of 1865. But the account for 1867 I have now before me, made up as I was kindly invited to do by Uncle Sam, and also up to this Lady Day 1868. This I could send you at once, if desired.

I do not press for it. Indeed if it is decided that I am to pay everything I will gladly do so, but I should like it to be decided one way or other whether I am to pay the rates, taxes and ground rent or whether my father is to do so. It is quite beyond my enfeebled powers of body and mind to hear what he says to me (every time I see him now) about this house and his buying it for me. The most curious part of it is that I have never once brought this upon myself by asking him for the "rates and taxes and ground rent" (although he said that he was to pay them). What he says to me is entirely gratuitous. Nor, as you are aware, did I ever ask him to buy this house for me.

I admit that I have been so overwhelmed this winter and spring with cares and sorrows and overpowering increase of business that I have felt at times as if I could not go on with the little calls upon my time and attention which the assessments and other claims (of having a house) bring upon me, my father and brother-in-law never really taking the smallest business off my hands. In haste.

ever yours

F. Nightingale

Editor: The next letters concern Uncle Sam's final illness and death in 1880, complicated by Shore's serious illness at the same time.

Source: Letter to Parthenope Verney, Wellcome (Claydon copy) Ms 9008/93

27 October 1880

. . . You will hear that Uncle Sam is dying, painlessly and calmly. But neither Aunt Mai nor Shore, who will be heartbroken at not being able to be with him at the last, know *how* ill he is. (He is conscious; everyone is recognized by him.) Nor indeed does Aunt Mai know how ill Shore has been. It seems cruelly sad that the two illnesses should have been together. . . .

Source: Letter, Columbia University, Presbyterian Hospital School of Nursing C130

Lea Hurst

29 October 1880

My very dear Mary [Bratby]

I am sure that "Aunt Mai" would wish you to know that God is calling him whom you and Bratby cared for so long to Him home. On

Tuesday the 19th there was a great change; he had been particularly well up to that day. Mr Taylor thinks that it is only the failure of the vital powers hastened by the sudden change to sharp frost, but that there may have been a slight stroke.

He lies quite peacefully for the most part, now and then speaking to whichever is by him. At times he speaks just like himself. He is now too weak even to have his bed made except with him in it. He suffers only from occasional restlessness and then he sometimes wanders. He takes only liquid from a cup with a spout, milk with brandy or soup or a pounded rusk in milk or cocoa.

Yesterday they were to have a nurse from London. Hawkins has been most attentive and has a bed in his room. Ellen Gilson sits with him when one or other of the family is not there by him.

Mr Shore is distressed beyond measure at not being with him and them at the last, but it was quite impossible. His progress is very slow and he has often had drawbacks, alas! (I don't think his mother realizes how serious his illness has been.) . . .

always yours sincerely

F. Nightingale

He sometimes speaks to Mrs Smith quite like himself, which is a great comfort to her. Miss Julia Smith was at Embley with two friends but considerately left for Ravensbourne yesterday. She saw her brother while he was asleep.

Source: Letter, Private Collection of Hugh Small, copy Balliol College; draft/ copy Add Mss 52427 ff85-86

Claydon

5 August 1887

Dearest Aunt Mai [Smith]

Thinking of you always, grieved for your suffering, hoping that you have still to enjoy. In this month thirty-four years ago you lodged me at Harley St. And in this month thirty-one years ago you returned me to England from Scutari. And in this month thirty years ago the work of the first royal commission was finished. And since then thirty years of work often cut to pieces but never destroyed. God bless you.

In this month twenty-six years ago Sidney Herbert died, after five years of work for us. In this month twenty-four years ago the work of the second royal commission (Indian work) was finished. And in this month this year it seems all to have to be begun over again. In this month this year the work at St Thomas' Hospital seems all to have to be begun all over again, changing matrons after twenty-seven years.

And in this month this year my powers seem all to have failed and old age set in.

May the Father almighty, irresistible, for love is irresistible, whose work and none other's this is, conduct it always as He has done, while I have misconducted it. May He do *in* us what He would have us do. God bless you, dearest Aunt Mai, as ever,

your old loving

Flo

Parthe's powers are wonderful but she suffers much. Sir Harry ages.

Source: Letter, Private Collection of Hugh Small, copy Balliol College

16 January 1888
7:00 A.M.

Dearest Aunt Mai [Smith]

Your dear letters are the greatest pleasures of my life. I am thankful to hear from you and of you, that you can say with such noble calm what you say of yourself and of God, that "everyone of us is to be helped to desire with all our hearts to serve God's ends in that *His* vast organization." *That* is the great help. When I think that we have to begin all over again some things in our sanitary administration, I am appalled. But when I think of what you say, *that* is the truth. It is such a different thing if they are *our* "ends" or "God's ends" that we have "to serve," even though those "ends" are apparently the same. We so often behave as if we thought that it is God who is to "serve" *our* ends, and we call upon Him to do so, not we who are to serve *His*.

I do so like that phrase I have met with: that we may become even here "one with Omnipotence," that is with almighty Love. (I think that the gospel came to substitute love for zeal; the Pharisees were very zealous.) But it is not that "Omnipotence" is to serve us, but we who are to serve "Omnipotence," almighty Love, as you say, "with all our hearts." Then, if we are doing this, why should we fear? Why should we be appalled? We are "about our Father's business"[74] as the twelve-year-old Christ said, *not* He who is helping us about *our* business, but we whom our Father employs about *His*. That makes all the difference. So can we "rejoice evermore." Mary said, "Behold the handmaid of the Lord,"[75] and so have I said in my youth. But I have

---

74 An allusion to Luke 2:49.
75 Luke 1:38.

wandered far, travel-stained. Perhaps we sometimes think absolutely as if "the Lord" were to be our servant.

We are all "to be helped" to be His servants "in His vast organization," as you say, and to be His children "about our Father's business." We say "Our Father" many of us every day of our lives, but we should, in saying that, always say, as the hymn does:

Lord, make me from this hour
Thy loving child to be.

No, there is no "final farewell." May God be thanked for it.
    your loving, ever dearest, Aunt Mai
    old Flo

Source: Letter, Private Collection of Hugh Small, copy Balliol College

10 South Street
Park Lane, W.
25 May 1888

Dearest Aunt Mai [Smith]

I fear that the summer comes into you only through your windows, the summer sun and the summer flowers. But the beautiful flowers and greeneries you so kindly sent for the Probationers' annual meeting at St Thomas' gave the most unbounded pleasure. With these, so fresh and green from Embley, and with flowering plants, their rooms were decorated. . . . So it was a most successful meeting, I believe. The gentlemen speechified, much to the pleasure of the audience. All the sisters and nurses came in from the wards as they could be spared. There was a large gathering of old pupils. It was the first "function" under dear Miss Pringle, our new and anxious matron, quiet as a great general, which she is—whom the patients used to call twenty years ago, when she was sister of our male accident ward, aged twenty—"the little general"—you know she is very small. . . .

In the naval work lately, at Plymouth, two war boats were making the "trial of speed," and were unhappily racing. The boiler of one of them burst. There were seven men on board: five were prostrated and could not move, but the man who, as it turned out afterwards, was the man most badly hurt, crawled up on deck and turned off the steam, thus saving all the lives that were saved. They were so disabled that they could not navigate the boat to shore. But he with the help of one other man managed to navigate the boat so as to reach the nearest vessel, to have food and cordials for the five prostrate ones, himself remaining without, and to take men on board from her to bring them to the naval hospital on shore, whose matron is one of ours. They arrived at 6:00 P.M. When they arrived he was almost in a state of collapse, but he *would* have the five attended to first. She poured beef tea down his throat—everything was done that could be done. He died that night, asking to his last moment how the five were. (He was scalded from head to foot. The accident happened at 11 A.M.) What heroism there is in the world.

What a hero is the German emperor. What a Greek tragedy might be written on the German Empire—a trilogy: the first part on the old emperor, the second on *this* good man, the third, and oh what a nemesis it will be, on the present crown prince, neither good nor gracious.[76]

Thank you so much for the beautiful rhododendrons so kindly sent me in early May. I have made them live till now.

Love to all. Sam [Shore Nightingale] is working *very* hard at St Bartholomew's. Rosalind went as delegate, after her visit to Cambridge, as you probably know, to the Co-operative Congress at Dewsbury. She has written a very good co-operative leaflet, which is published, and has translated some Michelangelo sonnets which my father was so fond of. *Not* printed, of course.

It was not for want of work that Louis lost the House of Commons clerkship, which you got for him. But there was really no time.

ever dearest Aunt Mai
your loving old Flo

Source: Letter, Private Collection of Hugh Small, copy Balliol College

10 South St.
30 July 1888

Ever dearest Aunt Mai [Mary Shore Smith]

Always I am thinking of you, but I have so much and such anxious writing to do, as your kindness well knows, especially now that we have a new viceroy for India and our new matron, St Thomas', Miss Pringle, at least only nine months old, that I cannot write my thoughts.

---

76 Later Kaiser Wilhelm II (1859-1941), declared war on England and abdicated at the end of World War I.

Have you seen *Gordon in Africa*?[77] I send it. I dare say the middle part is commonplace. I have not read it, but what speaks to me is the beginning and the end.

P. 18 "And do we question: 'Shall the end be thus?' " to the end;

the ceaseless strain
the songs of sorrow, hope,* doubt, fear and pain
Who guide us and reveal to mortal sight
The soul's Ideal on the heavenly height x x

*For "hope" read *trust* or faith, you will say.

I think we try too much to chase away "doubt" and "fear" as enemies, whereas they are stepping-stones, "guides" to truth, the "Ideal," love. Not *abject* "fear" but the old forefathers' phrase, the "fear of God." Don't we repudiate too much these rather tiresome guides?

I have so much to hear and to say. I hope to write again.

I have been reading in two or three places lately that, "however our own frames may change, or our powers of comprehension vary, He remains the same yesterday, today and forever."[78] It is an old truth, but it is a great comfort to me to be constantly reminded of it. God bless you, ever, dearest Aunt Mai.

your loving old
Flo

Source: Letter, Private Collection of Hugh Small, copy Balliol College

Claydon House
Winslow, Bucks
7 September 1888

Let me say, dearest Aunt Mai, what I cannot say, how much I am always with you, especially during the last month, in spirit. On 12 August I was with you all the day remembering how thirty-five years ago you brought me up to Harley St. On 7 August how you brought me back to Lea Hurst thirty-two years ago.

God bless you and He does bless you. Fare you very well, as we may say in sorrow and in care as in joy, perhaps more. But I always try to remember how you said that we must not be so *impudent* as to usurp the care and responsibility which are God's. Anxiety is impertinent you said. And it is *God's* past and not our own, and no doubt it is God's *future* and not our own.

---

77 A long poem by Arthur Waugh, *Gordon in Africa*.
78 A paraphrase of Heb 13:8.

I have but a very, very poor account to give of Parthe, but her courage is unfailing. I must stop now.

ever your old

Flo

Source: Letter, Private Collection of Hugh Small, copy Balliol College

[printed address] 10 South Street
Park Lane, W.
6 November 1888

Dearest Aunt Mai [Smith]

I think of you always, but my failing strength has been so pressed and is so still by the new viceroy going out to India. (This is the eighth viceroy since I began work at the India Office. Sir John Lawrence was the second.) Lord Lansdowne is extremely favourable to our objects and so is his wife, in her way, to Lady Dufferin's objects. But we are come to a "mauvais pas." And there is the Army Sanitary Commission to be reorganized. You know that Dr Sutherland has retired, and took no part for many months before his retirement. . . .

Here is how we start, and we have no one of weight on our side to fight our battle, the excellent W.H. Smith,[79] who was war minister and would have done it, having been taken away from the War Office, which no one but he could do to lead the House of Commons, which no one can do. Still we are in the lifeboat, and may steer through.

Sometimes, though not so often as I used, I am base enough to wish I had not lived to see this—but then I remember how you say: "it is a poor way to live, to wish it were over." And I cry, like Joshua, Be not dismayed.[80] I mean to write more another day to one of whom I am always thinking, if I may. My love to Blanche, and to those who are with you. I have not been able to see Arthur and Sam since I came back and they came back, but I shall.

God bless you and He *will* bless you, as you used to say, dearest Aunt Mai,

ever your loving
old Flo

---

79 W.H. Smith (1825-91), a liberal-conservative MP who took up social causes, served in various Cabinet posts, including secretary of state for war and first lord of the Admiralty (when he was satirized in Gilbert and Sullivan's *HMS Pinafore*).
80 A paraphrase of Josh 1:9.

Source: Letter, Private Collection of Hugh Small, copy Balliol College

10 South St.
New Year's Day 1889

Dearest, ever dearest Aunt Mai [Smith]

I do wish you a blessed New Year, as I am sure you wish me. The little book I send reminds me so much of things you used to say. These lines on the other side were written, I believe, by Lady Aberdeen, on a portfolio which came from her as a New Year's gift to my lady secretary (for I am now a miserable!? old woman with a typewriter).

"Let every dawn of morning be to you as the beginning of life, and every setting sun as its close, then let every one of these short lives leave its sure record of some kindly thing done for others, some goodly strength or knowledge gained for yourself."

The first two lines especially I thought you would like, the latter lines you do not need. My temptation is, I feel, to look too far ahead. Let me thank you for the pheasants, which come in so handy now, for the continual stream of sand which I always thank you for in my heart, and for the great pleasure your beautiful evergreens have given. Forever may God bless you.

ever dearest Aunt Mai
your loving old Flo

Source: Letter of Arthur Clough to Nightingale, Boston University 5/21

[printed address] Embley
Romsey
Wednesday [16 January 1889]

Dear Aunt Florence

I hope it will not last very long now. She lies with her eyes closed, coughing a good deal and finding it difficult to breathe. She has hardly spoken since Monday morning and could scarcely now make herself understood. They think however that she knows people a little when they speak to her, but she hardly opens her eyes.

Mr Taylor says she cannot live through the night. One can only wish that she had been spared the last few days, incessant restlessness and discomfort and choking. They are all here.

You will have heard that I went off yesterday by an earlier train and so missed your books. They came however by this morning's post, but I am afraid they have now nearly given up reading to her, for the last day or two.

your affectionate
A.H.C.

Source: Memorial to Aunt Mai, ADD Mss 45793 f225

Farewell, farewell, our dearest friend
And it does fare well with thee
O lovely, loving soul
O humble mind of high & holy thought
gone home unto thy Maker
unto the high & lofty One that inhabiteth eternity
in the high & holy place
that dwelleth within them also that are
of a humble & contrite spirit
to thy blessed memory this cross & crown
Mary Smith
Florence Nightingale
17 January 1889

Cousin William Shore Smith

Editor: There is only a modest surviving correspondence with "my boy Shore," but this includes some of the most interesting and revealing letters of the entire collection. One reports a dream; others discuss Nightingale and Shore's respective missions in life, the nature of angels, Greek literature, science and family responsibilities. Eleven years her junior, Shore was Nightingale's double cousin and heir to the Nightingale fortune. From childhood on he was for her more like a beloved younger brother than a cousin, and indeed he assumed the role of son to Frances Nightingale in her old age. Nightingale and Shore saw each other frequently, at Embley and Lea Hurst when they were children, and later when Shore inherited the estates and took Mrs Nightingale into his home in London, precluding the need for letters for lengthy periods. The letters below show how fond and how anxious Nightingale was for her cousin's welfare (in body, mind and soul), as does much correspondence about him not reported here. In 1845 Aunt Mai suggested to Nightingale's mother that Nightingale might take on Shore's education, "carte blanche, to teach him mathematics, algebra, trigonometry, astronomy, German . . . wishing however to let no stitch drop of his classics."[81] Evidently Nightingale did do some tutoring as the first letter shows.

Correspondence after he inherited the estates takes up business matters, notably coffee rooms around Lea Hurst and the local school.

---

81 Letter of Mary Shore Smith to Frances Nightingale 1845?, Wellcome (Claydon copy) Ms 9038/35.

Nightingale was evidently well aware, later in life, of the financial difficulties of maintaining Lea Hurst and Embley (Shore had to let Embley for extended periods; it was sold in 1896, after his death). She took great care to make his time at Lea Hurst as enjoyable as possible, aware of his negative feelings about it. A letter she wrote to Harry Verney tellingly states that "the only way of tempting Shore to Lea Hurst will be my being there. And I should be there some time before him to do some business."[82] Letters to Shore and Louisa in the 1870s on Bosnian refugee relief, on which all three worked with Paulina Irby, are in *Society and Politics*, as is an early letter on Derby elections and one on Siberian anthropology; letters regarding Italian politics appear in *European Travels*.

Source: Letter, Wellcome (Claydon copy) Ms 8992/72

Friday [1843-45]

My dearest [her sister or a cousin?]

... Shore and I potter a little at *simple* mathematics ... but as he is very languid, I do not use the rack and thumbscrew *much*. I am reading Undine[83] to him, at his own desire, as he began it in English at home. But I am obliged, like Pellico, when I come to certain canticles, to substitute some high moral sentiments of my own, of which he then requires to have the German respectively pointed out to him word for word, so that "singular instances of presence of mind" is constantly exhibited every night on my stage. But as it *is*, my dear, I am always standing on my head in convulsions for fear of being a forcing pit to his hothouse feelings. When we came to Hildebrand's unkindness to Undine, he wrapt me up, he held my head in his hands, he put out his arms as if to protect me from any imaginary evil and to say that such hard hearts should never come here, during which I remain as stern as a post and attentively look out in the dictionary, Lästigkeit [troublesomeness], a cosine, Bewegnung [movement], the use of the globes. Hildebrand showed Bertaldu a perfect use of the globes.

I suppose, beloved, it will now be many days before we see you. ...

ever thine

F.N.

___

82 Letter to Harry Verney 7 September 1881, Wellcome (Claydon copy) Ms 9008/174.

83 Undine was a sylph who married and received a soul, but caused great consternation to her family and eventually the death of her husband, in Friedrich de la Motte Fouqué, *Undine*, 1811.

Source: Incomplete, unsigned letter probably to Hilary Bonham Carter, Well-come (Claydon copy) Ms 8992/68

[1844]

. . . Shore too is gone today, but I cannot write about that. How is it, my dear, that the intercourse between boys seems always to bring out all the evil and none of the good. I think, if this were discussed, it would bring out a great deal that is useful, but it is as impossible to ask the question as it is to ask anything about inspiration. When you inquire with a cordial and sincere desire to know what people think of it, they answer, Oh then you don't believe the Bible, in one case, and in the other, Oh then you think you can keep boys in cells like nuns and that I can tell you, young lady, can't be. I do so wish I could know other people's observations on the subject, but they never will give them. If the physician does not know the cause of the disease, he gropes about in the dark, and does great damage. People say rightly, you cannot bring up a boy in a cell, and why will not they examine then *what* the cause of the harm is. I could torture them, as Nero tortured Caesonia,[84] to make her say why he loved her. The Bible never blinks the question but, with its usual daring, boldly declares at the risk of all misrepresentation how dangerous "the world" is. Now why does (not only *bad* company) but *all* company seem to call out mostly the bad in young people?

My dear, Hughie [Bonham Carter] is charming, and I love him already de toute mon âme [with all my soul]. He does and thinks and says many things I wish my boy [Shore] did, and I was quite touched by his joy and tenderness this morning when it was settled he was to stay.

Well, my dear, from the moment he came, Shore was méconnaissable [unrecognizable], I did not know what was become of him, everything was forgot, everything neglected, even his prayers. Oh is it possible that the happier we are, the less we wish to think of Him, the giver. Everything was altered, even his voice, for his voice to Hugh was like a bulldog's and his manner to him so coarse and untender. And, curious! since Hughie has been here, Shore has used a word which I never heard him use before, and which Hughie did not use. My dear, there was nothing left of him! Now is not this an anomaly? and one which ought to excite our *curiosity* if *nothing* better. Little pieces of self-ishness and temper came out, which I had no idea of and I saw Aunt

---

84 Roman Emperor Nero tortured his wife, Caesonia.

Joanna was in a constant state of uneasiness and irritation. I doubt too whether they make one another happy; they did not seem to do so.

I doubt that it is all up about our going to London. I cared less about it, because I hoped to the last to have kept my lad, but he is gone and gone, I am afraid, not to a better place; he seems to me to get so little at Mr King's[85] and to be so far from happy there and his mother wrote her desire that he should stay here.

It seems my fate to be always not exactly the Boys' Own Girl, but the Boys' Own Grandmother. Here is another individual come to be not *coach*ed but *cart*ed, but it is anything but my "adjustment" to look down, though it has been my fate all my life to have a junior. One feels such a constant inclination to look up, that we idealize for the sake of being able to regarder au plafond [look up], even where the qualities are not there. We have such an unconquerable desire to be led that it seems to me the measure of happiness is the measure of admiration one feels for those with whom one lives. How happy Aunt Jane is, for instance. I do not think we can love downwards, when the soul is below one's own, I mean. If we raise it, it is our own work; we may love our own work, but we are no longer prostrate before the accomplished being, the ideal which God had created for us.

What an anxious future Shore's is. I never felt it so much in parting with him. He is all impulse, and though all his impulses are good, God seems to have ordained that all greatness, moral or otherwise, all characters, should be built up of habits *and* not of impulses. A man without a shadow fares badly, but a man without a conscience, how fares he the while? Shore is still all the child in his total imprévoyance [lack of foresight], the child without care for the morrow which it does not look forward to, without regrets for the past which it does not remember, the child without anxieties, without melancholy, without repentance, always ready to leave a vexing thought to look for a new happiness. And yet, my dear, do you know es schändet mich [it makes me ashamed] to go and dig, after awakening that conscience, lest it should drag these feelings after it, to try and light that little rush light within, which sometimes becomes such a consuming fire afterwards, always, unless it grows into a warmth-giving sun.

One does so respect happiness here, where are so many suffering hearts, that it seems too sacred a thing to touch, unless one can be sure of their having instead of happiness, finding blessedness, the blessed-

---

85 Shore boarded at Dr W. King's, Montpellier Rd., Brighton.

ness of the poor in spirit. We are so apt to substitute blessed are the *strong in heart* for blessed are the p[oo]r in spirit.[86] Oh if I could but think that the link between the infinite Spirit and the finite was established in him, that he could find constant comfort in the society of God and strength, that *that* Jacob's ladder[87] was his (so seldom raised by us till solitude, suffering and disappointment have built it for us) down which the invisible Consoler descends and communicates with His children and angels come and minister to them. It is all my hope, all my desire for him, or he will learn to know the day which so many of us have known, when we say, there is but One who can do that for me, but I do not know Him. Oh how I have felt with poor Esau and cried with a great and exceeding bitter cry: Bless me, even me, also, O my father,[88] but he never has. Shore has religious emotions, but not the deliberate religious feeling. Oh how is he to make the acquaintance with God which is so necessary; he has the *poetical*, but not the *intimate* feeling towards Him.

The shadows, which present to our spirits the things we know but too certainly to be true, but it is a melancholy thing, piling together miscellaneous experience for oneself. The discernment of better knowledge should protect us from despair at the error, but on the limit between the discerning of the new knowledge and the despair at the mistake, the soul dies. There are but three sorrows which excite the sympathy of mankind, and all other sufferings are classed under the one great head, *imaginary*, but do not you believe that, when the secrets of all hearts shall be open, when shall be known all that may be borne and never told by hundreds, with whom we have been living cheek by jowl all our lives, that the remorse, the anxiety, the irritation, the shame and the doubt of human beings will be found to be the [Bremer's illeg] sword in the scale, Vae victis [woe to the defeated], and the other weights to be the false ones.

Have not wiser men than we believed that, in the future state of suffering, none but these "imaginary" evils will be used, no calamity of circumstances employed as punishment, but the mind only left to work out its own misery? And will the world then sit down and coldly and judgmatically pronounce the sufferings of this future state to be fancy? What does our whole life consist in? In ideas, in the meaning

---

86 An allusion to Matt 5:3.
87 An allusion to Gen 28:12.
88 Gen 27:34.

which we give to things. This is so, even in those who live the most in the brilliant realities which surround them. We make our ideas our household gods, and carry them out of burning Troy through the forty years wandering in the wilderness of Sinai. We live for them, die for them, die of them. George Forster died of a broken heart, because his ideas were not answered, as he expected, by the French Revolution. Charles V laid down the crown of the world for the same reason.[89] When we give up our ideas, we confess that our tree of life was rotten. Where we had found shade, there is nothing left but a desert, a naked spot, where had been the singing of birds in the branches. And shall the tree of knowledge of good and of evil[90] console us for this?

What is life? It cannot be merely a gaining of experience; it is freedom, voluntary force, free will and therefore must be a hard-fought battle in order to make a choice. There must be evil and good to choose from. I sometimes think, too, that we may be expiating in this life the sins of a previous existence, that the disgusts and weariness some people feel may be the natural and inevitable consequence of a reckless ministering, in some previous state, to the morbid cravings of the heart for excitement. Is there anything so very fantastical in this? We look forward to it, in our next state, push the process one step back, and some of us may be in one of our "next states" already. We talk of another world and are not considered dreamers; this is another world to the stars. In our next, it will perhaps be considered as fanciful as in this, to be imagining a previous existence.

But I must stop because it is a shame to send so much scribbling. I should have sent some yesterday, but what with cutting up Turkey carpet for Shore's flies, and with the boys damming up the stream, I really had not a moment even to send the worsteds, I have not a very clear idea of what amber is. I wrote, as you desired me, to Louisa Mackenzie one night, from ten to twelve pages of Moral Reflections adapted to the Use of *Cheerful* Youth, and have had a most melancholy answer. There is a great deal of illness and suffering about just now, and I was pleased the day before yesterday when Shore and I made a round, to see how much interest he took.

I hope, my dear, you will not think that I am sorry to have Hugh, because really I am very glad to make an alliance with him. He is very

---

89 Charles V (1500-58), Holy Roman Emperor, abdicated his claims to the Netherlands and Spain in favour of his son and brother respectively.
90 An allusion to Gen 2:17.

charming, but you know how difficult it is to me to turn the channel of my affections. They run sluggishly, but otherwise I am sure Hugh and I will be very happy together. It is frightful to think how much better one can always express a slight impression than an intense one. And in the same way, I am sure, that if our affections were matters of tariff, which were calculated by the rule of three at their worth, we should take the moderate much better than the exclusive affections, which give much less happiness, and alas! are generally a torment to both sides. For an exclusive devotion serves neither him who gives nor him who takes. The one always bears with difficulty the obligation, the other rarely forgives its being ill-returned.

Ah it is terrible to think how little a violent feeling does good when a look casts one down, and a word raises one. But still I believe at the end of one's life one blesses God for having been able to devote it to another love than that of oneself. A soul, which should be pure and devoted enough to love without the need of being loved, must be happy. And that I believe, my dear, is the secret of your happiness. How true it is that our own imaginations are the real world we live in, and the world about us but a vision, our occupations [breaks off]

Source: Incomplete, unsigned letter, Wellcome (Claydon copy) Ms 8992/76

Saturday 8 February 1845

My dearest [Parthenope Nightingale]

Shore is come and when I look at his pale thin face, I feel a little foreboding at my heart, but when I hear his cheerful voice and spirit full of interests, I think that a spirit once born into the world can never be lost to us. Once make a tie with it and it can never be broken, and it does not much signify where it is then. . . .

Source: Letter to William Shore Smith, ADD Mss 46176 f3

We were in Henry's den in Lincoln's Inn some days ago—such a perfume of sanctity! I felt less of a reprobate every moment I stayed there, but law, I believe, is the only thing to soften the heart and strengthen the affections. I go a good deal to see a friend of mine who married a lawyer, who as yet gets no law. She lives on four little pork chops in a house like a very clean hackney coach upside down, the only furniture in her bedroom two little plaster cherubs hung up aloft by their waists to keep watch for the soul of poor Jack. All the flowers of virtue flourish there, law having planted and poverty watered them. . . .

Source: Letter, ADD Mss 46176 ff5-6

Tuesday
[21 April 1846]

Dearest [William Shore Smith]

I have only time to send you a paper of the eclipse, which please return. I have bought pieces of green- and red-coloured glass to look through, as I think glass which one smokes oneself never answers. I advise you to do the same. Which part of the eclipse, as the paper recommends, do you mean to observe? The "beads" which are mentioned in the paper mean that some astronomers have thought that the edge of the sun, as seen beyond the moon, just before the annulus becomes complete, was not a continuous line but a series of beads. Thus [diagram of four beads curved] this you are desired carefully to observe. We shall be in a capital position at Embley (where we go home on Friday) for seeing the annulus. What a sell [disappointment of high expectations] it will be if the morning is one like this!

Anybody's observations upon this are so valuable that, if you will write yours down, I will forward them to Professor Powell, the man who drew up the enclosed paper, and who begged that any might be sent him. In great haste

thine ever
F.N.

Source: Letter, ADD Mss 46176 f7

Embley
29 April [1846]

Dearest [William Shore Smith]

I present thee a little birthday offering on the knees of my heart, but, as I have written thee a long letter, thou shalt not have here four pages more of this "gong and cymbal" work, only the dearest wishes of

thy old Bos

Source: Letter, ADD Mss 46176 ff8-9

Embley
15 May [1846]

My dearest lad [William Shore Smith]

It seems to me long since I have written to thee, but not the less have I thought of thee. Thy mother is with us now, so will thy father be tonight. Our two little cherubs, Edith and Gertrude, thrive, though as, upon consulting the "Hebrew Greek," we find *cherubim* to mean *knowing ones* or fullness of knowledge it may be doubted whether *my* cherub (big one or little one) according to strict etymology, can be called or entitled by the term of a knowing one. Nature, who has provided all other animals with the talent of self-preservation, cats with claws, and us with thick sculls, has allowed my animals to indulge in all sorts of saltatory exhibitions, leaving to me the entire care of the Vital Spark during the same, and baby is covered with bruises, in all the stages of black and blue.

Never trouble yourself about writing to me, my dear friend, when you don't want to. I never measure the extent of your love by the number of the envelopes which come through the Romsey Post Office— that would be weighing it by grains or rather SCRUPLES (which last weight was invented by the apprentice of the great druggist Satan).

I look upon love as the gift of a God of Love, the *free* gift, and consequently can neither have the feeling that it is mine by right, nor any weak distrust, that such happiness *can* be meant for *me*, because the gift is always measured by the substance of the Giver, not of the receiver. One ought not even to look the gift horse in the mouth.

But when a letter does come, it is always very welcome from thee. I rise while it is yet night, as friend Bathsheba evidently did, by her son's account, put on my hunting pink and boots, and gallop downstairs to be in at the death, i.e., the bagging or rather the unbagging of the fox, the letters. But as the maids are generally dusting (according to the true meaning of the term, *covering* with dust) I am obliged to remain in the passages, where, if discovered, I appear to be attentively engaged in observing the habits of the flies upon the ceiling, till the solemn procession of butler and bag emerges from the Penetralia [inner shrine], when I capture my part of the spoil and rush out of doors with it, singing an ode in honour of Mercury, the god of letters, till the time for breakfast-making arrives, when the goddess of keys, that's me, re-appears. (A procession of one, a term not generally employed by Johnson, but everybody knows that a well-bred butler is an *embodied* procession of one, as much as the schoolboy who split himself trying to walk two and two to church in the holidays.)

How does chemistry and Co. get on? Or do you say:

Astronome
It puzzles me
And Optics drive me mad;
Mensuration
Is vexation.
But *all* science is as bad.

I should think, dearest, that the unfolding angel in you, in *1946*, may have attained that most beautiful ideal of a light heart in a serious mind, perhaps even in this world it may. There is a most lovely character given of d'Alembert's,[91] the great mathematician's, light-heartedness, which I will show you some day. It says that it is the exclusive privilege of the exact sciences to enjoy everyday some new truth which comes to reward one's work.

Teazer [a dog] sends his love. He has made a bargain with a great jack hare, who promenades slowly up and down the terrace, that if it'll let him alone, he won't hunt it. But I must have done with all this "cymbal and gong" work, reaching through two sheets, as it does, or I shall not be alive to "*rite my own tail*" and with best love to Hughie, am ever

thy old Bos

Source: Letter, ADD Mss 46176 ff10-11

Embley
Wednesday [27 May 1846]

My dearest mannie [William Shore Smith]

Very glad was I to see the sight of thy hand again. I read thy little scratch by the rose garden, on a morning with its lights and smells and warm breath, such as one can never forget. But letters are to me lovelier than the breath of the roses, than the song of the winds, more kindly than the freshness of the dew, than the light of heaven, for they are to me like the spirits of my loves.

The babs [babies] left us this morning and we are now a very small party. Lady D'Oyley, a very nice old lady, who has lived all her life in India, and is full of curious stories about the Indian begums, and curious drawings she made herself, that is, all the drawings she was allowed to make but she knew the wife of Tippoo Saib (the widow, I mean) ninety-six years of age, and *she* would not let her take her portrait, because, she said, some man might see it. And if any man could say that he had seen the face of the wife of Tippoo Sultan, what an eternal disgrace to her. Even the patterns of costumes, which Lady D. begged from some of the Indian princesses, were sent to her sewn up in TWO silk bags, lest any man should peep at them, and under a solemn vow from her that they never should be seen by mortal (male) eye.

---

91 Jean le Rond d'Alembert (1717-83), co-editor of the *Encyclopédie*.

I am very sorry you do not like Mr Sortain [?]. I think that sort of preaching is disagreeable, too, but still one gets new ideas from any sort, so that I do not much mind. I have been trying to find out lately all the Bible tells us about angels, and there is a good deal, much more than I thought. It calls them ζῷα (living ones) which we choose to translate *beasts*!![92] In the Revelations, seraphim (burning ones), cherubim (knowing ones), morning stars[93] θρόνοι κυριότητες ἀρχαὶ δυνάμεις ἐξουσίαι.[94]

I was rather amused at one sermon I was reading about them, where the preacher calculated the angelic pace at so many miles an hour by Gabriel's journey to Daniel (chapter 9[95]) he boiled a gallop, you see, which brought him from the terminus in the supreme heaven to this earth *between* the *beginning* and the *end* of Daniel's prayer. It was active certainly, the pace was good, but is that all Gabriel's engine can do, simmering along at a few million miles a second? And can we ask *where* a spirit is at all? Can we speak of the migration of a spirit at all? All that we can say of a mind, is it not rather that it has laid down one system of relations to the external world and taken up another? All the *where* we can speak of is of the system of relations it has here—it is as easy to conceive the hand obeying the volition of a mind at the moon as of a mind in the head.

When I speak of the *where* of this very obstinate iron pen, I can say that it is bounded on the east by my cold finger, on the west by my very stiff thumb, on the south by this aggravating paper, on the north by the immediate contact of my nose, and that I trust it will very speedily be bounded on all sides by its box. But how can I do this of a spirit? *It* cannot touch anything—it has no *where*—the question is absurd.

---

92 The King James version indeed translates Rev 4:6, 8, etc. "beasts"; later revised versions use "living creatures."

93 Rev 22:16 "I Jesus have sent mine angel to testify unto you these things in the churches. I am the root and the offspring of David, and the bright and morning stars."

94 Nightingale seems to be joining together verses from Romans and Colossians, that neither "death, nor life, nor angels, nor principalities, nor powers . . . " could separate us from the love of God in Christ (Rom 8:38-39), and that all things were in Christ "whether thrones, or dominions, or principalities, or powers . . . " (Col 1:16).

95 In Dan 9:22 Daniel was praying when Gabriel, whom he had seen before in a vision, "being caused to fly swiftly," told him he had come to give him "skill and understanding."

I remember Lady Catherine Long saying once, that there is a moment when you must be in the room with a spirit, viz., at the instant of death, when it leaves the body. I turned my tongue seven times round in my mouth and said to my left-hand cheek, it is plain she thinks a spirit is a thin white ethereal pinafore, which slips off and flies up from the bed through a neat slit in the ceiling and goes—she does not know where—when it is *out of* the body. But can she tell me *where* the spirit was when it *was in* the body (as she thinks) or anything about it excepting its system of senses and relations, by which it makes itself manifest? Gabriel, it strikes me, needed no celestial railroad. I have no reason for saying he is not here at this moment; there is neither time nor space to spirits. You might as well count the seconds it takes you to bring back your thoughts from Borneo to Montpellier Road,[96] or the room your mind took in Australia just now, when you were thinking of Mackworth Shore. My spirit *is* at Montpellier Road now, dearest man, though you do not know it, and so may Gabriel's be, and into his care I resign thee.

thy loving Bos

Give my love to Hughie and tell him that I hear that Fan is pretty well again now, and that Hilary and Jack are perhaps coming down here next Saturday. We go to London on the 8th and on the 13th to Lea Hurst.

Fare thee well my dearest friend, or rather *no* fare thee well but au revoir, for, according to my theory, I admit no such thing as absence (when we can think of one another). Au revoir then tonight, when I go to bed, and not tonight only but every night and morning too.

Source: Letter, ADD Mss 46176 ff16-17

Lea Hurst
16 August [1846]

My dearest friend [William Shore Smith]

I think it is time to write and tell how fared the Solitary Grand of the Glorious Apollers when homeward bound alone. Mariette [her maid] and I returned in the bus with two old ladies, a great dog and a pussycat in a basket, a beast of a dog for a pet, with a string round his neck. The old female, who made him a pet, must have had no vision, but a *moral* vision, left in her head, for we will take it for granted that he was as good as he was ugly, 'ansum, but not near so 'ansum as his

---

96 Shore was a pupil at Dr William King's, Montpellier Rd., Brighton.

brother were, could only be here applied in a *spiritual* sense. This saint was encircled by an appropriate glory, a cloud of homely little animals, which are now greatly endamaging my tranquillity and endangering my sitting as calm as coffins. (N.B., just taken up two and committed 'em to prison.)

I hope that you have modestly scratched at Aunt Anne's door, 104 Marine Parade, but you will hear that from Aunt Joanna, who, I understand, went with you to Brighton still in search of houses. Houses are, I suppose, like the Fata Morgana; one seems to see just a few in this populous land, but when one approaches them, they *apperiently* vanish away. Your simple but useful invention might be a way of fixing them.

I have just had your note and thank thee. I have thanked Aunt Evans from you, and will again, because it will please her, for the 5/. The patent escritoire in young Henstock's ear has not yet disposed of its stationery but has moved somewhat nearer the door, wherefore I am in hopes for that young gentleman and squirt madly round the corner. We are just going down to Cromford Bridge to see if our jackets are buttoned.

The railroad is planning a new line, which will run, if carried into effect, all the way from the tunnel to the aqueduct *between* the river and canal, space no object: earth, air and sea all the same to it, but fire would be preferred, if agreeable, and a comfortable home in a salamander's pocket.

Uncle Sam, Hilary and Arabella Shore went on Friday to see Mlle Rachel in Camilla, the sister of the Floratri [?]. They were delighted, and I do not wonder, for she is stupendous, but the feelings she represents are not deep, but loud, passionate, but not fervent. Those calm and healthy heroics, the Greeks and Romans, never behaved themselves in that way, not even Hermione (whom she does), much less the Antigones and the Electras. There is an awful reality in all Mlle Rachel says and does, but the reality is awful because it shows us the emotional and animal, not the spiritual, part of our nature, as you would call it (i.e., the heart and not the soul, as I should say) under the focus of a strong, burning glass. We are unaccustomed to see it, so unveiled, so unmistakable in its primary colours, with us it melts off into such neutral tints.

So *our Lord's death* brings before us the true nature of passions (of all of which we may find the echo in our own hearts) in their startling reality and the most enormous of their consequences. The excuses which Judas made to himself have probably been made by all of us in questions less momentous—but what have the circumstances in which we are placed to do with the sin in our hearts? That is the same, and not an affair of criminal police, regarded under the point of view of there being different penitentiary systems in Rome (and in England). The love of power of the high priests, the fear of a row of Pontius Pilate, the inconsiderate "following the leader" of the people, are everyday feelings in our hearts, just as is the jealousy, which brought, under a different system of police, Abel to the grave.

But our Lord's death was necessary to show them in their real shapes, like Ithuriel's spear, the touch of which made Evil start up in its own likeness. So the circumstances of the crucifixion, viz., sin "aux prises" with a perfectly holy being, and struggling for its own life or death, were like a solar microscope to the waters of bitterness we are drinking every day, to show us what they really contain. There is a fable of a modern Prometheus, who made a man eight feet high in order that he might see to do the fiddling work without spectacles. So a colossal scale is necessary for our old eyes, worn out by familiarity with sin, unless indeed they are furnished with those best of lenses, the tears of experience.

On the Greek stage everything was colossal. So our Lord's death was a grand event, destined to show us, not darkly,[97] but on a gigantic scale, the real tendencies of those *little things* (?) which place themselves so naturally in our lives, and round themselves in so easily, that we are hardly conscious of what they are, till some great consequence stares us in the face. Or else some great epitome of sin, some very compendious analysis (like our Saviour's death) prophesies it to us: truly for the transgression of my people was he smitten—to show us the real nature of a lawless heart and its dark and restless way of life.

But I must stop. I miss thee much and am,
ever thine, Bos
My best love to Hughie and many a kiss to thee.

Source: Letter, ADD Mss 46176 ff51-52

Scutari
Barrack Hospital
20 January 1856

My dearest friend [William Shore Smith]

Our paths have taken us so wide apart in life that I can only say, in answer to what your mother told me, that I have always felt that we

---

97 An allusion to 1 Cor 13:12.

were each of us striving to do the work for which God had made us, that I have always felt, and it has been one of my principal pleasures to feel that we were both of us doing our own work and not playing at it, that I have never placed, or wished to place, my selfish gratification in merely seeing you or seeing you help *me*, in comparison with the much higher gratification, to me, of seeing you do the work you liked, and for which God had made you, that I am satisfied, perfectly satisfied, in this, and that, if we ever meet again, we shall meet again in this most perfect love and confidence. I have never wished for your laying aside your own work to help mine.

In our perfect uncertainty here as to what will happen next, whether peace or war, I can say nothing as to anyone coming out this spring. Since I "joined the Army" I am like a soldier ready to troop at an hour's notice. But what you say has given me the greatest joy I have had since I came out.

I believe that no greater calamity than this war could befall Europe except a peace at this moment. I feel more than I can say though hearing everybody here, while the civilization and freedom of Europe are trembling in the balance, thinking of nothing but "getting home" and that "a peace will let *them* go."

You are and always will be one of my best and dearest friends. And I am ever

your old Flo

Your mother seems to thrive here though I don't know what upon but her own goodness.

Source: Signed statements, ADD Mss 45795 ff34-35

Combe Hurst

2 September 1859

I engage to produce a surveyor's certificate that the house in which I live shall be thoroughly drained with pipe drains and that there shall be no hazard of the sewer gases being forced into the house up the suites or by the rise of the tide. I will moreover declare that the situation shall be open and airey and not nearer the riverbank than half a mile and that there shall be no mews or other nuisance and no canal or drain near it.

W. Shore Smith

I have already Shore's promise that Dr Sutherland is to see the house and that without his consent it is not to be taken.

Florence Nightingale

Source: Letter, Add Mss 46176 ff57-60

Embley

Romsey

12 April 1872

My dearest boy Shore [Smith]

I suppose you are about flitting now. And I cannot but say what I have always in my heart to feel, that, whatever sorrow I may have at your leaving your work, about which necessity I do not pretend however to be able to form an opinion, I can see nothing to regret, but on the contrary everything to be proud of, at your having kept at it so long. You have done a noble, useful work, in some respects a thankless one, amidst a good deal of discouragement, a great deal of untowardness and difficulty, which would have deterred ninety-nine men out of one hundred, for twenty years, done it in the best possible way, considering all things, been useful to a very great many workmen, developed your own powers of command, resource and perseverance, and lived a life as far as the poles apart from the ordinary, magazine-y aimless life of the aesthetic idiots of the present day. (I don't want to curse and swear about this. I am an old woman and getting cross, I dare say, but still experience, actual fact, is telling that, in the last ten years—I having now been eighteen in government offices—administration has deteriorated so much as to have become almost imbecile. And the House of Commons, in usurping the powers of the administration—such as they *used* to be fifteen years ago—has lost its own: all, the result, as it appears to me of the literary, critical magazine-y, not really hardworking spirit of the day.)

Were I advising a young friend of twenty-one or twenty-two at the present day, I should say: keep out of the. . . .

I think your life for the last twenty years has been not only comparatively 10,000 times more noble and useful than most men's lives between twenty and forty, but also in itself noble and useful. I am sorry, as you are sorry, that you have not made the money you wished and by no means disagree with the Neapolitan gypsy who prays to the Demòn Gorgòn, Manda pecunia, Nel mio Barzon [? Demon Gorgon]. Still, money is about the last thing in your case to distress yourself about, when there are other things "made."

I have not an idea what you are going to do and feel rather anxious to know. I hope Louisa and baby are thriving by the sea. Are the others with her?

I was really thankful that Aunt Mai was here so long and without cares. She grew twenty years younger and I hope will repeat the experiment (she is much younger than I). God bless you and He will bless you, and believe me

ever your

old Flo

Burn. I believe Emily Verney's case to be very bad indeed. They have shilly-shallied so long with this dreadful Malta fever, increasing enormously the lung mischief, that now they are frightened and no longer say, "Oh it's all her own fault." God grant it may not be too late! She is a girl, or rather a woman, of uncommon power and would have done great things. (If you are going to Combe, you may tell this to Aunt Mai, who is always kindly interested about her—and that the last account I have had of her is the worst.)

Source: Letter, Derbyshire County Archives

28 August 1878

My dear Sir [Dr C.B.N. Dunn]

If, after having seen *Mr Shore Smith's* ankle, you think he ought not to go tomorrow, would you kindly tell *me* as well as him? . . .

yours sincerely

F. Nightingale

Source: Letter, Derbyshire County Archives

Lea Hurst
20 September 1879

Private

My dear Sir [Dr C.B.N. Dunn]

First of all, let me thank you very much for your analysis of the Limbs' well water. I wrote without losing a moment by the same morning's post to Mr Shore Smith, giving him your information and asking what was to be done. He answered that he would write to Mr Yeomans, and, if the well belonged to the estate, it should be cleaned and the top made so that no dirty water could run into it. He fancies that the excess of chlorides is from dirty water coming into it, but, he says, "a dirty pail or pan will poison the best water more than a good deal tricking into a well." But may not there be *percolation* from some privy or *cesspool* into the well? That is the commonest cause.

As Mr S.S. says: "if this is the cause it is satisfactory to have found it out and I should not anticipate any difficulty in making it right." But I am afraid the Limbs' cottage does *not* belong to the estate. I think it belongs to Buxton. . . .

Source: Letter to Parthenope Verney, Wellcome (Claydon copy) Ms 9008/95

Lea Hurst
1 November 1880

. . . Shore makes progress, slow, and, as Louisa says, "talvolta indietro, ma pur si muove" [sometimes backwards but one still moves]. Of course the not being able to go to his father has been much against him (agitated him much).

F.N.

Source: Letter, Derbyshire County Archives

Lea Hurst
27 November 1880

Coffee Room Whatstandwell
My dear Sir [Dr C.B.N. Dunn]

Mr Shore Smith informed me of the conversation which you and he had had this afternoon on the proposed Coffee Room at Whatstandwell, and showed me Miss Hurt's kind letter.

Mr Shore Smith and I agree, I am afraid, that the buying up of the "Wheatsheaf" [a pub] scarcely offers enough inducement to balance the cost. To buy the license would probably take money enough to build three coffee rooms would it not? And who is to secure us against another license being obtained and another "public" being set up in the "Wheatsheaf's" place? . . .

Mr Shore Smith thinks that we might get a corrugated iron building, such as are made for schoolrooms, etc., containing possibly a bedroom for a manager, to put up. . . . What do you think?

ever yours faithfully
Florence Nightingale

Source: Note on a dream, Add Mss 47722 ff68-69

26 September 1889

W.S.S. I dreamt a strange waking dream between waking and sleeping, all night waking every two minutes. And it seemed as if my dearest Shore had to fight someone with swords at Lea Hurst, and there was no practice or training in swordsmanship to be had (any more than there was training in nursing to be had in my day). And we had something to do with it. Somehow it was my fault that this sword duel had to come off with a frightful Giant Swordsman and filibuster like Goliath. But David was victorious, thus so Shore. In simplicity and serenity and undismayed he went his way singing:

Art thou afraid His power shall fail
When comes thy evil day?
And shall an all-creating arm
Grow weary or decay?[98]

The contest was long and tedious. There were not what are erroneously called the "sinews of war," namely money, on the righteous side, erroneously, for some of the greatest victories have been gained by soldiers actually in rags and half starved. But by degrees it, the righteous side, gained ground, and in the end was wholly victorious. The victory was his and emphatically his own and immense good was done which could have been done in no other way.

Editor: This late letter, from Shore to their mutual cousin, Benjamin Leigh Smith,[99] shows the suspicion of the Nightingales for the Verneys. Nightingale in fact gave money to the Verneys for various things (including nursing care for Emily Verney), for the Verneys' money problems were obvious. From the next letter it is clear that Nightingale had not visited Embley since her father's death in 1874, and her mother's forced removal on Aunt Mai and Uncle Sam's becoming the owners, or not until after her mother's and sister's deaths. Of course she saw the Shore Smiths in London and Lea Hurst.

Source: Copy of letter by William Shore Smith, Chiddingstone Castle 6

> [printed address] Embley Park
> Romsey, Hampshire
> 25 August 1891

My dear Ben [Benjamin Leigh Smith]

Florence has been with us here for three weeks, I am glad to say, and I think it did her good. She had not been here since her father's death in 1874. She has left us today, as unfortunately we have been obliged to let the place again for the shooting season and the people come in this day week.

I told her of your very kind offer of Scalands [Sussex] to her and I told her how exactly suited the place was for her requirements. She was greatly pleased and obliged to you, but said she was obliged to go

---

98 A prayer by Margaret Ogilvy shortly before her death, in J.M. Barrie, *Margaret Ogilvy*, by her Son.

99 Benjamin Leigh Smith (1828-1913), Arctic explorer, on whom more below, son of Uncle Ben Smith.

to Claydon to be with old Sir Harry Verney. I greatly object to her going there but it is no use and she is gone there today. All they want is her money and they worry her to death, but I could not persuade her not to go.

She said to me today that she wished to write and thank you and I gave her your address. I hope you are doing well up there. Here it rains day and night and our magnificent crops are entirely ruined and I with them I fear. There is no use trying to farm in such a beastly climate. Adieu,

your W.S.S.

Source: Letter, Add Mss 46176 ff67-68

[printed address] Claydon House
Winslow, Bucks
27 November 1891

Dearest Louisa [Shore Smith]

Do you remember a Miss Man Mohun Ghose of Calcutta whom you, I believe, kindly visited at her school near London? Is she still there and what is the name of the school? Miss [Anne] Manning would know. Fred Verney is going to India in a few days with his Siamese Prince Damrong. I have given him an introduction to her delightful parents at Calcutta and he would go and see her previous to leaving England.

Thank you for your most welcome note. My love to all the children. I wish I knew Miss Llewellyn Davies. How is my Rosy getting on? I never hear from her. And is Shore the better for Folkestone? I expect to be back in ten days or so.

Yesterday I spied here in a servants' passage leads to the door opening on the back stairs (first floor) the forest scene with large trees and autumnal tints: Copley Fielding,[100] which hung on the left side the fireplace in the breakfast room at Embley (opposite which I have so often done my lessons with my father). Over it hung the De Wint,[101] I *think*, which was over the fireplace in the breakfast room, and left-hand side again was another picture: same size as the De Wint which also hung somewhere at Embley. I never saw them before because you only do see them going to the back stairs and I scarcely ever leave my rooms. *Nobody* sees them.

---

100 Anthony Van Dyck Copley Fielding (1787-1885), British watercolourist.
101 Peter de Wint (1784-1849), British landscape artist.

Would you like me to ask for that lovely Copley Fielding *for you to copy*, and one other? I do so wish you had taken them when Parthe offered them so gladly.

ever and always your

F.N.

The Siddons' engraving hung quite in the dark which was in the music room. They are so lost here. I am so glad you are painting.

Source: Letter, part in another hand, part by F.N., Hampshire Record Office 94M72/F586/2

[printed address] 10 South Street
Park Lane, W.
30 January 1893

Dearest Shore [William Shore Smith]

Thank you for your very kind letter. As to the pecunia, you have no call to be reckoning it up in that way; I haven't. As we agreed, we can fight and squabble about it in another and a better world. I am your debtor, not you mine. Not only as the day approaches for the anniversary of my dear mother's death, but always my thoughts dwell on your love and kindness to her and how all the happiness of her last years was due to you and yours. I feel that nothing I could say or do could at all express my thankfulness, and hers, I am sure.

I thank God that you are so much better. Don't be cross and ill-natured to your head. You will see he will get better, too. As for me, it is years since I could bear two people in the same room at once, which is sometimes very awkward. And I was shocked to find out that I could not bear a young lady playing the violin in my room—Mendelssohn's "O rest in the Lord," which I had much wished to hear. But I believe your head will get better soon, and then you will bless Bournemouth and the endless pleasure of the sea, and enjoy, I trust, some other place. But don't be in a hurry to go abroad. That will come in time.

You were so good as to telegraph an inquiry to me the day of the house being burnt in our street. When the danger was over, I wished you could have been here to see what I did. The two upper storeys of the house next door but one to this, and under repair, were in flames before the alarm was given. But then to see the fire gods rushing and roaring up the pass, i.e., Park Lane, to see each dissolve into seven or eight demigods with helmets on, as it arrived. You heard no order given; everybody, even the horses, seemed to know exactly what to do. The scaffolding in front of the house, that is, the tops were already alight. Four demigods flew up like eagles and, with their axes, slashed off the tops into the street. Others stood below and trampled out the fire with their boots. I suppose if the scaffolding had really taken fire, nothing could have saved the five houses, two on each side.

Now if you call this penny-a-lining, I shall bite you. The discipline of the men, all acting like one, yet each with his eyes and ears awake to the smallest thing—you should have seen the intentness of their faces—set to their work. I assure you there is nothing in Hindu or even in Greek mythology equal to the fire gods here. I could not help thinking how we waste our time in criticism. These gods did not waste a moment in thinking what idiots the workmen were who went to their breakfasts leaving a fire burning near pitch, but up and on to their work in a quarter of a second.

The police worked well, though they were late on the scene. They ranged the traffic on both sides Park Lane so as to let the fire gods pass, seven of them. The hose was all along the middle of the street. They drew a cordon at the mouth of Park St., and of South St. and on the other side the five houses, one of which was so hot that a lady and a nurse, half dressed, carrying babies came out, and afterwards went to live at Dorchester House. The next day the skylight at the top of their house fell in from the heat upon a woman, but she was not much hurt.

All was discipline on this side, all was indiscipline on the other, maids standing at their doors, akimbo, gabbling and giggling, but it was a grand sight. I am interrupted, but will write again if I may.

ever dearest Shore
your loving old F.

Editor: These next letters concern Shore's impending death, in September 1894, and condolences thereafter.

Source: Letter to Margaret Verney, Wellcome (Claydon copy) Ms 9014/126

Embley
24 September 1893

. . . I have been here at a sad leave-taking. Shore very ill, has been obliged, through poverty, to let this, his home, for 3½ years. . . .

Source: Letter, Add Mss 46176 ff69-74

10 South St., W.
5 November 1893
Inkermann Day

Dearest Louisa and Shore [Shore Smith]

Thanks so many for Louisa's dear letters and telegrams, so gratefully received by a hungry heart. I think I told you that we sent on the morning of your departure from London, and found you were flown "on the wings of the morning to the uttermost parts of the sea," which I translated Waterloo Station to be. Since then I have received many delightful letters from you, for which eternal thanks.

Mr Jowett was at Lea Hurst when the news that he would be elected Master of Balliol reach[ed] him. He was sitting in the balcony room with me. He got up and leaned his elbow on the mantelpiece and prayed: "O spare me that I may recover strength before I go hence and am no more seen." I do not think that he in the least remembered that I was in the room. (Except General Gordon, I don't know that I ever knew anyone who so far *realized* that there was no one but God in the room.) This was on 2 September 1870. God did "spare" him for twenty-three years. But I think he might have lived two years longer, if he had known how to manage himself.

I had such a beautiful letter from Lord Lansdowne about him, speaking of him as though he was with us still, only not visible to our eyes. There is rather a nice brochure published by the Westminster Gazette Office which I will send you if you have it not. But none can give the wonderful power of the man's individuality. (I liked him *least* when he epigrammatized on the young men.) How much a few can do. It is always the minority that works the great reforms—never the majority. One can't reconcile this with party government, just as one can't reconcile the "survival of the fittest" with Christianity (or what Christianity means, namely the goodness of God). (Vide Shore.) It is thirty-nine years today since Inkermann: "the Soldiers' Battle" when a mere handful (a few) saved the Army, perhaps saved Europe, thirty-nine years yesterday since we landed at Scutari. I always remember you on Inkermann Day, even more than on other days, because I once spent Inkermann Day with you at Lea Hurst.

How little real history there is even in contemporary history or biography. The sources of action are never known or told. When the Russians poured 100,000 men long before daylight in a dense November fog up a steep gully on to our plateau, we were completely taken by surprise. There was an hour and a spot which a mere handful of men, without officers and without orders, were holding. Eleven times the Russians took this spot; eleven times they were driven back by the handful, till the trench was full of Russian dead. It was greater than Thermopylae.

Very few were the survivors on our side. But it gave time for succours to come up. Had it not been for the pluck of these men and similar men, had the Russians broken into our lines, not only might our Army have been lost, but the Russians might have overrun Europe. This is not reflecting on our officers: their conduct in *fighting* is always splendid. When the succours came up there was more than one regiment that went into action with its full complement of officers and came out commanded by the junior ensign. But the men: "how well they kept the post, In the brave days of yore," THEY fought only for their comrades and their duty—their names were never known—they had no hope of winning— they only meant to sell their lives as dearly as they could for the right. That is the way God means *us* to fight.

Then the French came up to help us. And they could be heard a long way off through the fog playing "The British Grenadier" and "The Campbells are coming," etc. (WE had no bands) and "See the conquering hero comes." And our men said: "O it was better for us to hear our tunes than twenty breakfasts!" They had had no food and had no Henry V.

They are having a great celebration of Inkermann at Aldershot and the toasts are to be: The Duke of Cambridge and the Duke of Connaught. The son of the Duke of Cambridge wrote to me for a subscription, and I sent one. But I could not stand this toasting, so I begged for a toast for the *men* that fell there and I told part of this story, taking care not to commit myself. And I heard afterwards that they had put my letter in the papers. Now came *my* punishment. A newspaperman called to ask for an "interview" to tell him the story. And a Welsh committee writes to ask me to write a letter for them. These plagues are always happening now. And I know but one person of that sort who is not tainted with this vulgarity and that person is a dog, B. Smith's dog.

Now I must not write any more. You see I have no news to give. So I am obliged to write of the past. I knew the story of the Duke of Cambridge at Inkermann: he could not bear his horse treading in the blood ("c'est aimable, mais ce n'est pas la guerre" [this is delightful, but it's not war]). So they had nothing to do but invalid him home. I saw him at Scutari as he went down. Such is life and some of its hidden sources.

The abominable November has begun here. Bright sunshine be yours, within and without. I have sent a paper to the Leeds Conference on rural hygiene, Boards of Guardians and rural health missioners. They worried me into it. May Dr Scott do his best!

ever yours and Shore's

old Flo

Source: Incomplete letter with envelope, Hampshire Record Office 94M72/F586/3

[printed address] 10 South Street
Park Lane, W.
Christmas Day 1893

Dearest Shore [William Shore Smith]

On Christ's birthday I must wish you and the darling people about you a happy Christmas, "not dragging our hearts along the earth but fixing our hearts on heaven," as Augustine,[102] I think it is, says, not meaning by "heaven," you know, any future state, for he expressly says *today.*

I see the beautiful child Jesus
a-coming down to me,
and in His hand He beareth
flowers so rich and rare.

Those were almost the last words I ever heard of Parthe's, the last day she was here, just a week before her death. And she looked up at the Dresden Raphael [Sistine Madonna] and asked the child Jesus to come down to her. And He *is* "coming down" *today* to give us "His flowers so rich and rare." And you are to tell me what they are, and we must not sadden His soul by anything.

One of the most striking things in Mr Jowett was his ever-abiding conviction that life was a splendid gift, and this was not the fruit of animal spirits, for he had none. On the contrary, he was too often depressed. What makes it a splendid gift? Not ease, not prosperity, but that the real virtues, the greatness, come out of evil, and the contrariness of life and even weakness. For as that great man, Paul, said, "when I am weak, then am I strong."[103]

---

102 Augustine (354-430), Bishop of Hippo.
103 2 Cor 12:10.

The "kingdom of heaven," which Christ certainly meant for that on earth, is given to the "poor in spirit"[104] and to those who are labouring for others and yet are not praised.

So Augustine says, "I have already torn myself from that hope of ours (that apparently of becoming friends of the emperor) and have settled to serve God, and this I begin from this hour in this very place."[105]

Needless to say that God and truth and love (working for our fellow creatures) Mr Jowett said meant all the same thing. He would not have us think that God was particular in being named *Himself.* "But," Augustine says further (still referring to becoming "friends of the *Emperor*") "if I choose to become a friend of *God* I can do it *here* and *now.*"

Dearest Louisa has been so good in writing and telegraphing to me and she has sent me a turkey. And how good it was of Vaughan to come down here. And now I think of you all as "serving" truth and love—all that dear darling party at Gangmoor assembled today. And we have only to say, "Da quod jubes et jube quod vis," as Augustine did.

Hoping to see you soon and that you will let me know the hour and the day and with express trains of love to all the *dear yours,*

ever your old Flo

Do you remember Mrs Holmes at Lea Hurst, my most particular friend, who used to give out the milk? She is very poor. She is lame and ill; her husband is almost blind. She has only one daughter left in England, who has had two operations. Yet she writes to me for Christmas, "I can't think how we can say, I fear, when God says, 'Fear *not.*'"

F.N.

Thanks for all the Christmas Day, charming, evergreens your munificence has sent from everybody.

Source: Letter to an unknown recipient, Woodward Biomedical Library A.72

13 May 1894

. . . Shore was very ill in June in London, and quite unable to go to the marriage [of his daughter Rosalind]. He has never recovered [from] that illness, though a great deal better, but he still has a trained nurse and Sam, the elder boy, who is a doctor, still lives temporarily with them to take care of him medically. They are now at

104 An allusion to Matt 5:3.
105 *Confessions* 8.6.

Embley till they can let the place. Shore's wife and Barbara[106] are, of course, included in "they." They describe the place as being most beautiful. Lea Hurst continues let. . . .

Editor: William Shore Smith died 23 August 1894.

Source: Letter, Wellcome (Claydon copy) Ms 9014/171

[printed address] 10 South Street
Park Lane, W.
12 September 1894

Dearest blessed Margaret [Verney]

. . . I gave your most kind message to Shore's wife. She was very much pleased; she is able to take a great deal of pleasure in receiving tributes to *him*. And today she was quite delighted in receiving twenty-seven messages of love and sorrow from twenty-seven workmen whom Shore had helped in the best way.

Shore lived to see his grandchild [Louis Nash], which is not six months old yet. He did not nurse or caress it as grandpapas often do, but he watched it. It made all the difference in his life. His death was good and simple like himself.

The boys are so good in helping. Indeed everybody has been so good in helping. I cannot say more. I feel one of them. Shore has been more or less my care since he was four months old. My love to all, Aunt Florence's. I am sorry I shall not see Ruth or Harry. But I hope to see Ellin and Lettice and your dear self. Shore was so good to my mother. Ever, blessed saint,

your humble devotee

Aunt Florence

In haste.

Uncle Oc, Aunt Jane, Cousins Frederick and Flora Smith

Editor: This fairly small number of letters includes a childhood letter to cousin Frederick Smith, and correspondence on his youthful death, on an expedition in Western Australia. Nightingale's visits to her Uncle Oc and Aunt Jane (Jenny) in London are reported in *European Travels*. There is then late correspondence on the deaths of Uncle Oc (condolences to Aunt Jane) and on her death. Uncle Oc had been the link between Nightingale's parents, the brother of her mother and fellow student at Trinity College, Cambridge, with her father.

---

106 Daughter Margaret Thyra Barbara Smith.

Source: Letter, Edinburgh University LHB1/111/13 1 [large and small hand]

[1829]

Dear Fred [Frederick Smith]

I am afraid that I cannot send you a cake since Mama is not well, and I don't like speaking to her about such trumpery things. Do not be offended, I beg.

Blanche was in such a good humour last night, I jumped along the passage, and she laughed so, and shook herself, and she jumped almost out of nurse's arms and when I play at peep-bo she laughs so. She does not wear a cap now.

your affectionate cousin

Florence N.

P.S. Miss Christie sends her love to you. Mama will send you *a cake*.

Source: Incomplete letter, Wellcome (Claydon copy) Ms 8992/11

[1840]

. . . By his account Fred [Smith][107] was perfectly rational and himself till the moment he left him, weak and languid more than the others. He suffered agonies from the change of food which produced such dreadful pain in the stomach that he used to lie down in the sea. Mr Walker's opinion of the cause of his death is that it was purely accidental. His account is that Fred became so disgusted with the men that, wishing for a night's rest alone, he remained behind, telling them he would join them in the morning. He probably walked on a short distance alone, then lay down and during sleep rolled partially off the sandbank, and the head dropping considerably below the body, apoplexy followed, Mr W. said.

Mr W. said, had it not been for this, I see no reason why he should not have returned with the others. *Ruston* returned in the morning to look for him but, unable to find him, and probably from exhaustion unable to trace the footsteps, supposed that he had gone inland and would join them. He added, but fortunately when Uncle Oc and Aunt Jane were neither of them in the room, that Fred went, "lest people should call him a coward, for I represented to him how very ill I thought of the expedition and offered, when he said that, to stay behind if he would." *Twice* Fred was the means of saving their lives,

---

107 Fred Smith was the only person to die on the expedition, which was led by Sir George Grey, coincidentally the person who later encouraged Nightingale to study colonial statistics. For an account of the expedition from his perspective see Edmund Bohan, *To Be a Hero: Sir George Grey (1812-1878)*.

once by the swimming on shore, after which he lay down and slept in a boat half full of water till the sea broke over and *washed him out*, and also by bringing his fishing tackle, the only one who did so, which was afterwards their only means of subsistence.

He mentioned his home, said Mr W., several times to me and his father and mother, not as wishing to convey any message to them "but as a burst of affection forcing itself out." He sent a piece of his hair this morning, which Aunt J. *intends* to send back! as having been evidently put up for himself. Aunt Jenny repeats, "Had he remained with Fred, there seems no reason now why he should not have been brought back to Perth with the others and returned here safe. If he had not been left with his disgusting companions as Mr W. describes them, and wished to be alone that night, he might have been saved." But this morning she has agreed that Mr Walker's account is not to be depended on, that he was evidently anxious to exculpate himself, which nothing could do more thoroughly than his representing Fred as perfectly rational. There was evidently a great deal to conceal and his manner was excessively con [breaks off]

Source: Undated letter, Edinburgh University LHB1/111/13 3

Burlington [St.]

Friday

Dearest Aunt Jenny [Smith]

I would not write to you till I had seen Uncle Oc, of whom perhaps a bulletin from a *fresh* person may be acceptable. I rushed up to see him this morning before breakfast, knowing that was the only time when I could see him without people of business. I REALLY thought him looking well and in good spirits. He told me a great many funny stories about [missing page] could we have expected, with such an accident, that there would have been so little wretchedness, so few miseries, so few distressing scenes. No, really it is all thankfulness that it is so well. As for the feeling of the public, that must go *against* this iniquitous verdict. I only received your dear letter yesterday, it having followed me here. I am so VERY glad you are going to stay awhile longer where you are.

yours overflowingly

Flo

Best love to dear Val and all. My people stay another day in town, i.e., my females.

Source, Letter, Edinburgh University LHB1/111/13 5

Lea Hurst
21 September [1847]

Dearest Aunt Jenny [Smith]

I *was* so glad to hear from Uncle Sam such a good account of you and of your capabilities, land and water. Truly we should be very thankful to Ardtornish, if it is able to perform such wonders. And have you had no more toothache? I trust that Uncle Oc will be able to return. How too unfortunate was it that this poor cricket should have happened just when he was enjoying himself. Mr Kroff, who has been staying here, whom I like so very much, says to me, "Mr Octavius—I did tremble to see him again. I did think he would look disfigured, but I think he do look so venerable, dat is, worthy of veneration. The eye is so prettily closed; he look like a general who has lost his eye in the love of his country, he really look like a hero." Mr K. has such a warm feeling for you all. "I do love Miss Flora[108] like my daughter" he often said.

Laura and Lothian [Nicholson] were here for a week on their way to Scotland; they surprised me while my people were at Lady Sitwell's. However, there was plenty of house room and I sent up into the village for ¼ lb of tea and they had to find the spiritual dinner themselves.

Mrs Plunkett has a little girl (I know that you are kindly interested about her) and, though her family desired a boy, yet they had been sufficiently anxious about her not to make much difficulty with Providence.

Our little visit from your two boys was very short and sweet. Poor Shore was desolated not to stay as long as they stayed. But I will say for your boys that, in all matters of conscience, they are the greatest moral heroes and moral helps I know. They really, when they know a thing to be right, they actually do it! And though it does not sound a very astonishing thing upon paper, yet it is in life, as we all know, the rarest of all astonishments. They always say to my boy, "Do what you think they will like," meaning his father and mother, and as *they* do it, it is not only words. They are the only boys I know who do say so to him.

You will be glad to hear that poor *Cupid*, whom you took so kind an interest in, is to be taken from her present Bible and muffins place,

108 Flora M. Smith, eldest daughter of Octavius and Jenny Smith.

and as she has given up her visions of the stage and announced her desire to be a dancing mistress, is to be apprenticed to a respectable dancing teacher.

Aunt Julia and Aunt Maria are again ensconced at Combe. But we mean to keep Aunt Mai and her children some time longer here, as we do not move south till the 1st. They are now at Grandmama's. I cannot help fancying that Beatrice is a little better. The railroad here is progressing, it makes sad havoc in Aunt (Evans)'s field, but not in her peace. With us, on the contrary, it destroys our peace, but not our field. . . .

Pray tell Willie that I am quite reconciled to your friend M Mohl.[109] I say "your friend" because I believe you harboured him more than all the rest of the family put together. He came here and I dragged him (as in duty-bound by Miss Clarke's command) all over the manufactories, and all over the workhouse and the Board of Guardians, and all the remark he made was upon a carpet in the governor's home, that, if a German governor had a carpet, he would be turned off for peculation. So said I in my head, you are a thorough man of the world, who are labouring under a delusion (you know they say we have all of us one mental delusion, some two; in some it takes the form of imagining themselves teapots, in others, Napoleons). Now M Mohl thinks himself a political economist. Besides, I was very angry with him for not seeming to interest himself about Miss Clarke. Well, since he went, he has written such tender letters about his brother's marriage, so full of eager curiosity about Miss Clarke, and of fraternal certainty that his brother will make her happy (having had no idea of the marriage, while with us) that I have put dust upon my head and eaten all my words, though they were many and tough against him.

But you are probably not quite so much interested about the Clarke marriage as we are. We went last month to hear Jenny Lind at Birmingham, though I scorn to be disappointed, she does not shine in a concert room.

. . . We spent one night at Mrs Bracebridge's lately; they were overwhelmed with delight at having just been able to buy Shakespeare's house at Stratford,[110] of which he had been the prime mover. I cannot quite understand this enthusiasm. Is not one line of *Julius Caesar* more a remembrance of Shakespeare than the house where his old clothes

---

109 Brother of Julius Mohl.
110 Near the Bracebridges' home in Atherstone.

lay? We have himself, we have his whole mind, and what do we want with the room where he passed the night? It seems to me like going to visit a friend's dirty linen when we have his own living self by our side. But you will be very tired of my own living self, wherefore believe me, ever dearest Aunt Jenny,

yours overflowingly

F.N.

Best love to the boys and all the children and to the dear Bab, of whom we were defrauded.

Source: Letter, Edinburgh University LHB1/111/13 4

Embley

11 October [1847]

Dearest Aunt Jenny [Smith]

I *was* so glad of your letter, you cannot think, though it was a week before it reached me and now I have scarce time to tell you how rejoiced I was to have any tidings of you. All I can do in return is to tell you about Uncle Oc.[111] He was very much pleased with the interview he had had the day before with the foreman of the jury, a most sensible man, who had been entirely against the verdict from the very first, but, as the others had declared they would rather be "starved out" than not give it, he "didn't choose to be made a fool of." The coroner too, you know, was against it, but as you have heard all that from Aunt Julia I will not trouble you with it. The article too in the *Economist* was very satisfactory and Uncle Oc, taking such a right view of the case. Of course you will see it.

Uncle Oc was in his tub when I arrived, so I had not so long time with him as I should have wished. . . . They have not the least fear about Heasman's trial which comes on about the 31st. It seems that the expense will come to between £2000 and £8000. I am very glad the boats are to be given up, as it was too much anxiety for him.

There is no very distressing case now except one boy who has lost his leg. A great many people have got new hats for old ones, good clothes for bad ones, and are really the better for it. Your Jews, who asked £10 a piece for a basket of fruit, are gone off satisfied with £5. The Irish widow I told you of appeared to think it a perfect godsend

---

111 There was an explosion 27 August 1847 on the boat Octavius Smith used to transport his workers to and from Thames Bank, which resulted in five deaths and many injuries.

which had rid her of her husband, whom she "wished she had never seen," although she had only been married eight months. Two of the others who are dead do not, by their deaths, reduce their families to poverty.

The person who is giving Uncle Oc most trouble is that beggarly attorney who was advertising in the *Times*. If it were not for the lawyers, he said, everything would have gone right—they have done all the mischief. However he sees now the end of his business and of his liabilities, as Friday had been the first day without an application. There were really supposed to be (although it seems impossible) 100 people in that part of the boat, which was utterly destroyed! When one thinks of this, one feels as if one could hardly be thankful enough!

Take courage, dear Aunt Jenny, you will see that all is for the best, *now* as ever, that the feeling of the public will be against the verdict, that the tide will perhaps have turned all the other way long before Heasman's trial, that Uncle Oc will ride out the storm courageously, as he always does, that everybody will come round to the belief that, if no risks are run, there can be no improvements, that if there be government superintendence, and everything go on in the same jogtrot way it has done since King Alfred's time, when we had not a "stool to sit on," there may be no accidents, but there will be no progress. We might as well say that the actual amount of happiness produced by the railroads carrying the public cheap and fast was entirely neutralized and annihilated by the few dreadful accidents there have been. People who never try to walk will never stumble, that is certain. And those who never try to benefit the public in any way will never be exposed to cantankerous juries and accidental failures. But they will never either have done any good in their generation.

You will have heard all this so much better from Aunt Ju that I am shy of inflicting more upon you. I wish, too, I could give you more facts but, during the short time I was with Uncle Oc, we talked about other things, too, about you and how glad he was that you and Val should have a little more Scotch air, how he hoped to get down to you, but I am afraid that is doubtful. He looked well. I missed Aunt J. by half an hour, for I could not stay as I was coming down here with my father. You will see, dear Aunt Jenny, that there will be nothing to regret after a while. So mind you do not let sad thoughts spoil the Scotch breezes. But I am writing before breakfast, and I must go, and instead of applying a fixed rule for the investigation of your thoughts, apply a fixed rule for the laying down of the carpets.

My friend's "little possession" is a dark-headed nice little strong affair, a stormy little bab, who I should think would box the maternal ears. "Thank heaven, I've got rid of you," she said. Poor woman, she never was more mistaken—she has only just begun with it, has she?

Fanny Hanford is to be married in the end of November (and Parthe is to be bridesmaid). She is very happy and the future Mr Fanny, with whom I had a long tête-à-tête, appears to me a most satisfactory person. One cannot say anything with her, poor dear, but what a relief generally, that she should be turned over to a wise and good protector (with such a father, I mean) but this man seems all that her strong sense and confiding spirit can require in order to be able to *look up*. I wish she were a little less delicate looking now.

Farewell, dearest Aunt Jenny. My next letter will, I hope, have a little more variety. Till then I am yours hastily, but

ever lovingly and gratefully

with best love to all

F.N.

Source: Letter to Douglas Galton on the death of Gerard Smith, son of Octavius and Jane Smith, Add Mss 45759 f15

23 September 1858

. . . You will have heard from Marianne of the terrible grief of the poor Octavius Smiths. He left England immediately after the inquest to tell Aunt Jane at Aix. The verdict at the inquest was a cruel and unnecessary one since there was ample evidence that there could be no intention, but only great imprudence, on the part of poor Gerard. He tried to cross the line immediately before a train and was killed on the spot. Uncle Octavius was more affected by the verdict than by all the rest. . . .

Editor: The next letter gives Nightingale's condolences to Aunt Jenny on the death of Uncle Oc.

Source: Letter, Edinburgh University LHB1/111/13 6

Embley
5 March 1871

Dearest Aunt Jenny [Smith]

I know not whether you can care to read another letter in your sorrow, *your* sorrow which one can think of only before God, as being too great for man to meddle with, but infinite and holy like Him. Ah you have had two such sorrows in your life, and alas many others. The

flood of recollections of your fifty-two happy years with him, for you
told me they were the happiest of years, in spite of all sorrows, perhaps because of all sorrows, comes back without you. *Yours* would
never be the unloving cry, "oh that I had died first."

Ah why need I bring to *your* mind all, or any of the great and noble
and affectionate things he has done since (since thirty years ago)?
fifty-two years of such married life as yours. How few, how very few can
show anything like it, how few can even know what it means. You said
once, in the midst of agony, that you were the "happiest of women." I
should not wonder if even at this moment, though it seems like a miracle, you might be saying the same thing.

I see you as you were when you showed me the little house, with the
cinders before it, where you first went, a newly married wife, almost a
girl, with him and which you told me was paradise, when Fred was
born. I remember your saying that, in the holy joy of that birth, you
felt the pain as nothing, nothing but a sort of cheerful excitement,
that 26 June 1820. Then I see you all as you were during that time
when I knew you all so well thirty-one years ago. How great, how
manly, he was, what a noble charm in all he did, doing great helpful
things for people which no one else could do because no one else had
his grace and strength of unselfishness and manliness in assuming the
powers and duties of responsibility. There was a primitive saying about
him, that he was "adored in the yard." But to us who knew the causes
of this and how justly it was so, the expression was a good one, for it
was so.

That agonizing but happy time in 1840—how can I, though I have
passed through such scenes since, such battlefields, such national
calamities and catastrophes, how can I ever forget? I remember your
saying, "While he is with me, while I have *him* to be with, I can bear
anything." And, once you said, "Since I married him, I have really no
will but the will of God. I never wish to do anything but what I believe
to be agreeable to God." About Fred, I remember your saying, "Oh
Flo, I had rather have him lying there, as he is, on the desert seashore,
than have him as so many people's sons living just from breakfast to
dinner and from dinner to tea."

I am sure that, though I can hardly imagine you without dear, dear
Uncle Oc, you can rather rejoice that you have lived to be without
him than that he should have lived to be. But I will not weary your
eyes, dearest Aunt Jenny, with telling you what you know, and so much
better than I. I thought of you so much in the last terrible wrench yes-

terday. I told my dear mother of her loss. She took it quite beautifully, but, I could fancy, has been a little more feeble since, and I was glad that she was quite quiet in her bed and alone to tell her. She has talked of you incessantly ever since. And each day I repeat to her all the particulars I know. She has said constantly, would they all come here? I do not know even that you are well enough, alas! to move.

Dear Gertrude's happy prospect[112] which we trust will bring a great joy to her and also to you, would also prevent you for a time. Still I mention what my dear mother has so frequently said. Do not think of answering it yet.

I know how you and Flora share the same thoughts and dear Val and Willy. God bless you, dearest Aunt Jenny, and support you all. I can scarcely fancy you without *him*, but then you are *not* without him. All yours and

ever yours in thought and heart

Florence Nightingale (your old Flo)

Source: Letter with envelope to Miss Flora M. Smith, 28 Prince's Gate, Hyde Park, W., Edinburgh University LHB1/111/13 7

[printed address] 35 South Street
Park Lane, W.
28 March 1871

My dear Flora [Smith]

I was very grateful to you for your kind note on Monday week about dear Gertrude and her baby, you may be sure. I have heard every day since direct from Onslow Square, as there seemed, alas! some cause for anxiety. But I would not trouble anyone to write at such a time, when I could have my news for sending for it. I felt so much interested about all the poor baby's perpatetics about its wet nurse.

I trust that now all anxiety is over and, though one is very sorry that Gertrude cannot nurse herself, yet we will hope that both new Mama and new baby have settled their affairs for the best for this time. The one who must have felt most of anxiety, dearest Aunt Jenny, I have thought of most. I fear that she has suffered from it. But in a short time she will, we may trust, be receiving the joy which the dear new mother and grandchild will be able to give her. Please give her my dearest love and thank her very much for sending me Mr Martineau's address.

If you have another copy to spare and would kindly send me one for my father, he would truly appreciate it. I do not like to give away

---

112 Their daughter Gertrude married A. Craig Sellar.

my copy, sent me by dear Aunt Jenny herself. I did not like to write and give you joy in answer to your note till all fears were over, but believe me, dear Flora,

ever yours

Florence Nightingale

Source: Letter on her father's death, Edinburgh University LHB1/111/13 9

35 South St.

9 January 1874

Dearest Aunt Jenny [Smith]

Your sympathy is very dear to us. My dear father was taken from us quite suddenly at 8 o'clock on Monday morning. He had got up at his usual hour. But it is not sad for *him*, it is *his* New Year. We are sure, could he have chosen, *he* would have had it so.

It is very dreary for us not to have seen him again, that he should have had none of us by him at the last, and we no last word or message. But one who saw him just afterwards told me that he looked so peaceful and happy in death one seemed only to wish that a like quiet dismissal from care and toil might be granted to oneself. No one knows what the break-up is to us, especially to me who never once thought that *I* should survive *him*. I thought he had ten years of life in him, I perhaps not one.

My dear mother is very sweet and gentle in her grief. She begged so to see him "and kiss him once more," but was persuaded to give it up, by being told that it was only his "old garment" lying there: *he* was not "there." They did not wish her to see him then, for by that time the grand old head was much altered, though there was not the least convulsive struggle in death. The breath ceased, just as if the burden had been suddenly removed and the rest came.

I am not to go down to Embley just now, for there are almost too many people there for my mother, but she is fond of Sir Harry Verney and Aunt Mary is everything to her. I am afraid though that Aunt Mary was to go back to Combe today. She is so overcome she could not bear to stay over the funeral, which is tomorrow.

I am sorry to hear that you are so unwell. I will write more tomorrow when the last of him will be hid away from us. *Your* own standing sorrow is never out of my head, ever, dearest Aunt Jenny,

your loving old

Flo

Source: Letter, Edinburgh University LHB1/111/13 11

Embley
Romsey
17 February 1874

Dearest Aunt Jenny [Smith]

You are so good to me that I venture to tell you that I am obliged to come up to London on *Thursday* and shall be at *Waterloo Station* at *4:32* P.M. If you are so kind as to send your carriage for me, and it is not inconvenient, I shall be truly obliged.

But please believe that, if it is more than usually inconvenient, I can quite well get another carriage, if you will kindly tell someone to write to me. I leave the Verneys here and shall probably return soon. My dear mother varies much: always gentle, but sometimes quite realizing her loss and saying what she wishes to put on his gravestone, with more of mental and spiritual insight than ever she had, at others, not able to understand that he is gone, and wandering, I hope less painfully to herself than to us. Sometimes, I think she may not live through the day, at others that she may live for years—she is so much stronger than I. For me, the place "all withered when my father died,"[113] but, for me too, it is here to lie expecting to hear his voice and his step coming in to the rooms below, expecting always and always disappointed. Aunt Ju is here. Believe me, ever dearest Aunt Jenny,

yours affectionately
Flo

I hope that you are tolerably well.

Source: Letter, Edinburgh University LHB1/111/13 12

Embley
Romsey
17 March 1874

Dearest Aunt Jenny [Smith]

You are very, very good in writing and calling to offer me your beautiful carriage. Parthe lent me hers so I would not trouble you, and took it to my cost. "Sarv'd you right," you will say, dear, kind Aunt Jenny.

My dear mother's welcome of me this morning was inexpressibly touching; she shed tears. She is so gentle, so gentle: what treasures of goodness there are in people. Often I think there is more of spiritual

---

113 From Ophelia, in Shakespeare's *Hamlet*, act 5, scene 2.

insight and generous tenderness in her than ever she had in her life. And sometimes I wish that God would take her so. Aunt Ju seems thriving. Poor William Nicholson—what a break-up to him. Do you hear how he bears it? In haste, ever, dearest Aunt Jenny,

your old

Flo

Source: Letter with envelope on the death of Jenny Smith, Edinburgh University LHB1/111/13 13

35 South St.
21 July 1878
6:00 A.M.

Dearest Flora [Smith]

I have not written but you and she are ever present with me. I think your house is ever before me, just as much as if I were in it, and her, as I knew her at a time when all those magnificent qualities of devotion and heroism ever in her shone forth: the time of Fred's death till after her confinement. You were a little child then. God bless you always. I was with her then for months. And now she has the peace which passeth understanding.[114] I give her joy. And I know that you take the joy too. I bless God that I have ever known her though I find it hard to bear life without her in it. How much more must you.

Thank you, dearest Flora, for writing to me. Do you know that she wrote to me twice, in her own clear beautiful hand, the last time but a fortnight before her death. She wished me a "farewell" and she spoke "in the name of the precious grandchildren." How dear they must be in her name and in their own to their mother and to you. May they have every blessing that *she* could wish them! And I know how their mother mourns, too, her mother, as well as you do. But I think of *her* you know, as saying how much better it is to be with God, what gain, what joy, but that that joy will be *greater* by thinking of you all gallantly braving life for God's sake and for hers and being made perfect through suffering.[115]

Dearest Flora, I cannot but give you joy because I know you have the joy in this which nothing can take away from you. It is such a thing to have lived, *to live* with her who *lived*, who *lives* in the Highest. And I think of dear Val too. You know I remember him before and soon after you were born, I know how he was "wrapped up" in her, so to

114 An allusion to Phil 4:7.
115 An allusion to Heb 2:10.

speak, and she in him. And I pray that he may feel the joy and the peace.

I should so like to know (if you would be so very kind as to tell me) what were those three prayers which she asked dear Gertrude to read to her, in Mr Martineau's *Common Prayer*[116] was it? It would be such a very great comfort to me to read over those often to myself that *she* chose if I knew what they were, and to have them from your hand would still increase their price.

Dear Flora, some day I should like to write you my recollections of her, of her love-creating heroism in her, at a time when you cannot recollect her. I trust that you are somewhat better. Fare you very well and God be with you as He is with her.

> ever your
> old Flo

I can scarcely hope that Gertrude remembers the time when at Embley with my dear father and mother she used to throw her arms round my neck: "my 'ife, my 'ife, my precious Foey." She was the most lovely thing I ever had and so I doubt not she is still. God bless her, but I must not run on.

> F.N.

I hope the "precious little grandchildren" will be well and not sorrow *too* much.

Cousin Beatrice Smith

Editor: Again there is remarkably little surviving correspondence with cousin Beatrice, but the fact that they saw each other frequently in early years may account for that. Their correspondence regarding local schools is in *Society and Politics.* Beatrice Smith recognized Nightingale's distress and depression from illness after the Crimean War. The following letter shows the practical measures she took, in writing to the great Victorian sanitarian, Edwin Chadwick, for his help in giving Nightingale encouragement to work again. Chadwick wrote a lengthy and effective letter in response, part of which is reproduced below (the part where he went on to propose what became *Notes on Nursing* is recounted in *Public Health Care*).

---

116 Martineau wrote services 9 and 10 in T. Sadler, ed., *Common Prayer for Christian Worship.*

Source: Letter by Beatrice Smith, ADD Mss 45770 ff254-55

Combe Hurst
Kingston, S.W.
18 September [1858]

Dear Mr [Edwin] Chadwick

Your kind note, for which I am very thankful, was forwarded to me here. The papers you kindly sent have been kept back by the Lea Hurst people for their benefit and will come to me in my turn. Florence will, I hope, let me go to her on Saturday next and you shall hear as soon as I can say anything of her.

I believe it is for her sake most earnestly to be wished that you may come into some immediate communication with her. It is your *faith* that her working days are not yet over, that she may work in another field, her own being now closed against her. I cannot find that any of those who have been with her lately would share this hope, less on account of her health than of her state of extreme discouragement. Perhaps the trouble you may take in the matter will end in something far *short* of her full co-operation being given to the work you have in hand. That she will be interested and soothed I cannot doubt, and that *something* will be contributed by her, if she and you can meet . . . pray believe me

ever gratefully yours
Beatrice A.S. Smith

Source: Letter from Edwin Chadwick to Nightingale, ADD Mss 45770 ff89-90

Richmond
Surrey, S.W.
8 December 1858

Dear Miss Nightingale

It should be a consolation to you that such sufferings as those which you have to sustain, you will have prevented as well as mitigated to many thousands, countless numbers of others, though your efforts may as yet have fallen far short of your wishes and the extent of the present needs of relief for afflicted populations. I am desirous of submitting to you one method of relief for mental disappointment, which I have tried, that is when the inert mass is immovable or beyond one's strength exerted in one direction, not to afflict oneself, or to despair, but to change the direction of one's thoughts and labours.

The truth is that my conception of Poor Law legislation was for prevention rather than repression, but, finding I could not move others beyond repression I directed my labours to measures for the prevention of disease. Hence the report of 1842 and subsequent sanitary reports. Having got a check on measures, finding the mass immove- able farther, I had begun to move measures of administrative reform and move the cry and more than many people are aware of, and I might almost have gone away from sanitary measures if you had not pushed me upon India. If I had been twenty years younger you might have driven me amidst the jungles and the marshes there.

Your acts have been observed, and appreciated as the manifesta- tions of a noble sentiment. But your words have not hitherto been heard so to speak, but they soon will be, but only to a select class, and on a professional subject, on hospital construction, for your great monogram of evidence is shut out from the people. . . .

Aunts "Patty" Smith and Julia Smith

Editor: Aunts "Patty" (1782-1870) and Julia Smith (1799-1883) were the eldest and youngest sisters of Frances Nightingale respectively. Both were unmarried. There are several charming letters to Aunt Patty from Nightingale's childhood and one as a young woman. It is regrettable that there is almost no surviving correspondence with "Aunt Ju," who had a keen mind, supported the abolition movement, travelled widely and corresponded with eminent people. One letter by Nightingale to her and several about her are given here.

Source: Letter in child's printing, Balliol College lot 295

Embley
Thursday [1827]

Dear Aunt Patty [Martha Frances Smith]

Will you write me a long letter? We have been twice to court and once to the theatre for the first time at Winchester. In Mr Borough's court, the criminal's court, we heard Snelgrove's trial, the man who lives at the farm. He has stolen beans of Mr Eastted, of whom he is the servant. He was transported for fourteen years.

We went also to the cathedral Tuesday to hear Mr Penton preach; the judges and the sheriff came. The organ was beautiful. The church was much crowded. We saw some boxes in which the bones of the Saxon kings were put.

Flo

[cross written and faint]

Dear Aunt Patty [Martha Frances Smith]

On these boxes were names of the kings in Latin. We made out Eldred and Edmund. We saw Cardinal Beaufort's statue and the Saxon font. Mr Brent is dead and poor Maria is in great grief, and very ill. Mr Long (Martha's uncle) is dead and a poor woman of the name of Roud was burnt very much in attending him, and died a fornight after in consequence. [T]here are such a quantity of [a]pples, currants and raspberries here. An apple tree, which is in my garden, is quite loaded, and bent down with them.

your affectionate Flo

Source: Letter, Balliol College lot 300, addressed to Miss Smith, at 36 Seymour Street, out of London in England, not in Europe

Sunday 4 July [1830]

Dear Aunt Patty [Martha Frances Smith]

Mr and Mrs Thornton[117] are here, with their two daughters, Eliza and Harriet, and their two sons, Frank, who is thirteen, and Edward, who is eighteen. They are very good natured boys. They go out fishing almost every day. Yesterday Frank caught twenty-six fishes; six he threw away; six died and fourteen he brought home alive and put them in the sink to catch pikes with. Six died last night and eight this morning. They were all gudgeons and roach.

Pa is pulling down our north garden wall. Master Edwarde ys goynge to Yndya yn syx monthes to staye ten years—two years at Calcutta, four at Dacca, four at the Himalayas. Sir Charles Ibbetson has been here with his daughter, Laura, aged five, and his son Frederick, aged seven, and their governess, Miss Salisbury, and their nurse, Louise Issot, a Swiss. Laura's ankles are so weak that she is not allowed to walk about, though she can. She is going to Scarboro' to bathe. (I should not have written on pink paper, as we are in mourning, only I thought your eyes were bad.) Miss Christie is very well.

your affectionate niece

Florence Nightingale

---

117 Edward Parry Thornton (1811-), Indian commissioner and author.

Source: Unsigned, incomplete letter, Woodward Biomedical Library A.1

Embley

28 November [1845]

I have just heard from Aunt Julia that you were to be found at Milan, dear Aunt Patty, and sit down directly to hope that you have not forgotten me.

I have been leading a very busy life since you left us. Grandmama Shore's threatened paralytic stroke took me to Tapton in the summer till her *perfect* recovery, at eighty-seven! Then my little lad (Shore) spent the two months of his holidays with us, till October, and till that time poor Gale had been rapidly sinking, but then tapping seemed to give her a new lease of life. She insisted accordingly upon coming here, and ten days afterwards she died, a hero as she had lived, sitting upright in her chair, her last words being, "Don't call the cook. Hannah, go to your work." She sank to rest so gently that, though I held her hand, I could not tell the moment when her gallant spirit sped its way on its noiseless journey, except that the hand lay so still in mine, which never before it failed to answer to, with such a warm hug. She fought the fight out, till overpowered by the material world, like a good *man* and true. And I believe her soul is now gone to animate the body of a moral Napoleon or a Mère Angélique [of Port Royal]. Nobody will ever know all she has been to us. She was so happy and happiness is *so* interesting. Deformed and a dwarf as she was, her great soul made her like a Titan and a Prometheus, and she did bring down fire from heaven, which warmed and lighted our house. Except for ourselves though, how can we have a regret that her Father has sent for her? I never saw a more beautiful expression in death.

I have saved a bit of her hair for Ludwine, of whom she was very fond. Pray tell Ludwine with my love, that I have had the pen in my hand a thousand times to write to her but though it sounds very absurd for me to say I have no time, I really have written to nobody these three months, scarcely even to Helen Richardson, whose increasing illness has alarmed her friends very much, but who is better now, I am glad to say.

The last time I saw Mrs Reeve was in your room. Ludwine wrote to me, which I was very much obliged to her for, from Dover, but did not tell me where to write to them. I hope I shall behave better in future. Poor Mrs Gaskell! You will be much shocked to hear of her sudden death from apoplexy, but Aunt Julia, who arrived at Thames House the very day after it, will tell you all the particulars.

We have had the Stewart Mackenzies staying with us at Lea Hurst: Louisa, a most interesting and very pretty, dark, Oriental-looking creature, with that sensitive trembling quivering underlip, which bodes such nervousness. We struck up a great friendship with her. Mme Mère was exceedingly affectionate and full of inquiries about you all, delighted to meet Uncle Sam. She looks handsome and queenly as ever.

Keith [Mackenzie] and his wife and baby just come back to England. I think we are all in statu quo, a charmed circle. We gave *that* column in the *Times* no work and we seem destined to give no other column occupation either, not even as among railroad committees. Our railroad in Derbyshire is almost settled, and goes, I am afraid, through Bon "Wood." But, as long as we have no station in our back parlour, I think we have no right to complain. It goes behind Aunt Evans's, and will be, alas, a nuisance to the dear old lady.

I will not pretend to tell *you* politics: the American Corn Law, New Zealand questions, will all be settled next spring, and everybody is in a stir about them. We should have put on half mourning for the potato losses, if we had not been engaged with graver questions. Beatrice (the littlest Sam Smith) gets no better. Blanche, who has had a slight illness, Elinor and she are the party at Brighton with Miss Rankin.

The eight Carters are at the eight points of the compass, going round with the sun: Harry is at Cambridge (doing very well), Jack in London, Elinor at Brighton, Fan has just left us, Alf at Alresford, Hugh at Bristol, Hilary at Liverpool with Aunt Ju, or rather now at Thames House. The Nicholsons have quite, I am afraid, given up their Rome plans, which is the *odder*, as William N. has no prospect of being ordered abroad yet, and would have gone with them. They are very gay, went up to town for the amateur performance of Messrs Dickens, Jerrold and Co. for the benefit of the sanatorium. Aunt Jane is the only one whom I cannot give a good account of, children in the measles, self very delicate, Miss Beevor going to be married to Ted Carter and, except for the three boys, who seem to make up to their mother for all troubles (they are such living waters of happiness). She is rather out of spirits at having to leave their beloved Thames Bank for a house in Bedford Sq. where however they will be near the boys at the London University.

Can I tell you of any marriages? At Margaret Arkwright's wedding with her cousin, Vice Chancellor Wigram's eldest son, we were present. Charlotte Eyre is to be married to a Captain Strange, but these will not interest you. We are this moment come back from Dr Fowler's where we have been spending the week, they as young and delightful as usual.

We dined at the Palmerstons the other day to meet Horaga, who denies the whole story of his shaking the Queen of Spain into signing papers, for which he was obliged to fly. But, as Lord Palmerston says, two years ago I remember Narvaez[118] in exile at Gibraltar and Espartero *Regent* of Spain, next year Espartero[119] in the *Regents* Park, and Narvaez minister of Spain, and in a year or two Horaga will be back home and in place again.

You will be sorry to hear of Frederic Stainforth's death, the John Thorntons' son-in-law. Mrs John will adopt all those children directly, that is, Eliza's two she has adopted already. Lady Holland's death will interest you and her bequest of £1500 a year to Lord John Russell [?], most unjustly cutting out her already injured son, Colonel Fox, injured I mean, by her having produced him before his *younger* brother Lord Holland.

We had a most kind letter from Miss Fanny Allen the other day asking after you, and bearing wonderfully the loss at once of brother and sister, Baugh Allen and Mrs Surtees. I am afraid this is rather a forlorn letter, but I seem to have nothing entertaining to tell you; we have paid no visits for some time till this one. Parsons is going to marry poor Gale's niece and we have hardly a household therefore at present, and except Aunt Joanna, Jen and Alf for ten days and Aunt Maria, who is coming tomorrow, we have been quiet at home for six weeks.

How I wish you could go to Pisa and see my friend Caterina Ferrucci,[120] wife of the Professor Ferrucci there—how delighted she would be to see you. She is a poetess and all that goes with that. We [breaks off]

---

118 General Ramon Maria Narvaez dominated the government of Spain during the regency of Isabella II.

119 General Baldomero Espartero shared the regency with the Queen of Spain's mother.

120 See *European Travels* for Nightingale's acquaintance with the Ferrucci family.

Source: Letter, Hampshire Record Office 94M72/F587/7

35 South St., W.
17 October 1872

Dearest Aunt Ju [Julia Smith]

Thank you so very much for being so glad to see Miss Torrance.[121] She will thankfully come to you for a fortnight or so tomorrow (Friday) by the train which reaches Cromford at 4:18. I thankfully accept your kind offer to order her a fly[122] for that train.

I am sure that you will like her—that does not trouble me at all— and that she will be made happy and well. But I hope that the necessary housekeeping will not trouble you too much. *Please* charge it all to me, *including flys* (fours-in-hand, powdered footmen and the rest) for which purpose I send £5, and will send as much more as you please to charge.

She ought to eat, sleep and run about morning, noon and night, and read fairy tales, which is a religious duty, or the like. Shall I send down some books of the kind? Or will you unlock your literary (fairy) stores and those of the house?

She is, I believe, a Scotch Presbyterian, but, though intensely religious and devoted, the most entirely *un*bigoted person I think I ever met with—for she is not bigoted either against or for any denomination. Her Bible classes are a lesson and study.

I send by her three bottles sherry and two pounds tea, for, though, dearest Ju, I agree with you that Derbyshire tropical productions are beyond any other, yet I do *not* think that it shines in its "*teas*." God bless you.

ever your
old Flo

Source: Letter with envelope, Hampshire Record Office 94M72/F585/10/2

10 South St.
Park Lane, W.
24 May 1882

My dear Alice [Bonham Carter]

I trust that I am not troubling you too much by writing to you about Lea Hurst furniture for Aunt Julia. I have waited till her return to Ravensbourne, in order that it might only make *one* trouble in your speaking to the maid, if you kindly will. (I have tried to make things as

---

121 Elizabeth Anne Torrance, matron of Highgate Infirmary.
122 A small, light, one-horse, covered carriage.

comfortable as I could in having all kitchen utensils retinned and everything "washed up." And I am going to send down by Aunt Julia's maid a new piece of some satin to renew some drawing-room furniture.)

You know Aunt Julia has a roomful of her own "things" and utensils there. I have directed Mrs Francis to give out, in the way of counterpanes, etc., kitchen utensils, etc., everything that Aunt Julia wants, but to take charge of the rest herself. Please tell the maid that there is to be no stint in anything that Aunt Julia wants.

I come now to what I know you will not think me ungracious in. It is because the Shores propose to go to Lea Hurst as soon as she leaves, and Shore's alas! repugnance to the place depends a good deal on what I am going to explain, whether it increases or not. (I always retin and renew the whole of the kitchen utensils two and even three times a year, once after Aunt Julia's servants, once after Shore's. That is a very small grievance indeed and I should never have mentioned it. I always renew all broken glass and china several times a year.) But the last time Aunt Julia was at Lea Hurst, her cook, I *think* her name was Philpots, not only used the kitchen utensils we always leave out for Aunt Julia, but broke open a large box, of course without Aunt Julia's knowledge, in which all our kitchen utensils, entirely new and clean, were packed by me for Shore's arrival. That again is a small grievance, but these were put back without an attempt at cleaning—black off the fire, many of them *burnt* through, all more or less spoiled. Shore's family followed unfortunately at once. And—je vous laisse à penser [I leave you to think about this]—they thought this was my way of receiving *them*, the Shores. (I unhappily did not follow that year till September.)

A room was also left in an incurably dirty state, carpet quite spoiled. This also was laid to my door, in spite of all I have spent upon the house. This again would be a very small grievance if it did not make Shore dislike the place more alas! than he does already.

You will know how very much I grieve to be troubling you about these petty cares, who have so many petty cares already, as well as great ones. All I want to say is this: I have not left any kitchen utensils out for Aunt Julia this time, not because I did not mean to do so, but because all of them were sent to be made good in preparation. If you would be so very good as to tell the maid that Mrs Francis, the woman of the house, *will give out all she wants*; there need be no difficulty. But if she, the maid, would be so kind as to see that charwomen are sent for, at my expense of course, *to clean up all the kitchen utensils* when Aunt Julia leaves, and especially if any are burnt through or otherwise injured *to have them sent at once to Cromford* (Mr Yeomans or Mrs Francis will manage it) *to be retinned or renewed there*, at my expense of course, I shall be very grateful.

What a long story I have inflicted on you, dear Alice. I earnestly hope that Aunt Julia's stay at Lea Hurst will be *most* successful. There are many waiting for her: Mary Bratby, Jane Allison, Mr Haywood— God speed her. . . .

ever yours affectionately and many beggings for pardon
with love
F. Nightingale

Source: Letter, Wellcome (Claydon copy) Ms 9009/236

10 South St.
22 December 1883

My dear Sir Harry [Verney]

Parthe knows how ill Aunt Julia has been. The end came, I would rather say the beginning of her new life, last night at half past eight. It is not grievous but joyous. She died quite peacefully. She had so prayed that she might not have to lead long an useless life and also she longed not to survive her keen sympathy. I don't mean that she used that word. From Sunday last till Wednesday she was so much better that they thought she might live for months. On Wednesday night the temperature rose again; there was, I believe, some rather distressing delirium. Last night she died quite quietly, the last of the generation who loved Lea Hurst so passionately, for Aunt Mai will never go there again. Lea Hurst will know them no more and I shall not know Lea Hurst, if indeed I ever go there again, without them.

She was the last, too, of those ten vigorous brothers and sisters who all lived to great old age. For Aunt Joanna, Mrs Bonham Carter, scarcely takes notice of anything. Ravensbourne was her home and we rather regret that she did not die there. But, as Mrs Fremantle said, one can go to heaven as well from a journey as from home. O how glorious it is for her now. God bless you both.

ever yours affectionately
F. Nightingale

She died as you know at Hastings, Beatrice, Miss Burnett and her maid with her.

Source: Letter on Aunt Julia's death, Chiddingstone Castle

[1883-84]

Dear Alice [Bonham Carter]

I am afraid you are at all times overtasked. Fare you very well.
ever your affectionate
Flo

I wonder whether you have told Aunt Joanna yet. I return Beatrice's letter with very many thanks.

Barbara Bodichon:[123] I trust that she has taken comfort and borne it calmly and well. She may be so very sure that everything was done for dear Aunt Julia, body and soul, that could possibly be done. Will you be so very kind, when you write to her, as to give her my heartfelt sympathy and cordial love?

F.N.

I read the glorious burial service with you at half past two. Dear Alice, we all think of you and thank you.

Source: Letter on the death of Julia Smith, Columbia University, Presbyterian Hospital School of Nursing C161

New Year's Day 1884

Dear Bratby

Your flowers were quite in time. I should like to tell you how Mrs Henry Bonham Carter carried the flowers and herself dropped them into the grave in Keston churchyard, and on Sunday morning last Miss Alice saw them *still looking fresh,* the flowers as well as the wreaths having *all* been placed on the outside of the grave, and the soft wreathing mists have laid their dews on it and kept the blooms all fresh.

Five of Mr Harry Bonham Carter's boys asked to come to follow their loving great aunt: Mr Shore and Sam, Arthur Clough, Mr Coltman, Mr Godfrey Lushington and Beatrice, Mr and Mrs Harry and Alfred and Hugh Bonham Carter, Miss Alice and Beavis, Aunt Julia's excellent maid, Miss Burnett and Mrs Moore and Mr Mason from Lewes, the women in a carriage, the men walking followed the coffin from Ravensbourne to the beautiful little Keston churchyard where the vault is dug in pure white chalk in the hillside and covered with flowers.

123 Née Barbara Leigh Smith (1827-91), Barbara Bodichon, daughter of Uncle Benjamin Smith and his common-law wife, Anne Longden, a leader in the movement for women's suffrage, education and employment.

Mrs Bonham Carter, who is ill, could not be told of her sister Julia's death till the Saturday after the funeral (Saturday 29th) when she asked for her, and Miss Alice told her. She took it quite calmly, but afterwards, when she realized her loss, was much agitated, shaken and distressed. Miss Alice was almost glad, when, on Sunday afternoon, she was too ill to remember her loss. . . .

yours sincerely

F. Nightingale

Cousin Rosalind Shore Smith

Editor: Nightingale was an honorary aunt to her cousin (once removed) Rosalind, daughter of Shore and Louisa Smith. "Rosy" went to Girton College, Cambridge, married a political activist, Vaughan Nash, and worked with him in the co-operative movement. Nightingale was clearly delighted with her "niece's" choice of a cause, though it was not her own. Rosalind's vegetarianism also challenged Nightingale, who promptly passed on advice, recipes and food parcels (see "Food" below). Various of the envelopes show that eggs, cucumber, gooseberries and strawberries were sent with the letter. Inquiries went out when Rosalind was giving birth, flowers sent with congratulations and inquiries made about the "princelet." The first is on her mother's death.

Source Letter/draft/copy, ADD Mss 45795 ff149-50

6 February 1880

Dearest Rosie [Rosalind Shore Smith]

I send you my favourite book which was my father's and then mine and which I never part with except to you, and I hope you will like it as much as I do, if that is possible. Please return it when you have done with it. I am trying to get one *for your own.*

Dearest Rosie, I can never tell you how good your father and mother have been to my mother. I thought your father's love to her was like God's. O no, it is *not* "we can only love the loveable." It *is* the loving only can love. And your mother's devotion and care, beautiful, beautiful care. It was so *very, very* good of her to send me last night the prayer and hymn book and I have so, so valued it, and the flowers. I hope they will not be very tired tonight after this most trying day. You must nurse them well. I am so glad dear Sam went.

And thank you, thank *you,* dear Rosie, for all your protecting care of my dear mother at the Hurst, and Sam too.

"Old man and Marquis no more." Do you remember in the history of Charles I's revolution, an old royalist Marquis keeps his fortress till the last and then dies in prison worn out, "old man and Marquis no more." Now my mother is in the Immediate Presence of God. Fare you very well and Miss Mochler dearest.

ever your

Aunt Florence

Source: Letter, Woodward Biomedical Library A.92

Christmas Day [1880]

Dearest Rosy [Rosalind Shore Smith]

Aunt Florence's best love to you and Sam and all, for this and every Christmas. How is Mama? And how is Uncle Burrowes? Mr Haywood, the schoolmaster, is here till Monday. Great love to all, dearest souls and thanks for water lilies.

Aunt F.

I found Plumer Ward's volume about the Norton ghost at Lea Hurst in the study after you were gone, and have it here. The Shore who married the Norton ghost's sister, Urith Offley, was Mr Shore (afterwards of "Meersbrook"), a noble old man, my great uncle, the eldest brother of my Grandfather Shore, noble in mien, in character and everything. I will tell you a great deal about him some day. Urith Offley brought him Norton which he gave up to his eldest son, Sam, and retired to Meersbrook. . . .

Source: Letter with envelope, Woodward Biomedical Library A.55

7 June 1881

Dearest Rosy [Rosalind Shore Smith]

If you write to Sarajevo, please *not* to mention what I told you about the possibility of Miss Irby going to Ragusa for a week, nor to anyone. I do not know why it should be a secret, but I find it *is*. I earnestly hope Miss Irby will soon be better. Please let me know if you hear. Do you know *how long* she HAD BEEN IN bed?

I want to adorn Barbarina's garden, but this is a bad time of year. Could we anyhow get her a geranium and *rose tree*, and "plant them out" in her garden? Next year, if she is there, we must begin betimes, and give her bulbs and cuttings. *When* ought hyacinths and tulip bulbs to be put in the ground?

ever dearest

your loving

Aunt Florence

Source: Letter with envelope, ADD Mss 45795 ff152-54

[printed address] 10 South Street
Park Lane, W.
22 August 1881

My very dearest Rosy [Rosalind Shore Smith]

Aunt Florence's heart is filled with you and your going to Girton. I can say nothing and, saying nothing, I would ask those greatest of the "heathens," Plato, Aeschylus, Thucydides, to say much to you. Aeschylus whose Prometheus is evidently a foreshadowing of, or, if you like it better, the same type (with Osiris of Egypt) as Christ, the one who brought "gifts to men," who defied the "powers that be," the "principalities" and "powers of evil," who "suffered for men" in bringing them the "best gifts," the "fire from heaven," who *could* only give by suffering himself, and who finally "led captivity captive."[124]

Have you Mr Jowett's *Plato*? Please read some time the introductions to, I think, the *Crito* and the *Phaedo*[125] (I will look and see which they are). I gave him the spiritual hints for those, not of course the critical. It seems to me that I see in nothing so much the *history of God-in-the-religions-of-the-world*, which M Mohl learnt Oriental languages in order to write as in these great "heathens," Persian, Chinese, Indian, Greek also and Latin too, but specially Aeschylus and Plato. Perhaps too, in physiology: the *greatness* of His work, the silence of His work, what spirit He is of, His "*glory*" and *poorness* of spirit, and that to be "poor of spirit"[126] constitutes His glory—if to be poor of spirit means utter unselfishness, perfect freedom from self and from the very thought of self and from affectations, and from "*vain* glory."

May we all pursue the work that He has given us to do in the way that He pursues it, with *greatness* and *poorness* of spirit. HE never thinks of self. And may we remember how deep is the meaning of the old, old words, "to be like Christ, Christ shall save his people," if these mean the spirit of love and self-sacrifice, which indeed, my dear child, I think you do. My very dearest child, fare you VERY well, very, very well is the deepest prayer

of Aunt Florence

---

124 An allusion to Judges 5:12.
125 Jowett used Nightingale's recommended changes in his second edition, *Dialogues of Plato*, 1875. See *Society and Politics*.
126 An allusion to Matt 5:3.

Source: Letter with envelope, Add Mss 45795 ff155-57 [addressed to Miss Rosalind Shore Smith, Girton College, Cambridge]

10 South St.

Park Lane, W.

5 December 1881

Dearest Rosy [Rosalind Shore Smith]

. . . Miss Irby was with me twice at Lea Hurst, looking much better than last year. We had a heavenly November at Lea Hurst and I received the village people for thirty-four afternoons. I could not persuade Miss Irby to go to Girton alas! this time. She is now at 17 Albemarle St.

Now I will say no more, dearest, but good speed, and remember that, when your brain is tired, it is not saving time to force it on, but rest it for 3/4 of an hour. Take a little brisk walk is best, or read an entertaining book or play a bit of Mozart. Tennis greatly to be approved of, but not for 1/2 hour's relaxation. All Aunt Florence's best wishes are with you, dearest

Auf Wiedersehen.

Never work directly after meals or *late* at night. Better the early morning, but you know all this, O wise woman.

Source: Letter, Woodward Biomedical Library A.61

10 South St.

30 December 1886

Dearest Rosy [Rosalind Shore Smith]

I am afraid "Mama" is pretty bad. It was so kind of her to call here on Tuesday, but I am afraid it was not good for her and now the weather is worse. I dare not ask any of you to come out today. But if you, dear soul, could come to me tomorrow at 5:00 or any day after that you could fix. And I hope now, weather permitting, to see you all, as my heart is longing for you. And please if Papa is coming or Louis or Sam,[127] remember the "neat double-bedded room" here.

My love to Barbarina,[128] and a Barbados stamp. She has a cold too, I fear. I have not heard from her yet about the pocketbook. And for you, darling, do you want a pocketbook, with almanac, only not ruled, or a simple notebook? The old year is passing away.

May every blessing, dearest, that God can give be yours in the New Year, a path to follow, an object of great worth, health and sympathy, a

---

127 Her brothers Samuel and Louis Hilary Shore Nightingale.
128 Her younger sister Margaret Thyra Barbara Smith, also a Girton student.

daily supply from Him who *is* Love. Aunt Florence's heart yearns after your happiness, but *His* heart, the eternal Father's, yearns yet more.

Source: Letter to Rosalind Shore Smith, ADD Mss 45795 f158

[printed address] 10 South St.
Park Lane, W.
14 March 1887

. . . Do you leave England on Thursday? "I very much applaud you for what you have done" in the matter of Italy. Would I could be with you! How delightful, how unique in its delight, is Rome, but I am afraid you will say "it has too many facts."

ever your loving
Aunt Florence

Source: Letter, ADD Mss 46865 ff22-23

10 South St.
9 November 1887

Dearest Rosalind [Shore Smith]

I send you six "vegetables." When the parental birds are away, the mice do play. Are you there?

I expect that you will meet my Calcutta friends at Claydon, Man Mohun Ghose and his wife, high-caste Brahmins, now Brahmo-Somaj[129] people, whom we were talking about. He is the man who wants to set up nightclubs in the country and lecture to the ryots on the simplest forms of government. She has brought her daughter, thirteen, to England to be educated. "In India she would have been married, O long ago," says the mother.

Would you be so very good as to take the small parcel I send to Mrs Davidson, Aunt Parthe's most excellent maid, at Claydon?

I send you the "High Caste Hindu Woman," which we were talking about. If you like to take it to Claydon, I should not wonder if Aunt Parthe would like to look at it.

God bless you, my dearest. Success to you always.

ever your loving old
Aunt Florence

---

129 A group of progressive, socially conscious, monotheistic Hindus.

Source: Note on envelope, Add Mss 46865 f25

2 April 1888

Dearest Rosalind, you would not like to have the Quetelet volumes, etc. now, would you?[130]

F.N.

Is Louis come back?

Source: Letter, Add Mss 46865 ff39-40

13 March 1889

"Pure Literature Society"

Dearest Rosalind [Shore Smith]

I send their catalogue of books, which I ought to have done long before, for your small societies. Please look at top of p 3. I am a "subscriber to the society" and, if the co-ops will condescend, would gladly help to raise the "£5" or "£10" necessary to get a "half-price library."

Both the Lea Hurst institutes have profited by this. At the same time, I don't suppose there are in this catalogue the "hard" reference books your *central* library affects. But I would gladly get you some of these too, if you will kindly give me names.

Please tell me your *plans*. And please tell me how you all are.

ever your affectionate

Aunt Florence

Source: Letter, Add Mss 46865 f49

10 South St.

9 July 1889

Dearest Rosalind [Shore Smith]

I hear that you are going to live under Blackfriars Bridge, perhaps immediately? Are you quite alone at the flat, without even a woman at night?

Aunt Florence

Very anxious to hear of you. I feel like a wretch who has been starving you and making you live on bread and butter and no grass.

---

130 Quetelet's *Physique sociale*. A note is appended that she gave them to Dr Karl Pearson "for their college," University College, London, in which archives they remain. For Nightingale's discussion of Quetelet see *Society and Politics*.

Source: Letter with envelope, ADD Mss 45795 ff179-81

[printed address] 10 South St.
Grosvenor Square, W.
8 February 1892

Dearest, very dearest [Rosalind Shore Smith]

My heart *is* full of you, but, immersed in very sour business, I find nothing to *say* worthy of your sweetness. I do give you joy for having found a man[131] whom you can so thoroughly love and esteem and work with. And I, of course, give him joy at having found you. And I give us all joy.

But please look to the shillings. We cannot live on sweets and we must live in order to work together. I know you think me very worldly but, you see, unfortunately, we live in the world. It is a great bore, but then you heroically set to mending the world. So I pray you to live.

This does not at all say what my heart is full of, dearest child. But I hope soon to hear from yourself what your heart is full of, that is, when your nursing of dear mother and father is finished. I am afraid both still want it, my love. May I send a message to Mr Nash? God bless you both.

ever your loving
Aunt Florence

Source: Letter to an unknown recipient, Woodward Biomedical Library A.72

[printed address] 10 South Street
Park Lane, W.
13 May 1893

Dearest ever dearest old friend

I was so glad to hear from you. So often I think of you, and hope that you are happy, you who have so done your duties in love. Thank you for remembering your old friend's poor old birthday and your dear kind note. I am glad if you are able to go to your sister's and to Edinburgh.

You say you like to hear of our "family events." You know perhaps that Rosalind, Shore's elder daughter, married last June a man, Mr Nash, who has everything to recommend him except money. They have taken a small house at 12/ a week to the east of the east of London, where they are enormously busy, workshops, visiting all sorts of trades and writing about them. They travel all over Scotland, England

---

131 Vaughan Nash (1861-1932), later secretary to Sir Henry Campbell Bannerman.

and are now in Ireland on the same quest. They telegraphed to me from *Donegal* on my birthday. If Rosalind had but health! They were married at Embley. . . . The Shore Smiths have taken the name of Nightingale.

ever yours

F. Nightingale

Source: Letter, ADD Mss 46865 f82

[printed address] 10 South Street
Park Lane, W.
16 September 1894

Dearest Rosalind [Nash]

I want very much to know how you are and Mr Vaughan Nash and Mr Louis Vaughan Nash, who, I understand, stays with you because his conversation is an assistance to his father in writing his newspaper.

And I want very much to know whether you will be able to get away on Tuesday. All blessing be with you. And I don't want to trouble you to write—a verbal answer will, as far as it goes, do, something to satisfy my voracious maw.

ever your loving

Aunt Florence

I thought the brother *wonderfully* well on Friday.

Source: Letter, Woodward Biomedical Library A.74

[printed address] 10 South Street
Park Lane, W.
9 October 1895

Dearest Rosalind [Nash]

I need not, indeed I cannot tell you, how grieved I am, but I do so very much wish that you would have a nurse to help you. There *are* very nice French nurses, though I know none now.

Say "God bless you" from my heart to hers and say that the throat does require so much rest when the larynx is affected. I ask it as a favour from her dear self. It IS unfortunate that Sam is away; he is worth twenty nurses.

ever your loving

Aunt Florence

Mrs S.N. ill at Boulogne.

Source: Letter with envelope, Woodward Biomedical Library A.80

22 September 1896

By express messenger. Ask particularly how Mrs Vaughan Nash and the baby are but don't ask them to write.

[printed address] 10 South Street
Park Lane, W.
24 September 1896

My dear Mr Vaughan [Nash]

I am so grateful to you for writing to me. And I trust that all is going on right today. Because it is probable that Little Boy has expensive tastes in dress and in milk, I offer as his birthday present, a sordid ten-pun-note I mean. Doubtless he keeps accounts. I offer to his dear mother tenderest love. Her little room looks south, I hope, and receives the sun, that sun which no one can buy, not even with a ten-pun-note. And I am sure you are a capital nurse and keep her in a delightful (not a morose) stillness.

your affectionate
F.N.

Source: Letter with envelope, Woodward Biomedical Library A.88

[printed address] 10 South Street
Park Lane, W.
20 December 1898

Dearest [Rosalind Nash]

Please admit a horse for little Louis [born 1896] and a white woolly dog for Christopher [born 1898] and our dearest love and blessings for Christmas for all.

from your loving
Aunt Florence

Source: Letter with envelope, Woodward Biomedical Library A.89, "*With a grouse, To inquire*"

[printed address] 10 South Street
Park Lane, W.
22 August 1899

Dearest [Rosalind Nash]

I am sorry that Christopher has been "feverish." I hope he has not been exciting himself with the Dreyfus affair.[132] (N.B. The French call

---

132 French Army captain Alfred Dreyfus, a Jew, was convicted of treason in 1894 and pardoned in 1899 after a concerted campaign. He was finally declared to have been innocent in 1906.

us "islanders." I should like to see any other nation which will put itself in a fever about foreign affairs.) It is not a good plan.

Please come at 5:30 tomorrow (Wednesday) if quite convenient to you.

ever yours

Aunt Florence

May I send you one grouse, just come from Scotland. Mr Christopher does not eat grouse I believe.

Blanche (Smith) Clough and Arthur Clough

Editor: See the biographical sketch in Appendix A. There is little surviving correspondence to her cousin, Blanche, and none on personal matters to her husband, A.H. Clough. Of course Nightingale would have seen her cousin frequently in their younger years, and Clough was a frequent visitor when he worked for the Nightingale Fund. There is extant business correspondence with A.H. Clough; possibly personal correspondence was destroyed?

Evidently Clough was not considered a suitable husband for Blanche Smith and Nightingale sought to ease the way by having him introduced to her family by a person they knew and respected, her own former suitor, Richard Monckton Milnes. The latter then misunderstood Nightingale's letter to mean that Clough was her intended. Nightingale corrected that misunderstanding in a follow-up letter, explaining that Clough wanted "to be my son-in-law."[133]

Source: Letter to Richard Monckton Milnes, Trinity College, Cambridge Houghton 18/126

20 March 1851

Will you forgive me for asking a favour from you? I believe you are acquainted with Mr A.H. Clough. If you like him enough to speak a good word for him, that good word spoken at Embley might save a good deal of suffering.

There will be six objections in the minds of my people:

1. An instructor of youth;
2. Without a sous;
3. Or a relation;
4. Or orthodoxy;
5. Shy;
6. "Bothie."[134]

---

133 Letter to Richard Monckton Milnes 25 March [1851], Trinity College, Cambridge, Houghton 28/128.

134 His poem, "Bothie, the Love Story of a Young Man," 1848, if tame by later standards, was then considered sexually frank.

Might I ask you to be his introducer to my people, did it happen conveniently? I would not have asked it in this formal way, if I had thought it likely that I should see you.

Florence Nightingale

Editor: There is next a letter in 1860 recounting a visit of their infant son and then several letters from shortly after Clough's death in Florence. Nightingale's fondness for both clearly extended in full force to their son, Arthur (for example, she quoted his father's poetry to him). The letters to him show that he reciprocated that love, consulting his by-then-elderly "Aunt Florence" (they were first cousins once removed) about his unhappy love life. Later correspondence shows that he married in 1893, presumably to someone else.

Source: Incomplete letter, Balliol College lot 306

Upper Terrace
Hampstead
1 September 1860

Dearest [Blanche Clough]

The little chaps arrived yesterday as you know. "It" came in in its flannel coat to see me. No one had ever prepared me for its royalty. It sat quite upright but would not say a word, good or bad. The cats jumped up upon it. It put out its hand with a kind of gracious dignity and caressed them, as if they were presenting addresses, and they responded in a humble, grateful way, quite cowed by infant majesty. (I washed the cats before it came.)

Then it put out its little bare cold feet for me to warm which, when I did, it smiled. In about twenty minutes it waved its hand to go away, still without speaking a word. I think it is the most beautifully organized little piece of humanity I ever saw. And I think you will get your pension from government. They passed a good night and have been out on the heath this fine morning. I think they have brought fine weather.

Fanny Keene is quite impressed with the necessity of feeding them. I believe she will kill beef every day and keeps a herd of cows in the garden. She is always baking seed cake for the "It," Prince Arthur.

F.N.

Source: Letter to Blanche (Smith) Clough, Balliol College lot 309

> [printed address] 32 South Street
> Grosvenor Square, W.
> [ca. November 1861]

Twice I have "desired with desire"[135] to eat this sacrament with you, but did not like to press it and I now learn that you would not have liked to have been asked. But let not my dear Blanche suppose that, because I have been silent, I have not felt, always as now, deeply now as ever, at every waking hour, night and day, the greatness of her loss and how immeasurably greater hers than anyone's. How well he loved you, who knew better than I? Indeed I know no husband's love greater than his. What he was, I knew, and therefore what his love must have been. For the greater the soul the greater the love. You have been like Mary at the foot of the cross.

But more than his memory, himself, is still with you. To have been once his is to be always his. And, as Mary was called the Blessed,[136] should not you be called the Blessed? Nevertheless the loss is bitter, deep and wringing. But you have his children. This letter calls for no reply. God bless you.

ever yours and his
Flo

Source: Letter with envelope, ADD Mss 45760 ff11-15

> 32 South St., W.
> 18 November 1861

My dear Captain Galton

Our Clough is dead and I know no one who, not of his immediate friends, will feel more about it than you. He died on Tuesday, 12 November, a little after midnight at Florence. He was quite conscious, kissed Blanche and his sister, who had arrived three days before, and sent his "love" to his children. But he spoke very little during this last illness. Blanche and his sister are coming home and desire not to be fetched. They have courier maids, who were sent out to them.

There goes another valuable life. He always seemed to be like a race-horse harnessed to a coal truck. For himself there is nothing to regret. He never could have recovered health and spring enough to make life again what it should be to a man of that stamp. "The righteous per-

---

135 An allusion to Luke 22:15.
136 An allusion to Luke 1:28.

isheth and no man layeth it to heart," none considering that he is taken away from the "*good* he might have done."[137] Now, hardly one man remains (that I can call a man) of all those whom I have worked with these five years. And I survive them all. I am sure I did not mean to.

He was a man of a rare mind and temper, did "plain work" so ungrudgingly and so well. He helped me immensely, though not officially, with his sound judgment and constant sympathy. Would you tell Mr Lowe, who cared for him and who ought not to see it first in the newspapers?. . . .

Bertha Coltman has not been very well. And they keep it from her. I tell you out of excess of precaution only. But I thought it just possible that some of yours might write to her. Sutherland has been heard of at Paris where he arrived on Sunday. He will be at home tomorrow or not till Wednesday, in which case I may not see him till Thursday. I mention this, because of the Trinidad papers.

ever yours most truly

F.N.

Source: Letter, Wellcome (Claydon copy) Ms 8999/42

5 December 1861

My dear [Parthenope Verney]

It occurs to me that if Mama would offer Lea Hurst to Blanche and Miss [Anne] Clough and the children, for the winter and spring, making such arrangements as would allow them space in the house, the only way to secure quiet to her (she has been very ill since his death) it would be the greatest boon to her possible. For she clings to Lea Hurst as the last place where she was with him and the children. Miss Clough has gone through more than anyone I ever knew and she *is* so like her brother. I have not the least idea whether Blanche would accept it, but I am sure that all would take the offer most kindly.

I think you might determine Mama to make it in such a way as that it could be accepted. For absolute solitude would not be good for Blanche and Miss Clough just now, and they ought to be able to ask anybody to see them. And, if the offer is made, let it appear to come from Mama and Papa direct, and not at my suggestion.

Blanche will be home not before Christmas, and then she must be some time at Combe so that it will probably not be till end of January

---

137 A paraphrase of Isa 57:1.

that she will consider where to go. Then I think Lea Hurst would appear to her like a haven of rest.

For three years my *Clough's* bi-daily visits of help and sympathy dragged me through the hardest work man ever did yet. Without him I could not have done it. Oh Jonathan, my brother Jonathan.[138] I would we could repay something to his widow and children.

ever yours

F.

Source: Letter, Private Collection of Hans Cohen, Amstelveen, Netherlands

10 South St.
Park Lane, W.
7 November 1893

My dear Blanche [Clough]

Thank you so much for you note on the death of Mr Jowett. Do you know that he sometimes felt glad in the society of "Clough" during his last illness? He was in London at the house of those dear Lewis Campbells[139] for doctoring and nursing from 16 September to 23rd. He was lying in the way he liked, silent, with Mr Lewis Campbell sitting beside him, when suddenly he opened his eyes and said, "O is it you? I thought I was with Clough."

On the 23rd he *would* go down—he was so much better—to Mr Justice Wright's at Headley, as you know. On the 25th the collapse came. People said he was "unconscious." We don't believe it. Many of his old friends came down to see him and were admitted—he always knew them. He liked them to come, but he rarely spoke. So it went till Sunday 1 October when the end came, or rather the new life.

One of the best known of his old pupils, now in India, wrote me such a beautiful letter, exactly as if it was only his "*bodily* presence" that had gone from us.

My love to Flossy,[140] please, and to Arthur and his wife. I have not seen her yet, but I hope for it this winter.

ever your affectionate

F. Nightingale

---

138 An allusion to 2 Sam 1:26.
139 Lewis Campbell, co-editor of *Life and Letters of Benjamin Jowett.*
140 Their daughter, Florence.

Source: Letter, Boston University 5/8/4

10 South St.
12 October 1885

My dear Arthur [Clough]

I am still encompassed round with "wild bulls of Bashan,"[141] and fear I have not a single day this week free. Try me again.

Thank you for what you say about Sam. I am so glad you try to see him.

ever yours affectionately

Aunt Florence

I had such a nice little "wild" (not "bull" but) cow-kin on Saturday, a young Irish lady who has actually undertaken 900 beds of the Belfast Workhouse Infirmary without a single *trained* nurse. She told me a great deal, alas! Very unsatisfactory of the enormous union schools. But I think these schools are pretty nearly as bad everywhere. And we call ourselves a civilized people!!

You will have to look to this.

Source: Letter, Boston University 5/20/19

[printed address] 10 South Street
Park Lane, W.
24 February 1889

Dearest Arthur [Clough]

Thanks very many for the two pictures of youth and age, so lovely. I have several precious things to return to you.

Grannie [Aunt Mai Smith], I believe, went on writing every morning till within the last two years. No doubt Mama has these sheets. Will you not look at them? They must tell something.

Aunt Florence's deepest sympathy is with you all.

Source: Letter, Boston University 2/23/5

[printed address] 10 South Street
Park Lane, W.
13 June 1889

Dearest Arthur [Clough]

You didn't take me in on Wednesday. Nor do I deserve any credit therefor. I know very well what you are feeling. And with joy and anxiety and all my heart I wait and hope for your perfect success. I too

---

141 An allusion to Ps 22:12.

cannot say, "Them's my sentiments." But my "sentiments" run strong and deep for you and your ladye love, and are in great suspense to know what comes. Thank you for telling me about this.

I have had so much sad and obscure business since I saw you as not to be able to write. But all the more and not the less I was thinking of and hoping for you, if that would do any good.

Won't you and Sam come and dine here soon? and after dinner you can enjoy a shindy with Aunt Parthe, who will trail, poor darling, her coat-tails, or you yours. I don't know which—all over Amerikay and green Erin for you or her to tread upon. Only don't let there be any scalp wounds, for we have enough of those in hospital after rainy bank holidays.

Rosalind dined here on Friday but Sam went to Embley, so on Saturday she took to herself another Nebuchadnezzar worse than herself, on their way to Ipswich to eat grass with her.[142] I did my humble best to collect grasses for them, such as London grows, mostly in N. Africa, which come with the swallows, and they were pleased to approve of my selection, in spite of outraging the Goddess of Simplicity. But of all the superstitions grass is the greenest!

God bless you, my dear Arthur. I have been writing since 4 A.M. and am idiotic and can't spell, but all the more and

ever your loving
Aunt Florence

Source: Letter, Boston University 2/23/6

10 South St.
20 June 1889

Dearest Arthur [Clough]

I don't believe that your ideas are "distorted," but I believe that this is a time of great suspense to you, to me and those who love you. The 18th was Waterloo Day: there are many private Battles of Waterloo fought in people's lives, many a day, of which the world knows nothing. I have been and am (often beaten) fighting them always. The day before yesterday two: one, the fate of a commission started by Sidney Herbert thirty-two years ago on that very day, the other the fate of a matron of 130 nurses. But I fight on.

You remember what your father said:

O only Source of all our light and life,
Whom as our truth, our strength, we see and feel,

---

142 Rosalind Nash was a vegetarian.

But whom the hours of *mortal moral strife*
Alone aright reveal![143]

Waterloo Days are good days for that. I think of you continually, but He thinks of you *always*. God speed your suit! Your father said, "Love is fellow service."[144]

ever, dear Arthur, yours
Aunt Florence

Why do you say Rosy S.S. is of the feud, feudy? She never was, always tried to prevent it.

Source: Letter to Thena Clough, Boston University 2/23 unnumbered

10 South St.
22 June 1889

I think of you all more than I can say, my dear Thena. Do you think it would be too foolish to send with him one red rosebud and a white rosebud to bloom during the voyage? Red is for love, white for purity and green for hope. If you think it too silly, keep them yourselves, please.

(An old sea captain friend of mine, who rescued two of our nurses from a total wreck on their way home across the Atlantic, always took with him roses, which kept fresh in a glass of water with salt, all through the voyage.) Ah, laugh at me—a laugh does good.

God speed him and you all. Give my love to Mama and Flossie.
Aunt Florence

Source: Letter, Boston University 2/23/7

10 South St.
16 July 1889

My dearest Arthur [Clough]

I am very sorry—grieved indeed. I think the loss is hers as much as yours. But as an old fellow I think the present finality better than a correspondence dragging on across the Atlantic, which is very wearing. I have understood that she is so fond of her country that she would not leave it now, even for a visit. This does not make one the less grieved and disturbed for you. But you will bear it like a man.

I only had your note late last night. Thank you for writing to me. I hope very much you will go to Lea Hurst—Burton wants you badly.

---

143 A.H. Clough, "Qui laborat orat," in *The Poems*.
144 Subtitle to a poem, "The Clergyman's First Tale," in *The Poems*.

Would you fix some day to dine here, either with or without Sam, and let me see you a little before, perhaps tomorrow (Wednesday). For I must not interfere with thy mother and Flossie, who, I believe, return Thursday, or perhaps after they are gone. God bless you.

ever your affectionate
Aunt Florence

Source: Letter, Boston University 5/20/23

> [printed address] 10 South Street
> Park Lane, W.
> 5 August 1890

I shan't send you Burton's letter, my dear Arthur, if you call him a "prig." He is a pedant. So am I. But a prig is one who cannot believe in anything above his own level.

Uncle Shore, who is severe, says that, though a "schoolmaster all over," he (Burton) knows well how to tackle the flimsy, smart young ladies, and that there is an *excellent* tone ever between these and him.

You see Fanny Burton is at *South*lands. My books are gone to *White*lands. I am afraid they are not one and the same? What shall I do? Return me Mr Burton with your hints. I go to Claydon tomorrow. Come too.

Louis goes as the guardian of youth with two Siamese princelings to Scotland for a month.

ever your loving
Aunt Florence

Source: Letter to an unknown recipient, Woodward Biomedical Library A.72

> 13 May 1893

. . . Arthur Clough was married the other day to a delightful person, Miss Freshfield, daughter of the Traveller. I hope they have every prospect of happiness. His mother was delighted with the marriage. I have always seen a great deal of Arthur, but I have not seen him since his marriage engagement, for my doctor has strictly forbidden my seeing anybody I could help. . . .

The Verney Family

Editor: The letters here deal only with family and personal matters. Numerous others are included in *Theology, Public Health Care, Society and Politics, Women* and the volumes on war, nursing and hospital reform (an enormous number of letters and drafts or copies are extant). The largest number of Nightingale's letters are to her brother-in-law, Harry Verney, a close collaborator on so much work. They show the slow development of good will over many years of collaboration that developed on Parthenope's marriage to him in 1858 (see the biographical sketch in Appendix A). There is a small number to Emily Verney, daughter of Harry Verney, who became a close collaborator of Nightingale during the Franco-Prussian War. Emily Verney's early death was another great loss for Nightingale, who saw her as the only person in the two families combined with the capacity and commitment to carry on her work. Nightingale took flowers to Emily's grave regularly on the anniversary of her death. There is a small number of letters to Frederick Verney, the youngest son. He was also a collaborator of Nightingale's, notably on rural health missioners, for which correspondence see *Public Health Care*. There are also a few to the middle son, George Hope Verney, with whom there was less contact, although he pursued a military career and shared some interests with Nightingale.

Many letters to the Verney heir, Edmund, and his wife, the "blessed" Margaret, will be introduced separately below. These are followed by a small number to Verney grandchildren: Lettice Verney, Ruth Florence, young Harry Verney, the fourth baronet, and Harry Lloyd Verney. (Ruth Florence and Harry Calvert were also godchildren so that correspondence concerning them appears with that of other godchildren later.)

The letters reported here, only a small proportion of those extant, nonetheless reflect the range of subjects discussed and general emotional tone of the correspondence from frustration, exasperation and disappointment, through to joy, wonder and delight. This personal correspondence covers births, marriages, illnesses, accidents, deaths, the perils of raising children, their schooling, careers and marriages. While there will be much fuller reporting on Nightingale's own illness elsewhere, it receives frequent mention here. The near-death of Harry Verney is extensively covered. Nightingale gave advice from time to time on the nursing her sister needed in her lengthy, terminal illness (a frequent subject also of letters to her sister above). These are very much family letters, with annoyance apparent in both directions.

Nightingale's fondness for adventure is evident now with the telling of cousin Ben's Arctic adventures to a Verney grandchild below. There are reflections on reading and the news of the day. Deaths of old associates are noted and their exploits remembered.

It will be evident how close and important the Verney connection was for Nightingale. She took breaks from London in their country home far more often than she visited her own cousins, somewhat to the latters' chagrin. With Harry Verney's death in 1894 the next generation, especially Edmund and Margaret and Fred and Maude, became mainstays in Nightingale's life. They, as earlier her parents, cousin Hilary Bonham Carter, Parthenope and Harry Verney were invited to share in "taking the sacrament" with her. The attending priest is no longer Benjamin Jowett but a priest at Claydon. Nightingale's last visit to Claydon, late in 1894, was as the guest of Edmund and Margaret Verney. Their visits to her in London, in her extreme old age when she did not go out at all, were among the last she received (with those of several cousins and the children of cousins, especially Rosalind Nash). There is charming correspondence (not reproduced here) from the Verney grandchildren to Nightingale, especially from Fred and Maude Verney's children (in ADD MSS 68882-90).

The correspondence of course is one-sided; we do not have the letters to which Nightingale was replying. Most of the material comes from the Claydon collection (copied at the Wellcome Trust), hence we know that these letters and notes were actually sent. Some may have been deliberately destroyed, but an enormous number remain, including letters with material the Verney family might well have preferred to keep private. One, for example, concerned Edmund Verney's imprisonment for a sex offence and another, soon after his release, the trial of a local vicar (under his jurisdiction) for sexual immorality (Nightingale gave tactical advice).

Finally, these letters give the best portrayal we have of Nightingale's advanced and considerably more mellow old age. The last of her "dated notes," related in *Spiritual Journey*, is from 1901. Here we see short letters to Verneys as late as 1905.

Brother-in-Law Harry Verney

Source: Letter, Wellcome (Claydon copy) Ms 8998/26

30 Old Burlington St.
26 June 1860

My dear Sir Harry [Verney]

From your account of the churchyard at Middle Claydon, it appears that the old ground is chiefly at fault. It does not appear that a new cemetery would be at all required. The smell from the old ground admits of removal. And, if you applied for an inspector, there would not necessarily be any cost, except that arising from the operation of preventing the smell.

If I might advise, it would be that you should go yourself to the "Burials Act" Office, 4 Old Palace Yard, and ask for Mr Baker. He would put you in communication with Grainger or Holland, who would probably be able to tell you what to do without a formal application to the Home Office.

From what you say, it appears that the removal of the new churchyard is not necessary, and the having an inspector does not at all entail a recommendation to close it.

Many thanks for your concluding kind words and believe me, dear Sir Harry,

affectionately yours

F. Nightingale

Source: Letter, Wellcome (Claydon copy) Ms 8998/27

30 Old Burlington St., W.

30 June 1860

Dear Sir Harry Verney

I find that, by a recent act, all that is necessary to do is to have Claydon Church, and churchyard, *inspected*. The secretary of state can issue an order to the church wardens to abate any smell and to take precautions regarding health, quite apart from providing new ground. The church wardens can present the bill to the Overseer of the Poor, who would pay the cost out of the Poor rates. The worst of it is that *you* are, I dare say, church wardens, overseer and ratepayers all in one. From all I hear from different quarters, I do believe that both old churchyard and church are very much in want of this measure, which will not necessarily entail any other.

yours affectionately

F. Nightingale

Source: Letter, Wellcome (Claydon copy) Ms 8998/29

30 Old Burlington St.
16 July 1860

My dear Sir Harry [Verney]

The wise foreigners[145] come here to breakfast every day this week at 8:30 A.M. Sometimes there are too many, sometimes there are none. I need not say that we shall be glad to see you any and *every* morning.

yours affectionately
F. Nightingale

Source: Letter, Wellcome Claydon copy Ms 8998/41

Upper Terrace
Hampstead, N.W.
28 December 1860

My dear Sir Harry [Verney]

. . . I am now doing a new hospital at Lisbon for the King of Portugal to the memory of his Queen, by Prince Albert's desire (the tracing I send you will be adopted there). . . .

I hope that you will favourably consider a request, which is about to be made to you, that you will become a member of the council of the Nightingale Fund! It will not take up much of your time and it will be a great favour, if you can grant it. . . .

ever yours affectionately
F. Nightingale

Source: Letter, Wellcome Claydon copy Ms 8999/11

[printed address] 30 Old Burlington Street, W.
22 April 1861

My dear Sir Harry [Verney]

I find that a kind intention has existed of suiting me with an apartment in one of the royal residences, but that with a most entire ignorance of the work I am engaged upon—Kensington [Palace] has been mentioned—without any kind of communication with me (who am the only person, I suppose, who can know) this plan has been arranged. I might just as well have been given in marriage without my own consent, for my work has been more to me than any marriage I have ever seen or heard of.

---

145 Delegates to the International Statistical Congress.

During the whole time of the sitting of Parliament and of War Office commissions, I might as well give up my work at once as live at a place which entails nearly eight miles (to and fro) from Whitehall. During the remainder of the year, there are other spots near London which would suit me much better, as to health. If the *first* question is returned to, I would state my requirements as to whereabouts. I must live to work at all, without, I am sure, thinking of *begging* from the crown. Please help me out of this scrape as fast as you can.

ever yours sincerely

F. Nightingale

Source: Letter, Wellcome (Claydon copy) Ms 9001/94

[1861]

My dear Sir Harry [Verney]

I have to thank you for the French translation, also for the Hebrew chair from M Mohl, also for a map of the Seat of War in America, which has been my constant and dreadful study ever since (sent me before you went abroad).

Also will you ask your gardener whether he would like to have back the root of a gorgeous red lily, which was in magnificent flower, four or five on each of two stems, for more than six weeks! (sent me from Claydon).

Also, could you insert into any periodical (or before any committee) the enclosed reprinted from *Evangelical Christendom?* I have canvassed repeatedly Sir C. Eardley and all the Evangelical Alliance.[146] They are so busy praying for me that they can't give a sixpence or even answer my letters.

ever yours

F.N.

Editor: From the following letter it appears that Harry Verney was approached about becoming Governor of the colony of New South Wales, but whether he discouraged the thought, declined the offer or it was never made we do not know.

---

146 On behalf of the Kaiserswerth Deaconess Institution; Sir Culling Eardley (1805-63), founder of the Evangelical Alliance.

Source: Letter, Wellcome Ms 9000/31

9 Chesterfield St.
25 April 1862

My dear Sir Harry [Verney]

I have considered very deeply the letters you have done me the honour to send me, and when I say honour, I feel it so. My first impulse is to say "go." But then you know I am what Lord Panmure called me, a "turbulent fellow."

There is not the least doubt that the post is worthy of you and you of the post. There is not the least doubt that governors of the adventurer class have done our colonies much harm, that what they want is an English gentleman of a high moral standard, that of all the men they are likely to get, there is not one who would do so well for them as you.

Had England understood her true interests, she would have got grants of land in our colonies for her younger sons instead of making them hangers-on of government offices and of the church. And our colonies would then have been very different places from what they are now.

Melbourne understands her own interests well when she says she wants a gentleman and not a professional man. You certainly would do great good there and so would an English lady. The climate is one of the healthiest in the world and would far outbalance any harm the voyage would do Parthe. As far as human foresight can see, you and she would probably come back no older than you and she are now. I do not think the consideration of leaving her father and mother and sister ought to weigh with her, though it will grieve her as also, it ought not, I am sure, to weigh with them.

You have of course consulted your brother [Frederick Calvert]. Ask him to weigh very naturally the saving (of money) it would be to you. This is the point I doubt most. Colonies are very jealous, as indeed this letter states, of having the whole of the income they give spent in them. I could tell you an instance of a man I know very well (and quite the best administrator I know), who is unpopular from this cause alone. He saves the income, *his* governorship. What you would save would be simply the cost of living in England and the rent of your house. Your younger children are provided for as well as, or better than, most younger children of their rank. I confess this would weigh with me much less than the moral reason for going, and would not weigh at all against the sacrifice of leaving English society for six years.

The post of a governor, worthily filled, as you would fill it, is, on the other hand, a very noble one. I wish it were more the custom for men of your moral rank to accept these posts. We shall miss you very much in all moral subjects connected with the House of Commons, the Army and the charitable societies.

These seem to me the main considerations. If Parthe would like to come and talk things over with me, I could see her tomorrow at 12:00 instead of waiting till Sunday. Unfortunately I have tomorrow *afternoon* a meeting of men here about the removal of St Thomas' Hospital which, though I shall not see them, I cannot put off.

ever your

F.N.

Source: Letter, Wellcome (Claydon copy) Ms 9000/137

Hampstead, N.W.

15 October 1863

Dear [Parthenope Verney]

Mr William Banting, the house agent, has sent me, "*by desire of Sir Harry Verney*," a pamphlet by himself on how to reduce corpulence. By dint of a meat diet, sufficient to give a boa constrictor a fatal indigestion, he reduces himself one pound per week. Will Sir Harry tell him that a course of Colonel Brown, combined with the War Office, will effect the same with much greater rapidity and certainty, but I implore him not to carry the experiment too far, as he might "die cured."

ever your

F.

Source: Letter, Wellcome (Claydon copy) Ms 9001/56

Hampstead, N.W.

26 August 1864

My dear Sir Harry [Verney]

... About Mr Watts,[147] I really have a scruple against sitting. I think we ought to do so as to be forgotten ourselves, and God only to be remembered. (When I was quite a girl, Sir C. Trevelyan pointed out to me that the noblest works of the Christian Church, the old hymns, Te Deum, etc., were by authors who had not even left their names.) I

---

147 George Frederick Watts, RA (1817-1904); the portrait of Nightingale was never finished.

only consented to the Steele[148] bust because the soldiers asked for it, and thinking of me makes them think of their wives and mothers. I was very much the worse for sitting for that bust. To sit even for half an hour takes an amount of strength from me which I must finish God's "unfinished work" with.

ever yours
F.N.

Source: Letter, Wellcome (Claydon copy) Ms 9001/133

34 South St.
Park Lane
24 June 1865

My dear Sir Harry [Verney]

I thank you and bless you for your most kind, feeling and considerate note. But it is not possible for me "to write one word 'yes' or 'no' " and so to decide about buying a house which I have never seen, of which I do not know whether it is furnished or not, and many, etc. (even if I were looking out for a prospect of twenty years' *good life*).

1. I have never taken and would never take a house (which I have never seen) *for six months,* much less for twenty years. There are fatal objections to many of these houses, or what ought to be fatal—to everyone but to me, an entire prisoner to the house—would be altogether final.

2. It would be *quite* impossible to me to furnish a house. It would just incapacitate me for work at the time I most want my strength, as the moving in here has very nearly done.

3. I presume that I should have to enter upon tenancy directly. So that I should have *in July,* THREE houses upon my overtasked hands, if I go to Hampstead, i.e., two London houses to arrange for, when I can scarce arrange for this, while I am at Hampstead. I [am] obliged to leave behind the only person who has a head, Lady Clarges's maid, here.

4. When the house-buying plan began for me, Parthe represented it to me (as I believed from yourself and my father) *as a good investment for Papa.* It is now represented as just the contrary. Indeed it seems even doubtful where the money is to come from. I must have these questions answered.

I do not say "No" to your most kind plan for me, dear Sir Harry. But it is indeed, it is impossible for me to write to you "to try and

---

148 Marble bust of Nightingale by Sir John Steele (1804-91).

secure" for me, without more ado, a house I have never seen. . . . I do not even know who is the agent, or how I could get a ticket to view, supposing I were able to see it (or Mrs Sutherland).

ever yours gratefully

F.N.

Please, when you come to London next week, bring up with you the freehold land scheme[149] *and* my letter to you, containing the legal opinion, in opposition to R. Palmer. I have no copy.

F.N.

Source: Letter, Wellcome (Claydon copy) Ms 9001/134

> [printed address] 34 South Street
> Park Lane
> London, W.
> 24 June 1865

My dear Sir Harry [Verney]

I have been so utterly overdriven with work this week and I wrote to you in such haste this morning, that perhaps I should explain a little more concisely what I feel. As to the amount to be paid for 35 South St. (if it is *un*furnished, if it is £10,000, as you told me, not £8000) this, for twenty years, would be much more than I have ever paid yet.

If my father thought it a fair speculation for himself independently of me, that would be another matter; I should certainly accept it. But it seems to me quite out of the question that the business part of the matter (i.e., the providing the money for the purchase) should be undertaken *by me or on my account. But* the probable furnishing—the certainty of having *one* house and possibly two, on my hands, during my autumn stay at Hampstead, really make it quite impossible that I should "try to secure this house at once," without even seeing it, although to decline it absolutely I am unwilling. But I must know more about it. If you are so good as to "try to secure" the *refusal* of it for me, so as to give me time to see it, that is another thing. I should be glad.

In addition to all other worries, we have had a most serious continuance of questions asked in the House of Commons against Dr Sutherland. Another question in the same sense comes on on Friday. I am asked to ask you whether you will ask a question in *our* sense on

---

149 Nightingale gave considerable attention, without success, to schemes for ordinary people to own their own homes; see *Society and Politics.*

t night. You see we have lost all in the Poor Law Board Continu-
ce Bill.

ever yours

F.N.

Source: Letter, Wellcome (Claydon copy) Ms 9003/1

Dr Johnson's

Malvern

Monday afternoon [12 January 1868]

My dear Sir Harry [Verney]

I have only just received your kind note. Let me say first, what I am sure you know, that my wishes and prayers and my poor blessings are with the happy marriage tomorrow [of Edmund and Margaret], and not only tomorrow, but many tomorrows. Had I known of it sooner, I should have taken the liberty of sending flowers. Do they go to Claydon for the honeymoon?

You are so good as to ask me whether you can do anything for me. The only thing I would trouble you to do is to look in at 35 and advise Burch about Mr Bismark—the white cat is lost, poor fellow! I have already written to her and Mrs Sutherland to advertise for him. Do you know whether it is any use putting a description of the beast in these cases in the hands of the police? Or does that only make the thieves, if he is stolen, send him out of the neighbourhood, or kill him for his skin? Temperance says, with tears in her eyes, if a stranger has detained him: he (the cat) will "feel it very much."

I have to thank you for a noble brace of pheasants and for Lord Carnarvon's letter. It seems to me sensible. At all events, I could not act in opposition to his advice. Many, many thanks. When we meet again, I hope, please God, to continue this subject with you.

I can't tell you how much obliged to you I was for your charming note from Embley. My dear father's main interest now is in his cottages and I don't think he does too much. I believe that more moral and physical good is done by improving the *dwellings* of mankind than in almost any other way. And if all the money that is spent on hospitals were spent on improving the habitations of those who go to hospitals, and (on prisons) of those who go to prison, we should want neither prisons nor hospitals.

I feel a little anxious about my dear mother. It was to me so entirely a new idea that both father and mother would not long survive me, that I have only lately resolved that I would not spend another year without seeing her at home. I did think very seriously whether I should not spend this month with her, but I was quite clear in my own mind that it was better and more desirable and more agreeable for her to have her present pleasant party.

Will you say to Sir B. Frere (he has called twice at 35) how very much pleased I was, and also at their remembrance of me in sending me Miss Frere's pleasant little New Year's Eve entertainment.

Should the subject of my business *not* come up, I would ask you not to say anything thereunto to Sir Bartle. But, should it come on the tapis [carpet], e.g., between him and my mother and you perceive any misunderstanding likely to arise, I should be so very much obliged to you if you would explain (as you know so well how to do) that *he* does not send me business *enough* to do. It would kill me if I thought that he would not let me do the business I have always been in the habit of doing for the India Office and Sir J. Lawrence, and which has taken so *much more* hopeful a turn since Sir Bartle has undertaken it.

What has happened this last year to me is totally distinct from the government business, which is what I live for. (I have got into the habit of letting people, e.g., the St John's Council, use me in a way which does them no good and which destroys me. I mean, please God, to do my best to reform this in my life. And so I will say no more about this at present.)

You know that St John's House is broken up. Miss [Mary] Jones and the sisters are to leave (this very day their notice expires) and from that day St John's House, the only Protestant attempt to found a good and successful sisterhood in the Church of England, comes to an end. Without Miss Jones, it will be just the twaddle that all other sisterhoods are (including the North London deaconesses, who are twaddles in chief). The Council have behaved shamefully and have also tried to use me against Miss Jones. The bishop [Tait] has been disingenuous.

I will not enter upon the long and melancholy history of the fall of this great hope, but only mention this, because even in my retreat, such calumnies against Miss Jones reach me. (Calomniez, calomniez toujours, il en reste toujours quelque chose.[150] [Slander, slander, there is always something that will stick]).

> ever dear Sir Harry
> affectionately and gratefully yours
> Florence N.

---

150 Beaumarchais, *Le barbier de Séville* III.13.

Editor: The following letter is included for the brief allusion to the possibility of Verney's becoming Governor of Madras. A letter in 1862 (above) shows Nightingale encouraging his accepting the position of Governor of New South Wales. Here there is no such encouragement and scarcely any comment, for she evidently doubted that he would go (perhaps even that the offer would be made). One suspects that Nightingale considered her brother-in-law quite suitable for a position in Australia, but not India, so that questions about climate, health and her sister's wishes would not need to be addressed.

Source: Letter, Wellcome (Claydon copy) Ms 9003/123

Embley
Romsey
11 November 1869

Private

My dear Sir Harry [Verney]

As you have been so good as to speak to me about that painful subject, the railways, I cannot help venturing to say to you what I have always felt in myself, that it is a very great misfortune—a misfortune rendered greater by its being shared, I am told, by the vast majority of all those in England who have had anything to do with railways, is beyond a doubt. But there is no evil really in what makes a man more of a man, in what is not occasioned by our own lust of riches or ease or power—our own bad passions.

As you may be perfectly sure that you did this for the good of the county and not for your own, I think that you should no more torment yourself about it than if you had lost a ship or an arm or a leg. Even Philip, with the loss of the Spanish Armada, was *greater* than this. Forgive me for saying this.

Many times, in a public course which does not yet number sixteen years, my life has been broken to pieces at my feet, as in 1861 when I lost both Sidney Herbert and A.H. Clough, who were all the world to me. And I have had, with broken heart and health, painfully to put the fragments of the wreck together again. At those times, I have felt that, had there been the smallest grain of any ambition but that of *God's service* in the work I did with Sidney Herbert, I must have died or gone mad. *Not* being this I could only feel that that which still appears to me the most mysterious dispensation: misery never-to-be-forgotten is not really a misfortune in God's sight. I think I have never spoken so much of myself before. Forgive me.

Were your trial to end in your going to Madras, to rule, for the good of the natives, a kingdom larger than Great Britain, I cannot but say that, if it were I, I should look upon your railway adventure as no evil but a great good—no misfortune but the reverse. As I doubt your going, I will say no more about *that*. Excuse what I have said and burn it.

ever yours
F.N.

Source: Postscript to letter to Harry Verney, Wellcome (Claydon copy) Ms 9003/132

17 December 1869

In relation to the governorship and to health for standing it, Sir B. Frere asked me your *age*. I did not exactly know it and I did not like to ask Parthe, because I thought she would think that I was furthering the matter, which I assure you I am not. It is much too vital an interest for me to meddle with.

yours
F.N.

Source: Letter, Wellcome (Claydon copy) Ms 9004/34

Embley
Romsey
17 April 1870
Easter Sunday

My dear Sir Harry [Verney]

This was the old letter of Sir R. Napier[151] which you lent me for the address and told me to return. It was abominable of me not to put it into my letter when I said I had and give you the trouble of looking. I had mislaid it. Please tell P. [Parthenope] that I returned her (honest) a copy of [her novel] *Lettice Lisle* when I left London and brought one down (honest) here for my mother. But they seem to be in great numbers here, so that, if she likes, I will filch it away again. We shall send her some flowers for her birthday [19 April].

Springs are late now. When I was a child, I always used to go as soon as it was daylight and bring some lilacs with dewdrops on them, which were always in flower for her birthday, from some particular

---

151 General Sir Robert Cornelis Napier (1810-90), 1st Baron Napier of Magdala, conqueror and governor of Sindh (now Pakistan).

lilacs in the American garden, to her when she awoke in the morning, but there is nothing of the kind now.

ever yours

F.N.

Source: Letter to Harry Verney, Wellcome (Claydon copy) Ms 9004/65

10 August 1870

Thank dear Emily for her most kind offer to help me. I shall always remember it, but I am afraid it is impossible. At present my "organs" are so weak that I cannot talk more than 1/4 hour a day so that when I see Mama, I don't, to my great regret, see Papa. I am afraid that no one could help me except by doing things *instead of* me, and that, of course, is impossible except to one (*who does not exist*) who has been engaged in my business for some time. But I shall ever remember her kind offer. . . .

F.N.

I never saw my mother better in her life.

Source: Letter, Wellcome (Claydon copy) Ms 9004/158

[printed address] 35 South Street
Park Lane, W.
5 December 1870

Most *private Immediate*

My dear Sir Harry [Verney]

We cannot be thankful enough (I need not tell you for I am sure you know it) for your escape from as we trust, the after consequences of your railway accident. "I sing unto the Lord a new song."[152]

I am the more sorry to have to say for your information something rather disagreeable. I do so because I believe I am the only person who will tell you. Colonel Loyd Lindsay[153] is "seriously annoyed" that your wife should have written (and be about to publish) an article on his "society from information obtained WITHOUT *his knowledge* or his wife's, partly from the secretaries."[154] He has spoken of it seriously,

---

152 A paraphrase of Ps 96:1.
153 Robert Loyd Lindsay (1832-1901), later Baron Wantage, MP and leader of National Aid Society (Red Cross).
154 Identified as by the author of *Stone Edge*, "The Miseries of War: Notes from Sedan and Bazeilles." By the date of publication it would seem that the article was cleared with Colonel Loyd Lindsay, or that this is quite a different article.

calmly, and as I think, justly, *as a matter of business,* to men of my acquaintance. I feel I should be wrong not to say to you that, from sixteen years of official and business experience, I should be of opinion that the above, *if* it is correct, *is a thing not to be done.* I say nothing of the merits of the article.

(You know how careful I have been—but you do not know what innumerable invitations I have had, also from all kinds of newspapers, foreign and English—*to publish absolutely nothing* and not to put into *anyone's power* to publish anything while the war lasts.) I have even less respect for my own opinion than you can have. But I could not reconcile it to any feeling of right not to say that, were Sidney Herbert alive, he or any administrative man I might consult, would say: *"Such an article ought not to have been written or published at all without having been previously submitted to the reading of the chairman. And, if this has not been done, Sir H. Verney ought now to withdraw it before publication at any trouble, at any expense."*

Do not, please, answer this letter. I do not hope to influence your judgment and I am totally unable to enter into any discussion.

The *least* evil arising from all this has been an entire stop to pleasant and useful communication arising between Colonel Loyd Lindsay and me (thanks to your introduction). Everybody says to me: "I suppose you knew all about it" (the article).

Private. The first intimation of it (but one) came upon me like a surprise, viz., what I have said above, and an advertisement which I saw. (The only *one* other information was that, about three months ago or more, you told me "Parthe was thinking of writing in the *Cornhill.*" I had actually put down what I meant to say to you on the subject in answer, but I thought I should hear more. I was in almost daily communication with you all—my opinion was not asked, either. I thought I had reason afterwards to think it, the article, was dropped, from the total silence and from my never seeing it in the advertisements. Also, it never entered my mind that an article would be written, as is now stated, truly or falsely, *without the chairman's knowledge and partly from* the secretaries' and others' communications.)

Dear Sir Harry, I am now so ill that two hours of the day I work, ten or twelve hours of the day I am prostrate from pain and weakness. You may judge that nothing but a strong feeling of the right would induce me to waste my small capital of strength in this kind of writing painfully. "Lord, if this cup cannot pass from me, except I drink it, Thy will, not mine, be done"[155] is now my constant cry, when I feel the little strength left which God has given me for His work frittered away in all kinds of things which *can* do no one any good, and are equally painful and useless. God bless you.

ever yours

F.N.

No one knows that I am writing to you. I need hardly add that I am sure, if you in your gracious graceful way, were to say to Colonel Loyd Lindsay that you both had withdrawn the article till he could see it, all would be right again. (I should like him to know, for the sake of any useful influence of mine, that I knew nothing of it. But that is *nothing, nothing at all,* in comparison with a schism between *you* and him, on a point in which he is technically, if not morally, in the right.)

F.N.

Source: Part of letter, Wellcome (Claydon copy) Ms 9005/117

35 South Street
Park Lane, W.
4 March 1871

My dear Sir Harry [Verney]

. . . Many thanks for Emily's nice letter, which I return. I greatly grieve at the result of her expedition as to health, owing to the abominable Malta nuisances.

ever yours

F.N.

Emily. I was extremely distressed by Emily's illness. She has suffered as everyone does who goes to Malta. They have allowed the rock to become a dirty sodden sponge and hence the fevers. But the question now lies solely with the local people. We have advised the home government to give them £30,000 as a contribution to the improvements, leaving them to find £50,000. But they prefer crippling their commerce by quarantine and this depraved taste has been no little pandered to by the health authorities here and at Malta. I did not answer Emily's letter because you told me immediately afterwards that she was "coming home by sea." Please let me know as soon as she arrives. . . .

---

155 A paraphrase of Matt 26:42.

Source: Letter to Harry Verney written 3 December 1870, sent with letter 29 April 1871, Wellcome (Claydon copy Ms 9005/53

With regard to the first of these rules, and the (P[arthe]'s) staying in this house I will only state now one thing: that the rings at the doorbell averaged one every five minutes, that the necessary references made to me, especially by a small household unused to deal with changes and interruptions which would puzzle a clubhouse, have been three in one page of important papers which I was writing to the Government of India by order.

No business could be transacted in this way in an office, even were I in perfect health, and this house *is* my office by the necessity of illness. *No* MAN could or would consent to do my work under such conditions. But I always know that your goodness will lead you to look upon any statement or resolution of mine with the kindest indulgence, knowing as you do that it is not made without prayer for guidance and humility in feeling my own many and great errors.

I will only add that you must not think that anything else which has occurred this 1870 is the cause of this letter. I have frequently been urged to write it to *you*. And for years and my *only* reason for not doing so is: the pain it caused me and causes me. God bless you, dear Sir Harry.

ever yours
F.N.

Source: Letter, Wellcome (Claydon copy) Ms 9005/113

Embley
Romsey
25 February 1872

My dear Sir Harry [Verney]
I believe that every inch of window-room at 35 is filled for Thanksgiving Day, i.e., if they all come, but as they do not all answer (which is very tiresome because I can neither provide "vittles" nor fill up their places which will be then wasted). You can, if you wish, you say "pray consider," disgorge some of your perhaps overfilled house upon 35.

I will tell you who are *coming*: Mrs Sutherland and two friends, Beatrice Lushington and M and Mme Rossel. *Asked*: Miss Torrance and Highgate nurses, maybe five or six; Henry Bonham Carter and children, maybe four with two nurses; Pastor and Mme Fliedner, who is in England. Each of my maids is empowered to ask two "wives" each (House of Commons phraseology) (I hope the "wives" won't be lovers) and dine them at my expense. I am in great tribulation about hours, because if, e.g., the Highgate nurses must be there the whole day, they must be fed. And nothing can be had at the shops, I suppose, but what is ordered on Monday?

There is a splendid safe leads or balcony *over* the upper bedroom (yours) at 35 which would accommodate many sightseers. And people might see standing *on chairs* on the dining-room leads.

ever yours
F.N.

Source: Letter to Harry Verney, Wellcome (Claydon copy) Ms 9006/30

14 March 1873

... I was so very anxious to hear of the dear little baby: dearer by nine months to the mother than to anyone else, as well as by all she has gone through for it.[156] I trust that "the Angel" will not visit us yet "to take the flower away." It has a wet nurse; it has the large Claydon rooms and every care and love.

Shore from four months old to two years was at death's door many times (he was at Embley). He had four wet nurses including his mother. He was able to walk, to talk, and to read before he was weaned. *And* to direct his nurse (when she was changed) how to wash and dress him in illness. He was not weaned till over two years old because he was, again and again, in that dying state when milk from a full woman's breast had to be squeezed into his mouth. He is now a strong man of forty-two. May we not hope that the Lord intends as much for our babe? God bless it and its patient mother.

Please thank Parthe for her news of it and her. ...

Source: Letter, Wellcome (Claydon copy) Ms 9006/34

Good Friday eve 1873
My dear Sir Harry [Verney]

This is a charming note indeed, "valuable" in every sense of the word. Thank you for letting me see it. I rejoice to hear that dear Margaret has again a hope of giving us a little Margaret or Edmund. May she only take care of herself! I shall be very anxious to hear what course is decided upon for her.

F.

---

156 Ellin Verney was born in 1873, the daughter of Edmund and Margaret Verney, granddaughter of Harry Verney.

Editor: The next letters concern arrangements for Frances Nightingale after W.E. Nightingale's death, 5 January 1874.

Source: Letter, Wellcome (Claydon copy) Ms 9006/65

> 35 South Street
> Park Lane, W.
> 7 January 1874

My dear Sir Harry [Verney]

Thanks to you and Parthe for letters. Please write again. Have you written to the people at *Pleasley?*[157] I know no one there now but Miss Fox (who is gone) or I should willingly have written. I wish I knew the Lea Hurst people now to write to those who loved *him.*

ever yours affectionately

F.N.

Mr Jowett has telegraphed to ask whether he can be of any use at Embley. I think I shall write to him not yet, but if you think otherwise, will you write to him at *Belgrave Road, Torquay.*

Source: Letter, Wellcome (Claydon copy) Ms 9006/68

> 35 South St.
> 16 January 1874

My dear Sir Harry [Verney]

You tell me by this morning's post that Aunt Mai has written to Parthe a letter "to the effect that her mother (mine) is to stay here (Embley) and not to be moved or disturbed in any way."

On Monday while you were with me I received an exceedingly painful communication from Beatrice (in a certain sense strongly remonstrating against this). As your communication with me in no way made it necessary, I spared you the pain of telling you of this letter (which I afterwards made her burn at my fire) and which has almost killed me.

I have on receipt of yours this morning requested Beatrice that any communication that she may wish to make on this subject as connected with Parthe's intentions may be addressed to Parthe and not to me. And that any communication which she may think it desirable to address to me on the subject of her last may be addressed through you and her own brother-in-law, being two of the executors. Or that if she prefers addressing it to me, I will forward it to you. I have written to Beatrice to tell her that I have written to you that you and Parthe will hear from her, that I did not mention her communication with

---

157 W.E. Nightingale was a major landowner there.

me to you, as yours with me was wholly in the opposite sense to what she assumed, and that I am glad that I made her burn hers to me, as otherwise I should now have forwarded it to you for I am wholly unequal to these communications.

your affectionate

F. Nightingale

Source: Letter Wellcome (Claydon copy) Ms 9006/74

35 South St.

21 February 1874

My dear Sir Harry Verney [Verney]

In answer to your memorandum of 19 February, stating what you "propose to do" for my mother (for six months after she leaves Embley), I gladly accept that "she shall come to" you "at Claydon early in June for three months." It will be quite impossible for me to leave my work in London during those three months to come to Claydon—this in answer to what you say that you wish to "know beforehand what these times" (of my coming) "will be."

At the end of those three months, I shall be prepared to take charge of my mother and reside with her for the next period of three months. The circumstances under which this shall be done had better be arranged at some future time, seeing the state of my mother's health, had not they?

I accede to what you say that my mother "should retain as her household an indoor manservant and coachman, as well as Grace." Her *future* "household" can be arranged in *future*. (I do not quite understand what is meant, that "she will have only to find a *kitchen* maid and housemaid," but that need hardly be discussed now, need it?) I have been unable to write before and am, dear Sir Harry Verney,

always your affectionate

Florence Nightingale

Source: Unsigned note to Harry Verney, Wellcome (Claydon copy) Ms 9006/76

25 February 1874

Since I wrote this I have seen today's *Times*. By the way, how few politicians have received such an acknowledgment as that leading article of today on your address?

Source: Letter, Wellcome (Claydon copy) Ms 9006/97

35 South St.
20 May 1874

Upper Housemaid

My dear Sir Harry [Verney]

I was in the act of writing to you to know, merely for the sake of my interest, chiefly in Mrs Crook and in Ruth (whom my father cared for), and in the page William, whether Parthe had decided to pay off the servants, all except Grace and the coachman, when my Harriet gave me warning (upper housemaid) in the most unhandsome manner. I have given her room for retracting till Saturday. In the meantime would you ask Mrs Crook to write to me whether the *upper housemaid* at Embley *would do for me*, especially to keep my house and a young girl *during my absences?* It is mainly, I believe, a question of temper: could she restrain her temper with me, which in a very small family is all important? Fanny, the housemaid, who would be under her, is an excellent girl.

Will James Moody and his wife keep Embley for the present? What will become of the *cats?* Would Mrs Crook like to have Topsy? or the lilac one? If not, please let instructions be given to Moody to supply them with *milk*. (Topsy especially has been so petted.) I would pay for the milk, a weekly sum. Please ask Mrs Crook to write to me what she has settled with *Dowding* on my account.

I am so driven just now, but will write to P. tomorrow. Forgive me for troubling you. I am sure that you are good enough to pray with my dear mother in her room every morning. She so enjoys it.

yours affectionately
F.N.

Source: Letter, Wellcome (Claydon copy) Ms 9006/106

[June 1874?]

My dear Sir Harry [Verney]

. . . George Pembroke [son and heir of Sidney Herbert] is going to marry Lady Gertrude Talbot: eleven years older than himself and madness in the family. She refused him several times on account of age. I try to think what his father would have thought of it. I can find no words to describe the nobleness with which George has acted— whether with wisdom is another thing. There are not likely to be any children. This he accepts without regret, saying that he had rather "Sidney's children" should inherit.[158]

---

158 George Robert Charles Herbert (1850-95), the 13th earl, in fact was succeeded by his younger brother, another Sidney Herbert (1853-1913).

He knows her faults and accepts them. Both are very broad church: he is a radical, reads a great deal of metaphysical theology, works very hard, as pure as a child, his book non obstante. He has made up £1200 a year to each sister, and I believe to all. Had I seen you, I meant to have told you this and much more about him.

your affectionate

F.N.

Source: Letter, Wellcome (Claydon copy) Ms 9006/122

Claydon

[9 or 10 September 1874]

My dear Sir Harry and Parthe [Verney]

I hope that Parthe is resting completely and I will try and give an account of what is passing. . . . I address some conversation out of the window to Dr Pusey, who is lying coiled up in sulky jealousy of a little dog who is barking affectionately at her puppy, quite as big as herself, which young Pusey is dragging a remnant of the church under a bush, the remnant consisting of a large and very dirty piece of sacking with a bone entangled in it. (N.B. I think somebody should speak to Dr Pusey, who does not appear in a spiritual frame of mind.)

Sundays I open my windows to hear the chants and hymns. I can quite follow the service. It is seventeen years since I have been to church, or within hearing of a church. This is a great pleasure to me and bring the tears into my old eyes. . . .

Sir Henry Storks's death, and how intimate I was with him at Scutari. He is the last of those I put on my first royal commission. Lord Panmure's death (in July) closes a book of my life.

Mother has been out every day but one: two Sundays and one cricket day in garden chair. Dr Pusey and young Pusey accompany, but half way out Dr Pusey makes a sign to his son, who gallops back as hard as his four short legs can carry him.

Lord Napier of Magdala: a very charming letter, urging me "confidentially" to some Indian reforms. M Mohl: on Monday for the day (much worried with law business with Mr Charles Frewen). . . . God bless you.

your F.

Source: Letter, Wellcome (Claydon copy) Ms 9006/124

Claydon
17 September 1874

My dear Sir Harry [Verney]

. . . I shall be very sorry to leave your beautiful place, its *silence* and peace, its trees, and these lovely and comforting rooms (I have not been able to go downstairs and see the library, but I have been into Emily's old room and daily hold communion with her).

F.N.

Source: Note to Harry Verney c1874, Wellcome (Claydon copy) Ms 9006/113

Tell Parthe how much I liked her paper in *Macmillan*—it is splendid.

Source: Unsigned letter, Wellcome (Claydon copy) Ms 9007/17

1 April 1876

My dear Sir Harry [Verney]

Do you know this little: "Will there be work for me where I am going?" I so constantly think of Emily and *her* work among the dusty packages at St Martin's Place. Several people have said to me that it "hastened her end." Her *beginning*, *I* say, her going *home* to the perfect work she longed for. . . .

Source: Letter, Wellcome (Claydon copy) Ms 9007/38

35 South St.
16 June 1876

My dear Sir Harry [Verney]

I cannot say my delight (or my surprise) at receiving a letter from your own dear hand last evening. The God of mercies, not of "battles," willed to save you, because He and we have need of you, a little longer for us and we are bound to thank Him, not only in heart and voice, as we with all our mights do but by your keeping quiet, not talking, resting. I hope and believe that there is not any danger now except that, *as long as* there is any painful catching of the breath, it is *impossible* to say that NO *mischief might be set up*.

To talk, while that lasts, is like walking on a sprained ankle or writing with a sprained thumb. One *must* breathe but one need not talk. Forgive me for preaching; I feel so anxious. May we all show our thankful hearts to God in the way He best likes!

Macaulay's *Life*[159] is coming down today, which is supposed to have a soporific effect.

Miss Williams (from Edinburgh [Royal Infirmary]) is staying with me; we are recommending her to the matronship of St Mary's Hospital, Paddington. We are also sending a trained matron and nursing staff to the Herbert Hospital.

"Follow my advice most carefully." You say you do. That is a course supremely wise. Thank God!

ever yours most affectionately

F. Nightingale

Source: Letter, Wellcome (Claydon copy) Ms 9007/56

Lea Hurst

4 September 1876

My dear Sir Harry [Verney]

I thought of you and your dear and noble child [Emily] yesterday on the fourth anniversary of her "birth" [death]. Can we wish her back again? I think of her doing God's glorious work in another "mansion," of His "house," where He has "prepared her place"[160] without the "earth-born sorrowings" of this.

I wish I could give you any introduction worth your having (you ask) at *Brussels*, but the grand old Quetelet, my dear old friend, is dead—he died the same month as my father. I have survived so many of my greatest friends and I know no one at Brussels now worth your knowing.

God speed the civilization of the interior of Africa[161] (but don't overdo yourself) is the fervent prayer of

yours affectionately

F.N.

Source: Letter, Wellcome (Claydon copy) Ms 9007/60

Lea Hurst

3 October 1876

6:00 A.M.

My dear Sir Harry and Parthe [Verney]

Welcome home! I was delighted to hear of your safe return (by last night's post, too late to write) from a very enjoyable trip, and not alto-

---

159 George Otto Trevelyan, *The Life and Letters of Lord Macaulay.*

160 Allusions to John 14:2.

161 Harry Verney was attending an anti-slavery conference in Brussels.

gether unsuccessful, I trust, as far as Sir Harry's health is concerned. May he be well set up for the winter! The Brussels African conference is a noble thing to do, if it can but be carried out.

My mother is enjoying the old house and old associations, the drives, the views from her own room, the drawing room and the balcony room, the quiet, the absence of street noise and the talks and prayers. She made me *tell* her the whole story of the crucifixion from the discourse before the Last Supper the other day, listening with rapt attention (I left out, of course, the more painful physical parts but put in all Christ's words).[162]

She says "it is impossible to have a more charming bedroom than I have; you could not wish for anything better." In such things as these two kinds she has a far more vivid conception and feeling than any other person *living* I now know. (There is a letter from Aunt Mai I read to her *every* day.) Shore is here. In haste to catch the early post (as I have been interrupted).

yours affectionately

F.N.

What a state of things: (Emperor of Russia's letter, fighting in Serbia). Since I remember anything, I remember no *more*, no *such* tremendous crisis in European affairs. The *Standard* correspondent may tell you (and truly) that "Mohammedan law" forbids "outrages on women." *Does he tell you how that law is kept?*

F.N.

Source: Note probably to Harry Verney, Wellcome (Claydon copy) Ms 9007/107

35 South St.

7 June 1877

I am always anxious to hear of you. Thank you for writing. The accounts from *Miss Irby* are terrible; I suppose you have seen the enclosed.

Miss Robinson writes to me to write something to be read at the Mansion House Meeting, enclosed;[163] *what should* YOU *write?* Though I

---

162 Nightingale did a list of events of the crucifixion initially at the request of Jowett, for a revision of the *School and Children's Bible*, then one in 1890 for Harry Verney (Wellcome Ms 9013/29); see *Theology*.

163 Nightingale's letter to Robinson, 12 June 1877, is in the Clendening Collection, University of Kansas Medical Center; she gave a £10.10 donation and permitted her name to be used, although she would have preferred privacy.

586 / Florence Nightingale: Her Life and Family

am no admirer of hers, I believe her *Portsmouth* work is a great one; no one does so much. They are now putting up coffee boilers at the embarkation jetty for her troopship work. As you know, I dare say the troops even *before* landing are beset as the ships come up to the jetty, with invitations TO BAD of ALL kinds.

Mindful of your desire about Lord Houghton's daughters, I have ordered a Jowett's *Plato* in English, which I thought would do for the elder, and Miss Irby's book for the younger. Please ask Parthe for the *Christian names of each* and for Lord Houghton's *address* in *London* to send the books to.

I long for the sunrise breath and the sunrise dew and the sunrise lights, and the morning prayer of the thrush, in the American garden, and for the sunrise sights and sounds and scents. But God's will be done.

F.N.

(I have a particular association with 7 June and my room at Embley.[164]) Love to all.

Source: Letter, Wellcome (Claydon copy) Ms 9007/164

Lea Hurst

2 September 1878

My dear Sir Harry [Verney]

I shall think of you tomorrow when our dear Emily will have been six years "with God." To me the dead are so much more alive than the living and perhaps so much nearer to us. As dear Margaret said, "How much she must know now: how much she must have enjoyed." I have her hymn book beside me and it opens at:

> Departed, say we? is it
>   Departed, or come nigh?
> Dear friends in Christ more visit
>   Than leave us when they die.
> What thin veil still may hide them
>   Some little sickness rends,
> And lo! we stand beside them:
>   Are they *departed* friends?[165]

---

164 It is not clear to what this refers. Nightingale's original "call to service" was 7 February 1837, and it seems that she often used the seventh day of the month for reflection.

165 W.B.R., in James Montgomery, *One Hundred Choice Hymns* 207.

There are so many things, misunderstandings, stupidity, absence, that part us more than death. I could, like Milton [sonnet 14], say that "earthly load, of death, called life, that us from life doth sever." God bless you.

ever yours

F. Nightingale

Love to all at Rhianva.[166] Miss Jones, formerly of King's College Hospital, her most valuable "sister," Mrs Girdlestone, widow of the Indian Major Girdlestone, and two other "sisters" were all badly hurt, Mrs Girdlestone *dangerously* in Saturday's railway smash at Sittingbourne. Pray for them in your family prayers.

F.N.

Source: Letter, Wellcome (Claydon copy) Ms 9008/145

23 April 1881

My dear Sir Harry [Verney]

I *will* go out for a little walk, as you are so good as to wish it. But I have only strength to walk if I am quite alone and unnoticed, and will therefore transfer your kind visit to me to 6:00 or 6:30, if that will suit *you* and if you will allow me.

I hope Parthe is not too unwell to take a little drive with you. I would have a little drive, as she kindly asks, either before or after hers. *Please say when* today.

Fred *has* kindly sent me his Irish Land Bill.

F.N.

I wish Colonel Gordon[167] would come and see me. Where are the Basutos?

Source: Unsigned letter to Sir Harry Verney, Wellcome (Claydon copy) Ms 9008/158

10 South St., W.

11 June 1881

Thank God that dear Margaret [Verney] is safe and we thank God too that she has a *boy* [heir Harry Calvert Verney]. I give you joy, my dear Sir Harry, and Parthe too, of the jolly little man who comes hurrahing into the world, like the Scots Greys into the Battle of Waterloo, a gallant charge, carrying all before him. Three cheers for him. And a

---

166 Rhianva, on the Menai Straits, Anglesey, home of Margaret and Maude Verney's family, the Hay Williamses.

167 For correspondence with Gordon see *Society and Politics*.

brave and a gallant man fighting against evil he will doubtless be and justify his creation in the heroic mould as in the brave days of old. God be praised. How many a prayer we shall put up for him. Edmund was so good as to write me word of the dear little welcome newcomer.

Truly do we grieve over the loss of Sir James Hope. I thought he had been better and did not know it was so near. The whole Navy will grieve over it. I remember him when he was like a fresh breeze of delightful sea, not chilly, no, but like a southern Mediterranean breeze, and before that, in China time, when I used to hear of him every day from some government man. The two widows, how forlorn they will be, Miss Hope and Lady Hope. Please, if you go to the last "lay him in the earth," say something for me to each of them. It is from the bottom of my heart.

Amicia Milnes[168] is married today.

Source: Letter, Wellcome (Claydon copy) Ms 9008/173

Claydon
3 September 1881

My dear Sir Harry [Verney]

I have been with you all day, and *her* [Emily Verney] this happy day for her. I have carried flowers and wreaths to the grave as a poor outward token of the constant love which is ever burning in our hearts for her, a wreath of barberries as an emblem of the love of God and a cross of white flowers as shadowing forth her "white robes." And I strewed the step with pansies and small flowers. But I could find no rosemary "for remembrance."[169] I will take in the wreaths tonight, if this December weather continues, that they may be fresh for Sunday, the resurrection morning.

I shall be very glad to see Mr Trelawny Saunders, if you are kind enough to ask him, and if I could see him before dinner, instead of after. He will tell me an immensity about Indian affairs. I wonder whether he is the Saunders who was discussed, with others, to write Lord Lawrence's *Life*. Mr Fred is here and the children are well, but I think they wanted their Papa. He came yesterday. I have heard from Parthe, a cheerful letter from Meurice's [Hotel], Paris, going on to Dijon.

Thanks for the enjoyment of this beautiful house and gardens.

ever yours affectionately

F. Nightingale

---

168 Daughter of Nightingale's major suitor, Richard Monckton Milnes.
169 Shakespeare, *Hamlet* act 4, scene 5.

Source: Letter, Wellcome (Claydon copy) Ms 9009/33

Claydon House
27 April 1882

My dear Sir Harry [Verney]

. . . I put my Easter wreath of blue forget-me-nots and white flowers on dear Emily's grave. The singing birds seem fast disappearing from your trees on both sides the tennis lawn. I cannot help fancying they have been shot, though not by Mr Phillips the gardener. . . .

your affectionate
F.N.

Source: Letter, Wellcome (Claydon copy) Ms 9009/112

21 November [1882]

My dear Sir Harry [Verney]

Please tell me how you are and how Parthe is and how the dinner was. Whom do you mean to vote for at the School Board election next Friday? I think I shall vote for Sydney Buxton and Arthur Hobhouse, but I should like to know who *all* the candidates are and whether I can vote *by proxy*. The polling places are the Board Room, Mount St. or 21 Old Bond St., where voting papers and information can be had.

You have not told me what I am to say to Lord Morley[170] about the information given you by the family as to the supposed want of food in poor Colonel Balfour's case.[171]

yours and hers
F.N.

Source: Letter Wellcome (Claydon copy) Ms 9010/2

10 South St.
19 January 1884

My dear Sir Harry [Verney]

Pray let me hear on Monday if you come up on Tuesday, and by what train? Or if on any future day. I mourn that our dear P.'s nights

---

170 Earl of Morley, under secretary of state for war.

171 A letter 17 November 1882, Wellcome (Claydon copy) Ms 9009/109, by Nightingale responded to Harry Verney's desire to have the case inquired into by the Army. It was found that Balfour died of pyemia while recuperating at his sister's; Nightingale did not think there were grounds for the accusation of insufficient food on the voyage home.

are still so bad. You will be glad to hear that our old friend, Mrs Cox, is better. I thank God that General Gordon is gone to the Sudan.

Thanks for the rabbits and all favours. Let me have some snowdrops. I wish I could hear your thrushes sing.

That was a charming letter of Lord Chichester's. Lady Amelia Jebb[172] was one of the salt of the earth.

ever yours affectionately
F.N.

Source: Letter, Wellcome (Claydon copy) Ms 9010/34

10 October 1884

My dear Sir Harry [Verney]

If Mr Watson is coming this morning (I do not know what time), would any other hour this morning suit you better than 12:00? I would make *any* hour do. God bless you and your meeting with Mr Watson.

I am so sorry not to be at your lovely dinner, as you kindly wish it. You should not give me the pain of refusing you, for it is quite impossible. When I leave Parthe, I could not sit up for two minutes together at a table nor talk. I often do not dine at all, unless there is something very easy to eat.

Doctors have always told me that I should not speak a word nor even open a letter after 6 P.M. It is needless to say I cannot adhere to this. But if I were to attempt such a thing as dining downstairs, I could not be with Parthe the next day.

But we must "take pleasure in our infirmities and necessities," great and small, because when we are "weak, then are we strong."[173] May it be so with us all. God bless you again and again.

ever yours affectionately
F.N.

Source: Letter to Harry Verney, Wellcome (Claydon copy) Ms 9010/38

25 October [1884]

Barnes: I have read Barnes's letter, and scarcely think what he asks is unreasonable. It seems you merely asked for him a "*porter's*" place (which I did not know you meant to do, for when you were so very

---

172 The Jebbs were Nightingale family friends; Sir Joshua Jebb, a long-time collaborator, died in 1863.
173 An allusion to 2 Cor 12:10.

kind as to write you agreed with me that you should ask for a *suitable place*). At your recommendation they have been so good as to desire him to attend at Euston *again* on Wednesday next to see if they can find him a place *"which will suit him."*

I think if you had the great kindness to write a note to the N.W. Railway, thanking them for their having entertained your recommendation, and expressing a hope that they *will* be able to find "a place that will suit him," as you understand they have been so good as to offer, it would look not like an encroachment but like a recognition of their kindness.

F.N.

Source: Letter, Wellcome (Claydon copy) Ms 9010/49

11 December 1884

My dear Sir Harry [Verney]

How are you? and how is Parthe? Are you going today?

My beautiful cat died in the night and her kitten is dying, the results of a veterinary surgeon's "wash"!! May I bury them in your garden? . . .

F.N.

Source: Letter, Wellcome (Claydon copy) Ms 9010/50

10 South St., W.
15 December 1884

My dear Sir Harry [Verney]

Many thanks for your letters. I am writing down what you ask. Will you ask Maude kindly to give you 6/ for my Pleasley ticket? I will take care to pay her.

You do not enclose any "letter from the Duke of Westminster" in yours, but I gather from yours that there is an intention of naming this street "Florence Nightingale St." Whenever that is done, I must, of course, remove at once and go to quite another street. If it is too late to avert it, I shall begin to move directly, let my house for the whole Parliamentary season, for which I have always half-a-dozen offers, and not return to it except to pack up. You will find me gone when you come up again here. Surely our dear P. must know this or she must strangely have forgotten me.

I have several things to write about, but not now. Miss Crossland is, I am sorry to say, come back to St Thomas', but quite unfit, in my opinion and that of others, to work. Miss Williams leaves for Torquay today. If you were kindly to invite Miss Crossland (in her place) to Claydon, it would be a great boon. But I shall not say a word of this to her or anybody, of course. God bless you both.

ever yours affectionately

F.N.

Source: Letter, Wellcome (Claydon copy) Ms 9010/53

10 South St.

3 January 1885

Private

My dear Sir Harry [Verney]

I have considered long and closely the letter of the Duke of Westminster which you were so good as to send me, and which I now return. It is impossible to say in words how kind, and more than kind, we must feel his letter to be.

It is also quite impossible to say how very, very difficult I feel my decision to be. The letter of course changes the whole "venue" of the question of my (and your) residence in London. You were so good as to tell me that you had been invited to stand for North Bucks?, but had declined, that you would therefore be out of Parliament by the close of this year, that you and Parthe proposed to take on No. 4 "for one year" and then "see." But the Duke's letter speaks of his being "quite prepared to let it (your lease) run for the term of your own and of Lady Verney's life," etc. Look at a table of the value of life annuities, and you will see that the cost of an annuity of £250 a year (the reduction of rent offered me from Lady Day 1886) would be, for a life aged sixty-seven, *£2362.10,* my life being sixty-*six* then, a little more. You can scarcely wish me to accept £2360 from the Duke. But I am prepared, in consequence of Parthe's strongly expressed wish when I saw her last, *and entirely for her sake and for yours,* to keep on my house till Lady Day 1887.

I hope to find myself able to do this, because I know how strongly you and Parthe wish to remain in South St., and this delay, for a considerable time on my part in leaving my house, would keep you where you want to be. I cannot consent to pay the Duke less than the £400 for the extra year. This sum I will beg, borrow or steal. I feel the difficulty of decision to be great indeed. The Duke's conduct is quite charming, so full of delicate feeling as well as of generosity. As to declining the proposed new name of the street, of course I must do this, if I am to live here.

ever yours affectionately

F. Nightingale

N.B. If all the leases of this street are falling in, we must trust that the Duke will refuse to renew the lease of the public house opposite. At this time of the year the scenes are disgraceful and, *after* hours, drunken bad women rolling in the *mud* in the street at night, drunken singing and never a policeman to be seen. One day three drunken women and a man got into a cab at the public house door and upset it at the door. Every night there is drunken screaming of bad women and men in Park Lane about midnight—no police. God bless you both, ever dear Sir Harry,

yours and hers affectionately

F. Nightingale

Thanks for lovely flowers, rabbits and books shared with our probationers. All are going on well, thank God.

Source: Letter, Wellcome (Claydon copy) Ms 9010/72

Ravensbourne
6 April 1885

My dear Sir Harry [Verney]

How thankful to know you better. Many thanks for your letter and all your and Parthe's lovely strawberries, lilacs and goodies. I send the signature as directed.

John 20 and the journey to Emmaus, Luke 24:13, and all that happened on that glorious day took place on our Sunday, consequently the Jews' Monday, supposed to be 9 April, and what took place on the day week after would be 16 April. God bless you.

ever yours and hers

F.N.

Source: Letter to Harry Verney, Wellcome (Claydon copy) Ms 9010/81

10 South St.
10 June 1885

. . . But I write now on business. You know you were so good as to take back my draft lease for this house (for another year at *£400* per annum) to have it made out properly. It has now been returned to me ready for signature for a year at *£150* per annum. I wrote to you just before you came to London in January, as you will remember, asking you kindly to decline the Duke of Westminster's munificent offer of letting me have the house at *£150* year by year, but promising you that I would keep on this house for one more year (from next Lady Day) at *£400*.

May I ask you kindly to let me know by return of post (as they are urging me to sign) what came of your reply to D. of Westminster's offer, how it now stands and what you wrote to him. I was quite taken by surprise by this lease at *£150*, after what I had said. God bless you.

ever yours affectionately

F. Nightingale

Source: Letter, Wellcome (Claydon copy) Ms 9010/110

10 South St.

2 October 1885

My dear Sir Harry [Verney]

I think of you so much in our loss of Lord Shaftesbury.[174] The notice of him in the *Times* was very nicely done, but the keystone of all the wonderful work he did lay in the one line: "Thine was the cause; it was Thy work I did." That was the strength of his indomitable courage and perseverance and hope, that and his own humility. Parthe will remember how our oldest friend, Parker John, told with tender reverence how Lord Shaftesbury left his bed and paced up and down at night, saying he was a "sinner." What a life's work he leaves behind him! the life's work of "faith and love."

A Mr Curtis, "organizing secretary of Ragged School Union," came here this morning, asking if you would be chairman *today*!! of a meeting on his death. I said how great was your affection for Lord Shaftesbury, how great your interest in ragged schools, but that you could not come up and it was quite impossible at short notice. God bless you.

ever yours affectionately

F.N.

Source: Letter, Wellcome (Claydon copy) Ms 9010/112

10 South St.

6 October 1885

My dear Sir Harry [Verney]

I am almost sorry that you are coming to London for Lord Shaftesbury's funeral. It is cold standing in the Abbey. I don't think he would like you to come, but I hope, if you do, you are sleeping in London. I wish I could offer you a bed, but I am full of matrons.

---

174 Antony Ashley Cooper, 7th Earl Shaftesbury (1801-85), an old friend and collaborator on many issues; for correspondence see *Society and Politics*.

Will you lunch here after the Abbey? Or are you lunching at Maudie's? Anyhow I hope to see you after 4:00. I am engaged unluckily.

ever affectionately yours

F.N.

Source: Unsigned letter, Wellcome (Claydon copy) Ms 9010/122

2 December 1885

My dear Sir Harry [Verney]

I return you Lord Iddesleigh's[175] most kind letter with many thanks. I often wish he were at the India Office again.

I also return Miss Buckley's letter and am thankful to say that she has been successful in getting an annuity of £20 from the Incurables Hospital. She is so grateful.

7 December 1885

It was a glorious victory, glorious in the highest sense of the word. And there should now be some lines on the father riding in to Buckingham on his white horse at the head of his sons, and the good fellows, 5400 of them, who had worked so hard and so well "and all for love and nothing for reward," as Spenser says.[176] And Parthe, like another Bess of Hardwicke, getting the church bells rung. Yes, it was a glorious day.

Do you know, the charming little note you sent me on Saturday, was sent to the National Liberal Club. And though it had a stamp on, an old soldier, a messenger there, but whose hours were over, said, "No, it shan't go by post; Miss Nightingale shan't wait for it till Monday morning," and walked here with it at night in a deluge and stood at the door, dripping and leaving a pool even on the swimming pavement, and would not come in because he was "too wet." There is glory in small sacrifices as well as in great.

---

175 Stafford Henry Northcote, 1st Lord Iddesleigh (1818-87), foreign secretary.
176 *Faerie Queene* (1596) Book 2, canto 8, stanza 75.

Source: Letter, Wellcome (Claydon copy) Ms 9011/33

10 South St.

26 June 1886

My dear Sir Harry [Verney]

At Bath Mr Fred seems to be making a noble, impartial fight of it, speaking up for Lord Hartington[177] and Chamberlain,[178] as he always does, rousing the meetings to feeling responsibility as well as enthusiasm, dwelling on the broad principles to be remembered in the fight, keeping clear alike of local squabbles, as he fortunately can, and of what is even worse, abusive election gossip, and bringing out that which you would say in principle constitutes true liberalism.

This is not what even the greatest men of the party have done. And we may give you joy that your sons have been among the freshmen who have kept a higher tradition, not truckling to meaner feelings among the constituents.

Kathleen sends me word that she is much better, and feels more like herself, since she moved into the next room. Ralph[179] says he takes long walks with Grandpa. Both he and Gw[endolen] seem in good plight, thank God, and please thank Miss Shalders for her welcome letter. I pray that our dearest P. may be prudent and improve, with improved settled weather.

ever affectionately yours and hers

F.N.

Editor: The unhappy tale of Harry Verney's not supporting his son Edmund's election campaign (they disagreed on Home Rule for Ireland) is related further in *Society and Politics*.

---

177 Spencer Compton Cavendish (1833-1908), Marquess of Hartington, Earl and later Duke of Devonshire, assumed leadership of the Liberal Unionist Party in 1886.

178 Joseph Chamberlain (1836-1914), Liberal Cabinet minister; both Hartington and Chamberlain opposed Irish Home Rule.

179 Kathleen (1883-1966), the second daughter; Ralph (1879-1959), the eldest son of Fred and Maude Verney.

Source: Letter, Wellcome (Claydon copy) 9011/39

10 South St.
14 July 1886

PRIVATE

My dear Sir Harry [Verney]

I will not say anything about your being away from home on your son's two days, because that would be impertinent—you and poor Morey whose heart and mind must be in North Bucks. But I know you wish me and most kindly press me to say all I can about Parthe. And that is best done now when you are away. You say she "pressed" you "continually" to go to Norwich. You told me when you were in London and afterwards, when you most kindly wrote to me about that most anxious subject, her and her nurses, that you should take advantage of this "pressing" to tell her that the only condition on which you could leave her would be that she should relieve your "anxiety" by doing what you asked her about her nurses. *Nothing* has been done. Or rather, something has been done and it is much worse than when I was at Claydon. It is impossible to feel too "anxious" about her nursing.

Housemaid Emma has not been employed at all about her, instead of being employed regularly and systematically to relieve the nurses. And she (Parthe—my dearest Pop—oh fatal blindness) runs the risk of losing the one, Davidson, she calls the best nurse she ever had, and justly so and Nurse Taylor, both being thoroughly worn out, nothing having been done to help them. I know you kindly wish me to recapitulate:

1. *Davidson on night duty* when it is called a *better* night; Davidson gets up, that is, is called thirty times in one night!! This is the count.

2. The one who is on night duty ought to have *at least from 2 P.M. to 10 P.M.*, for sleep, exercise, etc., to herself.

3. Housemaid Emma, whom my poor Pop likes, and who is an excellent little nurse, ought to be, we should say, the whole day in attendance, to help with the needlework (which became entirely out of order in Phebe's time and which Davidson now does in the afternoon, *when she ought to be in bed*) to help in lifting, and turning Parthe, to give her her meals in the afternoon, and the thousand and one things which keep the nurses jumping up every two minutes.

4. My dearest Pop thinks that Davidson has time to do the needlework. She never has an uninterrupted two minutes. Nay, neither she nor Nurse Taylor scarcely ever have a meal in peace.

5. When Nurse Taylor is on night duty, *mutatis mutandis*; the same thing is to be said, the same rule laid down.

6. *Day duty*: It is impossible to keep a woman the *whole* day on duty—it is done neither with private nor hospital patients—and keep her contented, efficient and healthy.

7. Both these women are on the eve of going if no difference is made. Yet both would like to stay with her. I am merely recapitulating, you will observe, what you have had the kindness to discuss with me.

8. My dear Parthe, like most other private patients who have never nursed private patients themselves, cannot understand that, though three nurses could nurse in a hospital many patients, yet less than three cannot nurse a patient who, like herself alas!, requires attendance night and day, much of this attendance by day requiring two together.

9. You have kindly encouraged, nay pressed me, to discuss these matters with *you*, the *only* person who can carry them with Parthe and I merely put on paper what you have said or written and assure you that there is *nothing more* pressing than to carry this out. I pray God that you may be enabled to do so. No more "anxious" crisis can possibly exist.

10. Though it is of importance that Emma should give the whole day to Parthe, yet rather than lose *all* we ask, as we are doing now, we *might* compromise the matter by her giving, say, half the day. But these must be *fixed* hours, when she should sit within call of Parthe and help in the needlework while waiting a call. (She won't *wait* many minutes. She will be called about every two or three.)

11. *In either case*, someone must be had in from the village to do her work. It is impossible to keep that great house clean without at least three housemaids, even when you are alone. Now God grant the power to bring this about.

12. I would willingly, gladly pay, without Parthe knowing it, Emma's wages and keep and you have another housemaid. I see Parthe's nursing rushing down to destruction, and wish to help you to save it. No one else can save it. May God give the power.

Yes, everyone must be glad Lord Hartington is in, and sorry Trevelyan and many another is out, even Goschen. We had always better have the chiefs of *every* party in than Tom, Dick and Harry. *I* am sorry Arch is out. Dadabhai Naoroji[180] is a great loss and so is Evatt.[181]

---

180 Dadabhai Naoroji (1825-1917), president of the Indian National Congress. See *Society and Politics* for Nightingale's support of his Parliamentary career.
181 Surgeon-Major George Evatt, a long-time ally on Army sanitary issues. See *Society and Politics* for Nightingale's endorsement.

But I am not here to talk politics. God speed you.

ever affectionately yours

F.N.

Most Private. You see, of course, that Captain [Edmund] Verney lost by only 71 in 8800 votes. I have no one to share my grief and disappointment.

F.N.

Source: Letter, Wellcome (Claydon copy) 9011/41

10 South St.

15 July 1886

My dear Sir Harry [Verney]

Yes it is a terrible distress, but, for all that, Margaret and Captain Verney are they that have obtained the victory and *not* their successful opponent.[182] Covent Garden should have sent all its roses to strew in her path, had I but had time after the telegram came. For Margaret is she "that overcometh"[183] and Captain Verney too. I sent more than once to 37 Cornwall Gardens yesterday afternoon, but only got one message, after they were gone (from a maid) that "Mrs Verney was very well but very much upset." I am afraid that means, very tired. They did not dine at Cornwall Gardens, and Captain Verney was not there at all. They were to arrive at Amiens in the middle of the night and stay there till this afternoon, as you know, perhaps the best thing for them to go abroad. "Be strong and of a good courage."[184]

ever yours affectionately

F. Nightingale

Source: Letter, Wellcome (Claydon copy) 9011/72

10 South St.

12 January 1887

My dear Sir Harry [Verney]

I thought you had a New Year's present for me but it has not come. You did quite right to stay in the country. There was nothing but fog to bring you to London.

---

182 Edmund Verney had finally been elected MP for North Bucks in 1885 but was defeated in the 1886 election.

183 An allusion to 1 John 5:4.

184 A paraphrase of Deut 31:6.

I have been so busy that I have been unable to write. Many, many thanks for dear Margaret's letters. "Do not be thinking of how little you have to bring God but of how much He wants to give you." That is at p 19 of *With Christ.* I am sure you will be pleased with pp 18, 19 and indeed the whole section 3.

The trifling and frivolity with which people treat a shuffling of ministers in the same Cabinet, a change of *administration* though not of ministry, is so wicked that I can care nothing about parties.

There is an end of all good administration. If secretaries of state change every four months, it is absurd to expect that they can lead the permanent officials, the India Council or the many departments of the War Office. One party is just as bad as the other in this respect. And the language of the *Times* and indeed all the papers is disgusting: "Lord Salisbury has now two offices to dispose of" as if they were "good service" pensions or sacks of flour. On *us* the calamity falls with a crushing weight. . . . Fare you both *very* well.

ever yours and hers
F.N.

Source: Letter, Wellcome (Claydon copy) 9011/142

10 South St.
22 June 1887

My dear Sir Harry [Verney]

Your jubilee day has, I doubt not, taken place with immense joy to all, as has, you will see, the London Jubilee.[185] But you will also see that there was very near being a terrible accident, owing to one horse which could not stand fire (that is the cheers), poor Lord Lorne's,[186] when riding in the Queen's "Escort of Princes" not 300 yards after she left Buckingham Palace. The horse reared and threw him. (They had been obliged to tie a handkerchief over its eyes.) One shudders at what might have happened if it had kicked after it had thrown its rider in the midst. Half a dozen princes might have been severely injured, as Captain Cody's Cowboy King was, before it could be caught.

(Lord Lorne walked back to Buckingham Palace, borrowed a horse and rode by himself straight to Westminster Abbey, but did not again join the procession.) The moral is: never take a horse or pony you are

185 The fiftieth anniversary of Victoria's accession to the throne, 20 June 1837.
186 The Marquis of Lorne (1845-1914), husband of Princess Louise, daughter of Queen Victoria.

not sure of into noises or crowds it will not stand. Pray lay this moral to heart about your pony and Aldershot.

Today the children in Hyde Park. I expect this will find you gone to Aldershot. God bless you and my sister and keep you.

ever yours and hers

F.N.

Source: Unsigned note to Harry Verney, Wellcome (Claydon copy) Ms 9012/47

20 August 1888

Ask the bishop[187] whether he knows anything of the state of the Negroes in *Haiti*, and whether it is so grievously disappointing, and whether Negroes from the Southern states ever migrate to Haiti, or from Haiti to America.

Source: Letter, Wellcome (Claydon copy) Ms 9012/56

Sunday 7 October 1888

My dearest Pop [Parthenope Verney]

That unmitigated villain, Sir H., means to spend the afternoon of his Sabbath, the Day of Rest, as follows:

Missionary Service here

      "   "   Steeple Claydon

starting from here at 5:00 and meaning to do on his way Eli Beckett, perhaps Mr Gough, and Perseverance Society (three services today). He is quite impenitent, but perhaps might be induced to take a square tea at 4:30.

your F.

Editor: The next letters concern a serious illness, which Harry Verney survived.

Source: Letter on Harry Verney to his brother, Wellcome (Claydon copy) Ms 9012/118

13 February 1889

To Mr Calvert:

There was a slight check on Monday night: the temperature went up to nearly 100° but did not pass 100°. He was rather feeble yesterday (Tuesday) and did not himself wish to go out of his room, but enjoyed

---

187 Probably Henry Codman Potter, Bishop of New York, social gospel advocate. Nightingale did a critique of hospital plans for him in 1864.

the sun on the snow. Dr Benson thought him "rather weak" but otherwise satisfactory. He took a good meal at 1:30 P.M. yesterday, the night of Monday-Tuesday good.

I hope and believe that this is nothing more than a small "down" which we must expect. They hope to get him into the next room today.

F. Nightingale

Source: Letter, Wellcome (Claydon copy) Ms 9012/124

18 February 1889
Dear Mr Calvert

It is difficult to give a decided opinion. Doctors disagree. Dr Benson thinks he is *not* weaker. Morey thinks he *is*. There appears no doubt that the lung has done wonders in repair since Sir A. Clark saw him. Sir A.C. has been most kind in continuing the correspondence and, in concert with Dr Benson, altering prescriptions. The cough, weakness and inclination to faint at times, and the want of appetite are the present anxious drawbacks. He is only too lively, and not the want of interest but the too great interest the difficulty. There is nothing languid about him in manner or voice, when read to, which both Fred and Maude have done.

Saturday was not a good day—very bad as regards food. But he made an excellent meal at 1:30 P.M. yesterday and went into the next room at 2:15. Nights as good as possible. Parthe's cough better, but otherwise very suffering.

F. Nightingale

Editor: The next letters date from just after the death of Parthenope Verney, 12 May 1890.

Source: Wellcome (Claydon copy) Ms 9013/53

10 South Street
Park Lane, W.
20 May 1890
My dear Sir Harry [Verney]

Your dear daily letters are the comfort of my life, that your grief should be so swallowed up in *her* joy and that blessed Margaret should be with you.

I want to tell you about a letter I had from Mrs Milsom, the gardener's wife, this morning, how grateful she felt for all Parthe's kindness to her. The very last time I saw Parthe she said to me, "I am like the diver who goes to the bottom of the sea, brings up a pearl he scarcely knows how. *I* have been to the bottom of the sea, the pearl I have brought up has been the being able to do a little good to that little woman, Mrs Milsom. I didn't want her gratitude" (with tears) "only to be allowed to be a little use." Mrs Milsom says in her letter, "I could not think of anything I could do in my gratitude for her ladyship's kindness, so my husband made a wreath of a few of her favourite flowers, some which she so often gave herself to the great and poor alike, wherever they would bring brightness, freely given. He placed it for me beside the coffin, and if she knew of it the little offering would give her pleasure."

Will you thank Mr Calvert for his very kind letter to me? Mrs Davidson and Morey will mourn for her longest of those not her immediates. How much they did for her! I wish you could kindly tell me, with blessed Margaret's help, something I could give to each of those two they would like, about 10 or 15 guineas each, and something for Beart, about 5. The last time I ever saw *her* I was struck with Beart's deftness about her with that terrible cough. And Janet too.

I will write again. May God bless you and He does bless you and thank you.

ever yours and hers
F.N.

Source: Letter, Wellcome (Claydon copy) Ms 9013/52 (2)

[printed] 10 South Street
Park Lane, W.
13 June 1890

My dear Sir Harry [Verney]

You were so good as to speak to me yesterday about the Pleasley coal pit. The dates are these:

The colliery started 1872;

My father died January 1874;

Parthe's will 1875.

The colliery was then in full operation. Property including Pleasley and coal pit, etc. left to you for life, remainder to Fred absolutely.

ever yours and hers
F. Nightingale

Source: Unsigned letter/draft/copy to Harry Verney, Add Mss 45791 ff214-15

12 January 1891

. . . New Year, after great trials nothing seems less impressive than the dates of the calendar. The flight of time increases with age, more so through afflictions we may well call blessed, as they draw us nearer to eternity. Days and years x x but small influence on our grief. Their chief influence is to show us progressively the coming nearer of that time which will be at last perfect peace. But first therefore may we be thankful for every New Year given to us by God. Is it not a step more and nearer? Is it not *the way down* which leads us on? Is it not the blessed tool given to the faithful workman to do his work in confidence and faith, awaiting the words of welcome when work is over and evening's rest will begin?

That God may bless 1891 for you, dear Sir H., is a wish deeply felt. I often wonder whether you feel how much has been granted to you in being able to do so much good by your words and principles. x x My eyes are very weak, but I have learned to thank God that, in giving me this heavy cross to bear, with so many others, He has prevented me from other illnesses and that I am still able to do my work and to fulfill my duties which are—who knows it better than you?—the only consolations for suffering hearts *believing* firmly *in God's love to mankind.*

Nurses: I think discouragement ought never to prevail, rather ought one to consider the difficulties, and "ups and downs" as given to us for the sake of proving that we think highly of this question. My heart is very sad, as sad as ever, but ever full of peace and quiet under God's leading and strengthening hand. Once more God bless you.

Editor: On 4 May 1891 Edmund Verney was sentenced to one year in prison for attempting to procure a minor (a nineteen-year-old woman, then legally a minor) for immoral purposes.[188] As well as the letter below there is another, in *Theology*, which urges Harry Verney to forgive his prodigal and repentant son.

---

188 The various stages of charges laid, through to conviction, sentencing, loss of his Parliamentary seat, etc., are covered in stories in the *Times* 4 April, 20 April, 1 May, 5 May, 6 May, 7 May, 8 May, 12 May, 13 May, 10 June, 27 June 1891.

Source: Letter, Wellcome (Claydon copy) Ms 9013/152

[printed address] 10 South Street
Park Lane, W.
28 May 1891

My dear Sir Harry [Verney]

I hear with such great distress from you that your "day is quite filled with letter-writing on Edmund's subject," that you answer every letter, even "anonymous" ones.[189] I do not wonder that the more you do so, "the less" you are "comforted," because it turns away your thoughts from the great reality, the wonderful miracle that God's mercy is working before our eyes: Christ and the blessed Margaret bringing back the lost sheep,[190] the only real comfort, his deep repentance, Christ's love to sinners, Christ's and the wife's victory.

Is it a tribute to God or to morality (which is the same) to write and even to telegraph as if you had just some faint hope, and no more, that the sinner *might* repent and God might *just* save him? Is that faith?

Your telegram on Parthe's great birthday was very distressing to me. We must not fall into that desponding way as if we had to uphold morality against repentance. N.B. Parthe always impressed upon me, though I did not need the warning, whatever you telegraph to or from here, Claydon, is known all over Steeple Claydon.

I think the Persian's prayer is better than many Christians':

Four things, O Lord, I have to offer Thee
Which thou hast not in all Thy treasury,
My nothingness, my sad necessity
My *fatal sin* and earnest penitence.
Accept these gifts, and take the giver hence.[191]

That is, to a better life in this world. Edmund his [illeg]. Do you know that Edmund sent a message to me: "Tell her *that I prayed* to God to stop me: to release me from this slavery" (to vice). God has answered his prayer. Faith is saying "yes" to God.

The trial is terrible. But let us say "*yes*" to God and never, never doubt that God has given to Edmund salvation through repentance,

---

189 In addition to the nasty letters the Verneys also received many supportive ones, notably from W.E. Gladstone, Catherine Gladstone and W.H. Smith; see Claydon House, Verney Papers Bundle 10/429.

190 An allusion to Luke 15:6.

191 Nightingale copied this prayer into the diary of Luise Fliedner at Kaiserswerth in 1850 and also into her own Bible.

never, never—it seems so churlish to God if we do not believe in what He is about. And while there is such an outcry against Edmund, as there is, let us express not our faint hope but our fervent faith that he is *at this moment* the repentant and *changed* sinner, that he will come out of prison purified, as there is no doubt.

Unless Margaret had thrown all *earthly* feeling aside, her position would be intolerable. But she has nothing left in her but the "indwelling God"[192] to do what He has charged her with. But oh her sorrow! You who are so kind and so chivalrous towards her; her main comfort is being with you. If you think that you must uphold morality by your letters, I assure you there is no danger of people thinking that you do not feel this bitter sin enough. Let people not think that his *father* doubts his repentance.

Thanks for your great kindness to me which allows me to write this.

ever yours, my dear brother, praying for you hourly

F.N.

Source: Unsigned letter, Wellcome (Claydon copy) Ms 9014/30

[printed address] 10 South Street
Park Lane, W.
25 June 1892

In answer to your kind letters
My dear Sir Harry [Verney]

I must give you joy that what you have so long wished to do for Steeple Claydon you are now enabled to accomplish. I am sorry that the water supply takes one of your best fields, but we want it to be associated with your name. (But is it not raal naughty of you to wish "the water had been found on any other land than" yours?) Have you not the opportunity now to do as you have always wished—to make Steeple Claydon into a model village instead of the place it is? With the new railroad, if it were made into a place with a good water supply, the first essential of a model village, etc., might not villas be built, and Steeple Claydon become a good liver and prosperous?

The water supply will be, I presume, leased from you. There is such a movement all over the country that Bucks must not be left behind. Lea Hurst rated itself, brought pure water from a moor, and it is brought within a few yards of every cottage, I understand. As for "blessed Margaret," it was *her warmest wish* that you should do these

---

192 An allusion to John 14:17.

things, and do them without waiting for her return. She *craved* that you should do them, i.e., should do the water supply and also the new cottages after Sir H. Acland's pattern, as you wished, which you can do without waiting for anyone.

As I understand, you will not, shall you? be called upon to pay anything for what you call "the government measures" for another six months, because of the delays of the sanitary authorities. And by that time you will have, shall you not? another half year of Mr Calvert's income.

Source: Letter, Wellcome (Claydon copy) Ms 9014/111

10 South St.
30 May 1893

My dear Sir Harry [Verney]

How can I thank you enough for your delightful letter—so generously and graciously giving me the bit of land in Lea Hurst called "Lane Croft" for Shore, and desiring to "sign any document that does this legally." It has been found impossible to get ready any such document for your signature today, but I shall gratefully send it on to you to Claydon when ready.

God bless you.
ever affectionately yours
Florence Nightingale

Source: Letter, Wellcome (Claydon copy) Ms 9014/123

[Claydon]
4 September [1893]

My dear Sir Harry [Verney]

You will come to me today at 12, will not you? And you kindly promised to take the sacrament with me tomorrow (Monday) from Mr Higham. Will you ask him today?

You will see my offering at Emily's tomb.
F.N.

Editor: Many of the last letters to her brother-in-law are of a religious nature, including Nightingale's last greetings to him on his birthday, her last Christmas greetings to him ("on Christ's birthday"), and are reported in *Theology*. The last case on which she asked his help is dated 20 January 1894. There are concerns over his declining strength and condolences on the death of a grandson. Harry Verney died 12 February 1894.

Source: Letter, Wellcome (Claydon copy) Ms 9014/122

24 August [1893]

Dear Sir Harry [Verney]

I am very sorry but I cannot—very, very sorry. You were quite exhausted yesterday. The last half hour you were nearly fainting and I could hardly keep my senses. I can do nothing for you and it kills me. I could not break your fall, as I did before, if you fainted.

F.N.

Source: Letter, Wellcome (Claydon copy) Ms 9014/128

27 October [1893]

My dear Sir Harry [Verney]

Dear Ellin is in good spirits and we must be glad that this necessary trip will be accomplished under such good auspices. We are all in the hands of God. There is, I believe, good reason to expect that you will get through this winter and see dear Ellin again, if only you take care, and perhaps much more than this winter.

God bless you all and He *will* bless you.

F.N.

Source: Letter, Wellcome (Claydon copy) Ms 9014/130

[printed address] 10 South Street
Park Lane, W.
27 November 1893

My dear Sir Harry [Verney]

I am scandalized at your *riding* out in the *cold*—I try to forgive you, but I don't know that I can. But I hail with joy your return to penitence and prudence. Remember, you have *promised* not to ride out in the cold. (Don't remember to *forget.*)

Indeed I do sympathize with, feel for and with you all in the terrible loss of dear Vortigern. How many of us could learn a lesson from him. He could do what he did not like *joyously*—that marks a boy (and a man). What influence he had, though only nineteen. And, as James[193] says, there is nothing but what is pleasant to look back upon in his life. If it was right to do, he could do it *gaily*. May we follow in his steps! . . .

---

193 James Hope Verney (1869-1909), eldest son of George and Morforwyn Verney.

Source: Letter, Wellcome (Claydon copy) Ms 9014/133

[printed address] 10 South Street
Park Lane, W.
6 December 1893

Dearest blessed Margaret [Verney]

... I hope to send three books tomorrow for Sir H.'s birthday which perhaps dear Ellin will put with any presents for him. I hope but fear about my choice. One is a book of some, I think, very beautiful short prayers which the maids and I often use at morning prayers. Two books are Kingsley's. I wished to have sent Kingsley's *Hermits* but was afraid. . . .

Source: Letter, Wellcome (Claydon copy) Ms 9014/142

[printed address] 10 South Street
Park Lane, W.
20 January 1894

My dear Sir Harry [Verney]

A son of *Dr. Armitage* begs your kind interference, i.e., *Dr A. begs it for his son. Lieutenant Cecil Hamilton Armitage* wishes to go out to the *Gold Coast Corps,* which *Lord Ripon* could grant at once. He is a Lieutenant of the S. Wales Borderers' Militia (the old 24th). His age is twenty-four. He is a thorough trained soldier, has certificates for the *Artillery* (Shoeburyness) for *Rifle Shooting* (Hythe). He is known to Lord Battersea. I should not think the government was embarrassed with applications from promising young men for the *Gold Coast Corps.*

You will perhaps remember that you were good enough to get one of Dr Armitage's sons into the Navy, who has turned out excellently. Perhaps you would be so very kind as to ask Lord Ripon to put this young man into the Gold Coast Corps. He would not be a failure.

ever your affectionate
Florence Nightingale

Emily Verney

Editor: Business correspondence with Emily Verney will appear in the volume covering the Franco-Prussian War. The letters here deal with Nightingale's assistance to her as a young woman seeking her way, her fatal illness from unsanitary conditions at Malta and her untimely death at age twenty-nine.

Source: Letter, Wellcome (Claydon copy) Ms 9004/43

Whitsun Eve 1870

My dear Emily [Verney]

First of all, I recommend your plan to God and feel sure that, if it is for His service, He will enable you to carry it out. Things which go easy don't often go well, when it is His work. And therefore? I (don't wish you plenty of difficulties, because I am not saint enough for that but) am afraid you will have difficulties. But God knows much better what He is doing than we know what we want.

2. I had a long talk yesterday about your matters with Beatrice Lushington. The thing which you want scarcely exists yet. In fact it has to be created. Perhaps it is God's intention to call you to be one of the creators. But of course this will increase your difficulties in learning, at the beginning.

3. Beatrice says that, so far as she knows, *that* Miss Buss?[194] on Haverstock Hill? is really the only person who has set up good middle-class female teaching, but that the premises are so bad, so over-crowded, that it is quite out of the question your going there yet. There is an idea of lending Miss B. money to set up on better premises. Then you could go.

4. But this says: wait. Then there is Miss Clough. Beatrice and I both agree that it would rather counteract than further your purpose for you to go to her school at *first*. The thing is only in a state of experiment. It has all to be organized. Later, it might be of use, but this again says: wait. Miss Clough knows so much about schools that it would be most desirable you and she should have a conversation. Beatrice proposes Thursday (the day after your wedding[195]) at her house. Beatrice does not know anything of the Richmond School you spoke of.

5. But there is an officers' (military) daughters' school at Bath, which you probably know about, under a Miss Kingdon. (This Miss Kingdon was a cousin of our cousin, the first Mrs Bonham Carter; she lived with her till her death, helping her with her children. After her death, Miss K. took charge of the children till J. Bonham Carter married again.) Miss Kingdon then wished to do something, just as you are doing, and she undertook this school and has had it ever since, as superintendent. . . .

---

194 Frances Mary Buss (1827-94), founder of North London Collegiate School.
195 The wedding of Fred and Maude Verney.

6. Beatrice will make inquiries whether any one of the schools founded by the late Dean of Hereford is in a sufficiently good state for you to learn at, and especially where that Miss Sailly, who was his pupil and whom I once was with, is. (Poor King's Somborne, where she *was*, immediately under the dean, is quite degenerate.)

7. B. will also make inquiries about Liverpool and Edinburgh but fears there is nothing. You see the fact is you have to create. (I believe myself that there is no country calling itself civilized where *middle-class female* education is so backward as in England.)

8. Then there is Germany. There is, we know, far better teaching in Germany of this class than in England. But the difficulty is to find out where you could go with health. Even if I were sure that the normal school at Kaiserswerth were in the same state as it was under Pastor Fliedner, I am sure that you could not stand the bad food, the absence of all English, cleanliness and privacy, etc.

9. Pastor Fliedner's second daughter, Minna, has set up a middle-class female school at Hilden, some miles from Kaiserswerth. But how are we to find out about that? what it *really* is?

10. Beatrice knows of an excellent female school at *Berne*, but she does not know it personally. She says we all know what the Berne climate is. She will, however, inquire.

11. The (Miss Whateley) Cairo plan sounds very well. But of that you know more than we do.

12. Then you know the admirable American Mission (Mrs Hill) schools at Athens. (Mrs Hill used to let me attend her lessons with her.) They are exactly female middle class. And Eastern Europe has a strong touch of the East, its amazing quickness and genius, its rapid falling-off at the least fancy, its want of steadiness, perseverance, its lofty aspirations, its disappointing falls. But then, the present state of Greece, the trying climate (cold and hot), modern Greek to be acquired, etc.

13. You have doubtless consulted your excellent German lady friend who once lived with you. She would know, I suppose, about any good normal female school of the day in Protestant Germany.

14. You know how good the Moravian Herrnhuter [brothers] schools are. There is one near Bonn, I think. But neither Beatrice nor I know it *personally*; Frances Bunsen would probably know. You see how little all this amounts only to this: the whole question (or rather practice) of female middle-class schools is in an elementary state here. There are one or two places in England (nothing very high) where two or three months would enable you to feel your way both as to your

own powers and as to judging afterwards where to go next. You must inquire, feel your way, wait and try and make mistakes *and succeed.* The whole thing is in its rudest state, as hospital and sanitary nursing was in England twenty years ago.

But the more difficulty, the more glory, as the hackney coachman said when he drove over a heap of stones. Or, as St Paul says: Thy strength is made perfect in weakness.[196] God bless you ever, dear Emily,

yours

F. Nightingale

Believe that I shall be most anxiously interested to hear what you do next. I wish I had recent information at your service. But, after all, the most we can do for each other is to enable another to clear up his or her ideas. Each must tread his or her own path of the cross. No one can really take the responsibility for another. My deepest sympathy, my warmest interest, if that could do you any good, you *have.*

F.N.

Source: Letter, Wellcome (Claydon copy) Ms 9004/45

35 South St.

12 June 1870

My dear Emily [Verney]

I will write without delay the few things which seem important enough to write to you after my conversation with my accomplice Beatrice.

1. "Home and Colonial": I feel very strongly what I should do in this case, were it my own child, as, e.g., dear Agnes Jones was. I do not think that you could go there unless (1) you had seen the place for at least a morning; and (2) you had made (and had had accepted by them) many arrangements. You see, unless you had seen something [of] the place beforehand, and unless above all they had made special arrangements for you, you might not like the place at all, might not wish to stay there a week. I am sure that Captain and Mrs Verney, who are so handy-minded and so devoted, will agree with me. (I understand what you said that you could not quite, while with Lady Monteagle, run about after things your own way. That is true. But far better, I think, lose a month or three months than go to a place as it were haphazard.) To me much considering, the *course* would appear thus (ask Captain Verney who has a compass). . . .

---

196 A paraphrase of 2 Cor 12:9.

That you should thus take three or four months there. Neither Beatrice nor I have a *very* high opinion of "Home and Colonial," though we both think that you will acquire there the practice of children, the *dodges* of teaching. Learn what you can like and what you can stand and that three or four months will thus be very profitably spent there, *if limited* as above. . . .

The Richmond school: we both think that it would not do for you to offer yourself *as a mistress* there and that it would tell rather badly for them, if they accepted you. You would not learn the art of teaching. You would only be tied down to teach certain particular subjects, as best you may. This is how it strikes us. . . .

N.B. Beatrice feels pretty sure that there is no school of the late Dean Dawes' [King's Somborne] worth your going to, now. But, first and foremost, get rid of your cough. (2) I don't think you or anyone at all can guess whether you are equal to the labour of teaching for even four hours a day without an experiment first. It is a disappointing thing, which one should always avoid if one could, to break down at first. God bless you.

ever your affectionate and anxious old aunt

F. Nightingale

N.B. Behold the miraculous effects of *bride cake*! As some of Mrs Fred Verney's had been kindly sent me, for the orthodox purpose as I supposed. I placed a crumb under my pillow *and dreamt*. And I dreamt that I was under secretary for India with a balance of 10 millions on the right side of my sheet and that I was irrigating Orissa and draining the deltas of Hoogly and Brahmapootra and famine was vanishing away and cholera almost extinct. Tell Mrs F. Verney.

Source: Letter, Wellcome (Claydon copy) Ms 9004/111

Lea Hurst
21 September 1870
7:00 A.M.

Dearest Emily [Verney]

Don't suppose me such a "beast" as to *wish* even to take up your time and strength with writing to me. I am the more obliged when you do write, for anything that you can tell me is more interesting to me now than everything else, you may be sure. I know that you have got your "business" [aid to the sick and wounded in the Franco-Prussian War] into capital order and I glory in your work. How I have longed that I could take my share in this war as in the Crimean War! But what use is it offering to serve God in one way when He asks one to serve Him in another?

It was a great relief to me hearing, too, that Sir Harry was well and I hope you are taking care to do the same. As for the rest of your note, what can one say but that it is the great trial of life to see inefficiency, amounting to the unprincipled, among good people, to see the "*no-taking-pains-ness*" about the most important things, when people will extenuate themselves in taking pains about a trifle. Ah my dear child, it is not the "contradiction of sinners against" good things, but the contradiction of *good people* against good things which makes life weary! (There is a sort of childishness among English women "in easy circumstances.") It has often been said that genius is nothing but an enormous power of taking pains. I assure you *that* is true. And I assure you that nothing is so wearing as to hear people, good people say: "Ah *you*, you can do it," when you know that, if they would but take pains, they might do it too. But they won't even try to *walk* and then they say they can't *run*.

The only thing for us to do is to remember that none can ever have had this trial like our Lord and St Paul: our Lord who found his best beloved disciple disputing for throne,[197] even just before His own death; St Paul, who said: "All they [which are] in Asia have turned away from me."[198] And this too just before his own end, when he must have thought all his plans were blasted and all his work destroyed.

Do you know that I have never known any real founder or leader of any good thing who had not the same idea about his or her work? But perhaps I ought not to tell this to a young thing like you. However the only way is to look upon this path as the path Christ Himself has trod, who says He is the way.[199] *Can* we be Christians and not wish to tread His way? (though I sadly confess, very often, that, even in my old age, I have learnt to tread it so badly that I am quite ashamed of myself), never to stop to consider what comes from man but only to look, always to look at it as coming straight from God (which is just what I don't do and so I have no business to preach). But I am not sure that it *does*, for the service of God to be so overflowing with kindness as that you cannot really distinguish between one person and another. That (which however is a very rare failing) incapacitates one almost as

---

197 An allusion to Mark 10:35-45.
198 A paraphrase of 2 Tim 1:15.
199 An allusion to John 14:6.

much for organizing, working with judgment and seeing what answers and what does not, and putting the right person in the right place as the defect of too much censoriousn[ess].

In practical work, "charity" does *not* "believe all things,"[200] nor would St Paul recommend it. The thing is to think what is best for the service of God and always to keep one's eye on that, in short, to go back to the old plan, of always keeping one's thought on Christ, to see what *He* would have done in such a case. Christ was so witty; we cannot at all suppose that *goodiness* is what is expected of us. . . .

ever your affectionate old aunt

Florence Nightingale

Source: Incomplete letter, Wellcome (Claydon copy) Ms 9005/14

8 February 1871

Dearest Emily [Verney]

You wrote to me some time ago about giving you my vote (I don't mean my "female suffrage" as a "householder" ([b]ut) to some "orphan" or "incurable."[201] I did not answer because I had no time. Now I answer, but you need not [r]ead unless you like it.

I cannot vote because I have no vote, and I have no vote because I have, for many years, decided after no little consideration that to give up any of my time to this new-fangled mode of British wisdom for satisfying its own conscience that it is doing charity would be wrong in me.

I never subscribe to any charity except on condition of having no vote, i.e., anonymously where the charity is conducted by voting. Some have impudently told me that my name was worth more than my money and that they should keep my name in spite of me, even though I withdrew my subscription. One actually did this. And every year I am beset with requests for my "vote and interest." But, even had I ordinary health and leisure, I would not employ it in this way. I would employ my health and strength in doing some real good business, not in canvassing for "votes," putting up envelopes and affixing stamps.

It is one of those things which a whole class falls into without thinking, though one would think that the smallest moment of consideration would suffice to protect people from such a mode [of] spending their time. Indeed it is a mere matter of arithmetic. Given the number

200 An allusion to 1 Cor 13:7.
201 For more on Nightingale's views of private charities see *Society and Politics*.

of hours which each lady who devotes herself to the "canvassing" business spends in it, given the expense of the printing of cards, the paper and envelopes, the postage stamps, multiply this by the number of ladies and does anyone really think that, if all that good time, to say nothing of the money, were devoted directly to the use of the "orphan" or "incurable" it is for, half the orphans would not be educated, half the "incurables" cured, half the poor governesses provided for?

(I remember my dear mother saying thirty years ago when this mode of charity first came into fashion—for it is the growth, I think, of the last thirty years—about the poor governesses, that she always looked down the list to see for the one who had *fewest* names to recommend or canvass for her and *always voted for that one*. I remember about the same time the daughters of one of the richest dukes in England canvassing for an "old governess," *their own*. And of course they won. I do think—this is a parenthesis—that *that* would be impossible in any country but England. Russians, Germans, French and Italians would as soon think of throwing an old governess or tutor of their own on the charity of the public as an old mother or father. However, that is beside the mark—it is not the *real* objection to the voting system.)

I had, two or three years ago, a very striking instance of this voting system. A maid of honour of the Queen's who allowed herself to be ordered about by members of the royal family (*not* the Queen) in doing this sort of work corresponded with me on business connected with it. A good deal of the experience came out. I am really afraid to tell you what it was because you will think I am inventing, and because I cannot trust "my" memory for the figures. But I know that the *daily* letters numbered by *hundreds*, that the writing them took up the *whole* time (occasionally for as much as sixteen hours a day) of one or more ladies for six weeks (she was not "in waiting" during those weeks). The work included canvassing for votes, getting up bazaars and other things which I have not even time to enumerate, much less to do. Twice she had worked herself into a dangerous nervous fever. (The only wonder to me was that she was not in a lunatic asylum.)

I sent her a subscription with the express condition that it was *not* to buy anything at her bazaar, that it was to go direct to her charity, that it was to be anonymous, that I declined to vote (I was a Life Governor). And I told her pretty much what I am saying now (for which she expressed a great deal of gratitude. I know not whether she is acting up to it), viz., that if all that good work, all those powers of organization—for considerable powers of organization are often shown in this way—of thought, all that money and time, for she spent what can one say but that the amount of good time, thought, work and money thus spent, wasted, a[s] I believe, as utterly as if you were to put it, like Ariosto's[202] ol[d], dead moons behind the "edge" of the world, would go far to do away with pauperism, to educate children, to reform criminals, to cure sick?

N.B. I think, with regard to election by vote (of orphans and incurables) it is an exasperating cruelty to those who are not elected, since the worst, the most friendless cases are those which have the least chance of election. The only comfort is that these institutions are really so bad that it is almost a mercy not to be elected.

But *would* they be so bad if the gentlefolk who spend their time in canvassing and voting for them spent that time in looking after them? and in qualifying themselves to look [after] them *well*? Excuse the experience, which I need not say you need not attend to of,

your affectionate old aunt

F. Nightingale

Many thanks for Mrs Cox's *too* instructive letter, which I will return shortly. I am so glad that you have Colonel Cox with you. Pray remember me most kindly to him. How I wish I had been able to see him! Tell me *all* he says, but I must not say *all.* The prospects of peace for France seem better, of civil war less.

I am glad that dear Margaret is able to drive out. I suppose she will soon go back to Rhianva. Were she not so brave, I fear she would then anew feel her loss. My best love to her, please. In great haste.

ever yours

F.N.

Source: Letter, Wellcome (Claydon copy) Ms 9005/92

Lea Hurst
Matlock
21 September 1871

Dearest Emily [Verney]

Both now and forevermore, whenever you wish it, please take in harmonium from 35. It is doing nothing there and I like to think of it with you. You and I shall have a long talk some day about pauperism,

---

202 Ludovico Ariosto (1474-1533), poet.

etc., and I shall long to hear all your experience. I have not time to write, but in the meantime let me say that, in the hurry of the last morning, you misunderstood me about Poor Law "doles" and workhouse tests. Those whom you compel to find work by offering them the workhouse instead of outdoor relief, and who do *not* accept the workhouse (but take the work) are just the persons to whom outdoor relief should *not* be given. But suppose it, the "[work]house," accepted, as, e.g., by a widow (who *can* do some work) with children, neither woman nor children will ever come out again; they are made paupers for life (this is universal experience). And these are just the persons (struggling to keep out of the "house") to whom it should never be offered as a test, to whom outdoor relief *should* be given, and who should be helped to do productive work.

Everybody can *produce* to some extent, that is, everybody out of the workhouse. Only *in* the workhouse can they do no (productive) work. That is why the "house" is so pauperizing. (This is what young reformers should understand, like you.) The unproductive labour test is absolutely demoralizing. To help everybody in his measure to *productive* work is the only real help.

Have you ascertained whether Maud Herbert[203] is to marry *Gambier Parry?*

ever your old and affectionate "aunt"

F.N.

Source: Letter, Wellcome (Claydon copy) Ms 9005/124

Embley

24 March 1872

My dearest Emily [Verney]

. . . An excellent man, the Chaplain of Colney Hatch, has just sent me a little address which he makes to the insane when they are discharged. Now, as *I* am a poor old pauper lunatic, though *you* are not, my dearest child, I can tell you it is eminently refreshing and to the purpose. He says, *Take short views of life,* that is, don't be always worritting yourself and others with what you shall do, *if - -* and what will happen *when - -,* etc. He is also the only man I know who really enforces the *duty* of *amusing yourself* as a medicine (not of amusing yourself as a dissipation), of looking out for little pleasures, of keeping yourself

---

203 Lady Elizabeth Maud Herbert (1851-1933), daughter of Sidney and Elizabeth.

"whole," body, soul and mind in health. Imprudence, thoughtless-
ness, heedlessness he "puts down" entirely as the greatest enemies to
his maxims, because, he says, heedlessness is one great cause of the
anxiety he preaches against. And thoughtful, prudent people have
less cause to be anxious. "Live for today! Tomorrow's light tomorrow's cares shall bring to sight

St Francis of Assisi did not like the ants because, he said, they were
"so anxious." But the birds, he said, were just right, industrious, I suppose he meant, but not anxious.

Victor Hugo[204] in his better days wrote:

Soyez comme l'oiseau,	[Be like a bird,
Perché pour un instant	Perched for a spell,
Sur un rameau trop frêle	On a twig too frail,
Qui sent ployer la branche	Who feels the branch sway,
Et qui chante pourtant	Yet who sings anyway
Sachant qu'il a des ailes.	Knowing he has wings.]

The thing is to *have* "wings." And now, *dearest soul*, I think I have
preached enough. Next time I hope to be more "amusing" as my
good chaplain "preaches." . . .

Source: Unsigned note, Wellcome (Claydon copy) Ms 9005/125

[printed address] 35 South Street
Park Lane, W.
Good Friday [29 March] 1872

Dearest Emily [Verney]

A few flowers (alas! the frost has cut off almost everything—these
are our best), with F.N.'s overflowing love and best prayers for the passion's hopes and every best Easter blessing.

Source: Letter, Wellcome (Claydon copy) Ms 9005/143

[printed address] 35 South Street
Park Lane, W.
31 May 1872

My dear Sir Harry [Verney]

What can one say? She [Emily Verney] was worth us all put
together and now she is dying. She might have done such a great work
in this world. She was the only young woman of our families who had

---

204 Victor Hugo (1802-85), French novelist and poet.

any aim or idea of doing a public work in God's service. I always thought she would have been my successor (I *don't* mean in *hospital* work) and done it better than I. I have rarely seen, if ever, such great administrative powers in a young woman, and without experience. And now she is dying: "Fair form, young spirit, morning vision fled."

You know that I would come down to Claydon any day, if you ask me, to see her once more. But I so entirely agree that, whether God spares her yet a little longer or not, she had better only see you whom she loves best in the world; and her uncle who no doubt raises her to unite in spirit with our Lord to accomplish his Father's will, and does not excite her; and Parthe, that I do not press this for one moment.

I have nothing to say about the medical part. No doubt Dr Newham would say if he wished Dr Walshe to see her again. We cannot really mourn her, but oh that she should have gone before me. Had she lived, she would have seen:

Rich dream by dream decay
All the bright sunbeams drop from life away
Thrice blest to go!
Now the long yearnings of thy soul are stilled
Home, home, thy peace is won, thy heart is filled,
Thou art gone home![205]

God bless you.
    ever yours overflowingly
    F.N.

Source: Letter, Wellcome (Claydon copy) Ms 9005/151

[printed address] 35 South Street
Park Lane, W.
4 July 1872

Dearest ever dearest Emily [Verney]

(I will not say *my* Emily for it is God's Emily). It seems unnatural not to write one word to you of whom I am forever thinking. Do not you think that that state of life which is, as it were, between life and death is particularly fruitful? There is scarcely any state where one can be more faithful to God. All comes from or *seems* to come more directly from the hand of God then: the illness, the remedies, the beginning, the end of each day. Each day is, as it were, lent us by God.

---

205 A paraphrase from Felicia Dorothea Browne Hemans, "The Two Voices," in *Poetical Works of Mrs Hemans.*

We take our answer from Him generously, as St Paul took his before his martyrdom in the way he says to Timothy [2 Tim 4:6] he did. Each day we take as a special gift from God. We do not make plans of our own long ahead and we unite ourselves each day to God's plans, whatever they may be. We think, too, of the successes we may have in another life and of what we may do for Him there, and how faithfully we may act up to His plans there too.

Then every moment is precious here. And for what regards the body we submit to its slavery cheerfully and patiently. Thousands and millions die without knowing what they have died or lived for and we thank God that He has given us to know what we live and die for, and that He who counts even the hairs of our heads[206] will in His own good time give even those thousands and millions the real knowledge worth having. We say as earnestly as if it were the last time: Father, into Thy hands I commend my spirit.[207]

Dearie, I cannot help like an old nurse sending you a "10 pun" towards the nursing. God bless you.

ever yours (and it is really "ever"
for you are "never" out of my thoughts)
F. Nightingale

Source: Letter, Wellcome (Claydon copy) Ms 9005/153

Embley
Romsey
27 July 1872

Dearest ever dearest Emily [Verney]

I must write a word to you who are always in my thoughts and much farther from you now that I am here. . . .

Somewhere in the Apocrypha it says, "The just man if he be prevented with death" may be at rest, because God will take care that his works shall be worked out, and that He himself shall work out His works in some other "mansion" of our Father's house.[208] In an old German Latin book of the thirteenth century it says that, in the *undecaying spring* of God's *eternity* ("in immarcessibili aeternitatis meae vernantia," if ever there is truth in words, it is in these): all good works will be continued and increase and grow and fructify for eternity by

---

206 An allusion to Matt 10:30.
207 Luke 23:46.
208 A paraphrase of Wis 4:7 and an allusion to John 14:2.

God's "*co-operation*," i.e., by our being *fellow workers with* HIM. (This is, of course, necessary and essential to every good work) *through eternity.*

Eternity always seems to me not a harvest, but a spring, a time of ever-increasing, never-ending *growth.* We need never lament, *provided* we have good will to be fellow workers with God. How little we have done here, any more than delicate people who are unable to do anything before breakfast, need tear themselves to pieces about this inability.

I like the books of the early centuries of this millennium (for every thousand of God's years is, in fact, his "millennium" or one of his millenniums) because they seem to me to rise so much higher than those, whether Protestant or R. Catholic or rationalist, of these later centuries, in the appreciation of how this life is only a little piece of an eternal education. They often take pains to show that, if one's state of mind is in conformity with this, what does the loss of all the "sacraments" in the world signify, or sudden or early death or, etc., loss of opportunities, etc.?

I have your little hymn book always by me and sometimes I repeat some of it to my mother. Fare you well, dearest, and God be with you.

ever yours

F. Nightingale

Are you not glad that Dr Livingstone is found? All honour to that young American.[209]

I like to watch the clouds; "the scenery of the sky," as Faraday used to say, is finer than any other scenery.[210] What an artist God must be, for the sky is almost all His own, almost the only scenery of His which we cannot spoil (except by our smoke) and that is always beautiful in all its changes, that and the sea, which I am always fond of and which I shall never see again. But the sky is always with us.

Edmund and Margaret Verney, Lettice Verney

Editor: Edmund and Margaret Verney were married in 1868 and Nightingale's correspondence with them begins with their engagement in 1867. The large number of surviving letters, more to her than to him, carry on into Nightingale's old age, the last dated 1902. They cover all sorts of family news, health problems, miscarriages, births,

---

209 W.H. Stanley, who rescued Livingstone.
210 The quotation remains unidentified. Nightingale could be recalling the speech she heard him give at Oxford to the British Association for the Advancement of Science, 25 June 1847; see *Society and Politics.*

schooling, deaths of relatives, holidays, the care of Claydon employees and tenants, bird-feeding in winter, faith and morals. Correspondence regarding the selection of vicars for the Claydon parishes is reported in *Theology* and that concerning Edmund's political career is mainly in *Society and Politics*, but both these subjects appear to some extent here. A few letters to their daughter, Lettice, have also been included.

Source: Letter, Wellcome (Claydon copy) Ms 9002/192

[printed address] 35 South Street
Park Lane
London, W.
2 December 1867

My dear Captain [Edmund] Verney

I must thank you for the great kindness of you and yours to our nurses. I saw each of those worthies separately both before and after the performances and I am sure they each and all of them went away in a holier and happier frame of mind and with a more earnest resolution to undertake their duties, as "approved unto God."[211] Two or three of them said to me that she "should never forget this day" and I don't believe they ever will. I believe they go to the threshold of a new life with something of the feeling (thanks to you all) with which we ought to approach a new life. Each of them said this to me after her own fashion. But the elder of the first two, who is a woman of strong religious feeling (but with a temper like "one possessed with the devil"), was particularly impressed. I hardly know any ones but you who would have taken such pains to give them a great pleasure and to do them good. And I too had the pleasure of hearing the music: "Nearer, my God to Thee" and "If some poor wandering child of Thine."

I really have a superstition against croaking my blessing on your promessa [fiancée] but I hope tomorrow afternoon I may be a little less hoarse. *I* can find no present worthy of her. Neither have *I* any claim to make her any present at all, except through *you*. Therefore I would fain give her the pleasure, greater than any other, of a present from *you*, if *you* will appropriate this little sum to it and thus complete your kindnesses to your affectionate old (Aunt?)

Florence Nightingale

who wishes you every blessing on *your* expedition into the New Land from all her heart.

---

211 An allusion to 2 Tim 2:15.

Source: Letter to Harry Verney, Wellcome (Claydon copy) Ms 9003/120

[printed address] 35 South Street
Park Lane, W.
22 October 1869

How terribly sorry I am for Captain Verney's misfortune[212] I cannot say. It is such a serious thing for a man enthusiastically fond of his profession and aspiring in it, and he is such a fine fellow. But all this you know. And *I* should be wanting in duty to mine (my profession: nurse to Her Majesty's Service) if I did not say that I think heroism as heroic in bearing wounds and amputations as in going into battle. It is a far more signal patience which bears loss of limb at home than in the excitement of war. If you would not think me a brute, I should say that it is well worth losing an election and losing a foot to show how a brave man and a good man can act in both these trials. For, after all, it is not the object to go into heaven with two feet but to go there "enduring hardness,"[213] tried in patience, courage and goodness to the heroic degree, that is, having taken one's degree in virtue. Edmund must certainly come out a master. I shall be very anxious to hear that he goes on well for the next few days, if someone will be so good as to give me a word. You do not say what day it happened—I gather it was the 19th (that is just fifteen years since I was made Superintendent-General to go to the Crimea).

With Edmund's kind of mind, I am sure that, if this unlucky gun was to go off, he is ten thousand times happier that it should have shot him than that it should have shot his friend. But nonetheless do I wish all shooting at the devil, though I believe that is foolish, for certainly Englishmen are a great deal better for their love of field sports and climbing Matterhorns. One thing I can say, that it is "no end" better for a young man (or woman either) to have even such a terrible accident as this, better for future health both of body and mind, than to have a long, consuming sickness.

I will send your bulletins on to Papa. I left my mother wonderfully well. In great haste.

ever your F.

---

212 Edmund Verney accidentally shot himself in the foot while out hunting.
213 An allusion to 2 Tim 2:3.

Source: Letter Wellcome (Claydon copy) Ms 9003/133

[printed address] 35 South Street
Park Lane, W.
31 December 1869

My dear Mrs Verney, or, may I say, Margaret?

On Tuesday, if you are in London, I hope to see you and Captain Verney at this house, if all the imps and spirits of Poor Law and public offices were here. Please say what time you will come and please say whether you will have luncheon or dinner and at what hour. Do you sleep in London? How I wish I could offer you beds, but I am myself turned out of my room (by a stupid accident or blunder) and am living at the top of the house. Please send all your parcels here (one is come already, for Captain Verney's servant). At least you can have the dining room and little parlour here to yourselves for your business for the day. How I wish we could save you any fatigue!

I will write tomorrow. In great press of business, with dearest New Year's love and my poor prayers for the best New Year's blessings on you and all you care for.

ever yours
Florence Nightingale

Source: Letter probably to Parthenope Verney, Wellcome (Claydon copy) Ms 9004/2

[printed address] 35 South Street
Park Lane, W.
4 January 1870

I write one line to say that "Edmund and Margaret" are off, looking as well and happy and active as possible. He is a little changed, I can't quite say in what, but looks in sound health. I preached a little but did not like to preach violently, lest she should be always sparing him and he should be always sparing her. But I told him that, though he has made one of the quickest recoveries that ever have been made, he is also making one of the quickest exertions that ever was made, that as long as the wound is not firmly healed, he must not think of any active exertion, must keep his foot up and not go into strange places and that, as long as he has any nervous pain in the stump (though he has much less than others) he must remember that the vital system has not recovered the shock and feel for it accordingly.

Du reste, the open air, anything which contributes to his health, to appetite and digestion enough to feed himself *well*, is the best doctor.

I am glad he saw Savory[214] today, who is a sound opinion, and I believe preached much in this sense. As for his wife, she is a sort of heavenly-minded young woman. I don't know that I ever saw anyone quite like her. . . .

ever your F.

"Margaret's" last words were "We have been *so happy* in our visit to Claydon" and I do believe this is true.

Source: Letter to Harry Verney, Wellcome (Claydon copy) Ms 9004/20

8 March 1870

. . . O to be in the desert about Cairo "for three weeks"! Tell them [Edmund and Margaret Verney] to report particularly how Ramesses II lying on his face in a pool at Memphis is, how he does—a colossal mutilated statue, one of the finest, if not the finest in Egyptian sculpture.

Source: Letter, Wellcome (Claydon copy) Ms 9004/36

[printed address] 35 South Street
Park Lane, W.
5 May 1870

My dear Captain [Edmund] Verney

I was immensely thankful to hear Mr Savory's account of you, because if he thinks you can take a ship in the autumn, he knows you are all right. But I dare say *that* sensible man told you to take precautions which you don't tell me.

I think you are rather hard upon poor "Stumpy." You treat him like a spoiled and troublesome child, whom you have undertaken the charge of, and whom you are in duty-bound to furnish with the necessaries of life, but whom you can't be expected to indulge. I feel much more kindly to poor "Stumpy." I am sure he behaved very well at first and if he did not so well afterwards, you ought to have shown him some of that kindness and indulgence for which you are otherwise so remarkable. I feel satisfied, if it had not been for Mrs Verney's protection and care, poor Stumpy's life would have been a weariness to his flesh.[215]

I was very much obliged to you for showing me your book of sketches, which I looked through with immense delight. and I shall hope to see

---

214 Probably Sir William Savory (1826-95), surgeon.
215 An allusion to Eccl 12:12.

it again. They are very original and fresh and bring the old places before me again. There are some of the Nile, especially one *all yellow*, which I will swear with any amount of asseveration you please is the place itself.

For three days I have been trying to finish this foolish note, but must send it as it is, if at all.

ever yours and Mrs Verney's

F. Nightingale

Source: Letter, Wellcome (Claydon copy) Ms 9005/3

35 South Street
Park Lane, W.
12 January 1871

Dear Lady Sarah Williams [mother of Margaret Verney]

I am so very, very sorry for dear Margaret and Edmund's disaster—I will not say how sorry—for that will do her no good and I am sure that she will be most brave and patient in the conviction that it is her first business now to make herself well and strong.

I saw a letter this morning from a French lady: "Quant à moi, après avoir confié mes enfants et tout ce qui les touche aux mains de Dieu, je n'ai pas voulu m'adresser la moindre question sur elle, *car je n'aurais pas* vécu—JE VEUX VIVRE!" [For me, after giving all that concerns my children into the hands of God, I did not want to occupy myself in the least question *or I would not have lived*—I WANT TO LIVE!] (She goes on to explain how many duties she has to live for.)

Alas there are mothers mourning the loss of all their sons, leaving young widows about to be confined, or with infants a few days old. I am very grateful to you for your kindness in writing about what interests me so very much. I shall not be able to help sending to inquire after dear Margaret, but shall only expect a verbal answer. Ever, dear Lady Sarah,

with most respectful sympathy
and love, yours
Florence Nightingale

Source: Letter, Wellcome (Claydon copy) Ms 9006/93

35 South St.

My dear Margaret [Verney]

8 May 1874

Sir H. told me that you would kindly come and see me. Shall it be *today* at *4:30*? But any other time would do.

I send him Sir Arthur Cotton's jeu d'esprit on Lord Napier[216] and a note from Sir S. Northcote, also three books on the "Cité d'Alsace." Please let them all be returned to me.

Is baby glorious?

ever yours

F. Nightingale

Source: Letter Wellcome (Claydon copy) Ms 9006/54

Lea Hurst

Matlock

My dearest Margaret [Verney]

2 September 1874

. . . Dearest Margaret, I pray with and for you night and day. I think almost more about your approaching happiness, please God! than you do yourself, casting all your care upon Him, for He careth for us.[217] I should like "it" to be born tomorrow and to be a girl. For then it would be like our Emily come back, to whom you were so very dear. God forever bless you and He *will* bless you.

your affectionate old aunt

(I should like to be your Lucina![218])

Florence Nightingale

Source: Unsigned letter probably to Harry Verney, Wellcome (Claydon copy) Ms 9006/149

16 February 1875

I am so very glad to hear of the little arrival from heaven [Lettice]. I know that Margaret wished for another daughter [after Ellin] and, as it has been stated to me that there will certainly be thirteen sons in the next thirteen years, I think that we will pardon her this aberration of a wish just this time.

---

216 A paper to the Edinburgh Literary Institute in reply to Lord Napier's address on the Indian famine.
217 A paraphrase of 1 Pet 5:7.
218 Lucina, or Juno, the Greek goddess who presided over childbirth.

The "Inspecting Commander of the Coast Guard, Liverpool Division," has also been so good as to write to me. I don't know when I have been so amused and enchanted as on reading that definition of his titles in the *Times* births of this morning.

"Where is now the gentleman?" is often asked: *not* in connection with "When Adam delved and Eve span."[219] *There* is now the gentleman: the "Liverpool Coast Guard"sman who prides himself and justly on that manly designation, and if he had been the Prince of all Wales, or the proprietor of all Wales, would have put himself in just the same as "Commander of the C.G. Liverpool Division."

May God bless Baby 2 and Baby 1 and all *their* parents.

I think that an Icelandic Growler, or other Pirate, should be paid to make an well-planned descent by night on the Liverpool coast, to surprise, in the proportion of ten to one, as at Inkermann, "Commander Edmund H. Verney, Royal Navy," who repels the enemy, and tows the gallant foe in chains into the Menai Straits to Baby's feet.

Source: Letter, Wellcome (Claydon copy) Ms 9006/150

35 South St.
Park Lane
16 February 1875

My dear Captain [Edmund] Verney

I am so delighted at the arrival of a second little daughter who comes from a heaven above to a heaven below (and therefore is not to be pitied) that I think myself worthy of asking for a special love to be conveyed to its dear mother, who I know wished for another daughter, and to itself from its old Aunt Florence.

You know that the Rape of a Lock[220] was mine from Ellin, then some three weeks old, now promoted to be a little Mama or elder sister. I shall expect a similar rape on my behalf from the little woman who now enlightens our hemisphere. God bless her and her Mama and her little Mama is the fervent prayer of

yours ever affectionately

Florence Nightingale

I will read the letter you enclosed and return and answer it to you, my dear "Inspecting Commander of the Coast Guard, Liverpool Division."

---

219 From a revolutionary sermon by John Ball on the outbreak of the Peasants' War, 1381.
220 Alexander Pope, "The Rape of the Lock."

Envelope: Thank you very much for your Liverpool paper of 26 January with the report of your "resolutions." F.N.

Source: Letter, Wellcome (Claydon copy) Ms 9007/35

35 South St.
Park Lane, W.
10 June 1876

My dearest Margaret [Verney]

I think so much of you and dear Lady Sarah [her mother] at this time. I am always thinking of you if that would do any good, but I don't seem able to say anything. How I wish there were something I could send which would give a moment's pleasure, but she is going home, home, home, where so many weary hearts are longing to go, *at home with God*. (What words those are!) It is not death; it is only the *shadow* of death, "of death, called life, which us from life doth sever."[221]

I venture to send you, if you have not seen it, "Our Coffee-Room,"[222] by my dear old friend, Sir Arthur Cotton, the India irrigation engineer, or rather by his daughter.[223] Its *real reality* of religion surpasses anything, I think, I ever met with. One may not agree with much in it, but I have read nothing which (from that very reality) has given me so much pleasure since Agnes Jones went "home."

I will not weary you with my poor words. Fare you well. May God be with us all. And He *is* with you, I know. May I call myself

your Aunt Florence?

Source: Letter, Wellcome (Claydon copy) Ms 9007/48

35 South St.
12 July 1876

Dear Margaret [Verney]

My thoughts are so constantly with you that I cannot help writing a word now and then. "*Almost well,*" as dear old Richard Baxter answered when on his deathbed, to someone who asked him how he was.[224]

---

221 Milton, sonnet 14.
222 Elizabeth R. Cotton, *Our Coffee Room*, with an introduction by A. Cotton.
223 Elizabeth R. Cotton, later married to Sir James Hope, Harry Verney's former brother-in-law.
224 Richard Baxter (1615-91), Puritan divine, in *The Autobiography of Richard Baxter*, Appendix I: "Last Trial and Death" 266.

To me it seems as if it were almost too much happiness after a divine life to be dying at home with one's loving children always by one, waiting to go to the other side the river where all the meetings again are, to us who believe that it is not Charon's boat[225] but Elijah's chariot waiting to carry us, *to be at home*, at the real home with God—it seems so much happiness that, as to the dying woman who cried, "The chariot of Israel" and added: "And oh how easy it is." We can give, to *her*, joy, our tears, her joy. And let *us* be strong to say, "To heaven, to heaven my love, and leave us in the storm." For life *is* a storm to most.

That was a brave thought and execution that Sir Harry told me of, your giving a seaside rest in Anglesey to overworked East End clergymen. I wish I could go there myself.

Miss Irby is come home; she wants to go out again at once to the sick and wounded Serbians, but there is no chance of her raising money for this. She will go out again at all events two months hence to her work, of which I enclose the paper, if she can raise money for *that*. Fare you well. God be with us all.

F.N.

Source: Letter, Wellcome (Claydon copy) Ms 9007/58

Lea Hurst
Cromford, Derby
9 August 1876

Dear Margaret [Verney]

Forgive this interruption. You are always in our thoughts and prayers. I know the glorious moment is drawing very near, perhaps it is come already [the death of her mother].

Death comes to set thee free
O meet him cheerily
As thy true friend!

How one's soul reaches forward in a great longing so that it seems to be with her who is gone to dwell with God. I always remember what you said about Emily: "How much she must know now, how much she must have enjoyed!"

I told my mother today about yours and what she had said to you. She, my mother, drank it all in. My father used to make me repeat to him incessantly those two verses:

---

225 In Greek mythology Charon ferried the dead across the river Styx; see especially Virgil, *Aenid*, and Dante, *Inferno*.

O change! o wondrous change!
Burst are the prison bars.
One moment here, so low,
So agonized
And now beyond the stars.
O change! stupendous change!
There lies the soul-less clod,
The Sun Eternal breaks,
The young Immortal wakes
Wakes with his God.[226]

For your loss, it is unspeakable, immeasurable. But not the less do we praise and thank Him that the chariot of Israel is come for her. May God be with us all.

F.N.

Source: Unsigned note, Wellcome (Claydon copy) Ms 9007/53

10 August 1876

Dearest Margaret [Verney]

Your letter received. *She has been two days in heaven.* Is it well with her? It *is* well. And with you too. I saw a book dedicated, "To - - now in heaven I dedicate this book with never-dying love."

Source: Letter, Wellcome (Claydon copy) Ms 9007/59

Lea Hurst
Cromford, Derby
1 October 1876

Dearest Margaret [Verney] (if you will allow me to call you so)

I am always glad to hear from you. About "Mrs Wright," I "never heard of poor Mrs Wright's existence," but I "never heard" of poor *Mr* Wright's existence, not as my "secretary"—I never had a "secretary," not even a female one, much less a male one. But I think it possible that, though I do not in the least remember the name, he may have had something to do with our stores in the Crimean War or, etc. At least I cannot think of any other possible connection with my "secretariat." If you could give me a glimpse of what he was, I should be very glad if I can to do something for his mother.

---

226 A paraphrase of Caroline Anne Bowles Southey, "The Pauper's Deathbed," in *Poetical Works* 102-03.

Ah dear friend, the priceless treasure of that tenderness. You *will* feel the loss of it more and more every day. Else it would be no true loss, but oh thank God that you ever had it, and that it never can be taken away from you. Do not speak as if it were hard to you to return to the home where she is not:

Where is the home where she is not?
She is gone from us, but to rest
More surely in each faithful breast
And duties, *griefs* and joys shall take
A tinge of sweetness for her sake.
So like an inspiration be
Forever thus the "thought of thee!"

These are some unpublished lines written by a friend of ours (who is dead) upon another friend who died, on *returning* to the *home*. They begin thus:

I see it all, thy home and thee,
The waving of the birchen tree,
The shining water, rocky ground,
The pleasant look on all around.
Yon sun lights up that water still,
The flowers and fruits their course fulfill
But thou, O where, invisible,
Art thou that lov'dst them all so well?
I miss the bright and cheerful eye
That put each thought of sadness by.
The touch of death is on the scene
It cannot be as it has been.
Yet it is dearer, dearer still,
I shed no tear; I feel no chill;
Methinks I breathe a purer air,
And meet thy blessed Spirit there.
O lovely in thy life, in death
Borne onward by a childlike faith,
The clogging load of earth laid by,
Without a murmur or a sigh,
Dispersing sweetness to the last
On all the present, all the past.
Already as a spirit free,
Who would not live and die like thee?
Thy home, across my thought again

It comes like some departing strain,
Its sun, its shade, its pure bright things,
Without its earth-born sorrowings.
Thy home, O far excelling thought,
Where is the home where thou art?
Thou art gone from us but to rest
More surely in each faithful breast,
And duties, griefs and joys shall take
A tinge of sweetness for thy sake.

And so on to what I quoted at the beginning.

Dear Margaret, I did not mean when I began to quote all this, but as I went on the image of you and your beautiful Rhianva home by the sea and your lost saint, no not lost but gone before,[227] so rose before me that the lines seemed written *for you*. God bless you.

F.N.

Thanks for your inquiry about my mother. She does so enjoy the old home, the old associations and our daily talks and prayers, and I have such a faith that the day of birth into the new life is as *exactly* calculated and prepared for by the almighty Father as the day of birth into this life (after the nine months) so that we must never talk of "release" or "loss."

Otherwise I could wonder why the Father leaves her here so long, but how can we tell but that this may be the most important experience of her life, if indeed where *all* is exactly weighed in the design of supreme Goodness and Wisdom, one can talk of one time being *more* important than another? Excuse.

Source: Letter, Wellcome (Claydon copy) Ms 9007/76

35 South St.

11 March 1877

My dearest Margaret, as I cannot help calling you (my dear Mrs Verney as I ought to call you)

I write because I cannot help it. Captain Verney keeps you constantly in the current of our fears and now, thank God! our hopes. But he does not tell you, I am sure, what an incomparable captain of the sickroom he makes, sickroom*s* indeed we must say, for he has had *two* patients. And, if it pleases God to grant Sir Harry to us yet again, it is mainly to Captain Verney that we owe it.

---

227 An allusion to a chapter in Margaret Gatty, *Parables from Nature*.

He looked a great deal less anxious yesterday and Parthe revives apace. Captain Verney says that *you* are "as wise as owls and as quiet as mice." This description is infinitely reassuring. I am bound to believe it. I give you joy of your husband, if that is not impertinent, and I hope that it is some reward for letting him go that we could not possibly have done without him. I think I never was so thankful for anything as to hear that he was arrived, that bleak morning. And you see I had cause. Fare you very well and Maude too.

F. Nightingale

Source: Letter about Margaret Verney, Wellcome (Claydon copy) Ms 9007/112

> Lea Hurst
> Cromford, Derby
> 25 August 1877

My dear Captain [Edmund] Verney

I grieve so deeply—I will not say *for* you, for I think I grieve as deeply *as* any of you can. I did so wish for this, not *for* you, but *as much* as you, and after so long an imprisonment it does seem hard. I can only thank God that nothing more than the usual risk seems to be feared for my dearest, brave and noble Margaret. How different it would be if we were fearing for *her*!

May God, whose friend she is, carry her well through is, I am sure, the *most* fervent wish and prayer of,

> hers and yours ever
> Florence Nightingale

I shall be very anxious to hear again. You are so good in writing.

F.N.

Source: Letter, Wellcome (Claydon copy) Ms 9007/158

> 25 South St.
> 25 June 1878
> 6:00 A.M.

My dear Captain [Edmund] Verney

I ought to have thanked you long ago for your help and kindness about Miss Perssè, but have been under such stress of business and illness. And I did not hear from her till last night (she is an even worse correspondent than I am).

She is extremely indebted to you and was just carrying her three precious letters. She was getting her work somewhat into shape but she has so many hindrances: the drainage of her nurses' house so bad, the nurses neither good nor strong, material sometimes altogether unsuitable. She has however done much in making them do their work more efficiently. She says she feels equal to any amount of work. She has found two people, a lady and a gentleman, who have undertaken the duties of "improved dwellings." She is trying to get the poor women to lay by a little money weekly for children's clothes and to get them to do needlework. She says your letters will be *very* useful to her.

(I shall be sorry if your people are away, but after all a few weeks do not make much difference in our work.) She says doctors and clergy give them better cases now; that is, *really* sick to nurse, not mere drunken beggars to relieve. She goes about and hunts them up. But - - she speaks of the frightful mortality amongst children, the "grave sin" and the "cruel cases" of the *"burial clubs for young children," which we all know ought not to be allowed.* What are *Liverpool magistrates* about? *You could find* a remedy.

I am so glad that you have been with that excellent Mr Rathbone and so glad that Mrs Verney approves (and attends) Miss Lees's lectures.

Thanks a thousand for your beautiful *Eurydices*.[228] I am afraid I have one more than my share. You cannot think how the men patients at St Thomas' Hospital are charmed with it. (I always like to pull *them* out of themselves.)

My love to Margaret, if she will allow me to call her so, and your children. I hope to see them before you leave London. Please thank Mr Fred for me, if you see him, for his last night's letter.

ever yours affectionately
Florence Nightingale

Source: Letter, Wellcome (Claydon copy) Ms 9007/222

[printed address] 10 South Street
Park Lane, W.
3 May 1879

My dear Mrs Verney

I am so afraid you must have been very tired on Thursday and I was so shocked to find that I had taken the carriage when you were going out to dinner. After all, in the pleasure of seeing you, I forgot the one thing Parthe charged me to ask you: she gave me the enclosed from Miss Thornton and hoped you would be so good as to answer it for her.

---

228 Edmund Verney, *The Last Four Days of the Eurydice,* a true story of a shipwreck off the south coast of England.

I know what the "memorial fund" is to which she alludes, though Parthe does *not* enclose the paper. It is to Mrs Nassau Senior,[229] whom I knew (you know she was a Poor Law Inspector). Her premature death was a national and irreparable loss. If she could but have held on a few years longer, she would have had successors and the Poor Law Board would as soon have been without *lady inspectors* for girls' institutions as we should have had *male* matrons. Now that is all over. I have so long made it a rule *not* to put my poor name "ornamentally," not to give name where I could not give *work* that I VERY much wish Miss Thornton would let me off. But if she *will* have it, I suppose I must submit.

I am so sorry to give you this trouble. I hope you have good accounts to give of *yourself* and of the dear little Mama expectant. God bless her and you. I heard from Sir Harry this morning.

ever yours

F. Nightingale

I would not have asked you to come if I had known how much you were doing.

Source: Letter, Wellcome (Claydon copy) Ms 9007/265

[printed address] 10 South Street
Park Lane, W.
Christmas Eve 1879

My very dear Captain and Mrs Verney

If I could send all the Christmas wishes and prayers with which my heart is full to you and yours by train, no train would be strong enough to carry them. Your great kindness in wishing me to come to Rhianva, beautiful Rhianva, out of this foggy London, fills me with gratitude and also almost with humiliation. But alas! when I really think of it, I know that it is impossible, though perhaps there is nothing left in this world that I should rejoice in so much as enjoying your kindness there.

It is the last straw that breaks the camel's back, and the Lea Hurst charge is my last straw. I will not take up this which should be a joyful letter with explaining. Perhaps I may see Rhianva in another world.

---

229 Jane (Mrs Nassau) Senior, first woman Poor Law inspector, appointed in 1874. Thirteen letters to her from Nightingale (not seen by scholars) were sold at auction December 2000 for £17,000.

It pleases me very much that you wish my dear goddaughter Ruth[230] to bear my poor name. May all God's best blessings be hers and yours is the most earnest prayer of

Aunt Florence

Source: Letter, Wellcome (Claydon copy) Ms 9008/39

10 South St.
Park Lane, W.
27 March 1880

Dearest Margaret [Verney]

I take leave to give you joy with all my heart and mind and soul and strength and to sing "Hail to you in the strength of the Lord" at this truly Easter uprising, as it seems to us, of the poor and the rough to their higher interests.[231] The beer and the bribing and the paid agents and the cabs are on the other side. On ours is the purity and the real interest in the grand political issues and the disinterested enthusiasm.

One feels that, whether we win or lose, the men who have *thus* taught the crowds and the voters are great teachers, great and noble reformers of the people. Electioneering thus conducted is a high and noble task. Elections are usually so unutterably disgusting that one feels towards them as to some horrible illness out of which the House of Commons, the grandest representative body in the world (saving and except the last House of Commons[232]) has to emerge. (I never can pass the House of Commons without taking off my hat and without tears in my old eyes.[233])

But this election is being fought on our side with such unparalleled good faith and high motives that we may well call down the best Easter blessings on you and yours from the God who loves liberty, truth and progress. And I do pray every day, and in our family prayers, that the heavenly Father will send us a House of Commons, that most important body of all, which will further His cause and serve Him in

---

230 Ruth Florence Verney (1879-1968).

231 Edmund Verney unsuccessfully contested Portsmouth in this general election.

232 See *Society and Politics* for Nightingale's loathing of the right-wing, hawkish Conservative government of Disraeli and Salisbury, and her support for Gladstone's Liberal *jihad* against it.

233 In a letter to Harry Verney Nightingale quoted Garibaldi as having said this, 18 March 1880, Wellcome (Claydon copy) Ms 9008/34.

spirit and in truth.[234] Depend upon it this awakening of the ruder classes to their higher interests—to something beyond beer—is a progress which will be pleasing in His sight.[235] Into His hands I commend you,[236] dearest Margaret, and all these elections, thinking it not ill that Easter tide should be *thus* passed.

I hope my goddaughter is dressed in her father's colours. I ought to send little Ruth a bow, but I don't know them. The best success will be ours. God bless you both again and again. Think how you are putting a weight on the right side in the balance of eternity for all these poor people. You have had a Sisyphus work uphill,[237] but they will thank you in eternity. I see the Angel or Archangel Raphael, whoever is commissioned as the Angel of the elections, standing and crushing down the dragon of bribery and beer. And he is bringing a green sod from heaven for Margaret to stand upon in the turmoil of Portsmouth.

Aunt Florence

Source: Letter to Edmund and Margaret Verney, Wellcome (Claydon copy) Ms 9008/40

Easter Day [28 March] 1880

Do you sometimes go and look at the *Soldiers'* and Sailors' *Institute* in the High St. (Miss Robinson's)? It would be sinful to ask you to do one thing more now, but when you are MP for Portsmouth, perhaps I may venture.

Miss Robinson wrote to me some months ago to ask me to write in the *Times* for her. It is impossible for me to do that, which so many ask. It was impossible for me then *even to answer her letter*. Also, I had not even a shilling which I could properly spare. After the elections I may ask you to speak to her and to tell her this, and to say *how deeply* I am interested in the Soldiers' Institute, which indeed I hope she knows, and kindly to give her a small sum which I will send you.[238]

---

234 An allusion to John 4:23.
235 A allusion to Heb 13:21.
236 A paraphrase of Luke 23:46.
237 In Greek mythology Sisyphus was forced to roll a rock up a hill, which rolled back just before reaching the top.
238 In 1877 Nightingale sent a donation and let a letter of hers be read out at a public meeting (see p 749 below).

Dearest Margaret, we may "rise again" today and pursue and do His work, even His elections, in the true spirit of the risen Christ. He himself made a turmoil in the temple,[239] but he was all the more Christ for that.

Aunt Florence

Source: Letter, Wellcome (Claydon copy) Ms 9008/43

10 South St.
Park Lane, W.
2 April 1880

Dearest Margaret [Verney]

"Some natural tears we dropt but wiped them soon."[240] You have not lost, you have won, won for eternity and even for time, won for the progress of the people in freedom and justice, won for a new era for the people, when their highest earthly interest, that of self-government, shall rouse them with only pure enthusiasm, not of beer but of principle. You have lost, that is won, for a principle. Fifty elections won on any lower standard would only degrade them. But a lost election, purely lost, will win for next time and for eternity. And the election, foully won, will be lost for right and for eternity. How gloriously the elections are going. And the Liberal majority is as much won by you who have lost as by those who have come in at the top of the poll. God bless the right.

I only hope that *you*, dear Margaret, have not suffered in health for all the turmoil. Please let me hear. Please ask Parthe or Sir Harry to let me have the *trades* of the "fifteen or sixteen committee men" who gave all their time for three weeks to return the Liberal side. There were three grocers, two farmers, one cabinetmaker, one baker and who else? We are fighting a Liberal battle (the mill-men) in North Derbyshire and I want to make known such a noble example. Indeed the state of England *now* makes me not ashamed of being an Englishman, but jolly beyond measure. Only, my "pearl" keep well and don't consider the Portsmouth canvass lost time. God bless you all.

ever yours
Aunt Florence

---

239 Mark 11:15-17.
240 A paraphrase from Milton's *Paradise Lost* Bk 12, line 645.

Source: Letter to Edmund Verney, Wellcome (Claydon copy) Ms 9008/157

10 South St., W.

9 June 1881

Thank God that Margaret, my dear, my very dear friends, is well through her lying-in—dear, noble, beautiful, brave Margaret, and her little son.[241] And may we not thank God too, as it is His own doing, that it *is* a little son at last. The little "he" will give so much pleasure to many and not the least to his grandpapa, his grandpapa who wished to live to see Margaret's son. And though Aunt Florence sticks by her god-daughter, yet she *must* give Margaret joy of her son. I give you all joy, my dear friends. Let us sing a new song of joy this Whitsuntide.

I am sure you will see the little man, come of such good stock, in future days, fighting as in the brave days of old, standing shoulder to shoulder and not alone, with other brave few, perhaps against heavy odds, in the good cause. Then God bless the little man lying in his little shirt on his nurse's knee with his queer little bundle of features or perhaps opening his eyes to the light by his mother's side in her bed.

Tell my little Ruth to send her godmother a detailed account of the young hero whose protector and guardian she now is. May all blessings attend you all. I always thought Margaret looked as if she had brought down a sod from heaven to stand upon.

ever yours

Aunt Florence

Love to Maude too.

Source: Letter probably to Edmund Verney, Wellcome (Claydon copy) Ms 9008/168

22 July 1881

. . . Delight in your christening festivities, ushering the child of many prayers among the people where we hope he will continue the good traditions of his race. Prayer to the heavenly Father for him for all His choicest blessings, love to his dear mother who lives already on a green sod from heaven, joy in the Holy Spirit: these are my wishes for you.

Three little Indian famine orphans sent me the following blessing: the love of God the Father, the grace of God the Son, the joy of God the Spirit be with you always. I say the same to you and yours tomorrow and every day. I shall be with you tomorrow and every day.

Aunt Florence

---

241 Harry Calvert Verney (1881-1974), 4th baronet, born after three girls.

Longmore,[242] not "straight," has talked of the confidential paper you sent him, communicated the contents of his letter to you, including his depreciation of Mrs H. One of the men, an Army surgeon, to whom he has done so, has written to me. I will not tell you more of a disagreeable subject on a joyful day. But some say you must write a few words to Longmore. Anon, anon.

F.N.

Source: Letter, Wellcome (Claydon copy) Ms 9009/130

14 December [1882]

My dearest Margaret [Verney] (if you will allow me to call you so)

Thank God you are come! There is nobody in the world who can do half for her [Parthenope Verney] that you do. If it is not bad for you to go out, I would most thankfully see you, as you kindly propose. Would half an hour hence suit you? as it would perhaps be advisable that we should consult before the new nurse comes?

ever yours gratefully

F. Nightingale

Source: Letter, Wellcome (Claydon copy) Ms 9009/142

St Thomas's Day
[21 December 1882]

Dearest Margaret [Verney]

This is indeed a severe disappointment, but still she is better since you came. We must not be like St Thomas on his day, "be not faithless but believing,"[243] your dear face says to me each time I see it. I shall be *very* anxious to hear what the doctor says. And he must change the "bhang" [hashish] pill, must he not?

As to Sant's Christmas cards, they are lovely, each one is worth all the whole store I have. You so very kindly say, "I may keep any I fancy." I am like the child to whom it is said, which will you have? and it says: all. But I must not keep "all." What will *you* do? I meant to send some Christmas cards, of course, to my dear little godchild, motherless for Christmas, and her sisters. I must not send the same as you. Might I have two more sets of Sant's beautiful angels? What shall I do about all the other beauties?

---

242 Thomas Longmore, later Sir, Professor of Military Surgery.
243 John 20:27.

I am afraid I ought to have written this before you went out. God bless you.

ever, ever yours

F.N.

Source: Letter to Margaret Verney, Wellcome (Claydon copy) Ms 9009/140

Christmas Day 1882

You are our Christmas blessing. *You* are our "glad tidings of great joy,"[244] dearest Margaret. God bless you.

F.N.

Source: Letter to Margaret Verney, Wellcome (Claydon copy) Ms 9009/143

29 December [1882]

She [Parthenope Verney] *is* better, dearest Margaret, thanks to you, who have the power of making the crooked straight and the rough places smooth.[245] One cannot feel at all content that *you* should "take the afternoons." And I write this before Dr Acland comes. Might we not try another nurse?

I cannot forego my privilege of seeing you this evening, if you will still give it me. I will not ask to see Dr Acland because he has you. And I shall have him (and you who are much better) in you if you kindly will come this evening.

I am so very sorry about dear Ellin, *and* penitent.

Messenger of peace, God bless you. I shall not try to see my sister today because she will be tired with Dr Acland.

F.N.

Source: Letter to Margaret Verney, Wellcome (Claydon copy) Ms 9009/147

New Year's Day [1883]

All God's choicest blessings rain upon you, dearest Margaret, on this day, the beginning of His new year, and every day, on you and yours. No greeting that I have received pleases me like yours, our hope, and your three *daughters'* (!!!) little letters are charming. I would gladly in penitence make myself into a holocaust for Captain Verney to kill and roast and eat, if it would do him any kindness. But I am afraid I should "eat tough." I enclose a 10/ bit for all your little ones, the only part I can pay, but for all your trouble with them and with us; who can repay but God?

244 An allusion to Luke 1:19.
245 An allusion to the Messiah in Isa 40:4.

Does Dr Ogle come today? And if not shall I come? and when? I am afraid I should not be able to come tomorrow. God bless you.

ever your grateful

F.N.

Source: Letter, Wellcome (Claydon copy) Ms 9009/160

10 South St.
24 January 1883

Dearest, very dearest Margaret [Verney]

I wrote a letter to you on Sunday (which I have never had time to finish) saying *with all my heart* how I thank you for your dear letters. How Aunt Florence hopes that Ellin has recovered her cough and that her knee is better, and that the joyful three, joyful in having their blessed mother, not excluding Herr Baby, are succeeding in all ways, that the "governess" will prove and do all that she ought to be and do for the sake of the dear mother, and that the friendly court-martial over the cook has resulted favourably for peace. I am infinitely touched by the brooches and my old hair shall accompany the return, with Aunt Florence's best blessing, as soon as she has time.

Private. I had begun a sort of medical history, which I must postpone. The trouble had returned about Julie at Claydon, as we must both have expected and Julie gave warning to Sir Harry. *That* is all patched up again by Sir Harry but for how long? I think we two are agreed both about the necessity that Sir Harry and Parthe should be left alone as little as possible and about the extreme difficulty attending any arrangement to provide for this. She has declined to have "Morfy."

About having dear Maude, there was a mistake on Sir Harry's part (which as Maudie was unhappily not well and *could* not go) I should not otherwise have mentioned. Parthe did *not* say she would not be too happy to have Maude, but only (in which I think she was right) *not* in the carriage with her on the railroad journey.

Private. My medical history was to have included how Parthe spoke of you, almost rising to the height of the subject, which warmed my old heart, how I never liked a man so much as I did Dr Ogle when he looked at *me* with unspeakable disgust and asked in a sepulchral voice, "Is she really gone?" meaning you. I am afraid my medical history is not really very good, though not bad.

Private. The last five days in South St. she was making no progress, and though, if any bodies had seen her, as I did on Monday and Tuesday before starting, they would have pronounced it madness to move her, I am sure the doctors were right. She cried very much, and I do think it was my reading her your letter that encouraged her. She dwelt so on you. Sir Harry looked almost worse than she did. Had I known that he was to be alone, I should have telegraphed for Shore Smith to come to him on that Tuesday morning. He knelt down by her bedside and said to her, "We have been very happy together." She asked me whether he thought she was dying—I could not tell her what I am sure was the case—that he thought *he* was.

The sons do not see him when they are not there as I do. He spoke to me of his money matters, said that he wished to make Morey house-keeper!! and the kitchenmaid cook! parting with Ellis, which I am sure you will agree with me would not do on any account and would drive P. frantic.

Private. (Had there been ten minutes more, I should have entered with him on what you were so good as to mention to me, that Captain Verney would help him in selling outlying land.)

Sir H. told me that Buxton, the carpenter's bill at Pleasley was £1000, over how many *years* does this extend? of which £500 have been paid. (My father and I have known Buxton's sterlingness for fifty years—I fear? his bill is correct and cannot be beaten down.) There are many other things over which we could talk for their sakes!

To continue the medical history, there have been great difficulties with the bowels at Claydon, no medical orders obeyed, injection resorted to at last. (I hear from Julie, Sir Harry and Dr Acland—the first tells most.) Now I must leave off. O dearest Margaret, how can I bless you enough? May *God*, the infinite Love, bless you and your children! I feel like a criminal in putting all these difficulties before you. Yet how can I help it? And I think you would wish it, *not* good-bye, au revoir.

ever your loving and grateful

Aunt Florence

The account tonight (Wednesday night) not very good, knee very painful. Dr Denton (for Dr Acland) painted it with iodine. Redness and inflamedness followed and they were obliged to poultice.

I should not omit to say that Dr Ogle told me, very decidedly, that it would be quite "three months" before she should attend to business. In this you/I concur. Parthe, without knowing this, told me that the reason she shrank from Claydon was *not* that she feared the journey, but she knew "business would come" to her there, that it "killed" her before; that she dreaded the "Verney Papers," also, she said this afterwards to Dr Ogle. Dr Ogle wisely said: "She must do nothing for three months but what she does here (South St.) under Mrs Verney." But *to whom will Sir Harry talk* during that time?

N.B. I do not at all think Sir H. has ten years before him, or the half, or the quarter.[246] I think too there are deeper things at stake than money matters, viz., his life and her mind. N.B. I have the most private answers to make to his letters. And I think of the *housemaids*! As far as I know, at South St., all his papers were left out in the dining room for Morey to pack up the next day.

Now I must really leave off—not too soon, you will say. God bless you again and again. You kindly ask after my "Indian papers." I have not even begun and am much driven by this W.O. committee. How good of you to remember me.

F.N.

Source: Letter, Wellcome (Claydon copy) Ms 9009/213

4 October 1883

Dearest Margaret [Verney]

I send the only portion I can pay of our immense debt to you (the £1.1 for the bed bath). How good, how very good, you have been about it and all!

You must not give Sir Harry a bad account of Parthe: two very fair nights and two days of much less pain, notwithstanding that she over-fatigued herself yesterday. We had some very comfortable reading together, besides Job 1 and John 17, and a good deal of poetry. But, dear Margaret, you would laugh if you were to see what a state of dismay I am in. Parthe has received a letter about homeopathic doctors from Miss Frere upon which *you* would not engage *a servant* and P. declares that she will go back to homeopathy upon this.

Pray, pray that we may be guided to the almighty Father. I only mention it now in case Sir Harry who, I believe, saw it, mentions it to you. And it is good little Fra [Frederica] Spring Rice[247] who has done this, though I think she was very sorry afterwards. O for the smallest amount of reason!

---

246 He in fact lived another eleven years.
247 Daughter of Lord and Lady Monteagle; she and her sister assisted Parthenope Verney with the editing of the Verney *Memoirs*.

Love to Ellin and Lettice and my goddaughter and Harry. Good speed to your Liverpool expedition next week. God bless and reward you ever.

ever your grateful

and loving F.N.

(In greatest haste) I will if I possibly can write you the contents of the homeopathic letter today. You will see that you would not engage a scullery maid, much less a doctor, upon it.

Source: Letter to Margaret Verney, Wellcome (Claydon copy) Ms 9010/9

10 South St., W.

2 March 1884

We are all thinking of you, very dear Margaret, who have seen Mr Owen Stanley go home. I hope he had time to know you and to feel your comfort before he went. But now he is above all our comfort and has the true joy. Sir Harry has felt Joseph's loss very much: forty-five years of faithfulness gone. I am so more than glad that your dear presence is coming to them.

The last fortnight I have thought my sister looking better than she has these two years, quite herself in fact. I am sure that she has the use of her right hand *much* more, much more than she knows herself. She sees many people, too many. She has the use of her mind and she is often without pain, thank God, for hours together. But I do not like people to say to her she is better; it seems to her unfeeling. She was not at all better when she first came to London. Then she had the quack; now she is recovering from the quack—how thankful we must be.

Will your dear kindness think me very troublesome if I ask whether the Peuthos [?] family is to be dispersed, there might be a housemaid for me. Mine is such a very dull place, no menservants, only me—so quiet and small. I want an upper housemaid who will take charge of house, linen and furniture and, above all, "mother" the under housemaid (who is at present Lizzie [Coleman] from Claydon). She must not be a girl. She must take charge of this house when I am away. She must be a very trustworthy person.

It is an easy place, but I have always two or three girls (now three)! and "mothering" seems gone out of fashion, such as I remember it in my young days. She must feel some sort of responsibility towards me for "training" her under housemaids and not be a gadder herself, a clean woman, with a head on her shoulders. Dear Margaret, forgive my troubling you.

My love to Ellin who, I trust, is better and all your dear flock. Maude's children thrive. Au revoir, I hope. God bless you always.

ever yours affectionately

F. Nightingale

Source: Letter, Wellcome (Claydon copy) Ms 9010/14

10 April 1884

Dearest blessed Margaret [Verney]

Many many thanks. "Now is our soul troubled"[248] but we know what our Father does is right.

I will come in with your leave between 1:00 and 2:00. Or could I be of any use earlier? Has the doctor been this morning? Do not trouble to answer this. Thank God you are here.

F.N.

Source: Unsigned letter, Wellcome (Claydon copy) Ms 9010/17

10 South St., W.
10 May 1884

My dear blessed Margaret [Verney]

Captain Verney looks much better. The funeral yesterday[249] is well over. Mr Calvert came this morning to see Sir Harry and was quite calm and at peace. He was very much overcome at the funeral, but seemed to have had great satisfaction in all the things which were there to show sympathy in his great trial: the attendance of the tenants, the pleasant order and beauty, the shower of wreaths and flowers, the beautiful reading of that beautiful service (which I was reading to Sir Harry at the same time) by Mr Greene[250] in the little church and by Dean Fremantle[251] at the grave. Mr Calvert has always come to Sir H. with a smile on his face and has never agitated him. The dean's holy gentle manner is delightful.

Sir H. is quite steadily convalescing, is dressed in clothes and is carried down into the drawing room today for the first time. Yet I would he were out of the house, at Onslow Gardens [home of Edmund and Margaret Verney] for a few days as they so kindly press. Captain Ver-

---

248 An allusion to John 12:27.
249 Of Lady Lucy Calvert, wife of Sir Harry Verney's brother, Frederic Calvert.
250 Vicar of the church at Middle Claydon.
251 W.H. Fremantle, former vicar at East Claydon, then Dean of Ripon, married to Sir Harry Verney and F. Calvert's sister.

ney does not agree with me, and he is so admirable a nurse that I am bound to tell you so. Yet nobody sees Sir H. as I do—he sobs so hysterically with me at my sister's appearance, and I have never seen her look so ill since Christmas before last—she looks sometimes as if she were dying. Nurse Dare, who has been away for a few days, is struck with the change. Her cough distresses him so, and *that* will do so more now he will spend the afternoons in the drawing room with her, instead of the change refreshing him. He is so tempted to get up in the night to "rub her," when he hears her crying, that I am quite alarmed as to the effect this may have on his brain.

My sister is certainly much worse. She has a bronchial cough which shakes her fearfully. The nights are worse than they have been for months, there is an aggravation of arthritis. I wish she could have the house to herself for a few days—she does not know how she distresses him, though she makes every effort to be merry—he does not know how bad he is for her just now. The heat of their two bedrooms is such now, her bedroom being never empty, for she goes down into the drawing room when she ought not, to leave her bedroom for him, that I wonder they are not worse than they are. He is so parboiled that he finds the nights cold! and has twice had a return of cough. Maude is most anxious that he should come to [breaks off]

Source: Letter, Wellcome (Claydon copy) Ms 9010/101

Claydon House
18 August 1885
6:30 A.M.

Private

My dearest Margaret [Verney]

My sister will be so distressed if you and Captain Verney do not sleep here the two nights *at least* before and after the Archaeological (she thought you were coming for a week now). *I* shall not see you, if you do not, till after you are an MP in London, and after the general election, which is an epoch that will make the next ten years perhaps the most interesting in English history to those who are young enough like yourselves to throw yourselves into the great progress (more impressive than the "progresses" of Q. Elizabeth). But, what is more important, my sister so hopes and believes that you are coming, you and yours and Captain Verney, as long as you can before the general election, to stay of course over the general election. And this is a matter of business, general election and preliminaries *must* be conducted from *this* house. (I told my sister that I would companionize her, if she were alone during August, and till you came with your far better company and then, if she wanted me, after the general election till their Christmas party. I merely mention this to facilitate matters. I see some little failure of memory in them both, dear people, about future dates. Therefore I wanted—you will *not* betray me to her—to tell you how the land really lies.)

I can report well of both. No one could believe my sister to be the same person whom *you* picked out of that terrible state now nearly three years ago, thanks be to God. She sits out on the lawn till 7 P.M., remains up till 10 P.M. If ordinary care were taken, such as not sitting out in the chill before sunset, etc., she might, I think, recover to do much more of work and to run much less of risk. But often she gets a bad cough and the poor joints of course get worse. Still she really enjoys.

God bless you all, and with kindest regards to Captain Verney and love to childer four (in haste).

ever your loving and grateful

F. Nightingale

Source: Letter to Margaret Verney, Wellcome (Claydon copy) Ms 9010/103

25 August 1885

If there are little things (*not* English) to be bought at Dieppe, would you allow Ellin to expend £1 for self and compagnie for their loving Aunt Florence?

Source: Letter, Wellcome (Claydon copy) Ms 9010/104

Claydon House
31 August 1885
7:00 A.M.

Private

My dearest Margaret [Verney]

How glad we should be if you were not quite knocked up on the archeological day. I am afraid I contributed to your fatigues on that day. Pardon me if I worry you. Interference is so seldom successful, but you will remember that you kindly told me what my sister had said about Captain Verney's (supposed) electioneering speeches, and that you thought "somebody had been making mischief." Also, of the speeches of Sir Harry in the villages.

It is therefore no news to you, and it may possibly be some help in contradicting it, what I now write and enclose: that Captain Verney promises the people that every man is to have twenty (or forty) acres apiece (it does not signify which figure is right, as it is all a lie), that there are to be no more labourers and that if he does not fulfill his promises they will not return him again. At this my sister stood up like a man, as she tells me, and said, "Perhaps he won't wish to be returned again if you - -" so and so.

I said, "But Captain Verney has been so particularly careful to make no promises" and I asked who has actually *heard* him say these things? I cannot quite make out and I have no doubt that there is a good deal mixed up in her head, from Greig and Agur [?] (the schoolmaster) she says, with what the haymakers said to her in the carriage, which I told you and, perhaps, some confusion with Mr Chamberlain's[252] speeches.

"But," said they, "We hear it from other parts of the county. We can show you a clergyman's letter." And last night Sir H. sent me up the enclosed. Nothing was said to me about privacy and I really think I ought to send it you. Pardon me if I am wrong, *and return it me* (you will say that a clergyman who thinks "feudalism" tempered with "Christianity" a proper form of government—"une tyrannie tempérée par une chanson [tyranny tempered with a song]"—not worth attending to). But I am not worth attending to by these dear people because I have not heard Captain Verney's speeches. Are there no *reports* of them? No *notes*? Has he no first lieutenant who could give a reliable account? Indeed it is very important that we should be able to contradict these lies authoritatively, is it not?

Has Mr Chamberlain made this sort of program? Captain Verney's seems to be confused with his. Please forgive me and give, not me but these dear people, the means of contradicting this. You well know them, and what impression this clergyman's letter would make upon them, with all the rest that has been told them. (I shall not tell them that I have sent it you.) In greatest haste, with dear love to the children and kindest regards to Captain Verney,

ever yours affectionately

F. Nightingale

---

252 Joseph Chamberlain, Liberal Cabinet member, former Mayor of Birmingham, supporter of sanitary reform and housing.

Source: Letter, Wellcome (Claydon copy) Ms 9010/105

Claydon
1 September 1885
7:00 A.M.

Private

Dearest Margaret [Verney]

Last night Sir Harry seemed to be beginning again to say that he would, if called up to speak, warn the labourers again against believing in "promises." So I said that *that* had been taken and alleged, as directed against Captain Verney, that it had done much harm, etc. He said at once that he had "not meant it for Captain Verney, of course," that he wished it, the allegation, had appeared in some newspaper, in order that he might answer it. I said, could he not recommend warmly Captain Verney as his successor at once? He said, Yes, he meant to do so at his (Buckingham) dinner. I said, "but at once." I think now I could ask him to send that £25 at once to the Liberal Association and write a warm letter. (I *don't* ask your leave for this.)

I asked but what *is* Mr Chamberlain's program that all this has been hung upon it? (partition of land, etc.) They said, we don't know that Mr Chamberlain *has* made any such program. Then I asked, but whom was it that you *did* mean when you said to the labourers, "Don't believe their promises"? He said, I meant nobody in particular (but afterwards, in the course of conversation, he said, I am afraid some of the Radicals *have* been making "promises." Let those whom the cap fits, etc.)

However, he is quite warm now that he never thought of Captain Verney as having made "promises" of this kind and my sister disclaimed it too. The thing is, how can he undo any harm that has unwittingly been done? Could he not only speak and write *warmly* of Captain V. *as his successor,* but refer to the true nature of his, Captain V.'s *meetings and addresses? and speeches? What has their true nature been?*

Can you read this pencil without bothering yourself? God speed the truth and He *will* speed it. I trust that you are not bothered and am

ever your loving

F. Nightingale

He asked, has this allegation appeared in print, that I may answer it?

Source: Letter, Wellcome (Claydon copy) Ms 9010/106

Claydon
16 September 1885

Private

My dear Captain [Edmund] Verney

A good canvass to you and God speed your election. The enlightenment of a number of men by your meetings is surely a thing worth doing. I have been so sorry not to be able to see you.

My love to Margaret, dear Margaret, and the children. Pardon me for making an inquiry: we have no active magistrate, no active police near Lea Hurst. You are an active Chairman of Sessions. What would you do in such a case? At Whatstandwell Bridge (and Station) two miles from Lea Hurst but not on the estate, there is (1) a respectable public house, (2) our coffee rooms, and (3) a public house notorious for nearly every kind of iniquity, the Wheatsheaf, within 200 yards all three of them.

Our coffee rooms at first nearly closed the Wheatsheaf, but afterwards he beat us at every kind of weapon. I have just heard this, "The owner of the Wheatsheaf, who lived on the premises, has been in treaty for sale with a brewery company and he has been giving some ale to the quarrymen and others to induce them to stay at his house, so that the brewery company might see the house was doing a good business. He has sold the house this week (you see it is *done*) and as a rule public houses belonging to a brewery company do not do the business, as other houses, on account of the tenant being what is called tied to have the ale, spirits, etc. from the brewing company, whether good or bad." What would you advise? Is there anything possible to be done in such a case? God bless you and yours.

ever yours affectionately

F. Nightingale

Source: Letter, Wellcome (Claydon copy) Ms 9010/123

10 South St.
2 December 1885

Private

My dearest Margaret [Verney]

I think I feel almost as anxious as you do about this election, but then you see *you* are working for eternity, to raise and ground the Liberal cause, that *is* the "saving" of men's minds, bodies and souls, that *is* being fellow workers with God. And will He let one of these efforts be lost? Not He. You are not working for petty party issues which can

be won by canvassing and Primrose Leaguers [Conservative support-
ers], though none feel more than I do the tremendous issues now at
stake, the enormous difficulties of the nation for the next few years,
win who may. But God is a "Liberal," we may say that without irreverence, and how can He be beaten? We *must* win in His cause, whatever
happens.

Mr Fred was so good as to come in last night on his way from the
station home. I could not help a tear or two before he came, but he
was so full of valiance. He had won, though he had lost. The victory
was his. He had "saved" 4000 people's minds, and without one influence except the highest, just like you, without asking for one vote. I
could only sing for joy, though deeply disappointed for ourselves and
for the new House of Commons.

Dearest Margaret, God bless you, God bless you both. I can only
ease my old heart by giving you both to the everlasting Arms[253] which
are under you. Can you sleep? Success and joy and peace! If you are in
London on Sunday, I will keep all my Sunday open, but can scarcely
expect you to have a minute to spare for me.

ever your loving

F. Nightingale

God speed and He *will* speed.

Source: Letter, Wellcome (Claydon copy) 9011/29

Claydon
8 June 1886

Most Private

Dearest Margaret [Verney]

Grievous indeed to us is the letter which appears to have been sent
you and without the knowledge of Sir Harry, or, I need not say, of me.
She [Parthenope Verney] is so very suffering, worse than when you saw
her, no sleep and consequently very irritable. We have been obliged to
get a third nurse. She really has no idea of what she writes, and less
than none of what effect she produces.

When your dear beautiful letter arrived, she said to me: "I have
had such a beautiful letter from dear Margaret. I did not know that
she would care so much (or some word to that effect) for what I
wrote." Since then, Sir Harry has shown me your letter to her saying,
"Oh how different it might have been, if Margaret had not been the

---

253 An allusion to Deut 33:27.

woman she is, a pearl of great price."[254] I was going to write to you, with Parthe's concurrence, when I received a scratch from her: "I find Harry *has* written to Edmund." That letter, written before he had seen yours, seems to have been almost as unfortunate as hers. (Sir H. showed me your two notes to him.)

As far as I can make out, they are now entirely reconciled by what you have explained to them with such kindness and wish, viz., to have the "formal official" committee meeting in the North Hall, with Sir H. as president, the dinner in the "tent," which Sir H. would not attend. (I am thankful to say he declines all dinners.) If Captain Verney wishes for any reason, such as last night's division, to put off this annual meeting of the Liberal Association, it should be because he wishes it (not they) as *he* judges best "for the interests of the Liberal cause" is all their wish. They are quite pacific, Sir H. tender.

I don't know whether you and Captain Verney are greatly disappointed with last night's division. My feeling is that if, as appears to be in the plan of Providence, that Ireland is within ten years to manage her own affairs, but with Parliament supreme at Westminster, Providence probably knows how best to manage it, and that *this is* the most direct course, though it seems to us an uncanny one.

Poor Parthe is so very bad today. If I were to tell you the bodily condition, which however is I trust, being removed, you would wonder at *nothing,* forgive *all* [as] you always do. We do so grieve about little Kathleen and the separation from you of Maude. May your own children be all bright, all well! Ralph, not a very good night, but thriving today. God bless you again and again, dearest Margaret, and with kindest love to childer and kindest regards to Captain Verney. In great haste, believe me,

ever and ever yours
in reverence and love
F.N.

Excuse this scrawl. Miss Shalders gone to bed in another room but quite well.

---

254 An allusion to Matt 13:46.

Source: Letter, Wellcome (Claydon copy) 9011/38

10 South St.

12 July 1886

Dearest Margaret [Verney]

God speed you, all good be yours, and it *will* be yours. I hope you slept last night. Here comes a small bottle of eye lotion and eyeglass. Might I have the pleasure of having another small supply ready for you on Wednesday when you go abroad? My very best love to dear Ellin and Lettice, who must be in a state of rapture, and to Captain Verney, if I may. The good cause will triumph. We never seem to think that God cares for the good cause, but we can trust Him.

I wish I could have heard more from you last night. God speed. God speed. I hope you are a little rested.

ever yours

F. Nightingale

I am afraid I shall not see you again for a long, long, time.

Source: Letter to Margaret Verney, Wellcome (Claydon copy) Ms 9011/40

10 South St.

14 July 1886

Such a grief and disappointment[255]—we don't know how to express it but no defeat—such a gallant fight, this new method of conducting a canvass: how many have been instructed, how many have been raised from sordid life by it, how much of the higher life has been given them. No defeat but a victory against all odds, a minority of only 71 in 8800 votes!

I predict a long life in Parliament to Captain Verney still. I would strew flowers in your way as "conquering heroes" if there were time as bridegroom and bride, going forth to run your course. God speed you both and give you a beautiful journey. Love to Ellin and Lettice and Captain Verney. . . .

ever and ever

your loving

Aunt Florence

Editor: Lettice Verney fell ill in Leipzig in September, 1886, on this trip; Margaret Verney stayed there until March 1887 to nurse her.

---

255 Edmund Verney was defeated in the election of 1886, after having won in 1885.

Source: Letter, Wellcome (Claydon copy) 9011/57

Claydon

9 October 1886

Dear, dear Margaret [Verney]

It wrings one's heart, how it must wring yours! your account of the darling child. Yet how deeply pathetic, beautiful and touching. May God bless you is our cry every moment of the day, and He *will* bless you. But for her wise mother and admirable nurse—what a nurse you are, God speed you, and for all the medical care and appliances so close at hand and so wisely seized upon, it might have been so much worse. I have never known a similar case; it must be a very uncommon one, I should think, but I have known cases of apparently less severity where there was raving delirium. And from this agonizing state you have saved her, I believe. The Father Almighty says:

I will take her in charge,
so you "abide in my love."[256]

And you do "abide in His love," dearest Margaret, and so we cannot doubt He has her in charge. He is very near you in the little Leipzig room, consecrated now to His love.

Darling Lettice, I live in Mother's beautiful rooms at Claydon and think of her and you and I keep her east window open at night and hear the birds whispering their morning prayers to God before the dawn. Then comes the dawn of another day and I think of Mother. Then the cock begins in the courtyard with his loud impertinent cry and all the hens, white, black and Oxford mixture, come out on the lawn to my indignation, for they grab about and feed on the lawn. And if a solitary thrush comes modestly in the corner under the trees for his worm, they run at him, and say: "That worm is ours." The thrush retires discomfited and I think of getting a peashooter and shooting peas at the hens, but I know they would only stop and pick them up. But, if I do but shake my window, they run away, for they know their conduct is greatly to be disapproved. Then, at 8:00 o'clock, as I have observed at Lea Hurst and wherever I have been, the singing birds stop their songs and twittering and go away somewhere to break-fast for half an hour.

---

256 An allusion to John 15:10.

9 October 1886

Thank you so very, very much for writing so fully. We hang upon your news. How occupied you must be, beloved nurse. But it is very good of you, *indispensably* so, to keep diligently to your little walks and runs. When you write of Lettice singing like a "little bird" to herself, then I think of the morning singing birds under your E. window here and God's carol in their voices. Grandpapa and Grandmama shed tears over your letter. Fare you very well, sweet saint, much tried one, God's daughter of wisdom.

ever your

F. Nightingale

Source: Letter, Wellcome (Claydon copy) 9011/68

[printed address] 10 South Street
Park Lane, W.
Christmas Day 1886

Ah dearest Margaret [Verney]

God has sent us the most beautiful Christmas loving gift through you, dear Lettice better. Thank God. God bless you. We read with tears of joy your lovely account of the Christmas tree.

ever yours

Aunt Florence

May I send the twelve months of the New Year to Lettice?

Source: Letter, Wellcome (Claydon copy) 9011/73

10 South St.
13 January 1887

My dear Captain [Edmund] Verney

I only heard late last night that you were in London and going to Leipzig today or I should have petitioned for a little visit before you see those dearest ones. All peace and every joy attend you, for we know what love you bring them and they you.

The Winslow meeting seems to have been successful. May you have many more such! I need scarcely ask you to give Aunt Florence's dearest and anxious love to the darling child and the beloved mother and to take this picture book to Lettice. Fare you all *very* well. I do not like to ask you to write a word in English to tell me how you really find them, for I know you write in shorthand to Maude and Mr Fred and they often kindly give me news.

You will know how painfully I have been occupied in consequence of the sinful frivolity of this shuffling of Cabinet offices, as if they were a pack of cards. Administration is almost at an end, when secretaries of state are changed every four months. Farewell, farewell. I hope you *are* well and will have a good passage. Fond love again and again to the dear ones at 88.

ever yours affectionately

F. Nightingale

How Maudie misses her Mervyn [her dog died]!

Source: Incomplete letter, Wellcome (Claydon copy) Ms 9011/74

10 South St.

14 January 1887

Private

My dear Captain [Edmund] Verney

I received your note last evening. I feel with you more than you can imagine—it is indeed the greatest difficulty that I remember in political life since 1832.[257] I am so sorry, so infinitely sorry for both sides. Fathers and sons are set against each other, brothers against brothers, and husbands against wives.

It is hard beyond measure then to diminish in any one particular the hearty and loyal support they always gave him. Will you not kindly think that a personal trust may sometimes fill up a gap created by unavoidable political differences, and is it not an essential part of the liberal creed to honour a divergence in political conviction when it is the result of careful and honest study?

I think many of my father's old friends for my father's sake feel that personal trust in his son which enables them to support him heartily, even where not agreeing with him entirely. I would fain hope that you and my father may perhaps do the same. You know or perhaps you hardly know how painful it is to me to pain you.

257 The great Reform Act of 1832 also divided families. The Verneys were divided by the sons supporting Home Rule for Ireland, while Harry and Parthe were "Unionists."

Source: Letter, Wellcome (Claydon copy) Ms 9011/83

10 South St.

13 February 1887

Dearest Margaret [Verney]

I am afraid there is a little drawback in dear Lettice's eye. Yours is such a great, such an unusual trial, and we were so sorry when you lost Captain Verney's company. But he always looks so much better when he comes back from you. I have never heard Sir Harry so cheery in his love of him, and so appreciative of him. I hope Sir H. writes to you in that sense.

I do so want to have books for our school on *plants* and *birds*, the common plants and birds they see every day, *not* on *botany* and *ornithology*. Ah could you but lecture to them on the fertilization of primroses and other common flowers! The most delightful little book in Bengali was written by a Dr Watt of Bengal, now in England, about all these manners and customs of the plants Bengali children see every day, almost as if the plants were beings. He lent me a copy in English. Could you tell me of any book which gives English plants and their fertilization in the simple delightful manner I am sure you did in your classes? I know of none.

About birds: I have Rev Wood's school Natural History Series, but was very much disappointed in the *manner* in which he tells how birds fly (by the lightness their hollow bones give them, etc.) and how they sing, their whole body being as it were breath. Could you tell me any schoolbook giving the birds graphically?

Your letters always have a wonderful effect. I don't think Sir H. is well. He always complains to me of feeling so much older than last year, and of feeling giddy and as if he "would tumble down." I am at once surprised and thankful my sister is not more uneasy. Her bodily health is extraordinary, but the poor limbs are worse. She sees strings of people and never seems tired.

Maudie felt the loss of Mervyn sadly. The three children have been all ailing, as you know. Tomorrow they go with their mother to Seaton in Devonshire.

I will not tell you how everything has run into party politics, how administration and government are ceasing out of the country.... W.H. Smith was a capital secretary of state for war, i.e., as capital as anyone is now. Just as we are getting the most needful things, for soul and body, for the Army, he (the least party man, except Lord Iddesleigh, of the whole) is changed to what he *can't* do, to his own regret. And all stops.

And so with India, but it is too sad. As for Lord Dufferin (this is quite between ourselves), one very high up said to me: "He thinks to rule the natives of India by cleverness, but they are cleverer than he." I should add, "And by courtesy." But his courtesy fails him, as in his visit to Bombay, when he does not carry all before him. I must stop, for I have no strength.

You will be distressed about Morey. I think him very ill, worse than they do. He told the doctor it was from having such a multitude of things to think about. I should have added, and of contradictory orders and of flurry and needless hurry. Sir Harry and my sister's kindness to him has been beyond gratitude; they have never even thought of the loss to themselves, but so unconscious are they, that the flurry and contradictory orders to him have been greater than ever. He is now at Exeter, worse than when he started. I cannot conceive what they will do without him, if, as I fear, he must be long away, or come back only to go away again. Excuse these silly cards. Aunt Florence's best love to the little chocolate maker. God bless you both and all.

ever your loving
Aunt Florence

Source: Letter to Margaret Verney, Wellcome (Claydon copy) Ms 9011/104

10 South St.
10 March 1887

Thank God, thank God, dearest, blessed Margaret, that you are safe at home again with the darling child. Brave woman! We cannot thank God and you enough, we have been so anxious. Dear patient little girl, you have been brave too and you have not "turned" into a "little German girl," you see, thank God. God bless you both.

ever your loving
Aunt Florence

We felt inclined to say:

God save, God save them
And see them safe to shore.
For such a gallant deed
Was never seen before.[258]

---

258 A paraphrase from Macaulay's Horatius, *Lays of Ancient Rome*:
"Heaven help him!" quoth Lars Porsena
"And bring him safe to shore;
For such a gallant feat of arms
Was never seen before."

And you see He *has*. Don't do too much, dear Margaret, these first and second days, pray.

F.N.

Source: Letter, Wellcome (Claydon copy) Ms 9011/173

Claydon
5 September 1887

Most Private

Dearest Margaret [Verney]

Many thanks for the proof. It is quite impossible that you should do otherwise, of course, than go to the "Liberal Brotherhood's" meeting and tea. Sir Harry means to go himself (and wishes to have the "copper" put in order and to give "milk." The first I believe cannot be done. The second I am afraid will not be done). But I trust in God that you will not find all the difficulty we expected here.

Last night she [Parthenope Verney] asked me to pray for her that she might be guided aright in these difficult circumstances or some words to that effect. I knew that she meant to pray for wisdom and love. She never said anything at all like it before and I never expected to live to hear her say it. God is so good that I think He must grant our prayer: "I will," He says. And I know that on your side it will be all love and forbearance. . . . God bless you all and He *will*.

ever your loving and grateful

F. Nightingale

Source: Letter, Wellcome (Claydon copy) Ms 9012/140

10 South St.
27 February 1889

Private

Dearest Margaret [Verney]

I cannot thank you enough for your full and most interesting letters. Alas! this is the last day, I fear, I shall find you at Claydon.

Would you thank Captain Verney very much for sending me the Brooklyn City Government, or "County Council." I don't "think" you "cowardly." I know too well the exhausting nature of Claydon's days and I know too well the exhaustion of the strain of listening to her [Parthenope Verney's] condemnations of people dear to one. Still you know I think there is more "rhetoric" in it than anything. It is not the less painful for that.

About the coming to London: I do feel so much for them both. I think Parthe really needs the intercourse of wits in London for the health of her mind, as you cannot give her yours. She fancies London good for him, but he really needs Claydon for the health of his body, and rest. When you are gone, I shall hear nothing about the "let." I wonder he has not had a "bid." Do you know whether there is any chance of Sir H. Acland being admitted?

My best of loves to Lettice and thanks for her dear little letter. I seem all questions, while you are all graphic. Have you any idea whether Dr Benson encourages this prospective move to South St.? I do look forward to her future life with such terror. If she is to drive away her true friends, Maude and Fred, and *you* cannot come, and dear Lettice is a true friend, and isolate herself, and if she is to consider the diploma of a doctor and of everyone else to be the affirmative answer to: Is he a Unionist? her life will become nothing but a barren encounter of wits. In London she sees only her own side. London is all very well, but there is nothing of family or affection in the people she sees. *He* is becoming aware of this, but it is too late. Goodbye, blessed Margaret. I cannot bear to part.

ever your loving
Aunt Florence

Editor: The next letters date from soon after Parthenope Verney's death, 12 May 1890.

Source: Letter, Wellcome (Claydon copy) Ms 9013/54

10 South St.
Park Lane, W.
20 May 1890

Dearest blessed Margaret [Verney]

Your letters and Maude's have been like letters from heaven to me. How can I thank you enough? And Captain Verney and Fred have been so kind. Sir Harry says in every letter, with all his sweet humility, what comforts and supports you all have been to him. With regard to *you* he says (what I am sure is quite true) that he should not have known but for you how the most necessary things were to be set about. But I am afraid it must have been a great strain upon you settling all *her* things. But how beautifully you have done it.

Pray do not think for a moment "of coming up to see" me, dearly as I should love to see you. I don't believe he could live without you a day at present. And pray don't think of "bringing up" my sister's trinkets "to show" me, as Sir H. proposes, either now or ever. As far as I am concerned, I want to think of *you*, dearest Margaret, as her "residuary legatee." I am sure she would like her children and grandchildren to have her things or the best part of them. She used to speak to me with tears of pleasure that you and Maude made the dear children think of her as their real Grandmama.

But do you know what occupies me most now is this: Fred and Maude's share in my sister's property. It is as if by some indescribable intense impression, *not* a voice, from her who is gone, she were always saying to me, night and day: "Pray let this be set right; I made a sad mistake, but I did not mean it." You know that Captain Verney has the generous intention, which he told me, of getting Sir Harry to make a deed of gift immediately to Fred, the income of it to be paid to Sir H. during his life, so that his income shall not be lessened (*immediately* because otherwise the money might be all gone).

I consulted her executor, William Coltman, the letters passing through Henry Bonham Carter, her trustee, that I might not misexpress and William Coltman replies:

> 12 Old Square, Lincoln's Inn
> 17 May 1890

It is, I think, very undesirable that Sir Harry should make a deed of gift to F. Verney till his affairs are settled. It would only complicate matters *and would not be available against creditors.* ("I am afraid Sir H. owes a considerable amount, etc.) "Of course there is no objection to Sir H. making a provision for F.V. by will, *and the sooner this is done the better.*"

He then says that this "view" might "perhaps be impressed" on "Captain Verney." I have not written it to Captain Verney, thinking it better to write to you, as your kind letter to me put things so plainly yesterday. I tried to write yesterday but it was impossible. I have no words to say how noble in their disinterestedness F. and M. are. As Sir H. loses his grief in *her* joy, so they lose all thought of themselves in their feeling for *her* and Captain Verney in his feeling for her and them. I feel as if my sister were pressing me on to right this, to try to set things right.

With regard to what you say that, "When F. [Fred] married, it was a very clear understanding that Mama was to settle something upon him, but Papa seems to know nothing about it"!! I think *that* is entirely defect of memory. (It will come back to him.) And as he says "confusion." I can bring no proof of it, but I think even as far back as when they were still at Embley, after my father's funeral, there was a sort of understanding that F. was to have Pleasley. Sir H. has continually told me lately that he was losing his memory, that his mind was all "in confusion." I thought it such a test of his angelic temper that, instead of being impatient with himself or with others, he said, "I *pray* that it may not cause inconvenience to others."

I cannot but feel (morally) sure that Sir H. knew all about it (the proposed settlement on Fred). As for my sister, she told me distinctly herself about her intention. And I cannot, I believe, be mistaken in thinking that *within the last two years*, that is *since* the will drawn up by Mr Farrer, she again mentioned it, in rather different terms. She never talked to me about her affairs, except sometimes about the worry of them, how anxious she was to keep up society for *him* (and all that) while he lived.

She was essentially *not* a woman of business, but I can the less be mistaken in remembering these intentions and that is why I am so anxious they should be carried out *as hers*. I doubt not that she is thanking God now for the tenderness and affection her husband's family are showing her, hoping that Sir H. will put things straight. Otherwise her joy in "home" would be so dashed. I cannot, indeed I cannot say in words but only in heart, my feeling of intense thankfulness, etc. to God, that he should have a family and such a family about him not only at such an hour but always, cheering and supporting him like that angel in Gethsemane and with as little thought of self and showing such great kindness to me. All might have been so different.

You tell me what Mr Robertson says and I am afraid the executors are sadly aware of the debts. I do pray, as you *said*, that you may be supported through all this bad time, worse than death.

You are very good to ask me for a list of her friends and relations to send some thing of hers to. I will tomorrow and return your list. May I put down first the Shore Smiths whose unfailing goodness to my dear mother for several years was the comfort of *her* life. But they will want only very little things, *close* remembrances of Parthe. Shore is poorly at Embley. Would you kindly give my love to Mrs Davidson and Beart and my kindest regards to Morey? I am going to write to them. You know where all her notebooks are in the library, better perhaps than I, if Sir Harry wants them.

I had a charming little letter from your Harry before he heard of this, but the bats, my dear (please tell Mr Calvert) he likes school very much but it's the bats that makes school delightful. God bless you.

ever yours gratefully

F. Nightingale

Source: Letter, Wellcome (Claydon copy) Ms 9013/42(2)

[printed address] 10 South Street
Park Lane, W.
29 May 1890

Dearest blessed Margaret [Verney]

I cannot thank God enough that this settlement of the Derbyshire property is effected. It is an unspeakable relief, not only for the sakes of Fred and Maude, but for the sake of her who is gone, who, I am sure, demanded as well as meant this settlement. She could not have been happy without it. I am sure, too, that it is a relief to Sir Harry. He writes rather in low spirits that his retirement is coming to an end (I hope it is not) but he says with his sweet candour that there was this important business to be done, which it was his "duty" to do at once and that he is sure he should have gone on delaying and delaying, unless William Coltman had come, whose visit was therefore "peculiarly acceptable" to him.

Fred is evidently very much relieved. I think those two, F. and M., have behaved like two angels and I hope their wings will grow. Thank you a thousand times for your dear letter. I do wish Sir Harry indeed would delegate more to you. But it will come.

Would you be so very good as to add *Lady Ashburton's* name to the *list* of those who would be so pleased to have something of Parthe's. We have known her since we three were in our teens and after ourselves, I don't think there was a greater lover of Parthe's. I ought to have remembered it before. Loving love to all of yours,

from yours ever

F.N.

I "kissed," as the children say, your scrap telling the good news. I didn't like to look at her laburnum out of the window before.

Source: Letter, Wellcome (Claydon copy) Ms 9013/210

20 October 1891

Dearest blessed Margaret [Verney]

. . . Did you see the strange and beautiful sunset last night, lasting so long? Yet it will be followed by rain. Is not this the "*Real Presence*," not attached to a bit of biscuit, nor anything to eat, but to give us an unearthly pleasure with His love, *just* to show us *His love*. . . .

ever your loving, overflowingly

F.

Source: Letter, Wellcome (Claydon copy) Ms 9013/217

30 October [1891?]

Dearest Margaret [Verney]

Could we finish our syllabus today? And must we not have a copy for the Forty Thieves tomorrow? I want a copy, please, for our enterprising Lea schoolmaster, who brings forward the subject at the Schoolmasters' Derbyshire Union *at once*. Also, I have a string of questions two miles long to ask you. Not magnifique but la guerre. Hurrah for Ellin off on a fine day, but fog this morning, I fear. Thank God for Été de St Martin [Indian summer]!

F.

Source: Letter, Wellcome (Claydon copy) Ms 9014/8

[printed address] 10 South Street
Park Lane, W.
13 February 1892

Dearest Margaret [Verney]

May I ask has any progress been made towards Sir Harry, in concert with you, planning the disposal of his -- clear? thousands a year, whether, as you said, in paying off debt on Pleasley, etc., as also in improving cottages, etc. on Claydon? It will never be done, if not now with you. But your own hands are so full, your anxieties so great, my blessed one, that I have hesitated to write.

Christmas is now long since past when Sir Harry made a solemn promise to do it, as soon as he knew what income Mr Calvert had left him. That income is £8200 a year. Sir Harry was so good as to show me his balance sheet. Would you think the time is come for me to write to Sir Harry? My excuse would be that since Mr Payne has taken my photograph, the plague of people has been absolutely incessant, to have my photograph and an interview with me, and a history of my life from myself, including the dolls I played with!! (sic). I can no longer say, There *is* no photograph. (The insolence of the people who propose is only equalled by the vulgarity of the people who accept.) That is not however the question.

You and I are so exceedingly anxious about Sir Harry's balance sheet; shall I write to him claiming his promise conditional on my having my photograph done at Claydon? I write in greatest haste.

ever your loving

F.

Source: Letter to Margaret Verney, Wellcome (Claydon copy) Ms 9014/14

10 South St.

20 April 1892

Yesterday was Parthe's birthday and I celebrate it by thinking of all you have done by bringing out the books during *his* lifetime, for which she was so anxious, for her.[259] I celebrated it, too, by having Rosalind Shore Smith, before her unique, singular marriage. With absolutely no *certain* provision, they are going to live in a cottage at the east pole of London, separated from us by five millions of people, but not from the easterns among whom they are going to labour.

They are called by respective relations the Naughties, the Babes in the Wood, the Early Christians. I have not told Sir Harry, because if he were to write to the parents recommending a house in Grosvenor St., he would send them stark staring mad, the one from indignation that it should be thought desirable, the other from regret that he is too poor to give it her.

Verily the world is full of the strangest and saddest contradictions, but if you like to communicate this note to Sir Harry, please do.

ever your loving

Aunt Florence

Editor: Edmund Verney was sentenced to one year in prison 6 May 1891 and seems to have been released in April 1892. Margaret evidently visited him in Pentonville.[260] Nightingale was supportive in sending her notes and messages and helping to effect Edmund's reconciliation with his father (see above). Lord Rosebery wrote Nightingale asking how he could write the "imprisoned captain." She invited him to send her the letter, for the severe rules at Pentonville permitted only a quarterly letter from his wife. His letter "would be opened and destroyed," but she would see that he got it later.[261]

---

259 Margaret Verney finished the editing and published the first two volumes of the *Memoirs of the Verney Family*, 1892, on which Parthenope had done many years' research. The last two volumes are Margaret Verney's.

260 Letter to Margaret Verney 8 July 1891, Wellcome (Claydon copy) Ms 9013/166.

261 Letter to Lord Rosebery, Scottish National Library Ms 10090 ff11-12.

Source: Letter to Margaret Verney, Wellcome (Claydon copy) Ms 9014/18

[ca. May 1892]

Aunt Florence prescribes warmth, quiet and a little brandy. Don't laugh if she sends a little of Sandeman's purest brandy prescribed by Sir A. Clark. Or rather you *may* laugh. Keep Messenger; I am sure you must want messages doing.

I should have asked dear Edmund to come and see me, if he would be so good. But, now the main thing is going home to Claydon, it is better to be quite quiet. Please, just a postcard in the course of the day to say: "Two people well."

F.N. . . .

Source: Letter, Wellcome (Claydon copy) Ms 9014/74

[printed address] 10 South Street
Park Lane, W.
Advent Sunday
27 November 1892

Margaret's book

My dear Sir Harry [Verney]

Thank you very much for your kind note. I know how uneasy you are about blessed Margaret's health, and her being so overdone with work, which yet she loves for your sake and others' and for God's right. You have often been good enough to talk to me about how necessary it is to spare her everything that is unnecessary trouble or that *any* person who can read and write well can do *for* her and to invite my suggestions. I know how anxious you are to get the third volume of the *Verney Memoirs* done, Margaret being the only person who can do it.

You have no doubt anticipated me in what I am going at your prompting to suggest, viz., that you should make it clear to her that she is to have, *at your expense*, EVERYthing she wants for the book, that she is simply *to order any books of reference* she requires and to *employ as many clerks* as she can find work for, that she *is to* do this and no dispute about it. *You are ready to give her at once* any book of reference necessary for her work or rather yours. And there must be several of these wanted.

And then it is simply killing her to let her do *any* scribe's work for herself, killing the eagle who lays the golden eggs, for it is all for nothing. You and I know that more than one learned man and practical in authorship has said: it is entirely *impossible* for her to write that book for you if all clerical work is not taken out of her hands directly. You know dear Margaret is only *too* scrupulous not to run you into unnecessary expense. You will judge whether it might possibly be easier and safer for you, as it would be cheaper, to give her a blank cheque so far as the book is concerned—Christ's work must be worked in us this day.

I pray God and you to save that blessed life, to enable it to do all the work that it alone can do. This and action in God's work and holiness is putting upon us the "armour of light,"[262] this blessed day when Christ's work is worked in us, and even external ceremonies may be "works of darkness" if they do not lead to bright action in the business of God. We have *no* business of our own. . . .

Source: Letter, Wellcome (Claydon copy) Ms 9014/75

> [printed address] 10 South Street
> Park Lane, W.
> Advent Sunday
> 27 November 1892

My dear Edmund [Verney]

I have written to Sir Harry by this post to beg him to do what is so important to provide all clerkship, all necessary books of reference for Margaret. I hope he will show you or her the letter and act upon it at once. But [I] wish you would be so good as to order "an extinct baronetage" directly for me. I should be *so* glad and honoured to give it her. I would order it myself but am too stupid to know its title. Thank you *very* much for your letters

I am so horrified about Mr Hannen, the builder, and Mr Robertson's house and shall be so anxious to know what you have done. Sir Harry, I should think, would never be induced to make Mr Hannen liable to legal penalties. It is unwise to disturb Sir H. too much, but Mr Hannen *must* be compelled to repair his neglect and his scamped work. Have you sent for a man from Mr Hannen to see to Mr Robertson's house directly? I am so glad you are there, because you do your "spiriting gently." . . .

Editor: The next letters date from shortly after the death of Harry Verney, 12 February 1894.

---

262 An allusion to Rom 13:12.

Source: Letter, Wellcome (Claydon copy) Ms 9014/146

[printed address] 10 South Street
Park Lane, W.
20 February 1894

Dearest blessed Margaret [Verney]

The Grand Duchess of Baden[263] desires me to: "Please express all my warm sympathy to all the family. I have sent some flowers wishing them to be laid on his grave as a token of gratitude from one he has always been so kind to. How much I valued his letters!" It is such a heavenly letter. I hope to send you some more of it. She has been very ill with influenza.

I was so glad to hear "all well" from Las Palmas. Please tell Morey with my sincerest kind warm regards how thankful I am. And if you have heard from Brindisi, I am sure you will tell me. Or I shall hear from Maudie.

About dear Davidson, I don't know that I can say any more, but that I think, if *you* are quite satisfied with her, we could raise the money, at least for a year. Dean Fremantle could never find her equal as district nurse[264]—she has such good sense and good judgment and sympathy.

I have thought of you so much. *This* time and the funeral day are the bitterness of death. With *him* was not the bitterness of death. Please thank Edmund for his letter.

ever with great love yours
F.N.

A fortnight ago today he was riding. Did Mr Battersby[265] preach a funeral sermon last Sunday?

Source: Letter, Wellcome (Claydon copy) Ms 9014/171

10 South Street
Park Lane, W.
12 September 1894

Dearest blessed Margaret [Verney]

Thank you very, very much for your delightful letter received this morning. I would not interfere for worlds with your taking Ruth back

---

263 Louisa, Grand Duchess of Baden, daughter of the Queen of Prussia.
264 Mrs Davidson, formerly Parthenope Verney's maid, in fact became a district nurse.
265 George Harford Battersby (1860-1921), Vicar at Middle Claydon 1887-97.

or your cycling about, but the truth is I cannot come to Claydon now. I am almost bedridden and my dear people take up all my time and strength. But if you will try me again about the end of the month, I should be so glad to see you again, if possible. I gave your most kind message to Shore's wife [on Shore's death]. She was very much pleased; she is able to take a great deal of pleasure in receiving tributes to *him*. And today she was quite delighted in receiving twenty-seven messages of love and sorrow from twenty-seven workmen whom Shore had helped in the best way.

Shore lived to see his grandchild,[266] which is not six months old yet. He did not nurse or caress it as grandpapas often do, but he watched it. It made all the difference in his life. His death was good and simple like himself.

The boys are so good in helping. Indeed everybody has been so good in helping. I cannot say more. I feel one of them. Shore has been more or less my care since he was four months old. My love to all, Aunt Florence's. . . .

your humble devotee
Aunt Florence
In haste.

Editor: These next letters date from Nightingale's last, four-month stay at Claydon, as the guest of Edmund and Margaret Verney.

Source: Letter, Wellcome (Claydon copy) Ms 9014/189

Claydon
15 November 1894

My dear Edmund [Verney]

I cannot thank you enough for your kind and sympathizing note, giving me the precious freedom of your house for the present. As for your hospitality, offering to hang your pigeons and suspend them to the mutton bone, it can only be surpassed by that of the Arab who killed his own horse, which lived in his tent and taught all his children to ride on its back before they were two, because he had nothing else to give a stranger to eat.

I do prize beyond words the opportunity of seeing blessed Margaret, more dear than ever. And I hope I shall see *you* soon. You are engaged in so many works of mercy of which instructing people in

---

266 Louis Vaughan Nash (1894-1974).

the use of parish councils (how will they turn out?) is certainly one. Vaughan Nash, Rosalind Shore's husband, works almost "night" and day now at the School Board *elections*, London, the "night" being for writing articles for the *Daily Chronicle*, in which she sometimes assists.

I hope your cold is quite gone. I am glad to hear of my dear god-child Ruth's approaching confirmation next February [at age fifteen]. I did not remember she was so far advanced in years.

ever yours affectionately, dear Edmund

F. Nightingale

Source: Letter, Wellcome (Claydon copy) Ms 9014/203

17 December [1894]

Dearest blessed Margaret [Verney]

How is Lettice? Cheerily, cheerily, as you always do. My heart is with you—that does not signify, but what signifies is that you and dear Lettice are "in the heart of God," as someone said long, long ago.

ever your loving

Aunt Florence

Source: Letter to Edmund Verney, Wellcome (Claydon copy) Ms 9015/8

26 January 1895

Mr Battersby will come tomorrow (Sunday) at 4:15 unless he hears "to the contrary." Will this suit you? and Ellin?[267]

Thanks, my dear Edmund, for your letter.

Aunt Florence

Would Ellin come and see me, without hurrying herself, for a bit before starting this afternoon?

Source: Letter, Wellcome (Claydon copy) Ms 9015/9

Claydon
27 January 1895

Dearest blessed Margaret [Verney]

We are expecting you home. The house looks like a "spelonca" [dingy hole] without you. But Ellin is efficient maternally. We look upon the first stage of convalescence not as an eagerness to do, but a willingness not to do. So may it be with dear Lettice.

The sea housemaid! We know there are sea nymphs, tritons, sea serpents, amphilrite and all her maids. But you have discovered the sea

---

267 Presumably this was to conduct a communion service.

housemaid, who sweeps up the snow, the foam, the shingle, shavings and paper, and deposits them in her dusthole, the hotel, and your bow window . . . heart's love to you and Lettice.

ever your affectionate

Aunt Florence

I've got a formal letter offering me the "first honorary membership" of the "Matrons' Council." Good luck. What fools we be!

Source: Letter to Edmund Verney, Wellcome (Claydon copy) Ms 9015/10

Claydon

30 January 1895

Thank you very much, my dear Edmund, for your note and your newspapers. I should have asked to see you, but I *have* a conscience, "though you may not think it." And that tells me that, as you are in the midst of experiments (*not*, I hope, explosions) today and are going tomorrow to Lettice, which will delight her, *I may not.*

Please don't say that Margaret looks "every inch an authoress" in her pretty gown. The hat of an "authoress," especially of a female journalist, is hideous to behold, the profile of her figure is ridiculous to contemplate. Say rather that Margaret is "every inch" a saint and a hero, a genius and a heart, and her beautiful gown was "according."

ever your affectionate

Aunt Florence

There are three or four blackbirds looking so miserable in the snow on the lawn now. I favour them as much as I can on my balcony, but the sparrows and the starlings drive them away. Could you give them something meaty somewhere?[268]

F.N.

Source: Letter, Wellcome (Claydon copy) Ms 9015/13

[Claydon]

2 February 1895

Dearest [Margaret Verney]

Will you accept a few flowers? you who have given me so many—from some sent me this morning by Shore's Louisa and the four children, on the anniversary last night of my mother's death fifteen years

---

268 Nightingale in fact paid to have the birds fed. A letter from Margaret Verney 3 February 1895 (Claydon Bundle 40) thanks her "a thousand thanks for the cheque, in which thanks the thrushes and squirrels wish emphatically to join; your pensioners increase daily."

ago. You know she died in Shore's house—he was the most faithful son to her in the days of her decadence as she was the most faithful mother to him in the days of her brilliancy.

your F.

I have heard from Fred. He says he is "practically well," Maudie not yet so. He says nothing about Seaford!! He sends me the accompanying proof (which *he* says is mine—I believe it is *his*) of the preface to the Sanitary Conference at Aylesbury. He desires me to send it on directly to the "editor" there, *if we approve it*. O Lady of my heart and sibyl of history, it bites me to take you away from "Volume 4" and ask you to read this, but I *must*. Might we not leave out the "Miss"?

ever your F.

Source: Letter, Wellcome (Claydon copy) Ms 9015/16

[Claydon]
6 February 1895

Dearest [Margaret Verney]

Thank God Mrs Battersby is going on pretty well. About Kate Jones: I am so provoked that you should have all this botheration about her being a dissenter—I would say "*Welsh* dissenter"—*you* know better than I what that is. I should say from what I heard, both from Kate and from my dear little Nelly Owen, that it was a much fuller and more serious preparation from their ministers both for confirmation, whatever they call it, and for the sacrament than any we give in the Church of England? But of course they were right to crucify *Christ* as He was not in the Church of Jerusalem exactly. Kate went (alternately with the cook) morning or evening on Sunday to OUR church; she also took the sacrament there and I had a regular certificate from her minister.

But when a cousin came to live in London I encouraged Kate going *with her* to the Welsh church *occasionally*, ONLY *occasionally* it was, she went to that? polluted? place. She spoke and read English imperfectly when she first came to me and I encouraged her to translate Welsh scripture and sermons and Welsh hymns to me. What a beautiful language it is!

Kate would *like* to be in *London* and I should like that sort of place for her, which I believe she is quite competent to fill better than any other.

F.

May I see you today?

Source: Letter, Wellcome (Claydon copy) Ms 9015/17

[Claydon]
10 February 1895

Dearest blessed Margaret [Verney]

I *approach kneeling*, as Sheridan recommends. Would you, could you, will you look over this letter asked for from me for the meeting (Lord Mayor's) to raise £100,000 for St Thomas' Hospital? I have written it out in pencil with the diabolical intention of asking for *your* criticism, *your* omissions—it is too long—*your* additions. Our secretary, Henry Bonham Carter, insists on my introducing myself, as you see. The only good part of the letter is yours.

ever yours with great love

F.N. repentant to her benefactress

The distress over the country with our unthrifty habits seems appalling. I receive cries for help from people I cannot refuse, including the Lea Hurst agent, who says the quarrymen are another industry out of work.

May I hope to see you today?

Source: Incomplete letter, Wellcome (Claydon copy) Ms 9015/19

[Claydon]
11 February 1895

Dearest benefactress [Margaret Verney]

It is a twelvemonth today (by the week) and tomorrow (by the month) since our dear Sir Harry's resurrection. Perhaps he is not far off us. . . .

Source: Letter, Wellcome (Claydon copy) Ms 9015/18

[Claydon]
12 February 1895

Dearest blessed Margaret [Verney]

I do indeed feel with you this day. And what a gallant fight you have made this last long year. I have a beautiful little St George (Fra Angelico) on my table. But that is nothing to the holy heroic Sancta Georgina whom I sometimes have the privilege to have in my room very alive indeed.

Thank you, dearest, for what you so kindly say about my staying till it is sanitary to go. Indeed I am quite virtuously disposed to do what I like (there's virtue?) and stay with my saint till I have no excuse for staying any longer.

What time do you expect Dr De'ath[269] tomorrow? And what time may I expect you today?

ever yours

F.

Source: Letter of Margaret Verney to Nightingale, Claydon House Bundle 334

14 February 1895

... This is a white day to us—white in Welsh means blessed. Our two dear children are very happy and have gone out together in the pony carriage. Ruth and I have had a very happy reading and have been through the service together. She delights in all her lovely presents, and Lettice admires her Persian rug so very much and will find it so warm. Your presence here today is such a blessing to us all, we feel your love all round us.

I hope I may see you for a moment after the bishop, if you are not too tired. We shall be starting at 6:30 for East Claydon evening service. I do hope your throat is better.

Four squirrels have been under the window, one of them on the ledge looking in at us; he sits up in the snow with his right paw extended, his left upon his heart, declaiming, we think, at the selfishness of the warm well-fed rich inside, then at the end of his speech falling upon a poorer brother who attempts to share his meal and pursuing him with most unreasoning fury to the foot of the cypress, then returning alone to munch and moralize. I am afraid hunger does not develop the highest type of character.

your loving

Margaret

Source: Letter to Edmund Verney, Wellcome (Claydon copy) Ms 9015/23

Claydon

20 February 1895

The tom-tits have sent to me a deputation headed by the little one who, if it were to take off its clothes, would find a roomy dwelling in a walnut. They present a humble petition that Sir Edmund will cause mutton bones with some meat and more fat to be hung up. They state that two gigantic black parties called, they believe, rooks, have feloniously carried off their two best bones.

F.N.

---

269 George Hanby De'ath (1862-1901), Medical Officer of Health for Bucks. See *Public Health Care* for correspondence.

"Haste for thy life, post haste, haste, haste." I dare say Margaret was so good as to ask Sir Edmund kindly to send a man to look after *three* chimneys for me at the Joseph Colemans', Steeple Claydon. The two poor old folks are both now, or ought to be, *in bed*, ill. Dr Benson orders a fire night and day. But if there is the least wind, they are obliged to wriggle downstairs because that room smokes mildly while the bedroom smokes furiously.

Aunt Florence

Source: Letter, Wellcome (Claydon copy) Ms 9015/24

Claydon
20 February 1895

My dear Edmund [Verney]

Thank you very much for your note and for your kindness in proposing to go yourself to the Joseph Colemans' about the smoking chimneys. Yes, I would gladly put in the "Marlborough" grate into their bedroom if that is the only way of curing it. The chimney is short and straight. They boil a kettle there. They sit *and* cook in the parlour downstairs, which has an oven for the purpose, and therefore the Marlborough grate would not, I suppose, do there. (They only use the kitchen fire when they do not require a fire in the parlour.) They themselves think that three chimney pots would do their business better than grates. Thank you a thousand times.

your affectionate
Aunt Florence

Source: Letter, Wellcome (Claydon copy) Ms 9015/33

Claydon
10 March 1895

Dearest blessed Margaret [Verney]

How good of you to let me see these letters. How sweet and peaceful they are, worthy of the good man sinking to rest: "The peace of God." I return in another envelope some more letters of yours. But you know I have, if I have not returned to you, a more precious letter, Dean Fremantle to Edmund. If not returned, it is all safe and you shall have it back again. I hope to see you this afternoon.

ever your loving
Aunt Florence
Do you remember Watts?

Just such is the Christian: his course he begins,
Like the sun in a mist, when he mourns for his sins,
And melts into tears: **then he breaks out and shines,
And travels his heav'nly way**.
But when he comes nearer to finish his race,
**Like a fine setting sun he looks richer in grace,
And gives a sure hope at the end of his days,
Of rising in brighter array**.[270]

Source: Letter, Wellcome (Claydon copy) Ms 9015/40

[Claydon]
Ash Wednesday [27 February] 1895

Dearest blessed Margaret [Verney]

Blessed saint to stay in bed and rest. Now mind you keep up your character. The children at Steeple Claydon were more pleased to see you than even to have their long-looked-for tea. Of that more anon. The audience last night were delighted with "Sir Edmund's beautiful address." Of that more anon.

I want to ask a question. Of course you will have to go to London on Monday if Ellin is to be presented [at court] on Tuesday. Can 10 S. St. be of any use to you? I think you will naturally want to get rid of me *before Monday* (do you know that I have been at your blessed home four months today?)

If you go on Monday I have some scruple about taking Lizzie away from her mother just now (I think the sister so sure to break down). And *I* am rather shaky. But this is the way I could easily manage: go up to London on Friday, keep Lizzie the night to unpack for me and get out some papers which have been asked for, locked up there, and send her back to her mother on Saturday. What sayest thou, my saint? I have some letters to show you by and bye.

ever your loving

and troublesome Aunt Florence

Zillah!!

---

270 From Isaac Watts, "A Summer Evening." The stanza is given as written, Nightingale's condensed version in bold.

Source: Letter to Edmund Verney, Wellcome (Claydon copy) Ms 9015/27

[Claydon]
1 March 1895

Burn

... Might I ask you—I know how careful of blessed Margaret you are, not to say a word to her today about it. People see her splendid heroic saint's armour. Few or none know how much she suffers within. She sent me word yesterday that she was "*thinking of nothing,* doing nothing," which she knew would please me. Whether it was true or not, I can't say.

As for my "going away without seeing her," I should have to borrow a knife to cut off my head.

your affectionate
Aunt Florence

Source: Letter, Wellcome (Claydon copy) Ms 9015/29

[Claydon]
3 March 1895

My dear Edmund [Verney]

I owe you all sorts of apologies, which I hope you will kindly receive. I wanted to hear more about blessed Margaret from you, who is I am afraid tired, last evening. Also, I suppose you have no tidings of Fred.[271] It will be a great pity if he is not on the London County Council, won't it?

But about the pigeons and the 2½ ladders: you were not at home, and I sent for Milsom!! because the only place he could see the two (apparently) banished creatures was from my window. The night before last, and I believe for some nights previous, a yellow pigeon had roosted on the bottom ledge *outside* the false balcony. A lilac pigeon, attending upon it and trying to keep it warm, roosted close to it and on the very rim of the ledge. The day time they spent, I regret to say, on my balcony. I thought the others had driven these two away. Yesterday the lilac attendant appeared in the greatest distress how to feed his friend. He flew after you, then he thought better of it and returned to his friend who I thought was ill (I have seen two pigeons die). I sent for Milsom, who proposed the ladders. But lo! the yellow lady had laid an egg in the false balcony. They will not follow their egg to the dormitory. Your pigeons are of the *aristocracy* and not of the

---

271 Frederick Verney was a member of the Bucks County Council for eighteen years, then elected to the London County Council.

parish council. This is a long story, but you must have been surprised to see Milsom crawling up your house.

ever your loving Aunt Florence

Ellin better this morning.

Source: Letter, Wellcome (Claydon copy) Ms 9015/36

[printed address] 10 South Street
Park Lane, W.
12 March 1895

Dearest blessed Margaret [Verney]

We came all night—very steady, beautiful day. But the wind here is east, the water supply still frozen and our hearts were wae [woeful] at leaving you. May you not be troubled with tomorrow. I think of you hourly before the Father, but there is no occasion to remind Him of His love for you.

Poor Mrs Fremantle will probably be rather glad that he will lie in the cemetery rather than in the churchyard. And I don't think he will have any objection to her, so near Sir Harry. But what does it matter after all where the cheerful old man, old no longer, lies, except for disturbing you? But I wish, oh how I wish, I could do anything to make your life less of an effort. But it is splendid, the way you live your life.

Mr Jowett used to say we ought to thank God for His magnificent gift of life. Aye, and thank Him every moment, not once but every moment, because He is caring for us, not once but every moment. "Dieu le voit, Dieu le sait, Dieu vous aime [God sees it; God knows it; God loves you]"—this was the only answer made [by a] French nun, a great friend of mine, who was laying her great trouble before her advisor and who told me this story herself.

But we might all learn a lesson from you. I will not take up your time now. You know, I dare say, the Bishop of Ripon.[272] He is a man worth cultivating. Fare you very well, and take care of your health, blessed Margaret.

Aunt Florence

Love to dear Ellin and Ruth [and] Let[tice].

---

272 William Boyd Carpenter, a noted preacher and advocate of "Christian altruism."

Source: Letter to Margaret Verney, Wellcome (Claydon copy) Ms 9015/38

[printed address] 10 South Street
Park Lane, W.
15 March 1895

How good you are, dearest blessed Margaret, to go away like a "lamb" (here view the real lamb with all four feet in the air) with Maudie. I hope it will be to *a* sea—somehow there is nothing like the sea to make one forget one's cares and one's arrangements. To see the big waves rolling in and know that all one's arrangements won't make the slightest difference in theirs is very soothing, provided it is not too cold. "Peace be with you," and let Him say, "*My* peace I give unto you."[273]

We have had the most comical upset. Yesterday was seen (luckily it was when everybody was up) the water trickling down the walls of my dressing room. The builder's man was in the house and instantly turned off the water, which was already in four storeys. Today they have been pulling down walls and pulling up floors till they found the rent (in the main pipe which goes through the body of the house).

The men were chivalry itself and cut out the peccant part of the pipe to present to me. (I thought of presenting it to E[dmund] for his lectures.) I believe there are Brobdignag fairies,[274] though they are not down on the map, and in these days they probably have their cutlery from Sheffield. The rent in the pipe was cut with the utmost precision, as neat a job as I ever saw, with a good curve. But many, many gallons would have passed through it in two minutes and in a short time every ceiling in the house might have been washed away. The men are working as hard as they can, putting in fresh pipe and hope to finish late tonight. They are obliged to deal with five storeys (including attics). There is a long story—we can't be too thankful it is no worse. The men say that for several weeks they have been working by relays night and day. Everybody was bursting pipes. In haste.

ever your loving
Aunt Florence

The drawing-room ceiling looks as if Mr Jackson's dog had drawn its dirty tail over some part.

---

273 John 14:27.
274 An allusion to Jonathan Swift's *Gulliver's Travels*.

Source: Letter to Edmund Verney, Wellcome (Claydon copy) Ms 9015/41

[printed address] 10 South Street
Park Lane, W.
17 April 1895

Thank you very much for your letters, my dear Edmund. It is only now a fortnight to the trial[275] and I trust the matter will then be settled in as just a manner as can well be. We must be very anxious to hear.

I have heard about the (so-called) strike at Steeple Claydon, that a number of men were engaged at 3/6 a day from 6:00 A.M. to 5:30 P.M. and had too little physique for the work. It is very pitiful, but at least they do not seem to have interfered with the liberty of others to work, as these boot men do. But I should like to know what you think about the strike. . . .

Source: Unsigned letter, Wellcome (Claydon copy) Ms 9015/42

[printed address] 10 South Street
Park Lane, W.
24 April 1895

Trial of Rev Llewelyn Davies

Thank you very much, my dear Edmund [Verney], for your letter. Its first part I hardly know how to answer, but may I say what I think men who love you would say? or rather suggest, viz., that you should as far as possible keep yourself in the background, e.g., not go into the court at all, not attempt to see anyone in connection with the case, but take a room within call (on the 30th), and leave entirely to the discretion of the counsel for the prosecution whether or not to call you. (The counsel should be told the reasons against your being called.) Then at any stage in the case you may be called, or the counsel for the prosecution may, in his judgment, say at the proper time that rumour has been busy with other names, and he may challenge the other side, if he thinks fit. Is not this the way that would seem most dignified, and most like the conduct of an innocent gentleman?

About Harry Lloyd, I regret more than I can say that *she* [his fiancée] is a Roman Catholic, but they are much in love with one

---

275 Rev Llewelyn Davies, Vicar of Steeple Claydon, was convicted of acts of incontinence with a female servant; Edmund Verney was the patron of the living. The delicacy of the situation arises from the fact of his having been convicted as a sexual predator himself in 1891.

another. Morfy is terribly distracted about it. And I think it *is* distracting, with her husband in this state, to be called upon to do wedding joy. Why should we not hope—we can't undo the engagement—that Vera may come over to her husband's faith.[276] But if all her family's backs are set up, there is the chance of *his* falling into their arms, is there not? instead of *her* into his. Anyhow, George's life depends upon his being kept quiet, does it not?

Source: Letter, Wellcome (Claydon copy) Ms 9015/43

[printed address] 10 South Street
Park Lane, W.
1 May 1895

Llewelyn Davies

Thank God, my dear Edmund [Verney] that that terrible trial is over, as far as we are concerned. Thank you for writing to me. As for the poor wretch himself, it is better even for him that he has been found out. I trust that blessed Margaret will be better.

ever your affectionate
Aunt Florence

Source: Letter, Wellcome (Claydon copy) Ms 9015/44

[printed address] 10 South Street
Park Lane, W.
25 May 1895

Dearest blessed Margaret [Verney]

Blessed art thou among women.[277] I do so rejoice at the good news that Mr Stow[278] has Steeple Claydon. I rejoice for them, for you, for us, for himself. It is like St Paul saying to us, "Rejoice and again I say unto you, Rejoice."[279] And so I suppose I must rejoice over George coming to you. He cried over your beautiful welcoming telegram. Then I had a note from Morfy, and she too seemed to have a heart full, as well she might, at receiving such extreme kindness from you. So, you see, I crumble into dust or rather I am melted by the sun of

---

276 He in fact later married another woman.
277 Luke 1:42.
278 Llewellyn John Stow, Vicar of Steeple Claydon after Davies was convicted, but promptly left for reasons of health.
279 A paraphrase of Phil 4:4.

your love to man. God will look after you. I hope Morey is come back to help in the house.

ever your loving

Aunt Florence

I will write a little note, as you wish it, to Mr Stow. I suppose he is not gone to Davos yet. But I will send it to you with your leave to direct.

F.

Source: Letter, Wellcome (Claydon copy) Ms 9015/48

[printed address] 10 South Street
Park Lane, W.
13 June 1895

My dear Edmund [Verney]

Thanks for writing to me. You would have been quite justified in claiming from me the £82 instead of £30. Pray let me send £50. Has the unfortunate man left Steeple Claydon? Is it true that he has been further punished? But it is perhaps as well not to ask. I thank God that it is over as far as Steeple Claydon and Margaret and you and yours are concerned.

I hope blessed Margaret is really resting. It is good that George is as much better as he is. Thank you for writing.

your affectionate

Aunt Florence

Has Mr Stow given up Davos? I have not written to him yet to congratulate all upon having him at Steeple Claydon but I will.

Source: Letter, Wellcome (Claydon copy) Ms 9015/53

10 S. St.
27 August 1895

Private

My dear Edmund [Verney]

It is indeed a grievous calamity Mr Stow's going. Is it necessary? Do you think he worries himself about his health?

I will of course, make any *inquiry* that is possible for a man for you to make *inquiries*. And I will not mention to anyone else the disaster, for it is a real disaster. But I am so unprovided with advisers now and the man I always depended upon [Jowett] to recommend a clergyman is dead. I may possibly write to a friend and confidant of his. I think if you knew Dean Paget of Christ Church,[280] though he is rather high church, he

---

280 Francis Paget, Dean of Christ Church, Oxford.

would be a good man for you to write to. You must not hope much from me, I am afraid. Would that Mr Stow would re-examine his decision!

You do not mention how Margaret is, the blessed. Poor George! I do hope he will be able to go to Falmouth. Pray give him and Morfy, dear Morfy, my love.

That is a sad story about the diphtheria at Calvert Station [near Claydon]. I should have thought it was of all places the place for a M.O. of Health and an Inspector of Nuisances to interfere. Or must they wait for the District Council? But perhaps I am talking nonsense. God bless you. Believe me

ever yours sincerely

F. Nightingale

Thank you for Morey's letter.

Source: Incomplete letter, Wellcome (Claydon copy) Ms 9015/55

[printed address] 10 South Street
Park Lane, W.
29 September 1895

Dearest blessed Margaret [Verney]

I was so glad to see your hand again. How good of you to write! Ruth has written me a very nice letter. She seems to have enjoyed Antwerp and Brussels thoroughly. Please thank her when you write. And please thank Ellin too. When I hear that you are really better and "swimming" it is like new life to me. I hope you had some nice conversations with the sea gulls. Animals, especially birds, are so much cleverer than we are. Only sea gulls won't stay still.

How good it is of you to think of me and to wish me to come to Claydon, where I think I must be such a burden. I should have liked to come, as you so kindly say, before "the weather gets so cold." But the object is to see *you*, but we have been much upset this year, as you know. Not that I care much who is "in" and who is "out." I think of the time when Sidney Herbert and the best Peelites worked just as much for one side as the other. But no one does that now. What is worse, there is absolutely no one who in the least takes Mr Gladstone's place in keeping up the worthiness and the responsibility of the House of Commons. Mr Balfour[281] is useless in that respect. The House is like nothing but a set of workhouse patients throwing their tin cups and plates across the wards at each others' heads. The consequence is that things have

---

281 Arthur James Balfour (1848-1930), later Lord Trapain, Conservative MP and minister.

been so put off. The Indian Expenditure Commission does not begin its sittings till 5 November (the "Gunpowder treason and plot"). And there is a good deal to do at St Thomas'. . . .

Source: Letter, Wellcome (Claydon copy) Ms 9015/57

[printed address] 10 South Street
Park Lane, W.
13 November 1895

Dearest blessed Margaret [Verney]

As the time approaches in which I hoped to find myself turning into a *good* old woman under *your* inspiration, you will know how grieved I am to feel that work I should be hindering the so desirable change by neglecting, will prevent me from leaving London this month and I fear not in the *early* days of next. But I shall ask you as soon as I can whether it will be quite convenient to your goodness to receive my badness. And you must answer truthfully, because you *know* it *may* be inconvenient. But I still hope, I hope I hope.

ever your dutiful

and loving Aunt Florence

We have another glimpse of St Martin's summer. But alas! every leaf is gone, even the green ones. I have known three great November storms, beginning with the storm in 1854, when a great steamship went down with every man on board and all the troops' winter clothing (and nothing was saved) within a hand's breadth of Balaclava, missing her way into the Bonbonnière. But I think I never heard the wind blow as it did for a few hours on Sunday night.

Love to Ellin. I have given the government book on public libraries, recommended by her, to the great Mr Louis, who appears to be properly inoculated. But I have no hope of getting the Lea Hurst people to rate themselves, where we have three private public libraries and not a "peasant democracy." When are we going to teach it?

I hope still to see the "graduate" (odious American word!) Lettice during her holidays.[282] *She* is to *write* for peasant democracies, and my goddaughter.

Aunt Florence

I had a nice note from Ralph, whom I know you patronize.

---

282 Lettice Verney attended Lady Margaret Hall, Oxford University.

Source: Letter, Wellcome (Claydon copy) Ms 9015/59

10 South Street
Park Lane, W.
14 December 1895

Dearest blessed Margaret [Verney]

My doctor has quite decidedly forbidden my moving now. Alas for me that I shall not see my saint, but I am not without hopes that your own movements may be facilitated by this.

Some great man says never give two reasons. I am disregarding this maxim when I say that business here is so pressing that I do not see how I could have gone away and left it. *You* would not, I am sure. Edmund tells me that the plans for commemorating Sir Harry by a monument in Middle and Steeple Claydon churches are nearly ready and will wait my arrival. *Pray* do not wait for me. *Your* own judgment is so much better than mine, but tell me what you decide upon when you have decided. I grieve not to see the children.

ever your loving
F.N.

Source: Unsigned note, Wellcome (Claydon copy) Ms 9015/60

10 South Street
Park Lane, W.
31 December 1895

Dear Lettice [Verney]

I hope they keep you warm and get you breakfast and lunch such as is fit for an ante dentist victim. I am afraid he is rather tiresome, but you are a hero.

I meant to get up to see you today but I have a rather bad cold in my throat.

Source: Letter, Wellcome (Claydon copy) Ms 9015/64

[printed address] 10 South Street
Park Lane, W.
14 January 1896

Dearest blessed Margaret [Verney]

I heard of your grand fete last Tuesday to the aristocracy, the carpeted and lighted porter's hall, the reception in the saloon, and how beautiful Lady Verney looked when she was receiving them at the saloon door, and the music. Then the dancing and the grand supper and then dancing again. I hope you were not very tired. Your Christmas and New Year's festivities I suppose are over.

I do so want to know about Mr Stow and Steeple Claydon. I have the strongest impression that he would stay if it was pressed upon him now. But perhaps, please God it may be so! it has been pressed and he is going to stay. Love to all, God bless you.

ever your loving

Aunt Florence

Source: Letter, Wellcome (Claydon copy) Ms 9015/66

[printed address] 10 South Street
Park Lane, W.
24 January 1896

My dear Edmund [Verney]

Thank you for writing. May you get all the benefit from Biskra that we can desire, and I hope Margaret will too, provided she does not caper about too much. I think what one reads of Biskra is nice and am of the opinion of the man in the poem:

I fly to the desert away from man.[283] Only there is much of man at Biskra, is not there? Anyhow, God speed you. You do not say where Ellin is going. You will give us your address at Biskra. With deepest love to ever blessed Margaret.

ever your affectionate

F. Nightingale

Source: Letter, Wellcome (Claydon copy) Ms 9015/67

[printed address] 10 South Street
Park Lane, W.
26 January 1896

Dearest blessed Margaret [Verney]

God bless you. You take our summer hence.
The flower, the tone
The music of our being, all in one
Depart with thee.[284]

---

283 Thomas Pringle, "African Sketches Afar in the Desert," in *Poetical Works*: "With that sadness of heart which no stranger may scan/I fly to the desert afar from man!"

284 A paraphrase from Dorothea Hemans, "The Two Voices."

But I hope you will both come back refreshed in body and mind. Remember to look out for the mirage. There are cases, are there not? of caravans losing their way and all but dying of thirst, and being rescued by this means. One romantic case was told of a lady who was to be married at Biskra to a traveller who did not appear there at the time expected, and she went up a hill and she saw the mirage and a figure she supposed to be his and she interested the French governor. She and her father set out with camels and Arab guides and water and all the rest and arrived in time to save his life, when he was at the last gasp, and that of his Arab guide's.

But don't *you* go camelling it about the desert. The Nubian Desert always had a great attraction for me. And now, my very dear, fare you very well for two months and the children and Harry the man will fare well. This is the prayer, with affection for Edmund, of

your ever loving
Aunt Florence

Source: Note on letter to Margaret Verney, Wellcome (Claydon copy) Ms 9015/70

10 South St.
10 April 1896
Anniversary of 1848 the Chartist Petition and of the Duke of Wellington saving London by putting every soldier out of sight, but ready for action, and swearing in upwards of 100,000 respectable men as special constables.

Pardon me who saw PARIS *and* London for saving up this wonderful reminiscence (Sir Harry was one of the special constables), Louis Napoleon another. . . .

Source: Letter, Wellcome (Claydon copy) Ms 9015/78

[printed address] 10 South Street
Park Lane, W.
15 August 1896
Dearest blessed Margaret [Verney]

If you were to ask me to stand on my head "between 12 and 1:00 on Wednesday" in order to see you, I should do it. And I hope as Li Hung Chang is invited by Mr Gladstone, you will "accept some refreshment."[285] I am so very glad that Edmund is able to go abroad,

---

285 Li Hung Chang was in the U.K. on Chinese government business regarding suppression of the opium trade.

with Harry as nurse, "philosopher and friend" to "complete his cure," but you do not tell me where. I am glad you go to Rhoscolyn. And thanks for Ruth's funny little note.

The House is up, as you see, having done everything that it ought not to have done, and nothing that it ought.[286] Lord George Hamilton[287] has been really abominable. India is overtaxed and overassessed to a frightful degree, as everybody ought to know. And Lord G. applauds the state of its finances!!

I have written to Claydon to catch you at one end or the other. I am afraid you did not have Nurse Murray at Buxton.

I am more free than when the House was sitting, when we had Hong Kong plague, Calcutta bad hospital and two Hindus here, each with a righteous demand of England. But I have still the terrible business of parting with the lever of St Thomas', Miss Crossland, and helping to install the new one, who is nothing like Miss C.

Embley is sold, or perhaps you know, and in November there will be a good deal of minor business about this. Louis [Shore Nightingale] enjoyed his visit to Claydon so much. God bless you.

ever yours
F.N.

Source: Incomplete letter, Wellcome (Claydon copy) Ms 9015/84

[printed address] 10 South Street
Park Lane, W.
Christmas Eve 1896

Dearest Lettice [Verney]

I was very glad of your letter. I send £2.2 for your Lady Margaret Hall Settlement [her college]—I wish it were more but we are rather hard up.

I do think the quotation from the Bishop of Rochester is so good, I copied out the first paragraph and part of the second for our board schoolmaster at Lea Hurst, who is, in his way, a missionary of the best sort, and I am sure is anxious for the future lives of his scholars when they [breaks off]

---

286 An allusion to the confession in the Book of Common Prayer.
287 Lord George Francis Hamilton (1845-1925), secretary of state for India.

Source: Letter, Wellcome (Claydon copy) Ms 9015/85

> [printed address] 10 South Street
> Park Lane, W.
> 26 December 1896

Dearest blessed Margaret [Verney]

How can I thank you enough for the splendid Holroyd book? It is very curious that Sir C. Trevelyan wrote to me from distant Northumberland that I *must* read it, but I should never have got it for myself. And it is such a good print. And thank you, thank you a thousand times, and Edmund for the glorious nosegay, the exquisite white chrysanthemums which make a sun in the room, and the beautiful reds, the Italian tricolor, and your dear letters.

We had an infinitesimally small dance last night. Glory to God in the highest and on earth peace, good will towards men.[288] How comes it (I ask *you* as the wisest woman I know), that instead of peace the wars of Christian times have been the fiercest we know and the bitterest quarrels have been between different Christian persuasions? Perhaps it is because these wars and quarrels have all been about dogma. Now Christ eschewed dogma. *His* dogma was unselfishness, love to God and man. (*I* can remember when a clergyman refused burial to a dissenter and when both universities were for *Church* of England undergraduates alone.)

Please give Aunt Florence's love to dear Harry. And who does he think danced at our little dance? A large, long-haired tom kitten. This cat always tries to do what we do and it insisted on waltzing round the room to the music with the dancers, a young maid good-naturedly holding its forepaws, and it dancing on its hind paws. (Now cats usually abhor music and won't be in a room full.)

Please thank Edmund again for so kindly arranging that the noble nosegay should come on Christmas morning. I should so have liked to have heard your book lecture.

ever your loving
Aunt Florence

---

288 Luke 2:14.

Source: Letter, Wellcome (Claydon copy) Ms 9015/87

10 S. St.

16 January 1897

Dearest [Margaret Verney]

Will you tell Lettice that I did order her Spencer, but that the booksellers have formed a conspiracy, for which they ought to be whipped, to sell cheap editions (detestable print) and hers is not the only one which has been sent me. I am expecting a better edition every hour, and it shall come to her. But I am sorry for the delay, for I think she wanted to read it before she returned to Oxford. The booksellers seem to keep Christmas till Parliament comes to town.

My Lizzie Coleman [her maid] has desired me over and over again to thank you very much for your kindness to her at your delightful dance and to say how very much she enjoyed it.

yours in humble love

F.N.

Source: Letter, Wellcome (Claydon copy) Ms 9015/88

10 S. St.

16 January 1897

Dearest blessed Margaret [Verney]

You ARE gallant to head the poll of the School Board,[289] and with such members on the board. God will grant you success. I only wish we had you in Derbyshire. We have the very best board schoolmaster at Lea I have ever known and some of the members of the board the very worst I have ever known.

Thank you, thank you about the American lady. The weather has been so *dark* in London, and I have had to write so much by lamplight that do you know I was only able to read her letter yesterday by a gleam of sunlight close to the window?

My dear, I am a fool, but was there ever such a fool in the world as these American ladies suppose me? (I have just had a similar letter asking me to write a short "life" of myself for her. And I have sometimes seventeen similar letters by one mail.) Your lady, after all these superfluous phrases about "soldiers," tops up with: that they are to be led by a photograph! Their general is to be—a photograph!!! Good luck! But, to please you, the fool will write a line. I cannot read her name.

F. for Fool

_____

289 Margaret Verney was elected to the local school board and was later co-opted to the Bucks Education Committee.

Source: Letter, Wellcome (Claydon copy) Ms 9015/90

10 South St.
31 January 1897

Dear blessed Margaret [Verney]

I am very sorry Mr Battersby is going, for I know how you will miss them, and new friends are not like old.

Thank you very much for the little book on the West End. I have already looked it through. One always wishes to know those things more and more, and I hope they will go on to tell us the proportion of children in workhouse schools who come back to the workhouse, and of prisoners who come back to prison, and how the elementary, etc. schools answer in afterlife, which I should have done if I had had money.

Sir John Herschel said that we English never look up the experience of the past, what has failed and what has succeeded and why this has failed and that succeeded, but are always starting fresh things. Government reports may tell something, but not in an inviting way that common people may read, and as a matter of fact they don't read them. Sir John Herschel had a pithy way of putting his remarks. He said we had no medical statistics. The first thing is, he said, to know *whether the patient has taken his medicine.* How often I have thought of that when I have heard doctors congratulating themselves on the effect of their medicine, and I knew the patient had not taken it. And the other extreme, the French extreme: "Il est *mort* guéri" [he died cured] (with exultation).

I was so delighted that you had enjoyed Rhoscolyn and felt well there and the children too.

You kindly ask after me. We have had and have a winter on the wings of misfortune. Two of our most important outlying hospitals have been outrageously thumped by their committees. One has been decided already, *against* right. The other, I hope, will float. We have lost one of our very best women, who died almost suddenly in Cairo, where she had gone on her tour of foreign service. I saw her as she went out and thought she would survive me thirty years. She had all the elements of a great mother, a great leader, a great teacher, which she showed first as a night superintendent at St Thomas', then in the military service with the orderlies. When the news of her death came they cried like little children.

We have no more such at present (that is, not already in hospitals). But the "earnest expectation of the creature waiteth for the manifestation of the sons (and daughters) of God."[290]

---

290 A paraphrase of Rom 8:19.

Our Lizzie Coleman is with her mother now, who is very ill, at Steeple Claydon. I send Lettice's book: Spencer's *Education*.[291] The type is princely, in comparison with the first copy they sent me, which was artistically framed to ruin the eyesight. But I am not satisfied and I send it to you that you may kindly *not* send it to her unless you approve.

Poor Mrs Callander is come out of the cancer hospital, better than when she went in and strenuous in her praises of the nursing, care and attention there, but with the disease slowly increasing. I am writing to the secretary. Mrs Callander's address is: Mrs Callander, Collingshanger Farm, Prestwood, Gt Missenden.

Aunt Florence's best love to Ruth. Could you kindly think of a present for her?

Source: Letter, Wellcome (Claydon copy) Ms 9015/92

[printed address] 10 South Street
Park Lane, W.
13 February 1897

Dearest blessed Margaret [Verney]

Indeed I do think of dear old Sir Harry (old and Sir Harry *no more*) on this day, and of your memorable words: "By his gentleness and courtesy, he kept the command of himself and his room till the last moment," and of your making his last years so happy, happier than my father's. Sometime after his death, I had to write an account of the opening of the Damoodah Canal (near Calcutta), of the delight of the people welcoming it with their intense feeling as if it were a divine Spirit, of the almost instant springing up of verdure and crops on its banks. I said to myself, that is my father in another world. And, in a somewhat different sense, you will say that is Sir Harry gone to another world—his life at Claydon is now intensified and full of blessing.

I am afraid I tired you on Sunday, but you are so good. (My father has been dead twenty-three years, and yet do you know I often find myself calling out to him, as if he were there, though in all my life, I never can remember him caressing me.)

Ruth's books are coming—the German ones.

ever your

F N.

---

291 Probably Herbert Spencer, *Education, Intellectual, Moral and Physical,* 1861 and various later editions.

Source: Letter, Wellcome (Claydon copy) Ms 9015/95

10 South St.
9 March 1897

Dearest blessed Margaret [Verney]

. . . What did you think of the "demonstration" in Hyde Park on Sunday? (It was attended by two of our relations!) without a thought of what an European war would be now, with all our tremendous engines of destruction, our long-range guns, our Maxims [machine guns], etc., our ironclads, which sink one another even on a fine day in peace *by mistake.* . . .

Source: Letter, Wellcome (Claydon copy) Ms 9015/96

[printed address] 10 South Street
Park Lane, W.
10 March 1897

My dear Edmund [Verney]

Thank you for your kind letter. You know how delighted I am at your success in getting the Claydons under the Public Libraries Act. I wish *we* could get our three *private* libraries at Lea Hurst under the Public Libraries Act. But it is said that the small ratepayers, of whom there is a large body there, are unwilling, and we have no one to canvass them properly. However, I hope we shall come to it at last.

Bust given me by the soldiers: about the *bust* of me by Steele of Edinburgh,[292] which is the one, I believe, at Claydon, it is after this wise—it was given me by the soldiers after the Crimean War and I sat for it. It is left in my will back to the soldiers, if it were not given back to them during my life, and inquiries have already been made where soldiers would like it best to be, whether at Aldershot, or where.

I do not know who told Lady Wantage[293] of this bust—it was not I, though she had previously written to me on behalf of Lady George Hamilton. When she, Lady Wantage, came to me, she knew about it and it was impossible for me to decline *lending* it to them for the Earl's Court Exhibition. (I have such a respect for Lady Wantage—she sometimes just reminds me a little of Margaret.) So I did promise it her. You perhaps know that I had previously refused all solicitations to give

---

292 Marble bust of Nightingale by Sir John Steele, 1862; a replica was made for Claydon.
293 Wife of Colonel Loyd Lindsay, Baron Wantage.

them "relics" of "me and the Crimean War" on the ground that the real "relics" were:

1. *Sidney Herbert's* royal commission and four subcommissions, which laid the imperishable seed of the great improvements in the soldier's daily life, direct and indirect.

2. The *training* of *nurses* both in character and technical skill and knowledge. The untrained nurses sent out to the Crimean War were— well, it is unspeakable what they were.

3. The *hygiene* and *sanitation,* the want of which in the military and medical authorities caused Lord Raglan's death and that of thousands of our men from disease.

That frightful lesson really, thanks to Dr Sutherland, Sir Douglas Galton, Sir Robert Rawlinson and others, began and continued the enormous strides which have since been made in (civil and military) science of life and death. Excuse this long story. I only wanted to be assured that the bust of me at Claydon was the original one which the soldiers started.

Revision of Old and New Testaments—I like to hear of it. It has always seemed that some of the alterations in the *New* are unpardonable, e.g., in the Lord's Prayer, "But deliver us from *evil*" is or was altered to the "*evil one.*"[294] We always want to shift everything on to the devil. That was a wise child who said to his little sister: "The devil wasn't thinking of you." Also in St Paul's conversion, they have omitted those memorable words which have saved so many: "Lord, what wilt Thou have me to do?"[295] How short the prayers in the New Testament are, how heartfelt.

Excuse again this long story. I did not have your letter till late last night because I had a lady with me and the servants were all at "Aladdin." But I hope this letter will be in time. A good journey to you and blessed Margaret. I am so glad she is "well" and love to all.

yours sincerely

F. Nightingale

---

294 Matt 6:13-14 in the Revised Bible (1881) reads "but deliver us from the evil one," with "or evil" in a sidenote.

295 Acts 9:6 in the King James, but not in the Revised.

Source: Letter, Wellcome (Claydon copy) Ms 9015/98

[printed address] 10 South Street
Park Lane, W.
28 May 1897

Dearest blessed Margaret [Verney]

How your blessed letter had a saving life for me. I wish you could have seen it. It was the spirit of Ascension Day. We have been so driven with the pressure of work and various anxieties increasing month by month that I have not had a moment's leisure to ascend in heart and mind. Your letter gave me a respite.

Do you know I have not had time to read but a very little of Mr Jowett's *Life*.[296] It seemed to me more of a book than a life. But when your dear letter came, I took up the second volume and read some pieces which seemed like life. I agree altogether in your criticism—the book is sadly broken up. It has not in consequence the warmth and livingness of the man who said, "Life is a splendid gift." But now I know you like it, I shall read it whenever I have a moment and feel like you.

ever dearest
your loving Aunt Florence

Source: Letter, Wellcome (Claydon copy) Ms 9015/99

[printed address] 10 South Street
Park Lane, W.
30 May 1897

My dear Edmund [Verney]

Blessed Margaret has been so good as to tell me some of the blessed things yourselves are doing or trying to do at and round Claydon. Success will be slow, but what ripens too fast, what is "forced," is not what lasts the longest. The people must always be the most essential part of our machinery—the people, but not fashion. May God speed you. Thank you very much for your last letter and for the copies of the abstract. Do you think I might have some more printed? They are very useful.

Thank you for the information about Greece. I have kept it quite private, and should be very glad of any more that you would be kind enough to give me. As for what I hear, it is all of the same complexion, the disastrous folly of the Greeks, only to be equalled by the folly of the London and Paris newspapers, hounding a vain people like the

296 Evelyn Abbott and Lewis Campbell, eds., *Life and Letters of Benjamin Jowett*, 1897.

Greeks on to war and ruin. Of course the Greeks thought that all Europe would back them. If Turkey had paid Greece to play into Turkey's hands, it could not have been better done.

The indiscipline of the Greek soldiers can only be rivalled by the fatuity with which nurses were sent out, picked up from every place, like specimens at an exhibition, without heads, without coherence of any sort, and now under a Mrs B.F.[297]

yours sincerely

F.N.

Source: Letter, Wellcome (Claydon copy) Ms 9015/100

[printed address] 10 South Street
Park Lane, W.
9 July 1897

My dear Edmund and Margaret [Verney]

God bless Mr Gordon,[298] and may he be all you hope and expect. He is like the spring; you have waited and prepared for him long.

Thank you very much for your offer of more copies of your "Rural Prosperity." And, if I am not too exorbitant, may I ask for fifty?

I have had a letter from a churlish, disagreeable, clever man, who cannot spell, but keeps a coffee room with meals, reading and newspaper room at an enormously growing place, all round Whatstandwell Station, two miles from Lea Hurst, where the masons and quarrymen, etc., besides passengers, "meal" with him. I sent him a copy and he is very much struck with it. He says it wants a good board school, to lead to its *practice*, and a workman's bank. We have no real power there and the landlord is an unenterprising man. But the Lea Board School is, thank God, almost all one could desire. . . .

I am so very sorry about the abolition of the health missioners of which Fred told me.[299] I seem to have a great deal more to say, but there is more still to do, which keeps me back. Goodbye, blessed Margaret and Edmund.

ever your loving

Aunt Florence

---

297 Ethel Bedford Fenwick (1857-1947), leader of the movement for nurses' registration.

298 Arthur Gordon, Vicar of Claydon 1897-1922.

299 Nightingale's work with Frederick Verney on rural health missioners is set out in *Public Health Care*.

Source: Letter, Wellcome (Claydon copy) Ms 9015/104

[printed address] 10 South Street
Park Lane, W.
19 November 1897

Thank you so very, very much, dearest [Margaret Verney], for offering to come up to me. It is so *very* kind, but I will not accept your kindness now yet.

I have had a charming letter from Maude, dated Girzeh, enjoying so much. But I dare say you hear from her very often. It takes me back to beautiful, absorbing Egypt, where I have been so deeply interested in Auld Lan[g] Syne—Egypt which never grows old. I am sure that she and Fred must have done the King a world of good, seeing them in an informal way. Will you, please, thank Edmund very much for his letter. I am so glad he likes Mr Gordon so much. Does Mr Gordon ever come up to London for a few days? I should like to see him some afternoon [for communion], if he does and if he likes it.

I am so glad Teneriffe has a P.O. (Has Ararat a P.O.?)

Ah my dear when a daughter marries,[300] the mother cuts out a bit of her heart, and with some of her heart's blood, gives it as Holy Communion at the wedding breakfast. (That is not profane, is it?) Aunt Florence's love to dear Ruth and thanks for her dear letter.

There is some daylight in London today for the first time for a long while. While they are all inventing electric light, could they not invent a little daylight? The birds don't get up now till afternoon tea. But I have a little tom-tit which goes round and round on the balcony rail and I hope will be faithful.

Best love to your twice a daughter, Lettice. I do so like to hear about your children.

ever yours
F.N.

---

300 Ellin Verney's marriage to William Henry Salmon took her to South Africa until 1901.

Source: Letter, Wellcome (Claydon copy) Ms 9015/105

[printed address] 10 South Street
Park Lane, W.
2 December 1897

Dearest Margaret [Verney]

Your birthday is a birthday of new joy to all of us. You were so very good as to offer to come and see me, and I was compelled to decline from pressure of work and engagements then. Would it be possible for you to come to London and to me this next week? I will make no new engagement till I hear from you. I hear of you scattering fruit and flowers over Wales.

In London 3:30 or even 3:00 only gives one half hour of daylight. Can you tell me a Christmas present for dear Ruth? Excuse pencil and haste.

your loving devotee
F.N.

Source: Letter, Wellcome (Claydon copy) Ms 9015/113

[printed address] 10 South Street
Park Lane, W.
24 February 1898

Dearest Margaret [Verney]

How good, how very good you are, always thinking of everybody. I shall be so glad to see Mr Gordon on Wednesday 2 March at 4:00 P.M., or 5:00 if that is more convenient to him, if he will kindly give us the sacrament at this house. I think of your confirmation today, but am so sorry that dear Kathleen could not be at it.

We parted with Sam Nightingale yesterday (elder brother of Louis whom you know and are kind to). Sam—he is a doctor—volunteered for Bombay. We were all very glad of his chivalry, though they had just taken a house for the two brothers and sister here. We understand now he is to be sent on to Madras, probably en route to some place where plague is worse. They are very chary of giving information where plague *is* worst.

We only knew on Monday evening that he was accepted (because he has also a *public health* diploma he was very acceptable, but he had to be examined) and he had to be off on Wednesday morning early. The age of chivalry is come when people *volunteer* NOT to kill but to cure.

Excuse interruptions. I am so hurried today but I will write again to you if you will allow me, enclosing a note to him. I don't like to lose my chance by delaying a day in answering your most kind note.

ever your affectionate

F. Nightingale

Source: Letter, Wellcome (Claydon copy) Ms 9015/122

[printed address] 10 South Street
Park Lane, W.
23 February 1899

My dear Edmund [Verney]

I have not yet thanked you for your most interesting remarks on the papers about workhouse nursing read at the Poor Law Conference and for your "draft" enclosed, by commenting upon them. But they do interest me very deeply and I hope soon to venture upon some comments, but of praise.

ever yours most truly

Aunt Florence

I do not remember whether you know Douglas Galton. I am sorry to say he is very ill.

I was so much obliged to dear Margaret for sending me her book.[301] She has done a great work. I am giving it to Miss Irby, who is in England, and to Shore Nightingale's widow, who is a woman who reads for a wonder.

F.N.

Today we really could see for a few hours. Otherwise London has been in darkness. Could not they invent daylight?

Source: Letter, Wellcome (Claydon copy) Ms 9015/124

[printed address] 10 South Street
Park Lane, W.
14 February 1900

All success be with you, my dear Lettice Librarian. I feel for your pangs, though I can't abide "specimens," "compendia" et id genus omne [all that sort]. As Macaulay says, every man ought to make his "compendium" for himself and the only "extracts" worth making are those that every man or woman makes for him or herself. When I

---

301 Volumes 3 and 4 of the *Memoirs of the Verney Family* were published in 1899, edited by Margaret Verney.

look at a big book called *Elegant Extracts,* which we had to learn from in my youth, I think it has left out all that is worth extracting and put in most of what is not. But it is not given to every man, woman, boy or girl to have time, money or taste to make extracts. Therefore I give in, specially as *you* recommend the work. You know a deal more literature than I do. And so I send £3.8, partly in order to save you wasting too much your precious time in canvassing.

I hear of your skating. I hope you don't follow the example of the man:

It so fell out
We *all* fell in;
The rest they ran away.

N.B. Did you ever, in choosing the extract to be read to the household at morning prayers, leave it to one to choose for herself because you were so hurried? She invariably chooses something odd, new or not to the purpose, instead of choosing one of the grand old bits in our sacred literature that the household *ought to* know. Adieu, my revered librarian.

ever your[s] affectionately
Aunt Florence

Source: Dictated letter, Wellcome (Claydon copy) Ms 9015/138

24 February [1900?]
Dear scoundrel of my heart [Margaret Verney]

Why won't you condescend to say how you are? I have a most touching letter of the Grand Duchess of Baden to show you, a most piteous one from Sir H. Acland, still harping on the Empress, one from Miss Crossland, who is well again, thank God. Miss *Beynon* was the lady, and now I remember all about her. And many others. O how I sympathize with you that I could do a good piece of work much more easily than answer all these letters, especially those which say the same thing month after month.

ever your loving
Wisdom of Solomon
and precious Bore
I want to show you, too, a letter from our schoolmaster.

Source: Note, Wellcome (Claydon copy) Ms 9015/127

[printed address] 10 South Street
Park Lane, W.
24 December 1900

To Margaret [Verney]

Best wishes to everybody from Florence Nightingale.

Source: Letter with postmarked envelope, Wellcome (Claydon copy) Ms 9015/128

[printed address] 10 South Street
Park Lane, W.
27 February 1901

My dearest Margaret [Verney]

Many, many thanks for your kind letter. I am afraid I am beyond doing anything, but you will do what you kindly say far better than I can. May I leave it to you?

I should very much like to see Ellin's letters, but could not read the shorthand. I cannot read scarcely at all myself now, but Ellin reads all my letters to me, and also papers or anything that might be sent to me. How very much dear Ellin must miss her baby. This war is indeed sad, and not near its end,[302] I fear.

How proud we are of dearest Ellin. What an admirable soldier's wife. Best love to all.

ever your loving
Aunt Florence

Source: Letter, Wellcome (Claydon copy) Ms 9015/130

[printed address] 10 South Street
Park Lane, W.
4 June 1901

Dearest Margaret [Verney]

I am returning with very many hearty thanks Ellin's letters, that is some of them—the last lot, which I have kept, to be read to me again. It is good to think, very good, that she is returning home [from South Africa].

My compliments to Dorothea.[303] You must indeed miss her when she is with her other Grandma. I wonder how she will welcome her Mama.

Now I must thank you very, very much, you and Edmund, for the exquisite beautiful roses you sent me on my birthday. They were loves.

---

302 The Boer War, 1899-1902.
303 Daughter of Ellin (Verney) Salmon.

I had a charming letter from dear Ruth on my birthday. She seems, I thought, very happy with Harry at Oxford.[304] With best love to all.

your ever loving

Aunt Florence

Source: Letter, Wellcome (Claydon copy) Ms 9015/132

[printed address] 10 South Street

Park Lane, W.

23 July 1901

Dearest Margaret [Verney]

How can I thank you enough for the lovely little photograph of Dorothea? She is indeed an angelic thing in miniature. It must be delightful to you to have Ellin and her together again.

In speaking of [the death of] Dr De'ath, one cannot express what his life has been, so full of self-sacrifice. One dare not think of what the loss will be to so many.

Thank you so much for all your interesting news—how kind of you to give it me. I am returning Ellin's capital S. African news. With much heartfelt love to all.

your Aunt Florence

Source: Letter with postmarked envelope, Wellcome (Claydon copy) Ms 9015/133

[printed address] 10 South Street

Park Lane, W.

14 November 1901

Dearest Margaret [Verney]

I am sorry not to have been able to write before my joy at the birth of dear Ellin's son. I trust that Ellin is going on all right, also her little boy [Christopher], and that Dorothea, whose approbation is essential, approves of her little brother. God bless them all.

I am now going to trouble you to do something for me. Would you get for me from Mr Payne five photographs of me? And if you would kindly send the bill on to me, I would then forward you the money. I hope I am not troubling you too much. With best love to all, hoping that you and all are well.

your loving

Aunt Florence

---

304 Ruth Verney passed her "Oxford University Examination for Women" in 1897 (Claydon House, Verney Collection 10/598).

Source: Letter with envelope, Wellcome (Claydon copy) Ms 9015/135

[printed address] 10 South Street
Park Lane, W.
10 March 1902

Dearest Margaret [Verney]

Many thanks for your very, very kind letter. I shall be more than delighted to see you on Wednesday 12th at 5. I am very sorry to hear that there is anything wrong with dear Ellin, but still I hope for good news from you.

It is indeed sad about [the death of] dear Mr Rathbone, and I must thank you dearly for your kind sympathy. With best love to Ellin and yourself.

ever your loving
Aunt Florence

Source: Letter, Wellcome (Claydon copy) Ms 9015/136

[printed address] 10 South Street
Park Lane, W.
24 April 1902

Dearest Margaret [Verney]

I shall be more than delighted to see Lettice on Saturday 26th at 5 o'clock. I am not quite sure whether I said anything to Ruth about coming on Saturday, but I am sure she will not mind my putting her off if I did so for Lettice, as I have seen Ruth so lately. And I will see her again the first opportunity. I was so pleased to see both Harry and Ruth. Hoping you are all well. With much love

your affectionate
Aunt Florence

Source: Letter, Wellcome (Claydon copy) Ms 9015/137

[printed address] 10 South Street
Park Lane, W.
15 May 1902

Dearest Edmund [Verney]

One little line to thank you and Margaret for the lovely flowers which you brought me on my poor old birthday. Thank you so very much. I am so glad that everything is so flourishing at the Claydons. With much love and so many thanks for all.

your affectionate
Aunt Florence

Frederick and Maude Verney

Editor: Nightingale took an interest in young Fred Verney's studies and career (first as a vicar, then a lawyer and later still an MP), as references in other family correspondence have already shown and see *Society and Politics* on his political career. Material on his lengthy trip (he was secretary to the Siamese delegation in London) with Prince Damrong of Siam in 1892 is also related in *Society and Politics*. Nightingale was evidently fond of Fred, his wife and their children. She accepted their invitation to use their country home, Pine Acres, for a two-week convalescent stay, alone, in 1887. The letters here, mainly about Frederick, begin with his childhood and schooling and go on to "business." Some correspondence with Maude Verney will appear in *Women*. The selection here represents only a very small fraction of the surviving correspondence: eight volumes in the British Library.

Source: Letter, Wellcome (Claydon copy) Ms 8997/80

Burlington St.

13 November 1858

My dear love [Parthenope Verney]

When you told me that your youngest boy [stepson Fred Verney] was going to Harrow, I had a very strong opinion on the subject, but I did not like to express it, because I did not know whether it was trustworthy. On comparing it however with that of men, of whom I am allowed to mention Clough, I find that other people's opinions are so exactly like mine that I think it may be worth mentioning. The opinion is that Harrow turns out nice boys but not manly boys, that Dr Vaughan's is not a manly mind, that he is devoured by the love of appearances, that he has a timidity which stands him in lieu of conscience, that he is an elegant scholar and most accomplished schoolmaster, but that vanities and not realities are his masters. The school is a far more aristocratic and expensive one than Rugby. Temple is Master of Rugby[305]—I should like much to send a boy to Rugby, rather to send one to Eton, not at all to Harrow. I should expect a man to come out of Rugby, a gentleman out of Eton, and a dilettante out of Harrow. I ought perhaps to add that my opinion of Dr Vaughn is formed from quite other sources than Mr Stanley's and that I don't know what, if any, part he took in that matter.

---

305 Frederick Temple (1821-1902), later Bishop of London and Archbishop of Canterbury.

I have no doubt that, if Sir Harry has made up his mind to Harrow, he has done it on quite sufficient sources of information.[306] Take this for what it is worth and no more.

F.

Source: Letter, Wellcome (Claydon copy) Ms 8998/32

23 August 1860

My dear [Parthenope Verney]

I hope Freddy [Verney] is not too grand to read Mr Clough's little Plutarch, much better saints these than some of the "saints" in the "calendar" and who have formed a much better English character than the latter have a French. I send it for Freddy's consideration.

ever your F.

Source: Letter, Wellcome (Claydon copy) Ms 8999/25

30 Old Burlington Street, W.
14 June 1861

My dear Sir Harry [Verney]

. . . I send a "tip" (£1) to my (step) nephew Freddy, believing that "tips" give a great deal of pleasure, which people do not think enough of giving in this life, and do very little harm. If it were not so near the holidays it should be more.

I hope your daughter is pretty well.

yours affectionately

F.N.

Source: Letter to Parthenope Verney, Wellcome (Claydon copy) Ms 8999/43

9 December 1861

Would Freddy at Harrow like one of my little cats? And would it have any chance of a quiet life with the boys?

I should send a tom because the ladies are too delicate.

F.

Source: Letter, Wellcome (Claydon copy) Ms 9000/64

13 December 1862

My dear Sir Harry [Verney]

I have not got you much information for Freddy's tutors. Mr Jowett wrote to Torquay to inquire. Mr Warner's (you have already heard of

---

306 Frederick Verney in fact was sent to Harrow.

it) he thinks good but too young for Freddy. He recommends highly the Rev G. Venables, Bonchurch, Isle of Wight (formerly curate to Archdeacon Hare, Herstmonceux), as a good and conscientious man, a good classic and who takes pupils to prepare for *Oxford.*

He adds sorrowfully, that *good* tutors are hard to find anywhere, more particularly if you are tied to a place. He will inquire farther.

ever yours

F.N.

Source: Letter, ADD Mss 68882 ff64-65

Embley
Romsey
9 February 1872

My dear boy Mr Fred [Verney]

I make an opportunity (of restoring to you a letter, which I think you told me "to keep till called for") to congratulate Middlesboro'[307] and the Lady Maude upon your great doings there. I knew you would be successful, in the higher success.

A clergyman without real thought about any kind of knowledge— human or divine, or personal interest in his fellow creatures—is sure to fail and ought to fail, however many bishops' hands he may have had on his head. For a clergyman may call himself a clergyman, but he will never really be anything unless he has a knowledge of business and of human nature and has worked out in his own mind some lessons or truths which he is able to impart to others (such as clubs and the like). But if he *is* a real clergyman, what glorious opportunities he has—call them secular, if you please—and the less he is bound to conventionalism, the better, whether like Bishop Patteson[308] he gives his life for the "little naked wretches" *he* was so fond of, whether he works nearer home, as you do, putting in light in our dark overgrown towns.

However, I'm not going to preach. And as an atonement, I send you two letters about your belongings, which please return to F.N. here.

I am greatly distressed about Emily's fever, which I fear she has not lost at Athens. She has suffered as everyone does who goes to Malta.

---

307 Where he served as a priest 1871-73.
308 John Coleridge Patteson, Missionary Bishop of the Melanesian Islands.

They have allowed the rock to become a dirty sodden sponge and hence the fevers. . . . My writing days are over and I will ask your leave to finish by being now as ever

your and Maude's loving
and admiring old aunt
Florence Nightingale

I must add, though I scarcely need to add, that I entirely agree with your Keble College friend that the "secular" duties must really be inspired by love of God and man, or they will be "drowned in bustle," but that the "reality" of that love is best shown and known among the "unconventional" and in all kinds of methods for raising them morally, "secularly" and spiritually, I also think.

Source: Letter, Wellcome (Claydon copy) Ms 9005/129

Embley
Romsey
13 April 1872

My dear Sir Harry [Verney]

My father and mother desire me to ask you to be so good as to say to Maude, Mrs Fred Verney, *how very much* pleasure it would give them if she would come and finish her convalescence here. There would be *no one* [to] disturb her quietude. She should be out of doors as much as she liked—the country is now lovely and the bright weather. She should come *at the time* she likes and stay *as long as* she likes and *do what* she likes. Pray promote this, if possible. In great haste.

ever yours affectionately
Florence Nightingale

Source: Postscript to a letter to Sir Harry Verney, Wellcome (Claydon copy) Ms 9008/144

23 April 1881

. . . I should like much if Fred will send me a copy of his review of the *Irish Land Bill.*

Source: Letter, Add Mss 68883 ff160-62

10 South St.
11 November 1885

My dear Mr Fred [Verney]

On Sunday next my doors will be closed to everyone but you. "Blow me if I let anyone else in, angelic or diabolical, but you." (I have already put off the Lea assistant schoolmistress coming up to London to me till a later Sunday.)

I am miserable because Sir Harry is so unhappy. It is his brother much more than P. who pitches into him about his candidate sons and the "church in danger"! And I can't help thinking that, if he, Sir Harry, could but see it so, it is a mistake, a hopeless confusion on both sides whether disestablishment includes disendowment, on Lord Grey's[309] side a more than hopeless confusion between disestablishment and "overthrow" of the church, including "overthrow" of all religion! (sic).

And, but I must stop—I read your address and like Warren Hastings[310] I think you must say: "I am astonished at my own moderation." I hope Sir Harry may see it so, but he complains of Mr Calvert's Toryism and then lets his "old Whiggism" be guided by it. If you could but be "moderate" with *him*!

He says he wishes so much to "exert himself for" Captain Verney and you, but, as he cannot, being an "old Whig" and you "radicals" he wishes he were "out of the way"!! He is quite miserable.

Some of the best friends of the church, and I think I am one, consider that her power for good would be increased by disestablishment! She must have a poor opinion of herself to be so frightened. But all must wish that this agitation had not come on now. . . .

Source: Letter, ADD Mss 68884 ff80-82

10 South St.
28 June 1886

Dearest Maude [Verney]

I was very glad to see Mr Fred, but afraid he had a slight cold, which however I hope will come to nothing. Or rather I think he is coming to great good; let what will happen.

We had so much to talk about that I did not mention to him that Surgeon-Major Evatt is "standing" on the Liberal side (Unionist Home Ruler) at Woolwich—Dr Evatt is *the* reformer of the Army Medical Department, of Army medical administration, a man of singular talent in the reforming administrative line, and in speaking. He asked me

---

309 Henry George Grey (1802-94), 3rd Earl Grey; see his letter on disestablishment in the *Times* 9 November 1885.
310 Warren Hastings (1732-1818), governor of Bengal, impeached in 1788 for "high crimes and misdeamours" but acquitted by the House of Lords.

for "a line," of course.[311] I know nothing of his chances (but should have liked to talk him over with Mr Fred) in unseating the present C[onservative] member, Hughes (?). I am all on the administrative "go" for India, for Army medical, etc.

Sir Harry comes tomorrow till Thursday, when he attends the Conference on Imperial Federation, on Wednesday the Gordon Boys' Home Committee. You saw the letter of the Prince of Wales to the Duke of Buckingham, prompted by Mr Fred, in the *Daily News*. Sir Harry has about eight meetings on Wednesday.

I am greatly alarmed. Sir H. is a magistrate and I think my sister will have me taken up. The *Pall Mall Gazette* has done worse than I hinted to Mr Fred. It has put in my letter to Dadabhai Naoroji, with a heading "Letter to the Electors of Holborn," too bad, and side by side with its own expressions of "hatred to Chamberlain" and "detestation of Lord Salisbury." Que diable allais-je faire dans cette galère?[312] [what the devil could I do in this mess?] Those "hatreds" are certainly not mine. I shall be imprisoned in a Claydon dungeon.

I cry Hurra! to you with all my might. Don't you hear me afar off? I think it is a grand thing to be making speeches on *principles*. Thank you so much for your lovely views of Bath. I cry again, Goodspeed!

ever your loving

Aunt Florence

I have two pieces of good news for you: one that a Home Missions clergyman, without a church but only a room, is making quite a reformation among the very worst in the circle round our St Marylebone Infirmary. He has something every day, not only on Sundays. Among other things he is forming a Provident and Temperance Union, called the Sisters of the Phoenix Society, which admits the very poorest women, and which is begun to be managed by themselves with a committee elected by themselves. *He* is as poor as a rat and has of course three children every year.

The other is that our nurses at St Marylebone Infirmary are reviving the desire of a Provident Union among all trained nurses, for granting pensions and for sick pay, *upon the principle of never drawing out their money*, but, whether they cease to subscribe, upon marriage, or giving up the profession, or not, leaving whatever they *have* subscribed in for the Common Fund. You may perhaps remember that our Edinburgh nurses said the same thing.

---

311 For Nightingale's letter of endorsement see *Society and Politics*.
312 Molière, *Les Fourberies de Scapin* II.5.

Source: Note to Maude Verney, Add Mss 45808 ff30-31

2 February 1888

Life: How tragic is this world and how comic, how grave and how grotesque—what dreadful things people do and what idiotic things—how our lives, our minds, our happiness seem to hang by a thread, and how awful this, did we not know that Infinite Love has spun this thread, irresistible as Love. What a commonplace trivial surface has this life and everywhere crop up under one's feet the most unexpected tragedies, which perhaps after all are less tragic than the trivialities and indifference over a volcano.

I remember when I entered hospital life half the nurses were fallen women and the other half deserted wives. Perhaps every one of those wives had her tragedy, though a sordid one, and every one of the fallen women, though a sinful one. The best wardmaster in Scutari had eight wives—I mean eight wives alive—at different stations. And he regularly sent home through me 5/ a week out of a scanty pay to the child of a ninth who was not his wife's, a mere schoolgirl out of Mrs Σ [Bracebridge]'s school. He was tried when he came home at Warwick Assizes for what was euphoniously called bigamy, but was octogamy. He was not a bad fellow—many honest wives are more maltreated than his.

There were nine tragedies in one opera comique. Everyone perhaps has a skeleton in the house or in the lunatic asylum or somewhere. The greatest sorrows are those one can never speak of, as has been said. I have known sorrows unspeakable in many a hospital, many a house, many a workhouse. I think madness is the worst. I must not take to moralizing [breaks off]

Source: Letter, Add Mss 68888 ff62-63

[printed address] 10 South Street
Park Lane, W.
29 June 1895

My dearest Fred [Verney]

You left your coat here last night, which I send. I hope you got some dinner sometime. You "is to take your beer reg'lar."

I do "pray" and "thank" for you, my dearest Fred. I have been so much struck by these Mohammedans' call to prayer. It is not, "Listen, God, I'm going to 'pray.' " Still less, "I'm putting on a new hat to go to church." It is imploring God to take the whole thing into His own hands. Like St John of the Cross, a Spaniard of the sixteenth century, who said: Prayer is not to ask God to do what we want, but to ask Him what He wants us to do. All success attend you.

ever your loving

Aunt Florence

What a curious selection: Lord Lansdowne for the War Office and Lord George Hamilton for the India Office.

George Hope and Harry Lloyd Verney

Editor: There is much less correspondence with George Hope Lloyd (1842-96), the middle surviving son of Harry Verney, who was married to Harriet Morforwyn Hinde and father of five children, notably of Harry Lloyd Verney, with and about whom there are several interesting letters. George Verney pursued a military career and even it seems occasionally provided Nightingale with information although the two were never close. Nightingale letters to him were sold at auction in 2001 and so far have not become available to scholars. Among the numerous descendants of George Verney's five children are two Florences, one born in 1977 and one in 1994 (there is also one Florence from the Fred Verneys).

Source: Letter to Parthenope Verney, Wellcome (Claydon copy) Ms 8998/39

2 December 1860

. . . I liked George much. Want of steadiness and vanity are written on his face. But there is more high purpose, more idea of doing the world's work, more knowledge of and interest in interesting things than there was in all our boys at his age. I am afraid their highest idea, when they had one, was getting a high class at Cambridge. I thought him also much more gentlemanlike than boys in general, even than boys in the Army, of whom I have seen a great deal. He asked me to write him any questions I wished to have answered, which of course I shall. Perhaps you will send me a proper direction.

Poor lad! he is going for ten years. We have numberless Indian returns already come in, of which he looked at some.

ever your F.

Source: Unsigned letter, Wellcome (Claydon copy) Ms 9001/195

[1865]

Dearie [Parthenope Verney]

I am afraid G[eorge Verney] is behaving like a lunatic. But I have a great sympathy for a boy in the Army who wants to marry, knowing as I do that all the other boys in the Army (and many out of it too) want to do something just the reverse, especially in India. I have no doubt there is, as you say, a misgiving that Miss H[inde] won't wait, but even this is more respectable than the more usual thing I won't particularly specify.

As for Emily writing to Miss H., it was a great imprudence but one excusable at twenty-one, much better than the contrary extreme of worldly prudence (which *combined with* immoral notions in the young people of this day is what *I* most often see!) *She* will be sure to come round.

Source: Letter to Margaret Verney, Wellcome (Claydon copy) Ms 9013/124

10 December 1890

. . . I was going to write Ellin such a cheerful letter about Harry *Lloyd* as they call him. But he had a little accident yesterday afternoon with gunpowder in his own room at Mr Higham's. The face is burnt and the wrists and the *upper* (only) part of the neck. One eye is certainly safe *and they believe the other,* but the eyelid is of course too swollen at present to see. He had a good night and is quite cheerful. . . . This morning he has scarcely any pain, but the face is all covered up of course. . . .

Source: Letter, Wellcome (Claydon copy) Ms 9013/134

Claydon
10 January 1891

Dearest Margaret [Verney]

. . . All the grandchildren have the recuperative powers of the dear Grandpapa, it seems. I say it is quite improper and "contrairy to scriptur, which says seventy is the proper age of man." There's that boy Harry Lloyd! He's reading the newspaper today!!! Wanting to get up, but forbidden!! Can't chew yet, or open his mouth or swallow anything but soup or bread and milk, but isn't to have the honours of a bulletin any more!! Contraction the real danger. . . .

Source: Letter to Margaret Verney, Wellcome (Claydon copy) Ms 9014/113

16 July 1893

. . . Everything is being done by you that can be done. Does his father's example, at the last of peace and trust and love move him at all? . . . Harry Lloyd writes to me: "When our dear father is taken away from us we shall only be able to remember him as the best and kindest of fathers that sons ever had. He has been far too kind and loving to us boys." . . . We must remember how much George's moral state has to depend on the physical state of the heart. But it is all Christ's work on the hidden life. . . .

Source: From a letter to Margaret Verney, Wellcome (Claydon copy) Ms 9015/9

27 January 1895

. . . Harry Lloyd came last evening, as you know. As he was moping in his own room I asked him to visit me. "O," says he, "Ellin is getting quite dissipated." "Ah," says I, in a tone of extremest melancholy, "She is not like you and me, quiet, steady people, who always stick to our work, and never go stravaging about the country after balls and parties." "Stravaging." What's that? Stravaging is - - stravaging. It's a word of high antiquity, before the time of dictionaries, probably derived from the Phoenician. Stravaging is Harry Lloyd and Harry Lloyd is stravaging. But no more nonsense now. . . .

Source: Letter to Margaret Verney, Wellcome (Claydon copy) Ms 9015/45

27 May 1895

. . . I have had a nice note from Harry Lloyd but, as you say, it is so difficult to help him. . . .

Source: Letter, Wellcome (Claydon copy) Ms 9015/74

[printed address] 10 South Street
Park Lane, W.
16 June 1896

Dearest blessed Margaret [Verney]

I am desired to send on poor Morforwyn's feeling letter to you. You must feel some happiness at what you were to that poor fellow who is gone [George Hope Verney], winning him to the paths of peace, and your work in God, God will now perfect Himself. And after you Ellin did him good.

It was curious what influence Ellin had over poor, poor Morfy. I sometimes thought Morfy consulted her as if Ellin were her grand-mama. Morfy, I think, will not want to shut herself up. She is so like a woman in the scriptures who collects all her friends to weep with her.

But the person perhaps I think most of is good Harry Lloyd. He wrote me such a nice little letter from the shaking train. O that he may rise now to the responsibilities of life—he has such good feelings. The world is a little better for him being in it, because he is so full of sympathy. But it ought to be a *great deal* the better for him and it isn't. He is too fond of popularity. My heart is full of them all, so please forgive me. With love to all, dearest blessed Margaret

ever your loving Aunt Florence

Source: Letter to Margaret Verney, Wellcome (Claydon copy) Ms 9015/75

20 June 1896

. . . I wish, oh how I wish that some life could be made for Harry [Lloyd Verney]. He has absolutely no application for anything but dancing. And he wants to play the rich young man and "bon parti." His father did not wish him to return to Vienna. And, as you say of the other, the things he, Harry, says make one's hair stand on end; he wants to be a private secretary, but of a Cabinet minister,[313] if you please!!! . . .

Source: Letter to Margaret and Edmund Verney, Wellcome (Claydon copy) Ms 9015/100

9 July 1897

. . . I have two letters from Harry Lloyd at the British Legation in Athens. He seems getting on very well and it sets him on his legs. I only hope the Turks are not set on their legs too. . . .

Godchildren and Namesakes

Editor: Quite apart from her many godchildren and namesakes from after the Crimean War, Nightingale had two godchildren before she became famous: Florence Howe later Hall (1845-1922), daughter of her friends Dr Samuel Gridley Howe and Julia Ward Howe, and Carl Fliedner (1853-1930), son of Pastor and Mrs Fliedner. For both of these children Nightingale was an official godmother, although she did not attend the baptisms (in the United States and Germany respectively). For Carl Fliedner she not only sent gifts and later organized references for a medical appointment, but she contributed money for his upbringing.[314] She had early declined to be godmother to a Herbert infant, for reasons set out in the letter to Pastor Fliedner below. Yet she did later become godmother to other Church of England families, notably the Edmund Verneys (Ruth Florence Verney and Harry Calvert Verney, with both of whom there is correspondence below) and Fred Verney's Kathleen. She stood godmother to the son of her colleague Florence Lees Craven, whose husband was a Church of England clergyman (to and about whom there is correspondence). She

---

313 In fact he held many posts in the royal household, was knighted, and was private secretary to Queen Mary.
314 Letter to Harry Verney 12 May 1869, Wellcome (Claydon copy) Ms 9003/105.

was godmother to a daughter of her favourite suitor, Richard Monckton Milnes, Florence Ellen. Nightingale met her and her sister occasionally, sent them books and inquired after them.[315]

Nightingale agreed in 1861 to become godmother to Herbert Galton, named after Sidney Herbert, the son of her cousin Marianne (Nicholson) and Douglas Galton, who had worked with Sidney Herbert at the War Office. Nightingale described the boy's unhappy death in 1862 as a deep loss to Galton (see a letter to her mother p 150 above). She is said to have been the godmother of Florence Paget, daughter of Frances Paget (1834-1912) and granddaughter of the Rev Richard Garth of Farnham, whom Nightingale knew through visits to the poor around Waverley Abbey, the Nicholson home.[316]

Nightingale became godmother to the granddaughter of her good friend and collaborator, Sir John McNeill, Florence (Stewart) Macalister. There is no surviving correspondence to her, but references only and messages. She wrote a biography of McNeill which includes correspondence with Nightingale.[317] It seems, from a letter below and a gift, that Nightingale was also godmother to a grandson of Sir John McNeill. According to Cook (*Life* 2:389), Nightingale was godmother to Malcolm, son of Hugh Bonham Carter, but there is no correspondence regarding this. She was godmother to another Bonham Carter, Edith, with whom there is nursing correspondence.

At least three children in her own extended family were named after her: Florence Anne Mary Clough, "Flossie" (1858-c1901); Florence Nightingale Shore, daughter of William Entwistle Shore, born 1863, but who died a few days later;[318] and a second Florence Nightingale Shore (c1864-c1919), daughter of Offley Bohun Shore, who was also a godchild (several of her letters have survived, but not Nightingale's replies). This last godchild expressed her childhood desire "to become a hospital nurse . . . probably inspired by your kind interest in being my godmother." In asking for advice on obtaining training she stated that her "ultimate hopes are to become an Army nurse as you were."[319] In fact she trained as a district nurse at the Bloomsbury

---

315 See correspondence with their father in *Society and Politics*.
316 "Florence Nightingale and Farnham," Museum of Farnham, Farnham Surrey.
317 Florence Macalister, *Memoir of the Right Hon Sir John McNeill, and of His Second Wife Elizabeth Wilson*.
318 Family tree, Sheffield City Archives, LC 171.
319 Undated letter, Add Mss 45811 ff166-67.

House for District Work. Nightingale met with her and and gave her a much-appreciated clock before she went to her first post in Reading. Florence N. Shore seems to have had some of the spirit of her god-mother, for she told her: "I do indeed mean to put my whole heart into my work and hope that I may be permitted to be of a little use and comfort to some of my fellow creatures."[320]

Many other children were named after Nightingale for whom she was in no way a godmother, and whether or not permission was sought is not known. Two of these namesakes were the children of close colleagues. There is only a brief exchange of letters with Florence Farr (c1862-1917), daughter of William Farr (with whom there is a great deal of correspondence), a successful actress, notably playing the heroine in George Bernard Shaw's first play in 1892, and the person for whom Shaw wrote his famous anti-war satire, *Arms and the Man.* Eleanor Florence Rathbone (1872-1946) was the daughter of her good friend and collaborator, William Rathbone, and herself a Member of Parliament. She was a leading and effective advocate for family allowances, worked on refugee issues and to improve the situation of women in India. There is no known correspondence with her.

Of the innumerable children named after her whom she did not know, at least one made contact to ask for help: Florence Nightingale Giles. Two letters regarding her appear in "Waifs and Strays" below. Other namesakes with less pressing needs also made contact, for example a Florence Nightingale Fleming from Toronto, who at age sixteen wrote asking for her autograph.[321] Here we report correspondence to and about godchildren. The order is chronological except that letters to the same person are kept together. It is not clear who the possible godchild of 1855 might have been as the date does not match those of any of the known namesakes.

Source: Unsigned letter, Wellcome (Claydon copy) Ms 8995/56

Castle Hospital
Balaclava
28 October 1855

... I declined being godmother to the child of my best friends, the Sidney Herberts (who were so good as to ask me) *because of* not mak-

---

320 Letter 9 December 1897, Add Mss 45815 ff456-47, and see 10 October 1897 ff334-34.
321 Letter 28 May 1898, Add Mss 45815 ff66-67.

ing a solemn promise where one has neither the power nor the right to perform it. It is a well-meant farce which one ought not to play in, so I cannot be the godmother now, though I am pleased and more than pleased to be remembered (out in Crim Tartary) at my dear own home. If they like to name the child after one who has struggled through and suffered disappointment and disgust such as I am fain to think falls to the lot of few (*can* fall, I should hope, to *very* few), I shall be pleased. It will not make the poor child be like me and I would not augur it such a fate. . . .

Source: Laura E. Richards and Maud Howe Elliott, assisted by Florence Howe Hall, *Julia Ward Howe 1819-1910* 1:112-13. A baptismal present of a golden cup was sent with the letter.

Embley
26 December [1844]

I cannot pretend to express, my dear kind friends, how touched and pleased I was by such a remembrance of me as that of your child's name. . . . If I could live to justify your opinion of me, it would have been enough to have lived for, and such thoughts as that of your goodness are great thoughts, "strong to consume small troubles" which should bear us up on the wings of the eagle, like Guido's Ganymede,[322] up to the feet of the God, there to take what work he has for us to do for him. I shall hope to see my little Florence before long in this world, but if not, I trust there is a tie formed between us which will continue in eternity—if she is like you I shall know her again there, without her body on, perhaps the better for not having known her here with it.

Source: Incomplete letter, Harvard University, Houghton Library

Embley
20 May [after 1845]

My dearest Friend [Julia Ward Howe[323]]

I have been too busy or too lazy (which is the same thing) to write this last month to explain that the Shakespeare Mr Mills[324] took for me

---

322 Guido Reni's painting, in Vienna.
323 Julia Ward Howe (1819-1910), author of the "Battle Hymn of the Republic" and "John Brown's Body," abolitionist and suffragist. Ward Howe visited London in 1887, at which time Nightingale wrote her, but the two did not meet.
324 Arthur Mills (1816-98) MP, family friend.

across the Atlantic, is for my little namesake (you see what wonderful precocity I expect from your offspring) and that the bracelet of my hair which you were gracious enough to ask for, and I ungracious enough to forget, is for you. (You will receive it by another opportunity; it was not finished in time to go by Mr Mills.) It is a very little one—I considering that there must be small room upon your arm occupied by souvenirs which have a better claim than mine, for another, and yet wishing for my own place there, be it ever so small, yet mine and irremovable, I had the prudence to have a very tiny one made, on the principle of that wise book, which explains the, to us otherwise unintelligible, "poverty of spirit" by telling us to use this world as not abusing it. Am I too presumptuous? . . .

How do your two little cherubim do? Though, as, upon consulting the "Hebrew Greek," we find cherubim to mean knowing ones or fullness of knowledge, it may be doubted whether your cherub (big one or little one) according to strict etymology, is entitled to the term of a knowing one. Nature, who has provided all other animals with the talent of self-preservation, cats with claws and us with thick sculls, allows these to indulge in all sorts of saltatory exhibitions, leaving to us the entire care of the vital spark during the same. They are perpetually throwing themselves off the eminence of a stool or a table into the arms of Providence, for I'm sure I don't know what else they trust to. I wonder if the day will come when I shall ever see them or you again. I am just having a seal ring engraved with a kneeling woman and the words Ich warte, and round the ring, Ich warte bis zum Tode, bis zur Ewigkeit [I wait until death, until eternity], which I think but too symbolical of my intercourse with you and yours. . . . Once more farewell and with all our best remembrances I am

ever yours, dear friends
Florence Nightingale

Source: Letter, Fachbibliothek für Frauendiakonie und Fliednerarchiv, Kaiserswerth FA II K b 3

Upper Harley St.
London
le 10 Septembre 1853

Lieber Herr Pastor [Dear Pastor Fliedner]

[trans. from French] I would be delighted to serve as godmother to your dear new arrival in the world. May God bless him and guide him in the way his father and mother have passed. I have always refused to be godmother in England, where neither our law or customs authorize us to do what we promise before God to do for our godchildren. But here, where I have no desire but that my godson follow his father's footsteps, it seems that I can accept with joy and appreciation what you have so kindly asked me. I bring him every day before God, of whom he is already a son.

I hope that his mother is well. Please give her my congratulations and affectionate regards. I am so happy that her hour of danger and pain is over. . . . Pray for me, dear Pastor, and accept my eternal gratitude.

Florence Nightingale

Source: Letter, Fachbibliothek für Frauendiakonie und Fliednerarchiv, Kaiserswerth

10 South Street
Park Lane, W.
London
19 November 1880

My very dear godson [Carl Fliedner]

I only received your letter last night. It was forwarded to me in Derbyshire where I am now. I have written pressingly to the Committee of the German Hospital in London by this morning's post as to your candidature for the house surgeoncy and have enclosed it to our secretary in London, urging him to send it to some influential member. I have also written to my brother-in-law, Sir Harry Verney, by this morning's post, who is well acquainted with the German ambassador here, who is a patron of the hospital, urging him to push your candidature.

The worst of it is that there is no time for anything more, if the election is on Monday or Tuesday next, for few people are now in London. I wish I had had a week or a fortnight to press it. You have, I assure you, my dear godson, my best wishes that you should succeed and I bid you "Godspeed" with all my heart and soul. But you must not be disappointed if you do not. For I take it there is a crowd of candidates, many of a good deal of experience. But God will provide.

Excuse me for writing in English. I am so hurried to save this post. Overwork and increased illness—and I have come into Derbyshire for *work*—keep up a severe pressure upon me, *but God is good.*

Source: Letter, Fachbibliothek für Frauendiakonie und Fliednerarchiv, Kaiserswerth Rep XII 8

10 South Street
Park Lane
London, W.
2 December 1880

My dear godson [Carl Fliedner]

I am truly sorry for the disappointment at the German hospital at Dalston. Sir James Paget who, with Count Münster, Baron Ernest Bunsen, the Committee, Dr Weber and Dr Wallbaum, was among those written to on your behalf, says: "There was for his father's sake as well as for his own a very strong wish that Dr Carl Fliedner may be elected." But, he says, Dr Weber has "greatly surprised me by telling me of the kind of men, including Dr Fliedner, men of really marked scientific ability, who are candidates for this post." As you will have heard, Dr August Schreiber of Augsburg, at present first assistant at the hospital at Munich, has been elected as the new Resident Medical Officer for this German hospital at Dalston.

I regret it the more, my dear godson, because it will deprive me of the pleasure of seeing you in London. But we will trust that God, who does all things right, will open a path for you to do Him much good service in the medical career, one of the noblest careers which exists.

Excuse me that I write in English. Give my best and most respectful love to her whom I always hold in remembrance, your dear mother, and all my friends at Kaiserswerth—dear old Kaiserswerth. God bless you. In haste.

ever your affectionate godmother

Florence Nightingale

I lost my dear mother this year in London—my father has been dead six years. She went to rejoin him this spring where I hope to follow in God's good time.

F.N.

God bless you and He *will* bless you and prosper your medical career. It is a noble one. In haste.

ever your affectionate godmother

(with warm and constant love and remembrance to the Pastorin [pastor's wife] Fliedner and all my friends at Kaiserswerth)

Florence Nightingale

Source: Letter, London Metropolitan Archives H1/ST/NC3/SU131

30 Old Burlington St.
London, W.
29 August 1860

My dear Sir John McNeill

. . . I send per book post to Mrs Stewart (which will you present with my love?) a copy of Mr Clough's translation of some of Plutarch's *Lives* for the infant original of the photographs, when he can read it.

I believe there are much worse "saints" in the calendar than there are in Plutarch, and did French boys read Plutarch, as we used to do, when I was young, I don't believe the present Emperor could be on the throne. . . . Ever my dear Sir John,

yours gratefully and affectionately

Florence Nightingale

Source: Letter to Margaret Verney, Wellcome (Claydon copy) Ms 9007/264

12 December 1879

God speed the dear mother and welcome the babe (Ruth). I give her joy and give ourselves joy with all my heart and soul. I only heard of the prosperous event yesterday. Thank God for it. My love to the God-blessed newcomer.

Great Aunt Florence

Source: Letter on small cards with envelope, Florence Nightingale Museum LDFNM 0546 to Verney, Rhianva, Bangor 8/11/83

[printed address] 10 South Street
Park Lane, W.
8 November 1888

Dear little Ruth [Verney]

I send you a portrait and an account of a friend of mine, the dog Bob, who came to see me here. He saved the lives of the men in the Eira, as you will see in the account.[325] The Eira was a ship which a cousin of Grandmama's and Aunt Florence's fitted out to go and make discoveries in the Arctic seas, where it is all snow and ice, without a blade of grass. And he, the man, not the dog, commanded the ship himself, as Father might do. They went on till the poor Eira was pinched in the ice and went down in an hour and a quarter. But Uncle Ben brought his twenty-five men and his dog, a cat, a bird and a

---

325 For an account of Benjamin Leigh Smith's Arctic discoveries and the shipwreck in 1882 see A.W. Greely, *Handbook of Arctic Discoveries* 200-01.

musical box safe to shore, I mean to ice. There they lived all the dark, dark, winter.

You will see how Bob caught their dinners. Uncle Ben told me: He came in like a gentleman and laid his head in my lap, and then lay down at my feet. I had a plate of milk for him, but the man (in the picture), who came with him, said he never ate out of hours and never asked for any of the dinners he got killed for the men, more than his share. Bob is as modest as he is brave. He could not bear being stared at by the people in the Fisheries Exhibition, where he was taken with the boat of the Eira. They were then obliged to leave him at home.

Goodbye, dear little goddaughter, Ruth, and Ellin and Lettice and Harry. Kiss Mother for
your affectionate godmother
Aunt Florence

Source: Letter to Margaret Verney, Wellcome (Claydon copy) Ms 9013/80

[printed address] Claydon House
Bucks
20 September 1890
7:00 A.M.

... [Ruth] told me about her longings to be a nurse, but I talk about birds and not nurses. ... I told Ruth about your teaching me botany. She says Harry knows more botany than she does, but she knows about leaves and pollen and bees. And we asked one another: do wasps carry pollen? ...

Source: Letter to Margaret Verney, Wellcome (Claydon copy) Ms 9013/97

21 October 1890

... My goddaughter *is* to practise *whistling intervals.* It is not "vulgar," she does not whistle, "My wife's at the Marquis of Granby." Perhaps she is a great whistling genius. I never heard anybody do it before, like a great singer practising difficult intervals. ...

Source: Letter, ADD Mss 45810 ff110-12

Claydon
5 November 1890
Inkermann Day

My dearest Ruth [Verney]

I am so glad the "paw" is better. Thank you very much for dear Lettice's nice letter. I have heard nothing this morning yet. You know I had a telegram last night from [your] mother, safe at Bridge St., having left Lettice, all safe, with [your] father. She sent her "dear love." She is not coming here, I am afraid, but is for Liverpool today. Perhaps we should have eaten her up, if she had come here.

This is a greater day than Gunpowder Treason Day [Guy Fawkes Day]. It is Inkermann Day thirty-six years ago. It is called the *soldiers'* battle because they, our men, were not able to go into action under officers and orders all planned the day before, or at least some hours before, as is generally the case with great battles. The planning was all on the Russian side. We were surprised. In a dark thick fog, some hours before dawn, the Russians with an immensely superior force came upon us. Yet every one of our men stood for himself, for his comrades, shoulder to shoulder and for his country. There was no confusion. Not a man expected to come out of it alive. But they were determined to stand to the last by their country and their God and God was with them. That is the way God expects us to fight, my darling, standing by one another, "with a purpose true" and with the truth of love, as Mother does, and is doing things possible and impossible for others, "without a thought of self."

Our men were without food. Of course our officers and regiments came up without food as fast as possible and the officers behaved magnificently. But there was no confusion even when we were first surprised. I told you how the French came up after to help us, playing *British* tunes, still in the dense fog, and what our men said.

ever your loving

Aunt Florence

Inkermann Day 1890. If it had not been for those handfuls of our men standing to their posts on that dark November morning, and holding their posts till success came up against the whole Russian Army, the Russians might have swept our Army away like flies into the sea, and, who knows? swept all over Europe. The whole course of history would have been changed.

Purpose *untrue*
Standing by a purpose *true*
Heeding God's command
Honour them, the faithful few
All hail to Daniel's band.[326]

---

326 Hymn by Philip K. Bliss, in *Sunshine for Sunday Schools.*

Source: Letter to Margaret Verney, Wellcome (Claydon copy) Ms 9013/106

14 November 1890

. . . My little whistler, Ruth, says she is never dull, but adds confidentially to me, "When I am dull, I begin to whistle." Don't you see her mother's child there? Far more promising than if she were always unthinkingly merry. She is always busy, interstices are filled up with the "hospital." O the power of children's imagination! In that hideous thing, a doll, they find an object to love and nurse and care for! . . .

Source: Letter to Margaret Verney, Wellcome (Claydon copy) Ms 9013/111

29 November 1890

. . . Ruth says to me confidentially, that she "hopes Father won't resign; she wishes him to be in the House of Commons; it is so much more interesting." She thinks he had "better not come home directly" (in which I cordially join the General. She and I sometimes talk "constituents"!! and she, for a little, would talk politics!! But I rather act extinguisher.) . . .

Could you tell me of an acceptable present for Ruth's birthday? Really when she sits by me, I feel ashamed of talking of trivial dolls and childish things, to a middle-aged lady like that, I should talk philosophically.

ever your/Ruth's loving

Aunt Florence

Editor: In 1881 Nightingale gave a Bible to a godson: "Offered through her dear mother, Florence (Lees) Craven. F.N.," inscribed on the flyleaf: "For my dear little godchild Waldemar Sigismund Craven, with his godmother's most earnest prayers that many, many New Years, both in this world and the next, may pour upon him, all the highest blessings that God can give and I can wish him and that the child Jesus may be born anew in all our three hearts, his, and his mother's and mine, than which there can be no better wish. Florence Nightingale, 1881."[327]

---

327 Columbia University, Presbyterian Hospital School of Nursing.

Source: Letter, Columbia University, Presbyterian Hospital School of Nursing C8

[printed address] 10 South Street
Park Lane, W.
25 October
Balaclava Day [1881?]

Dear Mrs Craven [Florence Lees]

I have been so busy that I have not been able to think or rather to *do* about my dear godson's books hitherto. May I take your hint about military books and send him now the *Victoria Cross*, which teaches soldiers splendid gallantry towards each other and their country: *Battle of Waterloo*, which teaches them how to win a losing battle, the genius of, the necessity of attention to *details* and the still greater genius which knows how to apply these details, and Mrs Ewing's two lovely stories about boy soldiers. My earnest prayers [are] that he may make a hero, even among unheroic circumstances; perhaps the greatest heroes of all are these.

May I ask you to give him the parcel if in London? to send it to him wherever he is, and to be so good as to tell me the expense of carriage?

ever yours and Mr Craven's
sincerely
F. Nightingale

Source: Letter, Wellcome Ms 5483/65

[printed address] 10 South Street
Park Lane, W.
22 November 1890

My dear Sir Douglas [Galton]

My friend Mrs Dacre Craven (you may possibly remember her under her maiden name, Miss Florence Lees—she was our first probationer and our first district nurse) writes to me about her son, my godson, Waldemar Sigismund Dacre Craven, will receive his commission as 2nd Lieutenant in the Royal Artillery next month (the youngest cadet, she thinks). He is very anxious to get appointed to a FIELD battery (instead of to a garrison battery) as a better chance of active service on "passing out from Woolwich."

His mother wants me to mention his name to the War Office authorities (or to Sir Evelyn Wood if I know him, *but I don't*); with Sir Evelyn Wood [do] these appointments rest? It is not a question of preferment or pay. There is immediate hurry if it is to be done at all, I am told. I am very anxious about it. Could you kindly help me? I don't know that I know anyone now at the War Office who would do it. Would not you?

ever yours

F. Nightingale

Source: Letter by Sir Evelyn Wood, Columbia University, Presbyterian Hospital School of Nursing 028

War Office
1 December 1898

Dear Miss Nightingale

As a patient of yours in 1856, I have great pleasure in telling you that we have been able to meet your wishes, and that your godson, Mr Craven, will be specially selected for direct appointment to the Field Artillery.

I am very glad that Sir Douglas Galton has given me this opportunity of being of any assistance to you.

yours very truly

Evelyn Wood

Source: Incomplete letter to godson Harry Verney, Wellcome (Claydon copy) Ms 9023/110

I have just been having a delightful conversation with Ralph about his new little sister. He repeated to me a lovely little hymn about his sister [Gwendolen] "two years old."

Aunt Florence

Source: Letter to Margaret Verney, Wellcome (Claydon copy) Ms 9013/70

13 August 1890

... Gwendolen who is, as you know, very sensible (when one can keep her off poor deathbeds and Kathleen's salvation) talks to me about your Harry, how patient an observer he is of bees and flowers, and insects and birds. And, she says, he writes stories. ... How much I hope that Harry may turn out an observer, writer and teacher on the habits and customs of plants and flower, insects and birds. ...

Source: Note, Wellcome (Claydon copy) Ms 9023/131

For our dear Harry
with Aunt Florence's love
and may each day
of this New Year 1895
be better and happier
than yesterday

And may the young boy
and the old woman make
and find this a better and a
happier year than any
that has gone before,
So help us God!
New Year's Day
1895

Source: Card, Wellcome (Claydon copy) Ms 9015/7

Claydon
21 January 1895

My dear Harry [Calvert Verney]

Ay de me, ay de me, for losing Mother and Lettice. "Let us sit upon the ground and tell sad stories of the fate of kings." How is your paw?

Please tell father that a Thomas Tit, rather smaller than an undersized walnut, comes to my windows for his luncheon, dinner and tea, but says he can find nothing which suits his digestion (which he is obliged to be very careful of), and he requests that a mutton bone, with a good deal of nutriment upon it, should be hung up for his special refreshment.

ever your loving Aunt Florence

Are you going to Father's lecture tonight, you and Ruth?

Source: Letter to Margaret Verney, Wellcome (Claydon copy) Ms 9015/80

30 September 1896

. . . Your Harry called here, Harry the good nurse, when he arrived in London, looking so tall and so well, my Lizzie said, shook hands with Lizzie at the door. When he went away produced a card case and handed out an elegant card for me, like a gentleman.

ever your loving Aunt Florence

DOMESTIC ARRANGEMENTS

Food Orders and Recipes

Nightingale was a nurse with strong views on nutrition. No ascetic, she served good food to her relatives, friends and co-workers and enjoyed it herself whenever possible. She had difficulties with food when ill, so that there is much concern about getting food that she could eat. The following items show all this: letters about meals, food for invalids and guests, orders for food both for her own household and as gifts, supplies to be sent in from Embley (for which she paid) and recipes, all in her own hand. England at the time was notorious (as it would remain for some time) for its bad food. Getting a good cook was a challenge. Yet Nightingale had lived on the Continent and knew what was possible. She averred that the cooking was "immeasurably better" in the most-poverty-stricken places in Germany, even at Kaiserswerth, than in England.[1] (The spartan fare at Kaiserswerth is described in *European Travels*.)

The material here is only a small selection, ordered chronologically. There are numerous surviving letters with food orders (especially for food hampers to be sent to sick nuns and colleagues). For example there were gifts to R.G. Whitfield, Manor House, St Thomas' Hospital (3 brace partridges, 1 hare) carriage paid, 15 August 1866; Douglas Galton (1 brace partridges, 1 snipe) 17 August 1866; W. Clode at General Register Office (2 brace partridges, 1 hare); Dr Farr (3 brace partridges); P. Holland, Burial Acts Office (2 brace partridges) 24 Septem-

---

1 Letter to Parthenope and Sir Harry Verney 26 January 1882, Welcome (Claydon copy) Ms 9009/5.

2 Note, Wellcome (Claydon copy) Ms 9002/53.

ber 1866.[2] Colleagues and government employees on whom Nightingale relied for information were routinely plied with game.

For the Convent of Mercy at Bermondsey, Nightingale asked for "*vegetables*, fruit (apples, figs) are always acceptable, *flowers*, particularly so, ham and bacon also, mutton or pork, rabbits, hares and a little game."[3] When Mary Jones and her community were nursing in a cholera epidemic Nightingale sent her "a brace of grouse in their mountain heather."[4]

Nightingale had a cook but no housekeeper, so that she herself did much of the ordering, writing out letters to grocers and butchers. Merchants evidently kept these letters, which now appear in state and university archives. For example there is a letter ordering "a forequarter of your best small mutton, well hung, and I prefer of course four-year-old mutton, if it is to be had."[5]

Source: Letter, Wellcome (Claydon copy) Ms 8999/4

30 Old Burlington St.
20 February 1861

Dearest Mother

Would you send me up in the weekly box any spring vegetables, if it were only salad? Also, anything which Burton may have made for luncheon for that day, such as a fricassee, or a bit of chicken dressed in salad or something sharp (just as you would send to the poor people, only not rhubarb and not potted meat). Mrs Gamp[6] used to fold up a prong of vegetable like an umbrella and cram it into her pocket. Such are the vegetables here.

Also, I should be ashamed if (in the worst of times) I had *ever* given *my* patients what they give me here. I am ashamed to write of nothing else.

ever dearest Mother
your loving child

---

3 Note, Wellcome (Claydon copy) Ms 9002/76.
4 Letter to Mary Jones 17 August 1866, London Metropolitan Archives H1/ST/NC1/66/14.
5 Typed copy of letter to Mr Welsh 15 March 1889, Add Mss 45809 f115.
6 Sairy Gamp, the notorious drunken nurse of Charles Dickens' *Martin Chuzzlewit*.

Source: Unsigned note, Wellcome (Claydon copy) Ms 8999/59

My dear [Parthenope Verney]   [1861]

Don't make Ruth cook for me something distinct at 5:00 o'clock. All cooks object (and justly) to doing this when they have another dinner to do. You know I never eat anything but réchauffés [reheated] so it is no grievance to me. Embley sends a small rabbit pie every Thursday, which lasts me three days. If I have a bit sent from your dinner, it will do for tomorrow. . . .

Source: Letter, Wellcome (Claydon copy) Ms 8999/44

32 South St.
12 December 1861

Dear Papa

As you ask me about the *food*, I have set my wits to think. (I have not known the taste between flesh nor bread since my poor Clough's death.) I think, then, that I am tired of the sight of the *purée* and the rissoles, good as they are. The gravy soup we generally make into gravy for my dinner, which it tends greatly to render savoury. The other soup we generally make into Dr Sutherland's lunch. This is very appropriate.

I don't know what to ask for instead of the purée and the rissoles, for Burton knows better than I what will keep so as to come up good. I may eat anything that I can eat, *except* sweet preserves, anything pungent, *not* salt. Fruit and vegetables are particularly recommended. If then Burton could send up a different variety each week of any little dish she may make, spicy or otherwise? . . .

ever dear Pa

your loving child

Editor: A letter soon after clarifies that " 'pungent' means 'made dishes,' things made with pepper and mustard and so forth, or with seasoning or stuffing, or what children call 'hot' or 'spicy,' something with a stimulating taste."[7]

---

7 Letter to W.E. Nightingale 18 December 1861, Wellcome (Claydon copy) Ms 8999/46.

Source: Letter to Frances Nightingale, Wellcome (Claydon copy) Ms 9000/102

[printed address] 4 Cleveland Row, S.W.

15 May 1863

. . . Do you think you would make up a fine hamper of home produce for Rev Mother of Bermondsey and send it to me by Tuesday? as on Wednesday I go, if I can, to Hampstead and I should like to send her the hamper on Tuesday. I generally buy her a flitch of bacon two or three times a year, a leg of pork, apples—nothing comes amiss. What I buy is not so good as what you send, and plenty of your American flowers to make a show for her children on Whitsunday, please.

ever dearest Mum

loving child

F.

Your yesterday box went to cheer poor Miss Jones, flowers and all.

Source: Letter, Wellcome (Claydon copy) Ms 9000/97

11 April [1863?]

Dearie [Parthenope Verney]

They have forgotten to send me a bottle of port wine from Embley. Could you send me *two* immediately? (*one* for poor Burton, who will think it tastes better, being out of your bins). . . .

Source: Letter, Wellcome (Claydon copy) Ms 9001/97

Wednesday [1864]

Dearest Mother

I am very poorly. I have had a third dreadful night and we are so busy now that no one has a right to have bad night.

The Friern Manor milk, thanks to Mrs Webb's promptitude, answers admirably. I took the opinion of Topsy the cat upon it, who is an excellent judge. And she considers it good milk and cream, though not equal to Hampstead. She is a good judge, because she is dainty and not greedy.

Could you tell me of a *good baker*, whom Papa likes? (Mitchell, 69 Park Street, I am giving up because the servants complain of his bread.) Aunt Mai recommended one in Curzon St. to Papa, but that is a long while ago.

ever your loving child

F.

Source: Letter to Frances Nightingale, Wellcome (Claydon copy) Ms 9001/122

[printed address] 27 Norfolk St.
Park Lane, W.
8 April 1865

. . . I remember what you say, dearest Mum, about keeping alive for this poor world. I have to thank you for many fine boxes. Don't mind about the game being over. I really *prefer* a leg of pork, sausages, pig in general, tongue, chicken *and above all fruit.* You have been so good as to send us pork several times, and bacon. Chickens are 9/the couple in London now!!

ever dearest Mum
your loving child
F.

Source: Letter, Wellcome (Claydon copy) Ms 9021/20

Wednesday [1865?]

My dear Sir Harry [Verney]

I am afraid that, to make you comfortable, we must ask you to bring:
4 tea spoons
2 dessert "
2 table   "
4 forks

We will take great care of them and return them with you when you go. My father always brings his silver and I am sorry not to have thought of this before. But I hope it won't trouble you.

Could you tell me *where* you get your sherry? and *what* sherry?
ever yours
F.N.

I enclose our *latch key* for you tonight.

Source: Unsigned letter probably to W.E. Nightingale, Wellcome (Claydon copy) Ms 9004/4

[printed address] 35 South Street
Park Lane, W.
9 January 1870

I have really had not a moment to answer yours which, as it is the *third* letter which states that I have "emptied your larder," I suppose desires an answer. May I state the facts?

1. £150 a year is the average sum I pay for my "boxes" from Embley *including carriage.* This annual sum is sometimes more, sometimes less.

(It would be wasting your eyes and my time to go into particulars.) Of these, the *washing* is, as you know, paid for out of the £150. Of these [?], every bit of *meat, bacon, chine,* and *chickens* is paid for. (Before I made the arrangement for mutton with Embley, I did not pay for the bits of bacon, etc. sent me. By my own desire these are now added to the *paying list,* which I pay you every quarter.)

On the day you last told me I had "emptied your larder," I received (not by my own desire) one saddle mutton in the hamper of evergreens for the Highgate Infirmary besides the ordinary weekly "leg." This was weighed by my cook and entered by me, as well as the "leg," in this quarterly account for meat kept by me against myself.

(Since I have been cooking at this house for my excellent deputy at the Highgate Infirmary, and sending it up cold, I have always had to purchase the *de quoi.* Whether I have bought it of you or of the London shops, I have always paid for it. This is now just over, because the Guardians have appointed the cook. But I had to provide the first meals of all our nurses there.) I have had also double (and more) allowance of game during this latter time (a fortnight). I offered some time ago to pay for the game. You told me it was intended as a present.

The only other "emptying of your larder" that I have occasioned that I know of is that some joints of meat were sent through me, addressed to destination unasked for, on St Thomas's Day. That is the only meat I am certain which has ever come from you, *unpaid* for, here. I wish I had weighed them at the time, but I can guess at the weight within a few ounces. I have already added them to the account I keep against myself, to be paid to you, at Lady Day (I should have paid for them before, but, as they were all directed to the persons for whom they were intended, I thought that they were meant as a present to these, and that the *carriage* simply was meant to be paid by me, which carriage amounted to £2 odd that week alone).

2. Of the mince pies and buns I have only the same thing to say. They were sent in hampers addressed to the persons for whom they were intended. Buns I could have bought at our baker's for 1d. a piece. Mince pies we could have made (and did make) in my own kitchen for my servants and *clients.* I paid for the carriage about six times as much.

Source: Letter presumably to Harry or Parthenope Verney, Wellcome (Claydon copy) Ms 9006/73

21 February 1874

I enclose a cheque for my board at Embley:

Self: 20 days at   7/ £7 0 0
Jenny: " " "   2/ £2 0 0
Fanny: 6 " " "   12
3 couples of fowls at 5/6 16.6
Eggs 3
Cheque for £10.11.6
    F.N.

Source: Letter, Wellcome (Claydon copy) Ms 9007/28

35 South St.
Park Lane, W.
26 April 1876

My dear Margaret [Verney] (if you will allow me to call you so)

I have been so very sorry to hear of your anxiety about Lady Sarah[8] and of her inability to take any but liquid nourishment. I have no doubt that every kitchen conundrum that I could suggest you have already practised. But I cannot forbear telling you in my anxiety what my experience is of *purée of meat*: meat POUNDED small with good gravy so as to be of the consistency of cold cream, *seasoned* according to the patient's taste, made of mutton, beef or chicken, as preferred and served in a small tea cupful. I have rarely known a delicate person refuse it. It is liked so much better than panada. You know that the FIBRE of meat, so important to delicate people, is *not* contained in beef tea, broths or gelatine, but is all preserved in the *purée of meat.*

At the same time, it is a curious fact that, *after* seventy, provided *some fibre of meat* is taken, much nourishment is not *so* important as stimulants, wine or brandy and water, or whatever the patient can best take. May God be with us all! Pardon this note and believe me,

  ever sincerely yours
  Florence Nightingale

---

8 Lady Sarah Hay Williams, her mother.

Source: Letter to Parthenope Verney, Ms 9007/70

Monday 29 January 1877

An *apple pudding* "so delicious that it tasted not in the least like an apple pudding" excited Mrs Wardroper's "convoitise" [covetousness] at your *lunch*eon *yesterday. Might I ask for the receipt?*
F.N.

Source: Unsigned letter, Wellcome (Claydon copy) Ms 9010/111

10 South St.
3 October 1885

Dearest Pop [Parthenope Verney]

The eggs, etc. have come, to perfection, since the new tin with divisions. Would Mr Robertson get a second beautiful tin like that, charging the two to me? The smashed eggs were, as I think I mentioned (you ask) those which arrived on the Saturday (19 September) and the Wednesday (23 September) after I left Claydon.

I have now to make a most humiliating confession. After some inquiry, I find that Lydia actually put the smashed eggs and soiled sawdust back into the tin, and sent them so. She is really very sorry, but the excuse she makes is that Mrs Greig told her (this last time at Claydon) that she did not believe the eggs were ever smashed (there had been a controversy about it) and she, Lydia, sent them back to show her. (She, Lydia, knew nothing of the change from Greig.)

I was very severe and told her she must write an apology. When it came up, it was inadequate, but as I was just sending them off for a long day at the "inventories," I had not the heart to keep her, and she is now writing another, which I shall enclose. Pray be so good as to make my abject apologies to Mrs Robertson.

Source: Letter with envelope, ADD Mss 45795 ff159-61, "with 2 eggs, Egyptian lentils, rice shapes, cranberry and apple compote and a lampshade for Sir H. Verney"

10 South St.
8 November 1887

Dearest [Rosalind Shore Smith]

I send you two "vegetables" in their shells. We shall have some more fresh ones tomorrow. A new potato is, I assure you, *not* a vegetable. It is a mare's egg, laid by her, you know, in a "mare's nest." No vegetarian would eat it. I send you some Egyptian lentils. I have them every night for supper, done in milk, which I am not very fond of. The delicious thing is lentil soup, as made every day by our Arab cook in Egypt, over a handful of fire not big enough to roast a mosquito.

Also, some cranberry (we can't get fresh blackberries now, and blackberry jam made in shops is a compound of many things) and apple, as we make it. Is it too sweet? Also: some rice shape; don't you admit rice to be a "vegetable"? Rice is not starchy. Arrowroot, sago, tapioca are. Might I ask you when you go to Claydon to take this lamp-shade which he admired to Sir Harry?

My best love to Sam. God bless you both.

ever your loving

Aunt Florence

Source: Notes for the care of Mr Jowett when ill, ADD Mss 52427 ff104-05

[1887]

Meals: The rule for luncheon and dinner is to give *a whole hour* at least to each, not for continuous eating but for that function and digestion, before resuming the business of life. This ought certainly to be adhered to. An amusing book interesting enough to prevent the thoughts from scraping about, but not enough to excite the labour of thought, may be taken, or conversation, answering to this, or after lunch a little easy walk, but never hurry over the meal in ¼ hour.

All young meat, such as veal, is difficult of digestion. Veal should be prohibited. Fish, game, poultry, mutton, were the articles put down for his dietary. Stewed fruit is desirable three or four times a week, but probably better with luncheon than with dinner. Fruit is gold in the morning, silver in the afternoon and lead at night is a proverb. But the main thing is to roll the food well about in the mouth till it excites the saliva and so becomes a pulp, incorporated with saliva before it is swallowed, and NEVER to drink with food in the mouth.

Toast or a crust of bread is indispensable, whether at breakfast or dinner or lunch, as *that must* be ground with the teeth and chewed before being swallowed. It cannot be swallowed whole or nearly whole. Avoid anything, including haste, that produces flatulence. I record with indignation that jelly, which is good merely to take a little of when there is a bad taste in the mouth, was bolted by Mr Jowett, standing up in a plateful after a dinner of fish, of course producing flatulence and sleeplessness.

I say again it matters very little what I think. It matters very much what nature thinks. Nature sends in her bill without asking whether you could help it or no. And that is a bill which always has to be paid.

This is a supplementary instruction merely to what has already been written.

Source: Note ADD Mss 45809 f96

19 January 1889

Dear Mrs Neild [her cook]

I am sure you will make me an easy and nourishing dinner to eat for today and tomorrow. I have had, I think, no meat for a week and I am so poorly. Did you mean to make the Irish stew of the mutton which made the haricot? If that was a fair specimen of it I fear I shall *never* be able to eat that coarse meat. The ribs of lamb are not fit for me to try again *yet*. *Pray think of something and get the material.*

You may make me, if you like, a little mutton broth, a couple of oyster patties, but then I must have some meat, please. For tomorrow a little mutton broth, a fried sole, but then I must have some meat, please. Also, I put down a great many entrées. Will one of those do, besides?

F.N.

Source: Note to Mrs Neild, ADD Mss 45809 f91

11 January 1889

Please make a nice dish for Miss Williams of rissoles, or fillets of sole à la maître d'hôtel, oyster patties, or fish cakes or macaroni au gratin or cauliflower au gratin or omelette aux fines herbes, chicken à la mayonnaise with aspic jelly or cutlets à la béchamelle, or any of those thousand and one entrées which I have no doubt you make so well.

Source: Note for Mrs Neild, ADD Mss 45809 f104

11 February 1889

Fresh, Meat Minced: Mince beef for dinner please. Cut all the sinews out of the beef, which must be from the undercut of the sirloin. Pass the meat through the mincing machine over a plate, which will catch the juices that fall. Put in a stew pan and stand on the hot plate to cook gently. Serve hot. Give it me, please, instead of the oyster patties.

F.N.

Source: Letter with envelope, ADD Mss 45795 ff174-76, "small bottle, a few prunes, 6 eggs"

5 February 1890

Dearest Rosalind [Shore Smith]

I send you some common prunes: you put about a dozen senna leaves tied into a little bit of muslin and stew them with the prunes. (The senna leaves were sent on Monday.) (2) I send magnesia: you put as much as will go on a shilling and take it just before meals, some say 1/4 hour before meals. (The fashion now, a very good fashion, is to take very small doses, instead of very large ones of aperients.) N.B. *Don't* mix all my medicines together and take them in the lump.

your loving

Aunt Florence

I am going to send one more thing: dandelion for the liver. You are to report to me what you've done and what *it has done*. . . .

Source: Recipes, ADD Mss 45845 ff243, 248-55

19 June 1894

Mrs Mary Leader: To warm up [meat]: to cut off slices and keep them moist with clarified butter and then warm them on a hanging gridiron before the fire. Then they come out so tender and moist. . . .

Haricot of Mutton: Put three cutlets in a stew pan. Let them brown on both sides. Season with pepper and salt. Add one pint of good stock. Thicken it with 1 carrot, 1 turnip, 1/2 an onion. Let it simmer gently for 2 hours. Cut up some carrots and turnips in shapes and 2 button onions. Boil them all (separate). When the haricot is dished up put the vegetables in the centre but no onions.

Roast Pheasant: Prepare a pheasant for roasting. First hang it a good distance off, before a bright fire, basting it well every minute or two with good butter for an hour.

Roast Chicken: Put down to roast before a bright fire a nice young chicken for 1/2 an hour. First dredge it all over with flour and then lard it all over. Put it down to roast, basting it all the time, every one or two minutes.

Stewed Roll of Veal: Bone a nice breast of veal and stuff with very light stuffing, a few bread crumbs and fine chopped parsley and thyme. Then lard and stew in good stock for 1 1/2 hours. When done serve with white sauce.

Braised Beef: 6 or 8 lbs of middle of brisket of beef, braised 8 or 10 hours *very gently* with onions, carrots and turnips, a bay leaf, a few cloves, very little salt, in light stock or water.

Roast Mutton: Choose a good neck of very small mutton, never above 6 1/2 or 7 lbs., not too thin (streaky fat in the lean makes good mutton). Half the battle is in the trimming; the fat *near the bone* should be left to soak down into the meat. A nice brisk fire, but it should be put a good way off the fire at first, 1 1/2 hours doing. Keep on basting every minute or two, but do it in the tasty old-fashioned way: a little salt, a little flour, butter.

Boiled Mutton and Turnips: Cut about 4 chops from the end of a neck of mutton. Trim off some of the fat and put in boiling water. Let it simmer for 2 hours. Add a little salt in the water. Put on to boil 6 turnips. When they are done, strain them and squeeze all the moisture from them. Pass them through a hair sieve. Add one gill of cream, mix of butter the size of a nut, 1/2 teaspoonful of sugar, pepper and salt. Make hot and put round the mutton in shapes, with little dice of carrots.

Brisket: 10 or 12 lbs. Brisket 10:30 A.M. to 8:30 or 9 P.M. hot plate. Cold water. Vegetables rough cleaned: carrots, onion, celery or tops of celery, little plants, little bundle herbs, peppercorns, little salt. Simmer. If too fast pull it back. If still too fast put [in] cold water. If one side is too hot, pull it over to the other side. Take bones out when you take it off. Put it between two dishes after trimming glaze.

Source: Recipe, Add Mss 45815 f208

[late 1890s]

Minced Beef on Toast: Scrape the beef raw. Put it in the stew pan greased with butter with a little pepper and salt and gravy. Put the stew pan on the hot plate for a minute or two. If the hot plate is too hot, of course, it makes it hard. Toast or fry the toast. Gravy over it.

Expenditures and Donations

Source: Notes, Add Mss 45847

Editor: There are several surviving account books Nightingale kept, for 1853 (Add Mss 43403A), 1862-64 (43403B), 1865 (43403C) and her diary for 1877, with interspersed pages for accounts (Add Mss 45847). These detailed accounts for 1877, while Nightingale was mainly at Lea

Hurst, show expenditures for food (groceries, many legs of pork, loin of pork, fowl, lard, old hens, spareribs, eggs, butter, bacon, potatoes, apples, biscuits, apricots); for drink (coffee, beer, soda water, seltzer, brandy, cocoatina); for supplies (coal, water, gas, wood, oil), for transportation services (carriages, invalid carriage, rail hampers, cab, cart, porter, wagonettes, messengers). For her regular domestic employees she paid not only wages, quarterly, but their fares to go to the dentist, medical attendance and nurses at home, Christmas presents (including presents for an employee's mother) and extras stipulated for the savings' bank. There are items of payment also for a draper, charwoman and sweep. Taxes were paid: Poor rate, general, local and metropolitan, a house tax and income tax.

There were payments for clothes, baby clothes, toys, candles, flannel, calico, silk, wool, shoes, washing, envelopes, umbrella, stationery, postcards, paper, stamps, twine, music, linseed, plants, cold cream, cups and saucers, forks and knives, brooms, brushes, coffee mill, counterpanes, night stool, buttons, sewing machine. There are items showing payment for the *Times, Daily News, Punch* and Rice's Library.

Nightingale contributed throughout her life to worthy causes, only a partial list of which can be given here. Gifts to nurses and hospitals will be listed (as much as they are available) in the volumes reporting that material. The list below is a miscellaneous one, of what has appeared in correspondence processed so far (a full list will be made available in the electronic edition). There are letters sending £1 to some worthy cause, with an encouraging letter. Letters over many years, not reported here, include payments for children at Lea School. As well, Nightingale managed a whole caseload of Lea Hurst needy persons, former employees, tenants, etc., sending food and clothing, "meat and milk," cocoatina, and providing housekeeping and nursing care for those ill (see for example the letters to the Bratbys below). The information for 1877 is the most complete as her diary for that year includes bookkeeping entries. In 1879 she estimated her donations to Lea Hurst people at £500 a year, "chiefly among the old and sick women and the children of widows; the doctor's bill alone was £160."[9]

Nightingale was sometimes sent money for her to give to a worthy cause. She was reluctant to do this, and sometimes returned the money, preferring the donor make the choice directly. Yet she sometimes acceded, going to some trouble to choose an appropriate char-

9 Letter to Frederick Verney 23 June 1879, ADD Mss 68882 f99.

ity. For example, on receipt of £5 for the memorial to Agnes Jones, or another nursing cause, Nightingale explained that money was not the problem, but lack of heads, hearts and hands. She split it between the London East End Emigration Fund and the Adult Industrial Home, which enabled "poor women, deficient in intellect . . . habits of temperance, who would be otherwise picking oakum in the workhouse or doing worse," to work for wages.[10]

1848-52: Nightingale paid a sum yearly for five years (20 scudi in 1851), from her clothing allowance, to support a girl at the school for orphans at the Sacred Heart Convent, Rome.[11]

1853: Nightingale heard that Mrs Chisholm, the "emigrants' friend," was living on 9d/day and not had meat for weeks, yet refusing money, to give £5 to a testimonial for her;[12] she gave £1.5 to the Petite Soeurs des Pauvres;[13] she gave £5 to Elise von Tunzelmann to assist her to emigrate to New Zealand.[14]

1854: and various years after, Nightingale sent money for the care of the illegitimate son of Mathilde von Raven, an aristocratic German woman who had been seduced by a nobleman in Germany and was dying at the Middlesex Hospital when Nightingale took her to 1 Upper Harley St. for her last days.[15]

1858: Nightingale sent £5 and asked her father to contribute £5 for the Dispensary for Ulcerated Legs in Bloomsbury, for which she broke her "usual rule of never being patroness where I cannot give personal assistance" and became president.[16]

---

10 Typed copy of letter to unnamed recipient 7 January 1869, State Library of South Australia.
11 Letter to Mrs Colyar 28 February 1851, Boston University 2/1/2.
12 Letter to Frances Nightingale 2 June 1853, Wellcome (Claydon copy) Ms 8944/26 and 13 July 1853, note in account book, ADD Mss 43403A f2.
13 28 February 1863 entry in account book, ADD Mss 43403B f11.
14 Letter 18 November [1853] to Elise von Tunzelmann, private collection of (descendant) Colin Bass, Nelson, New Zealand.
15 Letter to H. Bence Jones 27 May 1872, Cambridge University Library Manuscripts and Archives ADD 8566/I/173; letter to Bertha Smith Boston University, 2/20/14.
16 Letter to W.E. Nightingale 23 September 1858, Wellcome (Claydon copy) Ms 8997/73.

1859: Nightingale gave £10 worth of games and a year's subscription to several periodicals, £5 to make the rooms comfortable to Gibraltar Reading Room.[17] She sent her "mite" to the Neapolitans, after consulting Monckton Milnes.[18]

1860: Nightingale paid £500, via Beatrice Smith, for the Lea School;[19] gave £10 to the House Fund of St John's House, Queen Square, Training Institution for Nurses;[20] twice sent cheques of £10 to Garibaldi[21]

1861: Nightingale sent £10, in her father's name, to a subscription for the defence of Jowett on charges arising from *Essays and Reviews*;[22] she sent a cheque to Mary Jones "to use . . . simply as I like;"[23] she gave £1 to the Brighton Branch, British Army Scripture Readers; and Soldiers' Friend Society;[24] she gave a donation, amount unspecified, for a school in Skye.[25]

1862: Nightingale sent £25 to the Fliedners at Kaiserswerth for mission work in Syria;[26] she paid £5.5 to the Chatham Institute and paid £30 and £6.18.4 for books for Montreal;[27] gave £50 to R. Hospital, but did not want to be a voting member;[28] sent £5 to Cotton Distress;[29] she promised £50 to £100 to the Winton Infirmary "if they made the hospital conducive to the welfare of the sick;"[30] she gave pictures and a

---

17 Extract of letter from Mrs Gaskell to Charles Bosanquet 7 November 1859, ADD Mss 45797 f76.
18 Letter to Richard Monckton Milnes 5 April 1859, Trinity College, Cambridge, Houghton Papers.
19 Letter 7 March 1860, Columbia University, Presbyterian Hospital School of Nursing C54.
20 Receipt 27 March 1860, ADD Mss 47743 f2.
21 Cancelled cheques 28 May 1860, ADD Mss 47458 ff28-29; ADD Mss and note 10; June 1860 ADD Mss 45794 f156.
22 Letter to W.E. Nightingale 20 December 1861, Wellcome (Claydon copy) Ms 8999/47.
23 Letter of Mary Jones 3 November 1861, ADD Mss 47743 f125.
24 Note to Samuel Smith ca. 16 October 1861, ADD Mss 45792 f247.
25 Letter of Matilda Wrench to Samuel Smith 11 June [1861], ADD Mss 45792 f174.
26 Letter to Samuel Smith 3 May 1862, ADD Mss 45793 f94, and note 30 May 1862 in account book, ADD Mss 43403B f2.
27 29 May 1862 entry in account book, ADD Mss 43403B f2.
28 Letter to Frances Nightingale 14 May 1862, Wellcome (Claydon copy) Ms 9000/39.
29 6 December 1862 entry in account book, ADD Mss 43403B f8.
30 Letter to W.E. Nightingale 23 January 1862, ADD Mss 45790 f245.

book of prints to the Sisters of Mercy at Bermondsey for them and the children in their schools[31]

1863: Nightingale sent £30 to Sister Cordero for work in Sardinia;[32] she could not give more although she had given money evidently on a number of occasions before;[33] she paid £1 to St Mark's School Club subscription.[34]

1864: Nightingale gave £30 to the Herbert memorial convalescent cottages, for which she did the plans, and £25 for the Aylesbury Infirmary, for which she revised the plans;[35] she gave £5 for relief after the Sheffield flood;[36] and apparently another £10 for the Mayor of Sheffield thanked her for her £10 donation and said, "We are touched by your allusion to our town and are proud to be styled your townspeople;"[37] she gave £3 for her mother's Rifles;[38] also £5 or £10 to her sister's Volunteers;[39] she paid an unspecified amount, plus £5 from her mother, to the Hill missionaries in Athens;[40] she paid £25 to the Church Commissioners' Fund, £10 to the Drummond Institute and £5 to the Soldiers' Bible Readers.[41]

1865: Nightingale collected £200 for the Fliedners; she contributed £200 to the Winchester Infirmary;[42] she gave £100 to Mary Jones's

---

31 Letter of Mary Clare Moore 24 July 1862, in Mary C. Sullivan, *The Friendship of Florence Nightingale and Mary Clare Moore* 97-98.
32 Letter to Hilary Bonham Carter 11 August 1863, ADD Mss 45794 f216.
33 Undated notes, ADD Mss 45794 f215 and f217.
34 31 December 1863 entry in account book, ADD Mss 43403B f16.
35 Letter to W.E. Nightingale 23 November 1864, ADD Mss 45790 ff327.
36 Letter to Frances Nightingale 25 March 1864, Wellcome (Claydon copy) Ms 9001/19.
37 Letter 30 March 1864, Wellcome (Claydon copy) Ms 9075/3.
38 Letter to Frances Nightingale 21 December 1864, Wellcome (Claydon copy) Ms 9001/89.
39 Letter to Parthenope Verney 28 September 1864, Wellcome (Claydon copy) Ms 9001/63.
40 Letter to Frances Nightingale 14 November 1864, Wellcome (Claydon copy) Ms 9001/89, and letter to Frances Nightingale 14 November 1864, Wellcome [Claydon copy] Ms 9001/82).
41 1 August 1864 entries in account book, ADD Mss 43403C f3.
42 Letter to Frances Nightingale 25 October 1864, Wellcome (Claydon copy) Ms 9001/72.

convalescent hospital, £50 to the Herbert Memorial and promised £25 to Swansea Hospital;[43] and gave £10 to an association for providing lodgings for soldiers' wives and families at Aldershot and to pay £10.1 for the Claydon Rifle Volunteers;[44] she paid £10 to Sister Gonzaga;[45] £20 to the Life Boat Institution and a 4/3 subscription;[46] she paid for church sittings for three servants, £2.1.9;[47] and gave an unknown sum of money for women's education.[48]

1866: Nightingale gave £5 to Catherine Marsh for convalescents from cholera;[49] she paid 10/0 for three pew sittings,[50] 10/0 for two pew sittings;[51] and £5 to the Consumption Hospital;[52] she sent two guineas as a contribution to the South London Industrial Exhibition, at the request of her colleague J.J. Frederick,[53] and acted as one of the guarantors to subsidize the South London Working Men's Exhibition.[54]

1867: Nightingale gave an unspecified sum of money to buy food for the Sisters of Mercy at Great Ormond St.,[55] and paid £15 to put a boy on the Chichester training ship.[56]

---

43 Letter to Frances Nightingale 29 September 1864, Wellcome (Claydon copy) Ms 9001/160.
44 Letter to Harry Verney 18 September 1865, Wellcome (Claydon copy) Ms 9001/155.
45 27 January 1865 entry in account book, ADD Mss 43403C f13.
46 Entry in account book ADD Mss 43403C f3.
47 31 May 1865 entry in account book, ADD Mss 43403C f11, or 30 June 1865??
48 Letter from Anne J. Clough to Nightingale 28 May [1865], ADD Mss 72824A ff69-70.
49 Letter to Mrs Chalmers 2 October 1866, Clendening History of Medicine Library, Kansas University Medical Center.
50 Entry in account book, ADD Mss 43403C f15.
51 April/July 1866 entry in account book, ADD Mss 43403C f17.
52 Entry in account book, ADD Mss 43403C f17.
53 Letter to George M. Murphy 26 March 1866, London Metropolitan Archives H1/ST/NC1/66/2.
54 Note to Parthenope Verney, Wellcome (Claydon copy) Ms 9001/199.
55 Letter probably to W.E. Nightingale 21 November 1867, Wellcome (Claydon copy) Ms 9002/187.
56 Letter to W.E. Nightingale 9 November 1867, Wellcome (Claydon copy) Ms 9002/183.

1868: Nightingale gave £2.2.0 for a memorial to Dean Milman;[57] she made a £1.1 contribution to the London National Society for Women's Suffrage.[58]

1869: Nightingale gave £50, the second of three gifts of £50 each, to the Derby Infirmary;[59] and gave £30, a wheelchair and wines, jellies, etc. for Mary Clare Moore's illness.[60]

1870: Nightingale gave £20, and forwarded £5 from her father, for aid in the Franco-Prussian War;[61] she sent £20 to Mme Schwabe for whichever society she thought best to aid starving people around Metz and Sedan;[62] she sent £5 for the Victoria Stiftung [Foundation];[63] she gave £2, via her colleague J.J. Frederick, to the Surrey Chapel Benevolence Society.[64]

1871: Nightingale publicly gave £5/week for four weeks, via the Lord Mayor's Fund for relief in Paris;[65] she gave £5 to Pastor Goulden at Sedan, for relief in the Franco-Prussian War;[66] she gave (publicly) £5 for the work of Dr Laseron in the Franco-Prussian War;[67] and £1.1.0 to London National Society for Women's Suffrage.[68]

1873 Nightingale sent £10 to support the Home for Incurables of St John's House.[69]

---

57 Letter to Harry Verney 12 June 1873, Wellcome (Claydon copy) Ms 9006/46.
58 Receipt 9 December 1868, signed Mentia Taylor, Add Mss 45801 f148.
59 Letter to W.E. Nightingale 2 December 1869, Wellcome (Claydon copy) Ms 9003/128.
60 Note in Convent of Mercy Annals, in Sullivan, *The Friendship of Florence Nightingale and Mary Clare Moore* 166.
61 Letter to Harry Verney 12 August 1870, Wellcome (Claydon copy) Ms 9004/71.
62 Letter to Mme Schwabe 15 November 1870, Columbia University, Presbyterian Hospital School of Nursing C100.
63 Letter 15 August 1870, Columbia University, Presbyterian Hospital School of Nursing C96.
64 Letter, 17 December 1870, London Metropolitan Archives H1/ST/NC1/70/17.
65 Letter to the *Times* 1 February 1871:6.
66 Letter to Harry Verney 1 October 1871, Wellcome (Claydon copy) Ms 9005/94.
67 Letter to Mme Schwabe 13 January 1871, Columbia University, Presbyterian Hospital School of Nursing C103.
68 Letter from Mentia Taylor with receipt 28 March [1871], Add Mss 47716 ff181-83.
69 Letter of Mary Jones 11 September 1873, Add Mss 47744 ff221-23.

1874: Nightingale gave £10 to the Bengal Social Science Association;[70] she gave Benjamin Jowett £100 towards a new hall at Balliol College.[71] Nightingale made a "generous contribution" to the memorial fund for David Livingstone.[72]

1875: Nightingale publicly, via the Lord Mayor, gave £10 for training sailor boys;[73] she gave £5 to J.J. Frederick "for any of your private charities that you choose";[74] she gave £50 to Bosnian and Herzegovinian Children's Relief Fund.[75]

1876: Nightingale gave £11 for the relief of homeless Bulgarians, adding this to other funds collected to a total of £40;[76] she publicly gave £5 for Indian famine relief, via the Lord Mayor.[77]

1877: Nightingale gave £10.10 for troopship work, with permission to publicize the donation at a public meeting;[78] made an unspecified donation to a fund for orphans, apparently in honour of Mrs Chisholm;[79] she sent £2.2 to the Crich National School and £1.1 for a memorial window for Mr Chawner at Crich Church.[80] Entries from her diary show a contribution to the Curzon St. school fête; for "grub" and oranges for the local school fête at Lea; for St Thomas' probationers' tea; for newspapers for a coffee room [to encourage non-alcoholic socializing]; maps for a reading room; a ragged school day in the country; firemen; a "starving Canadian"; a "crippled child"; a choral society and fifteen concert tickets and Christmas boxes of oranges and lemons. Nightingale paid subscriptions to the East India Association and to an association for charity reform voting.

70 Letter to Harry Verney 1 June 1874, Wellcome (Claydon copy) Ms 9006/102.
71 Letter from Jowett thanking her 5 February 1874, in Vincent Quinn and John Prest, eds., *Dear Miss Nightingale: A Selection of Benjamin Jowett's Letters to Florence Nightingale 1860-1893* #327.
72 Letter with receipt from Bartle Frere 9 April [1874], ADD Mss 45780 f246.
73 Letter to the *Times* 11 January 1875:5.
74 Letter 19 February 1875, London Metropolitan Archives H1/ST/NC1/75/1.
75 List of Donations Received, ADD Mss 45795 f85.
76 Letter to Rev J. Long 18 October 1876, Wellcome (Claydon copy) Ms 9007/61.
77 Letter to the *Times* 22 August 1877:6.
78 Letter to Miss Robinson 19 June 1877, Clendening History of Medicine Library, Kansas University Medical Center.
79 Letter to Nightingale from Octavia Hill thanking her, 29 November 1877, Woodward Biomedical Library B.34.
80 Letter to Wm. Acraman 26 September 1877, Boston University 2/2/5.

She gave money to Miss Irby, probably for printing expenses or a direct donation for Bosnian relief work. Her church donations include "Mr Smedley's chapel" (with a note of "two maids"), a contribution for the sixteenth anniversary of Lea Chapel, a Bible subscription for Mr Wildgoose, a payment for "Polly sacrament" and "church sittings for maids," presumably payment for a pew.[81]

1878: Nightingale gave £25 to the Russian Sick and Wounded Fund;[82] publicly gave £10.10 to the Eastern War Sick and Wounded Relief Fund;[83] gave £10 for shares in the Coffee Tavern Co. to provide non-alcoholic meals and lodging;[84] one sovereign to the local nurse for clothes for Patty Cottrell;[85] sent a cheque for £25 to a sisterhood in difficulty, offering another in two or three weeks' time, for "added to your terrible anxieties, you should not have money anxieties;"[86] £25 to the Relief Fund for Sheffield, to be applied to providing work for the poor women;[87] £2.2 towards a communion table at St George's, Hanover Sq.;[88] she wrote a cheque to Shore Smith for her subscription to the Holloway Reading Room;[89] gave £1 to Mr Headlam's Fund, anonymously as she did "not agree with some things;"[90] and gave £1 for the Eurydice shipwreck fund.[91]

1879: Nightingale sent £2.2. to Mr Acraman for school subscriptions;[92] she sent £5 to James Martineau's schools.[93] she gave a legacy left her

---

81 Diary, Add Mss 45847.
82 Letter from Stopford Brooke 20 January 1878, Woodward Biomedical Library B.38.
83 Letter 16 August 1878 read by the Earl of Harrowby at a public meeting, in Dorothy Anderson, *Miss Irby and Her Friends* 124.
84 Letter to F.C. Barnard 4 April 1878, Columbia University, Presbyterian Hospital School of Nursing C120.
85 Letter to Mrs Swann 23 March 1878, Wellcome Ms 5483/13.
86 Letter to Sister Frances [Wylde] 5 September 1878, London Metropolitan Archives H1/ST/NC1/78/2.
87 Letter 25 December 1878, Add Mss 45805 f119.
88 Copy of letter to Rev R.P. Oldham, vicar, 5 September 1878, Grosvenor Chapel.
89 Paid cheque 14 February 1878, Florence Nightingale Museum 0557.
90 Letter to Frederick Verney 16 April 1878, Add Mss 68882 f96.
91 Letter to Harry Verney 31 May 1878, Wellcome (Claydon copy) Ms 9007/52.
92 Letter to Dr Dunn 12 April 1879, Derbyshire County Archives.
93 Letter to Louisa Shore Smith 19 February 1879, Add Mss 45795 f129.

by a woman in Naples for use in schools there;[94] and gave £5 to Mme Werckner, having given £50 the previous year.[95]

1880: Nightingale sent £5 to pay for various items of clothing for Lea Hurst people;[96] she sent £2.2 to Mr Acraman's Curates' Fund;[97] gave £1 for stay in Dover Convalescent Home of William Hedges.[98]

1881: Nightingale gave £20 to the Soldier's Institute, Portsmouth;[99] gave a "kind gift" to the Association for Promoting Trained Nursing in Workhouse Infirmaries and Sick Asylums;[100] sent £3.3 to Mr Acraman to use wherever he felt most needed.[101]

1883: Nightingale planned to give £100 to the Farr memorial fund, and was willing to do so publicly if this might encourage other contributions (for the support of the unmarried Farr daughters, to whom she left legacies in her will);[102] she gave £5.5 for the Parkes Museum;[103] a "small coin" towards an altar cloth at a Wellow church;[104] and gave £6 to A. Crooks to pay a year's rent and have £1 to start.[105]

1884: Nightingale sent £1.4.2 to the schoolmaster to pay various expenses and undertook to pay for another pupil;[106] she gave 6/ for a Pleasley ticket.[107]

---

94 Letter to Mrs Schwabe 4 February 1879, Columbia University Presbyterian Hospital School of Nursing C125.
95 Letter to Harry Verney 31 May 1879, Wellcome (Claydon copy) Ms 9007/238.
96 Letter to Miss Mochler 19 August 1880, Boston University 2/2/8.
97 Letter to Dr Dunn 18 December 1880, Derbyshire County Archives.
98 Letter to Mrs Rusher 11 February 1880, Mt Sinai Hospital, Gerald P. Turner Nursing Department, Toronto.
99 Letter from S. Robinson 24 June [1881], ADD Mss 45806 ff178-79.
100 Letter of Louisa Twining 7 August [1880], ADD Mss 45806 ff61-62.
101 Letter 26 November 1881, Columbia University, Presbyterian Hospital School of Nursing C138.
102 Letter to H.H. Janson 25 June 1883, Farr Collection, British Library of Political and Economic Science 1/78.
103 Letter to Douglas Galton 14 June 1883, ADD Mss 45765 f214.
104 Letter to Louisa Dinah Petty 30 January 1883, Girton College, Cambridge, GCRF 9/1/12.
105 Letter to Edmund Verney 7 December 1883, Wellcome (Claydon copy) Ms 9009/233.
106 Letter to Mr Butler 27 September 1884, Boston University 2/13/1.
107 Letter to Harry Verney 15 December 1884, Wellcome (Claydon copy) Ms 9010/50.

1885: Nightingale sent 16s to the schoolmaster for subscriptions for various people to the institute;[108] she sent £25 to the North Bucking-hamshire Liberal Association;[109] she gave £3.3.0 to the Gordon Memorial Fund;[110] and gave a "generous" donation to the Belfast Hospital for Sick Children.[111]

1886: Nightingale gave an unspecified amount to the Gordon Boys' Home;[112] gave a generous gift to Octavia Hill for use on her "far" flock;[113] and gave a "little" contribution for the work of the Convent of Mercy at St John's and St Elizabeth's Hospital;[114] and sent £5 to buy a globe for Lea School.[115]

1887: Nightingale gave "another" £20 for a cause of S.C. Hall;[116] sent the Lea schoolmaster £2.5.4 for her "account, sent £5.5 for a "meat tea," adding £1.1 to provide non-alcoholic beer[117] and a cheque for £2.5.4 regarding a government examination;[118] she was asked for a renewal of her kind donation to the Paddington and Marylebone District Nursing Association for providing trained nurses for the sick poor;[119] and gave 10/ for "poor old Moss."[120]

1888: Nightingale contributed £50 and a letter of support to an appeal for a hospital for women in London;[121] and subscribed to a bed at the Ascot Priory;[122] she gave a "mite" wishing it were 20 times as much to the Convent of Mercy at St John's and St Elizabeth's Hospital;[123] and

---

108 Letter to Mr Butler 23 December 1885, Boston University 2/14/18.
109 Letter 13 May 1885, Wellcome (Claydon copy) Ms 9010/79.
110 Letter 11 September 1885, Bodleian Ms Eng.lett.e.9.
111 Letter from secretary 26 December 1885, ADD Mss 45807 ff203-04.
112 Letter to Harry Verney 26 June 1886, Wellcome (Claydon copy) Ms 9011/34.
113 Letter 5 July 1886 to Nightingale from Octavia Hill, ADD Mss 59786 f84.
114 Letter to Sister Stanislaus Jones 30 December 1886, Archives, Convent of Mercy, Birmingham.
115 Letter to Mr Butler 8 October 1886, Boston University 2/15/27.
116 Letter to Harry Verney 29 June 1887, Wellcome (Claydon copy) Ms 9011/144.
117 Letter to Mr Butler 3 June 1887, Boston University 2/16/33.
118 Letter to Mr Butler 10 October 1887, Boston University 2/16/37.
119 Letter 14 January 1887, ADD Mss 45808 f1.
120 Letter to Parthenope Verney 9 December 1887, Wellcome (Claydon copy) Ms 9011/204.
121 Louisa Garrett Anderson, *Elizabeth Garrett Anderson 1836-1917* 246.
122 Letter from Sister Bertha Turnbull 26 July 1888, ADD Mss 45808 ff170-73 f170 and receipt f173.
123 Letter to Sister Stanislaus Jones 25 December 1888, Archives, Convent of Mercy Birmingham.

paid the third part of her 50 guineas to the Paterson Memorial Fund.[124]

1889: Nightingale assisted Arthur Clough in raising money to pay for the education of a boy, and presumably contributed herself;[125] gave £5 for books for Prince Cheroon's tutor;[126] and gave a "little sum" for a prize for games at the Gordon Boys' Home.[127]

1890: Nightingale gave an unspecified "mite" to the Gordon Boys' Home;[128] she gave £1 to pay the fare of Philip Tomes to get to St Thomas' Hospital for treatment;[129] and an unspecified amount for work in the East End of London.[130]

1891: Nightingale gave £3.3 to a scholarship for Cornelia Sorabji to study at Oxford University,[131] and gave graphics to the Gordon Boys' Home.[132]

1892: Nightingale gave £10.10 to Dr De'ath for his objects in public health;[133] and £5.5 to the Convent of Our Lady of Mercy, Saint Joseph's, Hunslet, Leeds, towards a building.[134]

1894: Nightingale sent a contribution to the Sir Henry Acland Memorial;[135] she sent £1 to the mother of a deceased nurse.[136]

1895: Nightingale paid to supply magazines for the Botolph Reading Room, near Claydon;[137] gave £5 to the Convent of Our Lady of Mercy,

---

124 Letter to Fred Verney 15 July 1888, ADD Mss 68886 f15.
125 Letter to Margaret Verney 2 November 1889, Wellcome (Claydon copy) Ms 9012/249.
126 Letter to Fred Verney 15 July 1889, ADD Mss 68886 f52.
127 Letter to Fred Verney 7 April 1889, ADD Mss 68886 f52.
128 Letter to Alex Devine 28 August 1890, Wellcome (Claydon copy) Ms 9013/73.
129 Letter to Mr Morey 16 August 1890, Harvard University, Countway Medical Library.
130 Letter from Sister Bertha Turnbull 2 April 1890, ADD Mss 45809 f310.
131 List of contributors, British Library India Office, Eur Mss F 165 folder 17.
132 Letter of Lydia Constable 28 August [1891], ADD Mss 45810 f242.
133 Letter to Dr De'ath 27 January 1892, Chiddingstone Castle.
134 Letter of Sister M. Benedict Joseph 9 August 1892, ADD Mss 45811 f129.
135 Letter to Mrs Lisketh [?] 29 December 1894, ADD Mss 45812 f231.
136 Letter to Miss Gordon 1 September 1894, Wellcome (Claydon copy) Ms 5476/47.
137 Letter to Mr Morey 7 March 1895, Harvard University, Countway Medical Library.

St Joseph's Hunslet, Leeds, for their school;[138] 5/ to Belfast for a nurses' fund;[139] she gave £30 and offered more for expenses regarding the prosecution or replacement of a delinquent priest;[140] gave £10 to Dr Evatt to reprint his sanitary pamphlet;[141] and made a contribution to Fred Verney to use as he thought best.[142]

1896: Nightingale gave £100 to St Thomas' Hospital;[143] she sent £25 via Lady Monteagle for the use of Miss Pringle in training nurses for Irish workhouse infirmaries;[144] gave £5, via Nurse Ekblom, for a new home for probationers in Helsinki;[145] she sent, via Lettice Verney, £2.2 to Lady Margaret Hall Settlement, Oxford University;[146] sent money to the Convent of Mercy for the jubilee of Sister Anastasia Kelly;[147] and gave 10/6 for the gardening boys at Lea School.[148]

1897: Nightingale sent £5 (£4 to pay for sports at Verney Junction and £1 to pay a bill), and offered to give 10/ towards the American organ at East Claydon Church and bell for the cemetery;[149] and gave an unspecified small cheque to the Convent of Mercy at St John's and St Elizabeth's Hospital.[150]

1900: Nightingale sent Lettice Verney £3.8 for something for a library, to save her time in canvassing.[151]

---

138 Letter of Sister Benedict Joseph, 10 December 1895, Add Mss 45813 f148.
139 Letter of A.L. Bristow 5 February 1895, Add Mss 45813 f7.
140 Letter to Edmund Verney 13 June 1895, Wellcome (Claydon copy) Ms 9015/48.
141 Letter to Douglas Galton 6 February 1895, Add Mss 45767 f132.
142 Letter 19 January 1896, Add Mss 68888 f160.
143 Draft letter to R.G. Wainwright 14 February [1896], Add Mss 45813 f179.
144 Letter 25 October 1896, Add Mss 47727 f219.
145 Letter 5 March 1896, Kupio University, Helsinki.
146 Letter 24 December 1896, Wellcome (Claydon copy) Ms 9015/84.
147 Letter to Sister Stanislaus Jones 21 October 1896, Archives, Convent of Mercy, Birmingham.
148 Letter to Mr Burton 30 July 1896, Clendening History of Medicine Library, Kansas University Medical Center.
149 Letter to Mr Morey 19 July 1897, Harvard University, Countway Medical Library.
150 Letter to Sister Stanislaus Jones 26 April 1897, Archives, Convent of Mercy, Birmingham.
151 Letter 14 February 1900, Wellcome (Claydon copy) Ms 9015/124.

Cat Care

Editor: Nightingale, although a bird lover, was a devoted cat owner throughout her life. The items begin with instructions (to whom is not stated) for the (deluxe) care of a particular cat, Mr Bismark. (Although undoubtedly named after Prince von Bismarck, the militaristic German chancellor, we distinguish the two by keeping the cat's name as originally spelled, Mr Bismark, and correct the name of the chancellor to the usual Bismarck.) Several letters follow on the search for an appropriate home for a cat and news about cats who have gone to other homes. Nightingale tried her medical/statistical colleagues for cat homes as well. Dr Farr was offered a Persian, non-thoroughbred 4½ months old, "for your young people."[152] She was amused by a legend that she kept seventeen cats, with a nurse to attend each, and that the cats were periodically sent into the country, with an attendant, for a change of air.[153]

Source: Undated note, ADD Mss 45845 f236

[Nightingale's cat] Mr Bismark has been brought up to go to a large pan with fine sand, which was always placed clean in the room where he was shut up at night, and also clean in whichever room he was in in the day. Of course he can be taught otherwise. Only at first if he has not a pan he must not be blamed for making dirt. Very clean cat—never makes a mistake.

He is always brought in and shut up at night in a room (our large pantry) cleared so that he can spoil and upset nothing, and has a bed—a piece of carpet or something warm. He feels the cold. Of course he will be happier if a lady cat-companion is there.

Fresh water in a clean white vessel, which will not upset, should always be on the floor for a cat to drink. He will be strange at first, and perhaps had better not be let out till he knows his house. He is so tame that he would rather follow his mistress out in the garden than not, and he has never roamed. He has been made a great pet of and is the most sensitively affectionate of cats, very gentle and really a lady. He has always been a great favourite with the maids but has lived in the room with me. He has been used to the luxury of a comb and brush.

---

152 Letter 22 December 1863, Wellcome Ms 5474/65.
153 Letter of Mary Elinor Wilson 16 May [1870], Add Mss 47758 ff45-46.

He has always a newspaper spread for him like a tablecloth on the floor for his meals, which he eats like a gentleman out of a plate.

breakfast, 8:30   milk, a little meat or chicken bones or fish, never *salt* meat, *never* sauce or melted butter or the remains of made dishes or of pie crust; no fat;

luncheon, 1:30   a little meat cut up small and mashed up with potatoes and cauliflower or carrot and with bread sopped up in beef tea or broth; asparagus tails are always good;

tea, 5:00   milk, a biscuit or a bit of bread and butter from his mistress's hand is always welcomed, or a little bit of rice pudding;

supper, 8:00   fish, chicken bones or a little meat and vegetables as above;

bed, 10:00   milk and a little meat are left on the floor.

Too much solid meat is not good for cats. Liver once a week is good for them, occasionally ground. Fresh grass should always be accessible to a cat. Ribbon-grass is greedily eaten.

Source: Letter, Wiltshire County Archives 2057/F4/68

Hampstead, N.W.
24 October 1860

Dear Mr [Sidney] Herbert

There are rats in the War Office, also a cat. There are seventeen months' minutes to apply for 6 pence a week for her: forty minutes say that she ought to live on rats, other minutes that she ought to have milk, but that 6 pence a week is too much, others again ask what she is to live upon in the meantime.

I am very anxious to know what is your decision, whether you have given *any* as yet, whether you think 5 pence, 3 farthings would be too much? I incline to 5 pence, halfpenny.

yours sincerely

F. Nightingale

This is fact, not fiction, but I would not be a War Office cat, even for a very great deal.

Source: Letter, Wellcome (Claydon copy) Ms 9000/51

18 June 1862

Dear Papa

Tom and Topsy arrived in perfect preservation. They are more like human beings in a low state of civilization than animals. They said they were neither hungry nor thirsty, tired nor dirty, shy nor wild. They were only curious, particularly about a new spring bed of mine, the construction of which they had never seen before and into which they mounted immediately on arrival, to examine the springs. They behave as if they had known us and this residence all their lives, greatly to the horror of big Pussie, who does nothing but snarl at them. I think Tom and Topsy the greatest beauties we have had yet, particularly Topsy. I must compliment Mrs Watson upon their excessively tidy habits. . . .

F.N.

Source: Letter, Wellcome (Claydon copy) Ms 9000/30

House of the fever compelling Erinnys
25 April 1862

Dearest Mother

I expect to have an analytical description of each of the three little cats, whether tabby or yellow. If Thomas was with his wife, Thomas may have killed two of his little cats.

I forget how long the cat's monthly nurse thinks they (the babies) ought to stay before they are weaned. But I think it is six weeks. It is better to send me the two biggest first, and the third a week after. Cats' coats are most often spoiled by their being separated too young, so that they cannot be licked either by mother or sister.

The mouse colour, which Mrs Sutherland has (please tell Mrs Watson), holds her own against a Maltese dog, a spaniel dog and a large immense tomcat. My present Pussie has been married twice and no signs of little cats.

ever yours, dearest Mum

F.

Source: Letter, Wellcome (Claydon copy) Ms 9000/152

14 December 1863

Dearest Mother

In re cats, I think *I* will only have the thoroughbreds (then Pet had made a mesalliance after all). But give away the *nots* as fast as you can, for the old cat will settle down much better when the kittens are gone.

And you know *I* am to have all her future families, if she marries Tom.
I am quite envious of Mrs Sutherland's cats. . . .

Source: Letter, Wellcome (Claydon copy) Ms 9001/59

15 September 1864

Dearest Mother

. . . Papa tells me of Pet, the cat's misdemeanours. Pray remember
that Pet is the handsomest cat we ever had, though the original tom
was the finest. If I were you, I would not give her to the washerwoman.
I can easily find people who would be delighted to have her and have
asked for her over and over again, if you are determined to part with
her.

She was always inclined to dirtiness and to climbing trees, but we
managed by care to prevent the first. As for the last, what does it signify?
If she came down at night, it was all right. If she did not, we placed food
at the bottom of the tree and she came down at last. I certainly would
keep her, if I were you, but if not, let me find a home for her.

ever dearest Mother

your loving child

F.

Source: Letter, Wellcome (Claydon copy) Ms 9002/31

[printed address] 35 South Street
Park Lane
London, W.
21 June 1866

My dear Sir Harry [Verney]

If *Mrs Young* would like my cat (it is a she, 3/4 thoroughbred) about
eight months old, I should be rather glad to send her down directly,
by rail, if you would kindly indicate the way, so that she should not be
left to be thirsty in a basket this hot weather longer than necessary. I
did not like to trouble *you* with her. She has just lost her kits, which it
was an act of the grossest immorality in her to have, at so tender an
age, at all. . . .

ever yours

F.N.

Source: Letter, Add Mss 45754 f24

[c1869]

F. Nightingale begs to say that the lost cat has been brought back. She
takes this opportunity of begging Lord Lucan's housemaid, should a

cat with a furry tail ever come upon their premises, either to put it out the way it came, viz., the garden side or simply to ring at her area door and let her maids know that the cat is at No. 36. She will be most happy to make remuneration for this small service.

F.N. can hardly help expressing her surprise at a pet cat being turned out in the street, as was done on Monday.

Source: Letter to Mary Clarke Mohl, Woodward Biomedical Library A.13

Dearest Friend   18 April 1870

. . . Tit, Mufti and Topsy are well. Tit is the kit you were so good as to bring last May. Mr Muff (as the servants call him) and Topsy, Mrs Dicey [Elinor Bonham Carter] brought in October. They are not so feeling as the Mr Tit I once had from you, who, when I was crying for dear Hilary, used to put his arms round my neck, and he not four months old. But all cats, bless you, have much more sympathy and feeling than human beings have. Don't you remember X. de Maistre,[154] after telling the offers of service, the professions of affection his friends have made him (who now never come to help him or remember his existence)? (Oh my dear, how I have felt that!) adds "Ma chère Rosine" (Rosine is his dog), "[qui] ne m'a jamais fait d'offres de service me rend le plus grand service [illeg]." I hope your *book* is *going on* and going on well.

ever yours, dear friend,
F. Nightingale (Flo)

Source: Letter, Woodward Biomedical Library A.17

[printed address] 35 South Street
Park Lane, W.
16 July 1870

Dearest Mme Mohl

O that I should write to you, and write only about a cat! and this when empires [the Franco-Prussian War] are rushing to their ruin! . . .

But about the cat: you were so good as to leave word with Temperance [her maid] today that you had "plenty of good homes for the cats," if I had any to spare! Could you recommend me a home for *Mr Muff at once?* He is quite too troublesome to keep, and he is very unhappy, poor fellow. (And I have had quite too much of policemen, and printing handbills, and offering rewards and paying them, for lost

---

154 Probably Xavier de Maistre (1763-1852), soldier, writer and adventurer.

or stolen tomcats in London.) He is very handsome, one of yours, thoroughbred, very good-natured, about nine or ten months old. I am very sorry to part with him.

ever yours, poor failing

F.

It, the home for Mr Muff, must be somewhere where they can let him run about or he will break away and be lost the first night. I could send him to Embley, but they always let my tomcats be shot or trapped, *not* by *our* keepers, a cruel death.

F.N.

Source: Letter, Woodward Biomedical Library A.18

[printed address] 35 South Street
Park Lane, W.
20 July 1870

Dearest Mme Mohl

I have found a home for Mr Muff (cat) near London and the lady comes to fetch him in her carriage! I hope *this* will come in time to save your writing to Miss Smith. If she really wants a cat, I can give her one *soon*, a lady cat (one of yours) and wait for an opportunity to send it her. For I suppose there *is* danger this weather of sending a cat by rail to be knocked about on a platform by a careless guard and perhaps go mad.

God bless you. I should have liked to have seen M Mohl's letters.

ever yours

F.N.

Source: Letter, Woodward Biomedical Library A.35

[printed address] 35 South Street
Park Lane, W.
27 November 1871

My dearest Mme Mohl

I am so sorry that you are ill that I cannot help saying: take more care. Health is easier lost than won. After this oracular utterance, I must proceed at once to cats: I assure you that I feel so entirely devoted to "combler" [fill] the gap you describe that my whole energies are bent upon sending one to Paris by somebody, even without the glittering bait you hold out, that of introducing the somebody to society. I think a kit is ready now to go. But I don't think it ought to have gone before. I am not quite sure yet which is *Miss*. As to the colours, I think in my letter to M Mohl, I told you what they were. None are "black" and none are "black and white," which you proscribe. But all, I am afraid, are rather too dark for your taste. All three are a dark ground, two with orange-coloured spots, and one with grey spots, as if it were in mourning. All have beautiful faces, not one has any spot of white. Mr Muff, their pape, is much lighter. But Temperance says, quite gravely: "I am sure, ma'am, that Mr Muff would not like Paris." He is grown handsomer than ever, and is like *two* Muffs. But then you don't want a tom. . . .

If you hear of anybody coming to Paris, I will send the kit to *any* station to meet its chaperon or escort. And *I* will be on the lookout for someone going. But you know how off the stage I live. . . .

Source: Letter/draft/copy ADD Mss 46385 ff17-19

> [printed address] 35 South Street
> Park Lane, W.
> 23 December 1871

My dearest Mme Mohl

Do you think that I did not bend the whole purposes of my soul to getting the little cat princess to you? Indeed and I did, no ministry choosing an ambassador more anxious than I. The moment I had your letter about Dr Liebreich I wrote to him and sent my letter by hand. But meanwhile arrived Mrs Simpson and her carriage, saying that Dr Liebreich was starting at once and would we send the little cat at once? Instantly the little cat was packed up in a "most respectable basket," as the maids call it (I believe it is yours) and with quite as many directions as if it were a child, it was sent off.

Not till after Mrs Simpson was gone did I hear that Dr Liebreich was going round by Bath and not leaving for Paris till Tuesday, but that, as he was not returning by London, he wished to take the little cat (whose name is Tit) round with him by Bath. I believe I should have let Tit go, even had I known this untoward circumstance. For the only other person going to Paris that I have heard of is a cousin of Miss Smith of Oxford (who had Mrs Tit, the mother of the famous Mr Muff, the father of this kit) who goes on the 5th or 6th through Paris, and could not carry the kit to Rue du Bac, but would have taken it to the Paris station. But how do I know that the world may not have come to an end before that? The "5th or 6th January" indeed, for an affair of this importance!

I should have sent a special train and lady-in-waiting with the catkin before that! No, I believe I was right to let the Tit go, even round by Bath (what business has Bath to have the kit even for a Sunday?) by Dr Liebreich.

Temperance [her maid] showered her conditions upon Mrs Simpson. The kit was not to be let out. It was "to have a room to itself" (at Bath) and by no means to be let out of it. It was to travel in the carriage with Dr Liebreich. It was to have milk three times a day and a little meat twice (while at Bath). Dr Liebreich will be a monster if he does not bring it you safe.

I would gladly have sent you a pair. If you don't like Tit, you can have one next family Mrs Topsy has by Mr Muff. It is a matter as weighty as a royal succession.

Little Tit is the cleanest kit I ever had—used to scramble into the "pan" before it could walk. But you keep no "pan." So it must be taught what to do. (And I am afraid the turn round by Bath will not be conducive to good habits.) But who am I—writing to a professor of the art?

However, I shall be very glad when you write me a line telling me that Tit is arrived safe, and that you like it. It is the most engaging little animal, very agreeable in conversation, but has never been out before and is shy. In haste.

ever your
old Flo

Source: Letter, Wellcome Ms 5483/4

Lea Hurst
6 December 1876

Dear Madam [Mrs George Wright]

"Mr Darky" will be taken to Derby tomorrow *Thursday* and will be started from there by the train which I mentioned to you before arriving at *Nottingham,* I think, *1:50,* if you will be so good as to have him "met." I enclose his "habits," according to your kind desire.

He will be strange at first, but I am sure he will soon attach himself to you; he is such a very affectionate animal. And if your servants are as fond of him as ours are, he will give no trouble. His conversation is very agreeable, though he is shy.

If you are so good as to write to me about him, please address: 35 South St., Park Lane, London, W. It is curious how human animals which live with humans become. He knows quite well that he is going away and is sad. But you, I am sure, will be patient with him and soon comfort him. In haste.

yours sincerely
Florence Nightingale

Source: Letter, Woodward Biomedical Library A.47

35 South St.
Park Lane, W.
20 January 1877

Dearest Mme Mohl

This is solely about *cats*. The tom kitten with a "pretty face," which you said you would like (your own descendant) when you were here, has been scrupulously set apart for you. He has now, I think, the longest hair I ever saw, is most affectionate and very clean. I was in hopes that you would have let me know any opportunity by which he could have been sent to you at Paris (as you did not summon him to go with yourself). Could you let me know whether you still wish to have him? His name is Biz, and whether there will *soon* be a safe opportunity *of someone going to Paris* who would *carefully take him to you.* I should think he would be greatly admired even in Paris (if he stops here, he *will be stolen or lost*). Dearest friend, no more today.

ever your
old Flo

Source: Letter to unnamed recipient, University of Iowa, Iowa City

9 March 1882

I am so very sorry—for you and for myself. I had five Persian kittens and now I have not one. There are four little graves in the garden: two black kittens, two tabby kittens. The fifth was a most beautiful white kitten—it is dead too. All thoroughbred beauties, three or four of them were promised.

F.N.

Source: Letter, Scottish National Library Ms 6103 ff120-23

[printed address] 10 South Street
Park Lane, W.
29 December 1884

Sir [Professor Sir T. Burdon Sanderson, MD]

I venture to hope that you will pardon me, though a stranger, for writing to you and not waiting for one of our many mutual friends to introduce my letter to your kindness. It is to ask you to be so very good as to tell me in whose charge is now Brown's Hospital for Animals (at Battersea?). It had, I know, the advantage of your great name and skill at its creation.

My reason for asking yourself, the fountainhead, to direct me, is my unhappy experience of what you would call the brutelike ignorance of veterinary surgeons in treating brutes, especially thoroughbred cats. Within the last month a highly recommended veterinary surgeon so treated the last of a famous breed of real tortoise-shell Persian cats (given me twenty-seven years ago by a foreign friend, now dead) that they died—a mother cat and her kitten—in thirty-six hours in tortures. Both were in perfect health before. The cat had scratched a small wound on her neck, occasioned, as he said, by "parasites." To destroy these parasites he destroyed the cats by, in spite of my warnings and entreaties to run no such risk, steeping both cat and kitten in a "patent dressing" which, he said, he "always used with success," and which turned out to be an extract of tar. Could any result possibly follow but what did follow, viz., a cruel death? (It was like the centaur's shirt which killed Hercules. We could not get the tar off.)

The cats' looks at me were pitiful to see. The kitten I was obliged to have put out of its misery. The maids sat up with them, they were such favourites. (I am myself an overworked invalid.) Every cat of mine whom he had previously treated died under his hands, though I could not say that they died of what he did but of his ignorance what to do.

This man is the veterinary surgeon of a large district near London with an immense practice among all kinds of animals. I was advised to prosecute him but do not wish to injure him, but I wish to save future animals from veterinary surgeons.

I am encroaching too much on your kindness by so long a letter. Might I ask you to be so very good as to give me such particulars of this Brown's Hospital, or of any other doctors for animals, of which your name alone would be sufficient guarantee, that I might make use of the information both for myself and others. It is not only for the sake of valuable pets but for the sake of all animals that I write. Pray believe me,

ever your faithful servant

Florence Nightingale

A tom kitten of mine, several months old, had taken the little kitten, about a fourth his size, under his protection. He nursed it, washed it—it used to lie between his paws—kept its food for it. Since its death he has been inconsolable; his mourning for it has been quite human.

F.N.

Source: Letter, Columbia University, Presbyterian Hospital School of Nursing C168

10 South Street
Park Lane, W.
17 September 1885
10:00 A.M.

To the Inspector, Euston Station

Sir

When arriving by the 2:30 train from Bletchley way, I saw you yesterday. You were good enough to take trouble about a Persian kitten we had lost on the other side Watford Station.

Last night I wired to the Watford Station Master and had a reply: "Cat found not hurt; will send it to your address 7:25 hence tonight." But the poor little cat did not come and I have heard nothing of it, either last night or this morning.

Might I trouble you to let me know whether you have received the cat? And, if not, what you would advise to do further? With many apologies, believe me

your faithful servant

Florence Nightingale

Source: Letter, Wellcome (Claydon copy) Ms 9009/205

10 South St.
22 September 1885

My dearest Pop [Parthenope Verney]

... We had a curious journey: the hamper of Quiz, the kitten, was ill-secured and, on your side Watford, she jumped sheer out of window on to the rail out of Lizzie's compartment. I would not stop the train, but fortunately it stopped (against Bradshaw) at Watford, where I summoned all the stationmasters in England to my assistance, the same at Willesden and all the stationmasters speaking the English language at Euston. Everybody was most kind. He of Watford sent back along the rail to find it. I telegraphed to him in the evening and the answer was: "Cat found: will send it on tonight." But no cat appeared and I gave it up, for I had promised heaven to every man Jack who would deliver it at my door. But no one at the station would believe but what it was killed by leap. However next day it appeared. It had been in the Parcels Office at Euston all night and, cramped by its basket, injured by its leap, could hardly move or speak. But it is alive and begins to kick and sing. ...

Source: Letter, Columbia University, Presbyterian Hospital School of Nursing C179

[printed address] 10 South Street
Park Lane, W.
1 September 1887

Dear Madam [Mrs Hales]

Herewith comes my pet cat, Quiz, who I am sure will find a happy home with you. And I hope she will be as affectionate as she has been with me.

I will send you some particulars tomorrow about the way she has been brought up, if you will allow me. Might I ask that you will let me know in two or three days whether she goes on well, and then, later on again, as you kindly proposed.

most faithfully yours
Florence Nightingale

Letters to, for and about Domestic Employees

Editor: The first set of letters concerns the finding, keeping and looking after domestic employees, a subject to which the Nightingales, Verneys and all their relatives and friends devoted many letters. Only a small fraction are published here. Then follow letters to long-time Nightingale employees, which show how close were the ties between the invalid stay-at-home employer and her domestic staff. Again the selection, chronologically arranged, with letters to the same person kept together, represents only a small fraction of the extant letters.

Source: Letter, Wellcome (Claydon copy) Ms 8998/9

Hampstead N.W.
14 December 1859

My dear [Parthenope Verney]

It occurred to me after writing yesterday (1) if you are going to set up a needlewoman under the housekeeper, Mary Jenkins, Bathwoman, Dr W. Johnson's, Great Malvern, has a niece, living at Oxford, a first-rate needlewoman, eldest girl of a very large family, who wants or wanted a place. If she is at all like my good old friend, her aunt, she would be a very valuable servant. Perhaps her needlework would be almost too good for your place. I believe she is a qualified "young lady's maid," though when I heard of her, she had never been "out," i.e., in service. Perhaps she has a place. I think it answers very well in a large house to have as much as possible done at home, as little as possible "put out."

2. You know Mary Bratby is almost *too* maternal. I mean you need not fear her thinking it a *trouble* to arrange and manage for the boys. She would take almost too much trouble for them, especially if they came down without you. You know, on all the health expeditions to the sea or elsewhere of Shore or of Beatrice, years ago, *she* was always sent with the sick sinner.

3. Bratby's health necessitates some outdoor work. He is a very good outdoor servant. If he is left in charge of Claydon when you are in London, I should think it would suit very well. I suppose there must be some man left in charge.

yours ever

F.N.

Source: Letter, Wellcome (Claydon copy) Ms 8998/42

[1859-60]

Dearest Mum

It is *quite* impossible for me to see dear Mrs Sutherland tomorrow, at *any* hour. But would you show her this note?

Nothing would induce me to take a maid recommended by Frances or any Bonham Carter, having had *five* of these "treasures" who were absolute incompetents and worse. As Bertha and Beatrice have been in a *perennial* state of hunt for me, I don't anticipate much from *that*. Indeed and indeed, all these have been asked and failed over and over again. But, as for poor Frances, I positively decline seeing anybody sent by *her*. *Marianne Galton is the only person* in the family whose *recommendation is worth anything*. Could you, dearest Mum, ask *her*?

ever your loving child

F.

Source: Letter, Wellcome (Claydon copy) Ms 9000/15

9 C. St.

28 March [1862]

Dearest Mother

I shall be very much pleased with a housemaid from Embley, if it turns out that you think she will do. I am in treaty with three others, so that they must stand over till I hear from you whether yours will do or not.

You know that the most scrupulous cleanliness is what I want, nicety, and order in *common* work so that she shall not need someone always standing over her, or two dustpans of dust will accumulate under an ordinary carpet, a thing I have just discovered here in a room supposed to be thoroughly cleansed. There is no *fine* housemaid's work to do as Mrs P. Ward put away everything that was worth anything.

Many thanks for the prints, framed and unframed, the curtains and all the rest out of the boxes. We shall look quite grand.

Perhaps next time Burton will make us a *pigeon* pie. And could you send us next time a sod with grass for the cat? Are you going to have any kittens?

ever dear Mum

your loving child

F.

Source: Letter, Wellcome (Claydon copy) Ms 9001/5

24 January 1864

Dearest Mother

Your letter to Walker came too late for me to write to you by post on Saturday night that I am alive. As for Walker, she is gone. The less said about this miserable affair the better, there being so little tangible. I was obliged to desire her to leave the room and to send her home for a month to recover herself. Farther consideration has induced me to have her written to, to tell her not to return, giving her a month's wages and board wages instead of a month's warning. I think you had better say nothing about it, because I can PROVE hardly anything against her.

ever your loving child

F.N.

Parthe will remember that I begged her not to write to W. though I had no idea then of parting with her so precipitately. . . .

F.N.

Source: Unsigned letter, Wellcome (Claydon copy) Ms 9001/46

[1864-65]

Dearest Mother

Pray put out of your own head, and don't put into the cook's head, that "so much is required" in my place. I know *no* place where so little is required and so much is given. (I was perfectly satisfied with a mere girl, Mrs Sutherland's cook, and she with me, and we should never have parted but for that wicked woman, whose sin the girl had found out.)

In any family consisting of two there is *more* cooking than in mine. I know no one but myself who will spare a servant for a week's holiday, or for three months, to nurse a mother, paying her wages and supporting the mother all the time. All that *is* "required" is that she shall be trusted neither to drink nor flirt, *not* having a mistress, and not having a capable head servant to enforce order. In your family you can depend upon yourself and you can depend upon your other servants to find out if anything goes wrong with one. *I have no one, not even myself.* With this one exception, I know no family where so little is required and so much is given, as my own.

As for her taking orders through my maid, she *must* consent to do it. But I see more and more it is impossible. I must see her every day myself and give my own orders. This is what Ann C. provided for me yesterday, *and nothing else. A patient's diet*: luncheon, *gooseberry* pudding (which I did not touch); dinner, *bacon* and beans, almost raw, which I did not touch; supper, a cold drumstick chicken, which I did not touch because there was nothing to touch. Saturday. *Burn this.*

Source: Unsigned, undated note, ADD Mss 45815 ff197-98

Mrs Reynolds

The kindest best good humour wanting in business, that is, in seeing how to carry out your wishes. I am sure in your kindness you will be glad if I point out a few things:

1. Our kitchen maid—are her little naughtinesses encouraged by a certain want of firmness with her, which runs through all?

2. I have given my housekeeper/you ten minutes in the morning. More than this tires me so much as to destroy half my morning's power of work. During this time of ten minutes, if she will be so good as simply take the orders, remember and carry them out, and if there is anything like an illness or repairs which must be attended to directly tell it as shortly as possible, leaving all stories about cats, zymotic diseases to the afternoon if I see her then.

3. If a dish, such as warming up from a joint, is found always uneaten by an invalid, try another way till it succeeds.

4. To take in nothing but the best from a tradesman is simply one of the first duties of the cook. To make excuses for the tradesman is the sign of a bad cook.

5. Nothing should have to be repeated by the mistress twice.

6. It is natural that the cook should think everything she does well done. But she should remember the old proverb: the proof of the pudding (or meat) and not in talking.

Source: Letter, Wellcome (Claydon copy) Ms 9002/66

18 October 1866

My dear Sir Harry [Verney]

I think I will hardly trouble you to speak to Lady Lucy Calvert[155] about the maid. Sir John McNeill said: "One must be in such very robust health to undergo the water cure." And I feel, "I must be in such very robust health to undergo" that maid. I kept her till yesterday hoping in vain to see in her some sign of efficiency or common sense. For I have no one else in view and feel now as if I really could not undertake the going on with the search. But there really existed no doubt in anyone's mind here that she "would not do." She could not remember, at first, having been with Lady Charlotte Montgomery *at all* (as you saw also in her letter). And afterwards she talked of her with tears in her eyes! And so about EVERYthing.

Also, her indiscretion!!! She told me a story about the husband of a lady she had lived with, which I believe to be false, which, true or false, should never have passed her lips, and which I would not have her tell my innocent maids for the world. I thought I would have waited to hear from Lady Lucy Calvert before I determined whether to give Mrs Rushforth her "coup de grace." But, as there will be still some delay, and as I feel so incapable of dealing as a mistress with Mrs Rushforth, I think I will write to her today and dismiss the matter. She is a good woman, I am sure, but "so funny," as all this household called her. . . .

ever yours
F.N.

Source: Letter to Parthenope Verney, Wellcome (Claydon copy) Ms 9008/28

7 March 1880

. . . Can you tell me of an upper housemaid, capable and responsible, and KNOWN to someone we know and can trust? You remember W. Hedges. I took him in from St George's till I could get him into Dover "Home." His wife was looking out for a housemaid's place and I took her. She was three months with child!! And just at this time I have all this on my hands.

---

155 Wife of Frederick Calvert, Harry Verney's brother.

Source: Letter, Lea Hurst RSAS Age Care

10 South St. W.

19 January 1885

Dear Mrs Broomhead

I do feel so very much for you at losing your son in the house, though he is not gone very far from you, yet it is not the same as having him at home. And you so suffering!

I am sure that kind Mr Wildgoose must have been very, very sorry to find himself under the necessity of consenting to this, as well, as one or two others, who had served their apprenticeship as mechanics, being sent away. But it must be a comfort to you to know that there was no fault; on the contrary that especially Samuel is a good steady young man, Mr Wildgoose however having obtained him a situation with the firm at Loughboro' who make the machinery, it is well for him in that respect. He ought to make even more money there than he did here.

I should hope therefore that your son will be able to do as well for you, and he will not be so very far away. The young men are, I believe, all lodging together with a Christian woman. And this must make the blow less hard to you. Our loving Almighty Father knows what it is to you not to have him at home. He will keep you as the "apple of His eye."[156]

I heard the voice of Jesus say
"Come unto me and rest:
Lay down, thou weary one, lay down
Thy head upon my breast."[157]

My eyes and health are so bad that I can only write this pencil brief letter. God bless you ever. With deepest sympathy.

yours sincerely

F. Nightingale

Source: Unsigned letter to Harry Verney, Wellcome (Claydon copy) Ms 9012/223

23 July 1889

Mrs Davidson [Parthenope Verney's maid] wants to go with her brother (who has only a fortnight's holiday) to Scotland on Thursday 1 August (*must* know on Wednesday 31 July). If she cannot go, she will give up going to Scotland. Her health is bad. Her right arm is painful. If she cannot have this rest now, she *may* have to leave Lady Verney.

---

156 An allusion to Deut 32:10.
157 *Hymns Ancient and Modern* 257.

Editor: Nightingale's maid Temperance Hatcher married the Russian lad Nightingale brought back from the Crimea, Peter Grillage, who had become footman to her father.

Source: Letter, Wellcome (Claydon copy) Ms 9014/96

[printed address] 10 South Street
Park Lane, W.
4 February 1893

My dear Sir Harry [Verney]

... Last night Temperance—you remember Temperance, now the mother of an eldest son of nineteen—came up from Plympton with the eldest son, a very nice lad indeed, and the two slept here. This morning the lad has gone on to his place as journeyman gardener in Lord Fitzwilliam's gardens at Wentworth in Yorkshire. The poor mother seemed almost heartbroken at parting with him, but Lord Fitzwilliam's house steward, Hatcher, is Temperance's brother and that comforts her. He is a man whom you so to say *made*: you took him as pageboy, because he was Temperance's brother, and he rose to be house steward to Lord Lansdowne in Canada, and was with him during his five years in Canada and Lord L. would have taken him to India. Then he went with Sir -- Loch to Africa. Now he is house steward to Lord Fitzwilliam. And nothing else would have induced Temperance to let the boy go so far from her. God bless you.

your affectionate
F.N.

Source: Unsigned note, Wellcome (Claydon copy) Ms 9014/202

16 December 1894

Dearest Lettice [Verney]

Could you or Mother kindly tell me of a really nice book for *Ada White*, nearly sixteen, a Claydon girl, Mrs Robertson's maid, who is going with her to her new place, and has often picked wild primroses for me. I would write to London for it *today* and get it by Tuesday. I should like to give her two.

Source: Letter to Margaret Verney, Wellcome (Claydon copy) Ms 9015/83

12 December 1896

... How very kind of you to ask my Lizzie Coleman to your ball and to offer her a much-prized bed. She was delighted. I will accept the ball for her, but not the bed, please, because of the uncertainty whether she will be able to come. She shall sleep at her parents the night before and the night after that great event, i.e., at Steeple Claydon, and I will see that she has a fly, if possible. May all joy attend your ball! . . .

Bratby and Mary Bratby

Source: Letter, Wellcome (Claydon copy) Ms 8998/8

Hampstead N.W.
13 December 1859

My dear [Parthenope Verney]

I think Bratby a most valuable servant and in every respect what you want. Trustworthiness is Mary [Bratby]'s name. As the moral head of a household [I] think her unequalled. She is the ONLY servant I ever knew who placed her honour in speaking the truth at all times and in everything, about others as well as herself. (I say this literally and not as a flourish.)

I do not think you would find her useful in *any* manual employment. She never was a good cook, housemaid or needlewoman. And "the little" goodness she had "hath been taken from her"[158] by her poor thumb. En revanche, she has a curious talent, which I never saw to the same degree in *any* woman, educated or uneducated, and which is more like a clerk's, of knowing where I had put any paper or report, of always bringing the right book, etc. This made her loss to me an irreparable one. I should think it would be turned to account in a large house, charge of furniture, etc.

There must be many details as to what they will have to do with you which make it impossible for me to give a more particular opinion. All the things you specify, *except the needlework*, I would trust Mary to do *exactly* as I would myself. (She is a *really* religious woman.)

I think I never saw a luckier marriage, for the things Mary is most deficient in are those best done by Bratby, and they are the most inseparable couple. I need not say that it would be a great relief to me, were Mary *well* settled.

F.N.

---

158 An allusion to Matt 13:12.

Source: Letter, Columbia University, Presbyterian Hospital School of Nursing C126

[printed address] 10 South Street
Park Lane, W.
26 April 1879

My dear Mary [Bratby]

I was very sorry to hear of your being poorly again, as Mr Dunn had already written to me, but I hope you are now pretty well again. Do you know we pray for your health at our family prayer night and morning?

I like to hear that Bratby wants to get into his garden, and I hope that at last spring is coming. It has been as bad weather in London as anywhere else: snow last week. Mrs Nightingale and Mrs Shore Smith have both had bronchitis, but both are better. We lost a young trained head nurse on Easter Monday.

Boy Sam has passed his entrance examination at Cambridge and goes up to Trinity College in October. It makes me think of his father, though he is not like a bit to his father. I hear very good accounts of the Embley people.

As soon as I had your letter, I wrote to order twenty-four tins of cocoatina to go down to you. Please let me know when it arrives. It was addressed to you, care of Mr Yeomans, Whatstandwell Station. Would you please give a tin of cocoatina to that poor woman, Mary Shardlow, who lives with her sister? She has written to ask for it. Mr Dunn attends her and thinks ill of her. She is neglected and miserable in soul and body. I am going to ask Mr Yeomans to give her milk. I hope the little Allison grandchildren are quite well. Mr Dunn has quite set up Jane Allison, and I trust she is continuing well.

Do you know that Mr Alfred [Bonham Carter] is going to be married to a lady some twenty years younger than himself?, Mrs Harry's [Bonham Carter's] sister (Miss Norman). You know, I dare say, that Mrs Grace is going to be married to Mr Poyser, a grocer of Wirksworth, a great misfortune to my mother at her age. And we are in all the misery now of making the change. Pray God the new maid may succeed.

With kind regards to Bratby, I am ever your much overworked and ill, but

ever affectionately yours
F. Nightingale

Editor: From the date of the following letter it is evident that it was written the very day Mrs Nightingale died, one of the first of many Nightingale sent to advise friends, servants, doctors, etc. of her mother's death. Nightingale wrote Mary Bratby later in 1880 about the impending death of Uncle Sam (see p 485 above).

Source: Letter, Columbia University, Presbyterian Hospital School of Nursing C128

[printed address] 10 South Street
Park Lane, W.
2 February 1880

My dear Mary [Bratby]

I am sure that you and Bratby will be thinking of us. Just after midnight my dear mother died quite peacefully. Since Thursday week she had had much sweatiness and painfulness, though not so much as during her attack at Lea Hurst. She was always, when it came near the last, and at all times, soothed when Mr Shore came in. She smiled a smile as if she said: "I'm dying; it's all right." She longed to go home. Up to the last, she always responded to or repeated her favourite hymn and prayer. Then it grew more solemn as if she saw God, when she smiled.

When Mrs Shore repeated the Lord's Prayer, after she could neither speak nor swallow, she put out her arm, and waved it gently over her head in triumph, as it were, as if she said: "I see God. I am going home." Then she composed her own self to death at 9:00 last night, folded her hands, laid herself down, closed her own eyes and in three hours she was gone home.

I will write again. Please tell *your* "Aunt Fanny" and Sisters Allen. God bless you, dear Mary.

ever yours affectionately

F. Nightingale

Mrs Morris was *all* kindness and mourns her as truly as a daughter her mother. Her attention to her was beautiful.

F.N.

Source: Letter, Columbia University, Presbyterian Hospital School of Nursing C156

Claydon House, Bucks
3 October 1883

Dear Bratby

I am very sorry indeed not to see you again this year, but Mr Shore will have told you how impossible it is for me to leave poor Lady Verney till I am obliged to return to London. At this moment there is nobody but me; Sir Harry is absent.

I owe you for a year's *Daily News*. And, could you go on with some of the things our dear Mary did for me? (1) There is *Martha Sheldon*, whom you and I talked together about. What would you advise to be done for her this year? (2) And there is *Widow Barton,* one of the best women that ever lived, whom Mr Nightingale was very fond of. She is *very* poor. Some flannel or warm shawl or gown for the winter, and three or four months of two lbs. meat a week from the butcher, perhaps, would be the best things for her. Could you see her and ask? (3) Then there is poor old *Lyddy Prince,* who might be so comfortable if Adam were a better man. I think she must want something of warm clothes for the winter. (4) And there is old *Mrs Brown.* She, too, must want something of the sort. Meat also? (5) And the *sisters Allen.* They are very proud. But perhaps you or your niece could make out from them what they want in the way of warm clothing. Pray tell all of these with my kindest regards how very sorry I am not to see them this year.

I hope you yourself are pretty well, and your niece, too, and her eyes. Pray give her my kind regards and would she be so very good as to send me a list of those who have cocoatina. And perhaps she would write me a list of what these our friends want, that I may send you the money if you will be so good as to undertake it.

If *Widow Barton* would like the meat, then I send an order on Walker for it to Mr Yeomans. And should Widow Brown be failing, then she might like 2 lbs meat weekly, too. And you must not forget to send a message of love to "Aunt Fanny," Mrs Wildgoose, for me, and tell her how sorry I am not to see her. How is she?

I think our dear Mary used to pay Lizzie Holmes for doing some knitting or crochet work for me. Would you kindly undertake that this year? I am particularly sorry not to see the Holmeses this year. They are such good people. I heard some talk of their going to America. I should be so sorry. And *Jane Allison*: we must do something for her.

And now, dear Bratby, goodbye. I am glad to have seen you in London.

yours ever faithfully

F. Nightingale

I seem to be making out the list as I used to do with our dear Mary.

yours and hers most faithfully

F.N.

You have had Mr Shore and Mr Sam and Mrs Shore and Miss Rosy and the other two, so you will not have missed me. You will be sorry to hear that our Fanny is still ill in bed here.

Source: Letter, Columbia University, Presbyterian Hospital School of Nursing C158

10 South St.

8 November 1883

Dear Bratby

I have sent off today by quick train (carriage paid) to you from St Pancras a package of which I enclose the list of contents, and for whom (you will of course charge to me the porterage, etc.). If you will be so very good as to give the things and ask all the people to write to me and tell me particulars of how they are, I shall be grateful to you.

I enclose on the envelope what the gowns ought to have for lining and braid, which can be got in Holloway, if you will be so very good as to arrange this, or give with each of the gowns 2/ each.

I hope you are keeping pretty well. I will write more, and send you some more money, please. But I have been very poorly since I came home. Fanny is still in bed, though going on well.

ever sincerely yours and dear Mary's

F. Nightingale

All the things come from the best manufacture in North Wales, and I hope *are* the best.

Source: Letter, Columbia University, Presbyterian Hospital School of Nursing C160

[printed address] 10 South Street

Park Lane, W.

7 December 1883

Dear Bratby

I am so very sorry that you are disabled again, and very much obliged to you for all you have done for the people. I ordered the cocoatina the same day that I received Mrs Brocklehurst's letter and hope that it has arrived. A cheque for £5 is enclosed, as I think you will be wanting money to go on with what you have kindly undertaken.

Pray remember me kindly to Martha Sheldon. I am very sorry she is so poorly. If she likes to have Dr Dunn, I will gladly pay for him for her. I am glad you told her to knit stockings—two pairs might go to *Lyddy Prince*; two pairs to *Mrs Broomhead*, who I hear is very ill, if she likes them; two pairs to *Mrs Barton*. Remember me most kindly to all.

I am very glad the memorial stone is finished. That is a very nice verse Miss Smith chose for it. God bless you and dear Mary, not poor but rich indeed. I am sure she thinks of you.

By dint of good nursing, Lady Verney is a trifle better, thank God. She can occupy herself more, but she will never walk again.

Fanny has been a terrible anxiety for ten weeks that she has kept her room, with doctors nearly every day. She has been restless all the time, and last Monday she went most eagerly to St Thomas' Hospital. And next day she wanted to come out again, however she is quieting down. They are as kind to her as if she were everyone's only child there.

I would have written before, but as you may fancy I am quite knocked down by all this and can hardly do the work which comes in so fast, and which dear Mary knew so well. God bless you always.

ever yours sincerely

F. Nightingale

I am always glad to hear from you and about all the people.

Source: Letter, Columbia University, Presbyterian Hospital School of Nursing C164

10 South St.

18 March 1885

Dear Bratby

I have thought a great deal of you during this severe weather and feared that you were suffering more. I trust that you have had Dr Dunn and are now better.

I have not heard much of Hannah Allen lately, though I wrote to her. As she has her niece living with her, which I am glad to hear, I should welcome a letter from her. Poor Mrs Broomhead! She is a terrible sufferer. How her life is prolonged! There is, however, no "cancer" in the case, as Mrs Brocklehurst supposes. I hear of her from Dr Dunn. Pray give my kindest regards to her and tell her I should like to hear from her son of her. Is she cheerful?

But you must tell them all, please, that though I think of them, I cannot write. They, and you too, must think of me as seriously ill, with a night nurse (which I have never had in my life before), and a doctor two or three times a day. They must pray for me as I do for them, and God bless you all, I say continually. And poor Mrs Brown, she has my best good wishes.

(The last time Mrs Brocklehurst told me she was so poorly, I sent word to Dr Dunn, and he went at once. But he found her "better than usual" so I was rather in a scrape.)

I am very glad you sent Mr Graves to poor Martha Sheldon, to whom my kind remembrances, and gave her "good beef tea" and "gin," or whatever Mr Graves ordered. And please go on.

Dr Dunn gives me a very deplorable account of Jane Allison, that is, of the state of her mind, and the worry her relations cause her. Do you ever see her? I hope Lyddy Prince is pretty well. Is Adam good to her? Or is he out of work this severe weather? Give her, too, a message from me. Is there anything you would like me to do for her? She does have an allowance from Mr Yeomans for me. I will send you £5, in case you want more money. I hope you get your newspaper regularly, and that your eyes are good.

Poor Lady Verney is still in much the same state, but it is astonishing how much she likes seeing people. They even give a dinner party, she seeing the company before and after dinner. My aunt at Embley has not been allowed even to sit up in bed during this very cold weather and she has had toothache and had a tooth out. But I hear from her often—her hand as good and her mind as clear as ever and she suffers less. Shore and his son Louis have been staying here for an examination of Louis. Shore is going down to Embley tomorrow. You know that Mrs Smith was ninety on 4 February.

Now I cannot write a word more. So, dear Bratby, God bless you.

faithfully yours

F. Nightingale

I am sorry that Mrs Brocklehurst is so poorly herself and much obliged to her for writing to me.

Source: Letter, Columbia University, Presbyterian Hospital School of Nursing C173

10 South St.

9 November 1886

Dear Bratby

I am very sorry to have been so long in writing. Thank God that you were the better for Ramsgate, but I am sorry the poor hands are not better.

I wrote to Mr Yeomans as soon as I had Mrs Brocklehurst's note, to whom my kind regards, asking him to send a load of coals to Mrs Barton, which I hope arrived. Could you tell me and whether she will want some more?

Martha Sheldon writes to me that, if I mean to give her work, I had better do so at once. Would you kindly do this? Stockings, I think you must order, but not for Sir Harry Verney, for he will not look at them. She has been nursing her brother. If you could tell me of anything I could do for her, I would do it.

I have a good account from Mr Dunn, on the whole, of our people. And I hope to hear from you again soon. But this must be a very short note. I saw Mr Shore last night and heard from Mrs S. Smith at Embley this morning, in her own clear handwriting all right.

Do you want money? Please tell me. Mrs Thomason is with me, as temporary cook. She looks well. My cook is ill.

ever dear Bratby

yours sincerely

F. Nightingale

I hope you go on with your *Daily News.*

Source: Letter, Columbia University, Presbyterian Hospital School of Nursing C174

10 South St.

3 December 1886

Dear Bratby

I hope you will be so good as to get a pair of blankets for Martha Sheldon. She seems to be behaving very kindly to her brother at last. The blankets to be had at Matlock Bath, or even at Holloway, are just as good, I have found, as here, so perhaps you will kindly get them for her.

I am afraid you must have had some snow yesterday. I ought to have written before, but I have been so ill and so overworked with the India Office and War Office, like what I was when dear Mary and you were with me, that I have scarcely been able to do anything else.

I hope you are pretty well and Mrs Brocklehurst. Please give her my kind regards and thank her for her letter. . . .

Mrs Smith is very well. Shore is going down to Embley today. Lady Verney, wonderful to say, has been better the last week or two, and very active. But you know she is quite helpless—every joint is bad. She cannot even turn in bed. God bless you.

sincerely yours

F. Nightingale

Sir Harry comes up on Tuesday for Lord Hartington's meeting.

Source: Letter, Columbia University, Presbyterian Hospital School of Nursing C175

[printed address] 10 South Street

Park Lane, W.

29 December 1886

Dear Bratby

I send for Mrs Broomhead a soft invalid gown, a flannel for drawers and singlets; Lyddy Prince an "active" gown; Mrs Holmes (who gives away the milk) a cloth gown. Please give to each of these who have gowns 2/6 for lining, etc. or whatever it was we gave before. For sisters Hannah Allen flannel for drawers; *Ann* red flannel for petticoats; for Mrs Barton flannel for drawers and singlets; for Mrs Brown flannel ditto. All with my kindest regards and hopes that the things, which all come from Wales and, I am told, are the best of their kind, will prove comfortable and good.

I am sorry not to do them up all in separate parcels for you to send, but we are such invalids in this house and I am so busy. Perhaps Mrs Brocklehurst would be so very good as to buy paper, charging it to me, and do them up, and particularly the gown for Mrs Holmes, if she would do it up carefully and direct it outside and send it. Pray give her my kind regards and best thanks.

I am so sorry that your shoulders are so bad. Still I can wish you happiness in the New Year in doing many a kindness to your poor neighbours. I always think of dear Mary.

ever yours and hers

F. Nightingale

What stirring times these are.

Source: Letter, Columbia University, Presbyterian Hospital School of Nursing C176

10 South St.

8 March 1887

Dear Bratby and Mrs Brocklehurst

Thank you very much for all your kindness to our dear old Mrs Barton, and for the letters about her. I am sure the end of her life was made much happier by your attention.

I was very fond of her, when she lived, a happy wife and mother at Leashaw Lodge. Mr Nightingale used to go and see them almost every Sunday afternoon. He used to sit on the three-legged table before the fire—she has told me this—and say: "Now, Barton, read us a bit of a chapter" (to her husband). "And the squire would sometimes choose the chapter himself, but most times he would say, 'Barton, you choose it.' "

She was a good woman, so patient, living her lonely life in Holloway and so industrious, as long as she could work at all. Mrs Brocklehurst has been very kind to her. And Mrs Holmes has contributed to make her end happy; I hope she died happy. Now she wants no more—she is happy now.

I have written to Mr Yeomans to continue her two milks, her meat and her eggs, to *that* daughter-in-law who was *kind* to her, and who, I believe, is much worn, till Lady Day. If you think help is wanted to wash up what the good old lady has left, will you kindly pay for that washing? I hope what is worth it will go to that daughter-in-law. I have ordered a black gown from Wales which I will send you for her mourning, please.

I am afraid the other daughter-in-law was the *contrary* of kind in more ways than one. But I hope she had some comfort in her sons.

Now the labourer's task is o'er,
Now the battle-field is passed,
Now upon the farther shore,
Lands the voyager at last.[159]

God bless you both.

Sir Harry Verney, I am sorry to say, is in bed with a cold, under Sir Andrew Clark's care. His bad illnesses, during which he has lain at death's door for weeks, have always been during the March, or March and February east winds, but we hope this will be nothing serious, having taken it in time.

yours sincerely
F. Nightingale

Source: Letter, Columbia University, Presbyterian Hospital School of Nursing C178

Dear Bratby   23 July 1887

Thank God you are so much better. I hope the Ramsgate expedition will come to pass, as you wish it, and Dr Dunn approves of it, and you have a friend to go with you. Your recovery is wonderful, thank God for it. I trust you have not much pain now, and that your cough is going, this very warm summer.

Your neighbours, I am sure, have wished you well and will rejoice to have you coming among them again. Give my kind regards and thanks to Mrs Brocklehurst, and tell her that I have not written because all this year I have been so poorly that I have barely been able to do the most pressing business. But I have corresponded constantly with Dr Dunn about you. At one time he very kindly wrote to me *every* day. And Dr Webb wrote to me too.

I should like to hear (when you can dictate a letter), how the sisters Allen are, and Martha Sheldon, of whom I have not heard for a long time, and Lyddy Prince and her naughty son, and poor Mrs Broomhead, and all my friends. Do you want money?

I hope you have been able to take interest in the jubilee doings lately.

Mr Shore, who has been a good deal at Embley lately, because his mother is far from well, I grieve to say, goes today to the naval review at Portsmouth with Sam, and Mrs Shore goes with her brother from London. Louis is gone to Germany for two months to read. Arthur Clough told me when he had seen you. Mr Fred Verney has sailed

---

159 *Hymns Ancient and Modern* 401.

today with the Siamese princes (he is secretary to the Siamese legation in London) for America, Japan, Siam, to negotiate treaties. It is a sacrifice and a risk and Mrs Fred Verney and her children remain behind. Now God bless you.

sincerely yours

F. Nightingale

Source: Letter, Columbia University, Presbyterian Hospital School of Nursing C182

10 South St.

Park Lane, W.

13 December 1887

Dear Bratby

I am afraid I did not send you the £5 you wanted; I thought I did. This was a great mistake on my part, but here it is. I fear you are very suffering this weather. Pray have Dr Dunn.

PRIVATE: Poor sisters Allen—I hope they have all they want while Ann is in this state. I have asked Mr Yeomans to give them £5 (£1 at a time) during the winter months. I hope Hannah does not sleep in the same bed with Ann in her present illness.

Will you kindly tell all my friends whom you see that I shall not be able to send them Christmas and New Year's cards this year, but I shall wish them my best wishes all the more, and to you, too. I am obliged by doctors' orders to go away for a time into perfect solitude in order to put off the complete breaking up, if it be God's will, and the loss of my eyesight.[160] But letters will be forwarded to me.

I have letters from my aunt at Embley, nobly and cheerfully calm, though she knows she will never leave her rooms while in this world. She writes just like herself and in a firm handwriting. God bless you and all my Holloway friends. Pray have Dr Dunn.

ever sincerely yours

with kind regards to Mrs Brocklehurst

F. Nightingale

---

160 Nightingale went to the Fred Verneys's home, Pine Acre.

Source: Letter, Columbia University, Presbyterian Hospital School of Nursing C184

[printed address] 10 South Street
Park Lane, W.
5 June 1888

My dear Bratby

I am very sorry that you are suffering so much and very sorry that your eyes are so bad. But Mr Shore, I hoped, would have suited your eyes with glasses. He wishes to take any pains to suit them, and I hope he will still be able to do so. Just now he is in Devonshire but going to Embley, I believe, this week.

I have sent you some cocoatina. I did not understand Mrs Brocklehurst's letter when she said you would want in three weeks, and did not say *what*. I meant to have written to inquire, but was too ill. Poor Lady Verney is very bad.

It is very, very kind of Mr Wildgoose to pay for Adam Prince at the hospital. I trust poor Adam will now leave off the drink entirely. I would go on with Mrs Smith's allowance to Lyddy Prince, if you think she needs it badly. I do make her a small allowance.

I am so very, very sorry that Hannah Allen's good niece has had to leave her. You know that H. Allen had a delusion that she was being poisoned. This went off for a time, partly, I believe, because I send her things from here. I wish I had known *beforehand* that the niece was going to leave her. Possibly I might have been able to prevent it, at least for a time. It is a thousand pities. Poor old Hannah Allen!

I am glad you do for Martha Sheldon. Pray give to all my kindest regards. I hope you will go on trying to get glasses that suit you. I believe it is not serious seeing "two swallows" when there is only one. It only means that one eye has a longer sight than the other. The two eyes see but one object when the sight is equal. My eyes are very bad. Glasses hardly help me at all. But the sight of one eye is very much shorter than the other.

I have only been out of bed three times in three months long, enough to have my room done, and don't seem to get much better. But we are very busy now.

Sir Harry is brisk, but older. He fainted in my room, which is a serious thing for one of his age. God bless you.

ever faithfully yours
F. Nightingale

Source: Letter, Columbia University, Presbyterian Hospital School of Nursing C185

10 South St.
6 July 1888

Dear Bratby

I hope you are not suffering much this very bad summer. I am so very sorry that Mr Wildgoose is going to leave Holloway, and sorry for you, too. You will miss them.

I have good accounts of Mrs Sam Smith *on the whole*. But you know she was downstairs for the last time on 24 May last year. She is now entirely in bed in the music room and is not now able to sit up in bed. But her mind is as bright as ever and she not seldom writes to me. She has suffered a good deal but not lately. She still has the same nurses, a day nurse and a night nurse, and still has the same power of attaching people to her so much.

I heard from Mr Shore this morning. He is in Devonshire with Mrs Shore and Rosalind and Louis. Louis is there from Oxford for his vacation. They are staying with an old cousin of Mrs Shore's who, having lost her only brother, is very lonely.

How is Martha Sheldon? Please remember me to her and to Jane Allison. How is she?

Mr Arthur Clough is very bright and active, and does famous work at the Education Office. Sam is studying at St Bartholomew's Hospital, as you know. The two young gentlemen come and dine here pretty often. When Rosalind was staying here, Sam came every day. Rosalind is extremely active in co-operation, and attended the Dewsbury Congress as a delegate!! There is no hanging back from work among our young people nowadays.

Thena Clough lives a great deal with her aunt, helping her—Miss Clough being the principal of a college for ladies at Cambridge,[161] as you know. The other principal is a daughter of Mr Gladstone's. You may have seen the opening of "Clough" Hall by the Prince and Princess of Wales in the newspaper (which I hope you can read) last month.

Lady Verney is very poorly, but they had all our probationer nurses down to Claydon for the day from St Thomas', which they enjoyed excessively, last Thursday. Sir Harry ages, but is very active.

Beatrice is at Stokke. I am scarcely able to leave my bed at all, but am able to do a good bit of work. Lately we have sent "sisters" to a

---

161 Anne Clough was the first principal of Newnham College, Blanche Athena Clough (1861-1960) a later principal.

Mohammedan hospital for women in Egypt, one to South Africa, with twenty-five *Hampshire* agricultural families, including 100 children, five Gordon boys, where Lady Ossington, an old lady of eighty-four, has contributed the funds, to form a settlement 140 miles west of Port East London, called the Tennyson Settlement. We have, besides, more hospital business than we can undertake. Mrs Wardroper, matron of St Thomas', has retired, after thirty-seven years' service. And Miss Pringle, one of ours, thirteen years lady superintendent of the great Edinburgh Infirmary, which has 1500 students, has succeeded her at St Thomas'. God bless you.

ever faithfully yours

F. Nightingale

7 July 1888

Please remember me to all my friends at Holloway and to Mrs Brocklehurst.

Has Adam Prince left the Matlock water cure? How kind of Mr Wildgoose to put him there. And how is he? and his mother? my friend Lyddy Prince. I hope you have Mr Dunn whenever you wish for him.

F.N.

Source: Letter, Columbia University, Presbyterian Hospital School of Nursing C188

Claydon House
Winslow, Bucks
2 October 1888

Dear Bratby

I hope your maid is going on well. If not, that you will send for Dr Graves. I believe Dr Dunn is away.

I feel very sorry for poor old Lydia Prince. And yet all one gives her is so much saved for Adam Prince to put into himself for drink. If you like to give her half a crown a week for two months, and to tell me what she wants most—flannels—for what? or a warm gown. She is very much to be pitied.

I hope you pay for your newspaper out of what money you have of mine.

Lady Verney is worse. And Sir Harry's brother, also above eighty, is come here completely broken up. There are only we four and yet we are not an uncheerful four. Yet it seems a strange four, without chick nor child. Mrs Verney is coming soon, and then I must return to South St. We have as much to do in London as when you and Mary were with me in Burlington St. and I am worse.

Dr Sutherland is dying—he has resigned his post. He is eighty and so is Mrs Sutherland.

Dear Aunt Mai at Embley no longer writes, but she reads letters. She is pretty comfortable. Shore was telegraphed for from Embley to nurse a poor old lady-cousin of his wife's in Devonshire, where they have been staying much this summer to be with her. He is so good. Mrs Shore and Rosalind return from Ireland this week. Rosalind is working hard at co-operatives.

To return to poor Lydia Prince. Do you know *what* doctor attends Adam? I suppose it is Dr Graves? Will you tell me if she had the "medicine" she asked for, which I sent before to Adam, and which is a cordial prescribed by a London doctor against drink? I ordered two bottles from London to be sent them.

I am glad that poor Martha Sheldon is spending her savings' bank money. She had better spend it when she wants it. Thank you for going to see poor Jane Allison, too. I have not heard from her. I asked her to choose a favourite hymn, and I mentioned one or two, and to repeat it every day and tell me she had done so.

It is very difficult now for me to write much besides my most pressing business. My kind regards to Mrs Brocklehurst and thank her for writing. God bless you.

ever sincerely yours

Florence Nightingale

Source: Letter, Columbia University, Presbyterian Hospital School of Nursing C190

[printed address] Claydon House
Winslow, Bucks
11 October 1888

Dear Bratby

Thank you very much for telling me of poor Martha Sheldon's death, "poor" no longer. And thank your scribe, please. Some forty years ago she was such a nice young woman. She was in my class of adult mill girls and I was fond of her. Some twenty years afterwards I saw her again and was shocked at the change—so wild and quarrelsome. I think during her last few years she was not responsible for what she did and said. "'Tis a loving Father calls the wanderer home" and I hope she is gone home. It was very gentle her last call. I am glad she was spared a long illness in bed, which would have been terrible, so suspicious as she was of everyone. Now that is all over:

The young immortal wakes,
Wakes with her God.[162]

Thank you for what you did for her. It was very sad, with her heart complaint (though Dr Dunn had never given me the least idea that she was in danger) that we could not get in a woman to clean and a woman to wash for her. Please thank Mrs Bunting for making her beef tea, and if you could make her a little present for me.

I think, as you say, that Martha's money ought to go for what she saved it for. I cannot think how her old brother will do for himself. Could you kindly make a message to him for me, telling him what a regard I had for his sister, and how glad I am she has now peace. It is a blessed change for her. I am afraid she had no joy of her life here. I have been thinking continually of you all, but have been so poorly that I have not been able to do any but the most pressing business. I am obliged to go back to South St. on Monday.

Lady Verney is not better, but Mrs (Captain) Verney is coming to her here. Sir Harry is well. God bless you.

sincerely yours

F. Nightingale

Mr Shore is at Embley. His mother is much the same but happy.

Source: Letter, Columbia University, Presbyterian Hospital School of Nursing C169

[printed address] 10 South Street
Park Lane, W.
16 November 1888

Dear Bratby

I am very sorry that I have not been able to write before. I have been so pressed for three weeks by Lord Lansdowne's leaving England as viceroy for India, and my eyes and health are very bad.

About Martha Sheldon's money, I have just seen Mr Shore Smith, who came up to London late last night, and came to see me this morning. Both he and I would like to know: had you any distinct order or authority from Martha Sheldon to pay for her funeral? If not written, spoken? Also, did she say or write anything as to what should be done with the remainder of her money? If not, William Sheldon ought to have it. I have written this to Mr Yeomans, and asked him to advise with you.

---

162 Nightingale has made the pronoun feminine, ''her'' God, from Caroline Anne Bowles Southey, ''The Pauper's Deathbed,'' in *Poetical Works* 102-03.

Poor old Lydia Prince, I am very sorry for her. Do you know how much arrears of rent she has to pay? I would continue, if you think well, the 2/6 a week for four weeks longer, after the eight weeks. I am glad she has the 3/ a week parish relief.

James Bunting has written to me to ask me to serve as his reference. I do not much like this, for I do not do this with our own trained matrons and nurses from our St Thomas' school, unless I have had personal acquaintance with them and their work. *That* is the only value of a testimonial. James Bunting refers me to *you*. I believe you have a very good opinion of him. And I will ask you, if this is the case, but not otherwise, to give him the enclosed.

Mrs Smith of Embley is still bright and cheerful when not suffering. She is carried into the south room most days, but does not sit up except in bed or on the sofa.

sincerely yours

F. Nightingale

Source: Letter, Columbia University, Presbyterian Hospital School of Nursing C193

10 South St.

17 January 1889

Dear Bratby

You will have been prepared, I hope, by what I told you, to hear that since last Friday, my dearest aunt's life at Embley has been only a question of hours, and alas! of more or less suffering. She went home this morning at 1:00 o'clock quite quietly, home to her God whom she had so loved and sought. She was apparently conscious to the last, but too weak to speak above a word or two.

They were all there: Mr Shore returned to her on Monday, Mr Arthur Clough on Tuesday. They will all feel her loss terribly, Shore most of all, but all of us. God bless you.

faithfully yours

F. Nightingale

Source: Letter, Columbia University, Presbyterian Hospital School of Nursing C194

10 South St.

7 May 1889

Dear Bratby

I send you £5, because I want you not to run short of cash, and because I want you to pay for your own newspaper out of it. Pray do this.

At this moment Mr Shore is in London and I think may very likely come to Lea Hurst, that is, to Matlock, for a few days. Mrs Shore is in

London, or rather taking back Barbara to school at Brighton. Rosalind is at Albert Hall Mansions, working hard. Sam is gone back to St Bartholomew's Hospital and Louis is at Oxford.

Mrs Clough and Flossie are staying at a friend's, at Lyndhurst in the New Forest. Thena is at Cambridge, Arthur not come back from America. I hope you are pretty well. God bless you.

ever sincerely yours

F. Nightingale

Source: Letter, Columbia University, Presbyterian Hospital School of Nursing C198

[printed address] 10 South Street
Park Lane, W.
25 February 1890

Dear Bratby

I am so sorry for your being so suffering. Please send for Dr Graves or Dr Dunn, and Dr Webb of Wirksworth, if you like it, to meet one of them.

Though Mrs Brocklehurst mentions that *Lydia Prince* is "much worse" and "very ill," I am disappointed that she does not say that you have got Lydia the pair of blankets which I was in hopes she would have had directly. Also, if she has "parted" with anything necessary to her, I should like to replace it. I want to make her comfortable. And if you could mention anything else (I don't suppose she can last long). I asked Mr Yeomans to pay any woman she would like to come in and clean for her. She must want someone now to do more than that for her. Could you settle something for her? And if you could hear what the doctor orders for Adam? I should like to do something more for them. Adam Prince must want some *books* now he is in bed. I asked Mr Y. to subscribe to the institute for books for him.

I sent the *cocoatina* because Mrs Brocklehurst asked me some time ago. I was very glad you gave some to - - Mrs Wheeler, was it?

I am able to write so little and we are so busy. I am glad Mrs Brown is better. Pray thank Mrs Brocklehurst for her letter. God bless you.

ever sincerely yours

F. Nightingale

Frances Groundsell and Messenger

Editor: Frances Groundsell and Messenger, both Nightingale employees, later married.

Source: Letter, Columbia University, Presbyterian Hospital School of Nursing C162

[printed address] 10 South Street,
Park Lane, W.
2 June 1884

Frances Groundsell

I promised that I would let you know when I should want you. And I should be glad for you to come of *Saturday next,* 7 June, on which day I understand that you will be at liberty. I trust that you will be comfortable here, and I earnestly hope that this will be a peaceful and happy home. God bless you.

Florence Nightingale

Source: Incomplete, unsigned letter with envelope, Columbia University, Presbyterian Hospital School of Nursing C172

Claydon
28 September 1886

My dear Frances [Groundsell]

I have no time to write as I had intended. I am so glad that you had had a nice holiday and are looking better for it. And I hope that you will take a little run in the park every day to keep you well.

I send your quarter's wages, and £2 for the savings' bank, hoping that you will be able this quarter to put in a [breaks off at end of first page]

Source: Letter, Columbia University, Presbyterian Hospital School of Nursing C183

Claydon
25 January 1888

Dear Frances [Groundsell]

I am so very happy that Mr Verney is getting so much better and I thank you for all that you are doing for them. They are very much pleased with what you do for them, Mr and Mrs Verney. I bless God, and so I am sure do you, that he is so much better.

This is the day of the conversion of St Paul, when he asked so humbly and generously, "Lord, what wilt Thou have me to do?"[163] And thirty years of labours and sufferings and persecutions made

----

163 Acts 9:6.

him only the more anxious to know and to do what Christ would have him do.

Lizzie is quite well. Lady Verney is very poorly. Little cat has tumbled out of a high window, but does not seem much the worse. I hope the cats have not disgraced us. Have they ever done anything wrong in any of their rooms? Or do they go into them at all? Or on the stairs? Quiz is the only one to be trusted.

I am glad the papers have been moved out of my bedroom. As to the rest, I am sure you do what Mrs Verney likes best. I hope Nelly and the charwoman and Messenger help you in carrying things upstairs. God bless you.

ever sincerely yours
Florence Nightingale

Source: Letter, Columbia University, Presbyterian Hospital School of Nursing C200

[printed address] Claydon House
Winslow, Bucks
25 September 1890

My dear Frances [Groundsell]

I send you your quarter's [wages] with my very best wishes.

I hope that you have been drinking the tintara wine. You may call at Dr Armitage's tomorrow morning (when you receive this) and he will see how you are, and whether he recommends you to have "a glass of ale every day at dinner." I hope you are quite strong and take a walk in the park every day.

Thank you very much for your very nice letter. I quite depend upon you, or rather let us be able to say: God depends upon you. I should like to hear how you are getting on, you and YOUR GIRLS. God bless you all. Perhaps Mrs Burge will like to send a message by you. Is she very tired when she comes home at night?

Sir Harry's health varies very much. But he is wonderfully active and he trusts in God.

ever, dear Frances
yours sincerely
F. Nightingale

Source: Letter, Columbia University, Presbyterian Hospital School of Nursing C205

[printed address] Claydon House
Winslow, Bucks
26 November 1891

Dear Frances [Groundsell]

Please send by today's post to me the exact address of your aunt (name and all), the name of railway and the station by which the flannel is to come from Bradford. I know you are a long way from any station and you will send her the money for the carriage from the station. God bless you.

Sincerely yours

F. Nightingale

Source: Letter with envelope, Columbia University, Presbyterian Hospital School of Nursing C206

Claydon House
Winslow, Bucks
15 December 1891

My dear Frances [Groundsell]

You have acted wisely and well, and though I was shocked to hear about Mrs Burge, it is a great comfort to me to think that all is safe with you. I should be glad if Mrs R. Codlin could sleep at the house, but I am not uneasy. Would you find out if Mrs Codlin, the mother, is at home and could come to us when I come back or before?

I have not heard from any doctor about Mrs Burge. I was very much obliged to you for Dr Roberts's address, and I telegraphed to him at once. But he merely answered that he had advised her removal to the hospital. I was very glad to receive Mrs Burge's address. I hope to hear more tomorrow.

Sir Harry is very poorly, I am sorry to say. Mr Fred is gone to India for a few months. I was intending to come home on Thursday or Friday but fear it will not be so soon. Kind regards to Kate. I hope you have prayers in the morning. I am sure you will manage well. God bless you both.

your constant friend

F. Nightingale

Source: Letter, Columbia University, Presbyterian Hospital School of Nursing C207

Claydon House
Winslow, Bucks
21 December 1891

Dear Frances [Groundsell]

Will you be so good as to order in from Allen's and from Welch's for Christmas Day:

	sirloin of beef
Mrs Thomason	8 or 9 lbs.
Messenger (how is he?)	8 or 9 lbs.
Mrs R. Codlin	7 or 8 lbs.
Mrs Zanelli	7 or 8 lbs.
Mrs Wilks	6 lbs.

and for yourselves a piece for Sunday. A turkey and some sausages will come for yourselves tomorrow or next day. Perhaps you will each of you like to ask a friend to dinner. Can you make a plum pudding and mince pies for yourselves? Mrs Burge had ordered in the materials. And you may give the materials too for a plum pudding to Mrs Thomason and to Messenger.

One hamper and two small hampers of Christmas greeneries will come from Embley. Take some out for yourselves. Give some to Messenger and Mrs Thomason and a few to the others. And please take a nice bunch to 23 Bloomsbury Square, and to 510 Edgeware Road,[164] and to Mrs Craven's rectory, 26 Great Ormond St., with my love. Kindest regards to Kate and a good Christmas to all. Glory to God in the highest and on earth peace, good will towards men.

yours sincerely
F. Nightingale

Source: Letter, Columbia University, Presbyterian Hospital School of Nursing C208

Claydon
10 January 1892

My dear Frances [Groundsell]

We shall be, please God, at Euston on Tuesday at 2:35, and I have desired Messenger to come to you in the morning and to meet us at Euston at 2:35. I was so sorry he had been ill. Mrs Burge and I shall be very much obliged to you to pack up her things and send them to her. I enclose her note.

---

164 Offices of district nurses.

You will be glad that Nelly Owen is coming to us as cook for a time to help us, on Wednesday 13th. She had better be in what was Mrs Burge's room, had she not?

I am sorry that perhaps Mrs Verney and Miss Ellin are *not* coming. Jubilee, the cat, will come back with us. You can order in things for us. We shall bring chickens, eggs and bacon.

I shall want a very little luncheon at 3:00, and dinner at the usual time. I know that Kate will do her best for me, so I do not order *what*. The chickens won't be ready for cooking probably. The girls will want dinner on arriving. You will order things, of course, from the usual places. I know that everything will look very clean and nice. Will you get some brown wool from Savory's?

God bless you.

sincerely yours

Florence Nightingale

Source: Letter, Columbia University, Presbyterian Hospital School of Nursing C215

[printed address] Claydon House
Winslow, Bucks
28 August 1892

My dear Frances [Groundsell]

With regard to your and Kate's holidays, I am most anxious to please you both and I know you are to please me. I think what I said to you both, before I went, was: settle between yourselves what you like best, and let me know—of course in time for me to say what I think best after considering it.

Now I can only say this: you think that you must be at South St. both when the men come in and when they have done, to arrange for me properly, as Mrs Broome is a stranger. If Kate goes on Wednesday for a fortnight's holiday, that will only leave one week for your holiday if I have to come back in a month.

Would you like to put off your holiday till a week after I come home; that will put off your holiday a fortnight? Please, both you and Kate answer this, either by return of post or by telegram on Monday morning if you want me to telegraph by return. And I wish you both a pleasant holiday. May God bless you. Do you read prayers?

your affectionate

F. Nightingale

Source: Letter, Columbia University, Presbyterian Hospital School of Nursing C237

10 South St.
3 January 1897

Dear Messenger

I wish you a happy New Year and should wish to know what book you would like for me to give you, and, if you would have your Christmas photograph framed after your own liking, and let me pay for it.

Do you want a book to read now?

F. Nightingale

Source: Letter, Columbia University, Presbyterian Hospital School of Nursing C247

[printed address] 10 South Street,
Park Lane, W.
11 November 1901

Dear Messenger

I hear from Ellin that you are going to be married next Tuesday to Frances. I wish you every happiness and the best of health. I should like you to have next Tuesday and Wednesday and longer if you require it. Also, I should like to make arrangements so that you have your Sundays entirely off, which can be easily done if I get a few more extra coal boxes that you may be able to get in a few more coals on Saturday.

With best wishes, I remain
yours truly
Florence Nightingale

Lydia Norman

Editor: The next several letters concern Nightingale's employee, Lydia Norman, who came from a Claydon family. They show a very practical concern for Norman's welfare, with messages to her parents and inquiries regarding the suitability of a prospective husband, Nightingale acting very much in loco (Victoriana) parentis.

Source: Letter, Wellcome (Claydon copy) Ms 9010/77

10 South St.
6 May 1885

My dear Sir Harry [Verney]

. . . You are so very good as to see *Lydia Norman's* father and mother. Will you please tell them that *Lydia's message* to them is that *she means to turn over a new leaf*, and mine that, still trusting in this, I will *try to keep her*. Will you also ask whether Mrs Norman likes the *meat*, as I now send it her, from Winslow, cooking it herself? Or whether it is not better for me to do as I did before, namely give her a meal at Johnny Co-op's ready prepared? the advantage of the latter being that her whole family does not partake of *her* meat, and that it is better cooked?

(I know not how to tell Lydia's parents this, viz., that her message was preceded by 1¼ hour's insolence, that she has been making herself intolerable in the house, both as a woman and a cook, and that I *cling* to trying her again, only because I have reason to know that she does not mean to go into service again. To be a barmaid—and then *worse*—appears to be otherwise her future.)

Tell her mother I pray for Lydia as she asks and as I am sure she does. Let us all pray for her and for all erring lambs. Lydia does not now go out late, she *cannot*, without our knowledge. Please tell her mother this. . . .

ever yours and hers

F.N.

Source: Letter, Wellcome (Claydon copy) Ms 9010/78

10 South St.

9 May 1885

PRIVATE

My dear Sir Harry [Verney]

. . . Thanks for seeing Lydia Norman's parents, but there must be some great mistake. Her message to them was that she "meant to turn over a new leaf," and mine that I was willing to try her. Any unsettling of her now would be disastrous. Her younger sister is going to her parents on Wednesday to stay, leaving her place. It was high time she did. Lydia wisely declines going home now. As for getting her a place in the country, she would not take it and she would not keep it. Your own remark was, "she would run away."

I have therefore written to Mrs Randal that there is no question of looking for a place for her now. I have also written to Mrs Norman, and sent it through Morey, fearing the Sunday post would not reach her, and fearing that she might meanwhile write to Lydia, unsettling her. As I shall have the great pleasure of seeing you on Tuesday, I will not explain more now. What *we all want* is to prevent "Lydia becoming a barmaid." As far as can be seen, the only way to prevent that is to keep her here. She will not take another service. God bless you both.

ever yours and hers affectionately

F. Nightingale

Source: Letter, Wellcome (Claydon copy) Ms 9010/107

10 South St.
18 September 1885

My dear Sir Harry [Verney]

I am always thinking of you both. So sorry I was to leave you both. The terrible accounts I hope are nearly done and I trust Parthe is less worried and overtired now.

I am going to ask you to do me the great favour of writing to Captain Loftus to make the inquiry specified in the enclosed. The girl of course is Lydia Norman. It was good of her to tell me, but I am bound to make every inquiry I can as to the character of this young man—I have such a dread of London footmen. What *can* a girl know about one?

I am always so sorry to ask you to write one additional line. But I know you are anxious, too, and I know you will forgive me. The difficulty is that Captain Loftus's intellects are said to be somewhat impaired. Still there is no one else to ask. He is said to be a very good man; he is unmarried. In haste. Pray give my love to Margaret and the children.

ever yours and P.'s
F.N.

Source: Unsigned letter to Harry Verney, Wellcome (Claydon copy) Ms 9010/108

18 September 1885

. . . *Charles Goodfellow,* age about twenty-one, was formerly a page in the service of Mrs Loftus, the mother who is dead, at 8 South St. He is now footman in the service of Mrs Bell, 32 Grosvenor Place. The family appears to be well known to Captain Loftus. Goodfellow, the father, was his coachman, and now keeps his lodge (Saybridge Lodge), the mother is also employed about the house. The aunt is still housekeeper at 8 South St. The younger brother is now in Captain Loftus's service as page or footman. All this sounds well, if it is all true, being what a girl in my service tells me who asks me to allow Charles Goodfellow to visit at my house and "keep company" with her. Would Captain Loftus be so very good as to take the trouble to tell you whether this young man (twenty-one and twenty, the girl's age, are so very young to be making marriage engagements) is perfectly steady; or if he has any reason to think that the young man is not "well-living."

What is his principal fault? And did he leave Mrs Loftus's service for any fault? Has he thought of saving anything so as to have a little beforehand? or is he asking a girl to "keep company" merely for his amusement? What about his sobriety? What sort of son to his parents? If Captain Loftus would be so very kind as to tell you what he knows about this Charles Goodfellow? anything he pleases to tell you would be "confidential" with us. Captain Loftus is supposed to be now at his brother's Crawley, Newport Pagnell (do you know such a place?) or a letter addressed to 8 South St., I suppose, would find him. Please put on envelope wherever you address: *Immediate/Please forward.* . . .

Nelly Owen

Source: Letter to Margaret Verney, Wellcome (Claydon copy) Ms 9011/14

16 April 1886

. . . Very glad I am of the prospect of having Nelly Owen. I have written to your good Mrs Thomas to send her up, if possible, on Tuesday or Wednesday, for later on the Easter trains are so crowded, let alone Easter excursion trains. She shall be met of course in London. . . .

What was done about Nelly Owen's beer? Had she either beer or beer money? Is she Church of England? As to wages, I propose to give whatever you gave for the first month, then to raise and to raise rapidly if she suits. I hope she will be happy. . . .

Source: Letter to Margaret Verney, Wellcome (Claydon copy) Ms 9011/153

31 July 1887

. . . You are so very good as to ask after Nelly Owen. She is to have a holiday and to go home for a fortnight this week. She is as good as gold. But I am almost glad to hear of her "slowness" before coming to me. I was afraid it was our fault. It is not only slowness but denseness and indifference. She did not even care to go home—I was obliged to press it.

She is now in perfect health (she was not when she first came). But there are only two things I can get a rise out of her for: (1) her dead father, (2) Miss Ellin and Miss Lettice. It is quite beautiful how her face lights up then.

The difficulty of getting her to take a walk in the park, or to dress for tea, or to care about church or class, or to make progress in cooking—she cooks and then falls back—she had rather grub all day and all evening in the scullery, or to read or make her own pretty frock. Of course a great deal of this must be our fault. . . .

Mr Morey, Claydon

Editor: William Morey was Sir Harry Verney's butler and a valued employee. Apart from the correspondence with him above regarding Parthenope Verney's last illness and the aftermath from her death there is much with him, excluded, about Harry Verney's health (he acted as nurse). Here only a small number of more personal letters have been chosen, which show how Nightingale depended on him for various sorts of practical assistance such as cashing cheques and mailing parcels to India. The involvement she had with his family is also typical of many relationships with domestic employees.

Source: Letter, Wellcome (Claydon copy) Ms 9008/107

9 January 1881

I shall be very much obliged to Morey and Bond to come and have supper and play on Wednesday evening. And if the maids' hearts are set on dancing, *would* they play SOME *dancing music?* . . .
F.N.

Source: Letter, Wellcome (Claydon copy) Ms 9008/108

10 January 1881

My dear Sir Harry [Verney]
Would you kindly send me the address where you get your *hams?* *at once.* The program of our Wednesday's entertainment is as follows:
Company come at 7:00 P.M. (a little tea and cake)
Dancing   7:30 till 9:00
Supper   9:00
a little music afterwards at 10:00
Breakup   at 11:00.
I should be extremely obliged to *Morey*, with your permission, if he would take the head of the table at supper, and if he would order from Grosvenor Hotel a sufficient number of *bottles of bitter beer* or ale for about seventeen or eighteen, and dispense it himself. (Three out of my four maids are not allowed beer by doctor's orders. I don't want to forbid it on this festive occasion but I only want moderation.)
I should be extremely obliged to *Morey* if, with your permission, he will engage *a fiddle to come at 7:00*, and play *dance music*. I don't like to ask Morey to play dance music, but we shall hope to have *his music too and Bond's*, both before and after supper. We hope to have from your house: Morey and Bond, Julie, Leonard and Phoebe, the housemaid. And if YOU would look in upon the festivities (as I can't) it would *more than double* their value. . . .

Source: Letter, Wellcome (Claydon copy) Ms 9008/110

11 January 1881

My dear Sir Harry [Verney]

The servants want to *dance* in the *pantry* (*not* in the dining room) and to sup in the dining room. Could you kindly come and settle this knotty point, or send Morey? Could Parthe kindly send me a little cold stewed beef, or anything you have had at luncheon, tomorrow, for my dinner at 6:30 please.

F.N.

Source: Letter to Parthenope Verney, Wellcome (Claydon copy) Ms 9008/111

13 January 1881

. . . Pray thank Morey: he was the life of the "party" and "thank you for my good dinner."

F.

Source: Letter, Harvard University, Countway Medical Library

[printed address] Claydon House
Winslow, Bucks
23 December 1891

Dear Mr Morey

I hope to see you today and ask more particularly how Sir Harry is, but I don't want to interrupt your skating.

Could you be so very kind as to have put up for me this parcel for Pune in India to go via Brindisi by the Friday mail (I presume, though it is Christmas Day, the mail will go?) There ought to be seventy copies. (If there are more, I shall be glad of the surplus.) I must put in an invoice and direct the parcel, on white paper. Ought it to be packed with cardboard? Thursday evening's post is soon enough for the Friday's mail, but, perhaps, on Christmas Eve it ought to go by the morning post on Thursday?? Apologizing for the trouble I am giving you.

sincerely yours
F. Nightingale

Source: Letter, Harvard University, Countway Medical Library

Claydon
28 February 1895

Dear Mr Morey

Could you kindly get me this cheque cashed by Friday or Saturday: £5 bank note, £13 gold, £2 silver, [total] 20. But as I have only sent it you at the last moment, please return it to me if inconvenient to you and tell me how to get it cashed.

Please post this letter for me in London. Thanks for all you have done for me. I shall hope to see you on your return.

yours sincerely

F. Nightingale

I have a book for Edith.[165]

Source: Letter, Harvard University, Countway Medical Library

10 South St.

24 February 1896

Dear Mr Morey

I am glad that you intend leaving Edith at Ventnor "til May." The spring is the most trying time for young girls with delicate chests and I don't wonder that she seems not to show "so much energy." Besides, the poor darling, I dare say, finds it rather dull without her own family. Is she allowed to walk on the seashore? When I was a girl, I remember we could pick up kinds of shells not common on the English seashore in the Isle of Wight, the Buccinum [whelk] and the [illeg]. But it is very many years that I have been obliged to give up conchology.

If you would tell me what sorts of books she would like to read, and give me her address, I should like to send her a couple of books.

Thank you very much for your kindness in paying my bills. I send £3 to keep you in hand. And I beg that you will accept the £5 for Edith's expenses.

I had a cheerful letter from Sir E. and Lady Verney at Biskra. Lady Verney is sketching every day. And they are so amused with the strings and caravans of stately Arabs and all sorts of camels and asses and horses. They already find the weather rather hot, but it is the dryness which is so healthy and delightful. With kind regards to Mrs Morey, pray believe me,

ever sincerely yours

F. Nightingale

I return the receipts you have kindly sent. You probably like to keep your receipts.

F.N.

---

165 For his daughter: Swinburne's *Atalanta in Calyden*, which Nightingale inscribed at Morey's request in a letter 7 March.

"Waifs and Strays"

Editor: The following correspondence is but a small sample from the vast number of surviving letters giving practical assistance and advice to the enormous range of people who called on Nightingale. Her assumption of a caseload began, as the first letters show, before the Crimean War and her fame. Obviously the demands on her increased enormously afterwards. Correspondence regarding the orphan child in Rome for whom she paid board and schooling 1848-53 is related in *European Travels*. Letters regarding civil service, nursing and other professional positions are reported in those volumes. The material below then reports Nightingale's miscellaneous caseload. The expression, "waifs and strays" comes from a wording she proposed in raising money for Bosnian refugees who were not orphans.[166]

Source: Undated, unsigned letter with printed appeal, Wellcome (Claydon copy) Ms 8993/66

Dearest Mother   [ca. January 1847]

This poor man [Ebenezer Rand], the master of Nuneaton School, was trying to improve himself and get a higher certificate for high school. When Mr Bellairs, the inspector, came round he gave him a theme to write, as is the custom. The poor man said his eyes were bad and might he answer viva voce? Or some compromise, I forget what. Mr Bellairs said he could make no difference; all the schoolmasters did it. The poor man set to work, wrote his theme and did it; the next morning he was stone blind. He is a capital schoolmaster and would make a good master for the blind if he could first serve an apprenticeship to a blind school.

The Bracebridges, who are always starving themselves for everybody, mean to place him at one at their own expense. *Would you send them £1 towards it?* or whatever you think fit? as we did not do what we intended to do about his church. I thought I was coming home, else I would have sent you this before. Mr Tremenheere is going to get him in at the blind asylum.

---

166 Letter to Shore and Louisa Smith 31 January 1876, ADD Mss 45795 ff38-39.

Source: Letter with envelope, Wellcome (Claydon copy) Ms 8993/40

30 Old Burlington St.
7 March [1851]

My dear Sir [T.K. Appleton,[167] Boston]

I wish Rowland Hill[168] had never existed; he has filled our fingers with pens and our eyes with letters and our time with correspondence. I wish the penny post were in California. The same wish I have no doubt is in your hearts in America. Nevertheless I am going to write across the Atlantic, and you I hope are going to read it, because I want you to help in a good work by advice and I know you are always ready in that way. The unlucky Hessians are crowding over to England, Cassel being chuckfull of the Austrian, Prussian and Bavarian troops and of their twin trio, "plague, pestilence and famine."

Among these poor people one family interests me particularly, whom I have known for many years, consisting of a very pretty young lady, by name Adelberg, her promesso, whom she cannot marry because of these dreadful circumstances, her brother and her mother. The promesso is a thorough artist; he understands drawing, modelling and particularly architecture and I think engineering. He has been employed, I know, in making the railroads. The brother is a good chemist and has for years superintended a large soda and sulphuric acid, etc. factory, i.e., the chemical branch of it. What would you recommend these two young men to do? Is there any opening for them in America?

The young lady would gladly undertake to be governess, or I have thought she might give private lessons in German, if there were any opening for that, and if her promesso could get something to do for them to marry upon. I shall be exceedingly grateful for any hints you may kindly bestow upon me. She is a remarkably elegant and clever woman. . . .

Whether this note will find you in America or Africa, I have not the least idea, but I suppose you will be among the visitors at the Crystal Palace. All we Anglicans run away and hide ourselves in the country. Pray forgive me for troubling you with my questions, but I believe you are one of those who have always time for every good deed. If you will answer me at your leisure, I shall be always your grateful

Florence Nightingale

if you remember such a person.

---

167 Probably Thomas Gold Appleton (1812-84), whom she met in Paris, poet, author and brother-in-law of Henry Wadsworth Longfellow.
168 Sir Rowland Hill (1795-1879), founder of the penny post.

Source: Letter to unknown recipient, Wellcome (Claydon copy) Ms 8995/48

Castle Hospital
Balaclava
23 October 1855

The enclosed is from an old patient of mine at Harley St., poor Mme Piccozzi. I liked her as well as I pitied her, more than any of that terrible lot. I used to lend her money and sometimes afterward used to go and see her and her sister, in a nasty lodging which never smelt, as did not they, poor creatures, of anything but gin. The nephew supported them, as none but a French boy will do.

I never saw the worthy boy and could not recommend him here, where one man's untrustworthiness, if he should turn out so, perils the lives of hundreds. But if you could do anything for him in London as a clerk? I have not told her that I have applied to you so she will not bother you if you can't. . . .

Editor: William Jones was a young seaman whom Nightingale brought home from the Crimean War (the circumstances become clear in the correspondence).

Source: Unsigned letter, Wellcome (Claydon copy) Ms 8997/31

Great Malvern
7 March 1857

My dearest [Parthenope Nightingale]

. . . I have arranged for William Jones to go to school at *Barnet* with 170 boys and girls immediately.[169] It was very good of Beatrice to keep him so long. I fear he has been very troublesome. This is a school for soldiers' and seamen's orphan children and they make an exception in my favour for Jones (who is neither) on payment of the same annual sum as the others. . . .

---

169 In a letter to her mother Nightingale reported removing Jones from Barnet, then having him apprenticed to a watchmaker: "He is a bad boy" (Wellcome [Claydon copy] Ms 8997/54).

Source: Letter, Clendening History of Medicine Library, Kansas University Medical Center

[printed address] 35 South Street
Park Lane
London, W.
2 October 1866

Private

Dear Madam [Mrs Chalmers]

Only a few days ago was a letter of yours, of 9 March, received by me. It was about William Henry Jones, a young man who died in the consumptive hospital early in March, and was most kindly visited by you. He had been a terrible anxiety to me. And, though I had had most satisfactory accounts of the "repentance and faith" he showed on his deathbed (through the kindness of Mr Dobbin, the secretary), I cannot tell you how touching and comforting it was to me to hear from yourself what he said to you and what you thought of his state.

He was a merchant sailor boy, and, when he was about fifteen he was put on shore at Balaclava in 1856 and taken into hospital there in a state equally corrupt of mind and body (if I may phrase it so). One leg was amputated and for nearly three weeks he was literally kept alive on champagne wine alone (I have never seen such another case). When he recovered, as there was not a soul to take any charge of him, I brought him home with me, with two other boys, one a Russian, both of whom have turned out admirably. Alas for poor William Jones. And yet not alas! if the mercy of God has been shown him, what better can be said of anyone?

It was touching to me that he said to you that he "hoped I had heard no harm of him." For he knew well, if I heard of him at all, there was nothing but "harm" to hear. Not to weary you with a very sad tale, William Jones was taken in first at my father's house with those two other boys, my father's servants being of a patriarchal kind, butler and housekeeper being husband and wife and with their own boy living with them in the house. But it was found impossible to keep William Jones from his inveterate habits of lying. He was then apprenticed, at his own desire, to a watchmaker, and subsequently to other trades, and furnished with a spring-cork leg.

From every successive home he ran away and from each I received letters calling upon me to pay his debts. I am afraid there was worse behind. But, not to enter into more detail, I was quite relieved to be able to get him at last a bed in the consumptive hospital, still more relieved when I heard (through Mr Dobbin) from chaplain, matron and nurse how much "repentance" he had shown. He told Mr Ross (an excellent man, formerly a non-commissioned officer, who never lost sight of poor William Jones, though wearied out with his backslidings, and who visited him to the last) that he had written me a letter (in the hospital) expressing "repentance and faith in the Lord and asking my forgiveness." This letter I never had. But I think it likely that, in the weakness of illness, there may have been some confusion, and that this was the message which you so kindly conveyed to me, and which I received only last week. I cannot tell you what a comfort it was to me.

I blame William Jones, poor fellow, less than myself. He was quite corrupted when he came to me. I think, if I had placed him in a good reformatory, he might have been alive and honest now. But I thought an honest trade would be as well. For, at that time, there was no overt act by which he could legally have been placed, except by his own will, in a reformatory of any kind.

But God has done better for him, the best. The two other boys are now, one, a steward on an excellent landlord's estate in Scotland, the other, a servant in my father's house—both steady and well-principled young men, though the Russian, when he first came to me, a poor little (*scalded*) boy of nine years old, when he was asked "who made you? by a female missionary of mine (in English, which he spoke perfectly) answered: "Miss Nightingale." And, after some further steps by the same lady in his religious education, when he was asked, "where shall you go to when you die?" answered, "to Miss Nightingale's."

I would not have troubled you with so long a letter but to show my gratitude, however imperfectly, for yours. You kindly ask after my health. I am an incurable invalid, entirely a prisoner to my bed (except during a periodical migration) and overwhelmed with business. I should not say "overwhelmed" for, of all the causes I have for the deepest thankfulness to God, there is not one I feel so deeply as that He still enables me to work for Him and leads me so plainly, though by a way I "have not known."[170]

I have heard with the greatest interest of Miss Marsh's good work,[171] which she has added to her many others, for convalescents

---

170 An allusion to Isa 42:16.
171 Catherine Marsh (1818-1912), home missionary. See *Theology* for correspondence.

from cholera. Might I enclose a small sum, £5, to help in it? With my most fervent thanks to her for her kindness to my poor boy. Pray believe me, dear Madam,

ever your faithful and grateful servant

Florence Nightingale

Source: Letter, Wellcome (Claydon copy) Ms 8998/18

Hampstead, N.W.

29 January 1860

Dearest Mother

A girl of nineteen, who was housemaid to the Cloughs for two years, and whom they parted with to Lady Emerson Tennent, merely because they wished for a better situation for her, was overdone with the too-hard work of the new place, and had prolapsus of the womb. Lady Tennent parted with her without any inquiry as to where she could go. The Cloughs took her back and nursed her and she is still in their house.

Her doctor recommends her to go into a hospital for six weeks, but admits that if she could have perfect rest in country air, with some medical treatment, it would be better. I feel certain that, if she were cured *locally* in a London hospital, it would be at the expense of her constitution, perhaps of her virtue, and that she would gain in one day in the country what she would not in two in London. If I were going to stay here, I would have her here. I feel certain that, if you were to see her, you would like to help her, besides helping the Cloughs, who have been so kind to her.

She will go on *Wednesday* into the hospital, if not otherwise provided for. Now I thought, if you would let her come down to Embley on that day for five or six weeks, it would be perhaps the difference to her of a painful, helpless, dependent life and of a healthy, active, independent one. She would require, I believe, to lie up entirely for six weeks. But Mr Taylor would probably see her and direct what she was to do. Nurse Watson, I am sure, would look after her while you were there, and Mrs Watson, if you went away.

She is a most properly-behaved girl in all respects. She is niece to the Cloughs' faithful nursemaid, Emily. If you will have her, I will take care that she brings down with her her doctor's account of her case for Mr Taylor. But I believe that fresh air, entire rest upon a hair mattress, are what she principally wants. As she is so young and unmarried, she may get quite well with care. She is not helpless and walks about, which she ought *not* to do, I believe.

Please direct your answer to me to Burlington St. I will take care to send for it, if I am not there, in time for her to go, if you will have her.

ever dear Mum

your loving child

F.N.

Source: Letter, Wellcome (Claydon copy) Ms 9003/83

[printed address] 35 South Street
Park Lane, W.
31 January 1869

My dear [Parthenope Verney]

I want Mrs Watson to send, if possible by Tuesday's box, some arrowroot or rice or rice blancmange made in a mould which was delicious. It is for a poor lady, the wife of one of the best of our War Office clerks (the man I used to call my Temple to Friendship), who has had a dreadful confinement in which the child's life was lost and almost her own. She was miserable at the loss of the child (the husband earning about £120 or £150 a year) and insisted on sending the poor little body into the country to be buried with her sister's children, as she could not bear it to "lie in a great London cemetery, all alone." I am now sending in wine and things, as she is ordered every kind of restorative and anything at once delicate and nourishing that Mama would contribute would be acceptable.

ever your F.

Source: Letter, Wellcome (Claydon copy) Ms 9004/171

[printed address] 35 South Street
Park Lane, W.
23 December 1870

My dear Sir Harry [Verney]

I trouble you with the enclosed letter from the excellent Mr Stephen Hawtrey and its enclosure from the young man, Truelove, because your name is mentioned in it and you might possibly be able and willing to help him to what he wants. I thoroughly believe every word it says.

Mrs Truelove, the mother, is the daughter of a dissenting minister and the wife of a small publisher and stationer in Holborn, a most curious but high-minded man, a positivist. I have known them for years, and always had them to see me at Hampstead.[172] The mother has a sort of genius. Mrs Congreve gives her lessons in French, etc. She is one of the most interesting women I ever knew.

She insisted on sending her son (the one who writes) to Mr Hawtrey's School of St Mark's—Mr Hawtrey recommended him to Murray, the publisher, who thinks very highly of him. As for his leaving Murray, with the largest literary connection in England, for *me* to get him some "secretary" situation, it is much as if Robert Robinson were to leave Lord Kinnaird to ask von der Tann, the Bavarian general, to give him a farm in the Beauce. (Please return me the enclosed letters.) . . .

Source: Letter, Cambridge University Library, Manuscripts and Archives Add 8566/I/173

[printed address] 35 South Street
Park Lane, W.
27 May 1872

Private

My dear Sir [Dr Henry Bence Jones]

I come to you merely in the light of a beggar to ask you to do me a great favour with regard to procuring the Certificate of Death or of Burial of one of your (and my) late patients at the Institution 1 Upper Harley St., in 1854.

Mathilde von Raven, a German young governess, whom I fished out of the Middlesex Hospital, and who died a few days afterwards under your kind care, and was buried on 29 April 1854, where? Though I provided and attended the funeral, I cannot tell. But I think it was at a burial ground not very far from Harley St. on the road to Hampstead. (Fortunately our funerals were not very frequent and I should hope therefore that this will not give you much trouble to discover. Neither do I remember the name of the undertaker's, though I attended at his shop to sign some certificate, as having been the only nurse present at the death.) But *you* gave the Certificate of the Cause of Death, that I can well remember.

I will try to recall to you the case. She showed during the few days she was under your care very remarkable cataleptic symptoms. You your-

---

172 Nightingale in 1861 gave Mrs Truelove an inscribed copy of Arthur Stanley's *Arnold's Life and Correspondence*, now at the Vancouver General Hospital School of Nursing Alumnae Association; she gave her *Notes on Nursing* in 1860 (Add Mss 45797 f147) and *Introductory Notes on Lying-in Institutions* in 1871 (Add Mss 45802 f270).

self raised her arm into the air and it stayed there. When she was dying, you whispered to me, "I should like to have a post-mortem." And I ran down to your house in the early morning to tell you that she had died an hour or two before. I attended at the post-mortem by your desire. And you told me, I think, that there was extensive tubercular disease both in chest and stomach, but nothing discoverable in the head, which you opened.

I come now to the really sad part of the case, a case by no means uncommon, and which I confided to your kindness. She was a woman of noble birth, had been seduced by a nobleman (at Berlin, I think) and the child, a boy, she had placed out to nurse, and came to England as a governess to support it. Then she fell ill. This she told me while she was sensible in her last moments. I wrote to Berlin and found it true. The child was exceedingly well taken care of by its foster parents. I contributed to its support for some years. He is now a fine young lad of eighteen or nineteen, and doing exceedingly well: Lucas von Raven, at Berlin. There was a debt owing to his poor mother, which could now be recovered for him if I could send immediately a "Todtenschein" (copy of Certificate of her Death or Burial) to Berlin.

I am entirely a prisoner to my bed from ever-increasing illness, and am ashamed to say how much overwhelmed I feel by every increasing business. So many of my friends have been removed by death, and nearly all the ladies of the committee of 1 Upper Harley St. whom I knew best, that I have scarcely any resource but that of troubling you.

You were so kind to those unfortunate governesses of the institution. Do you remember one Fox, seduced in the same way, and you made the seducer provide for her at the lunatic asylum, Warneford, near Oxford? (She had, I had almost said fortunately for her, become a lunatic.) I remember saying to you that I knew hardly any man but you who would undertake these kinds of responsibilities and your answer: "that it made the difference between man and man whether he would or would not take responsibility."

Now I have tried to recall your interest in that poor girl, Mathilde v. Raven, so solitary and forsaken, in order to make it less burdensome to you, if you would be so very good as to procure me a copy of her death certificate, attested for legal purposes. Excuse this long scrawl, and pray believe me

ever yours sincerely

Florence Nightingale

Editor: Nightingale had evidently been asked to intervene to obtain admission to a school of a boy somehow connected with the famous singer, Jenny Lind, who had raised money for the Nightingale Fund among other worthy causes.

Source: Letter, Wellcome (Claydon copy) Ms 9005/166

Embley
Romsey
30 November 1872

My dear Sir Harry [Verney]

Need I say that I have not the slightest means of getting at the Duke of York's School, or any other? But that if you are so good as to use your influence, you may truly say (Parthe asks me to say this) that I exceedingly desire the admission of this boy.

Everybody must reverence Jenny Lind. But I am peculiarly bound to her. God bless you.

ever yours
F. Nightingale

Source: Unsigned letter, Wellcome (Claydon copy) Ms 9006/164

Lea Hurst
Cromford, Derby
12 August 1875

My dear Sir Harry [Verney]

... The old *coachman Moss* has written to me (doubtless to you also) to help to get him into the Winchester (St Cross) Almshouses. Will you tell me what you and Parthe thought of him? What was the reason for parting with him? How many years he was with my father? (eighteen, he says).

Source: Unsigned letter Wellcome (Claydon copy) Ms 9007/32

35 S. St.
5 May 1876

Wellow School Work

My dear Sir Harry [Verney]

Might I trouble you to give the enclosed £1 to Mr Empson (at the rate of 5/ a week) for needlework done or to be done at *Wellow School*? and to *ask whether I shall send them more work,* mending, which I have to do? But to say that I rather fancy they don't *want* work, as they have had some of mine four months and have it still? (I have therefore just sent some of mine to Lea Hurst.) Also to say that I find "Mrs

Crook" has sent some of *my mother's* work, as they have to Wellow School and probably not paid for it. . . .

Source: Letter to Harry Verney, Wellcome (Claydon copy) Ms 9007/86

Easter Day 1 April 1877

. . . You know that Mrs Chisholm, the emigrants' friend, (and alas Mrs Nassau Senior both) died last week. They are trying to get Mrs Chisholm's pension of £100 continued to her unmarried daughter, who has nothing (Major Chisholm, who still lives, having only his pension).

Sidney Herbert, had he lived, would have done this. It is greatly to the credit of the Chisholm family that they have literally no fortune.[173] Everything was spent in the work. (She died last Sunday in London after a long illness.) If you and Lord Houghton thought well to write to Disraeli about the pension, I should think it would be done.

F.N.

Source: Incomplete letter, Wellcome Ms 5483/6/1 and /2

London
19 May 1877

Dear Madam [Miss Ellice Hopkins]

I am quite sure from my own experience in long past years that the way indicated in your little book, *Work in Brighton*,[174] and in your letter which accompanies it, is the only true way. I agree with Mrs Vicars, whose work will be immortal like herself, that to begin with penitentiary work is like beginning at the *end*.

I could back your and her much-larger experience with my own of past years, when, for example, being a young woman, I tracked a motherless girl of thirteen years, ran her to earth in a vile row of houses in the suburbs, left a fly standing at the end, and entered one of those vile houses after another till in the last I found my girl. She let me take her hand, and so lead her down the row, put her by me in the fly and drive her off to a home, not a penitentiary, where late at night we were taken in.

I cannot think how "ladies" can call it "loathsome work." Those were blessed days to me (but our heavenly Father ordered my path otherwise). What is "character" given to us for but to help those who have none?

---

173 Nightingale's contribution to a fund for Mrs Chisholm in 1853 has already been noted (see p 744 above).
174 Jane Ellice Hopkins (1836-1904). Nightingale wrote a preface for it.

I bid your work of "Associations of Ladies for the Care of the Lost" "Godspeed" with all my heart and soul and strength. It is the one true way, the only way of reaching and putting the lost into safe places, where salvation may reach them. (To smuggle them into servants' situations at once is to lose them and to destroy others.)

I will give your little book *wherever* I see a chance of its being useful. . . . To give my work is simply impossible. With illness increasing every month (I am entirely a prisoner to my bed; it is difficult to me to find strength even to write this letter) with duties already ten times as great as a person in robust health should undertake, I should be a "foolish fool" to take anything more to do, fancying I could do it to any purpose.

May I send my earnest love and greetings to Mrs Vicars and again bidding Godspeed and the strength of God, *not my* poor speed and strength, to your "Associations for the Care of the Lost," pray believe me,

ever your faithful servant
Florence Nightingale

Source: Letter, Wellcome Ms 5483/13

London
23 March 1878

Dear Mrs Swann

I am always glad to hear of you and I hope you are quite strong now. I had heard from Mr Haywood, the Lea schoolmaster, that good little Patty Cottrell did not come to school (which I was almost sorry for, as I hoped, now especially that attendance at school is compulsory, she would be let go to school till she was thirteen years of age). But if she has a good place and is likely to keep it and if they look after her to keep up her reading and writing, I hope she may do well.

I will give a sovereign to help her with clothes, and you will judge best whether to spend half for her now and half six months hence, IF she keeps her place. I will send the money to Mr Dunn.

I am glad that Mrs Cottrell goes on improving. I wonder whether the house is any way improving (I have not heard before from you; you ask). . . . I have had a very heavy winter. God bless you.

yours sincerely
F. Nightingale

Source: Letter, Derbyshire County Archives

Lea Hurst
Cromford, Derby
22 October 1878

My dear Sir [C.B.N. Dunn]

Old Lyddy Prince: I saw her last night and she expressed the greatest gratitude for your kindness to her. There is some magic medicine of yours (for "palpitations" she says) which to have another "bottle" of she prays.

It would be extremely desirable if she were not to put off any longer applying for parish relief. The Guardians would then compel her three sons, who can well afford it, to do something for her. She has supported *herself* for fifty-three years. She does not like to ask you to say whether she is "past work." But if you could give her your medical opinion on this point, or a line of medical certificate, it would greatly facilitate any application of hers. (I have spoken to Mr Yeomans as a Guardian). . . .

yours sincerely
F. Nightingale

Source: Letter, Wellcome (Claydon copy) Ms 9007/253

Lea Hurst
Cromford, Derby
30 September 1879

My dear Sir Harry [Verney]

. . . ROBERT ROBINSON would be only too glad to meet you at *Pleasley* whenever you go there. He would gladly accept anything: a clerkship at the coal mines, anything, temporarily. . . .

Source: Note, Wellcome (Claydon copy) Ms 9009/45

[c1882]

Philip McCarthey: About twenty-four or twenty-five, carman and previously car*boy* in the service of the Midland Railway, St Pancras Station, son of an old soldier who was in India under Sir F. Roberts, now an attendant in a lunatic asylum, from Ireland, born in India, a teetotaller, not a R. Catholic, inclines to the "Salvation Army," might—I know what character he bears as to sobriety, steadiness, etc., a teetotaller—very good.

Source: Unsigned note, Wellcome (Claydon copy) Ms 9023/102

[May 1882]

Sir Harry Verney, MP

Can anything be done for these poor Miss Farrs[175] with Mr Gladstone? (daughters of Dr Farr). . . .

Source: Letter, Private collection of Drs Quita and Mark Cruciger, San Francisco

10 South St., W.
20 July 1884

Dear Sir [Mr Turner]

May I trouble you to be so very kind as to give me information about a poor woman giving her name as Mrs Keith, 11 Beaun St., Park St. (I know nothing of her) who called here last night after 10:00 o'clock asking for assistance?

She told a rather confused story of her mother having been "discharged incurable" from St Thomas' Hospital (disease: cancer) and having got an order for Eastbourne, whither she must go tomorrow (Monday) morning or lose her turn. To get her mother there she asked for help. In your thoroughly-looked-after district probably all is known about this poor woman and I will gladly contribute to this kind of help, if it is thought well to give it her. But it is quite impossible for me from increase of illness and overwork to inquire into or look after the case myself.

Again asking your pardon for troubling you and trusting in your kindness, believe me,

yours faithfully

Florence Nightingale

Excuse pencil which I am obliged to use.

Source: Copy of letter previously held at Chiddingstone Castle, Kent; current location unknown

10 South St.
7 January 1887

Dear Mrs Robertson

I grieve that even now you cannot give a "well" account of yourself. It is such a trying illness and made worse by bad weather.

Thank you for all the trouble you have taken, but do not ever trouble to *buy* butter for me. I get our butter from one (who lived with me as a soldier boy in the Crimean War, and was the faithfullest servant I ever had) in Warwickshire where he farms, not prosperously. I could

---

175 Emily and Mary Farr, unmarried daughters at home, to each of whom Nightingale left £100 in her will.

relieve you of sending me butter altogether if you liked. Mr Robertson, I hope, thinks Sir Harry well. I am always so glad to hear about your family and I trust that you will be getting quite well soon. With kind regards to Mr Robertson and many thanks, pray believe me,

ever faithfully yours

Florence Nightingale

Source: Letter, Wellcome (Claydon copy) Ms 9012/249

[printed address] 10 South Street
Grosvenor Sq., W.
Dearest Margaret [Verney]   2 November 1889

You know, I dare say, a great deal more about Mr Tuckwell than I can tell you. And I believe he spoke for Captain Verney at the last election. I do not know whether he receives anything for this.

Young Arthur Clough, the most unenthusiastic externally, the most enthusiastic inside, and differing from Mr Tuckwell in politics, was so moved by the man's energy, especially in practice, and difficulties, and so anxious to do something for the boy (Maurice) who was getting no regular education and whom A.H. Clough thought highly of, that he set on foot a little (very private) fund to educate him, and chose a college for him, Mason's College, Birmingham, as set forth herein. This fund is now *all but exhausted* and they are trying to raise another sum, also privately, for the purposes set forth herein also.

I am afraid your election has been sadly expensive and very likely you have contributed to Mr Tuckwell already. But I told A. Clough, when he asked me, that I thought you would care to know of the existence of this need and this fund. I hope you will take no notice unless you particularly wish it; you must have enough to do.[176] I thankfully return Fred's letter. I have had a nice little one too, speaking of Maudie's improvement in health, owing to autumn leaves!! and in spite of stuffy bedroom cars. With love to all.

ever yours

F. Nightingale

And don't kill yourself.

––––––––

176 A letter of Nightingale 8 November 1889, Wellcome (Claydon copy) Ms 9012/250, thanks Edmund and Margaret Verney for £5, "a good and friendly sum," for the fund.

Source: Incomplete letter to Harry Verney, Wellcome (Claydon copy) Ms 9012/31

[c1889]

. . . Do you remember the woman, wife of a soldier in the reserve and in the fish business, Florence Nightingale --?, born in my lying-in ward, whom you kindly brought from Buckingham to see me? Her husband having failed, she has removed from Buckingham with her mother, to Kentish or Camden Town (she sends me her address) and writes to me for work for herself and for knitting for her mother. What *can* I do? . . .

ever *yours and hers*

F.N.

The number of persons who "express a great desire to see" me is rather flabbergasting to my weak old mind. "Come up: bring all your brothers."

Source: Letter, Wellcome (Claydon copy) Ms 9013/33

[printed address] 10 South Street
Grosvenor Square, W.
13 April 1890
8:00 A.M.

"Florence Nightingale Giles"

Dear Mr Morey

. . . In answer to Captain Verney's inquiry about *Mrs Florence Nightingale Giles*, what I know of her is this: in January 1888, I think, a woman giving that name wrote to me from *Buckingham* saying that she was born in my lying-in ward (we had at that time a training school for midwifery nurses), that she had married a soldier, had two (or three) children; they were trying to live on a small fish shop in Buckingham, she, her husband, her mother and the children, that she had worked a piece of canvas for slippers for me, which she enclosed.

I asked Sir Harry to inquire at Buckingham into her character, in which inquiry I believe you kindly joined. I was at Claydon in that month and Sir Harry was going over to Buckingham with the carriage. The inquiry had previously elicited nothing but what was honest and honourable in both husband and wife. I remember that Sir Harry was particularly pleased to find that, at a loss to themselves, they refused to sell stale fish. Sir Harry saw the soldier (retired) and was much pleased with him. On this day he, Sir H. with his extreme kindness, said to the woman: "Jump into the carriage and I will take you to see Miss N." and she jumped in just as she was. I had a long talk with her and liked her very much. I gave her a little temporary relief, but no more.

The next thing I heard of her was that, the poor little fish shop having failed, they had removed to London. She wrote to me, asking me to find them employment. I would gladly have done so, but it was totally impossible for *me*, busy and overworked and ill, and she pointed out no way. The being born in a "lying-in ward" is not usually an introduction to acquaintance, nor is it usually to the credit of the mother. But it should not operate to the discredit of the child, which certainly could not help being born.

We saw and heard nothing but what we liked about these people, the Gileses. And they appeared industrious, independent, *not* helpless people. I should be truly glad if Captain Verney thought well to help them in the way indicated. I return "Florence Nightingale Giles' "'s letter as requested. . . .

sincerely yours

Florence Nightingale

Source: Letter, Wellcome (Claydon copy) Ms 9013/77

[16 September 1890]

Dearest Margaret [Verney]

The year before last I *think* Mr Battersby [the vicar] took a deaf Claydon boy to an aurist in London. (The aurist sent him back, said "nothing could be done for him.") Would you think well to ask Mr Battersby? He took the boy to the aurist's own house and the aurist was a man of note. I am telegraphing.

F.N.

Source: Unsigned letter, Wellcome (Claydon copy) Ms 9013/81

23 September 1890

My dear Sir Harry [Verney]

I am happy to say that I have a very long letter from Mr Devine,[177] and grieved that the cause of his silence is that he has five lads in scarlet fever. His housekeeper was away on holiday, his mother and sister away. He had no money for a nurse, so nursed them himself night and day. The money (the £10.10) came just in the nick of time, for he was actually hard up. And he thanks you gratefully.

His love for his "lads" is really like that of a mother. He never thinks them de trop but is really "in love and charity" with them each and all (one of the sick boys was a prostitute's child).

---

177 Alex Devine, head of Gordon Boys' Home, Manchester, on which see *Society and Politics.*

On Thursday there is a meeting of the City Justices to consider the money question for the Home. He cannot get away till after all is settled, but he is very anxious to get away. I should think, in his present state of health, he might fall an easy prey to any disease.

Source: Photocopy of letter, Private Collection of Cyril Leafe, Lea, Derby

[printed address] 10 South Street
Park Lane, W.
August, 189- [1891]

Dear Mrs Ashworth

I enclose you an admission to St Thomas' Hospital under the very doctor I wished for you.

As you cannot be admitted till 11:30 in the morning, I think you had better sleep here, where I will tell my housekeeper, a very kind woman, to take care of you and see you off to the hospital in a cab in the morning. You had better come as soon as possible after bank holiday. Please send a postcard to my housekeeper: Mrs Burge, 10 South St., Park Lane, London W., so that she may receive it the morning of the day you come.

I send you a cheque for four pounds. You will not of course pay anything at my house. This is for your journeys.

I am sorry to say I shall be gone, but I shall hear of you from St Thomas' Hospital. [ends here]

Source: Letter, Wellcome (Claydon copy) Ms 9013/234

3 December 1891

Dearest blessed Margaret [Verney]

. . . I see with horror that the boy from London who died there was *Leonard Hedges*, the son of a respectable butler whom my mother brought up from the age of two, because he was the orphan nephew of one of my Crimean nurses. It could not have been more than a week before that his father wrote to me for a nomination to a great charity school. . . .

Source: Letter, Columbia University, Presbyterian Hospital School of Nursing C214

[printed address] 10, South Street,
Grosvenor Square, W.
23 August 1892

Commissionaire No. 1216 William Magee[178] has been in my service since January. He has been uniformly sober, punctual and attentive,

---

178 Nightingale left him £45 in her will, if he was still in her service.

both in his indoor work and messages, scrupulously honest, doing his best, handy in many things, clean, quiet and very obliging, careful of my interests.

I have reason to be satisfied with him and should wish to have him again.

Florence Nightingale

Source: Unsigned letter, Wellcome (Claydon copy) Ms 9014/35

2 September 1892

Joseph Coleman's Cottage, Steeple Claydon: Might Mr Robertson be asked to look at Joseph Coleman's cottage, or Philip Tomes sent to look at it? It is one of two cottages at Steeple Claydon, standing back from the road, near the Post Office, opposite the grocer's shop, Tibbits, bottom of hill of which vicarage is at top. Joseph Coleman is getting worse because of the dangerous draughts and the outer door lets in wind all round. Could not the door be moved to the other side the large window, made to open the other way, a screen put, a small window put where the door now is? J.C. could then lie or sit on the side of fire nearest the light with his back to the window, and read or do something, instead of, as now, lying in the dark and the draught on the other side the fire?

Source: Letter to Harry Verney, Wellcome (Claydon copy) Ms 9014/93

19 January 1893

. . . But tell me what I want to know. How are the earth closets getting on for Steeple Claydon? And is the pool where the cows of Mr Ingram (your farmer and the Guardian of the public health) drink, and their milk is sent up to London, abolished? And is the drain from your stables and laundry finished? And poor Mr Robertson's house?. . . .

Source: Letter to Margaret Verney, Wellcome (Claydon copy) Ms 9014/101

15 March 1893

. . . Would you kindly take back to Claydon for Mr Robertson the three volumes of the Cottage Register which he filled up and kindly sent to me? And will you not have a look at them? There appear to be 109 cesspool privies to 132 cottages.

I trust Mr Robertson's house will be (undone and) done. . . .

Source: Letter to Margaret Verney, Wellcome (Claydon copy) Ms 9014/102

28 March 1893

It is more distressing than surprising about Mr Robertson's house. No one ought ever to live in it more, the saturated beast. If it were possible to feel this more strongly, it is because this might be an epidemic year, that is, illness will claw hold of such a lovely nest.

Sir Harry wishes to have a "competent opinion." But the name of the competent opinions is Legion, the illnesses *are* the "competent opinions" alas! If Sir Harry thinks some other necessary, would he have Mr Best? Long ago the house should have been pulled down. . . . [179]

Source: Letter, Wellcome (Claydon copy) Ms 9014/137

[printed address] 10 South Street
Park Lane, W.
29 December 1893

My dear Edmund [Verney]

I write in haste on a subject where I hope, if you think well, you will give me your kind help. You remember the house of Joseph Coleman, father of my Lizzie, where you were so kind about their smoky fireplace. It is very much dilapidated, very unhealthy, has only the one fireplace.

Sir Harry told them, and he told me too, that he would give them Quainton's house in the Upper Village, almost opposite the Police Station. Sir Harry at first said of his own accord that he would give it them at the same rent. But I don't want to hold him to that. Indeed I would not accept it. Quainton moved out of that house yesterday. It is a good house with, I believe, three bedrooms and I dare say more than one fireplace. I would gladly pay any rent £6, £7 or £7.10 a year, I should guess, Sir Harry chose. The Joseph Colemans are most respectable cultivated people—he was a gardener.

They are all three—father, mother and daughter—invalids from living in such an unwholesome house. The daughter has to carry the water every day some distance. (They were impoverished by one of those too common stories of the club to which the father had paid in

---

179 There is further on Robertson's house (Ms 9014/104) in *Theology*, where Nightingale asks "how can one say 'God bless you' if not doing the utmost to secure His blessing of health?"

for years closing.) Would Sir Harry fulfill his promise now of giving them that house? The old house smokes as badly as ever.

ever your affectionate

Aunt Florence

Let your kindness pardon me if you think me interfering.

Source: Letter, Wellcome (Claydon copy) Ms 9014/173

10 South Street
Park Lane, W.
9 October 1894

Dearest blessed Margaret [Verney]

I always think it so grievous of me to lay another straw upon your "camel's hump," v[ide] [see] your kind letter to me. But you have probably heard of the bad accident to Leonard Wiggins, the black-smith's son, and a wheelwright, last Saturday night. My maid, Lizzie Coleman, has been fiancée to him for more than eleven years. And she is of course very uneasy. I should think everything depended upon his being kept quiet. If you thought well to have Mrs Davidson for this case, I would so gladly pay for her.

If you thought Dr De'ath should be had to consult with the Winslow doctor who attends him, I would so gladly pay Dr De'ath. They are not needy people, as you know, but they would probably not even think of these two things, much less pay for them. Leonard's mother is no use as a nurse. I only heard of the case this morning. Leonard had seen my Lizzie Coleman's sister and the only thing he said was, "Was I coming? and was Lizzie coming?" Of course *I would send Lizzie* for a few days, if I knew it to be safe for *him*. But she is not the least bit of a nurse. (She might come back to pack me up, if I were so happy as to come to you. And then she would be at Claydon and seeing him as much as was desired and safe.) . . .

ever your loving

F.N.

Source: Letter to Margaret Verney, Wellcome (Claydon copy) Ms 9015/40

Ash Wednesday [27 February 1895]

. . . If you go on Monday I have some scruple about taking Lizzie away from her mother just now. (I think the sister so sure to break down.) And *I* am rather shaky. But this is the way I could easily manage: go up to London on Friday, keep Lizzie the night to unpack for me and get out some papers which have been asked for, locked up there and send her back to her mother on Saturday. . . .

Source: Letter, Wellcome (Claydon copy) Ms 9015/115

[printed address] 10 South Street
Park Lane, W.
26 April 1898

My dear Edmund [Verney]

I am writing to you about a thing for which it is inexcusable in me to write at all. "Lizzie Wiggins," who was once a maid of mine, writes to me from Steeple Claydon that she and her husband Wiggins "have applied for a house at Botolph Claydon which is just empty—some people of the name of Coker have been living there. Leonard" (i.e., Leonard Wiggins, her husband) has asked Mr "Robertson for it and he says there have been several applicants for it but that he (Leonard) should hear from him (Mr Robertson) again."

I think it is very unlikely you should choose to interfere for such a reason as my writing to you but they ask me to give them "a chance." Ever, dear Edmund, with love to all,

your affectionate
Aunt Florence

Source: Photocopy of letter, Private Collection of Cyril Leafe, Lea, Derby

[printed address] 10 South Street
Park Lane, W.
26 August 1898

Dear Mrs Holmes

I am so grieved and sorry for the mishap about the meat, and so is my cook. It was quite fresh meat when it set out, but the weather is too hot.

I send a cheque for £5 which Mr Yeomans, or anyone, will cash for you, and I hope you will get a bit of meat or anything you like *whenever* you like. And I hope you will get someone to help you—you who have helped so many. It would be an honour to help you.

I must not write more, if I am to get this letter off today. My kindest regards to your husband. God bless you both and He *will* bless you. He *does* bless you.

ever yours sincerely
F. Nightingale

APPENDIXES

APPENDIX A: BIOGRAPHICAL SKETCHES

S hort biographies of the most important people in Nightingale's life are provided in Appendix A of most volumes. For this first volume the sketches consist of members of her family, beginning with short notes on the Nightingale, Shore and Smith families generally.

The Nightingale Family

The Nightingales were a north Derbyshire family. Peter Nightingale (1705-63), of the mining town of Wirksworth, seems to have made the family fortune, in lead quarrying and smelting. He bought Lea Hall, an old manor house first recorded in the Domesday survey of 1086, or possibly he provided the money to do so. It may have been this Nightingale (otherwise probably his son) who endowed Lea Chapel as a Dissenters' Chapel in 1732,[1] although Derbyshire County Council records indicate a "Thomas Nightingale" endowing the chapel in 1690.

The son of Peter Nightingale and Ann Cheetham was another Peter Nightingale, known as "mad Uncle Peter" (1737-1803) for his habit of reckless horse riding, his addiction to drinking and gambling, "a typical dissolute man of the landed classes of the time" (4). He inherited Lea Hall and rebuilt it, adding a Georgian frontage of five bays in 1754. This Peter Nightingale built a factory at Lea Bridge for producing cotton, driven by water from Lea Brook. The venture proved to be unsuccessful however and the factory was leased to John Smedley, who converted the mill to wool spinning. Peter Nightingale also built a house, which was used as a cottage hospital, and a row of cottages at Lea for estate workers. This became the present-day inn, "The Jug and Glass," used for rent collecting (the excessive drinking

---

1 Norman Keen, *Florence Nightingale* 9.

there prompted Florence Nightingale to support temperance measures and coffee rooms).

"Mad Uncle Peter" was a respected landowner, including the manors of Cromford, later sold to a prominent local family, the Arkwrights, and Wakebridge, a farm. He died a bachelor, leaving his money to the son of his sister Mary (née Evans), William Edward Shore, who in 1815 changed his name to Nightingale.

The Shore Family

The Shore family were respectable business people in south Yorkshire by the eighteenth century and active supporters of the Unitarian Church.[2] Nightingale's grandfather, William Shore (1755-1822) and his brother John (1745-1832) were bankers, the brother a founder of Parker and Shore's Bank, Sheffield's first bank, which failed in 1843.

William Shore built a country house, Tapton Hill, also known as Tapton Grove, in the township of Ecclesall. He married Mary Evans, of Cromford, niece and heir of Peter Nightingale. There were two surviving children, William E. Nightingale and Aunt Mai. Another daughter, Anne, died in infancy. Nightingale visited her grandmother at Tapton and loved the place.

The religious affiliation(s) of the Shores in the nineteenth century remain unclear. Aunt Mai referred to her father as "a dissenter and a Unitarian" who attended Norton Chapel every other Sunday.[3] The fact that he was buried at the (Church of England) parish church does not belie this, for there were not then separate burial grounds for dissenters. Yet Nightingale's grandmother Shore attended the Church of England, in fact one that was then, and still is, strongly evangelical, Christ Church, Fulwood.

The Smith Family

Samuel Smith (1728-98), Nightingale's great-grandfather, was a prosperous London merchant, celebrated for his humanitarian acts, notably assisting Flora Macdonald when she was a prisoner in the Tower.

---

2 On the family history see Barbara Stephen, "The Shores of Sheffield and the Offleys of Norton Hall."

3 Undated letter of Mary Shore Smith to W.E. Nightingale, Wellcome (Claydon copy) Ms 9041/52.

William Smith (1756-1835), his son and Nightingale's maternal grandfather, was also successful in business and a supporter of liberal causes in a long Parliamentary career 1784-1826.[4] He worked with William Wilberforce on the abolition of the slave trade. A prominent Unitarian, he was an avid advocate of rights for all "dissenters," other Protestants outside the established church. In the Napoleonic era he opposed war with France. Unusually for the time he supported legislation against cruelty to animals. He was lampooned as a supporter of worthy causes:

> At length, when the candles burn low in their sockets,
> Up gets William Smith with his hands in his pockets,
> On a course of morality fearlessly enters,
> With all the opinions of all the dissenters.[5]

Before purchasing an estate, Parndon, Essex, the Smith family lived in Clapham Common, so that William Smith was identified with the Clapham Sect, of Church of England evangelicals, although Smith was a lifelong Unitarian. Smith was also an astute patron of the arts and art collector. For many years in London the Smiths lived in 6 Park St. (now 16 Queen Anne's Gate, offices of the Council for Museums, Archives and Libraries), from which house the Nightingale parents were married. A historical plaque describes him as a "Pioneer of Religious Liberty." William Smith's dedication to social reform instead of looking after his business interests in time cost him his fortune. Parndon Hall and the house in Park St. had to be sold and the family thereafter had to stay in rented quarters or with son Benjamin Smith.

Father: William Edward Nightingale (1794-1874)

Nightingale's father changed his name from Shore to Nightingale in 1815, when he turned twenty-one and inherited "mad Uncle Peter's" property. He was educated in the classics at Edinburgh and Trinity College, Cambridge. In 1818 he married Frances Smith, a woman six years his senior, and the two soon after set off on an extended European trip. He was a cultivated, easy-going man who enjoyed the life of the country gentleman. He is often referred to as "WEN" in biographies, although his wife's nickname for him was "Night." WEN kept

---

4 Richard W. Davis, *Dissent in Politics 1780-1830: The Political Life of William Smith, M.P.*

5 Cited in the *Dictionary of National Biography*.

an excellent library and supervised his daughters' education. He was exceptionally liberal in politics for his status as a country gentleman, the consequence probably of his Unitarian antecedents. He supported democratic reform, declining to stand for Parliament (gentlemen did not *run* for Parliament) until after the Great Reform Bill of 1832 was passed. He was a candidate in 1835 under the new rules, which effectively franchised the middle class and eliminated the worst abuses of the old system. He was defeated, apparently because he refused to bribe voters, and did not stand again.

WEN was the family member most supportive of Nightingale's aspirations, yet even he vacillated, giving in to his wife and older daughter's insistence that she remain at home and follow the usual manner of life of her gender and class. (When Nightingale finally began nursing in 1853 it was a full *sixteen years* from her first "call," and nine years from her first attempt to study nursing in Salisbury, when her father made inquiries but did not permit her to go.) In 1853 he provided her with an annuity of £500, and later raised it, to permit her to take the position at Harley St. WEN gave his daughter his blessing when neither his wife nor other daughter would.

WEN was responsible for Florence's early political education as for so much else. He took her to the local town, Romsey, to hear Lord Palmerston speak on foreign policy. The young Nightingale was hooked, and Palmerston himself in time became a good ally in political causes. After the Crimean War WEN was mildly supportive of her various social reform efforts (she hoped for more). Many of Nightingale's best letters on political reform were written to her father. He was also an intelligent and sympathetic correspondent on matters theological. Yet even late in life Nightingale felt his failure to support her during her early efforts to carve out a career. An unpublished note records: "It was his utter indifference to me. He never cared *what I was* or what *I might become.*"[6]

Jowett also realized that her father, though "very proud and pleased about your work . . . did not understand it." Jowett once told him that "to have a daughter who would keep alive his name was better than to have many sons. He was greatly taken by this."[7] Nightingale was much saddened by her father's death, especially as it was sudden and there were no farewells or last messages.

---

6 Undated note, Add Mss 45845 f136.
7 Letter 8 January 1874, Balliol College 323.

Strains between the Shore Nightingales and Smiths appear on occasion from the time of the Nightingale wedding in 1818 to the end of Frances Nightingale's life in 1880. Woodham-Smith reported that the Smiths, her parents, disapproved of the match, considering WEN "indolent" and lacking in "character" (4). The wedding took place, nonetheless, only months later, although his parents, the Shores, were not invited. Was there disapproval also of his family? The plot becomes more complicated with an exchange of letters between "Fanny" Smith and her father in 1816 regarding an earlier suitor, James Caithness, son of the Earl of Caithness (an Army officer without wealth). William Smith explained the facts of financial life to her and she acquiesced. Yet WEN with his fortune was not immediately accepted.[8]

It is evident from references in correspondence that there was little contact with either set of parents after the wedding (effectively after the Nightingales' return from Europe in 1821). WEN was evidently a reluctant visitor to his mother's deathbed (Florence Nightingale and Aunt Mai were there). Parthenope Nightingale hardly knew her own grandmother Shore, in contrast with Florence Nightingale who evidently took the initiative to visit when she was old enough to do so. On their mother's death Nightingale objected to "the cousins" following her coffin, with the exception of several she named: Shore and Louisa, William Coltman. . . . Florence Nightingale did not visit Embley after her aunt and uncle inherited it (and her mother had to vacate it) until after her mother's death. It is perhaps also worth noting that when William Shore Smith inherited the Nightingale estate the family changed its name to "Shore Nightingale," dropping the "Smith" entirely.

Mother: Frances (Fanny) Nightingale (1788-1880)

Frances Smith, Nightingale's mother, was one of the eleven children born to Frances Coape and William Smith. Her father (above) was a Member of Parliament and a supporter of reform causes for decades, but she shared none of these concerns. The Nightingales moved into Lea Hall, and then the larger Lea Hurst when it was built, on their return from Florence. Frances Nightingale, however, was not happy with the more rustic life of north Derbyshire, and her numerous

---

8 Letter of William Smith 21 January 1816 and undated reply of Fanny Smith, Chiddingstone Castle.

brothers and sisters lived in the south. It was she who promoted the purchase of Embley Park in 1825, near Romsey, Hampshire, where the family lived for most of the year, continuing to spend several months in the summer at Lea Hurst. They used rented accommodation in London for stays there. According to Woodham-Smith, Frances Nightingale was pleased with her husband's plans to run for Parliament in 1833, as this would mean having a house in London (15). Her fierce opposition to her daughter's becoming a nurse has already been described in the introduction.

The Smith family's Unitarian background has been noted above. At least with her marriage, however, Frances Nightingale became a member of the Church of England, from all evidence a devout one. Commentators have been unsympathetic to Frances Nightingale even on matters quite other than her refusal to allow her daughter to nurse. The contention that her move from the Unitarian Church to the established church was made for reasons of social prestige is addressed (and evidence to the contrary shown) in *Spiritual Journey*. Certainly Nightingale herself took her mother's faith at face value, as so much of the correspondence shows. A note by Jowett records a statement by Nightingale that "her mother had a gift of praying and preaching, and used to go and pray among the cottagers,"[9] hardly what one would expect from a social-climbing Unitarian.

Nightingale's "Lebenslauf" (see p 90 above) gives credit to her mother for attracting the best of company, "clever intellectual men, all very good society . . . they never talked gossip or foolishly." When a marriage partner came who "fulfilled all my mother's ambitions—intellect, position, connections, everything," yet she did not ever try to influence her. Nightingale herself was tempted, and marriage would have been "such an easy escape out of my difficulties." Clearly Frances Nightingale supported her daughter's scruples and did not press her.

Frances Nightingale only reluctantly gave way on her daughter taking the position of superintendent at the Establishment for Ill Gentlewomen in Harley St. She apparently initially declined to subscribe to the institution but later relented and gave £5.5. Post Crimea Nightingale let her off the hook, on the grounds that she supported so many other charities.

On her return from the Crimean War and establishment in her own rooms Nightingale kept her mother (and sister) away. Proposed

---

9 Jowett Papers, Balliol College, 1 H 41 January 1880 f37.

visits were declined on grounds of illness. Correspondence shows little meeting of minds, only occasional discussion of ideas among extensive letters about relatives and friends and the traffic in gifts and produce from Embley or Lea Hurst to town. Frances Nightingale kept her daughter well supplied with fresh vegetables, game, fruit, flowers, etc., much of which was sent on to St Thomas' or King's College Hospital. Nightingale also sent specific requests to her mother for things to be sent to needy persons, and her mother often obliged.

It seems that her mother later in life was able to reflect on the differences between them. A note Florence Nightingale made at Lea Hurst records her mother telling her: "What must you think of us, we whose lives have been all self-indulgence, you whose life has been all self-denial, all effort? What should you have wished different in your education? I have never thought of anything but my ease all my life."[10]

Frances Nightingale suffered from some form of dementia for the last ten years of her life. Nightingale was the daughter who had to take the main responsibility for her care, even leaving London for months to stay with her. Nightingale also went to her mother's aid on her father's death, when Frances Nightingale was required to leave Embley. Nightingale helped her to make the move to Lea Hurst and continued to have the responsibility of interviewing servants for her mother and generally overseeing her care. In her will Frances Nightingale left legacies to her two daughters, naming Florence Nightingale as the executor.

It is obvious that Nightingale always admired and respected her mother, and never doubted that her opposition to her nursing mission was based on a genuine, if mistaken, belief that she was acting in her daughter's best interests. The evidence is overwhelming that the affection was strong both ways. The correspondence shows Nightingale's high regard for her mother's kindness, her charitable work and contributions and general good judgment and wit. Correspondence in *Society and Politics* shows how she was influenced by her mother's practices in dealing with private charities. Another lasting legacy from her mother is evident in Nightingale's style of correspondence: her use of the old-fashioned "thee" and "thine" for family members and even "child" for a sister; amusing and exaggerated comments on friends and acquaintances, with warnings that they are "private"; and a predilection for signing letters to family and close friends with her initials, for both mother and daughter were "F.N."

---

10 Note 1868, ADD Mss 45845 f194.

Sister: Frances Parthenope, Lady Verney (1819-90)

"Parthe," or "Pop," christened Frances Parthenope, shared her younger sister's excellent education, which she took advantage of later in her own way. She was a gifted visual artist who painted and sketched well. For years Parthenope Nightingale, with her mother, blocked her sister's aspirations to become a nurse, becoming hysterical and even ill at the mere mention of the possibility. She was treated by the Queen's Balmoral physician, Sir James Clark, in Deeside; Nightingale herself went up to Scotland to bring her home.

It was Nightingale who introduced Sir Harry Verney, then a recently widowed Liberal MP, to her sister. The two married in 1858, but whether or not he had first proposed to Florence Nightingale is not sure. He was a keen supporter of progressive causes generally and nursing in particular, both of which Parthenope Verney took up as well to some extent. She joined him in giving hospitality to Nightingale student nurses and visitors. In London for years the two sisters lived next door to each other on South St.

In her mature years Parthenope Verney wrote stories and articles, publishing in such respectable journals as *Fraser's*, *Contemporary Review* and *Cornhill* (a complete list of articles and books is given in the electronic text, those cited in this volume in the bibliography). These are competent articles on women's education in France, women in the medical profession, the Franco-Prussian War, nature and country life. Two collections of them were published as books after her death: *Essays and Tales* and *The Grey Pool and Other Stories*. Correspondence with her publishers shows she was treated seriously as an author. She published several novels, both serially first and then as books (*Stone Edge* and *Avonhoe*). Her research on peasant life in Europe was also published both in periodicals first and then as a two-volume book: *Peasant Properties and Other Selected Essays*. For many years she worked on the Verney family papers in the Civil War, finished and published posthumously by Margaret Verney: *Memoirs of the Verney Family during the Civil War*.

Yet her sister continued to do all the wrong things as far as Nightingale was concerned. Soon after Sidney Herbert's death Parthenope sent Nightingale "eight closely written pages of worry, worry, worry" (see p 249 above). When Nightingale rejected Queen Victoria's offer of an apartment in Kensington Palace, because it was too far away from the political action, the Verneys pushed her to accept it. "Where should I have been now in any part of my life's work had I followed any part of her life's advice?" Nightingale rhetorically asked her father (see p 247 above). Nightingale felt that her sister was obtuse also in going along with plans for their street, South St., being named in her honour, which would have required her to move.

Even when her sister had begun to do serious things with her life Nightingale was slow to relent. Interestingly Parthenope Verney was keener than Nightingale on women becoming doctors; Nightingale's rather disdainful letters to her on the subject are vehement about the *different* role she wanted for women in medicine. It seems that her sister continued to miss the point on matters that Nightingale considered vital. An exasperated entry in Nightingale's diary of 1877 shows that Parthenope had written the Indian expert, Sir Bartle Frere, to put him off visiting, when Nightingale very much wanted to see him— this then required further correspondence to re-invite him (2:444).

Reconciliation was gradual as Parthenope Verney made an independent life for herself. Nightingale came to spend months at a time at Claydon. She had her own room where she could work, brought her documents and even had visitors on business there. Parthenope Verney suffered from two painful diseases in her old age: cancer and arthritis. Nightingale called her a "hero" for her endurance. In her last years Parthenope Verney spent Sunday afternoons visiting her sister in London (she had to be carried in). She died on Florence Nightingale's seventieth birthday and was buried on Ascension Day at Claydon. There is a plaque in the church commemorating her, but no marker in the graveyard itself. Sir Harry Verney was buried with his first wife and youngest child. Parthenope Verney left her sister £500 a year on her death in 1890, interestingly the same sum that WEN had provided for Florence Nightingale in 1853, which permitted her to become a nurse without losing social standing by accepting pay.

Uncle Samuel and Aunt Mary Shore Smith

The Shore Smiths were doubly related to the Nightingales: "Aunt Mai" (née Mary Shore) (1798-1889) was the younger sister of WEN and wife of Frances Nightingale's younger brother, Samuel Smith (1794-1880). Indeed Mary Shore had been first engaged to the oldest Smith son, Benjamin, but William Shore forbade the marriage on grounds of his being of bad character.[11] Nightingale attended their wedding at

---

11 Reminiscence of Nightingale to Margaret Verney, October 1890, Claydon Bundle 390.

Sheffield Cathedral, 26 June 1827. Samuel Smith was largely a sympathetic relative for Nightingale although strains are obvious when the Shore Smiths inherited Embley and Lea Hurst. Uncle Sam handled much of the banking for Nightingale during the Crimean War. He served also as her emissary to ask her parents' consent for her to go to the Crimea.[12] It seems that the Shore Smiths made the transition from Unitarianism to the Church of England as had the Nightingales, but perhaps more gradually and less thoroughly. Their daughter, Blanche, described herself as "evangelical" when she was sent to Maria Martineau's (Unitarian) school in Liverpool. When she reported favourable views of James Martineau this made for hostile treatment at Embley.

Aunt Mai was a devoutly religious woman, very much a kindred spirit to Nightingale, who poured out her heart to her in the anguished years of girlhood. Aunt Mai also encouraged the speculation that led to Nightingale's *Suggestions for Thought* (she was probably the source of the extreme determinism in it). She helped to rescue Nightingale in the years of struggle against her mother's and sister's opposition to her becoming a nurse. She was "a true mother" to Nightingale when her own mother was not. Aunt Mai's services include concerted appeals to Frances Nightingale to allow her daughter to obtain nursing training and live on her own. When Nightingale finally left the family home it was Aunt Mai who found her separate accommodation. Her aunt went out to the Crimean War to be her companion when Mrs Bracebridge left (the Bracebridges had accompanied her out). Nightingale returned from the war incognito, travelling as "Miss Smith" with her aunt.

In Nightingale's severe illness after the Crimean War Aunt Mai stayed with her for extended periods, acting as household manager and problem solver. Nightingale, who admittedly was painfully ill at the time, appears churlish and ungrateful in reproaching her aunt for abandoning her when she moved out, although she was getting older and had other family responsibilities. Cordial relations were soon restored, however, although it was not until much later that their ardent discussions on religion were resumed. It seems that Woodham-Smith is responsible for the preposterous and much-repeated statement that Nightingale refused to see, speak to, correspond with or forgive her for nearly twenty years (355).

---

12 Letter to Elizabeth Herbert 14 October 1854, ADD Mss 43396 f10.

There were difficulties with Aunt Mai and Uncle Sam also thanks to the terms of "Mad Uncle Peter's" will, for it was she who inherited the entailed property on the death of WEN, obliging Frances Nightingale to vacate her home of more than fifty years. Aunt Mai and Uncle Sam moved to Embley and assumed the duties of major landowners and acted as patrons of the local parish as the Nightingales had.

Benjamin Jowett in 1880 recorded a conversation with Nightingale "that the Shore Smiths would not have more than £5000 a year and could not keep up two places on that. He [Uncle Sam Smith] disliked Lea Hurst and would sell it with the consent of his son, which he could obtain in two years' time. He was very intelligent and well educated, but wanting in pluck and character. She thought that his son had better be a land agent."[13] Uncle Sam and Aunt Mai, it seems, did not take the Nightingale name on inheriting as WEN had. It was only in 1893 that the next generation of "Shore Smiths" adopted the name "Shore Nightingale," although they privately continued to use "Shore Smith" and Shore particularly the initials "W.S.S." With the deaths of Shore's sons, Samuel Shore Nightingale and Louis Hilary Shore Nightingale, who did not marry, the name died out.

(Sir) Harry Verney (1801-94)

To understand the dynamics of Nightingale-Verney relations it must be realized that the Verney family became prominent in the Civil War when the then Edmund Verney served as royal standard bearer. Interestingly the Verney father and son were politically divided, the father remaining loyal to the king, although privately he supported Parliament, while the son, also an MP, fought for Parliament. The Verney pedigree indeed goes back to 1216, although the baronetcy was recent. Harry Verney's father, then Harry Calvert, became the second baronet in 1826, assuming the name Verney.[14] The Verneys socially outranked the Nightingales, although the Nightingales by the mid-late nineteenth century apparently had more money. (The Nightingales also had money problems, but a little later. Or possibly the costs of running Embley and Lea Hurst were less than the more magnificent Claydon House.) Whatever the explanation, the Verneys by the mid-

---

13 Jowett Notes, Balliol College Archives 1 H 43 1880 f52.
14 See *Burke's Peerage and Baronetage* and the obituary in the *Morning Leader* 13 February 1894.

nineteenth century were short of cash, and money problems are in evidence throughout the correspondence. Claydon House, with its 6700 acres of grounds, is now a National Trust property in Buckinghamshire. The charming house, rebuilt in the reign of Henry VII, dates to the Verney acquisition of the property in 1465.[15]

Harry Verney early pursued a military career and then undertook adventurous travels in South America. He was on his way to a position in India when he became ill and had to turn back. When he inherited the Verney title and property the estates were in poor condition from long neglect. He set out to be a model landlord and succeeded in making substantial improvements, but was always hampered by inadequate revenues.

Sir Harry Verney was a widower and a respected Liberal MP when he first met Florence Nightingale. There had been Verneys in Parliament since 1472, always on the liberal side, in eighteen Parliaments before his first election in 1832 (1:327-28). Harry Verney sat nearly continuously for fifty-two years. He was never in Cabinet but was honoured with membership in the Privy Council in 1885.

Nightingale's initial opinion of Harry Verney was not positive. Indeed she described him to Sidney Herbert as a "pompous princess,"[16] but she soon changed her mind, gradually asking him to work on various causes with her (often giving him detailed instructions and tactfully getting him to reword letters or statements. By late 1857 Nightingale was writing Harry Verney about hospital plans.[17] In February 1858 when he visited Nightingale at Malvern to discuss hospital engineering he was described as "ignorant but *agog*."[18] In 1860 she asked him to serve on, and he later chaired, the Nightingale Fund Council. By 1861 she was asking her brother-in-law to help in the House with estimates, and following up on information sent her from his son.[19] She indeed came to respect his judgment and rely on it on numerous issues of social welfare reform, the Contagious Diseases Acts, Army Medical Service and aid in the Franco-Prussian War. He asked questions for her, went to committee for her, read her letters and papers at

---

15 F.P. Verney, *Memoirs of the Verney Family* 1:1.
16 Undated, unnumbered note, Pembroke Collection, Wiltshire County Archives.
17 Letters 26 November and 2 December 1857 Wellcome (Claydon copies) Ms 8997/49 and 51.
18 Letter to Sidney Herbert 9 February 1858, Pembroke Collection, Wiltshire County Archives 2057/F4/67.
19 Letter to Harry Verney 8 June 1861, Wellcome (Claydon copy) Ms 8999/22.

congresses and public meetings, arranged introductions to experts and was a conduit of information from Nightingale to senior Liberal politicians. This was facilitated by the fact that they were next-door neighbours in London on South St. The Verneys helped entertain Nightingale's visitors, took them to see the House of Commons and gave them carriage rides and dinners.

After her sister's death Nightingale spent several months in a visit of condolence to Claydon House. This prompted a new project, local health reform in Buckinghamshire, with which she worked with a Verney son, Frederick. She was assiduous in giving advice and practical assistance during Harry Verney's illnesses in old age. Much of the late correspondence concerns care for him, and their shared religious interests (reported in *Theology*).

Verney's first wife had four children who survived her, who became Parthenope Verney's stepchildren, and for whom Nightingale became an honorary "Aunt Florence." Nightingale's great fondness for Emily Verney is clear in *Theology* and the war volumes (they worked closely together during the Franco-Prussian War). Nightingale worked closely also with the youngest son, Frederick Verney, who was married to Maude Hay Williams, sister of Edmund Verney's wife (on whom see below). Fred Verney earned Nightingale's esteem first of all by becoming a clergyman, later a lawyer, politician and supporter of sanitary reform. Correspondence in *Theology* shows Nightingale wishing she could be his curate in Middlesborough, a working-class Yorkshire parish, while Maude herself was welcomed into the family with "star of the morning, handmaid of the Lord."[20] Fred, Maude and their children were important supports to Nightingale late in life. Their son Ralph himself was knighted in 1928 and made a baronet in 1946. The Verney son George Hope (1842-96) posed more problems for the family, but he also married an admirable woman, Harriet Morforwyn Hinde, from whose uncle they inherited an estate, Clochfaen and changed their name to Lloyd-Verney. The two raised five children who also were dear to Nightingale, notably Harry Lloyd Verney. George Hope Verney had a military career, which earned him Nightingale's respect, and he, too, sent her useful information from his experience.

---

20 Letters 1 May 1870 and 16 April 1871, ADD Mss 68882 f1 and f56.

Edmund Hope Verney (1838-1910) and
Margaret Verney (1844-1930)

Edmund Hope Verney, the eldest son and heir of Sir Harry Verney, pursued a respectable naval career, including service in the Crimean War and Indian Mutiny. He was captain of the *Growler* when in 1862 it delivered unmarried women to Victoria, BC, which suffered from a serious undersupply.[21] In 1868 he married Margaret Maria Hay Williams, of Rhianva, Menai Strait, Wales, and then headed the Liverpool Division of the Coast Guard in the 1870s. His first attempts to gain a Parliamentary seat in 1874 and 1880 were unsuccessful; he had to run where he was not so well known while his father continued to hold the Bucks seat. When Sir Harry finally retired Edmund won the North Bucks seat, in 1885, but lost it in 1886. He won again in 1889 but was forced out when he was convicted of attempting to procure a minor for immoral purposes, for which he was sentenced to one year in prison. Edmund Verney represented Brixton on the first London County Council, but also had to resign it on his conviction. On completion of the prison term society forgave him but he did not run again.

The offence for which he served a year was not serious: he induced a nineteen-year-old woman to meet him in Paris, but she declined to have sexual relations with him, and he paid her fare home. He later paid her £400 restitution. The case, however, revealed that he had been living a double life as a "Mr Wilson," and had obviously succeeded in seducing other young women.

Edmund Verney's many positive accomplishments include the publication of several books. Nightingale, who was very fond of adventure stories, especially liked his shipwreck tale, *Last Four Days of the Eurydice*. He was a collector of books and early editions of the Bible. He gave lectures to workingmen. He shared Nightingale's views on Russia and the czar and more than humoured her on bird care. He succeeded his father as baronet in 1894 to become a responsible landowner and patron of the church. Edmund Verney was clearly gracious, kind and helpful to Nightingale, who obviously liked him enormously.

Margaret Verney was a woman of enormous talent and deep, practical faith. She was an excellent administrator at Claydon, effective and tactful. Her difficulties with pregnancy appear frequently in

---

21 See Edmund Verney, *Vancouver Island Letters of Edmund Hope Verney 1862-65*, for interesting observations on the colony.

correspondence, but she eventually managed to produce three daughters and a son and heir. Her expertise in botany, and ability to make it live for children, greatly impressed Nightingale. On Parthenope Verney's death Margaret Verney not only finished the first two volumes of the Verney *Memoirs* for her, but published a collection of Parthenope Verney's articles, with a memoir by herself. In 1899 she produced the last two volumes of the series, reissued in 1923. She published several other historical books, wrote a school text, served on the local school board and the Bucks county education committee. She started a program for loaning pictures to schools, was a founding member of the Court of Governors of the University College of North Wales at Bangor, a member of the Court of Governors at the University of Wales and deputy chancellor. She was awarded an honorary LLD by that university.

Blanche Smith, Arthur Hugh Clough and Arthur Clough

Nightingale met Arthur Hugh Clough (1819-61) when he became engaged to marry Nightingale's (double) cousin Blanche Smith (1828-1904). Clough in turn introduced Nightingale to Jowett by sending him her *Suggestions for Thought.* Clough was a gifted poet as well as a classical scholar with a fellowship at Oriel College, Oxford when he lost his faith amid the Tractarian controversies of the 1840s. He felt duty-bound to resign the fellowship in 1848. He travelled on the Continent, visited the United States at the invitation of Ralph Waldo Emerson and returned to London in 1853 to take a position as an examiner with the London School Board, which enabled him to marry Blanche Smith. "My dear Clough" accompanied Nightingale in the nightboat to Calais on her way out to the Crimean War.[22]

After the Crimean War AHC held a modestly paid post as secretary to the Nightingale Fund in addition to his School Board work. He not only did the practical tasks of arranging tickets and dealing with blue books but accompanied Nightingale on trips to the country, corrected her proofs and negotiated with printers. Clough was adept at administration and easily made the transition from the genteel world of Oxford and poetry to hospital construction and barracks organization. He was a sounding board when Nightingale was writing her great

---

22 Letter to Frances Nightingale 6 October 1864, Wellcome (Claydon copy) Ms 9001/64.

tomes on religious philosophy, *Suggestions for Thought*. Nightingale cited his poetry in both her published writing and her journal notes, although only his poetry of faith—she ignored his later expressions of agnosticism. When she thought she was dying she left a note stating her wish that the money that would come to her on her parents' deaths should go to Clough. He was also the recipient of her instructions for her own last days and death.

Clough in fact predeceased her by nearly fifty years. He was still a young man when he fell ill of malarial fever in 1860. He went to Florence, Italy to recuperate but died there in 1861 (he is buried in the Protestant cemetery). Nightingale mourned his loss deeply, remembering the anniversary of his death almost as often and painfully as she did Sidney Herbert's. The late twentieth century saw an upsurge of interest in Clough's poetry, so that reprints, two volumes of correspondence,[23] a critical edition and biographies[24] of him have appeared.

After his death Nightingale described him warmly as "a man of a rare mind and temper, though more so because he would gladly do 'plain work.' To me, seeing the inanities and the blundering harasses which were the uses to which we put him, he seemed like a racehorse harnessed to a coal truck. . . . He helped me immensely, though not officially, by his sound judgment and constant sympathy. 'Oh Jonathan my brother Jonathan, my love to thee was very great, passing the love of women.' "[25]

Nightingale remained friendly with her cousin Blanche and the Clough children. She left money to her and their son, Arthur Clough, whom she also named as an executor and with whom she had a fond relationship.

---

23 *The Correspondence of Arthur Hugh Clough.*
24 Katharine Chorley, *Arthur Hugh Clough: The Uncommitted Mind, A Study of His Life and Poetry*; Robindra Kumar Biswas, *Arthur Hugh Clough*; Rupert Christiansen, *The Voice of Victorian Sex: Arthur H. Clough 1819-1861.*
25 Letter to Sir John McNeill, 18 November 1861, London Metropolitan Archives H1/ST/NC3/SU143.

Appendix B: The Rise and Fall of Florence Nightingale's Reputation

Nightingale returned from the Crimean War in 1856 a national heroine and remained a revered figure throughout her long life and for decades thereafter. In 1918 Lytton Strachey published his iconoclastic essay in *Eminent Victorians*, but it was whimsical rather than hostile and did not purport to be a scholarly analysis of Nightingale's work. The debunking of Victorian heroes and heroines that became fashionable in the 1970s, as well as postmodernism more specifically, probably also contributed to the new, and hostile, treatment of Nightingale. For example, Nightingale was described as being "dictatorial, neurotic, demanding, obsessed, morbid," and of driving "poor Sidney Herbert nearly demented."[1] Strachey himself had asserted, without any evidence, that Sidney Herbert "would not have perished" if Nightingale had been "less ruthless,"[2] a point often quoted, again without evidence, by later writers. Yet another critic held that, "Of all the Victorian viragos we have considered, Florence Nightingale, who hated women and wanted the co-operation only of men, was a neurotic all her life."[3]

The real shift in opinion occurred in 1982 with F.B. Smith's *Florence Nightingale: Reputation and Power*, which claimed to represent scholarly research with its copious endnotes of primary sources. Smith's book largely received favourable reviews, in effect making it "the true story" that was to replace the false accounts of earlier naïve biographers and historians. For example, the reviewer for the *American Historical Review*, who called the book "carefully researched," bought its argument that it was "power itself" that motivated Nightingale, that "she sometimes sacrificed a reform . . . to score in petty intrigue or to boast

---

1 Elizabeth Burton, *The Early Victorians at Home* 198.
2 Lytton Strachey, "Florence Nightingale," in *Eminent Victorians* 105.
3 Karen Armstrong, *The Gospel According to Woman: Christianity's Creation of the Sex War in the West* 147.

of her influence," that she was "ruthless with opponents—discrediting evidence, blocking publication, smearing reputations . . . authoritarian and vengeful."[4] Another review states that "nearly every page offers evidence of her manipulative methods, her dishonesty, her disloyalty, and her hunger for power."[5] The reviewer of the *History Workshop Journal*, wrote that Smith provided "abundant evidence of her fantasies, paranoia and lack of scruple,"[6] although the same reviewer warned of Smith's "misogyny" and "doubtful veracity" when dealing with Victorian women reformers (155). The review in the *Bulletin for the History of Medicine*, on the other hand, is highly critical of Smith, noting his "prejudice against Victorian reformers" and "antipathy" to female reformers," "his biases and malice."[7] These reviewers cite his "double standards of evidence," ludicrously high for anything good about Nightingale, while "little evidence—often none at all" is required when condemning her (287). Yet even these reviewers, although concerned about the "rampant prejudice," were at least willing to entertain Smith's accusation of "lying" and "cruelty" as true (290).

None of the above reviewers checked Smith's claims against the material he cited as support in his endnotes—nor are reviewers expected to do so. Yet many citations simply do not correspond remotely to the inferences drawn from them and in some cases indicate the opposite. Further, although Smith's primary sources include several major collections, they exclude the two largest collections of family material: this omission did not, however, stop him from commenting on family relationships.[8] I accordingly caution readers of Nightingale material not to use Smith's *Florence Nightingale: Reputation and Power* unless they can check the sources themselves.

Since Smith's publication in 1982, negative portrayals, including inaccurate and even preposterous accusations, have become common,

---

4 John M. Eyler, Review of *Florence Nightingale: Reputation and Power*, *American Historical Review* 88,2 (1988):398.

5 M. Jeanne Peterson, Review of *Florence Nightingale: Reputation and Power*, *Victorian Studies* 27,3 (Spring 1984):381.

6 Anne Summers, Review of *Florence Nightingale: Reputation and Power*, *History Workshop Journal* 14 (Autumn 1982):153.

7 Eileen and David Spring, "The Real Florence Nightingale?: An Essay Review," *Bulletin of the History of Medicine* 57,2 (1983):286.

8 For numerous examples of discrepancies see Lynn McDonald, "Florence Nightingale Revealed in Her Own Writings," *Times Literary Supplement* 5907, 8 December 2000:14-15.

many of them clearly acknowledging him. These hostile statements, now scattered throughout the secondary literature on Nightingale, are now routinely cited themselves as sources. For example, Martha Vicinus, in *Independent Women* in 1985, described Nightingale's "ambitiousness" and "ruthlessness" as facts needing no documentation or even a single example. Vicinus then criticized earlier biographers for not including these (assumed) characteristics, explaining that they "did not fit public assumptions about women."[9] While Nightingale is said to have inspired many women to enter nursing, she is accused of failing to help "the average poorly educated," and of generally having a "low" opinion of women (72).

Mary Poovey cited Smith on Nightingale's failure "at nearly every nursing scheme she devised," listing several examples. The last consisted of her efforts to reform workhouse nursing, which were said to have yielded "only a cruel parody of her original grandiose scheme."[10] Poovey and Vicinus, not so incidentally, have both produced editions of Nightingale's work (a selection from *Suggestions for Thought* and selected letters, respectively).

A bishop at the General Convention of the American Episcopal Church contended that Nightingale was mentally unbalanced and had died, apostate, from syphilis.[11] (The American Episcopal Church subsequently addressed the issue in detail and voted at its General Convention in 2000 to add Nightingale to its list of "lesser saints.") A subcommittee of the Anglican Church of Canada, working on a revision of the church calendar, voted to remove Nightingale from its list of commemorated persons, but the motion was not proceeded with and so Nightingale remains. The description of Nightingale this subcommittee approved, however, includes such unequivocal and undocumented statements as "her personality became increasingly unbalanced" and she "deliberately wrecked" the careers of those who disagreed with her.[12] After much pressure, a later committee declined to withdraw the motion, but did agree to remove the insults. It also declined to mention anything positive about Nightingale's spirituality or its relevance to her social reform work, which itself goes unmentioned.

---

9 Martha Vicinus, *Independent Women: Work and Community for Single Women 1850-1920* 21.

10 Mary Poovey, "A Housewifely Woman: The Social Construction of Florence Nightingale" 197.

11 Julie A. Worman, "Even Church Calendar Was Cause for Argument" 12.

12 Stephen Reynolds, *For All the Saints* 166.

Newspaper articles present Nightingale as a drug addict.[13] One journalist, ostensibly defending Nightingale against charges of not being "ideal" or "politically correct," even has her "a lesbian and a feminist. . . . she experimented with drugs and became an addict."[14] Rumours indeed abound that she was "crazy" and had syphilis. (One can count on normally sober scholars raising such questions at any conference where a Nightingale paper is presented, and some do not ask but rather inform listeners that Nightingale was mad, an addict and died of syphilis.) American- and Canadian-trained nurses tell of "learning" in their courses, taught at reputable, publicly funded institutions, that she was a nasty woman who succumbed to venereal disease, "because she loved the soldiers." Yet there is no evidence that any of this is true and much to the contrary; conditions at the Barrack Hospital at Scutari were such as to make assignations with soldiers unlikely for even the most determined sexual predator. None of Nightingale's symptoms correspond with those of syphilis. Moreover she lived to ninety, an unlikely age for a syphilitic. Her death certificate, signed by Louisa Garrett Anderson, states "old age and heart failure."[15]

A British nursing union, Unison, voted in 1999 to remove Nightingale as the model for nursing, as her image represented "some of the most negative and backward thinking elements in nursing." Her crimes were said to include subservience to doctors and tyrannical treatment of her staff, keeping her nurses "not so much under her thumb, but under the boot," and turning out "robotic acolytes" from her training school.[16]

---

13 James LeFanu, "What Bugged Florence Nightingale?" *Sunday Telegraph* 19 May 1996:4; Ashley Walton, "A New Light on Lady of the Lamp's Shady Secret," *Daily Express* 20 March 1996:3.

14 Jane Kelly, "Feminist, Rebel and the Ideal Role Model," *Daily Mail* 28 April 1999:25. I have begun the practice of asking authors who make assertions beyond the facts for their sources. Kelly gave as her source for lesbianism a reference in a biography to a "passion" for her cousin Marianne Nicholson (Cecil Woodham-Smith, *Florence Nightingale* 33), a point with no sexual connotations whatsoever. The drug-use source was a newspaper article on *medical use*. Reynolds gave no sources when I contacted him. The American bishop is deceased.

15 Somerset House records.

16 David Brindle, "Nurses Snuff Nightingale Image," *Guardian* 27 April 1999:8.

The report on a Nightingale session at a convention of the Royal College of Nursing in Edinburgh in 2000 was negative. Without any comment on the substance of any of the papers,[17] it regretted that one of the first conference sessions dealt with Nightingale, noting with approval that the conference then moved on to other "significant, new and interesting matters" (66) and looked forward to history moving on "past the dominating image of Florence Nightingale" (68).

A BBC2 program 17 July 2001 included such egregious errors as identifying Nightingale, who was a left-leaning Liberal, with Margaret Thatcher, a right-wing conservative, describing her religion as merely a front for her political activity, and asserting that she opposed the vote for women when she supported it. As for the other examples above, there is abundant evidence to the contrary on all these points.

---

17 Elizabeth J.C. Scott, "Significant Steps Forward for History of Nursing: History of Nursing Millennium Conference," *International History of Nursing Journal* 5,3 (Summer 2000):65-68.

APPENDIX C: FLORENCE NIGHTINGALE'S FAMILY TREE

This (partial) family tree gives our best estimates in cases of conflicting or unclear information. Previously published family trees, reference books, privately held family trees, obituaries, local archives (notably the Sheffield City Archives for the Shore family) and the Florence Nightingale Museum (for the Bonham Carter family) were consulted. Asterisks indicate cross-references by marriage.

The Shores and Nightingales

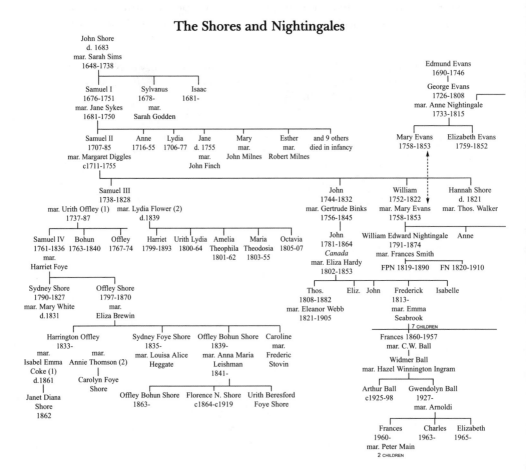

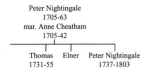

Peter Nightingale
1705-63
mar. Anne Cheatham
1705-42

Thomas   Elner   Peter Nightingale
1731-55   1737-1803

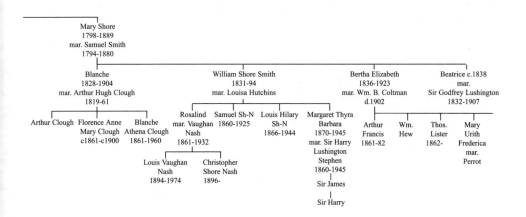

Mary Shore
1798-1889
mar. Samuel Smith
1794-1880

Blanche
1828-1904
mar. Arthur Hugh Clough
1819-61

William Shore Smith
1831-94
mar. Louisa Hutchins

Bertha Elizabeth
1836-1923
mar. Wm. B. Coltman
d.1902

Beatrice c.1838
mar.
Sir Godfrey Lushington
1832-1907

Arthur Clough   Florence Anne   Blanche
Mary Clough   Athena Clough
c1861-c1900   1861-1960

Rosalind   Samuel Sh-N   Louis Hilary   Margaret Thyra
mar. Vaughan 1860-1925   Sh-N   Barbara
Nash   1866-1944   1870-1945
1861-1932   mar. Sir Harry
                                    Lushington

Arthur   Wm.   Thos.   Mary
Francis   Hew   Lister   Urith
1861-82   1862-   Frederica
                          mar.
                          Perrot

Louis Vaughan   Christopher
Nash   Shore Nash
1894-1974   1896-

Stephen
1860-1945

Sir James

Sir Harry

The Smiths

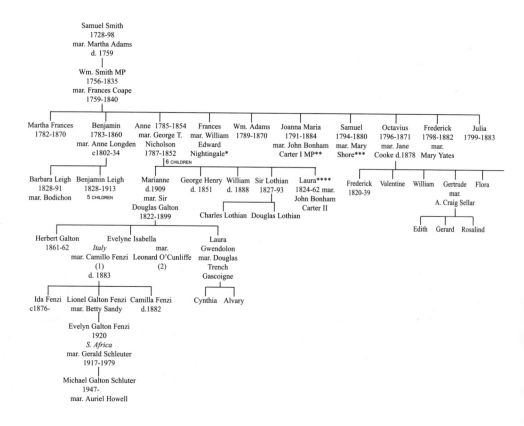

The Bonham Carters

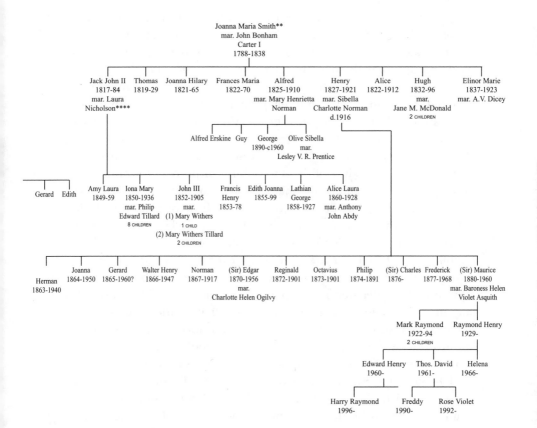

Joanna Maria Smith**
mar. John Bonham
Carter I
1788-1838

| Jack John II 1817-84 mar. Laura Nicholson**** | Thomas 1819-29 | Joanna Hilary 1821-65 | Frances Maria 1822-70 | Alfred 1825-1910 mar. Mary Henrietta Norman | Henry 1827-1921 mar. Sibella Charlotte Norman d.1916 | Alice 1822-1912 | Hugh 1832-96 mar. Jane M. McDonald 2 CHILDREN | Elinor Marie 1837-1923 mar. A.V. Dicey |

Alfred Erskine Guy George 1890-c1960 Olive Sibella mar. Lesley V. R. Prentice

Gerard Edith

| Amy Laura 1849-59 | Iona Mary 1850-1936 mar. Philip Edward Tillard 8 CHILDREN | John III 1852-1905 mar. (1) Mary Withers 1 CHILD (2) Mary Withers Tillard 2 CHILDREN | Francis Henry 1853-78 | Edith Joanna 1855-99 | Lathian George 1858-1927 | Alice Laura 1860-1928 mar. Anthony John Abdy |

Herman 1863-1940 Joanna 1864-1950 Gerard 1865-1960? Walter Henry 1866-1947 Norman 1867-1917 (Sir) Edgar 1870-1956 mar. Charlotte Helen Ogilvy Reginald 1872-1901 Octavius 1873-1901 Philip 1874-1891 (Sir) Charles 1876- Frederick 1877-1968 (Sir) Maurice 1880-1960 mar. Baroness Helen Violet Asquith

Mark Raymond 1922-94 2 CHILDREN Raymond Henry 1929-

Edward Henry 1960- Thos. David 1961- Helena 1966-

Harry Raymond 1996- Freddy 1990- Rose Violet 1992-

APPENDIX D: FLORENCE NIGHTINGALE'S LAST WILL AND CODICILS

Source: Probate Registry, York

I, Florence Nightingale, spinster, declare this to be my last will revoking all wills by me heretofore executed. I appoint my cousins, **Henry Bonham Carter**, **Samuel Shore Nightingale** and **Louis Hilary Shore Nightingale** (sons of my late cousin, William Shore Nightingale) and **Arthur Hugh Clough**, to be the executors of this my will.

I give my executors all my books, papers (whether manuscript or printed) and letters relating to my Indian work (together with the two stones for irrigation maps of India at Mr Standfords, Charing Cross and also the woodcut blocks for illustrations of those works at Messrs Spottiswoodes) upon trust in their absolute discretion or in that of the survivors or survivor of them to publish or prepare for publication such part if any as they or the majority of them for the time being may think fit and I give them a sum of £250 for those purposes. And without limiting the exercise of such discretion I should wish my executors to consult my friend, Sir William Wedderburn, in the matter of such publication. And I declare that if my executors within three years from my death have taken no or only partial steps to publish or before that time have decided not to publish anything the said sum of £250 or any unexpended part thereof shall fall into the residue of my estate. And subject to the foregoing I authorize my executors to destroy all or any of the above-mentioned books and papers, stones and blocks or otherwise to dispose of the same as they may think fit.

I bequeath to the children of my late dear friend, Arthur Hugh Clough, and his widow my cousin, **Blanche Mary Shore Clough**, the sum of £7000 to be divided between them in the following proportions: to the said **Arthur Hugh Clough** £2000, to **Blanche Athena Clough** £2500 and to **Florence Anne Mary Clough** £2500. I bequeath to each of them, the said **Samuel Shore Nightingale** and **Louis Hilary**

Shore Nightingale, the sum of £3500. To each of them, **Rosalind Frances Mary Nash** and **Margaret Thyra Barbara Shore Nightingale** (daughters of my said late cousin William Shore Nightingale), the sum of £1500. I bequeath £500 to the said **Henry Bonham Carter** as a tiny sign of my gratitude for his wise and unfailing exertions in connection with our training schools for nurses and also the portraits of Sir Bartle Frere, Mohl, Hallam, Bunsen and the Sidney Herberts. And I also give to him a further legacy of one £1300 for his objects and to **Joanna Frances Bonham Carter** a legacy of £100. I give to **Francis Galton** £2000 for certain purposes and I declare that the same shall be paid in priority to all other bequests given by my will for charitable or other purposes. I give £100 to **Mary Ureth Frederica**, the daughter of William Bachelor Coltman and Bertha Elizabeth Shore Coltman, his wife, and £50 to each of their sons, **William Hew Coltman** and **Thomas Lister Coltman**.

I bequeath £300 to **J.J. Frederick**, Secretary of the Army Sanitary Commission; £300 to **Sir Douglas Galton** of Chester Street London. I bequeath £100 each to **Mary and Emily**, daughters of the late Dr William Farr of the General Register Office; £250 to **Mother Stanislaus**, Reverend Mother of the Hospital Sisters in Great Ormond Street, for her objects; £100 to **John Croft**, late Instructor of the Nightingale Training School at St Thomas' Hospital and £250 to the **Mother Superior** at the time of my death of the Devonport Sisters of Mercy.

I direct my executors to purchase out of my estate an annuity of £60 on the life of **Miss Crossland**, late "Home Sister" of the Nightingale Training School at St Thomas' Hospital and also an annuity of £30 on the life of **Miss Vincent**, now Matron of St Marylebone Infirmary. And I bequeath to each of those ladies respectively the annuity so purchased on her life absolutely, each annuity to commence from the date of my decease. I bequeath £100 to **Miss Styring**, now Matron of Paddington Infirmary; £100 to **Miss Spencer**, now Lady Superintendent of Edinburgh Royal Infirmary; £100 to **Mme Caroline Werckner** who nursed the French prisoners in the Franco-German War at Breslau (now at Lymington); £100 to the daughters of Margaret, wife of Sir Edmund Verney, in equal shares; £100 to the daughters of Frederick W. Verney (youngest son of the late Sir Harry Verney) in equal shares; £500 to **Paulina Irby** of Sarajevo, Bosnia for her objects; £150 to **Peter Grillage** (from Balaclava) and **Temperance** his wife, whose maiden name was Hatcher, now at Ridgway, Plympton, Devon to be

equally divided between them and in case one of them should predecease me the survivor to take the whole £50; to **Fanny Dowding**, now
McCarthy, formerly in my service £100; to **Robert Robinson**, now
residing at 101 West Street Grimsbury, Banbury, £175; to my servant
Elizabeth Mary Coleman, if living with me at the time of my decease,
and to **Ellen Pearce**, £25 under the same condition; £100 to **William
Rathbone** MP as a feeble sign of heartfelt gratitude for his unbounded
goodness to the cause of trained nursing and to me; £250 to the said
Sir William Wedderburn for certain purposes; £100 to each of my
executors as an acknowledgment of his trouble in executing the provisions of my will. In addition to any other legacy left to him, I bequeath
£100 to **Mr William Yeomans** of Holloway House with thanks for his
kindness to the people of Holloway for me. I leave £20 for a small
gold cross or crucifix to be chosen by the said Henry Bonham Carter
for **Miss Pringle**, formerly matron of St Thomas' Hospital.

I give and bequeath the following specific legacies (namely): the
jewels from the Queen and the bracelet from the Sultan and the other
medals and orders, together with my engraving of the ground round
Sebastopol to the managers for the time being of the Reading Room
at Herbert Hospital, or at Netley, or at Aldershot or at some other place
where soldiers may see them as my executors may in their absolute discretion decide. All my prints framed or otherwise (except those that I
may otherwise dispose of) and including those of the Queen and
Prince Albert given me by the Queen at Balmoral in 1856 and of
Landseer's Highland Nurses to my executors to be distributed by
them amongst the Nightingale Training Schools for Nurses and those
connected with us in such manner in all respects as my executors may
in their absolute discretion decide: the framed Michelangelo photographs, the portfolio of Venice, photographs from Mrs Bracebridge,
the two lovely watercolour sketches of Embley and the copy of
Turner's Rock by Louisa Eleanor Shore Nightingale, my father's
watch and spectacles, the bookcase in the drawing room given me by
the said William Shore Nightingale and Louisa Eleanor, his wife, the
portrait of Sir John McNeill; the little Scutari clock and the box
(Miss Coape's) with all the "stuff" in it, i.e., annotated in pencil by
Mr Stuart Mill and Mr Jowett with their letters, etc. upon it to the **children of the said William Shore Nightingale** living at my death to be
divided amongst them in such manner as they shall agree upon and in
default of agreement as my executors, other than the said Samuel
Shore Nightingale and Louis Hilary Shore Nightingale, shall deter-

mine; the cutlery given me by the town of Sheffield and any tallboy or bookcase or tall stand for papers he may choose to the said **Samuel Shore Nightingale**, the "Colas" bronze of Sophocles, all copies of the printed three volumes entitled *Suggestions for Thought*, the three volumes of Quetelet given me by Mr Quetelet with my Ms papers in the same parcel, and my Dante in three volumes quarto with illustrations to the said **Rosalind Frances Mary Nash**; the sketch of the older Parthe to **Mrs Hawthorn**; a bookcase or tallboy and the picture of the head of Christ with the Crown of Thorns (Nazarene) in my own room to the said **Louis Hilary Shore Nightingale**; the Titian Virgin with the two sides of Angioletti and the (rare) cast of the Avignon Crucifix to the said **Margaret Thyra Barbara Shore Nightingale**, to each of them, the said **Samuel Shore Nightingale** and **Louis Hilary Shore Nightingale**, **Rosalind Frances Mary Nash** and **Margaret Thyra Barbara Shore Nightingale**, such six of my books as they shall select, the picture of Gordon in "The Last Watch" to the said **Louisa Eleanor Shore Nightingale**, the Bible given me by Pleasley to the said **Frederick W. Verney**, the Michelangelo Sistine Chapel ceiling stretched on two screen poles and my chatelaine with the blue seal ring, etc. upon it to the said **Bertha Elizabeth Shore Coltman**; the desk given me by Lea to **Beatrice Lushington** during her life and after her death to the said **Louis Hilary Shore Nightingale**, the framed "Nile" given me by the said Henry Bonham Carter and the models of Highgate Infirmary and Chapel made by patients there to **Sibella**, the wife of the said Henry Bonham Carter, the prints which belonged to dear Hilary, namely the Correggio Magdalen and Christ in the Garden, the large Michelangelo of Isaiah (all framed), also a packet of papers of Hilary's (in my despatch box) to be divided between **Alice Bonham Carter** and her sister, **Elinor Dicey**, or, if either of them should die before me all the said articles to the survivor, but if neither of them should survive me I direct that the said papers shall be burnt; the large framed photograph of her father, Sidney Herbert, given me by his wife to **Mary Herbert**, now Baroness Hugel; the large framed Madonna di San Sisto (with a little secret between us about Gwendolen's likeness) to **Maude**, wife of the said Frederick W. Verney; such of my blue books, War Office, India and statistical and hospital reports and books as he shall choose to the said **J.J. Frederick**, and the remainder of them to the said **Sir Douglas Galton**; the volume of Prince Albert's speeches given me by the Queen with her autograph in the book to the said **Henry Bonham Carter**; the *Life of the Prince*

Consort given me by the Queen with her autograph in it and the Athens photograph book given me by Emily Verney to the said **Margaret Verney**; the Illustrated New Testament and Prayer Book to my two little goddaughters, **Ruth**, child of the said Margaret Verney, and **Kathleen**, child of the said Frederick W. Verney; the Roman Catholic books in English or French, some of which were given me by the Rev Mother Clare of Bermondsey who died in 1874 to the said **Mother Stanislaus**; my Schiller to **Miss Shalders**, formerly governess to the children of Mrs Frederick Verney; and to **Blanche Mary Shore Clough** some article to be selected by her out of my personal chattels not subject to other destinations.

I give and bequeath all my remaining books, clothes, furniture, trinkets and personal chattels to my executors requesting them thereout to give some remembrance of me to their children and to the **children of my deceased friend, the said Arthur Hugh Clough** the elder, and Blanche Mary Shore Clough, his widow, the children of the said Bertha Elizabeth Shore Coltman, of the said Sir Edmund Verney, of the said Frederick W. Verney, of George Lloyd Verney, and of Henry Bonham Carter and Sibella, his wife, to the widow of the said George Lloyd Verney and to **Mr Burton** of Lea School.

To my beloved and reverend friends, **Mr Charles H. Bracebridge and his wife**, my more than mother without whom Scutari and my life could not have been, and to whom nothing that I could ever say or do would in the least express my thankfulness, I should have left some token of my remembrance had they, as I expected, survived me.

I further request my executors to distribute the whole of the remainder of the said articles, including the useful furniture and books amongst the matrons, home sisters, ward sisters, nurses and probationers trained by us for whom they know me to have a regard, particularly remembering the hospitals of St Thomas and of Edinburgh and the infirmaries of St Marylebone and Paddington, and including the successor of Miss Jones formerly Superior of St John's, now at 30 Kensington Square. And I declare that the gifts hereinbefore directed or authorized to be made by my executors out of the articles aforesaid shall be entirely in the uncontrolled discretion of my executors, both as to the selection of the gifts and of the donees other than those mentioned by name.

I request that all my letters, papers and manuscripts (with the exception of the papers relating to India and the other exceptions hereinbefore contained) may be destroyed without examination, also that the pencil notes in the pages of any religious books may be destroyed together with the books, and I appeal to the love and feeling of my cherished friends and executors and earnestly entreat of them entirely to fulfill these my last wishes.

I declare that every legacy hereinbefore given to a legatee for his or her objects or for certain purposes shall be considered in law as an absolute gift to such legatee and that every power of appropriation user or application hereinbefore contained shall be exerciseable by the legatee on whom the same is conferred without any liability to account for its exercise. I direct that all legacies, annuities and bequests given by this my will or any codicil thereto whether pecuniary or specific shall be free from duty which shall be paid out of my residuary personal estate.

In case any of the children of the said Arthur Hugh Clough, the father, or of the said William Shore Nightingale, shall die in my lifetime then I give and bequeath the legacy or legacies (specific or pecuniary) hereinbefore given to such child to his or her children (if any) who shall be living at my death, and if more than one in equal shares.

I devise and bequeath all the residue of my personal estate and effects whatsoever and wheresoever and all my real estate of every tenure and wheresoever situate unto and to the use of the **children of the said William Shore Nightingale** who shall be living at my death and the child or children then living of any deceased child of his absolutely, and if more than one in equal shares, but so that the children of any deceased child of his shall take equally between them only the share which their parent would have taken had he or she survived me.

I authorize my executors to determine what articles pass under any specific bequest contained in this my will or any codicil hereto and to determine all questions and matters of doubt arising under this my will or any codicil hereto. And I declare that every such determination whether made upon a question actually raised or implied in the acts or proceedings of my executors shall be conclusive and binding on all persons interested under this my will. And I declare that all powers, authorities and discretions hereby expressed to be vested in or given to my executors shall be vested in and exerciseable by the acting executors or executor for the time being of this my will. And I declare that my executors may employ the said **Louis Hilary Shore Nightingale** professionally if they think proper and that if so employed he shall be entitled to charge and be paid all usual professional or other charges for any business done by him and whether in the ordinary course of his profession or business or not.

I give my body for dissection or postmortem examination for the purposes of medical science and I request that the directions about my funeral given by me to my uncle the late Samuel Smith be observed. My original request was that no memorial whatever should mark the place where lies my "mortal coil." I much desire this but should the expression of such wish render invalid my other wishes I limit myself to the above-mentioned directions praying that my body may be carried to the nearest convenient burial ground accompanied by not more than two persons, without trappings, and that a simple cross with only my initials, date of birth and of death mark the spot.

In witness whereof I have to this my last will and testament contained in six sheets of paper set my hand this 28th day of July 1896.

Florence Nightingale

Signed by the said Florence Nightingale, the testatrix, as and for her last will and testament in the presence of us who, at her request, in her presence and in the presence of each other, all being present at the same time have hereunto subscribed our names as witnesses, the erasure of one line in the 3rd sheet and the interlineation on the first sheet having been previously made, F.H. Janson 41 Finsbury Circus Solicitor, Leslie Blunt, his clerk.

I, Florence Nightingale, spinster, hereby declare this to be a codicil to my will which bears date the 28th day of July 1896: I revoke the legacy of £2000 bequeathed by the clause numbered 3 of my said will to **Francis Galton** for certain purposes; I bequeath to my cousin, **Henry Bonham Carter**, in addition to the legacies bequeathed to him by my said will the sum of £2000, which I request him, but not so as to impose any obligation on him, either legal or equitable, to pay or apply to or for the benefit of such one or more of his sons, and in such proportions as he shall in his absolute discretion think fit. If the said Henry Bonham Carter shall predecease me then in lieu of the said legacy, I direct my executors to divide the sum of £2000 equally among his sons surviving me.

I bequeath to **Miss Pringle** named in my said will the sum of £100 for her objects in addition to the legacy bequeathed to her or for her benefit by my said will; and I bequeath the sum of £50 to **Mr W.J.P. Burton**, schoolmaster at Lea Board School, Matlock Bath in the County of Derby, if he shall be schoolmaster at the said school at the time of my death. I give and bequeath the bust of me given me by the soldiers to the manager for the time being of the Reading Room at Herbert Hospital, or at Aldershot, or at Netley or at some other place where soldiers may see it, as my executors may in their absolute discretion decide.

I declare that the clause numbered 7 of my said will shall apply to the legacy by this codicil bequeathed to the said Miss Pringle and to any legacies which may be bequeathed by any subsequent codicil to my said will to a legatee for his or her objects or for certain purposes as well as to the legacies so bequeathed by my said will. In all other respects I confirm my said will. In witness whereof I have hereunto set my hand this 23rd day of August 1897.

Florence Nightingale

Signed by the said testatrix as a codicil to her last will and testament in the presence of us both present at the same time who in her presence and that of each other have subscribed our names as witnesses, Eustace H. Barchard, Clerk to Messrs Janson Cobb & Co., 41 Finsbury Circus EC, Solicitors, H. Perinet Smith, Clerk to Messrs Janson Cobb & Co., 41 Finsbury Circus EC, Solicitors.

I, Florence Nightingale of 10 South Street, Park Lane, in the County of London, spinster, declare this to be a second codicil to my will which bears date the 28th day of July 1896. I give all my interest in my house, 10 South Street, aforesaid to my cousin **Henry Bonham Carter**. I revoke the paragraph numbered 5 of my said will so far as it relates to the remainder of the articles thereby bequeathed (including the useful furniture and books after giving thereout the remembrances of me referred to in the same paragraph and I bequeath the said remainder of the said articles to my said cousin Henry Bonham Carter. I revoke the paragraph numbered 6 of my said will and bequeath the letters, papers, manuscripts and books which I thereby requested might be destroyed and the majority of which I believe should be destroyed to my said cousin, Henry Bonham Carter.

I bequeath to **Elizabeth Mary Wiggins** the sum of £20 and my cats, and to my maid **Ellen Kate Sugby**, if she shall be in my service at the time of my death, my parrot and the sum of £205 with my best thanks for her loving service, and to my messenger, **William Magee**, if he shall be in my service at the time of my death, the sum of £45 with my best thanks for his faithful service. I revoke the legacies bequeathed to **Miss Pringle**. In all other respects I confirm my said will and the codicil thereto dated the 23rd day of August 1897 dated this 4th day of April 1901.

Florence Nightingale

Signed by the testatrix, Florence Nightingale, as and for a second codicil to her will in the presence of us both present at the same time, who in her presence and in the presence of each other have hereunto subscribed our names as witnesses, T. Hugh Cobb, J. Gerard Cobb, 22 College Hill London EC Solicitors.

I, Florence Nightingale, of 10 South Street, Park Lane in the County of London, spinster, declare this to be a third codicil to my will which bears date the 28th day of July 1896. Whereas by the paragraph numbered 2 of the second codicil dated the 4th day of April 1901 to my said will I have given all my interest in my house 10 South Street to my aforesaid cousin **Henry Bonham Carter**, now I hereby revoke the said paragraph numbered 2 of the said second codicil. Whereas **Florence Anne Mary Clough** has lately died, now I declare that the legacy of £2500 bequeathed to her by my said will shall fall into my residuary estate and shall not go to increase the legacies of £2000 and £2500 bequeathed to her brother and sister respectively. In all other respects I confirm my said will and the codicils thereto dated respectively the 23rd day of August 1897 and the 4th day of April 1901, in witness whereof I have hereunto set my hand this 27th day of June 1901.

   Florence Nightingale
Signed by the testatrix, Florence Nightingale, as and for a third codicil to her will in the presence of us both present at the same time who in her presence and that of each other have hereunto subscribed our names as witnesses, T. Hugh Cobb, 22 College Hill EC, Solicitor; Ellen Kate Sugby, 10 South Street Park Lane.

On the 31st day of October 1910 probate of this will and three codicils was granted to Henry Bonham Carter, Samuel Shore Nightingale, Louis Hilary Shore Nightingale and Arthur Hugh Clough, the executors.

Be it known that Florence Nightingale of 10 South Street Park Lane in the County of Middlesex, spinster, died on the 13th day of August 1910 at 10 South Street aforesaid. And be it further known that at the date hereunder written the last Will and Testament with three codicils of the said deceased was proved and registered in the Principle Probate Registry of His Majesty's High Court of Justice, and that administration of all the estate which by law devolves to and vests in the personal representative of the said deceased was granted by the aforesaid court to Henry Bonham Carter of 5 Hyde Park Square in the County of Middlesex, Samuel Shore Nightingale of 11 Rudall Crescent, Hampstead in the said county: Louis Hilary Shore Nightingale of 1 Devonshire Place Portland Place in the said County and Arthur Hugh Clough of Castletop Burley Kinwood in the County of Hants, the executors named in the said will. Dated the 31st day of October 1910.

    Gross value of Estate   £36,127.16.8
    Net Value of Personal Estate   £35,649.16.9

APPENDIX E: RESEARCH METHODS AND SOURCES

The acquisition of source materials (microfilms normally, sometimes photocopies) began with known, major collections (British Library, Wellcome Trust, London Metropolitan Archives) and then proceeded to other known, sizable collections. A list is given below of all archives used in the whole project, over 150 archives and private collections as this volume goes to press. The listing of the National Register of Archives (Historical Manuscripts Commission) in London was a useful source yielding five printed pages of sources, mainly in the U.K.[1] A directory of the International Association of Archives was used to send letters of inquiry to a large number of plausible sources, i.e., European state archives and other places known to have a Nightingale connection (to little result). Many American sources were found on the Internet. The list of the Library of Congress and a Canadian directory of archives were used. An email network of professional archivists generated some ten heretofore unknown holdings. A Canadian military email network turned up one source. The project's own website and media interviews prompted numerous sources. Undoubtedly there are further letters still in private hands, among the descendants or heirs of Nightingale correspondents, which it is hoped will be made available to us.

One of the great complications of working on this project is the fact that a substantial proportion of Nightingale's letters have been privately owned by descendants of her sister's husband. They are housed in an archive, with a professional archivist, at Claydon House, Middle Claydon, Buckinghamshire, but are accessible only by appoint-

---

1 Regrettably, some important collections are not registered there, notably the Royal Collection at Windsor Castle. Some entries are misleading or wrong, notably the description of the holdings at the Wiltshire County Archives as being correspondence with Lord Pembroke (they are owned by Lord Pembroke but the letters are with Sidney and Elizabeth Herbert).

ment, on payment of a fee, roughly one day a month. Most, but not all, of this material has been copied to the Wellcome Trust in London. There is no list of the holdings at Claydon House or of the copies in the Wellcome Trust but only approximate descriptions by folder (Wellcome) or by bundle (Claydon). The Wellcome folders are largely chronological in organization and thus easier to use. The 460 Claydon bundles were sorted by Sir Harry Calvert Verney, the fourth baronet, who was not a professional archivist but Nightingale's godson. The bundles are organized in an idiosyncratic manner, to say the least. Annotations include some helpful information, but many erroneous dates and odd guesses. Worse, Harry Calvert Verney gave away a number of letters, without keeping copies or even a list of what or to whom.

A further complication arises from the fact that some Nightingale letters at Claydon are housed in the massive Verney Collection, where letters are organized by recipient instead of by writer, and which have not been copied to Wellcome. As a result of these difficulties it was impossible to do all the checking that would have been desirable against the originals (I could not expect to live long enough with such infrequent access). It is quite obvious that there are gaps in the Wellcome copies, as well as unnumbered items and repeat numbering in some cases.

Some of the difficulties in the availability of Nightingale material devolve from long-standing differences between the Nightingales and the Verneys. Parthenope Verney inherited the substantial collection of Nightingale material held by her parents and left it to Margaret Verney; both kept it away from Nightingale for fear that she would destroy it. On Nightingale's death Margaret Verney wanted to publish a memoir but was informed by her executors that she would require their permission and did not proceed. Nightingale descendants then gave their collection(s), in stages, to the British Library while the Verney material remained and remains at Claydon. However, another set of Verney material (from Fred, Maude and their children) was held separately and much later made its way to the British Library.

There is no detailed listing of the British Library's substantial collection. Most of the volumes are identified as correspondence with particular named persons, and further divided by date for major correspondents. Yet there are twenty volumes identified only as "General Correspondence" (ADD Mss 45796-815), divided only by date and with no indication of the correspondents or subjects of correspondence. These volumes include letters from such important people as viceroys of India, General Gordon, Harriet Beecher Stowe and Earl Grey. British Library indices list three series of family papers, the third misleadingly noted as being the "final." Yet there is a fourth series of eight volumes with another set of Verneys, Frederick, Maude and their children, which were added to the British Library collection only in the index for 1986-90.

Without a catalogue a researcher must create his or her own from the volumes published every five years and the printout of the latest accessions. An electronic listing has been available since 1999, but it is not complete. There are thirty-five printed volumes to consult for Nightingale correspondence 1860-2000 (most from after her death). The largest number of letters and notes belong to the three large gifts of the Nightingale family, the source typically used by scholars. But other letters and notes are scattered throughout the British Library's holdings. One suspects, since the material arrived at different times, some quite late, that some letters and notes were deliberately held back. The very personal correspondence with her beloved cousin "Shore" arrived at the British Library (ADD Mss 46176) only in 1959 and her highly self-critical reflections on the fiftieth anniversary of her "call to service" (ADD Mss 52427) only in 1981.

While most of Nightingale's letters to members of her family are held either at Claydon House or the British Library, some have been sold to collectors and are scattered throughout county and university archives, and every other sort of collection all over the world. Some letters held by correspondents were returned to the family, and thus are housed with family letters, largely at the British Library. Letters to colleagues, servants, friends, doctors, neighbours, merchants and persons asking Nightingale's help on a great variety of matters were sold or given to archives.

Copies of any original letters exported from Britain must be deposited at the British Library, but the exporter need provide no information as to where they have gone. There is an embargo period of seven years (unless the exporter waives it, which rarely happens) during which these letters may not be consulted. Such provisions make it possible for scholars to see many letters no longer in the U.K., but the British Library cannot provide copies. The fact of the continued export of letters is another reason that there can never be a cut-off date for a project of this sort. At the time of writing this appendix there were numerous notations of exported letters still within the embargo period.

It must be realized that in Nightingale's time the papers of government members were treated as their private property and there was no requirement to leave them with the Public Record Office. Some Nightingale letters are thus still in the hands of her correspondents' descendants (e.g., the Marquess of Salisbury, the Earl of Pembroke and the Earl of Derby) who, fortunately, have permitted access. Other papers made their way through sales and auctions into collections around the world. Thus there are letters to the Duke of Newcastle on Colonial Office business in the University of Nottingham Archives and to the Earl of Derby on India Office business in the Woodward Biomedical Library at the University of British Columbia in Vancouver, BC.

Public archives often house privately owned material. Sometimes the owner requires notification to give permission for any access, sometimes only for copying, but in all cases this adds to the time and trouble of seeing sources. As well, public archives put their material on display, so that particular letters may be unavailable for inspection or copying when requested. Archives lose letters, so that actual holdings often do not correspond exactly to whatever list of holdings is provided. Few provide adequate lists of holdings.

Some sources were found by chance, aided by persistent inquiry. Wherever I travelled, and wherever I sought information on Nightingale, I also checked for possible original letters. Material emerged through social contacts and the networks of persons involved in the project. Sometimes archivists suggested other collections. I am very grateful to a large number of archivists for their valuable assistance on this and many other matters.

The processing of texts began with transcription, according to precise instructions, to achieve as close a rendition of the original as possible. Some archives would not provide copies of their material so that transcription could only be done on their premises (Royal London Hospital, British Red Cross, Reynolds Historical Library, University of Alabama at Birmingham) and for some the cost of copies was so high it seemed better to transcribe (some of the Bodleian papers). A great deal of checking had to be done with the original sources, for some folios could not be read in reproduction and some archives sent copies with items missing. The final stage of checking entails verification with one person reading the material to another.

Once a substantial amount of material had been processed it became possible to fill in blanks and correct errors in archival information. Letters to an unnamed recipient could sometimes be identified from letters in other collections. For example, an important letter to William Rathbone about nursing at the Liverpool Workhouse Infirmary is unidentified in Boston University's collection, but is clearly a response to one of his to Nightingale at the British Library. A letter at Columbia University with no identification within it, but listed as being to Cardinal Newman, is obviously to Henry (later Cardinal) Manning. Other important sequences of letters could be put together by drawing on the full range of archival sources. For example, on the Contagious Diseases Acts Elizabeth Blackwell's letter to Nightingale asking for advice on a submission to a royal commission is in the British Library (ADD Mss 45802 ff222-23), while Nightingale's reply is in Radcliffe College's Schlesinger Library. Together they both make a great deal more sense. Several letters to Julia Ward Howe and Samuel Gridley Howe were published in the *Yale Review* (reported above), without the whereabouts of the originals being noted. Harvard University's Houghton Library has another Howe letter, addressed to "Dear Friend" and not identified as being to Howe, yet by internal evidence was clearly to her.

Other errors and omissions in archive catalogues that emerged include an important letter by Nightingale on women in medicine to Dr Emily Blackwell, but listed as being to Elizabeth Blackwell (at Radcliffe College, Schlesinger Library). Elizabeth Blackwell's letter to Nightingale introducing her sister, and asking for advice regarding her medical career, is an unnumbered item at Claydon House.

The *Collected Works* makes it possible to deal comprehensively with subjects heretofore examined with only very partial sources. To trace Nightingale's work on public health care without missing essential points one needs to use material in the British Library, Wellcome Trust, London Metropolitan Archives, City of Liverpool Archives, Cambridge University Archives and Boston University Archives. Letters on colonial statistics are widely scattered from the British Library and Wellcome in London; the Royal College of Nursing, Edinburgh; the University of Nottingham; the Flintshire County Record Office, Wales; to the Auckland Public Library and the Alexander Turnbull Library, Wellington, New Zealand; the State Library of New South Wales in Australia; and Boston University in the United States. Nightingale's vast correspondence with Dr Dunn on the medical and other care of Lea Hurst locals is split among the Derbyshire County Archives, Boston University, Columbia University Presbyterian Hospital School of Nursing, London Metropolitan Archives and the Wellcome Trust. To follow Nightingale's *European Travels* one must draw on letters at the Wellcome, British Library, Claydon House, the Hampshire County Record Office, Florence Nightingale Museum, Boston University, University of British Columbia Woodward Biomedical Library, Columbia University Presbyterian Hospital School of Nursing, Edinburgh University and the Kaiserswerth Deaconess Institution in Germany.

Standard references works were used for biographical information: the *Dictionary of National Biography, American National Biography, Burke's* and *Debrett's Peerage and Baronetage, Grove's Dictionary of Music, The Dictionary of Art, Medical Directory, Dictionary of Christian Biography, Munk's Roll of the Royal College of Physicians of London, Encyclopedia Britannica, Catholic Encyclopedia*, etc. The London *Times* was frequently used for dates.

Electronic Data Bases

Information from transcriptions, which will be made available later in the electronic publication, was copied to two major data bases: names and chronology. Information from the annotation process was similarly copied into the names data base, and much material from secondary sources added. The chronology lists all major events, publications and dated letters and notes. It facilitated the identification of persons and events in numerous letters and notes. For example, a journal entry in a British Library volume asks for wisdom in speaking to "her," who is not identified, nor is the obviously delicate problem. The mystery appears to be solved with the chronology, which shows that two days earlier Margaret Verney's husband was arrested for a sex crime, for which he later served a year in prison. The chronology helped to date many undated and often out-of-order items in the Claydon copies at Wellcome. The chronological data base permits cross-references between Nightingale's reading and annotations, publications and events.

Data bases have also been created on the books and articles Nightingale used (those in her own library, those she purchased or borrowed, cited or gave away); works of art (those on which she commented, or bought and gave away reproductions of); battles and wars (on which Nightingale actively worked or at least commented); hospitals and convalescent institutions (to which she gave assistance or advice on plans, staffing, etc.); nursing and nursing training institutions (with whose nurses she met, or to which she gave or asked advice or to which she sent nurses); and charitable causes (those to which she publicly or privately gave money, encouragement or advice). These data bases will facilitate further scholarly work in their respective areas. They all bring together material from the entire range of archival holdings around the world.

Annotations

The goal is to provide explanatory material wherever possible: full names, dates and relevant material for persons mentioned, publication details for articles, books, etc. cited, dates and brief details for battles, clarification on places visited, works of art, etc. referred to. Much of this work was done with regular library resources and, increasingly throughout the project, the Internet and CD-Roms. The material is stored in the data bases referred to above.

I travelled to the places important in Nightingale's life, saw where she lived and worked, read the books and articles she read, visited the churches where she worshipped and viewed the art she had seen. Thus I visited Lea Hurst and her haunts around Derby, Embley and East Wellow, Hampshire, South St. in London, the Verneys' Claydon House in Buckinghamshire, the Bracebridges' home at Atherstone, Warwickshire and her grandparents' home at Tapton near Sheffield, the Convent of Mercy in Bermondsey. I visited the places she wrote about (Scotland, York, the Midlands cathedral towns and the south coast where she practised "conchology"). I checked out graveyards where Nightingale relatives were buried, took down information from memorial plaques in churches, consulted marriage records and wills and found obituaries at local archives. (Where there was a conflict between a printed source for dates and a gravestone, the gravestone won.) I visited Kaiserswerth-am-Rhein, where the Deaconess Institution is still going strong. The building where Nightingale lived while there is now a seniors' residence. The hospital is named after her.

I travelled to Rome and viewed it using Mary Keele's *Florence Nightingale in Rome* (especially useful for the Sistine Chapel and the Vatican Museum). I visited the convent where she made her retreat and saw where she lived (near the foot of the Spanish Steps). Naturally it is not possible to do all the things Nightingale did (even apart from the Crimean War): I did not have a personal audience with the pope, nor was I accorded an afternoon at the Sistine Chapel with no other visitors. The nuns at Sacré-Coeur no longer hold vespers. I visited her territory in Paris from the splendid Place Vendôme, where the Nightingale family stayed on their visit, to the humbler building where she stayed in the rue Oudinot when nursing with the Sisters of Charity (now a daycare centre). The building where Nightingale stayed with the Mohls in the rue du Bac, almost next door to the Sisters of Charity mother house, is still elegant. In all the places I visited I checked out archives, consulted archivists and librarians and obtained local printed material on relevant points as well as "absorbing the atmosphere."

A considerable amount of primary material on Nightingale relatives, colleagues and friends was consulted as well, some of it transcribed, but more often used more selectively. The substantial Verney Papers at Claydon House were an excellent source for correspondence to Nightingale family members from political figures, friends and visitors. (There is, for example, interesting correspondence from Cardinal Manning and Benjamin Jowett to Parthenope Verney.) Unpublished Jowett papers at Balliol College, including his sermons and journal notes were also used, as were journal notes of Richard Monckton Milnes at the Wren Library, Cambridge University. Memoirs and published letters of important Nightingale correspondents and collaborators were extensively consulted.

This appendix on research methods is intended also as a reply to those individuals and institutions who dismissed the *Collected Works* project on the grounds that it did not constitute "research," but a merely mechanical copying of material better consulted in the archives themselves. This appendix we hope demonstrates the need for an assembling of material worldwide. While I remain convinced that Cook's official biography of 1913 is still the best, this *Collected Works* shows that even it missed some important information. More cheerfully, we can hope that the *Collected Works* will prompt new biographies and analyses now that scholars will be able to draw readily on all of Nightingale's writing and take advantage also of the massive research materials in the electronic data bases.

Archives

Major Collections

British Library, London: 180 volumes in the Nightingale Collection, plus letters scattered throughout numerous other collections: Gladstone, Ripon, etc.

Claydon House, Bucks: 84 bundles of letters mainly by Nightingale, 376 bundles of letters to her or by or to members of her family, plus scattered letters in the Verney Collection.

Wellcome Trust for the History of Medicine, London: 14 folders of original papers, 39 folders of copies of Claydon material, 18 folders of copies of material in other collections (for this material, however, copies were obtained from the original sources).

London Metropolitan Archives, London: a substantial but unnumbered Nightingale collection largely of material from St Thomas' Hospital, plus letters scattered through other collections.

Other British and Irish State Archives/Libraries

Royal Archives, Windsor Castle; Public Record Office, Kew; India Office, British Library (including Marquess of Salisbury Collection), Scottish Record Office, Edinburgh (including Earl of Wemyss Collection); Northern Ireland Public Record Office, Belfast; Scottish National Library, Edinburgh; National Army Museum, Chelsea Hospital, London; National Library of Ireland, Dublin.

British University Archives

Oxford University: Balliol College (including Mallet Family Collection), Bodleian Library; Cambridge University: Cambridge University Manuscripts and Archives, Girton College, Trinity College.

University of London: British Library of Political and Economic Science (Farr Collection), University (Senate House) Library (Seeley Papers), University College Library (Chadwick Collection).

Universities of Liverpool; Edinburgh (Lothian Health Board); Birmingham; Nottingham; Guildhall University (Fawcett Library); Durham; Southampton (Palmerston Papers); Bradfield College.

British County and City Record Offices/Archives

Wiltshire County Archives (Earl of Pembroke Collection); Liverpool City Archives (including Earl of Derby Collection), Archives of Buckinghamshire, Derbyshire, Leicestershire, Flintshire, Hampshire, West Yorkshire, Bristol, Lincolnshire; City of Westminster Archives; Probate Register, York.

British Hospital/Medical/Nursing Archives

Florence Nightingale Museum, St Thomas' Hospital, London; Royal College of Nursing (Edinburgh and London); British Red Cross (Wantage Papers); Royal London Hospital, Whitechapel; Radcliffe Infirmary (Oxfordshire Health Archives), Radcliffe Guild of Nurses; Royal College of Obstetricians and Gynecologists; Royal Liverpool Infirmary; Royal College of Physicians, London; Royal College of General Practitioners, London; Glasgow Royal Infirmary.

Other British Sources

Lea Hurst RSAS Age Care, Derby; Convent of Mercy, Bermondsey, London; Convent of Mercy, Birmingham; Ascot Priory, Berkshire; Royal Bank of Scotland; Sudeley Castle, Gloucestershire; Victoria and Albert Museum, London; Royal Institute of British Architects, London; Grosvenor Chapel, London.

Other European Countries

Kaiserswerth Diakoniewerk, Germany; National Archives of Malta; Royal Library, National Library of Sweden, Stockholm; Kuopio University, Helsinki, Finland;

United States

Library of Congress, Washington, DC; Columbia University, Presbyterian Hospital School of Nursing, New York City; Radcliffe College, Cambridge MA (Schlesinger Library); University of Alabama at Birmingham (Reynolds Historical Library); University of California at Los Angeles; Emory University (Pitts Theological Seminary), Atlanta, GA; Harvard University (Countway Medical Library and Houghton Rare Books Library), Cambridge, MA; Boston University; Clendening History of Medicine Library, Kansas University Medical Center; Duke University (Rare Book Library and Medical Center Library); University of Chicago; Johns Hopkins University, Baltimore, MD; Yale University and Beinecke Rare Books and Manuscripts Library, New Haven; University of Iowa; University of North Carolina, Chapel Hill; Northwestern University, Chicago; University of Virginia.

Canada

Archives of Ontario, Toronto; University of Toronto (Thomas K. Fisher Rare Book Library); University of British Columbia (Woodward Biomedical Library), Vancouver; Vancouver General Hospital

School of Nursing Alumnae Association; Mt Sinai Hospital, Toronto; McGill University Nursing Alumnae.

Australia
State Library of New South Wales; State Library of South Australia.

New Zealand
National Library of New Zealand; Auckland Public Library; Dunedin Public Hospital; Alexander Turnbull Library, Wellington; Nelson Hospital.

India
Nehru Museum, Delhi; Pune Sarvajanik Sabha, Pune.

Other Countries
St Luke's Hospital, Tokyo, Japan; Public Archives of South Africa, Capetown; Turkish Land Force First Army, Istanbul.

Small Private Collections
Small private collections in London, Derbyshire, Dorset, Oxford, Northamptonshire, U.K.; Nelson, New Zealand; Netherlands; Toronto, Guelph, Windsor, ON; North Vancouver, BC; Fredericton, NB; San Francisco, CA; Providence, RI.

Published or Printed Sources and Copies
In some cases only previously published, or otherwise printed, microform or microfilm copies of letters were available; i.e., the original letters have been sold and for practical purposes disappeared or have been lost. In some cases photocopies of handwritten letters, sometimes only handwritten copies of letters believed to have been written by Nightingale, are available but the location of the original is unknown. Thus we have copies of correspondence previously held at Chiddingstone Castle, Kent; and in a private holding in Holloway, Derby. The Adelaide Nutting Historical Microform Collection was especially useful as a backup source in this situation. All non-original sources are indicated where they are used.

Other Archives and Libraries
In addition to the archives listed above from which original material was obtained, numerous other archives were visited. Although the search for original material was unsuccessful, most locations furnished some information: Bibliothèque Nationale, Paris; Archives of Missions étrangères, Paris; City of Florence Archives; Archives of the Convent

of the Sacré-Coeur, Rome; Sheffield City Archives; Muniment Room and Library, Westminster Abbey; Central Catholic Library, London; Dr Williams' Library, London; London Library; Durham Cathedral Library; General Assembly of Unitarian and Free Christian Churches, London; Museum of Farnham, Farnham, Surrey; Manitoba Provincial Archives, Winnipeg; Conrad Grebel Library, Waterloo, ON; Widener Library, Harvard University; Robarts Library (with much help from its electronic data bases) and Trinity College Library at the University of Toronto. My own library at the University of Guelph, with its affiliated libraries at the University of Waterloo and Wilfrid Laurier University, and its inter-library loan services, found an enormous amount of printed material for the project.

BIBLIOGRAPHY

BIBLIOGRAPHY

Abbott, Elizabeth. *A History of Celibacy.* Toronto: Harper Collins 1999.

Abbott, Evelyn, and Lewis Campbell, eds. *Life and Letters of Benjamin Jowett.* 2 vols. London: John Murray 1897.

Abbott, Jacob. *The Corner-stone, or, A Familiar Illustration of the Principles of Christian Truth.* London: T. Ward 1834.

———. *The Way to Do Good: Or The Christian Character Mature.* London: T. Tegg & Son 1836.

Abel-Smith, Brian. *The Hospitals 1800-1948: A Study in Social Administration in England and Wales.* London: Heinemann 1964.

Alcott, Amos Bronson. *R.W. Emerson: Philosopher and Seer.* London: Elliot Stock 1889 [1888].

Aldrich, Lizzie. "Florence Nightingale," in *Great Men and Famous Women,* ed. Charles F. Horne. New York: Selmar Hess 1894 6:369-77.

Allen, Donald R. "Florence Nightingale: Toward a Psychohistorical Interpretation." *Journal of Interdisciplinary History* 6,1 (Summer 1975):23-45.

Anderson, Dorothy. *Miss Irby and Her Friends.* London: Hutchinson 1966.

Anderson, Louisa Garrett. *Elizabeth Garrett Anderson 1836-1917.* London: Faber & Faber 1939.

Armstrong, Karen. *The Gospel According to Woman: Christianity's Creation of the Sex War in the West.* London: Elm Tree 1986.

Atkinson, Henry G., and Harriet Martineau. *Letters on the Laws of Man's Nature and Development.* London: John Chapman 1851.

Baly, Monica. "Shattering the Nightingale Myth." *Nursing Times* 82 (11 June 1986):16-19.

Barfoot, Mike. "To Catch a Nightingale: Nursing Reforms at the Royal Infirmary of Edinburgh, 1872-1900," in *New Countries and Old*

Medicine: Proceedings of an International Conference on the History of Medicine and Health, Auckland NZ 1994, ed. Linda Bryder and Derek A. Dow. Auckland NZ: Auckland Medical History Society 1995:256-62.

Baxter, Richard. *The Autobiography of Richard Baxter,* abridged J.M. Lloyd Thomas, ed. N.H. Keeble. London: Dent 1974.

Berquin, Arnaud. *L'Ami des Enfans, etc..* New ed. 4 vols. London: J. Johnson 1798.

Biswas, Robindra Kumar. *Arthur Hugh Clough.* Oxford: Clarendon 1972.

Bohan, Edmund. *To Be a Hero: Sir George Grey (1812-1878).* Auckland: Harper Collins New Zealand 1998.

Bolster, Evelyn. *The Sisters of Mercy in the Crimean War.* Cork: Mercier 1964.

Bunsen, Frances von. *A Memoir of Baron Bunsen Drawn Chiefly from Family Papers by His Widow.* 2 vols. London: Longmans 1868.

Burton, Elizabeth. *The Early Victorians at Home 1837-1861.* London: Arrow 1974.

Butler, William Francis. *Great Lone Land: A Narrative of Travel and Adventure in the North-West of America.* London 1874.

Calabria, Michael D., and Janet A. Macrae, eds. *Suggestions for Thought by Florence Nightingale.* Philadelphia: University of Pennsylvania Press 1994.

Cavanagh, Terry. *Public Sculpture of Liverpool.* Liverpool: Liverpool University Press 1997.

Chorley, Katharine. *Arthur Hugh Clough: The Uncommitted Mind, A Study of His Life and Poetry.* Oxford: Clarendon 1962.

Clay, Walter Lowe. *The Prison Chaplain: A Memoir of the Rev John Clay.* Montclair NJ: Patterson Smith Reprint 1969 [1861].

Cohen, I. Bernard. "Florence Nightingale." *Scientific American* 246 (March 1984):128-33, 136-37.

Cook, Edward T. *Life of Florence Nightingale.* 2 vols. London: Macmillan 1913.

Cotton, Elizabeth R. *Our Coffee Room.* 3rd ed. London: James Nisbet 1876.

Davis, Richard W. *Dissent in Politics 1780-1830: The Political Life of William Smith, M.P.* London: Epworth 1971.

Diamond, Marion, and Mervyn Stone. "Nightingale on Quetelet." *Journal of the Royal Statistical Society* (Series A) 144 (1981):66-79; Part 2 "The Marginalia" 176-213; Part 3 "Essay in Memoriam" 3:332-51.

Donnison, Jean. *Midwives and Medical Men: A History of Inter-Professional Rivalries and Women's Rights.* New York: Schocken 1977.

Dossey, Barbara M. *Florence Nightingale: Mystic, Visionary and Healer.* Springhouse PA: Springhouse 2000.

————. "Florence Nightingale and Her Crimean Fever and Invalidism." *Journal of Holistic Nursing* 16,2 (1998):168-96.

Eastlake, Elizabeth. *Five Great Painters: Essays Reprinted from the Edinburgh and Quarterly Reviews.* 2 vols. London: Longmans 1883.

Edge, Frederick Milnes. *A Woman's Example and a Nation's Work: A Tribute to Florence Nightingale.* London: Ridgway 1867.

Escott, Thomas Hay Sweet. *Social Transformations of the Victorian Age.* London: Seeley 1897.

Essays and Reviews. London: Parker 1860.

Evans, Alfred S. *Causation and Disease: A Chronological Journey.* New York: Plenum Medical 1993.

Faber, Geoffrey. *Jowett: A Portrait with Background.* London: Faber & Faber 1957.

Fauriel, Claude-Charles. *Histoire de la poésie provençale,* ed. J. Mohl. 3 vols. Paris: Benjamin Dupont 1846.

Ferrand, Antoine. *Éloge historique de Madame Elisabeth de France.* 2nd ed. Paris: Desenne 1814.

Forster, Margaret. "Florence Nightingale 1820-1910," in *Significant Sisters: The Grassroots of Active Feminism 1839-1939.* New York: Knopf 1985:92-129.

Gaskell, Elizabeth. *Sylvia's Lovers.* London: Dent 1964 [1863].

Gatty, Margaret. *Parables from Nature.* 2nd series. 2nd ed. London: Bell & Daldy 1858.

Gladstone, John Hall. *Michael Faraday.* London: Macmillan 1872.

Greely, A.W. *Handbook of Arctic Discoveries.* Boston: Roberts 1896.

Green, John Richard. *Short History of the English People.* London: Simpkin, Marshall 1875. Rev. ed. by Alice Stopford Green. London: Macmillan 1888.

Griffin, Eric R. "Victims of Fiction: Research Notes on 'The Love Story of Florence Nightingale and John Smithurst.'" *Wellington County History* 5 (1992):45-52.

Grote, George. *History of Greece.* 8 vols. London: John Murray 1846-56.

Harte, Bret. "The Luck of Roaring Camp," in *Prose and Poetry and Other Sketches.* London: Routledge 1872:1-25.

Hartil, Rosemary, ed. *Florence Nightingale: Letters and Reflections.* Evesham: Arthur James 1996.

Helmstadter, Carol. "Robert Bentley Todd, Saint John's House, and the Origins of the Modern Trained Nurse." *Bulletin of the History of Medicine* 67 (1993):282-319.

_____. "Passing of the Night Watch: Night Nursing Reform in the London Teaching Hospitals, 1856-90." *Canadian Bulletin of Medical History* 11 (1994):26-29.

Hemans, Felicia Dorothea Browne. *Poetical Works of Mrs Hemans.* London: Frederick Warne n.d.

Herschel, John. *A Preliminary Discourse on the Study of Natural Philosophy* 1831.

Hill, Frederic. *Crime: Its Amount, Causes and Remedies.* London: John Murray 1853.

Hopkins, Jane Ellice. *Work in Brighton, or Woman's Mission to Women.* 2nd ed. London: Hatchards 1877.

Johannson, Bertil, ed. *"God Bless You, My Dear Miss Nightingale": Letters from Emmy Carolina Rappe to Florence Nightingale 1867-70.* Stockholm: Almqvist & Wiksell 1977.

Kaye, John William. "Our Indian Heroes: I Sir Henry Lawrence." *Good Words* (1865):69-80.

Keble, John. *The Christian Year, Thought in Verse for the Sundays and Holydays Throughout the Year.* Oxford: J. Parker 1835 [1827].

Keele, Mary, ed. *Florence Nightingale in Rome: Letters Written by Florence Nightingale in Rome in the Winter of 1847-1848.* Philadelphia: American Philosophical Society 1981.

Keen, Norman. *Florence Nightingale.* Ripley, Derbyshire: Footprint Press/ Derbyshire Heritage Series 1982.

Kopf, Edwin W. "Florence Nightingale as Statistician." *Publications of the American Statistical Association* 15 (1916-17):388-404.

Litchfield, Henrietta, ed. *Emma Darwin: A Century of Letters 1792-1896.* 2 vols. London: John Murray 1915.

Long, George, trans. *The Thoughts of the Emperor M. Aurelius Antoninus.* 2nd ed. London: G. Bell & Son 1883.

Macalister, Florence. *Memoir of the Right Hon Sir John McNeill, and of His Second Wife Elizabeth Wilson.* London: John Murray 1910.

Mackenzie, Morrell. *The Fatal Illness of Frederick the Noble.* London: Sampson 1888.

Martineau, Harriet. "Miss Martineau on Mesmerism." *The Athenaeum* Pt 1 No. 891, 23 November 1844:1070-72; Pt 2 No. 892, 30 November 1844:1093-94; Pt 3 No. 893, 7 December 1844:1117-18; Pt 4

No. 894, 14 December 1844:1144-45; Pt 5 No. 895, 21 December 1844:1173-74.

McDonald, Lynn. *Early Origins of the Social Sciences.* Montreal: McGill-Queen's University Press 1993.

―――――. *Women Founders of the Social Sciences.* Ottawa: McGill-Queen's University Press 2001 [1994].

―――――. "Florence Nightingale Revealed in Her Own Writings." *Times Literary Supplement* 5907, 8 December 2000:14-15.

―――――, ed. "Florence Nightingale," in *Women Theorists on Society and Politics.* Waterloo ON: Wilfrid Laurier University Press 1998:165-202.

Montgomery, James. *One Hundred Choice Hymns.* Edinburgh: James Taylor 1873.

Moss, Arthur W. *Valiant Crusade: The History of the R.S.P.C.A.* London: Cassell 1961.

Newman, John Henry. *Apologia pro sua Vita,* ed. David J. De Laura. New York: Norton 1968 [1864].

Nightingale, Florence. The Institution of Kaiserswerth. London 1851.

―――――. *Subsidiary Notes as to the Introduction of Female Nursing into Military Hospitals in Peace and in War.* London: Harrison & Sons 1858.

―――――. *Suggestions for Thought for Searchers after Religious Truth.* 3 vols. London: Eyre & Spottiswoode 1860.

―――――. *Notes on Nursing,* ed. Victor Skretkowicz. London: Baillière Tindall 1996 [1860].

―――――. *Observations by Miss Nightingale on the Evidence Contained in Stational Returns Sent to Her by the Royal Commission on the Sanitary State of the Army in India.* Report 21 November 1862.

―――――. *Observations on the Sanitary State of the Army in India* (reprinted from a Report of the Royal Commission). London: Stanford 1863.

―――――. *Introductory Notes on Lying-in Institutions.* London: Longmans, Green 1871.

―――――. "Hospital Statistics and Hospital Plans." *Transactions of the National Association for the Promotion of Social Science.* August 1861.

―――――. Army Sanitary Administration and Its Reform under the Late Lord Herbert. London: McCorquodale 1862.

―――――. "How People May Live and Not Die in India." Paper, National Association for the Promotion of Social Science, Edinburgh 1863. London: Emily Faithfull.

―――――. "Introduction," in *Organization of Nursing.* Liverpool: Holden 1865.

_____. "Note on the Aboriginal Races of Australia." Paper read at the National Association for the Promotion of Social Science, York 1865 [1864].

_____. "Una and the Lion." *Good Words* (June 1868):360-66.

_____. "A Note on Pauperism." *Fraser's Magazine* 79 (March 1869): 281-90.

_____. "The People of India." *Nineteenth Century* 4,18 (August 1878): 193-221.

_____."A Missionary Health Office in India." *Good Words* Pt :2 (August 1879):565-72.

_____. "Health and Local Government." Introduction to *Report of the Bucks Sanitary Conference October 1894.* Aylesbury: Poulton:i-ii.

_____. "Sick-Nursing and Health-Nursing." *Woman's Mission: A Series of Congress Papers on the Philanthropic Work of Women.* Chicago Exhibition 1893.

Palgrave, Francis Turner. *Palgrave's Golden Treasury: The Best Songs and Lyrics in the English Language.* London: Senate 1994 [1861].

Payne, Karen, ed. "Florence Nightingale and Her Mother Fanny, 1851-62," in *Between Ourselves: Letters between Mothers and Daughters 1750-1982.* Boston: Houghton Mifflin 1983:99-111.

Pellico, Silvio. *My Prisons,* trans. I.G. Capaldi. London: Oxford University Press 1963 [1832].

Pickering, George. *Creative Malady: Illness in the Lives and Minds of Charles Darwin, Florence Nightingale, Mary Baker Eddy, Sigmund Freud, Marcel Proust, Elizabeth Barrett Browning.* London: Allen & Unwin 1974.

Poovey, Mary. "A Housewifely Woman: The Social Construction of Florence Nightingale," in *Uneven Developments: The Ideological Work of Gender in Mid-Victorian England.* Chicago: University of Chicago Press 1988:164-98.

_____, ed. *Florence Nightingale: Cassandra and Other Selections from Suggestions for Thought.* Washington Sq: New York University Press 1993.

Pringle, Thomas. *Poetical Works of Thomas Pringle.* London 1839.

Quinn, Vincent, and John Prest, eds. *Dear Miss Nightingale: A Selection of Benjamin Jowett's Letters to Florence Nightingale 1860-1893.* Oxford: Clarendon 1987.

Reynolds, Stephen. *For All the Saints.* Toronto: Anglican Book Centre 1994.

Richards, Laura E. *Samuel Gridley Howe.* New York: D. Appleton-Century 1935.

————, ed. "Letters of Florence Nightingale." *Yale Review* 24 (December 1934):326-47.

Richards, Laura E., and Maud Howe Elliott, assisted by Florence Howe Hall. *Julia Ward Howe 1819-1910.* Boston: Houghton Mifflin 1916.

Sadler, T., ed. *Common Prayer for Christian Worship.* London: Williams & Norgate 1879.

Savonarola, Ierolamo. *Poesie di Ierolamo Savonarola.* Florence: Tommaso Baracchi 1847.

Schimmelpenninck, Mary Anne. *Narrative of the Demolition of the Monastery of Port Royal des Champs.* 3 vols. London: J.&A. Arch 1816.

Showalter, Elaine. "Florence Nightingale's Feminist Complaint: Women, Religion, and *Suggestions for Thought." Signs: Journal of Women in Culture and Society* 6,3 (1981):395-412.

Simpson, Mary Charlotte, ed. *Letters and Recollections of Julius and Mary Mohl.* London: Kegan Paul 1887.

Small, Hugh. *Florence Nightingale: Avenging Angel.* London: Constable 1998.

Smith, F.B. *Florence Nightingale: Reputation and Power.* London: Croom Helm 1982.

————. *The People's Health: 1830-1910.* Aldershot, Hants: Gregg 1993.

Smith, Robert Angus. *Air and Rain: The Beginnings of a Chemical Climatology.* London: Longmans, Green 1872.

Sorabji, Cornelia. *India Calling: The Memories of Cornelia Sorabji.* London: Nisbet 1934.

Southey, Caroline Anne Bowles. *Poetical Works.* Edinburgh: Blackwood 1867.

Spender, Dale. *Women of Ideas and What Men Have Done to Them.* London: Routledge & Kegan Paul 1982.

Spiegelhalter, David J. "Surgical Audit: Statistical Lessons from Nightingale and Codman." *Journal of the Royal Statistical Society* A 162, Pt. 1 (1999):45-58.

Stark, Myra, ed. *Cassandra.* Old Westbury NY: Feminist Press 1979.

Stephen, Barbara. "The Shores of Sheffield and the Offleys of Norton Hall." *Transactions of the Hunter Archaeological Society* 5, Pt. 1 (January 1838):1-17.

Sticker, Anna, ed. "Florence Nightingale Curriculum Vitae." Kaiserswerth: Diakoniewerth 1954.

Stolley, Paul D., and Tamar Lasky. *Investigating Disease Patterns: The Science of Epidemiology*. New York: Scientific American Library 1995.

Stone, Richard. "Florence Nightingale and Hospital Reform," in *Some British Empiricists in the Social Sciences 1650-1900*. Cambridge: Cambridge University Press/Raffaele Mattioli Foundation 1997.

Strachey, Lytton. "Florence Nightingale," in *Eminent Victorians*. New York: Weidenfeld & Nicolson 1988 [1918].

Strachey, Ray. *"The Cause." A Short History of the Women's Movement in Great Britain*. London: Bell 1928.

Sullivan, Mary C., ed. *The Friendship of Florence Nightingale and Mary Clare Moore*, Philadelphia: University of Pennsylvania Press 1999.

Summers, Anne. *Angels and Citizens: British Women as Military Nurses 1854-1914*. London: Routledge & Kegan Paul 1988.

Surgeon-General [Confederate Army]. *Directions for Cooking by Troops, in Camp and Hospital, Prepared for the Army of Virginia*. Richmond VA: Ritchie & Dunnavant 1861.

Taillandier, Saint-René. "La suisse chrétienne et le dix-huitième siècle." *Revue des deux mondes* 38 (1862):420-67.

Trevelyan, George Otto, ed. *The Life and Letters of Lord Macaulay*. 4 vols. Leipzig: Bernhard Tauchnitz 1876.

Tuson, Penelope, ed. *The Queen's Daughters: An Anthology of Victorian Feminist Writings on India 1857-1900*. Reading, Berks: Ithaca Press 1995.

Verney, Edmund. *The Last Four Days of the "Eurydice."* Portsmouth 1878.

_____. *Vancouver Island Letters of Edmund Hope Verney 1862-65*, ed. Allan Pritchard. Vancouver: University of British Columbia Press 1896.

Verney, F.P. *Stone Edge*. London: Smith Elder 1868.

_____. *Lettice Lisle*. London: Smith Elder 1870.

_____. *Peasant Properties and Other Selected Essays*. 2 vols. London: Longmans 1885.

_____. *Essays and Tales*. London: Simpkin, Marshall, Hamilton 1891.

_____. *The Grey Pool and Other Stories*. London: Simpkin & Marshall 1891.

_____. *Memoirs of the Verney Family*, ed. Margaret M. Verney. London: Longmans, Green, vols. 1-2 1892; vols. 3-4, 1899.

_____. "The Miseries of War: Notes from Sedan and Bazeilles." *Saint Pauls Magazine* 8 (September 1871):509-24.

_____. "Peasant Proprietors: Jottings in France in September and October." *Contemporary Review* 41 (January 1882):1-26.

————. "Old Welsh Legends and Poetry." *Contemporary Review* 27 (February 1876):396-416.

————. "Autumn Jottings in France: Peasant Proprietors." *Contemporary Review* 41 (April 1882):560-82.

————. "Peasant Properties in Auvergne." *Contemporary Review* 42 (December 1882):954-72.

————. " 'Little Takes' in England versus Peasant Properties in France and Germany." *Contemporary Review* 47 (May 1885):675-82.

————. "Foreign Opinions on Peasant Properties." *Nineteenth Century* (November 1885):794-803.

————. "Peasant Properties in France, 1787-1887." *National Review* (December 1887):549-64.

Vicinus, Martha. *Independent Women: Work and Community for Single Women 1850-1920.* Chicago: University of Chicago Press 1985.

————, and Bea Nergaard, eds. *Ever Yours, Florence Nightingale: Selected Letters.* Cambridge MA: Harvard University Press 1990.

Waugh, Arthur. *Gordon in Africa.* Oxford: Shrimpton 1888.

Wedgwood, Julia. *John Wesley and the Evangelical Reaction of the 18th Century.* London: Macmillan 1870.

Woodham-Smith, Cecil. *Florence Nightingale 1820-1910.* London: Constable 1950.

Worman, Julie A. "Even Church Calendar Was Cause for Argument." *Episcopal Life* (September 1991):12.

Young, D.A.B.. "Florence Nightingale's Fever." *British Medical Journal* 311 (23-30 December 1995):1697-1700.

INDEX

INDEX

S pace limitations required some compromises in the index. It includes most proper names, omitting those of acquaintances, employees and others appearing briefly and not readily identifiable. Most of the names for God are included, but not all the synonyms for the Holy Spirit. Entries are grouped as much as possible. Names in Nightingale's will and major entries in the bibliography are indexed, while those in the family tree are not. Biblical references are indexed by book under "Bible." Items with identifying information are shown in italics.